TENTH EDITION

Techniques and Guidelines for Social Work Practice

Bradford W. Sheafor
Professor Emeritus, Colorado State University

Charles R. Horejsi
Professor Emeritus, University of Montana

PEARSON

Boston Columbus Hoboken Indianapolis New York San Francisco Amsterdam
Cape Town Dubai London Madrid Milan Munich Paris Montréal Toronto Delhi
Mexico City São Paulo Sydney Hong Kong Seoul Singapore Taipei Tokyo

VP and Editorial Director: Jeffery W. Johnston
Acquisitions Editor: Julie Peters
Program Manager: Alicia Ritchey
Editorial Assistant: Andrea Hall
Executive Marketing Manager: Krista Clark
Marketing Coordinator: Elizabeth Mackenzie Lamb
Operations Specialist: Maura Zaldivar-Garcia

Art Director: Diane Ernsberger
Cover Art: ©robsonphoto/Fotolia
Media Producer: Allison Longley
Full-Service Project Management: Integra/Anandakrishnan Natarajan
Composition: Integra Software Services
Printer/Binder: Edwards Brothers Malloy
Cover Printer: Phoenix Color/Hagerstown
Text Font: 10.5/13, Dante MT Std

Credits and acknowledgments borrowed from other sources and reproduced, with permission, in this textbook appear on appropriate page within text.

If you purchased this book within the United States or Canada you should be aware that it has been imported without the approval of the Publisher or the Author.

Library of Congress Cataloging-in-Publication Data

Sheafor, Bradford W.
    Techniques and guidelines for social work practice/Bradford W. Sheafor, Professor Emeritus, Colorado State University; Charles R. Horejsi, Professor Emeritus, University of Montana.—Tenth edition.
        pages cm
    ISBN 978-0-205-96510-6 (alk. paper)—ISBN 0-205-96510-5 (alk. paper)
    1. Social service—United States.   I. Horejsi, Charles R.   II. Title.
HV91.S48 2014
361.3'2—dc23
                                                                        2014019725

10 9 8 7 6 5 4 3 2 1

ISBN 10:   0-205-96510-5
ISBN 13: 978-0-205-96510-6

To the next generation of social workers,
*who have chosen to devote their time and talents to the service of others
and the struggle for social justice,*

and

To our families,
*Nadine, Laura, Brandon, Perry, Christopher,
Gloria, Angela, Martin, and Katherine,
for their love and support*

Contents

PART 3: TECHNIQUES COMMON TO ALL SOCIAL WORK PRACTICE   111

PART 4: TECHNIQUES AND GUIDELINES FOR PHASES OF THE PLANNED CHANGE PROCESS   161

PART 5: SPECIALIZED TECHNIQUES AND GUIDELINES FOR SOCIAL WORK PRACTICE　419

Preface

Many people are influenced, directly and indirectly, by the decisions and actions of social workers. Working in courts, clinics, hospitals, schools, businesses, private practice, and a myriad of private and public social agencies, social workers deliver a wide variety of services directly to clients while also striving to promote positive community and social changes. Improving the quality of life for an individual, a family, or the people of a community ultimately impacts society as a whole and elevates the health, happiness, safety, and productivity of all its members.

This book is about what social workers actually do when helping their clients solve problems and/or enhance their functioning. Although many books describe social work's basic principles and theory, *Techniques and Guidelines for Social Work Practice* focuses on a more specific and concrete level. It describes 154 techniques and guidelines that social workers use in everyday practice.

Most social workers have been exposed to a variety of practice theories and conceptual frameworks described in the literature and taught in programs of social work education. Although that knowledge base is essential, practice is much more than a set of beliefs and ideas about how people can be helped. In reality, social work practice is a set of actions and behaviors by the social worker. Clients are not directly affected by the worker's theory; rather, they are influenced by what the worker actually does—by the social worker's specific actions and behaviors. We do not intend to suggest that attention to the techniques can or should replace attention to theoretical frameworks. Rather, techniques and specific guidelines complete the package of knowledge and skills needed by the social worker.

Plan and Structure

Understanding the design of a book helps the reader make use of its contents. This book has five major parts.

Part I, "Social Work and the Social Worker," reviews the background knowledge and characteristics we believe a social worker must possess, including:

- A clear conception of the domain of social work and the competencies the social worker is expected to bring to the change process (Chapter 1)
- An understanding of the challenges a social worker faces in merging his or her personal life with professional roles and responsibilities (Chapter 2)
- The native talents necessary for perceptively creating and entering into the interpersonal relations that are at the heart of practice (i.e., the art of social work), as well as a commitment to draw on and apply the science of social work—that is, the profession's knowledge base and its ethical principles (Chapter 3)

Part II, "The Building Blocks of Social Work Practice," stresses the need for the social worker to become familiar with the central features of effective helping. To serve clients ranging from individuals to communities, a social worker must have these qualities:

- An understanding of the varied roles performed by social workers in delivering human services and the specific functions associated with these roles (Chapter 4)
- A deep appreciation for the profession's fundamental practice principles and a commitment to be guided by those principles (Chapter 5)
- A basic knowledge of the various perspectives, theories, and models that have proven useful in practice (Chapter 6)
- The ability to use critical thinking to select the best possible knowledge, values, and skills to help clients make sound decisions about how they might improve their lives (Chapter 7)

In Chapters 8 to 16 we present numerous techniques and guidelines, each of which has a number and a title (e.g., 10.4: Making a Referral). In this example, *10.4* signifies the fourth item in Chapter 10. This system of numbering is used to refer the reader to related information in other parts of the book.

Several paragraphs describe each technique or guideline and its application. In addition, we present a Selected Bibliography, which usually lists two to four books or articles that we consider particularly useful for obtaining more in-depth information related to the topic discussed.

In Part III of the book, "Techniques Common to All Social Work Practice," we have included techniques that strengthen the social worker's performance regardless of agency setting and irrespective of whether the client is an individual, family, group, organization, or community. Underlying our selection was the belief that the social worker must have these basic skills:

- The interpersonal competence to communicate effectively and engage the client in a set of basic helping activities (Chapter 8)
- The ability to address ethical issues, handle organization-related details of service delivery, and effectively manage her or his time and workload (Chapter 9)

Part IV, "Techniques and Guidelines for Phases of the Planned Change Process," lists techniques and guidelines for both direct and indirect practice in chapters organized around the five phases of the planned change process. Although social work authors use differing names for these phases, we have elected to use the following:

- Intake and engagement (Chapter 10)
- Data collection and assessment (Chapter 11)
- Planning and contracting (Chapter 12)
- Intervention and monitoring (Chapter 13)
- Evaluation and termination (Chapter 14)

When introducing these five chapters, we describe what should be accomplished during that particular phase of the planned change process. These general concepts are then elaborated to more clearly describe the direct-practice applications (Section A) and the indirect-practice applications (Section B) in those chapters. A worker can readily examine several suggested techniques or guidelines by identifying the phase of the change process, determining if the activity is a direct or indirect intervention, and then locating the most applicable technique or guideline.

Part V, "Specialized Techniques and Guidelines for Social Work Practice," includes some items that cut across the five phases of the planned change process and thus did not fit into the classification system used in Part IV. To address these issues, we created two chapters containing items related to serving vulnerable client populations (Chapter 15) and the items related to maintaining a social work position and enhancing one's professional performance (Chapter 16).

Definition of Terms

Writing about social work practice inherently presents some language problems. One has to read only a few social work texts or articles to become at least a little confused when various authors use terms somewhat differently. Unfortunately, some commonly used terms lack a precise or an agreed-upon definition. Perhaps that is to be expected in a profession that focuses on complex and dynamic human and social interactions. This book cannot overcome these long-standing problems of terminology, yet the ideas presented here will be more readily understood if we make the meanings of several terms, particularly those in the title of the book, more explicit.

A **technique** is viewed as a circumscribed, goal-oriented behavior performed in a practice situation by the social worker. It is a planned action deliberately taken by the practitioner. The application of a simple technique (e.g., making the first telephone contact) may take only a few minutes, whereas more complex techniques (e.g., assessing a client's social functioning) may require several hours or more.

Guidelines, by comparison, are a set of directions intended to influence the social worker's behavior and decisions. Guidelines are essentially lists of do's and don'ts. They might be used when working with a specific type of client (e.g., a child or a client with mental illness) or when carrying out workload management tasks (e.g., recording or writing reports).

Social work is a term applied to a specific profession that is committed to improving the quality of life for vulnerable people by helping them deal more effectively with the challenges they face and/or helping to change the social and economic conditions that create or exacerbate individual and social problems. In our introduction to Part I, we more fully spell out our perception of social work.

Practice is a term used when speaking about what social workers actually do, as in the phrase *social work practice*. The word *practice* infers action and performance by the social worker. The word *practice* also implies that social workers always are learning from what they do, always open to new insights, and never content to do what they have always done. Thus, social workers take the viewpoint that they are continually practicing, evaluating, and improving their craft.

In addition to terms in the book's title, the reader should be alert to the varied meanings of the term *client*. Common usage implies an individual who is the consumer of services. However, as used in this book, the term has a broader connotation. The **client** of the social worker may be an individual, a family or another form of household, or even a small group, committee, organization, neighborhood, community, or larger social system. Throughout the book, the term *client* is occasionally expanded to mention clientele, clients, client groups, or client systems, reminding the reader that the traditional narrow definition of *client* is not intended.

Finally, the term **intervention** is sometimes confusing to someone new to social work. The practice of social work is all about change—for example, change in the client's thoughts, perceptions, and actions, as well as change in the environment that affects or impinges on the client. The word *intervention* suggests that the social worker enters into and guides the client's search and struggle to deal more effectively with some particular challenge or problem.

New to This Edition

Techniques and Guidelines for Social Work Practice has been carefully updated to provide students with easy access to current information on fundamental techniques required for social work practice from the generalist perspective. Virtually every chapter and every item has been revised to add new understanding, to delete outdated material, and so far as we are able, to offer clear descriptions and explanations. In addition, new features of this tenth edition of *Techniques and Guidelines* include:

- The brief descriptions of intervention approaches commonly used by social workers (see Chapter 6) have been expanded to include dialectical behavioral therapy and various trauma-related approaches.
- Several new items related to direct-practice interventions are included in this edition: clarifying roles and responsibilities, the meaning of work in social functioning, assessing a client's needed level of care, mandated reporting of abuse and neglect, understanding the family life cycle, accessing evidence-based information, and providing support for caregivers.
- We have also added two new indirect-practice items: conducting community assets assessments and participatory action planning.
- An item on measuring client change with frequency counts was added to Chapter 14 to complement the items on measuring with individualized and standardized assessment scales.
- In Chapter 15 new items related to the client with a personality disorder and the client or family experiencing an adoption have been added.
- With each new edition of this text it has been necessary to delete some items in order to make room for new content we believed was important to include. Many of these deleted items are quite relevant today and we are making them available by indicating through marginal notes how to access them. The notes appear near related content in this current edition.

Supplements for Instructors

For instructors using this book in their classes, we have created an Instructor's Manual and Test Bank to assist them in using this text. This manual can be obtained from your campus Pearson representative or by writing to Pearson Education (One Lake Street, Upper Saddle River, NJ, 07458).

Acknowledgments

Social work practice involves many different activities with a wide variety of clients having many different problems and concerns. Moreover, social work practice takes place within a wide spectrum of organizational settings and social environments. Consequently, social work practice entails a vast array of knowledge and skills. This book is ambitious in the sense that it describes techniques and guidelines used by social workers practicing in different settings and with many differing types of clients and situations. That goal and broad scope calls for more expertise than that possessed by its two authors. Consequently, in preparing this book we asked more than 65 colleagues and former students in social work practice and social work education to critique our drafts of the items included in the book. We thank them for enhancing the quality of this publication, but take full responsibility for the final product.

We would also like to acknowledge the following individuals, who reviewed this tenth edition and offered suggestions for improving this publication: Kathleen Belanger, Stephen F. Austin State University; Rosalyln Deckerhoff, Florida State University; Kimberly Delles, Aurora University; Lettie Lockhart, University of Georgia; and Patricia Magee, Pittsburg State University.

Bradford W. Sheafor
Charles R. Horejsi

PART 1

SOCIAL WORK AND
THE SOCIAL WORKER

Social work is an indispensable profession in our complex and ever-changing society. But it is an often misunderstood profession, in part because it is a profession characterized by considerable diversity. Indeed, social workers engage in a broad range of activities within many types of settings and with many different people. Some social workers deal intensely with individuals and families, whereas others work with groups, organizations, or whole communities. Some deal primarily with children, others work with older persons. Some are counselors and psychotherapists, others are supervisors, administrators, program planners, or fund-raisers. Some focus on family violence and others specialize in how to provide housing or medical care to the poor. This variety is what makes social work so challenging and stimulating. But it is because of this diversity of both clients and activities that it is so difficult to answer the simple question: What is social work?

The task of concisely defining social work in a manner that encompasses all of what social workers do has challenged the profession throughout its history. At a very fundamental level, **social work** is a profession devoted to helping people function as well as they can within their social environments and, when necessary, to changing their environments to make positive social functioning possible. This theme of improving person-in-environment functioning is clarified and illustrated throughout this text.

The authors' perspective of social work is captured in the following three-part definition of a social worker. A social worker

1. has the recognized professional preparation (i.e., knowledge, ethics, and competencies) and the requisite skills needed to provide human services sanctioned by society, and

2. especially to engage vulnerable populations (e.g., children, older people, the poor, women, persons with disabilities, ethnic groups) in efforts to bring about needed change in the clients themselves, the people around them, or related social institutions,

3. so that these individuals and groups are able to meet their social needs, prevent or eliminate difficulties, make maximum use of their abilities and strengths, lead full and satisfying lives, and contribute fully to strengthening society.

In order to be a responsible professional, the social worker must understand and function within the profession's accepted areas of expertise. Throughout its history, social work has been portrayed as both an art (one's personal characteristics) and a science (a base of knowledge and skill required to be an effective professional). Part I of this book addresses the most fundamental elements of social work practice—the blending of the person and the profession. These elements must be clearly understood before a social worker can most effectively use the techniques and guidelines described in the subsequent parts of the book to assist vulnerable and disenfranchised people as they seek to prevent or resolve the complex social problems that arise in their daily lives.

1

The Domain of the Social Work Profession

LEARNING OBJECTIVES

At the conclusion of this chapter, the reader should be prepared to:

- Describe the unique place of social work among the several helping professions.
- Identify that the improvement of people's social functioning and changing detrimental social conditions are the dual responsibilities of social workers.
- Recognize that social work's person-in-environment focus requires the social worker to address issues and problems ranging from those of the individual to those impacting the community or society as a whole.
- Identify the merging of client, social worker, agency, and social policies and programs during the process of planned change.

When a person sets out to help others, he or she assumes a serious responsibility. The responsible helper from every profession must practice within his or her **professional domain** (i.e., the profession's area of expertise) if clients or patients are to receive the most effective services that the professional is prepared to provide. Indeed, professional helpers can harm those they intend to help if the helpers' activities extend beyond their professional boundaries because these boundaries identify and encompass the services its members are best prepared to deliver. These boundaries also determine the content of professional social work education and training.

This text is concerned with the profession of social work and how social workers assist people in addressing a variety of different problems and issues that confront them. Thus, understanding the professional domain of social work is prerequisite to helping clients address their issues.

Social work is, indeed, a curious name for a profession. In times that emphasize image over substance, it is clearly a title that lacks pizzazz. In fact, the use of the word *work* makes it seem burdensome and boring. Social work is a title that many social workers have wished they could change, possibly without understanding where it came from in the first place.

The title is attributed to Jeffrey Brackett (1860–1949), who served for nearly 30 years on the Massachusetts Board of Charities and later became the first director of what is now the Simmons College School of Social Work. In the early 1900s, Brackett argued that the word *social* should be part of this developing profession's title because it depicts the focus on people's interactions with important forces that shape their lives, such as family members, friends, or a myriad of other factors, including their relevant cultural or ethnic group, school, job, neighborhood, community, and so on. He added the word *work* to differentiate professional practice from what he considered the often misguided and self-serving philanthropic activity of wealthy volunteers. Brackett believed including *work* in the profession's title emphasized that its activities were to be orderly, responsible, and disciplined—not something to be engaged in by volunteers or those simply curious about other people's problems.

Social work, then, is an accurate title for a profession that applies helping techniques in a disciplined manner to address social problems. During the years since Brackett convinced early helping services providers to accept this title, the domain of social work has expanded and its methods have been reshaped by knowledge drawn from the social and behavioral sciences. Yet the title continues to describe this profession's central focus today.

THE SOCIAL WORK DOMAIN

It is important for the social worker to carefully examine the domain of social work (i.e., to understand its purpose, focus, scope, and sanction). This is critical for students because educational programs divide the study of social work into units, or courses, and this can lead to familiarity with the parts without necessarily understanding the whole. Yet the practice of social work requires attention to the whole of the profession's mission.

Another reason for understanding the social work domain is to help guard against **professional drift**, which is the neglect of a profession's traditional purpose and functions in favor of activities associated with another discipline. This happens most often in clinical settings when social workers align themselves too closely with models and theories used in medicine, psychology, and other disciplines that tend to minimize attention to social policy and social justice issues. These individuals may come to define themselves as their job title first (e.g., therapist, probation officer) and social worker second—or perhaps not as a social worker at all. Professional drift is also seen among administrators and managers, too, who were trained as social workers but identify primarily with the existing procedures of specific organizations rather than also introducing the perspectives of the social work profession. When professional drift occurs, it is a disservice to one's clients, social agency, and community, for it diminishes the unique commitment, perspective, and competencies that social work brings to the helping process.

A precise and generally agreed-upon understanding of the boundaries that mark the several helping professions does not exist. Different disciplines (e.g., social work, clinical psychology, school counseling, and marriage and family therapy) have claimed their domains without collaboration or mutual agreement about where one profession ends and another begins or where they appropriately overlap. This problem is further complicated by the fact that each state that licenses the practice of these professions is free to establish its own definitions of professional boundaries. It is important, therefore, to approach learning about social work's domain with recognition that the boundaries between professions are sometimes blurred.

Social Work's Purpose

An understanding of the social work profession begins with a deep appreciation of humans as social beings. People are, indeed, social creatures. They need other people. Each individual's growth and development requires the guidance, nurturing, and protection provided by others. And that person's concept of self—and even his or her very survival, both physically and psychologically—is tied to the decisions and actions of other people. It is this interconnectedness and interdependence of people and the power of social relationships that underpins social workers' commitment to improve the quality and effectiveness of those interactions and relationships—in other words, to enhance clients' social functioning and, at the same time, to improve the social conditions that affect social functioning.

Improved Social Functioning

The concept of social functioning is a key to understanding the unique focus of social work and distinguishing it from the other helping professions. *Social functioning* relates to a person's ability to accomplish those tasks and activities necessary to meet his or her basic needs and perform his or her major social roles in the society. As Maslow (1970) suggests in his *hierarchy of human needs*, the most basic human needs concern having adequate food, shelter, and medical care, as well as being safe and protected from harm. At an important, but not quite so critical, level, people need to feel that they belong within their social networks, experience some level of acceptance and respect from others, and have the opportunity to fulfill their own potential (i.e., self-actualization). Indeed, one aspect of the diversity in the profession of social work is that social workers are prepared to help clients improve social functioning related to all levels of these basic human needs.

Another illustration of the diversity of human situations social workers address relates to the fact that their clients typically are expected to simultaneously perform several social roles, including, for example, those of being a family member, parent, spouse, student, patient, employee, neighbor, and citizen. Depending on the person's gender, ethnicity, culture, religion, abilities, occupation, and so on, these roles may be vague or quite prescribed. Furthermore, they may change over time, leading to confusion, tension, and conflict in families, at school, or at work. Thus, the concept of improving social functioning includes the wide range of actions that social workers might take to help clients strengthen the match or fit between an individual's capacities to perform these multiple social roles, and resolving the sometimes conflicting demands, expectations, resources, and opportunities within his or her social and economic environment.

Although the social work profession is concerned with the social functioning of all people, it has traditionally prioritized the needs of the most vulnerable members of society and those who experience social injustice, discrimination, and oppression. The most vulnerable people in a society are often young children, the frail elderly, persons living in poverty, persons with severe physical or mental disabilities, persons who are gay or lesbian, and persons of minority ethnic/racial backgrounds.

To carry out their commitment to improving people's social functioning, social workers are involved primarily in the activities classified as social care, social treatment, and social enhancement. **Social care** refers to those actions and efforts designed to provide people in need with access to the basics of life (e.g., food, shelter, and protection from harm) and opportunities to meet their psychosocial needs (e.g., belonging, acceptance, and self-actualization). In social care, the focus is on providing needed resources and/ or helping the client be as comfortable as possible in a difficult situation that either cannot be changed or modified in the immediate future. Examples of social care would be efforts to help older people adjust to the somewhat restricted lifestyle of living in nursing homes, adults who experience a serious and persistent mental illness, and persons who face a terminal or life-threatening situation.

Social treatment involves actions designed to modify or correct an individual's or a family's dysfunctional, problematic, or distressing patterns of thought, feeling, and behavior. In social treatment, the focus is primarily on facilitating individual or family change through education, counseling, or various forms of therapy. In some cases (e.g., children in foster care, hospice work), the social worker may provide both social care and social treatment to the same family.

A third form of intervention seeks to enhance, expand, or further develop the abilities and performance of persons who are already functioning well. **Social enhancement** services emphasize growth and development of clients in a particular area of functioning without a "problem" having necessarily been identified. Some examples of enhancement-oriented services are youth recreation programs, well-baby clinics, marriage-enrichment sessions, and job-training programs.

Improved Social Conditions

Social work's second broad area of emphasis is on shaping and creating environments that will be supportive and empowering. Underpinning this goal is one of the most fundamental social work values: a strong belief in the importance of social justice. **Social justice** refers to fairness and moral rightness in how institutions such as governments, corporations, and powerful groups recognize and support the basic human rights, dignity, and worth of all people. A closely related principle is *economic justice* (sometimes called *distributive justice*), which refers to basic fairness in the apportioning and distribution of economic resources, opportunities, and burdens (e.g., taxes, bank loans, business contracts). Social workers often favor the use of various laws, public policies, and other social and economic mechanisms to ensure that all people are valued and treated with fairness and that all have reasonable opportunities for social and economic security and advancement.

Very often, political controversy has its origin in differing conceptions of what is truly fair and just and in differing beliefs about whether and how society should assume responsibility for addressing human needs and problems. Most social workers would argue that social and economic policies must recognize that all people have the right to have their basic needs met—not because of individual achievement, but simply by virtue of one's inherent worth as a human being. Among those *basic human rights* are the following:

- The right to have the food, shelter, basic medical care, and essential social services necessary for one's survival
- The right to be protected from abuse, exploitation, and oppression
- The right to work and earn a sufficient wage to secure basic resources and live with dignity

- The right to marry who one chooses, to have a family, and to be with one's family
- The right to a basic education
- The right to own property
- The right to be protected from avoidable harm and injury in the workplace
- The right to worship as one chooses—or not at all, if one chooses
- The right to privacy
- The right to associate with those one chooses
- The right to accurate information about one's community and government
- The right to participate in and influence the decisions of one's government

Social workers would also argue that rights and responsibilities necessarily coexist. With every right comes a responsibility. For example:

- If a human has the right to the basic requirements for survival, then others have the responsibility to make sure that each person has food, shelter, and essential medical care.
- If people have the right to be protected from abuse, exploitation, and oppression, then others have the responsibility to create social programs and take actions that will provide this protection when required.
- If a person has the right to work and earn a living, then others have the responsibility to make sure that employment opportunities exist and that those who work are paid a living wage.

Situations of injustice develop when people are concerned only about their own rights and have lost a sense of responsibility for others and for society as a whole. Not infrequently, social workers become advocates for those who whose rights have been ignored or abused. And in many situations, social workers provide a voice for the vulnerable and oppressed.

More often than other helping professionals, social workers seek to bring about changes in the environments in which people must live and function. When working with individuals and families, these changes are often termed *environmental modifications*. An example would be efforts by a school social worker to prepare students for the return of a former classmate who was badly scarred in an automobile accident. Another example would be special training and guidance given to a foster mother so she can provide a calming and protective atmosphere for a young vulnerable foster child who is fearful of new people.

Even when working with an organization or a community, a social worker may seek to modify its wider environment. That may entail efforts to influence local decision-makers, businesses, political leaders, and governmental agencies so they will be more supportive and more responsive to a community's needs and problems. Such interventions may involve the worker in social research, social planning, and political action intended to develop and improve laws, social policies, institutions, and social systems so they will promote social and economic justice, expand opportunities for people, and improve the everyday circumstances in which people live. Specific examples would be expanding the availability of safe and affordable housing, creating incentives for businesses to hire people with disabilities, amending laws so they better prevent discrimination, and helping neighborhood and community organizations become politically active in addressing the issues they face.

In some situations it is possible to prevent a problem from developing or from getting worse. **Prevention** consists of those actions taken to eliminate social, economic, psychological, and other conditions known to cause or contribute to the formation of human problems. To be effective in prevention, social workers must be able to identify the specific factors and situations that contribute to the development of social problems and then select actions and activities that will reduce or eliminate their impact (see Item 12.13). Borrowing from the public health model, three levels of prevention can be identified:

Level 1: Primary prevention. Actions intended to deter the problem from ever developing

Level 2: Secondary prevention. Actions intended to detect a problem at its early stages and address it while it is still relatively easy to change

Level 3: Tertiary prevention. Actions intended to address an already serious problem in ways that keep it from growing even worse, causing additional damage, or spreading to others

Social Work's Focus

Social work is certainly not the only profession concerned with how individuals and families function, nor is it the only profession interested in social conditions and social problems. However, it is social work's *simultaneous focus* on both the person and the person's environment that makes social work unique among the various helping professions. This pivotal construct is termed **person-in-environment**.

Social workers strive to view each individual as a **whole person**, having many dimensions: biological, intellectual, emotional, social, familial, spiritual, economic, communal, and so on. It is this concern for the whole or the complete person that contributes to the breadth of issues addressed by the social work profession—for example, the individual's capacity to meet basic physical needs (food, housing, health care, etc.), the person's levels of knowledge and skills needed to cope with life's demands, the person's values about what is important in his or her own life and how others are viewed, the individual's goals and aspirations, and the like. It is important to note the person-in-environment construct uses the word *person*, not *personality*. Personality is but one component of the whole person. A focus only on personality without attending to other influences on that person would be incongruous with the domain of social work and slant it toward the domain of psychology.

A person always lives within a particular environment. As used here, the term **environment** refers to one's surroundings—that multitude of physical and social structures, forces, and processes that affect humans and all other life forms. Of particular interest to social workers are those systems, structures, and conditions that most frequently and most directly affect a person's day-to-day social functioning (i.e., the person's *immediate environment*). One's immediate environment includes the individual's family, close friends, neighborhood, workplace, and the services and programs he or she uses.

Social workers devote major attention to helping clients improve aspects of their immediate environment. In addition, they are also concerned about what can be termed the client's *distant environment*. These more remote influences have to do with what people need for healthy growth and development, such as clean air, drinkable water, shelter, and good soil to produce food. And because biological well-being is a prerequisite to positive social functioning, social workers must also be concerned with problems such as prevention of disease and pollution.

Because social relationships are of central concern to their profession, social workers must understand the power of a social environment—both its potentially helpful and harmful influences. Humans are social creatures with a strong need to be accepted by others. Achieving what others in our environment do is a powerful force for change—either positive or negative. Social workers also understand that if a person's environment changes to become more supportive and nurturing, that individual will be more likely to make positive changes in attitude and behavior.

Social Work's Scope

A profession's **scope** can be thought of as the range of activities and involvements appropriate to its mission. One way of describing social work's scope involves classifying the intervention by the size of the client system. Practice at the **micro level** focuses on the individual and his or her most intimate interactions, such as exchanges between husband and wife, parent and child, close friends, and family members. The terms *interpersonal helping, direct practice,* and *clinical practice* are often used interchangeably with *micro-level practice.*

At the other extreme, **macro-level** practice may involve work with and efforts to change an organization, community, state, or even society as a whole. Macro-level practice also deals with interpersonal relations, but these are the interactions between and among the people who represent organizations or are members of a work group such as an agency committee or interagency task force. When engaged in macro-level practice, the social worker is frequently involved in activities such as administration, fund-raising, proposed legislation testimony, policy analysis, class advocacy, and social resource development.

Between the micro and macro levels is **mezzo-level** (midlevel) practice. Practice at this level is concerned with relationships and interactions that are somewhat less intimate than those associated with family life but more personally meaningful than those occurring among organizational and institutional representatives. Examples of midlevel practice would be the change efforts with and within a self-help or therapy group, among peers at school or work, and among neighbors.

Some practice approaches address more than one intervention level. For example, the generalist perspective requires the social worker to be capable of practice at the micro, mezzo, and macro levels (see Chapter 6).

Social Work's Sanction

The concept of **sanction** refers to the authorization, approval, or permission needed to perform certain tasks or activities—ones that can have a significant impact on someone's life and possibly cause harm. Three sources provide sanction for social work practice. One of these is legislation at the state and federal levels that explicitly or implicitly recognizes and approves social work activities. This is most apparent in the state licensing and regulation of individual social work practitioners. Sanction is implicit in various forms of legislation that creates social programs and allocation of funds for social work activity.

A second source of sanction is the many private human services organizations (both nonprofit and profit-making agencies) that endorse social work by recruiting and hiring social workers to provide services or by purchasing services from social workers who are in private practice or employed by other agencies. Indirectly, then, the community sanctions and pays social workers to provide specific services.

Finally, the true test of public sanction for practice is the willingness of clients to seek out and use services offered by social workers. In order to win the trust of clients, social workers must demonstrate on a daily basis that they are capable of providing effective services and conduct themselves in a responsible and ethical manner.

In return for this sanction, both individual social work practitioners and the profession, through its professional organizations and through state licensing boards and accrediting bodies, are obliged to make sure that social work practitioners are competent and adhere to the *NASW Code of Ethics* (see Item 9.5).

AN OVERVIEW OF SOCIAL WORK PRACTICE

Indeed, many factors shape the work of the social worker. Figure 1.1 presents a model of the key factors that influence social work practice and shows how the content in the 16 chapters of this book fits together to reflect the whole of social work. The overlapping circles in the center of the figure depict the client (or client system) and the social worker as joined in an effort to bring about a desired change in the client's functioning or situation. This **planned change process** involves several phases during which the client and social worker move from their decision to initiate action to improve some aspect of the client's social functioning, through assessment and action phases and on to an evaluation of its success and a decision to terminate the helping activity. Although the social worker is expected to guide this process, the client must ultimately decide that change is needed and commit to utilizing the helping resources identified by or provided by the worker.

"The Client" side of Figure 1.1 indicates that the client's problem or concern is, most likely, the product of a combination of personal and environmental factors. Each client has a unique set of *personal characteristics* (e.g., age, gender, ethnicity, life experiences, beliefs, strengths, limitations, needs) that may have contributed in some way to the situation being addressed. Some of these personal characteristics will be important resources during the helping process.

Clients do not exist in isolation. Their *immediate environment* might include friends, family, school personnel, employers, natural helpers, neighborhood or community groups, or even other professional helpers, to mention just a few. In some cases these environmental influences have contributed to the client's problem and may need to become targets for change and others may be potential social supports and resources.

"The Social Worker" side of Figure 1.1 suggests that the worker brings unique personal characteristics and a professional background to the change process. These are experienced by the client through what the social worker actually does (i.e., the worker's activities and application of skills and techniques). What the worker does is a function of the specific professional role he or she has assumed and the conceptual framework(s) he or she has selected to guide practice. The social worker's *personal characteristics* encompass many factors. For example, the social worker's unique perspectives on the causes of human suffering, as well as her or his particular values, are inevitably introduced into the change process. Those perspectives will have been shaped by the social workers' unique life experiences of family, community, socioeconomic background, gender, age, sexual orientation, and the like. All of these characteristics to some degree affect the social worker–client relationship.

At the same time, the practitioner brings the special contribution of a *professional background* to social work, which differentiates the social worker from the client's friends, family, and the professionals representing other disciplines who may also be working with the client or have attempted to help in the past. What is this professional background?

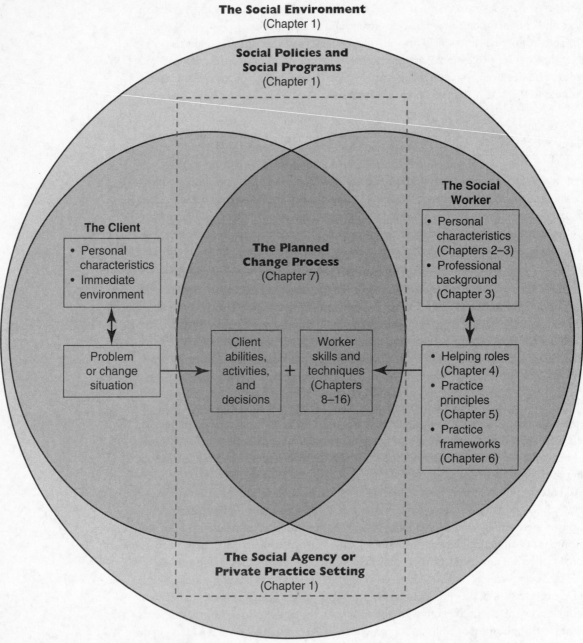

Figure 1.1
An Integrative View of Social Work Practice

First and foremost, the social worker brings the belief system, values, ethical principles, and focus on social functioning that are common to social work. Through education and experience, the social worker develops the "artistic" part of his or her helping skill (i.e., the practice wisdom and the natural ability to use his or her personal characteristics, special talents, and unique style to help clients). In addition, the social worker brings the "science" of social work (i.e., the knowledge about people and their social interactions, as well as knowledge about how to help them make changes in their circumstances and functioning).

As social workers carry out their responsibilities, they perform various *helping roles*. Indeed, social workers must be prepared to perform a wide variety of roles and functions, ranging from linking clients to appropriate resources, to assessing case situations and providing direct services, to planning and conducting social action.

The social work profession has a long history of adopting and using many different approaches in its efforts to provide needed and effective services. Although there is no established social work practice approach or strategy that fits all practice situations, some tried-and-true guidelines have evolved. These have been reduced to a set of *practice principles* that are, perhaps, the most universal directives for how a social worker should conduct her or his practice.

Another important element of the social worker's professional background is knowledge of the various *practice frameworks* that guide one's practice decisions and the change process (e.g., practice perspectives, theories, and models). The social worker must master several of these frameworks in order to select the most appropriate and effective approach for each client situation.

Finally, the social worker's *skills* and mastery of *techniques* are his or her most observable contribution to the change process. The skills or techniques selected by the social worker will depend, of course, on the nature of the client's problem or concern, the expectations of the practice setting, and the worker's own competence in using them.

Returning to Figure 1.1, it is important to recognize that social work practice usually takes place within a particular **social environment**—namely, the context of a social agency. For the client, this agency is a type of *distant environment*. Typically, the agency has been shaped by local, state, and/or national social policies and its programs are a reflection of society's values and beliefs. Commitment to the social welfare of its members varies among societies; within the United States, it even varies among regions, states, and communities. Having sound **social policies** aimed at improving the well-being of all people is essential for a just, healthy, and productive society. Yet, every social worker knows that the country's social policies leave much to be desired.

Through its legislative and other decision-making bodies, society creates **social programs** intended to help certain people. These programs take three basic forms:

- *Social provisions* involve providing tangible goods (e.g., money, food, clothing, and housing) for persons in need.
- *Personal services* include intangible services (e.g., counseling, therapy, and learning experiences) intended to help people resolve and/or prevent their problems.
- *Social action* programs are concerned with changing aspects of the social environment to make it more responsive to people's needs and wants.

The particular philosophy on which social programs are built has a significant bearing on how smoothly they operate, how effective they are, and how they affect both the client and the social worker. The two dominant competing philosophies of social welfare, a safety net or a social utility, are at the heart of considerable debate about how to provide human services.

Historically, the prevailing philosophy in the United States contended that, ideally, private charities (e.g., nonprofit agencies and churches), with the aid of voluntary donations, should address such problems as poverty, lack of health care, homelessness, hunger, dependent children, and the like. If public tax-supported social programs were to exist, they would serve only as a *safety net*, providing a minimal level of assistance to those who are in desperate economic straits and who can demonstrate "real need" by meeting strict eligibility criteria. In other words, these public programs would be a last resort for those who are in a dire situation. It was gradually recognized that private funding could not come close to meeting the income, health, mental health, and other needs of the most vulnerable members of the society, and so government-supported agencies are increasingly providing the bulk of the human services for people experiencing serious social issues.

A second philosophy of social welfare, the *social utilities* conception, considers public tax-supported social programs to be first-line functions of society (similar to a public education, libraries, highways, and law enforcement). In other words, this view is that social welfare is a fundamental government responsibility and it should make these programs available to all of its citizens, usually without a means test and without having to prove the existence of a genuine emergency. If a fee is charged for a particular service, the amount it is minimal or easily waived. Such programs are able to place an emphasis on prevention and early intervention.

Social welfare benefits, services, and programs are typically provided through a **social agency** or an organization created for this purpose. For the most part, social work is an agency-based profession and most social workers are agency employees. A social agency might be a public human services department, mental health center, school, hospital, neighborhood center, or any of a number of differing organizational structures. It may be a *public agency* supported by tax funds and governed by elected officials, a *private nonprofit agency* operating under the auspices of a volunteer board and supported primarily by fees and voluntary donations, or a *private for-profit agency* providing services under the auspices of a corporation. Regardless of the structure, the basic functions of the agency are to administer social programs and to monitor the quality of the helping process.

To perform these functions, the agency must secure money, staff, and other resources; determine which people are eligible for its services; and maintain an administrative structure that will meet targeted social needs in an efficient and effective manner. The most important ingredient of a social agency is its people. Receptionists, custodians, administrators, and service providers all must work together to deliver successful programs. Often, several helping professions are employed in the same agency. In such interdisciplinary programs, each profession brings its own perspective on helping—as well as the special competencies appropriate to the domain of that profession.

Social workers are also increasingly providing services through **private practice**. These private practitioners maintain an independent practice, as is typical in medicine and law, and contract directly with their clients to provide services. Unless the practice is large and involves several social workers and/or professionals for other disciplines, it functions more as a small business than a social agency.

CONCLUSION

Social work is one of several human services professions that have been sanctioned by society to help improve the quality of life for its people. Other such helping professions include clinical psychology, drug and alcohol counseling, marriage and family counseling, school psychology, medicine, rehabilitation counseling, nursing, and so on. The uniqueness of social work among these professions is its focus on the social functioning of people and helping them interact more effectively with their environments—both their immediate and distant environments. Social workers perform this role by assisting people in addressing issues in their social functioning and working to prevent social problems from emerging or, if they already exist, from getting worse.

Increasingly, conflict and competition arise among the various human services professions over issues of the domain (or turf) of each. These squabbles and power struggles tend to center on competition for jobs, salary, status, and control, as well as disagreements over which profession is most qualified to perform certain tasks. To minimize the effect of this head butting on service delivery, it is important for the members of these professions to engage in **interprofessional collaboration** as they provide their services. However, each discipline must avoid letting its practice activities drift into the areas of expertise of the other professions.

Social workers have historically claimed they represent the profession best prepared to help people resolve problems in social functioning and to guide social change efforts that can prevent problems from occurring or growing worse. It is important that social workers maintain their focus on these central features of their domain.

SELECTED BIBLIOGRAPHY

Maslow, Abraham H. *Motivation and Personality*. New York: Harper and Row, 1970.
National Association of Social Workers. *Code of Ethics*. Washington, DC: NASW, 1999.
Sheafor, Bradford W., Armando T. Morales, and Malcolm E. Scott. *Social Work: A Profession of Many Faces*, 12th ed. rev. Upper Saddle River, NJ: Pearson, 2012.

2

Merging Person
with Profession

LEARNING OBJECTIVES

At the conclusion of this chapter, the reader should be prepared to:

- Recognize that being a social worker can be both personally rewarding and, at times, discouraging and frustrating.
- Recognize that social work is a career that can affect the social worker's personal life.
- Identify tasks a new social worker should be prepared to complete in order to develop a positive professional reputation.
- Identify the importance of a social worker being prepared to address issues in agency functioning and/or community conditions that compromise or threaten the quality of life for residents of the community.
- Demonstrate commitment to being fit for social work practice and seeking help in periods of stress or when addressing personal problems.
- Describe the importance of not taking oneself too seriously and enjoying the practice of social work by maintaining a sense of humor about the trials and tribulations of social work practice.

Social workers' professional roles and responsibilities are always, to some degree, intertwined with their personal lives. They will try to keep professional concerns separate from their personal and family lives but the very nature of social work makes this difficult.

The social work profession views the individual client as a whole person, with many dimensions to consider such as the physical, emotional, psychological, social, spiritual, and the intellectual. This, of course, also describes the social worker, for he or she responds as a whole person to the demands of the job and profession. Thus, a social worker's beliefs, values, physical and emotional well-being, and all other dimensions of living will both influence and be influenced by what the social worker encounters each day in his or her professional practice.

The social worker views the client as always functioning within a particular situational and environmental context. Social workers, too, function within various professional and organizational contexts. Also, they have numerous roles and responsibilities in addition to those associated with their jobs. For example, a social worker is part of a family or household, often a spouse or partner, often a parent, part of friendship and social networks, and a resident in a particular neighborhood and community. Moreover, he or she may be a member of an ethnic group, affiliated with a religious denomination or faith community, a member of a special-interest group or political party, and a member of one or more service organizations. Given this multitude of connections and contexts, the social worker is challenged to cope with the tensions and conflicts that can easily arise between personal matters and professional obligations.

Although this book focuses primarily on the activities that occur during the hours that the social worker devotes to her or his profession, this chapter examines how the realities of practice may impinge on the worker's private life. The observations presented here are intended to assist social workers in striking a healthy balance between their personal needs and responsibilities and the demands and responsibilities of social work practice.

SELECTING SOCIAL WORK AS A CAREER

People's lives are shaped by the choices they make. Because choosing social work as a career has some unique implications for self and family, those attracted to this profession must consider (and periodically reconsider) if social work should be their life's work. There must be a good fit between the person and his or her occupation. A mismatch can cause stress and threaten one's health and well-being. A person who feels trapped in the profession cannot bring the desired energy and commitment to the helping process, and consequently, clients will be poorly served.

Social Work as a Life Companion

An individual considering a social work career must be satisfied and comfortable with his or her answers to the following questions:

- Is being a social worker a meaningful and worthwhile way for me to live my life?
- Will the practice of social work be an appropriate use of my special gifts, abilities, and skills?
- Do my personal beliefs, values, ethical standards, and goals in life fit well with those of the social work profession?
- What impact will my career in social work have on my family?
- What impact will this career have on my physical and mental health and the overall quality of my life?

Each person needs to identify what is truly important. The work and rewards that accrue from being a social worker should be consistent with those priorities.

Earning a Living as a Social Worker

People do not choose the social work profession because of the money they will earn, but they cannot devote their time to the practice of social work unless they can earn a decent living. Social work has never been a high-paying profession and in contrast to some occupations, the earning power of social workers does not rise rapidly or continually as they gain skill and experience. Social workers earn a modest income and have limited opportunity to climb the economic ladder. However, the satisfaction of doing something truly worthwhile and making a difference in the lives of people is often viewed by social workers as an offsetting form of compensation.

Most entry-level social work jobs involve the provision of services directly to clients. After several years in the direct services, many social workers seek positions in supervision and administration as a way of increasing their incomes. This may be a wise move for those attracted to management tasks such as budgeting, policy development, public relations, personnel selection, and staff training. It may be an unwise decision for those whose job satisfaction comes primarily from direct contact with clients.

Those entering social work should expect to change jobs from 5 to 10 times during their working years. Sometimes a job change is prompted by an agency's staff reductions, but most often it is a matter of personal choice. Among the reasons why social workers change jobs are the following:

- Desire for higher salary, better benefits, or job security
- Desire to learn a new field of practice and work with clients having a different set of problems or concerns
- Desire for more discretion and control over practice decisions and methods
- Desire to work in a setting that embraces new ideas and innovations
- Desire for a less stressful or a safer work environment
- Opportunity to receive better supervision or additional training
- Desire to remove oneself from conflicts with a supervisor or agency administrator
- Need to adjust work schedule due to changes in personal or family life (e.g., a marriage, divorce, birth of child, illness)

Those preparing to enter social work are advised to identify their personal and career goals and formulate a plan for reaching those goals. Examples of goals include becoming skilled in work with certain client populations, having the opportunity to design an innovative program, becoming an administrator of a certain type of agency, conducting research on a particular topic, and so on. In these times of rapid change, it can be difficult to develop such a plan and even more difficult to follow it. However, career planning provides a framework for making decisions about what experiences and training to pursue.

The School-to-Job Transition

Social work is a rewarding career but it is full of challenges. For many social workers these challenges will become apparent as they transition from the role of student into that of being a paid professional within an agency setting. Many new social workers will experience a reality shock. For example, in describing her new job, a very capable recent graduate told one of the authors: "I had no idea that my clients would be so troubled, my job so difficult, and that my agency setting would be so complex."

Those beginning their first social work job soon realize that there is seldom enough time to do all that needs to be done. Many discover that in far too many social agencies, core social work values and ethical principles have taken a backseat to the forces of political pressure, administrative expediency, budget limitations, the fear of lawsuits, and the day-by-day struggle to cope with the workload. Many find that some colleagues have lost their enthusiasm and are too fatigued and demoralized to be effective. If the workplace environment is rushed and stressful, it can be a challenge to maintain one's professional ideals and standards.

Every new social worker is somewhat frustrated by the slowness of change, whether that change is by individual clients, organizations, or communities. They discover that identifying or knowing what needs to change is relatively easy compared to actually achieving that change. Programs of social work education teach about the process of change and the techniques for facilitating change, but they cannot teach the personal qualities of patience, perseverance, tenacity, and tolerance so necessary for turning good ideas into reality.

New social work graduates who were high academic achievers may face a special challenge as they move into agency-based practice. Simply put, they are accustomed to doing grade-A academic work and they expect to do high-quality work on the job. They often discover, however, that there is not enough time for perfection and probably only enough time for C-level, or average, work.

Some of the agencies and organizations that employ social workers provide a superb work environment for their employees, but far too many work settings are noisy, crowded, and even dangerous. Dissatisfaction with such conditions has led many experienced social workers to enter private practice in search of a more agreeable work environment and more control over what they do and how they do it. Although this is an understandable response to frustration, it has the effect of drawing talented social workers away from the profession's traditional commitment to serving the poor and oppressed. Throughout their careers, social workers must struggle to reconcile their desire for adequate income and a decent work environment with their concern for the poor and a commitment to social and economic justice.

Many new social workers are surprised to discover that office or organizational politics plays a significant role in the decisions and functioning of their agency settings. Within every organization—whether a business, a social agency, a religious body, or a professional association—people use their power and authority to move the organization in directions they perceive as desirable. Thus, all organizations are inherently political to some degree. Social workers, however, must guard against becoming so absorbed in the politics of the workplace that they lose sight of their agency's real purpose and the people it is to serve.

ESTABLISHING ONESELF AS A SOCIAL WORKER

It is not enough for the new social worker to carry his or her credentials and skills into a job and simply assume that everything will fall in place for a satisfying and effective career. The social worker must first demonstrate to clients, colleagues, and other agencies in the community that he or she is competent and trustworthy.

Acquiring a Reputation

Every social worker will acquire a reputation within his or her agency, within the local human services network, and among the clients he or she serves. That reputation will have a significant impact on his or her work with clients, professional communications, interagency cooperation, and whether the worker is considered for promotion or offered other social work jobs. Social workers should regularly review how their statements, decisions, behavior, and associations are shaping their reputations.

One need only sit in on a few support group meetings or spend an hour in an agency waiting room to realize that many clients talk freely about the social workers, doctors, teachers, and other professionals they know. They tell friends, neighbors, and other clients about how they have been treated and who does a good job and who to avoid. Clients are especially sensitive to whether social workers really listen to what they are saying, are available when needed, and fair in the decisions they make.

Within an agency, each social worker acquires a reputation as an employee. Over time, the other agency employees form an opinion about the worker's competence, whether she or he is honest and dependable, and a good team member. That reputation will affect the willingness of the other employees to offer their support, assistance, and cooperation.

Reputation is a determining factor in whether a private practice or a fee-for-service program will succeed. If they have a choice, people will select a professional with a good reputation and avoid using agencies and professionals who have poor or questionable reputations. In addition, those who are in a position to refer clients to a social worker will select a practitioner who has a reputation for being competent, ethical, and effective.

A good reputation can take years to develop but can be quickly destroyed by others. For this reason, many cultures consider slander and the spreading of gossip that can ruin a person's reputation to be among the most reprehensible of moral transgressions.

Conflict over Agency Policy

Every social worker comes to her or his practice setting with a set of beliefs, values, standards, and expectations. It is inevitable that she or he will, from time to time, disagree with agency policy and administrative decisions. How is a worker to respond in such situations? The decision on what to do must be based on a thoughtful examination of the issue or conflict. One might begin this examination by seeking answers to the following questions:

- Which of my beliefs, values, or standards is threatened or violated by this agency policy or decision? Is my concern or conflict a matter of principle or possibly arising from my own bias or perhaps from a difference in professional or administrative style?
- Why has my agency administration taken this position? What are the arguments for and against this position? What political and economic forces and circumstances gave rise to this position?
- What impact does this position or policy have on those served by my agency? How will it affect those most at risk and most in need of agency services?
- What impact does this position or policy have on the community? Does it enhance and strengthen the functioning of individuals, families, and the community? Does it recognize the obligation of communities and society to promote the common good, expand social and economic opportunities, and provide assistance to those unable to meet their basic needs?
- Does the position or policy recognize the dignity and worth of every person as well as the basic right to self-determination? Does the position recognize that every competent person is responsible for his or her own actions and must accept the consequences for violating legitimate laws?

If the worker concludes that this is, indeed, a serious matter and is clearly unfair and harmful to clients, he or she should seek guidance from trusted, knowledgeable, and experienced peers on how it might be changed. If the problematic situation cannot be changed, the worker must ponder his or her future with the agency. In extreme cases and when there is no acceptable alternative, the worker may need to seek employment elsewhere.

One of the most painful situations social workers can experience is to discover that they are employed by an organization that does not really respect its clients, value professional competence, or expect ethical conduct. Such situations can arise when an organization's administration is more concerned about politics, cost cutting, or profit than providing needed services.

If the worker is expected or asked by his or her agency to perform a task or take an action that would violate his or her professional or personal moral standards, the worker should voice these concerns, document them in a letter to the administrator, and formally request to be excused from having to participate in the questionable activity.

All organizations develop a culture consisting of its values, expectations, and group norms. Once formed, an organizational culture tends to perpetuate itself while exerting a pervasive effect on its employees who are rewarded when they accept this culture and ostracized when they do not. A social worker employed by an organization with a destructive culture will need to work to change that culture or else look for another job.

When issues are complex, knowing what is right is never easy and doing what is right is always difficult.

Promoting Social Justice

Most of the individuals attracted to social work are somewhat idealistic. They want to make the world a better place. As discussed in Chapter 1, the social work profession and social workers strive to create a more just and humane society. Social workers seek to establish **social justice**, a condition where everyone in the society shares in the same rights, opportunities, and protections.

All considerations of social justice rest on the core beliefs that every human being has inherent dignity and is intrinsically valuable. Moreover, every individual possesses certain inalienable rights. This worth of the individual person is not something that must be earned or proved, nor is it a privilege obtained because of one's skin color, nationality, gender, income, social status, health, education, political affiliation, occupation, or other life circumstances. Simply by virtue of being human, every person has a right to be treated with fairness and respect, protected from abuse and exploitation, and granted opportunities to have a family, secure an education and meaningful work, and have access to basic health care and social services.

A multitude of economic, political, historical, and social forces can give rise to unjust and dehumanizing conditions. Because an injustice can be woven into a society's dominant belief systems and into social and economic structures, situations of exploitation, oppression, and discrimination may go unnoticed by all but those who are directly harmed. Social workers must be always open to the possibility that they or their agencies may unintentionally and unknowingly contribute to or perpetuate a social injustice.

Usually we do not feel personally responsible for the existence of social and economic injustice. When an injustice is brought to our attention, we are likely to conclude that it is the fault of society and beyond our control. We may feel helpless and conclude that we are too small a force to make any real change in the situation. Social injustice is indeed a societal problem, but the responsibility to oppose injustice rests with the individual.

Achieving social justice is a complex undertaking, and even among people of goodwill and compassion, there will be different perspectives on what is truly fair and what actions move us toward a more just and humane society. Social workers must pursue social and economic justice in ways that recognize legitimate differences of opinion while maintaining respect for those with whom they disagree.

In order to correct an injustice, people must become politically involved, speak out, and propose practical solutions. However, those who seek social reform must also understand that they will likely pay a price for challenging powerful individuals and groups that stand to lose money, power, or position if the status quo is altered. Those who work for justice may be ridiculed, lose their jobs, or, in extreme cases, subjected to physical threats and injury.

Political Involvement

Efforts to advance social and economic justice require participation in the political process. **Politics** is the art of gaining, exercising, and retaining power. Some social workers are attracted to politics; others find it distasteful. The degree to which one becomes involved in political activity will reflect such factors as level of interest, available time, and temperament. Being an informed and conscientious voter is, of course, essential, but more is required of social workers if they are to remain true to the "soul" of their chosen profession. A social worker's participation in the political process will usually involve one or more of the following activities:

- Assessing the impact of an existing or proposed law, social policy, or program on people, especially the most vulnerable members of society
- Participating in the development and formulation of just and effective social policies
- Educating the public about the social dimensions and ramifications of existing and proposed laws and policies
- Entering into the public debate and advocating for needed changes
- Working for the election of those who will advance social and economic justice

As social workers become involved in the political process, they must decide where they stand on complex issues. This can be difficult because there are usually some valid arguments on all sides of the debate. Most social workers tend to be on the liberal or progressive side of the conservative-to-liberal continuum. However, it is a mistake for social workers to assume that they must choose between being either a liberal or a conservative. Rather, they may need to be a little of both. Everyone who is intellectually and spiritually alive is liberal in the sense of being open to the truth, regardless of its source; desirous of needed change; and accepting of governmental action if it will expand opportunities and improve the lives of people. Similarly, every thoughtful and responsible person will be conservative in the sense of wanting to preserve those values, social arrangements, and approaches that have been fair and beneficial to people. The newest idea is not necessarily the best one and, not infrequently, there is a negative side to government intervention. Thus, depending on the issue, a social worker might line up on either the liberal or conservative side of a debate. The merits and wisdom of a proposal, and not political ideology or political party, should determine one's stance on an issue.

The political health of a nation, state, or community depends on informed citizens debating the issues and finding feasible ways of achieving social and economic justice and advancing the common good. Such a debate requires not only mutual trust and goodwill among all involved but also a respect for diversity, a common language and terminology, and an agreement on core beliefs about people, society, and government. Those presenting or arguing their viewpoints should presume that those on the other side of the issue are acting in good faith and merit respect and a genuine effort to understand their opinions and reasoning. People destroy the possibility of finding common ground and a workable compromise if they replace dialogue with monologue, reason with slogans, and civility with coercion.

Political involvement can be tiring and frustrating. Some lose heart when confronted with setbacks. In order to continue working for justice and needed changes, year after year, social workers must develop the personal qualities of patience, perseverance, and tolerance. They need to present their positions without being shrill and offensive. They must hold to their core beliefs and principles without becoming narrow and partisan. They need to guard against being manipulated and refrain from manipulating others. And they need to focus on what brings people together rather than on what divides them.

Social workers are often in a position to directly observe the impact of a social policy or program on the lives of people. Such observations are seldom available to the politicians who write the laws and the administrators who design programs and formulate operating procedures. Thus, the social worker has both an opportunity and the obligation to document the real impact of legislation, policies, and administrative decisions, as well as to offer ideas on how policies and programs can be made more humane, effective, and efficient. Social workers who are skilled speakers and writers can make valuable contributions to the education of legislators and the citizenry.

THE INTERPLAY OF ONE'S PERSONAL AND PROFESSIONAL LIVES

Social workers frequently meet people who have overcome great obstacles and who care deeply about their families and communities. Getting to know these individuals is an inspiring and uplifting experience. At the same time, social work practice can be stressful and requires a heavy commitment of time and energy. Those demands affect the social worker and his or her family.

Being Changed by Your Clients

In every type of practice, social workers will meet clients and other people who are truly remarkable because of their courage, wisdom, compassion, and generosity. Many will have faced great challenges and hardship. Social workers have the awesome opportunity of learning from these individuals. At a deeper level, many professional relationships are an exchange of intangible gifts and both the social worker and the client stand to be changed by what they give to and receive from each other.

One cannot begin to really know a client without coming to understand how the client thinks and feels about life. In many cases, the client's perspectives, beliefs, and values will be significantly different from those of the social worker. This may challenge the worker to rethink his or her own life experiences and reevaluate priorities.

A social worker may be nudged toward further self-examination by a client's criticism. A client might, for example, accuse a social worker of being rushed, insensitive, or unfair. The worker must remain open to the possibility that a client's uncomplimentary evaluation is accurate and, if that is the case, strive to modify the attitudes and behaviors that have offended the client.

The clients who cause a social worker to feel anguish and inadequacy are a particularly painful source of a worker's self-examination. Not infrequently, the worker's skills and the available resources are insufficient or ineffective in helping a troubled client modify destructive behavior. In such situations, the worker will feel powerless and help-less as these clients make bad choices that disrupt family relationships, damage their health, or get them into trouble with the law. These humbling experiences teach the social worker that she or he is but one small influence in a client's life.

Personal Responses to Clients in Need

Many of the clients served by social workers live in poverty and experience misery because they cannot pay for even the basics such as food, shelter, and health care. By comparison, the social worker, with only a modest income, seems quite well off. This situation confronts the worker with a troubling question about his or her individual responsibility. Once a social worker has done all he or she can do as a professional and as an agency's representative, what, if anything, remains as a purely personal responsibility? Should a social worker ever spend his or her own money to address a client's emergency?

Some would quickly answer no and argue that meeting people's basic needs is a community and governmental responsibility. For a social worker to do so, even occasion-ally, would be unreasonable. Moreover, it might make it too easy for the community or government to ignore and avoid its responsibilities. On the other hand, some profession-als might argue that even when social welfare systems fail to meet basic human needs, the social worker still has a personal moral and ethical responsibility to respond in certain cases. It can be argued that a social worker, because of his or her knowledge, has a unique obligation beyond that of the ordinary citizen.

Ultimately, one's answer to this complex question is a matter of conscience and a judgment call as to what action would be helpful to the client and reasonable for the social worker. The social worker might consider the following questions in formulating his or her response:

- What situations, if any, require some extraordinary and essentially personal response by the professional that is above and beyond what the agency provides? What if the situation involves a person who is especially vulnerable and at risk of imminent harm?
- Given that social workers may encounter desperate and emergency situations on a daily basis, is it realistic to even consider using one's personal financial resources to address these situations? If a personal response is not reasonable, is some type of political or community action required of the worker?
- If a social worker decides to make a personal contribution to deal with some client emergency (e.g., to buy food, pay for a night's lodging, pay cab fare), how is this to be done? Can it be done in a way that keeps the donor's identity confiden-tial so the client does not feel awkward or beholden to the social worker? What personal, ethical, and legal pitfalls might result from making a cash contribution directly to a client?
- Should agencies have a policy on whether, when, and how a personal contribution can occur? Would it be appropriate for the workers of an agency to create and donate to a special emergency fund that is separate from the agency's budget?

The Social Worker's Family

It is difficult to keep work-related concerns from affecting one's personal life and family relationships. It is also difficult to keep one's personal and family responsibilities from affecting professional performance. Nevertheless, social workers must strive to maintain a healthy separation and protect his or her family from being adversely impacted by work-related concerns.

Those who provide direct services to seriously troubled and dysfunctional clients will observe behaviors and situations that may be extreme, depraved, and cruel. Long-term exposure to such behavior and circumstances can distort a worker's sense of normality and moral compass. In an adult correctional setting, for example, the daily exposure to intimidation, violence, and manipulation can dull one's sensitivity and stretch one's tolerance for and acceptance of abuse and inhumane treatment. Skewed views on what is acceptable behavior, if brought home to one's family or into one's friendships, can strain those relationships.

Like everyone else, social workers experience personal and family problems. When the worry associated with personal concerns is added to the stress of social work practice, the worker may feel overwhelmed. During these times, she or he needs the support of colleagues and must be open to guidance provided by those able to see more objectively what is happening.

A SELF-CARE PROGRAM FOR THE SOCIAL WORKER

To be of maximum assistance to clients, a social worker must maintain a proper boundary in professional relationships. The worker's own need for meaningful relationships and friendships must be met outside of relationships with clients. In addition, effective practice requires that the worker be intellectually alert and physically, emotionally, and spiritually healthy.

Friendships and Community

Good friends provide us with support and encouragement, and help us to examine our assumptions, test reality, and maintain perspective. Good friends also provide constructive criticism when we behave inappropriately.

Because people tend to choose friends who are similar to themselves, many friendships develop within the workplace. Although this is a natural occurrence, it has a downside. It can, for example, limit one's exposure to differing points of view. If a social worker's friends are mostly other social workers, he or she may come to believe that only another social worker can understand his or her concerns and frustrations. In some cases, a narrow circle of friends gives rise to an "us against them" mentality. The social worker should cultivate friendships with people from outside the profession in order to attain varied perspectives on life, the community, and society.

Unfortunately, the feeling of belonging and the sense of community are often missing in our fast-moving society. A genuine sense of belonging to a community is something that grows slowly as individuals share what they have—time, energy, creativity, or money—with others in order to reach a common goal. Long-term associations, personal sacrifices, trust, mutual respect, and loyalty are the building blocks of community and a sense of belonging; there are no shortcuts.

Social workers often find a spirit of community and camaraderie through participation in professional associations such as the National Association of Social Workers. Professional organizations are important because they advance the profession. However, social workers should not limit their involvements to professional groups and organizations. They should also participate in neighborhood and local community events, projects, and activities.

Self-Worth and Self-Image

Social work is not an esteemed profession. To a large extent, this is because its purpose and activities are not readily apparent to the public. Also, social workers often call attention to problems and social conditions that many in society would prefer to ignore and deny. Because so many of the people served by social workers and social agencies are devalued and avoided (e.g., the poor, parents who abuse their children, the mentally ill, individuals addicted to drugs, the homeless), social workers are, by association, also devalued.

Given the types of concerns they address, it is not surprising that social agencies and social workers become targets for criticism by politicians and others who do not want to be reminded of unmet human needs, injustice, and the inadequacy of existing programs. Not infrequently, social workers are blamed for systemic and societal problems that are beyond the control of any one person, profession, or agency. Social workers understand that such criticism is unreasonable or misdirected, but it is still painful and frustrating. Social workers, like all people, want to be understood, valued, and respected.

In order to counteract feelings of being devalued and misunderstood, social workers must possess a strong sense of personal worth, self-confidence, and mission. This derives from a belief in the importance of their work and the value of the services they provide. If the social worker doubts his or her own worth or the importance of the profession, he or she is easily demoralized. No one should feel apologetic for being a social worker; the profession's mission and values are truly noble and reflect the very best of the human spirit.

Physical and Emotional Well-Being

There must be a suitable match between a person's physical and emotional stamina and the demands of her or his job. Thus, when selecting a particular type or field of practice, a social worker needs to consider his or her temperament, physical limitations, and any health problems. In addition, the worker must consider the normal developmental changes that will occur during the years of work. As people grow older, their level of stamina decreases and they often experience some degree of loss in vision and hearing. These ordinary changes can affect the performance of specific social work tasks. Family and group therapy, for example, require excellent hearing. Also, one's age can make it either easier or more difficult to build relationships with clients who are in certain age categories.

For the most part, social work is a sedentary occupation. Physical inactivity can place the worker at a greater risk of heart disease and other health problems. In order to counter this risk, it is important for workers to adhere to a program of regular exercise.

The expression of empathy and compassion by the social worker for the client is necessary to support and encourage the client during the change process. However, those efforts to "be with" and to "feel with" the client are sometimes exhausting and even painful. The social worker must strive to strike a healthy and realistic balance between empathy for the client and maintaining the emotional distance, objectivity, and personal boundaries appropriate to a professional relationship.

Social workers must be able to cope with and respond appropriately to the intense feelings and emotions (e.g., sadness, anger, fear) they encounter when working with clients who are in gut-wrenching situations such as, for example, the father who has abused his child or the family that has lost a member to suicide. The frequent and long-term exposure to the distress of others can contribute to *compassion fatigue* and a numbing or hardening of the worker's own feelings (see Item 16.4).

Many clients are so overwhelmed by their problems that they develop *learned helplessness,* a pervasive feeling of hopelessness and a belief that no matter what they do, their pain will continue. Social workers who meet these clients on a daily basis are vulnerable to developing this same sense of helplessness. Social workers who have not satisfactorily resolved issues in their own family relationships or who carry emotional baggage related to traumatic life experiences may sometimes distort and mishandle a professional relationship when clients are struggling with issues similar to their own. In extreme cases, vulnerable workers have been so knocked off balance emotionally that they could no longer function as professionals. It is critically important that social workers become aware of their emotional weak spots and, if needed, obtain professional help (see Item 16.3). If that is not possible or successful, they should arrange for work assignments that will avoid handling those cases and situations that might threaten their emotional well-being.

Life-Long Learning

The risk of intellectual stagnation exists in every profession. Learning must continue throughout one's life and career. People put themselves in touch with new ideas in a number of ways, such as reading, listening to presentations by experts, and participating in thoughtful discussions with family, friends, and colleagues. It is helpful to place oneself in situations that will generate pressure to study and think through the matter in more depth, such as making a presentation to a professional organization, teaching a class, or writing an article (see Item 16.10). Ideally, every new social worker will find a mentor who provides encouragement and direction as the worker seeks to learn a new job or develop his or her knowledge and skills (see Item 16.9).

"Learning From a Book or Article" from 1st edition

"Learning From an Oral Presentation" from 1st edition

Learning, especially learning during adulthood, requires a special effort to let go of comfortable and familiar ideas. In order to learn, people must first feel unsure about what they "know" and be willing to examine new and sometimes disturbing ideas. Learning begins with a question and an inner dissatisfaction with one's level of understanding or skill. It continues as the individual searches for answers, either alone or with others.

It is hard to imagine a type of work that can evoke as many truly significant and challenging questions as does the practice of social work. The situations that social workers encounter each day raise questions about justice; human rights and responsibilities; moral and ethical behavior; the causes of individual, family, and organizational problems; and the nature of personal and social change. However, social work is not an academic discipline, nor is it a pure science wherein the search for knowledge is driven primarily by the excitement of ideas and the joy of discovery. Those who want most of all to grapple with theoretical matters and knowledge building are usually not content in the role of a social work practitioner. Social workers spend much of their time trying to patch together practical solutions to very serious but fairly common human problems, dilemmas, and crises.

Religion and Spirituality

What motivates an individual to pursue a career in social work? Undoubtedly, there are a variety of answers, but many social workers would say that it has something to do with their spiritually and religious beliefs and values.

Both religion and spirituality involve a sense of the sacred—a sense that we are part of some indescribable and incomprehensible mystery or ultimate reality that transcends the familiar and usual. Both wrestle with the really big questions of life such as: Does my life have some ultimate purpose and meaning? How should I live my life? How do I decide what is right and wrong? Why is there so much evil and suffering in the world? Why is there so much good and love in the world? Is there an afterlife? Is there a God? What is God?

These are not questions that the scientific method can answer. Rather, they are matters of spirituality, faith, and choice. The major religions of the world offer some answers and perspectives that have been meaningful to countless people over thousands of years, but, ultimately, each individual must choose her or his own spiritual path.

Although religion and spirituality are intertwined, it is helpful to make a somewhat arbitrary distinction. A **religion** is a way of life organized around a set of beliefs, traditions, stories, and practices that nurture particular forms of spirituality and provide a conceptual framework for spiritual life. Religions are passed from one generation to another through various forms of leadership and institutional structures. The usual elements of a religion are public prayer and worship, various rituals that mark transitions in the life cycle or the spiritual journey, a moral code, and reverence for certain sacred writings and sacred places.

As compared to a religion, which is public and institutional in nature, **spirituality** is more a quality of the inner self or soul—that deepest recess of our being, where we encounter our "true self" and judge ourselves in light of what we believe to be ultimately worthwhile, right, and wrong. An individual's spirituality is his or her unique way of interpreting and assigning meaning to life. Our spirituality is revealed in our everyday decisions and actions such as how we treat people, what we do with our money, and how we react to success and setbacks. Deeply spiritual persons are often described as compassionate, real and genuine, self-aware, kind, nondefensive, unpretentious, joyful, generous, grateful, forgiving, accepting of others, and cognizant of the interconnectedness of all that exists.

Spiritual growth is a process, a lifelong journey. Spiritual leaders and guides underscore the importance of occasional solitude for reflection and meditation, being of service to others, striving for self-knowledge and self-discipline, and having patience with themselves and compassion for others. They also identify common barriers to spiritual growth such as a desire for control, power, prestige, and possessions, and the fear of change.

One's spirituality needs to be durable in the sense that it provides meaning, direction, and a sense of hope during both good times and bad, throughout the life cycle, and especially as the person faces suffering and death. It is difficult to develop a healthy and durable spirituality without the ongoing support of a group or community that provides guidance, encouragement, and challenge. Also necessary is what some have termed a "sacred technology" (i.e., prayer, meditation, solitude, ritual, study, fasting, etc.) that helps the individual remain conscious of his or her spiritual ideals and values. As people grow spiritually, they realize that they are capable of great love and generosity. They also become more aware of their "shadow side" and their tendencies toward selfishness, small-mindedness, and self-deception.

Every day, social workers meet people who have been hurt by injustice, dishonesty, prejudice, and violence. Every day, social workers encounter people who have unmet needs for food, shelter, and health care. How do social workers make sense of such a harsh reality? In order to avoid being consumed by frustration and in order to maintain a positive attitude, the social worker must strive to develop a hopeful spirituality—one that views all people, including those who cause harm to others—as having inherent worth and dignity as well as being capable of positive change. The social worker needs a spirituality that celebrates the basic goodness of people. (For more information on spirituality see Item 15.18.)

Artistic Expression

Another piece of the social worker's self-care is artistic expression. There is evidence that effective social workers are often creative people. It is not uncommon to meet social workers who are talented in various forms of artistic expression such as music, painting, acting, creative writing, sewing, photography, dance, woodworking, and so on. Social workers need to cultivate and share their artistic talents. The exercise of creativity can be a diversion from the stress of social work practice and a gift that enhances the quality of life.

HAVING FUN IN SOCIAL WORK

Human beings need to play and have fun. Adults often satisfy this need by introducing various forms of humor (e.g., jokes, playful pranks, and silly antics) into their work environment. How is a social worker to reconcile this need for fun with the serious business of social work? In many ways, the practice of social work is a rather grim and heavy endeavor. Many clients are often in truly desperate and tragic situations. Although human distress is not a laughing matter, humor can be a counterbalance to the frustrations experienced in practice.

Without an active sense of humor, social workers can be boring and social work practice can be unbearable. Social workers must take their work seriously yet acknowledge and appreciate those things that are genuinely funny about themselves, their jobs, and the situations they encounter. They must allow themselves to laugh at the absurdities of life and to temporarily slip out from under societal demands for conformity and the many restrictions they place on themselves.

"Using Humor in Social Work" from 6th edition

The use of humor with clients is always somewhat risky, but given proper precautions, it has a place in helping relationships. It is always wrong to laugh at clients, but it may be appropriate and even helpful to laugh with them as they describe the humorous aspects of their experiences. Often, it is the clients who teach the workers to find humor in the clients' situations. Many who live with harsh realities come to appreciate humor as a way of achieving a degree of detachment from their painful situations. Humor is an essential coping mechanism that should be affirmed and supported.

CONCLUSION

When an individual chooses social work as a career, he or she is faced with all the challenges involved in blending or merging a unique human being with a set of professional responsibilities. The social worker, as a whole person, has many dimensions, including the physical, emotional, intellectual, social, and spiritual. These dimensions both affect and are affected by social work practice and the workplace environment. The social worker's family is affected by the modest earning capacity associated with the profession and by how the social worker handles the everyday demands and stresses common to social work practice.

A social worker may attempt to keep his or her personal and family life separate from professional responsibilities but this is inherently difficult. Each social worker must strive to achieve a healthy balance between his or her personal and professional lives.

SELECTED BIBLIOGRAPHY

Austin, Michael. *Social Justice and Social Work.* Thousand Oaks, CA: Sage, 2013.

Cox, Kathleen and Sue Steiner. *Self-Care in Social Work: A Guide for Practitioners, Supervisors, and Administrators.* Washington, DC: NASW Press, 2014.

LeCroy, Craig. *The Call of Social Work: Life Stories,* 2nd ed. Thousand Oaks, CA: Sage, 2011.

Meisinger, Sarah. *Stories of Pain: A Social Worker's Experiences and Insights from the Field.* Washington, DC: NASW Press, 2009.

Payne, Malcolm. *What Is Professional Social Work?* Chicago: Lyceum, 2007.

Reichert, Elisabeth. *Social Work and Human Rights,* 2nd ed. New York: Columbia University Press, 2011.

Rosenberg, Jessica. *Working in Social Work: Real World Guide to Practice Settings.* New York: Routledge, 2009.

Whitaker, Tracy. *The Results Are In: What Social Workers Say about Social Work.* Washington, DC: NASW Press, 2009. (For updated materials from NASW Workforce Center see http://workforce.socialworkers.org.)

3

Merging the Person's Art with the Profession's Science

LEARNING OBJECTIVES

At the conclusion of this chapter, the reader should be prepared to:

- Recognize that a social worker's personality and values (i.e., his or her art) must include a strong sense of caring about others and concern for achieving social justice.
- Demonstrate appreciation that successful helping must be underpinned by the application of the best available knowledge (i.e., the science of social work) related to human and societal behavior, social work intervention techniques, and social policy development.

The previous chapter described the merging of an individual with the roles and responsibilities of being a professional social worker. This chapter focuses on another type of merging—namely, the blending of the artistic with the scientific, or the merging of a social worker's unique creative gifts with the knowledge component of the social work profession.

Professional education cannot teach these artistic features, although it can help the learner identify such strengths and develop the ability to apply them in work with clients. Professional education can also assist the person entering social work in developing a beginning understanding of the knowledge (or science) that is necessary for effective practice. This merging and blending of one's art and the profession's science is initiated in social work education programs, but it is a lifelong activity, as social work knowledge is constantly expanding and the worker is being continually changed by life experiences.

THE SOCIAL WORKER AS ARTIST

A social worker's **art** is the application of his or her intuition, creativity, and natural aptitudes and skills for helping people. One need not look far to observe that some people have an unusual capacity to build trusting relationships and engage others in an effort to bring about a needed change. People who enter social work typically possess a healthy amount of this natural ability and find personal satisfaction in being able to assist others.

There are numerous ingredients of this artistic ability that each social worker must possess, although each worker may hold the components to varying degrees. It is helpful for each social worker—or potential social worker—to consider the following elements of the art that is prerequisite to effective social work practice.

Compassion and Courage

One essential component of the artistic ability found in social work is the social worker's compassion. The word **compassion** means to suffer with others; it refers to a willingness to join with and enter into the pain of those who are distressed or troubled in order to address that difficulty. Although most people see themselves as compassionate, it is important to recognize that a high level of compassion is not typical of most people. In fact, it is quite natural to want to avoid involvement in the pain of others. A social worker who lacks compassion is likely to distance himself or herself from client concerns.

Social work also demands **courage**, not in the sense of being bold or daring but rather in being able to confront on a daily basis human suffering and turmoil and, not infrequently, negative and destructive human behaviors. Day after day, case by case, the social worker must be able to respond constructively to people who are directly affected by illness, disability, violence, neglect, sexual abuse, addiction, criminal exploitation, poverty, chaotic family life, separation from a loved one, loneliness, abandonment, and other types of human suffering. Moreover, the social worker must be able to respond constructively and with respect to people who have directly or indirectly inflicted injury and suffering on others. They must be able to deal with sometimes appalling human problems without becoming distracted or immobilized by their own emotional reactions. Over time, an individual can develop this fortitude or courage, but it is not something that can be learned from books or in a classroom.

Professional Relationship

A bond of trust must exist before people are willing to risk that difficult human experience—change. The most fundamental tool of the trade is the use of a **professional relationship** to help people become open to the possibility of change and engage in the always uncomfortable change process. A positive relationship is a precondition for effective work with individuals, families, or groups of clients, and also in working with the people who make up organizations and communities.

Following Lambert's (1992) literature review and research, he concluded that there are four factors that contribute to successful helping:

1. *Client factors* (e.g., the quality of the client's participation in treatment, satisfaction with what the worker is doing, the client's personal strengths and resources)
2. *Relationship factors* (e.g., the trust and connection between client and helper)

3. *Expectancy factors* (e.g., the client's positive expectations from the helping process)

4. *Model/technique factors* (e.g., the specific practice approach used by the worker)

Lambert's research indicates that client factors account for about 40 percent of successful outcomes, relationship factors for 30 percent, expectancy factors for 15 percent, and helping approach the remaining 15 percent. This research suggests that of the two variables the worker can most directly affect (i.e., relationship and intervention approach), relationship is the most significant. It is important, however, to recognize that the intervention approach (see Chapter 6) can be the added contribution to the helping process that makes the difference in a successful outcome.

There are several essential qualities of a successful helping relationship that are discussed more fully in Item 8.1. First, one must understand the client's thoughts, beliefs, and life experiences from that person's standpoint. To accomplish this *empathy*, a social worker must temporarily set aside her or his own values, attitudes, and judgments, so far as possible, in order to take on the other person's perspective. Empathy is needed, for example, to understand the fear and anger of a battered wife and yet her continuing concern for the man who hurt her; to be sensitive to the anger and guilt of an abusive parent; to appreciate the difficulty of a teenager risking criticism by peers for speaking up in a group; or even to hear out the frustrations of an overworked staff member.

Warmth is another quality of relationship that communicates respect, acceptance, and interest in the well-being of others. However, warmth is much more than just saying "I care," although at times that is important. Warmth is transmitted in many forms of communication, from a reassuring smile to an offer of tangible assistance. Warmth is an artistic quality that is expressed differently by each person, but inherent in all expressions of warmth is acceptance of the other person and a nonjudgmental attitude.

Linked to warmth and empathy is the quality of *genuineness*. Trite as it may sound, the social worker must behave like a "real" person and must truly like people and care about their well-being. The social worker may know the correct words to say or the proper action to recommend, but the client will assign them little value if the worker appears phony.

Creativity

In addition to a trusting helping relationship, **creative thinking**, the integration of diverse facts and information leading to the formation of original ideas, is central to effective helping. Creativity is important in social work because each client's situation is unique and constantly changing. So-called textbook answers to human problems cannot accommodate this uniqueness.

One aspect of creative thinking is having the *imagination* to identify a variety of ways to approach and solve a problem, whereas the unimaginative social worker identifies only one or two options—or perhaps none at all. For example, one area in which the social worker must be imaginative is in interpreting and implementing agency policies. Policies are created to serve the typical client, yet people are characterized by infinite variety. Although the social worker cannot ethically (or sometimes legally) ignore or subvert agency policy, he or she can often find creative ways to adapt a policy to meet unique client needs. The social worker who is bound by a literal interpretation of "The Agency Manual" is simply not able to make the system work for some clients.

Flexibility is also a dimension of creativity. Helping others to cope and change requires an ability to continually modify and adapt prior plans and decisions. The social worker making a foster home placement, for example, must have the flexibility to adapt his or her thinking to the often differing perspectives of biological parents, foster parents, the child, the court, the agency, and even the neighborhood. To align oneself rigidly with any of the affected parties limits the social worker's ability to help resolve problems and conflicts. At times, one needs to be supportive; at other times, it is necessary to challenge the client; and at still other times, the social worker must be hard-nosed, be directive, or exercise legitimate legal or professional authority. The effective social worker must have the flexibility to shift from one tactic to another and correctly decide when a shift is needed and appropriate.

One additional characteristic the creative social worker must possess is *persistence*—the capacity to continue on a course of action, despite difficulties and setbacks. Working with clients to translate creative ideas into action does not always work on the first try, but continuing to attempt new approaches can often lead to successful outcomes.

Hopefulness and Energy

The motivation of a client to work for change, especially when the prospect of change is anxiety producing or painful, is often a reflection of the social worker's ability to communicate the possibility that by working together the worker and client can improve the client's situation. Two characteristics the social worker must communicate to increase client motivation are hopefulness and energy.

Hopefulness refers to communicating a firm belief in people's capacity to change in positive ways, and in encouraging them to work cooperatively with others for the common good. Clients have typically been unsuccessful when attempting other avenues to address their issues or they would not be seeking professional help. Consequently, they often approach professional services with a carryover of skepticism. Given the serious and intractable nature of many of the situations encountered in practice, the social worker, too, is vulnerable to feelings of discouragement. The worker's hopefulness makes it possible to approach each practice situation with a genuine sense that this time the helping effort can make a difference.

Hopefulness, alone, is not enough. There must also be the infusion of energy to support movement toward change. **Energy** is the capacity to move things along, get results, and bounce back from mistakes and failures. The social worker's energy is needed to activate the client and counteract the client's hesitation. The worker's willingness to commit time and effort to the change process can encourage clients to also invest themselves in that activity. The worker should be careful, however, to avoid communicating a false or counterfeit optimism.

Judgment

The complex nature of the helping process and the uniqueness of every client's situation require social workers to make difficult judgments. **Judgment** is the ability to make distinctions among varied and sometimes conflicting information, identify how factors interrelate, choose between alternatives, and arrive at decisions on how to proceed. Judgment is at the very core of such professional activities as assessing client situations, formulating intervention plans, choosing techniques or procedures to utilize, and deciding when to terminate services. Ultimately, professional judgment depends on clear and critical thinking by the social worker.

Needless to say, some people are better than others when it comes to forming judgments and making decisions. Some make poor judgments because they act more on emotion than on careful and logical thinking. Discipline is sometimes required by the social worker to slow down the process and make sure that the client's situation has been thoroughly analyzed and sound judgments have been reached before moving forward with an intervention. One's life experiences and wisdom acquired from working with clients facing similar issues helps inform the social worker's judgment, but nothing substitutes for well-informed and thoughtful decision making.

Every responsible social worker strives to be free of prejudice that could adversely affect clients. However, every thoughtful social worker is aware that he or she may retain some degree of bias and prejudice, yet must make difficult and sometimes gut- wrenching decisions that may be affected by personal bias. It is the responsibility and the burden of professionals to make these difficult decisions, even when painfully aware that they can make mistakes because of their humanness and fallibility.

Personal Values

The reasons one might enter social work are varied, but the motive is almost always a concern for others and a desire to make the world a better place. However, it is important to remember that when a person becomes an instrument for change, there is in that person's mind some notion about what constitutes a desirable and good life for people. In other words, social workers, like all people, possess personal values. A **value** is a consistent preference that affects one's decisions and actions and is based on that person's deepest beliefs and commitments. Values are a person's fundamental beliefs about how things should be and what is a right and worthwhile way of acting.

A *value dilemma* arises when there is a difference of opinion over what is "right." The social worker's view of the "right" outcome or the best course of action may be different from the client's, and both may differ from that of the agency that employs the social worker or of other persons in the related community. Is it "right," for example, to encourage a single mother to find employment if having a job necessitates placing her young children in day care? Is it "right" to refer a woman to an abortion clinic? Is it "right" to withhold further financial assistance from a client who has violated an agency rule by not reporting income from a temporary job? Is it "right" to force homeless people to reside in shelters against their will? Whose "right" is right? Whose values are to be followed?

Given that one person's values cannot serve as absolute guides for all others to follow, is it appropriate to expect the client to conform to what the social worker or his or her agency considers desirable or the right thing to do? Logic would answer no, but many clients feel pressure to go along with what they think the agency or social worker expects. If a social worker accepts the principle of maximizing clients' self-determination, she or he must allow clients to make the decisions and to move toward outcomes the clients believe are most desirable. And apart from those values codified in law and universally recognized moral principles, the social worker should hold his or her personal beliefs and values in abeyance in favor of client self-determination.

This is not to suggest that the social worker is always to remain neutral with regard to client behaviors or decisions that are socially irresponsible, self-destructive, or harmful to others. A social worker is of little help to a client if he or she sidesteps or avoids discussing moral and ethical issues directly related to a client's concerns. Laws, basic moral principles, and even the rules of civility do matter. They are an essential and important aspect of the client's social functioning. However, when such issues are discussed, it must be done in ways that are respectful of the client's perspective.

As value conflicts arise, it is important for the social worker to consider what she or he believes about the situation and why, lest her or his personal values are inappropriately forced on the client. It is useful in a social worker's personal life to regularly discuss value-related issues and various moral dilemmas with family, friends, and colleagues to obtain alternate views that might contribute to refinements in his or her thinking.

It is desirable for the social worker's personal values to be compatible with the values of the social work profession. If these two value systems are in conflict, one of two things is likely to happen: (1) the worker will go through the motions of representing professional values, but because her or his heart is not in it, the lack of genuineness will be apparent to both clients and colleagues or (2) the worker will reject the profession's values and principles as a guiding force and respond to clients entirely on the basis of personal beliefs and values. In both instances, the client and the employing agency will lose the benefit of the social work perspective.

What values characterize professional social work? The *NASW Code of Ethics* (NASW, 1999) is predicated on six core values that drive this profession:

1. *Service.* The primary purpose of social work is to help clients deal with issues of social functioning. The obligation to serve clients takes precedence over the workers' self-interests.

2. *Social justice.* As social workers engage in efforts to change unjust societal conditions, they are particularly sensitive to the most vulnerable members of the population (i.e., those individuals and groups who have experienced poverty, illness, discrimination, and various forms of social injustice). Social workers, then, are committed to promoting public understanding of the effects of the oppression of vulnerable populations and encouraging an appreciation of the richness to be gained from human diversity.

3. *Dignity and worth of the person (and the society).* Social workers are committed to considering each client a person of value, and therefore treating the client with respect—even when his or her behavior may have been harmful to self or others. At the same time, social workers are committed to improving societal conditions and treating others with respect while attempting to resolve issues in the broader society that negatively affect clients.

4. *Importance of human relationships.* Social workers understand that relationships are central to human development as well as to a successful helping process, whether serving individuals, families, groups, organizations, or communities. Further, clients are hesitant to risk change unless they are true partners in the helping process, feel supported by a meaningful relationship with the social worker, and maintain as much control as possible over the decisions about how to achieve change.

5. *Integrity.* A helping relationship cannot be sustained unless clients can trust social workers to be honest and to respect the clients' rights to privacy. Moreover, workers are obligated to assure that any human services agency with which they are affiliated treats clients and information the clients reveal in an appropriate and professional manner.

6. *Competence.* Social workers are committed to bringing the best knowledge and skill possible to the helping process. They are obligated to practice within their areas of expertise, to search for the best knowledge and skills related to the practice situation (i.e., evidence-based or evidence-informed practice), and to contribute to the profession's knowledge base.

None of these values is unique to social work, but the effect of the combined set of values differentiates social work from other professions.

Professional Style

Each social worker is a unique human being and therefore has a unique style of practice. A **professional style** is how the social worker does his or her work, not in the technical sense, but in how the work is an expression of his or her personality, manner of communicating and relating to others, level of energy, creativity, sense of humor, wisdom, and judgment, as well as his or her passion and commitment to addressing the client's concern and other social issues. Personal and professional uniqueness is also expressed in one's choice of clothing and hairstyle, one's posture and manner of speaking, and in a hundred other choices and behaviors that send out messages about who they are and what they believe about themselves and others. One's style can open up and facilitate the helping process or shut it down, depending on how it is viewed by the client. A given client my be attracted to one style and put off by another.

One's professional style must be adapted to be appropriate to the situation being addressed, the clients served, and the agency setting. For example, a worker might dress casually when working with children and families but should dress more formally when making a court appearance in their behalf.

A social worker's practice style emerges as she or he balances individuality with the behaviors required for practice. Inherent in the process of becoming a member of a profession is pressure to conform. The need to balance expectations of profession, agency, and clients with one's individuality is an issue for every social worker. The social worker must ask: How far am I willing to compromise my individuality and personal preferences in order to serve my clients and meet agency expectations? An answer is that so long as clients are properly served and not alienated or harmed, one has considerable latitude. In fact, the profession is enriched by the varied styles of its members.

THE SOCIAL WORKER AS SCIENTIST

Social workers must use both heart and head when interacting with clients and providing services. With his or her individual artistic abilities as a foundation, the social worker builds professional capacity by drawing from the available knowledge about the clients to be served and the most effective methods of helping. One form of knowledge, *practice wisdom*, is derived from the worker's personal observations and the collective experiences of several generations of social workers who informally share their understanding with colleagues.

Although practice wisdom is valuable, professionals prefer to use **scientific knowledge** when it is available. This is knowledge derived by way of the scientific method, the most accepted approach for building knowledge in Western societies. We often think of science as a particular type of information but, more importantly, science is particular way of thinking about problems, a way of asking questions, and a method of finding answers. In its most rigorous applications, the *scientific method* involves carefully identifying and isolating the problem under study, precisely defining all concepts and terminology used, formulating hypotheses to be tested, following appropriate sampling procedures and an established protocol for gathering data, using control and experimental groups for comparison, applying valid and reliable tools of measurement, and, finally, submitting the research findings to scrutiny by professional peers so they can replicate the study and either confirm or repudiate the findings. Although the use of the scientific method is not the only source of knowledge, it is one that helps to minimize errors of judgment caused by bias and subjectivity.

For a variety of reasons, it can be difficult to apply the scientific method to social work practice. For example, many of the problems that concern social workers cannot be easily quantified, client confidentiality may limit the collection of needed data, and identical client situations seldom exist for rigorous comparison and testing. Also, for ethical reasons, social workers and agencies cannot assign vulnerable, at-risk clients (e.g., an abused woman or a child who is being bullied) to a no-treatment or control group. Single-subject designs may be used to study the relative effectiveness of two or more interventions (see Item 14.7), but seldom can the effectiveness of an intervention be directly compared to doing nothing at all.

For practical and ethical reasons, social work may never be a completely scientific discipline, nor should it be. Practice wisdom, values, and beliefs will inevitably shape the social worker's practice. Nevertheless, the worker must strive to be scientific in his or her thinking and seek out the best scientific knowledge to guide his or her practice (i.e., evidence-based practice). Social work is not a science to the same degree as, for example, physics, botany, or chemistry. However, social work can be said to be scientific in the following ways:

- It gathers, organizes, and analyzes data drawn from both social work practice and other disciplines.
- It uses its observations, experiences, and formal studies to create new techniques, formulate new practice guidelines, and develop new programs and policies.
- It uses data as the basis for formulating propositions and conceptual frameworks that guide social work interventions.
- It objectively examines its interventions and their impact on the social functioning of people.
- It critically evaluates the ideas, studies, and practices of social workers and communicates those findings to others in order to improve the outcomes of social work practice.

To the extent that social work is scientific, it should be viewed as an **applied science** rather than a pure science. And like many other professionals, the social worker is more a technologist than a scientist. For example, as a technologist, the physician draws from and applies the findings derived from the biological sciences; likewise, the mechanical engineer applies knowledge derived from the science of physics. The social worker, too, is a technologist who draws from and applies the knowledge derived from the social and behavioral sciences. Whereas the primary goal of the scientist is to understand, the primary goal of the technologist is to apply knowledge to facilitate change.

Social workers need to understand the client systems with which they work (e.g., individuals, families, groups, organizations, and communities). And, because social workers are also concerned with the social environment of people, they must also be knowledgeable about the social conditions in communities, agencies, and the human services delivery system. Finally, they need to have knowledge of the social work profession, its legal and societal context, and the various approaches and interventions used in practice.

Knowledge of Social Phenomena

Social workers are concerned with interactions between and among people, as well as interactions between people and the systems that deliver social programs. Thus, as described in Chapter 1, social work requires an exceptionally broad knowledge base.

In preparation for practice, it is important for the social worker to first understand the interrelatedness of the various system levels and the kind of client situations typically being addressed in the worker's place of employment. Then the worker must understand the individual person to whom she or he is providing services, which requires basic knowledge of both normal and atypical human development. The social worker must also understand the functioning of families and other households, as the family has long been a dominant point of intervention for social workers. With the increase of nontraditional family structures, understanding alternate living and intimacy patterns has more recently become especially important. Furthermore, a considerable amount of social work practice takes place with small groups, including support groups, therapeutic groups, and the myriad of committees that operate in organizations and communities. Thus, the social worker needs to understand small-group behaviors and processes.

Most social work practice takes place under the auspices of a formal organization, such as a social agency, school, hospital, or correctional facility. The social worker must understand how clients and other members of the community view these organizations and how people are affected by the functioning of these organizations. To work effectively within an organization, a social worker must understand organizational development, different types of authority structure and funding mechanisms, efficient and effective methods of operation, and successful communication patterns. Indeed, the social worker is required to possess substantial knowledge regarding the people and organizations with which he or she works.

The social worker must further understand cultural and religious perceptions related to ethnic identity, cross-cultural interaction, and the impact of oppression and discrimination on vulnerable population groups. Since people are influenced by the neighborhoods and communities in which they live, the social worker must also be familiar with, for example, theories of community decision making, resolving intergroup conflict, and facilitating community change.

Knowledge of Social Conditions and Social Problems

Social workers must not only understand the problems commonly brought to the attention of social agencies but they also must recognize how human problems (e.g., family violence, adolescent crime, school dropout, poverty, substance abuse) cluster together and overlap. The interrelatedness of these problems is an inescapable fact.

As background for dealing with social problems, the social worker should be familiar with the "big-picture" factors that contribute to the overall quality of life on this planet. Some of these are the need for clean air and water, a safe and sufficient supply of food and energy, stable political and economic conditions that support personal freedom and social justice, new technologies that improve human welfare, success in controlling communicable illnesses and promoting wellness, and a world free of racial hatred and war. In short, the well-informed social worker must have a grasp of current events and an awareness of the changes and developments that are impacting her or his country and the world as a whole.

Social programs and services delivered by social workers are particularly influenced by conditions at the national or regional level. When practicing in the United States, for example, the social worker must understand the beliefs, values, and organization of U.S. society and its governmental, political, and economic systems. Resources to meet client needs are expanded or contracted by political decisions, and social workers must be prepared to advocate for client needs when these decisions are being made.

Although some social conditions and problems are national and international in scope, others are a function of regional and state characteristics. For instance, regional drought conditions or low prices for farm products can directly affect people in the agricultural states of the Midwest or Rocky Mountains differently than people in urban centers or coastal cities. Also, efforts to respond to social problems may vary from state to state, just as value differences about the responsibility for caring for vulnerable people may vary across state borders.

Finally, some social conditions affect local communities but not whole states or regional areas. The well-publicized crime rate in Chicago, and the high incidence of gang activity in Los Angeles have dramatically affected those cities, whereas towns a few miles away may be relatively free of those problems. Rural areas may also experience social and economic problems caused by, for example, high fuel prices and an associated decline in the timber harvested in Montana or the closing of a small town's single industry in Alabama.

When social conditions are perceived as either harmful to people or a threat to the community or the society, social policies may be formulated and social programs created to address the problem. The actions taken will largely depend on how the problem is perceived and understood by those who have political power and decision-making authority. Essentially, a **social policy** is a set of principles, usually expressed in law and governmental regulations that guide the assignment of specific benefits and opportunities or provide for regulation of certain harmful behaviors. Social workers must be familiar with the policies that most strongly influence the programs with which they work and understand how these policies affect the clients served by those programs, as well as how the policies might be changed, if necessary.

Social programs consist of three major elements: organizational structure, benefits or services, and providers. Social programs must be delivered through some form of organization that determines who is eligible, how the program will be designed, who will deliver it, and what resources are required. Thus, social workers must be knowledgeable about the fiscal, administrative, and organizational aspects of service delivery.

The benefits and services provided by a social program can take the form of social provisions, personal services, and/or social action (see Chapter 1). The social worker must understand the programs offered by his or her own agency and be familiar with those provided by the agencies to which clients might be referred.

Finally, social programs require providers—the people who are in direct contact with the clients who are the consumers of the services and benefits. Providers may be volunteers, but most often they are paid professionals. Social work is only one of the professions that delivers services and benefits. Teachers, psychologists, physicians, nurses, occupational therapists, and others also help provide a wide array of human services. Each profession has its own focus but there are areas of overlap. Understanding the competencies of each profession, as well as the dynamics of teamwork and interprofessional cooperation, is an important part of developing the social worker's knowledge.

Knowledge of the Social Work Profession

The social worker must understand the functions that her or his own profession performs in society as well as the benefits and responsibilities that accrue from this status. When society grants professions the authority to provide the specific services that fall within their domain, in essence, a monopoly is given to that profession to determine the qualifications of its members (e.g., educational and experiential prerequisites). In return, the profession is charged with monitoring and policing its members to protect the public against abuses of that monopoly.

Social workers have devoted considerable effort to identifying their knowledge base, creating professional organizations, staking out their domain, clarifying their ethical obligations, specifying criteria for identifying qualified social workers, and taking other steps to become a valued profession. The requirements for recognition as a professional social worker have changed through time. Today, the entry point is through the completion of a baccalaureate or a master's degree from a social work education program that is accredited by the Council on Social Work Education. To move to more advanced or more specialized levels of recognition, one must gain experience, and through demonstration of appropriate levels of knowledge and competence, he or she can receive one or more specialized certifications through the National Association of Social Workers. Additionally, all states have some form of licensing or certification for at least some social work practice activities.

Closely linked with professional recognition is the social worker's compliance with the profession's ethical principles. Workers must be both competent and ethical in their practice if the profession is to maintain the public trust. Thus, it is essential that each social worker possesses a thorough understanding of the ethical principles that guide practice. **Ethics** are concerned with what is morally right or, in a profession, what is the correct course of professional action. Perhaps no single document is more important to the practice of a social worker than the *NASW Code of Ethics* (NASW, 1999). When a social worker joins the NASW, he or she pledges to practice within the profession's ethical code. Should there be charges of unethical practice, the NASW uses the Code as a standard for determining if charges have a basis.

Knowledge of Social Work Practice

In a profession such as social work, it is not possible to separate theory from practice or concept from action. In fact, **professional practice** is the process of using knowledge and applying theory in order to bring about specific change. A practice uninformed by theory tends to become repetitive and sterile, whereas theory uninformed by the realities of practice tends to be merely interesting, but often irrelevant.

By selecting from the theories, models, and perspectives discussed in the social work literature, the social worker constructs the conceptual frameworks that guide his or her practice. A **conceptual framework** is composed of a coherent set of concepts, beliefs, values, propositions, assumptions, hypotheses, and principles. Such a framework can be thought of as an outline of ideas that help one to understand people, how people function, and how people change. Consider the following purposes for having clear conceptual frameworks:

- They provide a structure for analyzing complex and often highly emotional human problems and situations.
- They organize information, beliefs, and assumptions into a meaningful whole.
- They provide a rationale for action and decision making.
- They promote a systematic, orderly, and predictable approach to work with people.
- They facilitate communication among professionals.

Social workers package a variety of theories, models, and perspectives into their **frames of reference.** Although these terms are often lumped together and simply called "theory," it is helpful to make some distinctions when describing these conceptual frameworks (see Figure 3.1). It is useful to consider that there are theories *of* social work and theories *for* social work. The **theories of social work** focus on the profession and explain its purpose, domain, and character within a society. They describe what the profession is all about and why it functions as it does. By contrast, the **theories for social work** focus on clients and helping activities. They explain human behavior, the social environment, how change occurs, and how change can be facilitated by the social worker in order to benefit clients.

Some theories provide the social worker with background understanding of the elements of the human condition that social workers are likely to address. These *orienting theories* describe and explain behavior and how and why certain problems develop. This knowledge is usually borrowed from other disciplines such as biology, psychology, sociology, economics, cultural anthropology, and the like. Examples include the various theories related to human development, personality characteristics, family systems, socialization, organizational functioning, and political power, as well as theories related to specific types of problems such as poverty, family violence, mental illness, teen pregnancy, crime, and various expressions of discrimination. Orienting theories, by themselves, provide little guidance on how to bring about change. For such guidance the social worker must construct his or her own practice frameworks that best represent the needs of the clients served and the capacities of the social worker.

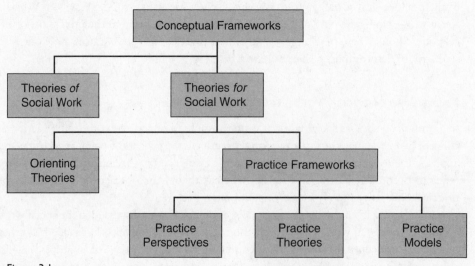

Figure 3.1
Types of Conceptual Frameworks

The three elements that typically make up a **practice framework** are practice perspectives, practice theories, and practice models. The social worker may select one or more of these elements for the practice framework used in any practice situation.

A *practice perspective* is a particular way of viewing and thinking about practice. It is a conceptual lens through which one views social functioning and it offers very broad guidance on what may be important considerations in assessing a practice situation. Like a camera lens, a perspective serves to focus on or magnify particular features. For example, the ecosystems perspective is commonly used in assessing relationships between people and parts of their environment. Or, the generalist perspective focuses a worker's attention on the importance of performing multiple practice roles and the possibility of various levels of intervention. Other perspectives, such as the feminist and the ethnic-sensitive perspectives, remind the worker of special challenges faced by certain groups in society.

A second element of a practice framework might be a *practice theory* that offers both an explanation of certain behaviors or situations and guidance on how they can be changed. A practice theory serves as a road map for bringing about a certain type of change. Most practice theories are rooted in one or more orienting theories. An example is psychosocial therapy, which is based primarily on psychodynamic theory and ego psychology. Another is behavioral therapy which derived from the psychology of learning.

A distinction is made here between a practice theory and the third possible element of a practice framework, a practice model. A *practice model* is a set of concepts and principles used to guide intervention activities. However, in contrast to a practice theory, a model is not tied to a particular explanation of behavior. For example, crisis intervention is viewed as a practice model rather than a practice theory because it does not rest on a single explanation of crisis situations. For the same reason, task-centered practice is termed a model. Most often, a model develops out of experience and experimentation rather than from a theory of human behavior.

The term *model* can be confusing because it is also used in a different context in social work (i.e., when an approach is patterned after another profession's approach). For example, when someone refers to an approach to change based on the medical model, she or he is describing practice activity that mirrors that used in medicine—one that places emphasis on the practitioner as an expert and an authority figure, the careful gathering and categorization of data (study), the application of a classification system to properly label the problem (diagnosis), and an intervention (treatment) dictated by the diagnosis. Similarly, social workers may refer to the legal model as a way of describing an approach to social action and client advocacy—one that involves competition and conflict among adversaries. The term *model* is also used to describe innovations in practice that are spread from agency to agency by borrowing or imitating the essential principles of a successful program. Thus, we hear such terms as the *self-help model*, the *grass-roots model*, the *12-step model*, the *case management model*, and so on.

Social workers will use many of the same techniques and guidelines even when applying different practice frameworks.

A **technique** is a set of specific steps one might take for accomplishing a particular outcome. Although a worker's frame of reference might lead him or her to select particular techniques more frequently, they are, for the most part, independent of specific theories. **Guidelines** are more general than techniques in that they are typically a mix of prescriptions (do this) and proscriptions (avoid this) that guide one's practice actions.

CONCLUSION

In order to perform effectively, the social worker uses a combination of art and science. It is recognized that a worker brings certain intangibles to the practice situation that affect both the process and the outcome—the art encompassed in building relationships, creative thinking, compassion and courage, hopefulness and energy, using sound judgment, and committing to appropriate values. At the same time, the social worker must combine his or her artistic abilities with the profession's knowledge and scientific base. Without art, the knowledge base is of little value. But without the knowledge, the art is of limited effectiveness.

The social worker merges her or his art and the profession's science into a practice framework. Chapter 6 provides descriptions of more than two dozen practice perspectives, theories, and models that commonly are included in practice frameworks. The intent is not to provide a comprehensive description of any of these approaches nor is it to provide a complete listing of all those available to the social worker. Rather, Chapter 6 is intended to supply enough information to suggest how the elements of a practice framework may differ and what might be included when constructing one's own orientation to practice. However, what goes into practice frameworks is contingent on the roles the social worker is expected to perform and that are further shaped by the established principles regarding how the social worker should perform those roles. Thus, the information provided in Chapters 4 and 5 make clear the context in which a social worker's practice frameworks are developed.

SELECTED BIBLIOGRAPHY

Lambert, Michael J. "Implications of Outcome Research for Psychotherapy Integration." In *Handbook of Psychotherapy Integration*, edited by John C. Norcross and Marvin R. Goldstein. New York: Basic Books, 1992.

National Association of Social Workers. *NASW Code of Ethics*. Washington, DC: NASW, 1999.

PART 2

THE BUILDING BLOCKS OF SOCIAL WORK PRACTICE

Once the social worker is personally and professionally prepared to engage in practice, at least four additional building blocks will shape the nature of that practice.

The first building block has to do with the various roles performed by the social worker, such as the roles of advocate, counselor/clinician, broker of services, administrator, social change agent, etc. Although other helping disciplines or professions perform some of the same roles, it is the breadth and variety of roles performed by social workers that distinguishes the social work profession and reflects its wide-ranging efforts to help people to function more effectively within their environments. The various roles are described in Chapter 4.

The second building block is a number of principles that have evolved over time that should guide each social worker's approach to practice activities. These principles provide the "bottom line" for offering appropriate and effective service to clients. To many social workers, the phrases used to communicate these principles have becomes almost clichés: "Begin where the client is," "Help the client help himself (or herself)," "Guide the process, not the client." The casual use of these phrases too often masks the wisdom of these principles. These basic principles of social work practice are described in Chapter 5.

Third, in helping clients formulate plans for addressing the issue(s) for which they seek help from the social worker, the worker draws on various conceptual frameworks that provide an overall strategy for the change process. There are literally hundreds of these conceptual frameworks, which we call *perspectives, theories,* and *models.* Each social worker must select or assemble a set of conceptual frameworks that can best address her or his clients' concerns and that are compatible with agency expectations. Chapter 6 presents brief descriptions of conceptual frameworks commonly used in social work practice.

The fourth building block is comprised of three elements essential to successful practice: (1) the social worker's critical thinking ability, (2) the worker's selection of the best evidence available to inform practice decisions and actions, and (3) the skill to guide clients through the phases of the change process. These elements are discussed in Chapter 7.

By examining these building blocks for social work practice, the foundation is laid for understanding and selecting the practice techniques and guidelines presented in the remaining chapters of this book.

4

The Roles and Functions Performed by Social Workers

LEARNING OBJECTIVES

At the conclusion of this chapter, the reader should be prepared to:

- Explain the five direct practice roles and the associated functions expected to be performed by a social worker.
- Describe the five indirect practice roles and the associated functions expected to be performed by a social worker.
- Explain the functions expected of a social worker in the role of a professional social worker.

Every occupation (e.g., engineer, teacher, farmer) is expected to perform a particular set of activities. For example, a physician is expected to conduct tests to diagnose a patient's condition, prescribe treatment, and monitor the results. Similarly, a social worker is expected to carefully analyze the client's situation, select and apply the most effective intervention, and assess the impact of that effort. Although there is individuality in how a social worker performs his or her job, there are also common role expectations for social workers that shape what they should be prepared to do.

Associated with each role are several job functions that can best be described as the activities one performs within a specific role. This chapter describes 11 roles and nearly 40 associated functions expected of social workers. In the course of a day, most social workers engage in several practice roles. Someone in a very specialized practice setting will typically perform a more limited number of these roles and functions, whereas the generalist worker will usually engage in a broad array of activities.

IDENTIFYING PROFESSIONAL ROLES

The roles and job functions expected of the members of a given profession are defined by social norms and historical traditions, by legal codes and administrative regulations, and by agency policies and procedures. In any practice role, the performance of several distinct functions may be required. Similarly, a specific job function may be applied in the performance of more than one role. For example, a social worker might engage in an assessment of a client's situation in the role of a broker of human services, a counselor or clinician, and a case manager. In the following text, however, each function is described only once.

The Social Worker as Broker

Social work's particular emphasis among the helping professions is to assist people in adapting and adjusting to change, and negotiating a more satisfactory situation and set of interactions within their social environment. That places the social worker in the position of being the professional person most likely to facilitate linkage between client and community resources (i.e., to bring together a person needing a service and a provider of that service). To carry out the **broker role**, the social worker identifies clients' needs, assesses their motivation and capacity to use various resources, and helps them gain access to those resources.

As a broker of human services, the social worker must also be knowledgeable about the various services and programs available, maintain an up-to-date assessment of each program's strengths and limitations, and understand the procedures for accessing those resources. These resources may include social provisions (e.g., money, food, clothing, and housing) and/or personal services (e.g., counseling, therapy, group interaction experiences, and rehabilitative services).

Functions

- *Client Situation Assessment.* The first step in brokering is to thoroughly understand and accurately assess the needs and abilities of the client(s). An effective broker should be skilled at assessing such factors as the client's vulnerability, culture, verbal ability, emotional stability, intelligence, and commitment to change.

- *Resource Assessment.* The social worker must also assess the various resources available to meet client needs, both within his or her own agency and other community agencies. It is important to be familiar with the type of services provided, the quality of those services, the eligibility requirements, and the likely cost to the client. Additionally, the social worker must know the best way for clients to gain access to those resources.

  The process of connecting clients to resources requires that the social worker make a judgment regarding the motivation and ability of the client to follow through and the likelihood that the resource will accept the client for service. Depending on these judgments, the social worker will be more or less active in the referral process. For example, sometimes the social worker will simply give the client information about the resource and suggest making an appointment. At other times, it may be necessary to physically accompany the client in connecting with that resource. A proper referral also entails follow-up activity wherein the worker checks to assure the client-resource connection is working to meet the client's needs. If there has been a breakdown, further action may be warranted.

- *Service System Linkage.* Brokering requires that the social worker facilitate continuing interaction between various segments of the service delivery system. To strengthen the linkage and cooperation among agencies, programs, and professionals, the social worker may engage in networking to strengthen communication channels, negotiate resource sharing, and/or participate in interagency planning, information exchange, and coordination activities.

- *Information Giving.* Brokering often requires the transmittal of information to clients, community groups, and legislators or other community decision makers. As a repository of knowledge about the effectiveness of the service delivery system, the social worker helps others by sharing this knowledge. Also, it is often important because the social worker may make the general public aware of gaps between client needs and available services as a way to correct evident deficiencies.

The Social Worker as Advocate

Advocacy is fundamental to social work's mission and is clearly embodied in the *Code of Ethics* (NASW, 1999). Section 3.07 of the Code calls for social workers to advocate for resources needed by clients and to assure that the resource allocation procedures are open and fair for all clients. Furthermore, Section 6.04 indicates that social workers are expected to advocate for social justice.

Advocacy involves supporting action on behalf of individuals, groups, or communities with the goal of improving a social condition or preventing a social problem from developing. Social workers must balance their methods of advocacy with the principles of maximizing client self-determination and client participation in the change process (see Chapter 5). To the extent possible, social workers should also assist clients to be their own advocates.

Advocacy within one's own agency or with the community service system is a necessary function performed by social workers. What is needed, however, is not always popular. The social worker must choose his or her battles with care and should be prepared for negative and even hostile responses to advocacy activities.

Functions

- *Client or Case Advocacy.* A common goal in this type of advocacy is to assure that the services or resources to which an individual client is entitled are, in fact, received. The first step is gathering information and determining if the client qualifies for the desired service. If so, negotiation, mediation, and, if necessary, more strident and confrontational tactics are used to secure the service. The client is helped to make use of available appeal procedures and, in some instances, to initiate legal action against an agency or service provider.

- *Class Advocacy.* The social worker must often serve as an advocate for groups of clients or a segment of the population that have a common problem or concern. Typically, class advocacy entails action intended to remove obstacles or barriers that restrict a group of people from realizing their civil rights or receiving benefits or services due them. It usually requires efforts aimed at changing agency regulations, social policies, or laws. Consequently, class advocacy requires activity within the political and legislative arena and building coalitions with organizations that are concerned about the same issue.

The Social Worker as Teacher

Much of social work practice involves teaching clients or client groups how to deal with troublesome life situations or how to anticipate and prevent problems or crises. Such knowledge is empowering to clients. The teaching role, as it plays out in social work, involves teaching clients how to adapt to conditions that negatively affect them. It also involves providing understandable information, advice, and descriptions of possible alternatives and their consequences to help clients make informed decisions about issues in their lives.

A fundamental purpose of social work practice is to help clients change dysfunctional behavior and learn effective patterns of social interaction. This may require teaching clients to adhere to the various rules or laws and norms of society, develop social skills, learn to function more effectively in specific roles (e.g., parent, employee), or gain insights into their own behavior. The teaching may occur informally during one-on-one interviews or in more structured educational activities such as presentations and workshops.

The teaching role also has a macro-level application. Social workers should be prepared to engage in activities that educate the public about the availability and quality of needed human services and the adequacy of social policies and programs for meeting client needs.

Functions

- *Teach Social and Daily Living Skills.* Teaching clients the skills of conflict resolution, time and money management, use of public transportation, adjusting to new living arrangements, personal care and hygiene, and effective communication are examples of activities regularly engaged in by some social workers.

- *Facilitate Behavior Change.* The social worker may use instructional approaches such as role modeling, values clarification, and behavior modification in teaching clients how to be more effective in interpersonal interactions. When dealing with larger social systems, the social worker may, for example, educate a board of directors about an emerging social issue or teach a client advocacy group how to redesign a change strategy that is failing.

- *Primary Prevention.* Throughout its history the social work profession has been mostly concerned with addressing and modifying serious human problems and conditions. However, the profession is also concerned with preventing problems from ever developing. Many such prevention efforts place the social worker in the role of a teacher or even a public educator. Examples include such activities as providing premarital counseling, teaching parenting skills, offering information on family planning, and informing the public of the need to address an emerging social problem or issue.

The Social Worker as Counselor/Clinician

Perhaps the most visible and frequently performed role in social work is that of counselor or clinician. The **counselor/clinician role** involves the application of evidence-based assessments and interventions to assist individuals, families, or small groups to address social and emotional issues in their lives.

In order to perform this role, the social worker needs knowledge of human behavior and an understanding of how the social environment impacts people, an ability to assess client needs and functioning and to make judgments about what interventions can help clients deal with these stresses, skill in applying intervention techniques, and the ability to guide clients through the change process.

Functions

- *Psychosocial Assessment and Diagnosis.* The client's situation must be thoroughly understood and his or her motivation, capacities, and opportunities for change assessed. This involves selecting conceptual frameworks to organize the information in ways that promote an understanding of both the client and the other people or factors in his or her social environment that affect social functioning. The social worker must also master the terminology used for labeling and categorizing various mental disorders and social problems. A basic knowledge of proper terminology is required for interprofessional communication, research, program planning, and obtaining third-party or insurance payment for services provided.

- *Ongoing Stabilizing Care.* The counselor/clinician role does not always involve efforts to change the client or social situation. Sometimes it consists of providing support or care on an extended basis. For example, counseling people who are severely disabled or terminally ill—or working with their families—may involve efforts to increase their choices and help them to more comfortably deal with difficult but unchangeable situations or conditions.

- *Social Treatment.* This function involves such activities as helping clients understand their relationships with other persons and social groups, supporting client efforts to modify these social relationships, engaging clients in problem-solving or interpersonal change efforts, and mediating differences or conflicts between individuals and/or between individuals and social institutions. Social treatment involves helping individuals, families, and small groups improve their social functioning as they cope with troublesome situations in their lives. Sometimes this involves treatment aimed at helping the client change his or her perceptions, attitudes, or behaviors. Or it could focus on helping change problem-causing factors in the client's surroundings. Often it requires both.

The Social Worker as Case Manager

The **case manager** role is of critical importance for clients who must utilize services provided by several agencies. As a case manager, the job of the social worker typically begins with identifying the type of help needed and moves on to exploring ways to secure those services, advocating for clients as they attempt to connect with potential helpers, and, on occasion, providing some of the services directly to the client. Finally, the worker monitors the success of the services plan on an ongoing basis and helps solve problems that may emerge. Effective case management requires a social worker to be goal oriented, proactive, and assertive.

Functions

- *Client Identification and Orientation.* This involves directly identifying and selecting those individuals for whom service outcomes, quality of life, or the cost of care and service could be positively affected by monitoring and guiding the change process.

- *Client Assessment.* This function involves gathering information and formulating an assessment of the client's needs, life situation, and resources. It may also involve reaching out to potential clients who have been referred for service but have not requested this assistance.

- *Service/Treatment Planning.* In concert with the clients and other relevant actors, the social worker identifies the various community services that can be accessed to meet client needs. This activity includes the work necessary to engage the clients, their families, and relevant professionals and programs in formulating a plan for improving the client's condition. Sometimes this involves assembling and guiding group discussions and decision-making sessions to design an integrated intervention plan.

- *Linkage and Service Coordination.* As in the broker role, the case manager must connect clients with appropriate resources. The case manager role differs, however, in that the social worker remains an active participant in the delivery of services to the individual or family and places emphasis on coordinating the clients' use of resources by becoming a focal point for interagency communication.

- *Client Support.* During the time the services are being provided by the various resources, the case manager assists the client and his or her family as they confront the inevitable problems in obtaining the desired services. This activity includes resolving interpersonal conflicts, providing counseling, supplying information, giving emotional support, and, when appropriate, advocating on behalf of clients to assure that they receive the services to which they are entitled.

- *Follow-Up and Monitoring Service Delivery.* The case manager makes regular and frequent follow-up contacts with both the client and the service provider to ensure that the needed services are actually received and properly utilized by the client. If not, action is taken to correct the situation or modify the service plan. Typically, it is the case manager who completes the necessary paperwork to document client progress, service delivery, and adherence to the plan.

The Social Worker as Workload Manager

Social workers must simultaneously provide the services needed by clients and engage in **workload management** to effectively and efficiently accomplish the agency's goals. In other words, they must balance their obligations to both clients and agency. Very often this requires the social worker to maximize the services provided within an environment of scarcity.

Functions

- *Work Planning.* Social workers must be able to assess their workloads, set priorities according to importance and urgency, and make plans that will accomplish work in the most efficient and effective way possible. This must be done despite a usually heavy workload.

- *Time Management.* If the social worker is to give each client proper attention, priorities for the use of one's time must be set and the available time carefully allocated. Time management requires that the worker learn to use the agency's computer systems and other time-saving office equipment.

- *Quality Assurance Monitoring.* The social worker should regularly evaluate the effectiveness of his or her own service provision and also be involved in the assessment of services provided by colleagues. These activities might include reviewing agency records, conducting job performance evaluations, and holding performance review conferences with colleagues.

- *Information Processing.* Social workers must collect data to document need and justify service provision, complete a variety of reports, maintain case records, and substantiate various expenditures. Further, information about agency regulations and procedures must be clearly understood, which requires that workers be skilled at preparing and interpreting memoranda, participating in staff meetings, and engaging in other activities that facilitate communication.

The Social Worker as Supervisor/Staff Developer

Social workers often serve in middle-management positions. In that capacity, they devote a part of their energies to maintaining and improving the performance of other staff members. That might involve working with secretaries, receptionists, and volunteers, but most often the **supervisor role** centers on maximizing the effectiveness of professional helpers.

Staff development requires many of the skills used in the teacher role. In this case, however, the knowledge is transmitted to professional peers rather than clients or the general public. Staff development is predicated on an accurate assessment of the training needs, with the training taking the form of individualized instruction such as job coaching, consultation, and/or conducting or participating in training sessions and workshops.

Functions

- *Employee Orientation and Training.* Orientation to the agency and training for specific job assignments are necessary for all new employees and volunteers. The tasks required to perform this function include specifying job expectations, orienting workers to organizational policies and procedures, and teaching practice skills and techniques used in the agency.

- *Personnel Management.* Personnel management activities may range from the selection of new employees to the termination of someone's employment. These middle-management activities, for example, might include monitoring the employees' workloads and resolving any disputes or complaints that might arise.

- *Supervision.* This function involves overseeing and directing the activities of staff members to enhance the quality of services they provide and make sure that agency rules and regulations are followed. It includes such tasks as making and monitoring caseload assignments, developing performance standards, and negotiating staffing changes to better address the needs of clients.

- *Consultation.* As compared to supervision, which is a part of the agency's administrative hierarchy, consultation is given on a peer level—from one professional to another. As opposed to supervision, the consultee is free to use or not use the advice offered by the consultant. Typically, consultation focuses on how best to handle a particularly challenging practice situation.

The Social Worker as Administrator

In an **administrative role** the social worker assumes responsibility for implementing the agency's policies and managing its programs. When performing this role, the social worker might be an agency's chief executive officer (CEO) or executive director. Or the social worker might be in a middle-management position, in which the administrative responsibility spans only the social workers in an agency or perhaps one program area (e.g., the child welfare division). The tasks one would be expected to perform might include giving leadership to program planning, implementing programs that have been adopted, and evaluating the effectiveness of the programs. At the same time, it is often advisable for administrators to carry a small caseload or otherwise engage in the primary work of the agency in order to have firsthand knowledge of the day-to-day issues in operation of the agency.

In the role of administrator, the social worker is responsible for implementing policies, programs, and laws made by others. Agency boards or elected officials typically define agency purposes, establish administrative guidelines, and allocate the funds required to operate the agency. Normally, either the governing board of a volunteer agency or, in a public agency, elected officials, appoint the executive director to administer the organization. The social worker in an administrative position in the agency may perform all or some of the following functions.

Functions

- *Management.* The management function calls for the administrator to maintain operational oversight of a program, service unit, and/or the entire organization. It includes such responsibilities as facilitating the work of the agency board, recruiting and selecting staff, directing and coordinating staff activities, developing and setting priorities, analyzing the organizational structure, promoting professional standards within the organization, adjudicating employee conflicts, and allocating the financial resources. In addition, management involves budgeting, documenting the use of resources, and arranging for the acquisition and maintenance of buildings and equipment.

- *Internal and External Coordination.* A primary task of the administrator is to coordinate the work within the agency. This involves developing plans for implementing the agency's programs in an efficient and effective manner, which may require negotiating among several units or programs or working with staff to assure that new programs are integrated into the agency's functioning. A second important task for an administrator is to serve as the primary representative of the agency to external constituencies. These external tasks include serving as a buffer to protect staff from external pressures, addressing disputes with consumers, and interpreting programs to the community in order to enhance viability and secure needed funds to support the agency's programs. Thus, the administrator is a key figure in the agency's public relations and its communication with consumers, other social agencies, and the general public.

- *Policy and Program Development.* The effective administrator is proactive. Although considerable time and energy must be devoted to maintaining established programs, an administrator should regularly assess the need for new or different services by conducting needs assessments, being knowledgeable about social trends, generating alternative policy goals for the governing body to consider, and translating new program or policy goals into services.

The Social Worker as Social Change Agent

Social work's dual focus on both the person and environment requires that the social worker facilitate needed change in neighborhoods, communities, or larger social systems. The role of social change agent in the social worker's repertoire of practice roles distinguishes social work from the many other helping professions.

When working directly with clients, social workers are in an excellent position to recognize conditions that are contributing to people's distress and the need for human services. When performing the **social change role** the social worker must take responsibility for stimulating action to create resources or change conditions that contribute to social problems. Social change does not occur rapidly or easily, and the authority to make the political decisions to achieve change is rarely held by social workers. Rather, change requires skill in stimulating action by influential groups and decision-making bodies that have the power to address the problems.

Functions

- *Social Problem or Policy Analysis.* A first requirement for social change is to understand the nature of the problem. Trends must be analyzed, data collected and synthesized, and findings reported in ways that are understandable to decision makers. Without this background work, change efforts have little chance of success. The tasks involved in such analysis include identifying criteria for the analysis, ascertaining the impact of the policy on clients and social problems, and analyzing community values and beliefs that may affect the issue.

- *Mobilization of Community Concern.* Translating one's understanding of problems into social change efforts requires mobilizing and energizing concerned individuals, groups, and organizations. This might involve encouraging clients, human services organizations, and/or other citizen groups to address and speak out on the problem. Mobilization for action might involve assembling interested parties and presenting an analysis of the situation, helping expand their understanding of the issues and identify goals they could achieve, aiding in the selection of change strategies, identifying the decision makers who can bring about the desired change, and planning and/or carrying out the activities necessary to induce change.

- *Social Resource Development.* The social change agent might also work toward the development of needed programs and services. Resource development involves creating new programs and services where they do not exist, extending or improving existing resources, planning and allocating available resources in order to avoid unnecessary duplication of services, and increasing the effectiveness and efficiency of services offered by a unit, an agency, or a group of agencies. This may involve lobbying and providing expert testimony to legislative committees or more informal communication with decision makers.

The Social Worker as Researcher/Evaluator

If it is to remain a viable contributor to the society, it is not sufficient for a profession to simply continue doing what it has always done. In today's rapidly changing world social workers must regularly conduct **research** and evaluate the knowledge, values, and skills that guide their practice; make use of new knowledge that is developing in related disciplines; and position themselves in the forefront of strengthening knowledge that specifically supports social work practice. To do that, the social worker must perform the role of a researcher and evaluator.

Functions

- *Research Consumption.* New knowledge is built on existing knowledge. Thus, before a social worker can engage in knowledge-guided practice or add new information to the profession's knowledge base, he or she must be skilled at consuming the knowledge that is already available. Some of that knowledge is in the form of theories of human behavior or the functioning of the social environment drawn from social work and related disciplines, but increasingly social workers require knowledge that has been empirically tested through scientific research. The social worker, then, must be competent to evaluate the merits of existing knowledge, both theoretical and empirical. This requires sufficient background knowledge to critically examine the many available theories and accurately select those that are most relevant to the social worker's practice. It also requires general knowledge of sound research design and the appropriate application of qualitative and quantitative research data.

- *Practice Evaluation.* Social workers are increasingly expected to engage in evaluation of their own work, both their direct practice activities with their clients (i.e., individuals, families, or groups) and the programs they deliver, to determine the relative success or failure of their efforts. Direct practice evaluation requires measuring client change on a case-by-case basis. This requires skill in selecting and using individualized and standardized tools to empirically measure change, as well as the ability to select appropriate formats for organizing the data (e.g., goal attainment scaling, single-subject designs). Program evaluation, too, is often a function performed by the social worker. She or he must monitor and evaluate the agency's programs and collect data that will help document the adequacy of the services and/or suggest actions that might be taken to improve them.

- *Research Production.* It is not enough for social work to depend on other disciplines to conduct the research that social workers might use, especially research related to the effectiveness of social work interventions. Thus, it is incumbent on the profession to produce social workers who can conduct research that advances the practice of social work. This research might range from a practitioner making a qualitative analysis of recordings from interviews with clients to a complex quantitative study funded by a major government agency requiring sophisticated data collection and analysis techniques.

The Social Worker as Professional

Basically, a **professional** is a person whose actions are thoughtful, purposeful, competent, responsible, and ethical. It is incumbent on the social worker to practice in a manner that reflects the highest professional standards. The social worker must constantly seek to develop her or his knowledge and skills, to examine and increase the quality of her or his practice, and to perform in a highly ethical manner.

As one who benefits from professional status, the social worker should actively engage in the enhancement and strengthening of the profession. Active participation in professional associations at the local, state, and national levels is an essential component of the professional role.

Functions

- *Self-Assessment.* The autonomy required for professional decision making carries with it the responsibility for ongoing self-assessment. Social workers in every type of human services organization (including private practice) and those performing every social work role are expected to devote substantial effort to self-assessment and engaging in their own professional development based on that assessment.

- *Personal/Professional Development.* The corollary to self-assessment is further developing one's abilities and addressing any performance problems that have been identified. Social workers are expected to regularly read articles in professional and scientific journals; seek critique of their practice from colleagues; and periodically attend workshops, seminars, and other programs intended to improve their knowledge and skills for practice.

- *Enhancement of the Social Work Profession.* Social workers should contribute to the growth and development of the profession and the expansion of its knowledge base. Maintaining membership in the National Association of Social Workers, for example, and contributing time and energy to the efforts of NASW to strengthen the quality of professional practice and support legislative initiatives are obligations of each social worker. In addition, social workers should contribute knowledge gained from their practice or research to colleagues through presentations at conferences and contributing to the professional literature.

CONCLUSION

The range of practice roles performed by the social worker is extensive and varied. The effective social worker must master at least the basic job functions associated with these roles. The specialist practitioner might develop more in-depth competence in fewer roles, but the generalist social worker, in particular, must continually seek to expand his or her competence in each.

SELECTED BIBLIOGRAPHY

Davis, John M., and Mary Smith. *Working in Multi-Professional Contexts: A Practical Guide for Professionals in Children's Services*. Thousand Oaks, CA: Sage, 2012.
National Association of Social Workers. *NASW Code of Ethics*. Washington, DC: NASW, 1999.

5

Guiding Principles for Social Workers

LEARNING OBJECTIVES

At the conclusion of this chapter, the reader should be prepared to:

- Describe the seven basic principles that focus on the social worker's own orientation to social work and social work clients.
- Display familiarity with the practice principles that provide guidance for how the social worker interacts with clients and carries out his or her professional responsibilities.

Within each profession there exist a number of basic principles that guide practice decisions and actions. **Principles** are guidelines that have evolved from observing successful practices that have stood the test time. They are perhaps the most fundamental and overreaching directions a professional might find to guide practice activities. By adhering to a profession's basic principles, it is thought that one cannot go too far wrong in serving his or her clients.

Social work's practice principles are grounded in the profession's philosophy, values, ethical prescriptions, and accumulated practice wisdom. Most are not supported by empirical verification nor are they compiled in a single document. Social work's practice principles are largely unwritten and are passed on informally from seasoned workers to those who are entering the profession. They are often expressed as clichés such as "Start where the client is" or "Accept the client as he or she is." Many of the principles seem so obvious to experienced workers that they often are not consciously taught in professional education programs or during supervision. However, they are central to effective social work practice and should be fully understood.

This chapter presents a synopsis of 25 fundamental principles that should guide social work practice. The first 7 focus on the social worker. The others are concerned with the social worker in interaction with clients—whether it is an individual, family, small group, organization, neighborhood, community, or even larger social structure.

PRINCIPLES THAT FOCUS ON THE SOCIAL WORKER

The Social Worker Should Practice Social Work

This fundamental principle seems so obvious that it appears trite. We expect the teacher to teach, the physician to practice medicine, and the social worker to practice within the boundaries of the social work profession. Yet it is not uncommon to find professionals extending their activities into the domain of another profession. This principle admonishes the social worker to do what she or he is sanctioned and prepared to do.

Social work is expected to focus on social functioning and helping improve the interaction between people and their environment—that is the social work domain (see Chapter 1). The requisite educational preparation equips the social worker with the knowledge, values, and skills to accomplish that mission, which is the unique contribution of social work among the helping professions.

Due to overlapping areas of knowledge and skill, sometimes determining which profession should provide what services to clients is unclear. The lack of clarity is magnified when a member of one discipline strays into another discipline's area of expertise. Although individual social workers may have special talents that exceed the profession's domain, the social worker who drifts from the profession's area of focus potentially deprives clients of a critically important perspective on human problems and associated change activities.

The Social Worker Should Engage in Conscious Use of Self

The social worker's primary practice tool is the self (i.e., his or her capacity to communicate and interact with others in ways that facilitate change). The skilled worker is purposeful in making use of his or her unique style of relating to others and building positive helping relationships with clients.

In professional relationships, workers reveal—verbally or nonverbally, directly or indirectly—their values, lifestyles, attitudes, biases, and prejudices. Workers must be consciously aware of how their own beliefs, perceptions, and behaviors may have an impact on their professional relationships, as these personal attributes will surely affect the ability to be helpful to clients. Part of the "art" that the social worker brings to the helping process (see Chapter 3) is his or her enthusiasm for helping people improve the quality of their lives. This personal commitment to serving others facilitates communicating energy and hope to the client.

The social worker must be comfortable with his or her unique personality and be at peace with whatever problems he or she has experienced in life. For most people, acquiring such self-knowledge and self-acceptance is a lifelong journey that requires a willingness to take risks, because taking a close look at who we are can be disquieting (see Item 16.3). Every social worker must discover and build on his or her special strengths and minimize the impact of deficiencies, identify the types of clients and situations that respond positively to his or her practice style, and develop a pattern of regular, objective, and nondefensive examination of how one's professional self is functioning.

The Social Worker Should Maintain Professional Objectivity

By the time most clients come into contact with a professional helper, they have attempted to resolve their troublesome situation themselves—by either struggling alone or seeking assistance from family, friends, or other helpers. Often, these efforts are thwarted by high levels of emotion and the conflicting advice they receive. This may only add to the person's frustration and preclude clear understanding and response to the situation.

The professional adds a new dimension to the helping process by operating with a degree of personal distance and neutrality. Maintaining this neutrality without appearing unconcerned or uncaring is a delicate balancing act. The worker who becomes too involved and too identified with the client's concerns can lose objectivity. At the other extreme, the worker who is emotionally detached fails to energize clients or, even worse, discourages clients from investing the energy necessary to achieve change. The social worker can best maintain this balance through a controlled emotional involvement.

Further, this professional objectivity is important to the social worker's own well-being. A degree of emotional detachment is needed, allowing the worker to set aside the troubles of clients and society and separate the professional and personal aspects of one's life. Professional objectivity is perhaps the best antidote to worker burnout.

The Social Worker Should Embrace Human Diversity

The practice of social work involves activity with and in behalf of people from virtually all walks of life, most racial and ethnic backgrounds, a variety of cultures and religions, a range of physical and intellectual abilities, both genders, as well as various sexual orientations and ages. Such diversity brings richness to the life experience. A failure to recognize and appreciate the many differences within the human family is a major obstacle in any type of helping and service delivery. The social worker must understand that what may appear to be unusual behavior from one perspective may be quite normal and appropriate given a different set of values and life experiences.

Respect for diversity requires sensitivity to the fact that various population groups have had differing experiences as they participate in the society. In addition, individuals within a particular group or class may have had quite different experiences from other persons in that same group. The social worker, then, must also be sensitive to the variations within any group and avoid making assumptions about any one person's cultural identity, beliefs, or values on the basis of that person's external characteristics or membership in a particular population or demographic group. Practitioners who respect diversity are careful to guard against making decisions based on overgeneralizations and stereotypes.

The Social Worker Should Adopt People-First Thinking

Words make a difference; they can shape our attitudes and opinions. All too often, the people who have a seriousness illness or disability are thought of with words such as, for example, *schizophrenic, disabled, mentally retarded,* or *brain injured.* Upon thoughtful examination, one sees that these words distract our attention from an individual's uniqueness, humanity, and personhood and, instead, imply that a disease or a disability primarily defines the person. A more accurate, sensitive, and respectful wording would be, for example: "She is an individual who experiences schizophrenia," "He suffers from the effects of a brain injury," or "Our program serves people who deal with mental illness." The phrases such as *a person with* or *people who have* keep the focus on the individual and properly view the illness or disability as only a secondary characteristic. Although the use of people-first or person-first language is at times awkward, it should be utilized by social workers in their speech, professional records, and correspondence to maintain the focus on the person.

The Social Worker Should Challenge Social Injustices

The true moral test of a society is how it treats the poor, the vulnerable, and the person who is an outsider, such as an immigrant or someone different from most members of the society. Central to social work is the recognition that many human problems are caused by discrimination, oppression, or more subtle social factors that limit people's opportunities or create difficulties for them. The failure of employers to accommodate the needs of persons with disabilities and paying men more than women for comparable work are just two well-known examples of social injustices. If not addressed, these injustices will continue to burden the individuals affected, as well as the society as a whole. Eliminating injustices will improve the quality of life for all and will prevent many social problems from occurring in the first place.

Challenging social injustices is a long-term proposition. The social worker cannot expect social issues that developed over time to dramatically be resolved with only short-term effort. Moreover, advocacy for social justice is often perceived as threatening by the powerful of a society because it challenges their wealth, privilege, and power. Unless social workers and other concerned citizens effectively identify, document, analyze, strategize, and have the courage to carry out social change efforts, social injustices will surely continue.

The Social Worker Should Seek to Enhance Professional Competence

Social work is a contemporary discipline. Its focus is on the here-and-now concerns of ever-changing people living in a dynamic environment. Helping people interact more effectively with their environments requires that the social worker be in tune with how others live their lives. One cannot be empathic and creative in working with a wide range of clients while holding a narrow and uninformed view of their social realities. The social worker must continuously seek growth and development—both personally and professionally.

The person who becomes immersed in social work to the exclusion of other activities and experiences actually limits the ability to be helpful by restricting her or his knowledge and awareness of broader issues that affect human functioning. To appreciate the infinite variety of the human condition, one must understand life from various orientations. Appreciation for history, science, the arts, travel, and interaction with a wide range of people is vital to the continuing development of the social worker.

The social worker must also be current with the latest professional information. The rapid change in the relevant knowledge requires constant updating of the social worker's knowledge base. New concepts, theories, and intervention techniques regularly appear in the literature and are presented at workshops and conferences. It is incumbent on the social worker to regularly participate in such activities in order to continue to grow as a competent social worker.

PRINCIPLES THAT GUIDE PRACTICE ACTIVITIES

In addition to the principles related to the social worker, a number of other principles are concerned with the social worker's interaction with individual clients and client groups.

The Social Worker Should Do No Harm

Social work practice is about the facilitation of desired change. However, there is always an element of risk in any effort to bring about change, no matter how well intended or desirable the goal. Because facilitating change is a very human process, the responsible professional must anticipate that mistakes will be made. By anticipating such possibilities, the social worker should have back-up plans for dealing with the things that can go wrong in an intervention. The social worker must strive to at least minimize any harm.

Professional actions and the programs social workers implement should in no way discourage or undermine responsible client behaviors nor erect barriers to appropriate social functioning. Furthermore, social workers engaged in efforts to change an unjust condition or unfair social policy must avoid or minimize creating other injustice to people affected by the change.

The Social Worker Should Engage in Evidence-Based Practice

At the very core of society's trust in professions is the expectation that professionals will bring to their work the latest knowledge and the most effective tools and techniques. Consciously using the best available evidence regarding the client condition and successful interventions in one's practice requires considerable discipline. With the pressure of heavy caseloads and busy schedules, there is a tendency to fall into a pattern of reacting to client situations without carefully considering what is known about people who experience similar conditions and what research has shown about the effectiveness of different intervention approaches related to this condition.

A social worker cannot possibly stay abreast of all the knowledge that relates to the many dimensions of social work practice. However, the worker is obligated to be familiar with the most current evidence that directly relates to her or his practice activities and to be able to retrieve needed knowledge from the social work literature, from the vast resources on the Web, from presentations at professional conferences, and from colleagues. After all, it is the clients who are most at risk if practice assessments and intervention decisions are based on faulty information. Each social worker should be prepared to engage in critical review of social work's theoretical knowledge and "best practices" research before adopting an approach to his or her practice activities (see Item 11.22).

The Social Worker Should Engage in Value-Guided and Ethical Practice

It is critical that the social worker make a conscious effort to identify and address relevant value and ethical issues in social work practice. Value choices and value conflicts are at the center of many practice situations. The social worker must recognize that one's values are powerful forces in human behavior and that helping clients clarify and understand value issues in their lives can be a critical step in bringing about change. However, in many cases, if clients are to change themselves or their situations, they must take some action to adjust or adapt their values to be more congruent with those of others in their lives—or help others adjust or adapt their values to be more congruent with those of the client. When working directly with clients, then, the social worker must be sensitive to the value issues and value conflicts that inevitably arise.

Organizations and communities also operate from values about who should be served, who should pay for the services, and how the services should be delivered.

When engaged in practice activities that relate to the agencies that employ them, the social conditions that exist in the community, or the social programs that are created at the city, state, or federal level, the social worker should attempt to understand the values that have influenced that situation. Societal problems are often a result of value differences, and an important step in finding solutions to those problems is to address the value issues.

Social workers must also be sensitive to their own values and beliefs and be prepared to suspend or set aside their own preferences and perspectives to avoid inappropriately imposing their beliefs on their clients. Social work practice, however, is not value free. At times, the social worker must take actions to protect the health and safety of others or achieve a broader social benefit than the self-interests of a single client. Making those practice decisions ethically requires careful consideration. The *NASW Code of Ethics* (NASW, 1999) provides a useful guide for making ethical choices in one's practice.

The Social Worker Should Address All Relevant Client Systems

Most professions focus on a single dimension of the person. Physicians are primarily interested in physical well-being, teachers focus on intellectual development, and psychologists are concerned with emotional and cognitive processes. Social work, however, is unique among the professions because of its concern for the *whole person*—biological, psychological, social, and spiritual. The social worker, then, must be concerned with the client's internal physical and psychological systems, as well as the external social systems that are relevant to the client's functioning.

Concern for the whole person requires attention to the client's past, present, and future; to focus attention on both the client's problems and strengths; and to look beyond the client's immediate or presenting problem and be alert to the possible existence of other issues, ranging from a lack of food and shelter to a lack of meaning and purpose in life. The social worker must attend to the client's symptoms as well as the causes of those symptoms. In keeping with the person-in-environment construct, the social worker must be concerned with the well-being of the client and also the many other people who may be affected by the client's behavior and by the worker's intervention. Finally, the social worker must be concerned with both the short-term and long-term implications of the change process for both the client and others.

The Social Worker Should Serve the Most Vulnerable Members of Society

From its inception, the profession of social work has concerned itself with those people most likely to experience difficulties in social functioning. This includes persons who are poor, mentally or physically disabled, from a minority race or culture, and who otherwise may be devalued and face discrimination, ostracism, and neglect by the dominant society. All too often, these individuals are treated as if society has little interest in their well-being. Needless to say, not every person who is part of a vulnerable population actually experiences problems and requires the assistance of a social worker. Yet many individual members of these groups are at risk and are frequently encountered by workers when delivering social programs.

Not infrequently, ill-conceived social policies and laws treat devalued groups unfairly and place them at a social and economic disadvantage. Social workers have often been champions of efforts to remedy these conditions, even though advocacy for (and with) these groups may be politically unpopular. Such advocacy, if successful, forces members of the dominant society to face the existence of social and economic injustice and the need for change in the social order. In fact, those who have power and privilege often benefit from the status quo and resist change. They may therefore dislike what social workers are trying to do and seek to discredit the profession. To be a social worker, one must be willing to accept the criticism that sometimes follows from service to devalued and disenfranchised groups and engage in the advocacy needed to accomplish social change.

The Social Worker Should Treat the Client with Dignity

Philosophically, the social worker must accept the proposition that each person or group deserves to be treated with dignity, respect, and understanding regardless of that person's behavior, appearance, and circumstances. Acceptance occurs when the worker views the client as he or she is, with all of the endearing and maddening characteristics that every human possesses. That means recognizing that clients sometimes make wise decisions and at other times make irrational choices that harm themselves and others. Nevertheless, the social worker is obligated to treat each client as a person who is valued and deserves to maintain her or his dignity throughout the helping experience.

Communicating acceptance and respect requires that the social worker avoid making moral judgments concerning clients. The worker's nonjudgmental attitude helps clients overcome the resistance to being evaluated and frees up the helping relationship for positive, rather than defensive, action. The need to treat each and every client with respect and acceptance does not imply approval of all behavior by a client. One can accept and treat the client with dignity without approving of, for example, illegal, harmful, or socially destructive behavior. The key to adhering to this principle is to remember that the purpose of social work is to help people make needed changes, and it has been amply demonstrated that acceptance of and respect for the person are prerequisite for change, while condemnation and being judgmental erect barriers to such change.

The Social Worker Should Individualize the Client

To individualize the client is to be cognizant of and sensitive to the uniqueness of the client and the uniqueness of his or her situation, concerns, history, and possibilities. The social worker must adapt his or her approach to this uniqueness and to the client's capacities, limitations, and readiness to participate in a particular intervention or change effort. What works well with one client may not work at all with another.

Closely related to the principle of individualization is the precept "Start where the client is." In other words, the social worker must strive to identify and tune-in to the client's current thoughts, feelings, and perceptions. The worker should always begin the professional relationship, an intervention, and each contact with the client by focusing first on the concerns, issues, and circumstances that are most relevant to and most pressing for the client. The client's highest priority or greatest concern may, of course, change from day to day or week to week. A skillful social worker will be alert to such shifts and adapt his or her approach accordingly. The process can always return to the primary purpose of the intervention when the current concerns are addressed.

The Social Worker Should Consider Clients Experts on Their Own Lives

Who knows more about a client than the client himself or herself? Too often, social workers and other helping professionals become enamored with their theoretical knowledge of human functioning and forget to consult with their clients to learn the actual circumstances of their lives. There are many things social workers will never know about their clients—and, in fact, many things in clients' lives are not the business of the workers. Where possible, clients should be viewed as the primary experts on their lives. Even the social worker with exceptional empathy may never fully recognize the many factors that shape the client's perspective. Ultimately, unless the perceptions are severely distorted, the client's judgment about his or her situation should be the starting point in making a professional assessment.

What, then, is the social worker's role in assessing a client's situation? The expertise a social worker brings is to help the client identify the factors that are influencing her or his life and situation, provide alternative interpretations of and understandings of those factors, discuss possible explanations of how these multiple factors are interrelated, help the client decide which of these factors can and should be modified, and to link this information to knowledge and techniques that can assist the client in making needed changes in their understanding and behavior. The client will be empowered when realizing that the worker recognizes her or him as the expert on her or his own life.

The Social Worker Should Lend Vision to the Client

A central feature of professional helping is to bring vision—new ideas, new perspectives, and more effective change strategies—to a problem situation. If an individual or group is to invest in the difficult process of changing, they must be convinced that the outcome will be worth the effort. The social worker must introduce and nurture a sense of hopefulness that change is indeed possible and that there may be new and better ways for the client to deal with the situation. The client will become more hopeful and more open to change if the worker displays a genuine belief and faith in the client's potential for change, in his or her power to overcome obstacles, and in the capacity to build working alliances with others who can become resources to the client.

While offering new perspectives, encouragement and support, and techniques for change, the social worker must also be realistic and honest about limits and possibilities. Clients are not helped by raising false hopes or by projecting unrealistic outcomes for the helping process. A tempered infusion of energy and vision allows the client or client group to make real progress toward achievable outcomes.

The Social Worker Should Build on Client Strengths

All too often, social workers and other human services professionals become preoccupied with client problems and invest considerable effort in identifying the specific limitations or deficiencies of a client or client group. Such an essentially negative way of thinking about clients and their situations is reinforced by the diagnostic labels now required for statistical purposes within many human service agencies or by insurance companies that pay for social work services.

For the social worker, it is the clients' abilities and potentials that are most important to build on in helping to bring about change. Since a change in social functioning is largely under the control of the client, it is important to help clients recognize and utilize their strengths. The emphasis on building on clients' strengths helps change the tone of the helping relationship from one of gloom over problems to one of optimism over possibilities.

The Social Worker Should Maximize Client Participation

"Help your clients to help themselves" is a principle based on the belief that if meaningful and lasting change is to occur for an individual, group, community, or other client system, the people who will need to change must be active participants in the change process. It is the responsibility of the social worker in guiding the process to be sure that, as far as possible, all relevant persons participate in identifying the problem, formulating a plan of action, and implementing that plan.

In order to maximize client participation, the social worker should "Do *with* the client and not *to* or *for* the client." For example, it does little good for the social worker to construct a sophisticated diagnosis of a client's situation if that client does not understand or accept those conclusions. Meaningful change will occur only when those who must change clearly understand the need for change and are willing and able to take action to bring about that change.

As compared to an attorney, who single-handedly presents a case advocating for the client, or a physician, who injects the patient with a chemical that can cure an illness with minimal patient involvement, a social worker must view himself or herself as primarily a collaborator, facilitator, and catalyst. Although situations do arise in which a social worker must act in behalf of clients, the social worker should always seek to maximize client involvement.

The Social Worker Should Maximize Client Self-Determination

The instruction to "Guide the process—not the client" captures another important principle. This principle maintains that those who must ultimately live with the outcomes of decisions should have the freedom to make those decisions. The job of the social worker is to help clients explore alternatives and the implications of various options but not to prescribe their final choices.

The principle of self-determination must, however, be qualified in its application. It assumes that the client is capable and legally competent to make decisions in relation to self and others. Sometimes that is not a valid assumption. Some clients may not understand the consequences of an action or may lack the mental capacity to make sound judgments and might therefore make choices that are clearly harmful to themselves or others. At times, the social worker must take on a decision-making role for these clients (e.g., children, the person who is mentally ill). This may involve persuading them to take a particular action, using the authority or power that the social worker's position might command, securing a court order declaring mental incompetence, or, in the most extreme situations, calling for police assistance in order to prevent a tragedy.

The social worker should reluctantly assume the responsibility for making decisions in behalf of clients and then only after careful review of the situation, after consultation with others, and always with the intent of returning that responsibility to the client as soon as possible. In the final analysis, the social worker should attempt to maximize the client's ability to determine her or his own destiny.

The Social Worker Should Help the Client Learn Self-Directed Problem-Solving Skills

Most social workers are familiar with the idea of helping people help themselves. Perhaps this should be extended to "helping people help themselves now and also in the future." Too often, the changes in social functioning made by a client with the assistance of a professional helper come unraveled unless the client is prepared to sustain that change over time. Ideally, a social work intervention helps prepare clients to cope successfully with future difficulties and to engage in self-directed problem solving when faced with another problem.

Hopefully, what the client learns during his or her interaction with the social worker can be applied to other concerns that emerge in day-to-day living. The admonition "Don't do for clients what they can do for themselves" relates to this principle of helping clients learn the skills needed to be independent and self-reliant.

An important aspect of preparing clients for the future is to teach them how to identify and make use of resources that might be found in their immediate environment. Such resources may include family members, friends, self-help groups, service clubs, and church, mosque, or synagogue groups.

The Social Worker Should Maximize Client Empowerment

Because social workers are committed to serving society's most vulnerable citizens, they regularly work with people who have been victims of various forms of discrimination and oppression. One especially helpful contribution social workers can make to their clients' social functioning is to help them gain increased power over their lives. Although some of the principles described here have the effect of giving clients more control over some dimensions of their lives (e.g., maximizing participation, maximizing self-determination, or helping to develop problem-solving skills), a principle that should guide all of a social worker's practice activity is the goal of empowerment.

Helping people, both individually and collectively, secure the power needed to gain control over how they live their lives has been part of social work's philosophy from its founding. The term *empowerment* reflects efforts to help people gain control over their life circumstances, to obtain needed information and resources, and to develop the skills needed to make the decisions and take the actions necessary to attain a higher level of self-reliance and modify one's social and political environment. In order to empower others, social workers place a special emphasis on the activities of encouraging, teaching, and facilitation, as well as collaboration and shared decision making within the professional relationship.

The Social Worker Should Protect Client Confidentiality

Individuals and families seeking help from a social worker often reveal very private aspects of their lives. In groups, clients may discuss secrets and self-perceptions that could be embarrassing or damaging if made public. The community worker, too, encounters instances when information about individuals, agencies, and organizations must be protected. All social workers must therefore be capable of handling private and sensitive information in a confidential manner.

There are two basic forms of confidentiality: absolute and relative. *Absolute confidentiality* refers to a situation when information imparted by the client can never go beyond the social worker. That degree of confidentiality is rare in social work practice. It is only under the protection of some professional licensing statutes that a client can claim a legal right to privileged communication. Most social work practice involves *relative confidentiality*, meaning that the most the social worker can promise is to treat information responsibly, as prescribed in the profession's code of ethics; adhere to existing laws; and follow agency policy concerning the handling of client information.

The degree of confidentiality that can be provided will depend on the type of information communicated, the nature of the agency where the practice occurs, the state and federal laws and regulations that govern its operation, and the existence of other legal requirements such as the mandated reporting of child and senior abuse. In correctional programs (e.g., prison, parole, probation), the client can expect little confidentiality. On the other hand, a client who receives social services within a hospital setting will have a much higher level of protection. But even here, a client's records might be reviewed by nonhospital personnel such as insurance companies, Medicaid or Medicare authorities, worker's compensation officials, hospital accreditation teams, and others who have authority to review patient records for purposes of quality control and establishing eligibility for certain benefits. The clients should be advised early in the helping process of the limits of confidentiality the social worker can guarantee.

The social worker must be prudent regarding what information is placed in agency files, and care must be taken in preparing clerical staff to respect the confidential nature of any materials they may type, file, inadvertently overhear, or have access to through agency computer networks. To protect confidential information, social workers must carefully plan the location of interviews and cautiously select the information to be discussed during professional consultations and in case conferences. Also, clearly separating one's personal life and work life is important in protecting against breaches of confidentiality that might occur when discussing work with family and friends.

The Social Worker Should Adhere to the Philosophy of Normalization

Many social work clients have evident mental and physical disabilities and often experience discrimination and social isolation. The philosophy of normalization is a powerful force in efforts to integrate persons who appear "different" into the life of the community and ensure that their lives resemble that of the so-called normal person as much as possible.

Normalization connotes helping people, especially those experiencing disabling conditions, to live their lives within an environment and in a manner considered typical and culturally normative for persons without disabilities. This approach has the effect of minimizing social stigma and increasing social acceptance of persons who are in some way different from most others. For example, a person with mental retardation should, to the greatest extent possible, live in a typical or ordinary home, attend a conventional school, and perform work that is useful and valued. His or her recreation, religious participation, clothing, transportation, and daily routines should be as conventional and mainstream as possible.

The Social Worker Should Continuously Evaluate the Progress of the Change Process

The practice of social work is far from an exact science. It involves working with ever-changing people and ever-changing situations. The objectives of helping activities, therefore, must be clearly delineated and regularly reviewed to be certain that they remain relevant to the client's needs. It is not enough to set the course of an intervention strategy and assume that the desired outcome will be achieved. Rather, a continuous monitoring and evaluation of the change process is necessary. To achieve this, both the worker and the client or client group must regularly collect and record data that are indicators of change and these data must be reviewed and carefully analyzed. If the desired change is not occurring, the worker is obligated to try another approach or redesign the intervention plan.

The Social Worker Should Be Accountable to Clients, Agency, Community, and the Social Work Profession

One factor that complicates practice is that the social worker must answer to a number of parties. Practitioners in some disciplines might feel that they are accountable only to the client, but the social worker—working at the interface of person and environment—faces multiple sources of accountability.

Social workers are obligated to give their best service to all clients at all times and therefore must be accountable to the individuals, families, and groups they directly serve. In addition, since most social workers are employed by a social agency or as part of a private practice group, they must be accountable to their employing organizations by carrying out their work as effectively and efficiently as possible. Furthermore, social workers must also be accountable to the community that sanctions them to practice in the first place.

The social work profession, as reflected in the *NASW Code of Ethics* (NASW, 1999), expects accountability to clients, colleagues, employers, the profession, and society. At times, practice situations place the individual worker in a position that makes it impossible for her or him to be fully and equally accountable to all audiences. In those situations, the social worker should attempt to maximize the accountability to each—but accountability to one's clients should be given priority.

CONCLUSION

The new social worker is often inundated with information that reveals, in bits and pieces, the knowledge and values that guide social work practice. Some of this information is formally taught in professional education programs, whereas other information, such as the principles described in this chapter, is typically transmitted in a more subtle and informal manner.

Practice principles reflect that combination of values and knowledge that should underlay all practice activities. If all else fails, the worker cannot go too far wrong if he or she is operating within these principles. They might be viewed as a fail-safe mechanism in social work practice. With these principles firmly in mind, the social worker is prepared to engage the client in a change process and to identify and select appropriate techniques for addressing the client's problems, needs, or concerns.

SELECTED BIBLIOGRAPHY

Colby, Ira C., Catherine N. Dulmus, and Karen M. Sowers, eds. *Social Work and Social Policy: Advancing the Principles of Economic and Social Justice*. Hoboken, NJ: Wiley and Sons, 2013.

National Association of Social Workers. *Code of Ethics*. Washington, DC: NASW, 1999.

Payne, Malcolm. *Humanistic Social Work: Core Principles in Practice*. Chicago: Lyceum, 2011.

6

Practice Frameworks for Social Work

LEARNING OBJECTIVES

At the conclusion of this chapter, the reader should be prepared to:

- Identify and explain the principles that should be considered when selecting a framework for use in social work practice.
- Identify and explain key features of the five practice perspectives that are frequently used in social work practice.
- Explain key features of several practice theories and models used in social work practice.

It has been said that there is nothing so practical as a good theory. Some social workers may question that notion when faced with the rather daunting task of trying to understand and sort through the multitude of theoretical orientations described in social work textbooks and journals and discussed at conferences and workshops.

At the end of Chapter 3, under the heading "Knowledge of Social Work Practice," the topic of practice frameworks was introduced and three types (perspective, theory, and model) were described. The reader may want to review those pages before proceeding. Basically, a **practice framework** is a coherent set of beliefs and assumptions about how human behavior and social systems can be changed. Some frameworks focus mostly on individual change, whereas others describe ways of modifying the functioning of families, small groups, organizations, or communities. This chapter suggests criteria for the selection of a practice framework and provides brief descriptions of ones commonly used by social work practitioners. Following each description are a few suggested readings related to that particular framework. The Bibliography at the end of this chapter lists references that are of a more comprehensive nature.

REQUIREMENTS OF A PRACTICE FRAMEWORK

A framework to be used in social work practice should meet the following criteria:

- It is consistent with the purpose, values, and ethics of the profession.
- Its key concepts, principles, and terminology are clearly described and defined.
- It provides practical guidance and direction to the change process.
- It rests on an empirical foundation (i.e., based on facts and observations).
- It helps the worker analyze and understand complex situations.

Because social workers practice in a wide variety of settings and encounter clients with many different types of problems and concerns, it is not possible to identify a single framework that is superior to all others. However, a practice framework is most likely to yield the desired outcomes for the client if it encourages the social worker to do the following:

- Build a collaborative worker–client relationship based on trust and on the worker's respect, empathy, caring, and compassion for the client.
- Assess and address the client's concern or problem within an environmental and situational context (e.g., view children's problems within context of family and family problems within a community context).
- Allow and encourage the client to make decisions related to the intervention's goals and the methods used to reach those goals.
- Recognize and build on client strengths and avoid focusing exclusively on limitations, deviance, and psychopathology.
- Be proactive and reach out to the client with offers of services that he or she considers relevant.
- Offer services and use approaches that are congruent with the client's values, culture, and religion.
- Offer services for which the costs to the client in time and money are reasonable, given the probable benefits or outcome.
- Achieve some initial success, even if a small one, so as to demonstrate the usefulness of intervention and maintain the client's motivation.
- Encourage the client to utilize social support networks and self-help groups.
- Facilitate the client's acquisition of knowledge and skills that will decrease his or her need for professional assistance and formal resources in the future.

GUIDELINES FOR SELECTING A PRACTICE FRAMEWORK

When selecting a framework, the social worker must grapple with the question: With what types of clients, with what kinds of problems, in what practice settings, and under what circumstances will a particular practice framework provide relevant and useful guidance? The utility of a given framework depends on the nature of the problems or issues receiving the worker's attention, the characteristics of the clients or consumers, the phase in the helping process, and the setting or organizational context of practice. For example, a framework that is helpful in guiding work with voluntary clients may be of limited value in work with mandated, court-ordered clients. A framework that is useful with teenagers may not be useful with older adults, and one that is useful with persons of one ethnic group may prove ineffective when used with persons with a different cultural background.

The choice of a particular practice framework can either enlarge or constrict the social worker's vision and options. Thus, critical thought must go into the worker's selection. The concepts, beliefs, and assumptions from which frameworks are constructed must be continually reexamined and tested against changing times and new research findings. Students and new workers especially must guard against becoming overly committed to a single practice framework, for this can constrict one's professional growth and ultimately it is a disservice to one's clients. An additional caution is important: Within the human services, the term *theory* is loosely used. For example, some people apply the term to ideas that have no empirical basis or are so vague that they cannot be tested. Sometimes, the ideas called a "theory" are little more than a description of someone's personal style.

In working with a specific client or client group, social workers may use several practice frameworks together or sequentially. They may shift from one to another as they move through the phases of the helping process (see Chapter 7). For example, the ecosystems perspective is most helpful in the beginning phases (e.g., problem definition and assessment), but less so during the later phases of planning, implementing, or evaluating an intervention. On the other hand, a framework such as behavior modification provides detailed guidance on implementing behavior change, but its application presupposes that changing a specific behavior will be the focus of the intervention. Questions that a social worker might consider when selecting a practice framework include the following:

- On what client system does the framework focus? The individual? A couple? Family unit? Peer group? Organization? Community?
- What type of client change is expected? Changes in attitude? Change in behavior? Acquire new knowledge or skill? Obtain access to a needed resource?
- Does the framework explain or describe how and why change may occur?
- When applying the framework, what is the role of the social worker? An advisor? Teacher? Counselor? Broker of services? Case manager? Administrator? Planner? Researcher? Advocate?
- What are the implicit or explicit assumptions concerning the preferred or expected relationship between the professional and the client? Consider these possibilities: The professional is the expert who knows what the client needs and what should be done, whereas the client is to follow the professional's instructions. Or the professional is to control and distribute services, whereas the client is to utilize these services in a cooperative and appreciative manner. Or, the professional presumes that clients will often know what type of intervention or service will prove beneficial and will therefore solicit suggestions and guidance from the client?
- What is the primary medium of communication? Does the framework rely on verbal exchanges? Writing? Reading? Expression through art or games? Formal or official communication? Spontaneous and informal exchanges?
- Does the framework specify when its use is appropriate as well as when its use would be inappropriate or possibly harmful? Is there evidence in the social work literature to suggest that this intervention approach may be successful with this client and the client's situation (see Chapter 7)?

- Does the framework recognize the importance of the client's cultural or ethnic background and religious values and beliefs? Can it be adapted for use with clients of various backgrounds?
- Does the framework presume a particular setting, such as an office in an agency or private practice setting? Meetings in the client's home?
- Is the framework applicable when the client is uncooperative, involuntary, or court ordered?
- Does the framework describe how it is similar to and different from other commonly used frameworks?
- Does the framework utilize a special set of helping techniques or skills that the worker must acquire or are they ones that are used also with other frameworks?
- Does the framework exclude certain individuals or situations, either explicitly or implicitly—such as an individual unable to pay a fee? A person who cannot meet in the professional's office during regular office hours? An individual who cannot read? A person with a physical or mental disability? An individual whose primary concerns are a lack of food, shelter, health care, protection from harm, and so on?
- Does the framework emphasize keeping the client within his or her family and usual social network? Or does it emphasize removing the client from the influence of family, friends, and peer group?

The social worker's choice of a practice framework is never a completely objective process. A worker brings subjective factors to the selection process, such as the feeling or intuition that a particular approach fits best with her or his personality and practice style or that it simply works better than other approaches. However, subjective factors alone are not sufficient. By passing the various practice approaches through a screen of questions such as those just described, a greater degree of rationality can be applied to the worker's selection of a practice framework.

SELECTED PRACTICE FRAMEWORKS

Typically, a social worker draws on several practice frameworks that offer guidance and direction in work with the various types of clients served. This repertoire of perspectives, theories, and models can be termed a **practice frame of reference**. When first developing one's frame of reference, the worker may adopt and utilize only a limited number of frameworks. Gradually, the number can be expanded to fit the needs of one's agency and clients and one's interests and abilities.

Presented next are brief descriptions of several commonly used frameworks that may be adopted individually or in combination with others. Each description offers a few key concepts or assumptions that set the framework apart from others. We begin with five perspectives: generalist, ecosystems, strengths, ethnic-sensitive, and feminist. Then a sampling of practice theories and models is provided, beginning with ones that are oriented mostly toward work with individuals and moving on to ones intended to facilitate change within families, small groups, organizations, and communities. The reader is reminded that most social workers draw ideas and techniques from several frameworks.

Selected Practice Perspectives

As identified in Chapter 3, a practice perspective is like a lens that focuses attention on certain factors or considerations when approaching a practice situation. One or more of the following (or other) perspectives might be part of the worker's frame of reference.

Generalist Perspective

The social work profession has been described as inherently generalist. The word *generalist* refers to a person with numerous skills and knowledge of many fields. Thus, the terms **generalist practice** and *generalist social work* refer to a practitioner who has broad general knowledge, a range of skills, the ability to draw on several perspectives, theories, and models, and is capable of moving with minimal difficulty from one field of practice to another. The opposite of generalist practice is one characterized by *specialization*, either by type of problem addressed, method used, or level of intervention.

The generalist perspective directs the social worker to approach every client and every situation with openness to using a range of techniques and a willingness to consider more than one level of intervention, from micro to macro. Such an orientation is especially relevant during the beginning phases of the helping process when the client's problem or concern is being clarified and assessed and when decisions are being made concerning the types of interventions that might be needed and effective.

The generalist social worker is prepared to engage and work with a variety of client systems; for example, an individual; a whole family; a group formed for a purpose such as therapy or social support; a committee or task group; a formal organization, such as an agency or a network of agencies; and legislators and policymakers who affect community decisions. In addition, the generalist is prepared to assume a variety of social work roles—for example, advocate, case manager, counselor or therapist, group facilitator, broker of service, fund-raiser, program planner, policy analyst, and researcher. The generalist expects to mold his or her approach to the client's unique situation and to characteristics of the local community, rather than expecting the client to conform to the professional's or the agency's preferred methods. Four elements most clearly characterize the generalist perspective:

1. *A multidimensional orientation that emphasizes the interrelatedness of human problems, life situations, and social conditions.* At the heart of this perspective is an appreciation for the interplay and interdependency of people and the various social systems that constitute the environment or context in which they must function. The primary level of an intervention (e.g., micro, mezzo, macro) is not selected until after a careful consideration of the various and multiple ways that a client's concern and situation might be defined, conceptualized, and approached.

2. *An approach to assessment and intervention that draws ideas from many different practice frameworks and considers all possible actions that might be relevant and helpful to the client.* The generalist perspective requires that the social worker be **eclectic** (i.e., draw ideas and techniques from many sources) and versatile enough to at least initiate relevant practice activities in a variety of situations. That is not to say that the generalist is expected to be an expert in the application of all theories and models. Rather, the generalist is knowledgeable enough to know when he or she can responsibly serve the client and when to refer elsewhere for more specialized interventions.

3. *Selection of intervention strategies and worker roles are made primarily on the basis of the client's problem, goals, situation, and the size of the systems that are targeted for change.* The generalist perspective calls for the social worker to adapt her or his practice activities to the client situation. Sometimes that may require working directly with the client, with key persons in the client's immediate environment, and at other times working to change agency and community factors that affect the clients or the delivery of services.

4. *A knowledge, value, and skill base that is transferable between and among diverse contexts, locations, and problems.* The more specialized frameworks may, implicitly or explicitly, prescribe or limit the type of settings where a worker can practice or the type of client, problem, or concern to be addressed. However, the generalist perspective can be applied in any human services organization or geographic context and used with a wide variety of clients and presenting problems. That transferability has job mobility value to the worker, but is a trade-off for the more in-depth knowledge and skills that are required in specialized settings.

The flexibility offered by this perspective is particularly useful when the social worker's job description demands the performance of multiple roles (see Chapter 4). However, it must be recognized that some agencies have missions, policies, and job descriptions that constrict the scope of a worker's activities (e.g., an emphasis on individual change, group services, community development). In such settings the generalist perspective would have less relevance.

Suggested Readings

Johnson, Louise, and Stephen Yanca. *Social Work Practice: A Generalist Approach*, 10th ed. Upper Saddle River, NJ: Pearson, 2010.

Kirst-Ashman, Karen, and Grafton Hull. *Understanding Generalist Practice*, 6th ed. Independence, KY: Cengage, 2012.

Miley, Karla, Michael O'Melia, and Brenda Dubois. *Generalist Social Work Practice,* 7th ed. Upper Saddle River, NJ: Pearson, 2013.

Ecosystems Perspective

The ecosystems perspective borrows selected concepts from both general systems theory and ecology and uses them as analogies and metaphors to describe ways in which people function and adapt within an ever-changing environment. It offers conceptual tools for describing the interactions between and among people and social systems. It also reminds the social worker that the process of planned change is both enhanced and inhibited by a myriad of forces and factors within the client's environment. This perspective is especially useful during the phases of assessment and planning.

A *system* can be defined as a functioning whole, composed of interrelated and interconnected parts and processes. The essence of a system is internal organization. A system has a hierarchic, multilevel structure. It is made up of numerous *subsystems.* And in addition, a system is usually a part of some much even larger system, a *suprasystem.* The term *focal system* identifies the system (e.g., a family, an agency program) being addressed by a social work intervention. If, for example, a social worker is helping a particular family (the focal system), the worker is aware that the family consists of numerous individuals and is also a part of larger systems such as a kinship group, a neighborhood, and a community. Within a typical family, several subsystems can be identified, such as the spouse subsystem (husband–wife relationship), the parental subsystem (parent–child relationships), and the sibling subsystem (child–child relation-ships). Within an organization, such as a social agency, one can identify a multitude of parts and subsystems (e.g., social workers, clients, administrators, support staff, programs). That agency's suprasystem(s) might be a particular community, a state government, or a federation of agencies.

All systems have a boundary. The outer skin of the human body is the physical boundary of an individual. The boundary of a social system (e.g., family, organization, community) is less obvious and more symbolic. The boundary defines or identifies those who are the parts of the system. When working with a family, for example, it is some-times a challenge to determine which individuals (e.g., parents, children, grandparents, significant others) are, in fact, the members of a functioning family system.

Because all parts of a system are interconnected, a change in any one part affects all other parts as well as the functioning of the system as a whole. A dysfunction in a part or subsystem will usually cause problems elsewhere in the system. Thus, for example, a social worker's assessment must anticipate how a given intervention might affect others within the client's family or social network. If an individual seeks help with a marital problem, the social worker will usually want to work with both the husband and wife, since a change by one will impact the other.

Systems are constantly changing, adapting, growing, and developing, but they resist radical change and will function in ways that preserve a dynamic equilibrium, "same-ness," or a steady state. If a system is not actively maintained, nurtured, and sup-ported, it tends to disintegrate. This tendency of a system to run down and come apart is termed *entropy*.

"The General Systems Perspecteive" a retired item from 8th edition

The ecosystems perspective also borrows concepts and principles from ecol-ogy, a biological science. It is important to understand that when concepts are borrowed from the hard sciences, their fit with social work will leave something to be desired. For example, a primary unit of study in ecology is the *ecosystem*, which consists of many interacting plant and animal species and their exchanges with their physical and chemical environment. Ecology is focused primarily on the adapta-tions and functioning of a species, not on the individuals of that species. By contrast, social work places a high value on the individual and considers environmental factors primarily as they impinge on the individual.

The ecological concept of *niche* refers to that combination of conditions and circum-stances (e.g., temperature, soil chemistry, food supply) needed by a particular species. When *niche* is used as a metaphor in social work practice, we recognize that clients will function better in some situations than in others. Many social work interventions are designed to help a client find a social niche in which the client can make the most of his or her particular abilities.

Each species within an ecosystem is constantly adapting to an ever-changing environment. If the environment changes rapidly or if the species cannot adapt, the species may be overpowered or replaced by a more adaptable species. One form of adap-tation is *specialization*. A species that is specialized in terms of what it requires to survive can be at an advantage because specialization usually reduces competition. However, a highly specialized species is vulnerable in a rapidly changing environment. As a general rule, specialization increases survivability in a stable environment but decreases surviv-ability in a changing environment. Such ideas might, for example, guide the thinking of professionals designing a job-training program. Is it better to train individuals for a highly specialized job or provide them with a broader and more general type of train-ing? Having specialized skills makes someone more competitive in a stable job market but more vulnerable to a layoff if the job market is in flux or if developing technologies could soon make a particular set of skills obsolete.

Because the resources needed by a species (e.g., food, water, space) are usually limited, a species must compete with other species. In this *competition* the most adaptive and flexible species tends to have the advantage. Moreover, when the resources needed by a particular species are scarce, the individuals of that species must, in addition, compete with each other. In that situation, the strongest individuals survive. The competiveness built into our economic system, job markets, and schools can be positive in that it may motivate people to work harder, stay focused, and realize their innate abilities. However, unbridled or unfair competition can be destructive and give rise to abuse, exploitation, and oppression. Needless to say, such factors as illness, disability, advanced age, immaturity, and lower levels of intelligence can limit a person's capacity to compete. If all the individuals in a society are to be valued and treated with dignity (a core social work goal and value), then various forms of cooperation and mutualism are needed to counterbalance the negative effects of competition.

The term *carrying capacity* is defined as the maximum number of individuals of a species that can live within an ecosystem. If the carrying capacity is exceeded, disease and starvation will decrease that population. Either a rapid expansion or a rapid decline in population numbers can upset the delicate balances necessary to the health of an ecosystem. Given the values and ethics of the social work profession, we cannot stand by and watch the raw forces of nature control human populations. However, these ecological ideas would be relevant to social workers and public health personnel when they anticipate the possible consequences of a large-scale refugee movement or the existence of crowded slums in economically depressed areas.

Although many more concepts from systems theory and ecology make up the ecosystems perspective, the ones that have been mentioned here illustrate how this perspective can stretch our thinking about human behavior and planned change. Social work's fundamental concern is the well-being of the "whole person," and its focus is on the "person interacting with his or her environment" (see Chapter 1). When viewed through the lens of the ecosystems perspective, the purpose of social work can be described as striving to enhance the adaptive capacities of people, remove environmental obstacles that limit their effective social functioning, and expand the availability of resources that meet the basic needs for those who cannot secure them through usual competitive means.

Suggested Readings

Andreae, Dan. "General Systems Theory." In *Social Work Treatment: Interlocking Theoretical Approaches,* 5th ed. Edited by Francis J. Turner. New York: Oxford, 2011.

Gitterman, Alex, and Carel Germain. *The Life Model of Social Work Practice,* 3rd ed. New York: Columbia University Press, 2008.

Mattaini, Mark, and Kristin Huffman-Gottschling. "Ecosystems Theory." In *Human Behavior and the Social Environment: Theories for Social Work Practice.* Edited by Bruce Thyer, Catherine Dulmus, and Karen Sowers. Hoboken, NJ: Wiley, 2012.

Walker, Steven. *Effective Social Work with Children, Young People and Families: Putting Systems Theory into Practice.* Thousand Oaks, CA: Sage, 2012.

Strengths Perspective

The strengths perspective directs the social worker to identify and build on client strengths. A **client strength** can be defined as any attribute, capacity, or experience that contributes to a satisfying life and effective social functioning. Strengths can take many forms, such a particular ability or skill, the desire to learn, personal integrity, and fortitude (see Item 11.6). This perspective presumes that all clients have strengths, even when the client's behavior is seriously dysfunctional. Strengths are presumed to exist in all environments, no matter how harsh they may appear. For example, within every neighborhood and community there will be individuals and groups that care deeply and contribute their time and resources to be of help to others. Creative efforts by the social worker can identify and mobilize those resources.

The strengths perspective offers an important counterbalance to the overemphasis on problems and pathology that characterize so many human service programs. Many models and theories used by helping professionals focus mostly on what is going wrong in a client's life. Such deficit-oriented approaches often overlook the positive and functional aspects of a client's behavior and situation.

When a social worker helps a client identify and build on his or her strengths, it has the effect of increasing client motivation, elevating the client's sense of hope and self-confidence, and reducing resistance to change. Although it is true that traumatic life experiences or an illness or disability can impose limitations on a person's functioning, even these circumstances can become a source of personal strength and opportunity. No one can know for certain the upper limits of a person's ability to overcome life's difficulties.

The strengths perspective presumes that clients will usually know what types of interventions will be most helpful in addressing their concerns. Thus, the professional helping relationship is intentionally collaborative and the practitioner's role is primarily that of a consultant to the client. The client is viewed as an expert on her or his situation and the social worker will always ask for and use the client's ideas on how best to proceed. The strengths perspective is relevant in work with all clients and during all phases of the helping process. It has much in common with the Solution-Focused Model, described later in this chapter.

Suggested Readings

Jones-Smith, Elsie. *Strengths-Based Therapy*. Thousand Oaks, CA: Sage, 2013.
Rapp, Charles, and Richard Guscha. *The Strengths Model*, 3rd ed. New York: Oxford University Press, 2012.
Saleebey, Dennis. *The Strengths Perspective in Social Work Practice*, 6th ed. Upper Saddle River, NJ: Pearson, 2013.

Ethnic-Sensitive Perspective

Given that people are shaped by their backgrounds and life experiences, factors such as a client's ethnicity, culture, religion, and socioeconomic class will strongly influence that client's thoughts, behavior, and values. These sociocultural factors also affect what an individual defines as a problem, whether he or she will seek assistance from a professional or human services agency, how he or she expects to be treated by service providers, and what types of services he or she considers relevant and helpful. The ethnic-sensitive perspective draws the social worker's attention to these important influences. This conceptual lens is especially important when the client is a member of an ethnic or minority group and whenever the client's presenting problem or concern is related to discrimination or oppression. It is applicable during all phases of the helping process.

It is important for every social worker to become a *culturally competent* practitioner—one who has the ability to work with a client in ways that are congruent with the client's beliefs, values, traditions, and expectations. In order to develop this ability, the social worker, must, first and foremost, develop self-awareness and become cognizant of how her or his own beliefs, values, and expectations have been shaped and molded by his or her own culture, ethnicity, religion, and social class. A social worker must be especially skilled in communications with people of various backgrounds. (For more information on cultural diversity, see Items 8.8, 15.18, and 16.3.)

Suggested Readings

Appleby, George, Edgar Colon, and Julia Hamilton. *Diversity, Oppression, and Social Function*, 3rd ed. Upper Saddle River, NJ: Pearson, 2011.

Diller, Jerry. *Cultural Diversity: A Primer for the Human Services*, 3rd ed. Independence, KY: Cengage, 2011.

Sisneros, Jose, Mildred Joyner, and Cathryne Schmitz. *Critical Multicultural Social Work*. Chicago: Lyceum, 2008.

Feminist Perspective

The feminist perspective heightens the practitioner's awareness of how societal beliefs and attitudes related to sex, gender, and sex roles may shape how a client views and explains a problem or situation and also the ways that a professional or agency respond to their clients. This perspective is especially important when one recognizes that male-dominated institutions have designed most of the laws, policies, and programs that impact women.

The terms *sex* and *gender* are often used interchangeably but they have somewhat different meanings. The concept of *sex* refers to the classification of people as either male or female, based on anatomy and a particular assemblage of the X- and Y-chromosomes. By contrast, the concept of *gender* has to do with the meanings that people assign to these biological differences and to ideas of femininity and masculinity. For example, in many societies femininity or being a female is associated with the qualities of compassion, cooperation, loyalty, intuition, caring, sharing, openness, and attention to human relationships. Masculinity, on the other hand, is often associated with rationality, competition, authority, leadership, courage, decisiveness, fortitude, honor, and attention to things and objects. Needless to say, many of the perceived or assumed differences between the sexes have their origin in historical forces and cultural and societal dynamics, rather than in biological differences.

The feminist perspective challenges the belief systems and social structures that give rise to the oppression and exploitation of women. Two examples are sexism and patriarchy. As a set of beliefs and attitudes, *sexism* presumes that one sex (usually the female) is inferior and should be subordinate to the other, thus resulting in an unfair ordering of roles and responsibilities and to social and economic inequalities. *Patriarchy* refers to a hierarchical system of societal organization in which men control the family, political, and economic structures. It, like sexism, rests on the belief that the male is inherently superior and naturally suited for leadership and decision making.

Central to the feminist perspective is the belief that the professional helping process cannot be limited to clinical or direct service activities; it must also emphasize political action and advocacy. Thus, a client's concerns or problems are assessed within a sociopolitical context with special attention to the sex-related power differentials within male–female relationships, marriage, family, and employment. An emphasis is placed on empowerment and building on client strengths (see Items 11.6 and 13.18).

It has a strong educational component, including teaching the client about sexism, sex-role stereotyping, discrimination, and the historical factors that have shaped societal attitudes toward women and also how women view themselves. The helping relationship is egalitarian with the professional taking the role of a partner or colleague, not an expert or authority figure. The professional willingly shares relevant personal experiences. A client is expected to be an active participant in the helping process and there is an emphasis on creating and utilizing women's social networks and support groups.

The feminist perspective is especially important in work with women and whenever a client's problems or concerns are linked to sexism and sex-role stereotyping. However, its emphasis on empowerment, social justice, and political action should be a part of practice in all settings and with all clients. It is applicable throughout the helping process and especially during the phases of problem definition and assessment.

Suggested Readings

Bricker-Jenkins, Mary, and F. Ellen Netting. "Feminist Issues and Practices in Social Work." In *Social Workers' Desk Reference*, 2nd ed. Edited by Albert Roberts. New York: Oxford University Press, 2008.

Valentich, Mary. "Feminist Theory and Social Work Practice." In *Social Work Treatment: Interlocking Theoretical Approaches*, 5th ed. Edited by Francis J. Turner. New York: Oxford University Press, 2011.

White, Vicky. *The State of Feminist Social Work*. New York: Routledge, 2006.

Selected Practice Theories and Models

A practice perspective does not stand alone; it is always used in conjunction with various practice theories and models. For example, a social worker operating from the generalist perspective may elect to use behavioral techniques, small-group theories, and/or theories of organizational change, depending on the practice situation. More specialized practitioners may draw on a smaller number of theories or models, but apply them with more depth of knowledge and skill. In the remainder of this chapter we offer brief descriptions of practice theories and models commonly used by social workers.

Behavioral Theory

Of all the practice frameworks used by social workers, behavioral theory is the most empirical and methodical. It is based on the laboratory study of the learning process. It presumes that most human behavior and even some types of emotional reactions are best explained by principles of learning. A core principle is that people repeat behaviors that are reinforced (rewarded) and abandon behaviors that are not rewarded or are punished. In other words, how a person behaves is determined by the consequences that a particular behavior elicits within his or her environment. Both functional (healthy) and dysfunctional behaviors (psychopathology) are learned this way.

The behavioral approach, often termed behavior modification, can be used to teach new skills or to eliminate dysfunctional behaviors. Its application begins with a specification of the behavior to be changed (i.e., the target behavior) and the collection of baseline data regarding how often and under what conditions the target behavior occurs. A change in behavior is defined as an increase or a decrease in the frequency, duration, or intensity of the target behavior. Ongoing data collection informs the practitioner whether a specific intervention is being effective.

Either the client or practitioner must have control over whether or how the target behavior is reinforced (rewarded). This approach is frequently used in residential treatment and correctional settings, where it is possible to closely observe the behavior of clients and also exercise control over the reinforcement they receive. In some applications, the client is taught how to modify his or her own behavior through the self-administration of reinforcers.

This approach can be used to improve the functioning of individuals, couples, families, and organizations. It is applicable in work with the nonvoluntary or mandated client if the professional has the authority to allocate or withhold reinforcements. It is usually not an appropriate approach when the client's concerns or problems are related to value conflicts, decision making, and distorted thinking. (For more information on techniques of behavioral change, see Items 13.3, 13.4, and 13.5.)

Suggested Readings

Bronson, Denise. "A Behavioral Approach to Social Work Treatment." In *Social Workers' Desk Reference*, 2nd ed. Edited by Albert Roberts. New York: Oxford University Press, 2008.

Martin, Garry, and Joseph Pear. *Behavior Modification*, 9th ed. Upper Saddle River, NJ: Pearson, 2011.

Sundel, Martin, and Sandra Sundel. *Behavior Change in the Human Services*, 5th ed. Thousand Oaks, CA: Sage, 2005.

Cognitive-Behavioral Theory

This framework integrates selected concepts from learning theory with ones drawn from the study of cognitive processes (i.e., how people interpret and assign meaning to their experiences and the interplay of thoughts, emotions, and behavior). Many personal problems and troublesome moods and feelings are caused by the person's faulty, irrational, and rigid thinking about the way things are or should be. We humans live at the mercy of our thoughts and beliefs. We react not so much to our actual experience as to how we have interpreted and think about that experience. In large measure, the degree to which we are happy and content in life is a function of how well what is happening in our life fits with or matches what we believe ought to be happening. A person's expectations and habits or patterns of thought (termed *schemas*) are largely formed during childhood. Basically, a *schema* is an enduring conviction about oneself, others, and what one can expect in life.

An intervention based on cognitive-behavioral principles will teach clients to recognize the content and impact of their cognitions (thoughts) and schemas, evaluate the validity of their beliefs, and to view events and situations with greater objectivity. As clients change how they interpret and understand their situations, they start to think, feel, and behave differently. Within this framework there are subdivisions, such as rational emotive therapy and cognitive therapy. Practitioners and theoreticians tend to differ on whether to emphasize the cognitive side or the behavioral side of the cognitive-behavioral construct and on the degree to which they attempt to modify fundamental cognitive process such as perception, memory, information processing, judgment, and decision making.

As a general rule, people strive to behave in ways that are consistent with their beliefs, values, and moral standards. When a person perceives a discrepancy or disconnect between his or her beliefs about what is right and appropriate and how he or she is actually behaving, the person experiences *cognitive dissonance* (i.e., inner discomfort, regret, or guilt). The person will then try to bring his or her behavior more in line with his or her beliefs and standards. However, sometimes people respond to dissonance by adopting new beliefs that fit their behavior. To take an extreme example, consider a soldier placed in a situation where he must kill others. But killing is repugnant because he has always believed that it was wrong to kill another human being. To resolve this inner conflict, this dissonance, the soldier may adopt beliefs that justify or rationalize the killing, such as: "If I don't kill the enemy, he will kill me," "The enemy is less than human and not like me," "The enemy lives in such a terrible society, he is better off dead." In this example, the behavior (killing) gives rise to a change in beliefs about killing.

The cognitive-behavioral approach is helpful in addressing problems of depression, low self-esteem, and various self-defeating patterns. The client must possess the requisite intellectual capacity and a willingness to invest the time needed to monitor and analyze her or his patterns of thought and behavior. (For more information on cognitive behavioral techniques, see Items 8.6, 13.6, 13.7, and 13.10.)

Suggested Readings

Beck, Judith. *Cognitive-Behavioral Therapy*, 2nd ed. New York: Guilford, 2011.

Corcoran, Jacqueline. *Cognitive Behavioral Methods: A Workbook for Social Workers*. Boston: Allyn and Bacon, 2006.

O'Donohue, William, and Jane Fisher, eds. *Core Principles of Cognitive Behavior Therapy*. Hoboken, NJ: Wiley and Sons, 2012.

Ronen, Tammie, and Arthur Freeman, eds. *Cognitive Behavior Therapy in Clinical Social Work Practice*. New York: Springer, 2006.

Dialectical Behavioral Therapy (DBT)

Dialectical behavioral therapy is an elaborated form of cognitive-behavior therapy. The word *dialectical* describes a tension that is built into the therapist's relationship with the client—a tension between acceptance and a push for change, between nurturance and challenge. On one hand, the client's thoughts, feelings, and situations are validated—just as they are—with empathy and understanding and without judgment. But, at the same time, the therapist challenges the client to reconsider his or her assumptions and to try out some different behaviors. The client is taught how to change what needs to change and can be changed and, at the same time, taught ways of accepting and living with those troublesome thoughts, emotions, and circumstances that cannot be changed.

Using both individual and small-group sessions, the therapist helps the client learn four sets of skills: (1) *Mindfulness skills* help the client stay focused on the here and now and avoid wasting energy on regrets from the past and unhelpful worry about the future. Many of the mindfulness skills are borrowed from spiritual practices common to Eastern religions, in particular Buddhism. (2) *Emotion regulation skills* help the client learn how to identify, manage, and control emotional reactions. (3) *Interpersonal effectiveness skills* are those that help the client better communicate his or her thoughts and feelings, become more assertive, and, in general, build more positive and meaningful relationships. (4) *Distress tolerance skills* help the client tolerate and cope with the unwanted experiences and circumstances that cannot be changed. This involves learning how to quiet one's emotions, accurately observe and size up one's situation, identify options, and maintain self-esteem and self-respect despite one's troubles and frustrations.

Ideally, a course of DBT has four components: one-on-one meetings between client and therapist (usually weekly), between-session client–therapist telephone consultations, client participation in a weekly small-group session with other DBT clients, and a weekly meeting between the therapist and her or his consultation team intended to keep therapists motivated, help therapists manage their own stress, and secure guidance from the team.

Dialectical behavioral therapy is increasingly utilized in the treatment of a variety of mental disorders. It is the one form of therapy that shows fairly good results with clients who have a borderline personality disorder, if these clients remain in a program of DPT for at least one year (see Item 15.13). Because of its structure and its emphasis on learning practical skills, the dropout rate tends to be lower than with other forms of therapy.

Suggested Readings

Koerner, Kelly. *Doing Dialectical Behavioral Therapy*. New York: Guilford, 2012.
Dimeff, Linda, and Kelly Koerner. *Dialectical Behavioral Therapy*. New York: Guilford, 2007.
Marra, Thomas. *Dialectical Behavioral Therapy in Private Practice*. Oakland, CA: New Harbinger, 2009.
Van Dijk, Sheri. *DBT Made Simple*. Oakland, CA: New Harbinger, 2012.

Exchange Theory

The principles of *exchange theory* are drawn from the fields of behavioral psychology and economics. This theory is built around the observation that self-interest is a key factor in human motivation. Self-interest frequently explains and usually predicts the behavior and decisions of individuals, families, groups, and organizations. Most people, most of the time, place their own wants and desires above those of other people and will behave in ways that move them closer to whatever they perceive to be of benefit to themselves. Moreover, people strive to protect or preserve that which they value. In short, people seek to maximize benefits and minimize costs.

A client's values are the key predictors of what he or she will define to be a benefit, advantage, or reward, and what he or she will judge to be a cost, disadvantage, or punishment. Various individuals and groups can have quite different ideas about what is desirable and important. For example, some people desire money, possessions, power, and status, whereas others may believe that personal freedom, honor, social approval, friendship, a sense of belonging, or the feeling of a "job well done" are of greatest value. For still others, adhering to a moral code, performing religious practices, and holding on to tradition may be more important than anything else. Similarly, costs are defined differently. Examples of costs are the loss of money or time, the loss of status or respect, dishonor, humiliation, or knowing one has done wrong. Understanding how clients' define costs and benefits is central to understanding their motivation, to predicting how they will behave in certain situations, and to formulating an effective intervention and outcome goal. Knowing how to appeal to a client's self-interest is an essential skill in work with all clients and especially with nonvoluntary and uncooperative clients.

Within micro-level social work practice, exchange theory suggests that a client will make use of a service (e.g., counseling) only if and only so long as she or he believes the benefits (e.g., feeling better, avoiding negative consequences) outweigh the costs. In this situation, costs might include fees, time, loss of privacy, and stress. Exchange theory also helps predict intergroup and interorganizational behavior. As a general rule, the desire to secure rewards and avoid costs determines whether people cooperate and collaborate with others or, perhaps, adopt a strategy of competition and conflict. For example, Social Agency A will cooperate with Agency B if doing so helps A get what it wants. But Agency A will compete with Organization C if it believes it will gain more through competition than through cooperation. If social agencies are expected to cooperate and work together, there must be advantages for them to do so. If there is no incentive to cooperate and collaborate, the agencies will compete for limited resources, such as funding, press coverage, status, staff, and the like. Among the basic principles of exchange theory are the following:

- When a client must choose from among various alternatives, the client will engage in the behaviors that she or he believes will secure the greatest benefits and incur the least costs.
- When a client concludes that all possible alternatives will result in about the same level of reward or benefit, the client will usually select the alternative that has the fewest perceived costs (i.e., disadvantages) and risks.
- When a client believes that all possible alternatives will have immediate outcomes that are about equal, he or she will usually select a course of action that may result in some long-term benefit.
- When a client believes that all possible alternatives will have long-term outcomes that are about equal, he or she will usually select a course of action that might provide an immediate benefit.
- When a client's values have been shaped by a Western, industrialized society, the client will usually choose a course of action that promises the greatest financial gain or the least financial cost.

Closely related to exchange theory is *rational choice theory*, based mostly on the principles of economics. Its core assumption is that people are rational and logical, and, when given a choice, will always choose those alternatives or behaviors that maximize their benefits and minimize their costs. Thus, it is possible to guide people toward desired social goals and choices by designing a system of incentives and penalties. This is the rationale behind many public policies in the areas of health care and social welfare. A weakness is this approach and other economic models is that they overlook the fact that people are not always rational and that they make many decisions on the basis of emotion, misunderstanding, peer pressure, tradition, habit, and many other psychological and social factors.

Suggested Readings

Allingham, Michael. *Rational Choice Theory*. New York: Routledge, 2006.

Appelrouth, Scott. *Sociological Theory in the Contemporary Era*. Thousand Oaks, CA: Pine Forge, 2011.

Robbins, Susan, Pranab Chatterjee, and Edward Canda. *Contemporary Human Behavior Theory*, 3rd ed. Upper Saddle River, NJ: Pearson, 2012.

Psychodynamic Theory

This direct practice framework focuses mostly on the client's deeply personal thoughts, feelings, and inner conflicts. It gives much attention to the power of intense emotions and feelings (e.g., fear, hatred, anger, guilt, lust) and the psychological turmoil they can cause. Psychodynamic theory presumes that many of our choices and behaviors are determined by forces that are largely unconscious or beyond our awareness.

The workings of the mind are conceptualized as the interplay between the ego, id, and superego. The **ego** is the reality-oriented, problem-solving, and decision-making component of the personality that mediates the conflicts between one's primitive drives and impulses (the **id**) and one's values, norms, and moral standards that have been absorbed from family and society (the **superego**). Largely unconscious *defense mechanisms* (e.g., repression, projection, rationalization) operate to minimize or mask the anxiety associated with these inner conflicts (see Item 11.8). The term *ego supportive treatment* refers to an intervention intended to maintain or enhance a client's ego strength and the capacity to make decisions, solve problems, and take needed action.

The psychosocial development of an individual is viewed as progression through life's phases, beginning in early infancy. Accomplishing the developmental tasks of a particular phase sets the stage for the next phase. Negative childhood experiences can disrupt development and result in various psychological problems. The concepts of *object relations* (people relations) describe how current patterns of thought, feelings, and behavior often reflect, at an unconscious level, one's childhood experiences with parent figures.

Change results from the client's cathartic expressions of conflict and feelings; from gaining insight (understanding) into how past experiences gave rise to current troubles; and from facing and working through one's inner turmoil. The change process requires an in-depth professional relationship wherein the client feels safe to express very private thoughts and feelings. It is presumed that the client will often act and feel toward the practitioner as he or she did toward other significant persons such as parents or persons who inflicted psychological trauma, a phenomenon termed *transference.* In some instances, the client is asked to examine this transference to gain self-understanding.

Social workers have adapted various therapeutic methods rooted in psychodynamics to the realities of an agency-based practice and to the social work profession's emphasis on viewing the client within an environmental context.

Recent contributions to this approach incorporate concepts drawn from the cognitive-behavioral approach and family therapy. As a general rule, however, a practice based on psychodynamic concepts gives more attention to the client's psychology than to social, situational, and environmental factors. A client is expected to be motivated, verbal, and willing to participate in numerous therapy sessions. This approach is seldom appropriate if the client has limited intellectual ability, is chemically dependent, or is overwhelmed by adverse social and economic conditions (e.g., poverty, inadequate housing).

Suggested Readings

Borden, William. *Contemporary Psychodynamic Theory and Practice*. Chicago: Lyceum, 2009.
Bower, Marion. *Psychoanalytic Theory for Social Work Practice*. New York: Routledge, 2005.
Brandell, Jerrold. *Psychodynamic Social Work*. New York: Columbia University Press, 2004.
Goldstein, Eda. *Object Relations Theory and Self-Psychology in Social Work Practice*. New York: Free Press, 2001.

Person-Centered Theory

The person-centered approach was borrowed from counseling psychology. With roots in humanistic and existential philosophy, it is constructed around a very positive and optimistic viewpoint that people are basically good, wanting to do what is right, and striving to discover and develop their full potential. It presumes that change will occur when the practitioner provides the client with a relationship that is validating, accepting, and nonjudgmental. Within such a relationship, clients will lower their defenses, examine their attitudes and behavior, and perceive themselves in a more realistic and positive manner.

For the most part, the helping process and the professional relationship is *nondirective*, meaning that the practitioner accepts the client's choice of issues to be discussed and does not guide the discussion toward any particular topic. Also, the helper refrains from giving advice, labeling, and diagnosing. The professional places much emphasis on conveying the qualities of acceptance, empathy, warmth, and genuineness and using the techniques of active listening (see Items 8.1 and 8.4). Within this safe and supportive professional relationship, clients can free themselves of the negative thoughts and feelings that block their innate potential for personal growth and self-actualization.

The person-centered approach presumes that the client will be voluntary, highly motivated, articulate, and interested in self-examination. It is most often used in individual counseling and in personal growth and human potential groups. It is not appropriate for clients who are manipulative, have an addiction, are highly dysfunctional, or burdened by adverse social and economic realities.

Suggested Readings

Holosko, Michael, Jeffrey Skinner, and Ra'Shanda Robertson. "Person Centered Theory." In *Human Behavior and the Social Environment: Theories for Social Work Practice.* Edited by Bruce Thyer, Catherine Dulmus, and Karen Sowers. Hoboken, NJ: Wiley, 2012.

Rowe, William, and Alicia Stinson. "Client-Centered Theory and Therapy." In *Social Workers' Desk Reference*, 2nd ed. Edited by Albert Roberts. New York: Oxford University Press, 2008.

Tudor, Keith. *Person-Centered Therapies*. Thousand Oaks, CA: Sage, 2008.

Interactional Model

As the name suggests, this approach primarily focuses on a client's interactions with others and with various social systems. This is one of the few practice frameworks that developed within social work, rather than borrowed from another profession. It grew out of experiences with typical social work clients in a variety of social agencies and it is applicable in work with individuals, families, groups, and organizations.

The interactional model approach gives primary attention to the client's here-and-now experiences and realities. It recognizes that people naturally seek connectedness, even though disputes, conflict, and ambivalence are a part of social interactions. The social worker becomes an active "third force" who functions as a mediator between individuals, groups, and systems, and seeks to resolve conflicts and expedite effective exchanges. Neither the client's relationships nor the client's problems can be understood apart from their social and environmental contexts. The model presumes that many social work clients will be struggling with concrete problems such as poverty, inadequate housing, and the lack of health care. It also presumes that many clients will be resistant to entering into a professional relationship.

This interactional model consist of four key elements: (1) the client, (2) the social systems and the individuals with whom the client interacts, (3) the interactions that are troublesome to the client, and (4) time. As explained in Item 8.4, this model views the helping process as occurring or unfolding in four phases: the preliminary or preparatory phase, the beginning contracting phase, the middle or work phase, and the ending or transition phase. The model offers specific worker skills that are applicable during each phase.

Suggested Readings

Shulman, Lawrence. *The Skills of Helping Individuals, Families, Groups, and Communities*, 7th ed. Independence, KY: Cengage, 2012.

———. *Interactional Supervision,* 3rd ed. Washington, DC: NASW Press, 2010.

———. *Interactional Social Work Practice*. Itasca, IL: F. E. Peacock, 1991.

Structural Model

The structural approach to direct practice rests on the belief that most of the client problems addressed by social workers are a manifestation of inadequate social arrangements and insufficient resources, rather than, for example, a manifestation of individual pathologies or deficiencies. A client who has a problem is not necessarily its cause.

The social work profession strives to maintain a focus on the person-in-environment. It is, however, inherently difficult to give equal attention to both the client and his or her environment. The structural approach instructs the practitioner to consider, first, changing the client's environment. Whereas other approaches to counseling and therapy focus mostly on helping individuals make changes in their own behavior and attitudes, the structural model aims to modify the client's environment so it can better meet the needs of the individual. Improving social conditions by modifying social structures is the responsibility of all social work practitioners and not an exclusive concern of those practicing in the areas of community organization, social policy development, and social planning.

The four major activities or roles of a social worker are those of conferee, broker, mediator, and advocate. It is assumed that the worker will move from one activity to another, depending on the needs of the client. This model rests on several fundamental principles: Be accountable to the client; identify and engage others who have concerns or problems similar to those of your client; maximize the supports that exist within the client's environment; proceed on the basis of "least contest" (e.g., take on the role of broker before mediator and mediator before advocate); help the client understand the social forces impacting on her or his situation; and teach behaviors and skills that will help the client take control of her or his life.

Suggested Readings

Mullaly, Robert. *The New Structural Social Work,* 3rd ed. New York: Oxford University Press, 2006.

Wood, Gale Goldberg, and Carol T. Tully. *The Structural Approach to Direct Practice in Social Work*, 2nd ed. New York: Columbia University Press, 2006.

Crisis Intervention Model

The crisis intervention model is used to help individuals who are experiencing an acute, psychological crisis. A *crisis* is defined as a time-limited period of psychological disequilibrium, usually set in motion by a personal loss or traumatic event. During a crisis the individual's usual methods of coping prove ineffective. Typically, this period of turmoil, anxiety, and disorganization lasts a matter of weeks, after which the person gradually regains his or her ability to cope. If the individual does not reestablish a pattern of effective functioning, he or she is at risk of developing more serious and long-term problems. Basically, crisis intervention provides "emotional first aid" to cushion the impact of a disruptive event and help restore a more normal level of functioning (see Item 13.14).

When using this approach, the professional is quite directive and will usually offer advice and guidance. Key elements of the model include (1) quick access to the client; (2) frequent contact with client during the crisis period (e.g., five to eight counseling sessions over a four-week period); (3) focused attention on the precipitating event and its subjective meaning to the client; (4) emphasis on helping the client make decisions, take action, and regain control of her or his life; and (5) drawing supportive persons from the client's social network into the helping process.

Suggested Readings

James, Richard, and Burl Gilliland. *Crisis Intervention Strategies*, 7th ed. Independence, KY: Cengage, 2013.

Kanel, Kristi. *A Guide to Crisis Intervention*, 3rd ed. Independence, KY: Cengage, 2012.

Roberts, Albert, ed. *Crisis Intervention Handbook*, 3rd ed. New York: Oxford University Press, 2005.

Task-Centered Model

Many clients know what they need to do to change their situation but are unable to plan and take the needed action. The task-centered approach is designed to help clients (individuals, couples, families, and groups) perform important tasks and activities. This model developed out of work with rather typical social work clients who were experiencing a wide variety of problems and challenges. The approach is especially useful with clients attempting to manage problems caused by a lack of resources. It is fairly effective with nonvoluntary clients.

A specific action or step toward change is termed a *task*. The tasks to be worked on can take many forms, such as making a decision, securing a needed resource, learning a skill, and communicating with another person. Large or complex tasks are broken down into several smaller ones so they are more manageable and so the client can experience some success and maintain motivation. Priority setting is used to limit the number of tasks to only two or three per week. The use of a clear and concrete plan of action and specific time lines for the completion of a task help the client stay focused on what needs to be done. The model is largely empirical, stressing the close monitoring and measurement of task completion (see Item 14.5).

The model's emphasis on taking action and the completion of tasks should not be interpreted as a lack of concern about clients' feelings or inner conflicts. However, this approach rests on the belief that people are more likely to change as a result action than from simply discussing their thoughts and feelings (see Items 12.1 and 12.2).

Suggested Readings

Epstein, Laura, and Lester Brown. *Brief Treatment and a New Look at the Task Centered Approach*, 4th ed. Boston: Allyn and Bacon, 2002.

Fortune, Anne. "Task Centered Practice." In *Social Workers' Desk Reference*, 2nd ed. Edited by Albert Roberts. New York: Oxford University Press, 2008.

Fortune, Anne, and William Reid. "Task Centered Social Work." In *Social Work Treatment: Interlocking Theoretical Approaches*, 5th ed. Edited by Francis J. Turner. New York: Oxford University Press, 2011.

Reid, William. *The Task Planner*. New York: Columbia University Press, 2000.

Psychoeducation Model

When faced with a specific problem or condition, such as a mental illness, both the client and his or her family need information in order to understand what is happening and what they can do about it. The psychoeducation model is designed to improve the functioning of individuals and families by educating them about the problems they are experiencing and about possible interventions. When people have accurate information, they are better able to make informed decisions, focus their efforts, and utilize services. This model originated within the field of mental health, but is now used in a wide variety of practice settings.

Psychoeducation is seldom a stand-alone intervention; rather, it is used to complement or supplement other therapies. As an illustration of psychoeducation, consider the case of John, a man recently diagnosed as having schizophrenia. Both John and his family need information about this disorder, its etiology, progression, prognosis, and treatment options so they can secure treatment and better cope with the bewildering symptoms associated with this illness.

A wide variety of problems or conditions might become the focus of psychoeducation sessions; for example, living with bipolar disorder, substance abuse, going through a divorce, parenting a teenager, coping with the death of a loved one, managing a child with attention deficit disorder, and so on. A program of psychoeducation lessens anxiety and worry, corrects possible misunderstandings, and teaches problem-solving skills and coping strategies. A social worker using psychoeducation must be clear on the goals for a session(s), what a client expects and needs to learn, and how this content can be presented so the client can most easily grasp and apply the information (see Item 13.33).

Suggested Readings

Brown, Nina. *Psychoeducational Groups: Process and Practice*, 3rd ed. New York: Brunner-Routledge, 2010.
Lefley, Harriet. *Family Psychoeducation for Serious Mental Illness*. New York: Norton, 2009.
Walsh, Joseph. *Psychoeducation in Mental Health*. Chicago: Lyceum, 2009.

Addiction Model

This practice framework addresses the challenges of helping a client gain control over an addiction. It rests on a number of beliefs about how addictions develop and their progressively destructive effects on a person's life. The model presupposes that most people with an addiction will usually deny that they have a problem and will resist entering a treatment program. When we think of an addiction we usually think of dependency on alcohol and drugs. However, other problems such as certain eating disorders, gambling, and compulsive sexual activity are appropriately viewed as forms of addiction.

In the beginning stage of an addiction, the individual uses the substance or activity mostly as a means of meeting some psychological need or as a way of coping with a distressing problem. When the substance or activity temporally makes the person feel better, its use has been reinforced or rewarded and, subsequently, it is used again and again. Over time, the substance or activity consumes more and more of the individual's attention and resources and displaces other relationships and activities. As the addiction spins out of control, the individual develops a system of denial, rationalizations, and behaviors that ensure access to the substance or activity.

During the process of successful treatment, an individual with an addiction must abandon denial and acknowledge that he or she has a problem, develop a sense of hope based on the awareness that people with similar problems have made a successful recovery, come to understand how the addiction developed and why it has gotten worse over time, acquire the resolve and social support necessary to make needed changes, and finally, battle the addiction. Even after the individual is able to function without the addictive substance or activity, he or she must continually monitor his or her thoughts, behavior, and lifestyle to avoid being drawn back into the addiction. Both one-on-one counseling and small-group experiences (e.g., 12-step programs) are usually needed to help the person gain control over an addiction. (For more information on chemical dependence, see Item 15.11.)

Suggested Readings

Capuzzi, David, and Mark Stauffer. *Foundations of Addictions Counseling*, 2nd ed. Upper Saddle River, NJ: Pearson. 2012.
Fetting, Margaret. *Perspectives on Addiction*. Thousand Oaks, CA: Sage, 2011.
Van Wormer, Katherine. *Addiction Treatment*, 3rd ed. Independence, KY: Cengage, 2013.

Self-Help Model

Alcoholics Anonymous, Parents without Partners, and Overeaters Anonymous are but a few of the many self-help groups that exist in most communities. Such groups rest on five assumptions and beliefs:

- People have a need to tell their story and to be heard by others. They are receptive to suggestions from those who have similar concerns and experiences.
- People are helped as they help others. We learn from others and have much to teach others.
- People are attracted to and feel most comfortable in small groups that are welcoming, informal, and noncompetitive.
- People are attracted to simple rules and principles that offer practical guidance on how to cope with day-to-day problems (e.g., "Live one day at a time," "Walk your talk").
- Helping and caring for others is a natural human activity and not a commodity to be bought and sold.

In order for the self-help approach to be effective, a participant must be willing and able to listen to others and honestly tell her or his own story. Self-help groups work best with voluntary participants but some groups will welcome nonvoluntary and even court-ordered participants. Self-help groups usually depend on leaders drawn from the group. Some groups rotate the leadership role among its members, although a few look to leadership by professionals or members who have received special training on how to facilitate group sessions.

Sometimes self-help takes the form of neighborhood groups and associations helping each other with, for example, home maintenance chores, child care, sharing transportation or tools, food co-ops, emergency financial assistance, or offering micro-loans to persons trying to start a small business.

Suggested Readings

Gitterman, Alex, and Lawrence Shulman. *Mutual Aid Groups, Vulnerable and Resilient Populations, and the Life Cycle*, 3rd ed. New York: Columbia University Press, 2005.
Kurtz, Linda. *Self-Help and Support Groups*. Thousand Oaks, CA: Sage, 1997.
Norcross, John, et al. *Self Help That Works*, 4th ed. New York: Oxford University Press, 2013.

Solution-Focused Model

A variety of influences, most of them economic, have forced social workers and agencies to do more with less. Insurance companies have even placed limits on the number of therapy sessions that will be covered. This reality has given birth to new forms of brief counseling and therapy. The solution-focused model is one of the more popular forms of short-term intervention. It is built on several assumptions and principles:

"The Clubhouse Model"
a retired item from
7th edition

- Real change and the resolution of problems can occur in a relatively short period of time; because of a ripple effect, even a small positive change can have a positive impact on other aspects of the client's functioning.
- It is not necessary to understand the cause of a problem in order to help resolve it. There are many possible ways of viewing a situation and many right ways of dealing with a problem.
- Clients are the true experts on their life and situation and are in the best position to know what will and will not work to solve their problems.
- Clients do not resist making a change if it seems reasonable and provides relief from distress.
- Clients have strengths and resources that can be identified and mobilized to address their problems.

This approach to working with individuals, couples, and families does not seek to identify or analyze the causes of the client's problem. Rather, the social worker strives to help the client identify what he or she is already doing that is at least partially effective in minimizing its effects. Various questioning techniques are used to help the client recognize that she or he already has some control over the troublesome situation and already possesses some good ideas on how best to resolve it. The client is helped to amplify or expand on those actions (solutions) that are currently making a positive difference, no matter how small it might be. Because this approach accepts the client's definition of the problem and invites her or his ideas on how to solve it, it is inherently more culturally sensitive than approaches that place the social worker in the position of identifying and diagnosing the client's problem. This approach can be quite effective in working with court-ordered, non-voluntary clients and those with substance abuse problems.

Suggested Readings

Greene, Gilbert, and Mo Yee Yee. *Solution-Oriented Social Work Practice*. New York: Oxford University Press, 2011.

Nelson, Thorana, ed. *Doing Something Different: Solution-Focused Brief Therapy Practice*. New York: Bruner-Routledge, 2010.

O'Connell, Bill. *Solution-Focused Therapy*, 3rd ed. Thousand Oaks, CA: Sage, 2012.

Narrative Model

The narrative model of therapy is applied in work with individuals and families. The model is built around the observation that individuals construct personal stories (narratives) in order to describe and explain their life and why things are the way they are. In short, people construct stories to make sense of what they experience and, in a certain sense, create their own reality. Moreover, people react to and are shaped by their own stories, whether factual or not. Narratives can determine whether people value and respect themselves, whether they are hopeful or discouraged, whether they feel adequate or inadequate, and what they expect of themselves and of others.

The stories or narratives that people construct are influenced by societal and community values and beliefs. They also incorporate themes and plots drawn from movies, magazines, and pop culture. And unfortunately, many people derive their expectations and evaluations of their own marriage, parenting, children, and job from the images and stories they see on television.

The therapist helps clients to voice and examine their stories and to understand how these constructed stories can generate unhappiness, misunderstandings, and disappointments. Clients are helped to unravel the assumptions and interpretations on which they have assembled their narratives and then to construct alternative interpretations (new narratives) that are more positive, less restrictive, and less painful.

In addition to careful listening and gently raising questions about the client's narrative, a key technique in narrative therapy is termed "externalizing the problem." This is an effort to separate the person from his or her problem or, more accurately, from his or her story about the problem. The negative narrative, not the person, becomes the target of change. A troublesome narrative may be named the "opponent" or "oppressor" as the client and therapist work to "combat" its effects.

Suggested Readings

Kelly, Patricia. "Narrative Therapy and Social Work Treatment." In *Social Work Treatment: Interlocking Theoretical Approaches*, 5th ed. Edited by Francis J. Turner. New York: Oxford University Press, 2011.

Freeman, Edith. *Narrative Approaches in Social Work Practice*. Springfield, IL: Charles C. Thomas, 2011.

White, Michael. *Maps of Narrative Practice*. New York: Norton, 2007.

Trauma-related Interventions

Several approaches are used to prevent or lessen the negative after-effects of having experienced a traumatic event such as military combat, a horrific natural disaster, a rape, or other violence. As examples, we provide brief descriptions of three types of intervention: Critical incident stress debriefing, exposure therapy, and eye movement desensitization and reprocessing.

Critical incident stress debriefing (CISD) is an intervention designed to prevent the development of post-traumatic stress in people who have been exposed to an extremely disturbing and traumatic experience. A CISD is often made available to police, firefighters, and emergency first responders. Typically, CISD is a one-session, guided group discussion led by an individual trained in this method. The participants come to understand that they are not alone in their reactions and the discussion gives them an opportunity to share their thoughts and feelings in a supportive and confidential environment. Ideally, the session is scheduled within 24 to 72 hours of the incident.

A CISD session will have the following phases: (1) *Introduction*, which outlines the sessions' purpose and ground rules; (2) *Fact phase*, in which the participants talk about where they were when the incident occurred, and what they saw, heard, and smelled; (3) *Feeling phase*, during which emotions felt at time of the incident and at present are shared; (4) *Symptom phase*, during which the participants share their physical symptoms such as vomiting, uncontrollable shaking, and depression; and (5) *Teaching phase*, at which time the leader provides information on alternative ways people react to extreme and abnormal situations. Participants are also given advice on self-care and told how to get professional help if needed. Last is (6) the *Reentry Phase,* when participants consider the possible need for a follow-up session.

Exposure therapy is a type of desensitization used to treat symptoms of post-traumatic stress disorder, phobias, and other anxiety disorders. A traumatized individual will often avoid situations that remind him or her of the trauma. For example, if a man was in a serious car accident, he may experience intense fear at the prospect of riding in a car. If a woman was raped, she may avoid being near men and steer clear of the location of the crime. Such avoidance behavior, if extreme and ongoing, interferes with normal functioning. Exposure therapy can lessen a person's fear and anxiety by assisting the individual to confront the source of his or her fear and avoidance. A couple of methods can be used to facilitate a confrontation with the feared situation, thoughts, or memories. For example, if the woman who was raped now avoids going to her place of work where the rape occurred, the therapist may accompany and support her as she gradually moves closer and closer to the feared location. Alternatively, a client can be encouraged to repeatedly imagine, visualize, and describe in great detail the traumatic experience. This has the effect of helping the client overcome personal fears and anxiety.

The therapy known as **eye movement desensitization and reprocessing** (EMDR) presumes that distressing after-effects of trauma arise when the intensity of the experience overwhelms the usual psychological and neurological coping mechanisms. When the brain does not adequately process disturbing thoughts, images, and emotions, it generates symptoms such as flashbacks, recurring nightmares, intrusive memories, and erratic emotions. This type of therapy helps the traumatized individual reprocess that experience and thereby eliminate or lessen the disturbing symptoms.

This unconventional approach consists of eight distinct phases. The core of the therapy entails recalling and describing thoughts and feelings associated with the traumatic experiences and, in later phases of the therapy, talking about the experience while being attentive to a side-to-side eye movement, tapping, or ear tones. It has been suggested that the eye movements mimic the rapid eye movements of healthy sleep so necessary to psychological health. Some individuals obtain dramatic symptom relief with EMDR. A therapist needs special training in EMDR to use it effectively.

Suggested Readings

Murray, Jennifer, ed. *Exposure Therapy.* New York: Nova Science Publications, 2012.
Parnell, Laurel. *A Therapist Guide to EMDR.* New York: Norton, 2007.
Shapiro, Francine. *Getting Past the Past: Taking Control of Your Life with Self-help Techniques from EMDR.* New York: Rodale, 2012.
Webber, Jane, and J. Barry Mascari. *Terrorism, Trauma, and Tragedies: A Counselor's Guide to Preparing and Responding.* Alexandria, VA: American Counseling Association, 2010.

Family Therapies

The use of a family therapy approach is appropriate when the purpose of an intervention is to modify the interactions among family members and improve the functioning of a family system. Family therapy is feasible if it is possible to assemble all or most family members for a series of sessions and if the members have at least a minimal level of interest in strengthening their family. Most family members should be voluntary participants, although it is expected that some members will have been pressured to attend by the more powerful family members.

Although there are numerous theories and models, they have much in common, such as the family system is the unit of attention, all or most family members are engaged in the change process, the focus is mostly on improving relationships, attention is on current behavior (here and now), the practitioner is especially sensitive to the subtleties of communication among the family members, and active techniques are employed (e.g., family sculpture, role-play, homework). The differences between the various approaches are mostly a matter of emphasizing certain concepts and procedures over others. A family therapist is usually eclectic and draws ideas and techniques from many sources. In order to illustrate how one approach might differ from another, a few of the key assumptions associated with commonly used approaches are presented here.

The **communications approach** presumes that family problems and conflicts are often caused by faulty communication. Change occurs when family members learn to listen to each other, to express themselves and speak honestly. The practitioner models clear communication and uses experiential exercises to demonstrate and teach the skills of effective communication.

As suggested by its name, the **structural approach** focuses primarily on a family's structure and internal organization. Special attention is given to the delineation and interaction of the spousal, parental, and sibling subsystems. Unhealthy alliances and splits among these subsystems and either overly rigid or overly flexible boundaries, rules, and roles are major sources of family dysfunction. Change occurs when the roles and responsibilities of family members are clarified and agreed to by all.

The **family systems** approach focuses on the struggle of family members to simultaneously be a part of a family and be an individual apart from that system. Problems arise when an individual either suppresses the self and is enmeshed with his or her family or, at the other extreme, rejects and disconnects from the family. This approach recognizes that families tend to repeat the patterns of prior generations (i.e., the intergenerational transmission of dysfunction) and are especially sensitive to the problems that arise in the various stages of the family life cycle.

An approach known as **strategic family therapy** gives special attention to the distribution and use of power within the family and to family rules (i.e., the often unstated family beliefs about how family members should think and behave). The word *strategic* connotes the active and directive role by the therapist in strategically selecting interventions that move the family toward behaviors deemed desirable and healthy by the therapist.

The **social learning approach** draws concepts and techniques from behavior therapy and behavior modification. It presumes that family conflicts and problems arise because the members have not learned basic skills such as communication and conflict resolution, and/or that positive and functional behavior is not being reinforced within the family system. Thus, the practitioner places a heavy emphasis on teaching. *Functional family therapy* resembles the social learning approach but also attends to the wider social and community context of family functioning. It also focuses on how family problems often reflect unsuccessful efforts by family members to cope with the struggles of dependence versus independence, freedom versus control, and intimacy versus distance.

The **narrative approach** to working with families focuses mostly on the personal and family stories and anecdotes that family members construct to explain and interpret their own lives, situations, and problems. (See "Narrative Model" in this chapter.)

As is true of psychotherapy in general, most approaches to family therapy grew out of work with middle- and upper-class families. Consequently, they may not be as effective when utilized with families that are economically poor or members of an oppressed minority group. Social workers are challenged to select approaches that can be adapted to agency-based practice and to their profession's emphasis on social functioning and the person-in-environmental construct. To help them make that selection, Kilpatrick and Holland (2013) offer a practical **integrative model** that ties the use of various family therapies or family interventions to four levels of family need and functioning. For example, the approaches recommended for a family struggling to meet basic needs (food, safety, equality, etc.) would be different from the ones recommended for a family having problems related to a lack of communication and intimacy. (For more information on work with families, see Items 11.4, 11.19, 11.20, and 12.7.)

Suggested Readings

Becvar, Dorothy, and Raphael Becvar. *Family Therapy*, 8th ed. Upper Saddle River, NJ: Pearson, 2013.

Collins, Donald, Cathleen Jordan, and Heather Coleman. *An Introduction to Family Social Work*, 4th ed. Independence, KY: Cengage, 2013.

Fenell, David. *Counseling Families,* 4th ed. Denver: Love, 2012.

Kilpatrick, Allie, and Thomas Holland. *Working with Families: An Integrative Model by Level of Need*, 5th ed. Upper Saddle River, NJ: Pearson, 2013.

Nichols, Michael. *Essentials of Family Therapy*, 6th ed. Upper Saddle River, NJ: Pearson, 2014.

Small-Group Theories

Work with groups occurs in a variety of social work settings for a multitude of purposes. For example, small groups are created and designed for the purposes of teaching and training, therapy, mutual support, social action, and recreation. There are a number of models in social group work. Differences among these approaches have to do with the purpose of the group (e.g., an agency planning group versus a treatment group); the role assumed by the professional (e.g., group leader, therapist, teacher, mediator, or facilitator); and whether the professional is focused mostly on the behavior of the individuals within the group or mostly on the functioning of the group as a whole or as a social system. Numerous orienting theories provide social workers with background knowledge on small groups and such matters as leadership, structure and norms, group cohesion, intensity of group conflict, stages of group development, and communication issues. For purposes of illustration, we will identify some applications of group work and a few of the practice frameworks used by social workers.

"The Family Preservation Model" a retired item from 7th edition

Task-oriented groups are formed for the purpose of carrying out a specified set of activities or to achieve a specific goal. Examples include committees and agency boards. These goal-oriented groups tend to be structured and formal. The group's leadership and officers are elected by the membership. Typically, a written agenda and *Robert's Rules of Order* guide the discussion and decision-making process.

When groups are used for the purpose of **teaching and training**, the social worker assumes the roles of leader and teacher. Depending on the topic being addressed (e.g., parent training, learning a job skill) and the number of times the group will meet, there may or may not be an emphasis on promoting member interaction and developing a sense of belonging to the group.

The **developmental approach** is used to promote normal growth and development, and the learning of ordinary skills for living. Many of the groups that are part of YMCA/YWCA programs, summer camps, after-school programs, and senior citizen programs are of this type. In these developmental groups, the worker typically assumes the role of leader, planner, and arranger of group activities and makes heavy use of programming (see Item 13.22).

The **group treatment approach** views the group as a therapeutic environment and a tool to change the behavior or attitude of the individuals in the group. The focus is mostly on the problems each is having outside the group. It is assumed that a member's behavior within the group will usually reflect or mimic his or her behavior and functioning in other environments such as family, school, or workplace. In a treatment group, the social worker assumes the role of a therapist, expert, and group leader. In some groups, such as those used in the treatment of sex offenders and persons addicted to alcohol or drugs, there is heavy use of challenge and confrontation and members are required to complete assigned homework and strictly adhere to established rules.

The **interactional model** places the social worker in the role of a mediator between members of the group and between the group and its wider environment, including the agency that has sanctioned the group's formation (see the description of the interactional model in this chapter). The worker gives attention to both the functioning of individual members and to the functioning of the group as a whole. This approach assigns a high value on client self-determination. (For more information on groups, see Items 11.21, 12.7, 12.8, 13.21, 13.23, 13.26, and 13.30.)

Suggested Readings

Garvin, Charles, Maeda Galinsky, and Lorraine Gutierrez. *Handbook of Social Work with Groups.* New York: Guilford, 2004.

Gitterman, Alex, and Robert Salmon, eds. *Encyclopedia of Social Work with Groups.* New York: Routledge, 2009.

Greif, Geoffrey, and Paul Ephross, eds. *Group Work with Populations at Risk*, 3rd ed. New York: Oxford University Press, 2011.

Macgowan, Mark. *Guide to Evidence-Based Group Work.* New York: Oxford University Press, 2008.

Toseland, Ronald, and Robert Rivas. *An Introduction to Group Work Practice*, 7th ed. Upper Saddle River, NJ: Pearson, 2012.

Organizational Change Models

Organizations must constantly adapt to their ever-changing social, political, and economic situations and environments. Various models of organizational development and change can be used to modify the functioning of a human services organization in order to increase its ability to address the needs and concerns of its clients and staff. A change effort may be the result of a lengthy and methodical process of analysis and articulating a plan for incrementally making needed changes (see Item 12.10 for information about strategic planning), or it may stem from concerns by staff members and/ or clients that some problem in agency functioning must be immediately repaired. In either case, the change effort will typically involve the agency's top administrative staff, the board of directors of a private agency, or elected officials and legislative committees if a public agency.

The complexity of organizational change becomes apparent when one recognizes that organizations are made up of numerous individuals, each with a unique personality and each with specific roles and tasks to perform; a set of formal and informal structures, procedures, and norms; and established power and authority relationships. Moreover, an organization is a legal entity whose purpose and functioning is tied to a charter and bylaws (private agency) or to certain legislation and statutes (public agency), as well as to its available resources (e.g., staff, facilities, funding).

Every social worker employed by an organization, regardless of position, must give some attention to how well it is functioning. A social agency must be efficient in using its resources, yet provide appropriate and adequate services to meet the needs of its clients. As one moves from line worker to supervisor or middle manager, or to agency administrator, the responsibility to engage in organizational maintenance and change activities increases. Such activities typically include informing upper-level administrators of staff concerns and client needs, proposing specific changes in agency policies and procedures, arranging for input from consultants, participating on committees to study specific aspects of the organization's performance, conducting program evaluations, and so on.

The selection of an approach to planned organizational change will depend on the nature of the organization, including its history and culture. Three models describe most organizations. The **rational model** assumes that those who are part of the organization are in agreement about its goals and committed to those goals. Thus, an organization is primarily a way of structuring the work that needs to occur in order to reach a goal. Given that view, proposed changes (e.g., restructuring, personnel assignments, adoption of new technologies, reallocation of resources) will be accepted if it becomes apparent that they would improve the organization's capacity to achieve its goals. Change following the rational model results from such activities as self-study, obtaining the advice of consultants, examining the complaints or suggestions made by clients or consumers (see Item 14.10), in-service training on new technologies, and so forth.

The **natural-system model** views an organization as a system made up of a multitude of individuals, roles, subsystems, and formal and informal processes striving to function and survive in a wider and complex environment. It recognizes that the personnel of an organization can be easily distracted from the organization's official mission by such things as job stress, unclear work assignments, and disagreements over duties and responsibilities. This model views an organization as needing to balance its goal achievement with maintenance functions. Change efforts emphasize the clarification of goals and objectives, improving communication, recognizing and addressing the social and emotional needs of personnel, morale building, and the like.

The **power-politics model** assumes that an organization is essentially a political arena in which various individuals, departments, and other units compete for power, resources, and personal advantage. Consequently, the achievement of the organization's official or stated goals may take a backseat to other agendas. To change such an organization, one needs access to persons in positions of influence and power and one must be able to persuade them that a specific change is in their self-interest. External forces such as media exposure, investigations by citizen groups, legislative oversight, and lawsuits might be necessary for modifying these organizations.

Depending on the organizational model that best reflects the agency, a social worker might adopt one or more of the following strategies or approaches for generating change in a human services organization. The **policy approach** achieves change by developing and adopting new policies that will guide the organization and its operation. Those working for change direct their efforts toward the groups and individuals who are authorized to make policy and allocate resources at either the local, state, or national level. They provide these decision-makers with data and new insights concerning a specific condition, problem, need, or issue, and advocate for a specific policy change (see Item 13.28).

A **program approach** seeks to change the organization by designing and introducing new or additional programs and services to better express and implement existing policy (see Item 14.9). Change efforts are directed primarily at people in administrative and managerial positions (i.e., those with authority to modify specific programs and alter the procedures and technology used in the work of the organization).

The **project approach** introduces change at the interface between line staff and the clients or consumers of the organization's services. Small-scale projects are used to test or demonstrate new ways of working with agency clients. Policies and programs remain the same but staff skills and performance are enhanced, often through in-service training and increasing sensitivity to clients' needs.

An approach termed **client-centered management** focuses mostly on the relationship between organizational procedures and client outcomes. It is predicated on the belief that an excessive emphasis on powerful decision-makers, funding bodies, interagency communication, and personnel issues diverts the attention of administrators from their primary purpose—assuring that the social agency provides high-quality services that truly respond to client needs. This approach strives to secure client input into agency decision making and planning (see Item 14.10).

The **teamwork model** is primarily concerned with the manner in which workers interact to implement agency programs. It is based on two premises. First, it recognizes that the typical bureaucratic organization places excessive control in the hands of administrators, which, in turn, reduces innovation and consensus among workers about how best to provide services. Second, it recognizes that given the explosion of knowledge and technology, specialization is increasingly required in almost every occupation, but with specialization comes the need for better coordination. The providers of human services must be able to coordinate practice activities since services to clients are often provided simultaneously by several disciplines and several different agencies. Unfortunately, the department structure used in many agencies may erect barriers to coordination because the lines of communication and decision making are organized by profession, role, and job title, rather than by the need for an integrated approach to service delivery.

The teamwork approach has proven especially useful as a means of retaining the specialized knowledge and competencies of the several helping professions, and at the same time, coordinating their practice activities (see Item 13.25). To make multidisciplinary teams viable working units, they are given the authority to plan and implement programs and to make decisions about the personnel and resources necessary to carry out their assignments. In this process, the teams become powerful forces for innovation as well as policy and program change.

Suggested Readings

Lewis, Judith A., Thomas R. Packard, and Michael D. Lewis. *Management of Human Service Programs*, 5th ed. Belmont, CA: Brooks-Cole, 2012.

O'Connor, Mary Katherine, and F. Ellen Netting. *Organization Practice: A Guide to Understanding Human Services*, 2nd ed. Hoboken, NJ: Wiley, 2009.

Patti, Rino J., ed. *The Handbook of Human Services Management*. Thousand Oaks, CA: Sage, 2009.

Community Change Models

Social workers are frequently involved in efforts to improve the functioning of a community and increase its capacity to address the concerns of its members. Whenever such a change is being considered, it is important to recognize that the word *community* can be defined in several ways. For example, a community might be defined as the people who live in a particular geographical area (e.g., neighborhood, town, or city) or the word *community* might be applied to the people who share a common interest, focus, or concern (e.g., people who are working to protect the environment or those who share a particular religious orientation). The selection of a particular approach to community change must be based on an assessment of the problem or concern targeted for change and, to a large extent, on political factors. If the social worker has the authority, responsibility, and/or support of others to work toward a specific community change, his or her efforts will be more likely to succeed. Yet, even under the best circumstances, community change is a slow and time-consuming process.

Social work embraces three models of community practice, and each rests on a different set of assumptions concerning how *community* is defined, the change process to be followed, and the role of the professional.

The **participatory engagement model** presupposes that the community consists of people who share a sense of belonging to their local area and can work together to reach a consensus on how to address community problems. It emphasizes broad citizen participation, sharing of ideas, democratic decision making, cooperative problem solving, and self-help. In the process of working on problems, people learn the practical and leadership skills needed to tackle other concerns of the community. In performing most community-level social work practice, the professional performs such functions as enabling, facilitating, coordinating, and teaching.

The model of change known as **social planning** focuses on specific social problems (i.e., crime, inadequate housing, lack of health care, etc.) and seeks to improve the responses of the human services delivery systems to these problems. It is a data-driven approach that recognizes the complex legal, economic, and political factors that must be addressed in solving a community problem. Although involvement by ordinary citizens is welcome, the key to community problem solving and change is involvement by influential persons, government officials, and organizations that have authority, power, and influence. This approach also recognizes the need to involve people and organizations from outside the immediate locality such as state and federal government agencies, and, on some matters, corporations that do business in the community. The social worker using this approach gives much attention to fact gathering, data analysis, policy analysis, sharing technical information, and program planning.

The third model, **social action**, is usually associated with efforts to correct a social injustice or achieve a needed change for a devalued or disadvantaged group (e.g., those living in poverty, those who experience discrimination). It views a community as consisting of diverse groups and special interests that are competing for power and limited resources. Thus, in order to bring about a change in human services programs, there must be a shift in the decisions of those who exercise power and influence—or new decision-makers must be given authority to take action (see Items 11.25 and 13.37). Since it is assumed that those in control will not easily relinquish their power, change requires confrontation with those who have power. The functions of the professional within this model include those of organizing, advocating, and negotiating.

Suggested Readings

Delgado, Melvin, and Denise Humm-Delgado. *Asset Assessments and Community Social Work Practice.* New York: Oxford University Press, 2013.

Hardcastle, David A. *Community Practice: Theories and Skills for Social Workers*, 3rd ed. New York: Oxford University Press, 2011.

Minkler, Meredith, ed. *Community Organizing and Community Building for Health and Welfare*, 3rd ed. New Brunswick, NJ: Rutgers University Press, 2012.

Netting, F. Ellen, Peter Kettner, and Steve McMurty. *Social Work Practice with Communities and Organizations*, 4th ed. Boston: Allyn and Bacon, 2008.

Weil, Marie, ed. *The Handbook of Community Practice*, 2nd ed. Thousand Oaks, CA: Sage, 2013.

CONCLUSION

As suggested by this survey of conceptual frameworks, the intervention approaches used by social workers have similarities but may differ in what they emphasize. Some differ in terms of basic assumptions about how and why change occurs (see Chapter 7 for additional ideas about the nature of change); others differ in the characteristics of the clients they are intended to serve. A lifelong activity of the social worker is to carefully select a configuration of perspectives, theories, and models that match his or her practice style and best meets the needs of his or her clients. The reader is reminded that no one approach is always or inherently superior to others and that a social worker needs to have a basic understanding of several. One's practice framework might include multiple perspectives and an ever-growing repertoire of practice theories and models. Since all frameworks are concerned with helping people change, the worker must always be cognizant of the whole person—humans are thinking, feeling, and behaving biological beings whose survival, growth, and development depend on constant interaction with others and their environment.

SELECTED BIBLIOGRAPHY

Beckett, Chris. *Essential Theory for Social Work Practice*. Thousand Oaks, CA: Sage, 2006.

Borden, William. *Reshaping Theory in Contemporary Social Work*. New York: Columbia University Press, 2010.

Coady, Nick, and Peter Lehmann. *Theoretical Perspectives for Direct Social Work Practice*, 2nd ed. New York: Springer, 2007.

Encyclopedia of Social Work, 20th ed. (in four volumes). Edited by Terry Mizrahi and Larry Davis. New York: Oxford University Press, 2008.

Oko, Juliette. *Understanding and Using Theory in Social Work*. Thousand Oaks, CA: Sage, 2011.

Payne, Malcolm. *Modern Social Work Theory*, 4th ed. Chicago: Lyceum, 2014.

Walsh, Joseph. *Theories of Direct Practice*, 2nd ed. Independence, KY: Cengage, 2010.

7

Using Evidence in the Change Process

LEARNING OBJECTIVES

At the conclusion of this chapter, the reader should be prepared to:

- Exhibit commitment to using evidence-based knowledge as a primary consideration when engaged in client and client situation assessment, selection of intervention approaches, and monitoring and evaluating practice activities.
- Recognize the importance of critically evaluating the relevance and validity of information being considered in relation to a practice situation.
- Recognize that each practice situation is unique and that a social worker must adapt the planned change process to the context of each situation.
- Discuss the several groups of actors that might be engaged to successfully complete a planned change process.
- Recognize that carefully moving through all phases of the change process (i.e., intake/engagement, data collection/assessment, planning/contracting, intervention/monitoring, and termination/evaluation) is likely to yield the most successful outcomes.

The admonition that the social worker should "Guide the process, not the client" is fundamental to effective professional practice, yet perhaps oversimplifies the complexity of guiding client change. One must first fully understand the client situation, help identify the change needed, engage the client in efforts to bring about that change, and, finally, evaluate the success of the change effort. To perform these tasks, the social worker must select the best knowledge and intervention strategies, engage in critical thinking about the application of that knowledge, and guide the client through the often difficult process of making a change in her or his functioning.

The issues that social workers help clients address are ones that frequently evoke strong feelings and emotional responses within clients, in other people affected by the situation, and even within the social worker. Intense and often irrational emotions can easily get in the way of achieving a clear understanding of a troubling situation and developing the best possible plan for addressing the matter. It is important, therefore, that the social worker insert into the practice situation a steadfast commitment to bringing an informed and rational perspective to the process. Critical to this effort is identifying and using approaches, procedures, and interventions that are supported by research and judged to be a best practice in addressing the client's problem or concern.

CONDUCTING EVIDENCE-BASED PRACTICE

Increasingly, social work and other helping professions are emphasizing **evidence-based practice**, a term suggesting that the practitioner is to draw on the strongest documented information to guide practice-related judgments and decisions. This orientation strengthens the scientific basis of practice and is consistent with the *NASW Code of Ethics* (1999), which calls for social workers to inform practice with empirical knowledge and within the framework of social work ethics. This approach calls on social workers to critically examine and evaluate their own practice, keep current on the professional literature, and remain open to the implications of new research.

In the past, many social workers assumed that their good intentions, compassion, common sense, and adherence to core social work values were sufficient to bring about desired changes. We now recognize that something more is required. Clients deserve social workers who will think critically about the concerns they want to address and will search out and apply interventions that have been evaluated and found effective.

Given their heavy caseloads and time demands, social workers can easily find excuses for not spending precious time searching professional journals, textbooks, and the Internet for information to guide their practice. All too often, those excuses provide only a short respite from the time crunch and, in the long run, create added time pressures because the most effective assessments and interventions were not applied and, as a result, the client's concerns or problems continue to occupy the worker's time. (Item 11.22 offers guidelines for accessing evidence to obtain the most applicable information to inform one's practice.)

It should be recognized, however, that because many client situations are unique and highly complex, not all social work practice can or should be based only on research findings and professional literature. Indeed, many decisions and actions must be based largely on professional values, ethics, legal statutes, agency policy, and court orders. Moreover, practice-related decisions must always consider such factors as the client's personal preferences and special circumstances. But, to the extent possible, social workers should strive to base their practice on the best evidence available.

Because *evidence-based practice* has become such a popular phrase in social work, it is often used without fully appreciating the different phases of the helping process where evidence should be sought and applied.

- When making an *evidence-based assessment,* the social worker seeks out and makes use of theory and research data that will expand his or her understanding of the practice situation. Two sets of data are utilized; one focuses on the client's specific condition or problem, and the other focuses on the client group or population being served.

  In social work education, the courses that fall under the heading of *human behavior and the social environment* provide knowledge about the development and functioning of individuals, families, groups, and communities. Although this information is extensive, it usually does not provide enough depth to adequately guide interventions related to a client's particular condition or problem. Thus, the worker must search the literature for more specific information to better understand, for example, the implications for a family if a child is diagnosed with Down syndrome, or if an older parent is exhibiting signs of dementia, or perhaps if a couple is experiencing sexual dysfunction.

Another aspect of evidence-based assessment seeks to learn more about the client population being served. For example, if the worker's client is an adolescent, what does the worker need to know about adolescence as a stage in human development? When working with a client who is a member of a vulnerable or oppressed group, the worker will want a better understanding of how prejudice and discrimination impacts the day-to-day life of an individual or family. Or the worker may need to find information about a religion that is central to a specific client's life.

Fortunately, much information on various illnesses, disabling conditions, social problems, and population groups is available online, and search engines provide links and easy access to relevant websites. Additional sources are, of course, social work journals, textbooks, and documents published by organizations that focus on particular conditions, social problems, and issues.

- Evidence-based practice also involves drawing on the most dependable information available about the many approaches for helping clients make needed changes (i.e., *evidence-based intervention*). But how does one decide which approach is most appropriate for a given client? To answer that question, the professions are beginning to engage in "best practices" research, in which intervention approaches are carefully scrutinized in relation to success rates when applied to specific client conditions or specific client populations. This information does not assure practice success, but it can clearly suggest intervention approaches the social worker should consider. Ultimately, it is the judgment of the individual social worker that should prevail.

- *Evidence-based evaluation* is a response to the obligation of social workers to evaluate and document the effect or impact of their intervention. For example, a managed care organization may refuse to pay for client services unless the social worker offers evidence that a particular intervention is both appropriate and effective when working with a specific client condition. Increasingly, social workers are expected to describe the changes or outcomes that they anticipate from a specific intervention and empirically measure these changes, a topic addressed in Chapter 14.

CRITICAL THINKING WHEN MAKING PRACTICE DECISIONS

The social worker's skills in critical thinking are also essential for successful practice outcomes. **Critical thinking** is a process used by social workers to make judgments regarding the accuracy and applicability of information about the client, the client's condition, intervention alternatives, and evidence of client change. It is not sufficient for a social worker to assume that a usual or common approach will be relevant and applicable to a specific client or situation. Rather, the worker must have the discipline and take the time to thoughtfully sift through the information available and make the best choices for each individual client.

The skills of critical thinking include the following:

- Clarifying and defining key terms and concepts and using them in a consistent manner
- Determining the credibility of an information source
- Differentiating relevant from less-relevant information
- Distinguishing between verifiable and unverifiable claims and statements
- Checking the accuracy of a statement or claim
- Recognizing proper and improper use of research and statistics
- Separating informed thoughts and logic from emotions and feelings
- Identifying biased, ambiguous, irrelevant, and deceptive arguments
- Recognizing logical fallacies and inconsistencies in an argument or line of reasoning
- Reaching conclusions about the overall strength of an argument or conclusion

Critical thinking is especially important in social work because all people develop beliefs or ideas that they draw on to interpret new experiences. Such frames of reference or conceptual maps are necessary to human thought and reasoning, yet are also a potential source of errors, bias, and distortion. A critical thinker, however, recognizes that all ideas (e.g., concepts, theories, definitions) are provisional and subject to reformulation. They are inventions constructed to describe and explain our understanding and judgments at a particular time. Critical thinking requires recognition that these inventions may not represent "truth" about the topic, are invariably incomplete, and are likely to shift as we have new experiences or acquire more information.

Critical thinking also requires an ability to distinguish between a fact, an assumption, an opinion, and a value. A *fact* is a statement of what is or of what happened that can be independently verified by empirical means. A fact is more or less solid, depending on how easily it can be confirmed. An *assumption* is an idea that is taken for granted or presumed to be accurate for the sake of making an argument but is recognized as possibly untrue or inaccurate. An *opinion* puts forward one particular interpretation or viewpoint when it is understood that other credible interpretations are also possible. An opinion based on critical thinking has some factual basis, is rooted in extensive experience, and is derived from careful judgment. A *value* is a strongly held belief concerning what is truly worthwhile, right or wrong, and the way things are supposed to be.

In our efforts to think clearly, it is also useful to distinguish between information, knowledge, and wisdom. The term *information* refers to a more or less random collection of concepts, facts, and opinions. *Knowledge* is an orderly and coherent arrangement of relevant and trustworthy information related to a specific topic. The term *wisdom* relates to the integration of observations and knowledge that has a truly lasting quality. Typically, wisdom is a distillation of key ideas and principles drawn from a broad base of knowledge, careful and in-depth examination, and based on substantial practical experience. Wisdom implies both having knowledge and knowing the limits of that knowledge. These distinctions help us realize that a person can possess much information but lack real knowledge. Also, a person can be very knowledgeable on a topic still but lack wisdom.

The critical thinker is aware of his or her susceptibility to self-deception. All too often, we rely on our perceptions and what is convenient and comfortable for us to believe. We tend to ignore facts and ideas that do not fit with our expectations and too often we hold tightly to whatever we already believe, even in the face of evidence to the contrary. Another aspect of self-deception is our tendency to seek knowledge until we find what supports our preferred ideas, positions, and personal agenda. Moreover, we tend to look harder for evidence that supports our view than for evidence that refutes it.

An important dynamic giving rise to uncritical thinking is our desire to be right and to convince others to agree with us. That is why we so often become defensive when our beliefs are questioned. The more fragile our self-esteem, the more likely we are to be threatened by new ideas, and the more likely we are to uncritically accept ideas proposed by others, especially the ideas that we want to believe.

When thinking critically about a claim or assertion, consider the following:

Purpose

- Who is making this claim? How reliable and trustworthy are these individuals or sources?
- Why do those making the claim or assertion want me to believe it?
- What motives or circumstances might cause them to make misleading, false, or erroneous claims?
- Do they have something to gain from my acceptance of this claim or assertion?
- Am I attracted to this argument or claim because I want to believe it or perhaps because it meets some emotional need?

Evidence

- Are the terms used to present the claim clearly defined and explained?
- Is the claim or assertion rooted in facts? Assussmptions? Opinions? Values?
- Does the claim or assertion recognize the complexity of the matter being considered, or is it an oversimplification or superficial understanding of the topic?
- Are the facts and figures used to support the argument correct and complete? Have relevant facts been omitted or distorted?

Interpretation

- Could the facts and figures be interpreted in other ways or assigned different meanings?
- Have irrelevant and extraneous facts been added to the argument in order to create confusion or divert the focus from the central question?
- Has the claim or assertion been framed or stated in a way that allows it to be subjected to independent verification, objective observation, and scientific study? Were the studies as free as possible from bias? Have the studies been replicated?

Critical thinking and a search of the literature for "best practices" are especially important when an unconventional intervention (such as rebirthing, aroma therapy, or crystal therapy) has been requested or suggested for use in a particular case situation. A social worker must first decide if this is a valid approach and make an informed judgment about its effectiveness and the risk of this approach for the client—and the social worker. Clearly, a social worker is more vulnerable to a malpractice suit if he or she is unable to demonstrate that an intervention or treatment is the one most effective and appropriate to the client's problem or situation (see Item 16.6).

Having the self-discipline to draw on the best evidence available and to think critically about that information is fundamental to responsible and ethical practice. Critical thinking need not occur in isolation. It is often strengthened through discussion of the available information with colleagues and supervisors.

GUIDING THE PLANNED CHANGE PROCESS

Change is inevitable. Humans and all of the social systems created by humans are constantly adjusting and adapting within their ever-changing environments. Many of the changes experienced by individuals and families are set in motion by the natural consequences of biological maturation and aging, and also by personal choices such as selecting a certain occupation, attending a specific school, choosing a particular person as a spouse or partner, raising children, or getting a divorce. Still other changes are imposed on people by illness, accidents, natural disasters, and even world events such as wars and shifts in the economy. These events and experiences change the way people think, feel, and behave, and they may constrict or expand their choices and opportunities.

Although many of the changes experienced by individuals, families, groups, and organizations are unplanned, unintended, and unwelcome, others are deliberately chosen and achieved through individual and group effort. Such intentional change can be called a planned change. Within social work, professional efforts to help clients bring about a planned change are called *interventions*. Interventions are designed to allow the social worker to temporarily enter into client's life, thoughts, and decisions to help alter some specified condition, pattern of behavior, or set of circumstances to improve a client's social functioning or well-being.

An intervention or a **planned change** is a *process*: a series or sequence of actions directed toward the achievement of a specific end. However, the use of the word process should not be interpreted to mean that the change effort, once underway, will naturally unfold and proceed on a predictable path toward its goal. Quite the opposite is usually true. Given the complexity of change, change efforts can easily lose momentum and movement toward a goal can easily be derailed.

In some ways evaluation of a planned change effort is similar to evaluating a scientific experiment. Based on knowledge and a working hypothesis, the social worker takes certain steps and then monitors the effects to determine what, if any, change has occurred. However, an intervention will usually have both expected and unanticipated outcomes.

Change—even if wanted and planned—is often difficult to achieve and requires a considerable investment of time and effort by both the client and the worker. Consequently, some degree of emotionally laden *reluctance* can be expected. The social worker who is helping others make a change must be ready to address this reluctance and be comfortable with the client's expressions of fear, frustration, and anxiety.

Resistance to change, too, is a characteristic of humans and their social systems. People tend toward preserving the status quo and resist change, particularly if it is rapid or especially upsetting to familiar patterns. The social worker must anticipate and be prepared to deal with resistance, even in a case where the client has expressed a strong desire to change.

Closely related to resistance is *ambivalence*, which is a condition of both wanting and not wanting a particular change. For example, an abused wife may want to leave her abusing husband in order to escape the abuse but at the same time not want to risk the loss of the financial security she has while married. Such a client is pulled in opposite directions and may become immobilized and unable to make decisions or take action to change the situation.

Helping clients sort through their perceptions of the risks and rewards associated with change is another important social work activity. If the potential rewards outweigh the risks, most clients will attempt the change. However, if the change involves high risk or promises few or uncertain rewards, clients may be reluctant to work toward change.

No one, whether professional or not, can make someone else change. In the final analysis, it is, of course, the client who alone must create or bring about the desired change. However, significant change is rarely something that can be accomplished alone. Almost always, change requires the help, assistance, and support of other people.

Success in making changes is largely a function of the client's motivation to change, capacity for change, and opportunity to change. *Motivation*, which can be viewed as a state of readiness to take action, represents the balance between hope for improvement and the desire to avoid discomfort. Clients will work toward change if they believe this change is truly possible (i.e., the pull of hope) and if they are sufficiently dissatisfied or distressed with their current situation (i.e., the push of discomfort). A client's level of motivation may vary over time and from one social context to another. Thus, a meaningful assessment of a client's motivation must be tied to some specified goal or action rather than being viewed as a personal trait or characteristic.

One's *capacity* for change reflects the abilities and resources that clients or other people in the clients' environment bring to the change process. These capacities include time, energy, knowledge, experience, self-discipline, optimism, self-confidence, communication skills, problem-solving skills, money, political power, and so on. Different types of change require different capacities. For example, the capacities needed by someone to perform successfully as a participant in a therapy group may be significantly different from those needed to communicate effectively with his or her teenaged son and different still from those capacities needed to adjust to the limitations of a chronic illness.

Change further requires *opportunities*—that is, various conditions and circumstances within the client's immediate environment that invite and support positive change. For example, consider the situation of a young man on probation who genuinely wants to find a job and stay out of trouble. His environment consists of his family, peer group, neighbors, law-enforcement personnel, and so on. In addition, his day-to-day life is influenced by community attitudes, economic conditions affecting the availability of jobs, and other social forces. All of these influences will have much to do with whether this young man finds a job and stays out of trouble.

When a social worker becomes involved as a facilitator of planned change, he or she adds professional resources and knowledge to the client's motivation, capacities, and opportunities. The role of the social worker can be conceptualized as taking action and applying knowledge and skills designed to increase motivation, expand capacity, and create or uncover opportunities for change.

THE CONTEXT OF PLANNED CHANGE

Whether the social worker's client is an individual, a family, a group, an organization, or a community, the client's concern or problem always exists within a wider context. A multitude of social, economic, cultural, legal, and political factors affect client functioning.

However, many of these factors are beyond the influence of both the client and worker. Reality demands that the client and social worker narrow their focus and zero-in on those aspects of the situation that can be influenced and changed.

For the purpose of further explaining the process of planned change, the term **client situation** is used here to describe that segment of the client's total existence, experience, and circumstances that are the focus of the planned change effort. The *observed situation* (or objective situation) is the client's situation as viewed by people in the client's environment and perhaps expressed by professionals using commonly understood terminology, categories, and classifications. By contrast, the *perceived situation* (or the subjective situation) is the situation as it is felt by and subjectively interpreted by the client. This perception reflects the client's hopes and fears, desires and aspirations, and usually the client's history and life experiences. The situation as perceived by the client may be significantly different from how it is viewed by professionals and others in the client's environment.

The importance of the client's perceived situation to the change process is recognized in the social work axiom "Start where the client is." The starting point for planned change is for the worker to understand the client's concern and situation from the client's subjective point of view. It is this element of subjectivity—the client's deeply personal and unique thoughts and feelings—that makes it so difficult to predict how clients will respond to a given intervention.

An awareness of the contextual and situational aspects of planned change yields several fundamental guidelines for social work practice:

- The social worker must give primary attention to the client's problem or concern as it is defined, perceived, and experienced by the client.
- The worker must focus primarily on those aspects of the situation and the client's environment that most immediately and directly affect the client.
- The intervention must address those aspects of the situation over which the client and/or the worker have some control and influence.
- The social worker must recognize the multitude of forces pushing and pulling on the client but understand that the actual impact of those forces is at least partially dependent on the client's subjective interpretation.
- The worker must be prepared to intervene at one or more levels (e.g., individual, family, organization, community), depending on the nature of the client's concern, the client's interpretation of the situation, what the client wants to do about it, and what the client can reasonably expect as an outcome.
- The worker should be prepared to use a variety of techniques, approaches, and services—whatever is done must make sense to the client, given his or her perceptions and circumstances. Preference should be given to approaches that reinforce, guide, and build on the positive forces already at work in the client's life (i.e., client strengths) and, at the same time, remove or overcome barriers that block change.

IDENTIFYING ACTORS IN PLANNED CHANGE

Efforts by a social worker to facilitate change typically involve numerous individuals, groups, and organizations. To be effective in working with these varied interests, the social worker must clarify the purpose and goal of each intervention and what is expected of each of the many actors in the change process. Drawing from the widely accepted conceptualization by Pincus and Minahan (1973), we suggest the following terminology to help make needed distinctions among the various actors:

- *Change agent system.* The social worker and the worker's agency.
- *Client system.* The person, group, or organization that has requested the social worker's or agency's services and expects to benefit from what the worker does.
- *Target system.* The person, group, or organization that is identified or targeted for change in order for the client system to benefit or overcome its problem. (In many situations, the client system and the target system are the same.)
- *Action system.* All of the people, groups, and organizations that the change agent system (e.g., the social worker) works with or through in order to influence the target system and help the client system achieve the desired outcome.

An episode of practice typically begins with the client system and the change agent system coming together and contracting to address a particular client concern. They identify the person(s), group(s), or organization(s) that need to change and then reach out to and involve them to help facilitate the change. For example, a single mother (the client system) may approach and contract with a human services agency to receive counseling from an agency social worker (the change agent system) on how to help her 10-year-old son who is withdrawn and socially isolated because he is ridiculed or teased by schoolmates. If both the mother and child need to change, both would be target systems. If the social worker draws the child's teacher, the school principal, and the school psychologist into the helping process, these become part of the action system. If the intervention also attempts to change the behavior of the other children at school, they are also part of the target system.

PHASES OF THE PLANNED CHANGE PROCESS

An intervention or planned change activity typically moves through several sequential phases, with each phase building on previous ones. The uniqueness of each phase is that the social worker is focusing on specific actions, information, decisions, or outcomes. If the social worker is to guide the change process, he or she must become an expert regarding the tasks that must be accomplished at each phase.

Descriptions of these phases have been a part of the social work literature throughout the history of the profession. In her classic book, *Social Diagnosis* (1917), Mary Richmond described several steps necessary in helping people. Forty years later, Helen Perlman (1957) echoed the same theme when describing helping as a problem-solving process that involved three major phases: (1) beginning with *study* that would ascertain and clarify the facts of the problem, followed by (2) *diagnosis*, where the facts would be analyzed, and concluding with (3) *treatment* that involves making choices and taking actions to resolve the problem. In subsequent years, various authors divided these phases into more discrete units, described them in more detail, and demonstrated their application in a range of helping approaches and in work with client systems of various sizes. Elements of the planned change process typically include:

- Identify, define, and describe the client's concern, troublesome situation, or problem.
- Collect data needed to better understand the client's concern or situation and its context.

- Assess and analyze the concern and situation and decide what needs to change, what can be changed, and how it might be changed.
- Identify and agree on the goals and objectives (outcomes) to be achieved by the process of planned change.
- Formulate a relevant and realistic plan for reaching the goals and objectives.
- Take action based on the plan (i.e., carry out the intervention).
- Monitor progress of the intervention and determine if it is achieving the desired outcomes and, if not, modify the plan and try again.
- Once goals and objectives have been reached, terminate the intervention and evaluate the change process to inform future practice activities.

The logical progression of these phases gives the appearance of a linear, step-by-step set of activities. In reality, change rarely proceeds in an orderly fashion; rather, it is more of a spiral, with frequent returns to prior phases for clarification or a reworking of various tasks and activities (see Figure 7.1). During each phase, the worker also anticipates future phases, tasks, and activities and lays the groundwork for their completion.

At any given time, it is helpful to be clear about where the client is in the process of planned change because the worker draws on somewhat different techniques to accomplish the tasks of each phase. What is helpful in one phase might be ineffective or even counterproductive in another. For example, it would be an error for a worker to discuss with an abusive mother her possible participation in an anger management group (i.e., planning and contracting) when she has not yet concluded that there is something inappropriate and harmful about how she disciplines her child (i.e., data collection and assessment).

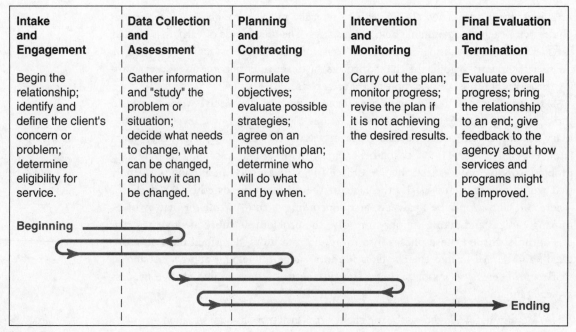

Figure 7.1
Phases of the Planned Change Process

CONCLUSION

Faith in the ability to change human interactions and social conditions to improve people's well-being is at the very heart of social work practice. This belief in the potential for positive change is more than wishfulness. It is a fundamental belief that planned change activities can indeed be successful.

When guiding a planned change process, the social worker makes several important contributions. She or he understands the whole process necessary for change and guides the client(s) through the several phases, being sure that the key decisions or actions to be accomplished at each phase are indeed completed. The social worker also contributes critical insights that the client would not normally be expected to possess. This includes seeking out and engaging in evidence-based assessment—in terms of drawing on the best evidence found in the literature regarding people with the client's characteristics, evidence regarding the issues to be addressed in the practice situation, and the relationship between the two factors. In addition, the social worker should have researched the "best practices" to use in that client's situation (evidence-based intervention) and should be competent in using that approach or skilled in referring the client to someone who is. Finally, throughout the process the social worker must monitor progress in the situation and engage in critical thinking that can lead to sound decision making to improve the chances of a successful practice outcome.

The five phases of the planned change process described in Figure 7.1 are an important part of the structure of this book. Because the phases reflect activities that should be accomplished as the practice episode unfolds, it is possible to identify various practice techniques and guidelines that are most likely to be helpful in each phase. In Chapters 10 through 14 more than 100 techniques and guidelines are presented. A description of the work to be done in each phase is provided in each chapter's introduction and the various items are divided into those most likely to be used in providing services directly to clients, and those that support the indirect practice activities in which social workers are typically engaged.

SELECTED BIBLIOGRAPHY

Drisko, James, and Melissa Grady. *Evidence-Based Practice in Clinical Social Work*. New York: Springer, 2012

Glissen, Charles A., Catherine N. Dulmus, and Karen M. Sowers, eds. *Social Work Practice with Groups, Communities, and Organizations: Evidence-Based Assessments and Interventions*. Hoboken, NJ: Wiley, 2012.

Holoako, Michael J., Catherine N. Dulmus, and Karen M. Sowers, eds. *Social Work Practice with Individuals and Families: Evidence-Informed Assessments and Interventions*. Hoboken, NJ: Wiley, 2013.

Perlman, Helen. *Social Casework: A Problem Solving Process*. Chicago: University of Chicago Press, 1957.

Pincus, Allen, and Anne Minahan. *Social Work Practice: Model and Method*. Itasca, IL: F. E. Peacock, 1973.

National Association of Social Workers. *Code of Ethics*. Washington, DC: NASW, 1999. (http://www.naswdc.org/pubs/code/default.asp)

Orme, John G., and Terri Combs-Orme. *Outcome-Informed Evidence-Based Practice*. Upper Saddle River, NJ: Person, 2012.

Richmond, Mary. *Social Diagnosis*. New York: Russell Sage Foundation, 1917.

Roberts-DeGennaro, Maria, and Sondra J. Fogel, eds. *Using Evidence to Inform Practice for Community and Organizational Change*. Chicago: Lyceum, 2011.

Rutter, Lynne, and Keith Brown. *Critical Thinking and Professional Judgment for Social Work,* 3rd ed. Thousand Oaks, CA: Sage, 2012.

Thyer, Bruce A., Catherine N. Dulmas, and Karen M. Sowers. *Developing Evidence-Based Generalist Practice Skills*. New York: Wiley, 2013.

PART 3

TECHNIQUES COMMON TO ALL SOCIAL WORK PRACTICE

The two chapters in Part III focus on techniques and guidelines that are fundamental to all of social work practice, regardless of agency setting or type of client served. This content lays a foundation for understanding and applying the more specialized techniques and guidelines that appear in Parts IV and V.

In every setting, the social worker must be a skillful communicator and able to develop relationships. Thus, several items focus on the skills and tools of effective communication and relationship building. Although many of the examples are drawn from direct service, most of the techniques are applicable in work with organizations and communities.

Few beginning-level workers are prepared to cope with the time pressures and paperwork they encounter. Thus, items in Part III offer information on maintaining client records, writing reports, time management, and managing a workload. Given an expansion of computer applications in social work, a worker must know at least the basics of information technology and know how to access online resources.

Because social work can be a stressful occupation, workers must be able to apply principles of stress management. Throughout her or his career, the social worker must strive to continually learn and grow as a professional person. The worker's ability to master these tasks often determines whether she or he will be successful and thrive in social work.

8

Basic Communication and Helping Skills

LEARNING OBJECTIVES

At the conclusion of this chapter, the reader should be prepared to:

- Identify the key characteristics or qualities of an effective helping relationship.
- Determine whether verbal messages are accurately communicated.
- Describe the importance of nonverbal behaviors in face-to-face communication.
- List and describe several helping skills that social workers might use in interviews with clients.
- Recognize the influence of human emotions on behavior.
- Identify several interviewing techniques that may be helpful when dealing with a client who is guarded, resistant, and/or defensive.
- Describe an example of a social worker exhibiting cultural competency in social work practice.

This chapter presents what might be called "the basics" of social work communication and relationship building. It focuses on generic communication and basic helping skills—those used with all clients, whether an individual, a family, a small group, an organization, or a community.

The purpose of a social worker's interaction with a client will determine what type of relationship he or she attempts to create and, of course, also his or her messages to the client. A worker providing direct services (e.g., case management, counseling) to individuals and families will strive to develop a professional relationship characterized by qualities known to positively affect the outcome of the helping process, such as acceptance, empathy, personal warmth, and genuineness. By contrast, the indirect-services worker who is, for example, interacting with the members of an agency board or a planning committee, will build relationships that are more formal and characterized by communications that are concise, precise, and task-oriented.

Essentially, **communication** is a process in which one individual conveys information, intentionally or unintentionally, to another.

Communication is a form of behavior, but not all behavior is communication. It occurs when a person attaches meaning to the behavior, verbal or nonverbal, of another. Communication is primarily a receiver phenomenon; regardless of what the sender may say in words or intend to communicate, it is the person on the receiving end who assigns meaning to another's words and gestures.

It is important to recognize the complexity and limitations inherent in our efforts to communicate. Because each individual has a unique personality and has had a particular set of life experiences, she or he possesses various perceptual filters and patterns of thought that affect how messages are sent and received. Thus, one individual may notice things that others overlook, and messages that are important to one person may be inconsequential to another.

Most communication involves the use of words. A word is but a symbol. A word may have somewhat different meanings to a variety of people, depending on their belief system, life experiences, capacity of abstract thinking, and familiarity with the language being used. The words of a language have literal, or denotative, meanings (i.e., dictionary definitions) and they may also have an implied or connotative meanings. The meaning of a word, phrase, or nonverbal gesture may depend on who is using it and the social or situational context.

Communication also depends on the functioning of the physical senses (e.g., vision, hearing) and the cognitive activities of the brain, which include **attention** (focusing on certain stimuli while disregarding others); **perception** (using pattern recognition and sensory memory to interpret stimuli picked up by our senses); **memory** (retaining information over time); **language** (interpreting, expressing, and remembering verbal and written words and symbols); **conceptualization** (organizing information and ideas into categories); **reasoning** (drawing conclusions from information); and **decision making** (choices based on an anticipation of future events). These cognitive processes are interrelated and overlapping. If the senses are impaired (e.g., a hearing loss) or if the brain has been damaged, the ability to communicate will be limited to some degree.

One of the most important factors affecting people's communication is their self-concept, or how they define themselves in relation to others (see Item 11.10). One's self-concept can affect how a message is understood and interpreted. For example, an individual with pervasive feelings of inferiority may be guarded and find it difficult to speak honestly and listen attentively to others. A defensive individual may find it difficult to accept direction, instruction, or constructive criticism.

The capacity to send and receive messages accurately is strongly influenced by one's emotional state and expectations. Not infrequently, we hear what we want to hear and what we expect to hear. People may unconsciously misinterpret the messages sent by others in order to avoid feeling inner conflict or emotional discomfort. Individuals with certain personality disorders are especially prone to twist and distort messages (see Item 15.13).

The lack of clear communication is a common cause of problems within families and organizations. In general, communication problems develop in these situations:

- We speak for others rather than allowing them to speak for themselves.
- We discourage or suppress another's communication by ordering, threatening, preaching, patronizing, judging, or blaming.
- We allow our prejudices to color our interpretations of what others are saying.
- We do not take the time or make the effort to really listen.

- We do not speak honestly or truthfully because we want to avoid disagreement and conflict.
- We assume that others already know or should know what we think.

8.1 CREATING AN EFFECTIVE HELPING RELATIONSHIP

The nature of a professional relationship is shaped by the reason why the social worker and client are meeting, the client's presenting concern or request, the agency's program and procedures, and the practice framework utilized by the social worker. A positive relationship between the social worker and the client is necessary, but by itself, it is not sufficient to facilitate change. The application of specific techniques is also necessary. Without a positive relationship, change is not likely to occur. With a positive relationship, the various helping techniques and skills are more likely to have their intended effect.

Some type of relationship will develop whenever a social worker and a client interact. It may be either positive or negative, depending mostly on the client's interpretation of the worker's words and actions. A social worker cannot make a positive relationship happen but can endeavor to be the type of professional that most clients find helpful. It is important to note that a positive and effective helping relationship is not free of tension. Because change is difficult and often resisted, a relationship intended to promote change will be somewhat stressful and taxing for both the client and the social worker.

A number of qualities characterize a helpful and therapeutic relationship. At the very heart of these relationships is **human caring**. A social worker must genuinely care about his or her clients. Clients expect a social worker to be knowledgeable, but they will not pay much attention to what the worker knows until they are convinced that the social worker really cares. **Trust** is always basic to the relationship. When clients trust a social worker, they have faith and confidence in the worker's integrity, ability, and character. Trust develops when the client experiences the social worker as truthful, dependable, and competent.

Empathy is the social worker's ability to perceive the client's inner experiences of thought and feeling. It is often described as the capacity to step into the client's shoes and see things from the client's perspective. A worker can convey empathy by giving the client her or his undivided attention and by applying the techniques of active listening to demonstrate that the worker understands the client's feelings and perceptions (see Items 8.4 and 8.6).

The quality of **unconditional positive regard** exists when the social worker views a client as having inherent worth and treats him or her with respect, regardless of what the client may have done or how he or she behaves during an interview. The word *unconditional* is meant to convey the notion that clients are to be treated with fairness and thoughtfulness simply because they are human beings, not because they have somehow earned the right to such treatment.

Unconditional positive regard is closely related to the admonition that a social worker should maintain a **nonjudgmental attitude** in work with clients. Whenever clients feel they are being judged or criticized, they become defensive and may withdraw from the relationship. Thus, in order to be helpful and to facilitate positive change by the client, the social worker must be able to suspend making moral judgments within the professional relationship. Needless to say, there are times when this is difficult to do. A social worker is most likely to become judgmental when the client has violated the worker's own cherished values and moral principles such as having abused a child or committed a murder or rape. When a worker has negative feelings toward a client, she or he must exercise self-discipline so as not to damage the professional relationship.

To say that the social worker should strive to be nonjudgmental is not to suggest that he or she cannot or should not make professional and objective judgments concerning the client's attitude, behavior, or functioning. Neither does it mean that the worker must condone harmful and inappropriate behavior. A client's inappropriate and destructive behavior will need to be discussed and confronted if it is related to the client's presenting concerns and/or the reason he or she is involved with the worker's agency. However, the unacceptable behavior must be discussed in an objective manner, not in a way that will belittle or disparage the client.

The relationship characteristic of **personal warmth** exists when the social worker responds to clients in ways that help them feel safe and accepted. Without the quality of warmth, the worker's words will sound hollow and insincere and have no therapeutic impact. Warmth and acceptance are conveyed mostly through nonverbal communication, such as a smile, a soft and soothing voice, a relaxed but interested posture, and appropriate eye contact.

The condition or quality of **genuineness** refers to a professional who is real and speaks from the heart. Social workers who are genuine and authentic are unpretentious and spontaneous. What they say matches what they do. They lack any hint of phoniness. However, genuineness is not the same as being totally honest about all things, for the worker must be sensitive to the needs and emotional state of the client. Those who are new to social work sometimes worry that they cannot behave in a professional manner and at the same time be real and authentic in their relationships with clients. That concern reflects a misunderstanding of professionalism. Being a professional has nothing to do with playing the role or trying to imitate some image of a professional person. A true professional is caring, knowledgeable, self-disciplined, responsible, ethical, and, most of all, effective. There is no conflict between those qualities and being genuine.

In addition to caring, trustworthiness, empathy, positive regard, personal warmth, and genuineness, certain other conditions are important to a helping relationship: **concreteness** (being able to communicate one's thoughts and ideas in ways that are understandable and clear to the client), **competence** (proficiency in carrying out professional tasks and activities), and **objectivity** (factual, impartial, and able to appreciate differing points of view).

In some situations the building of a professional relationship can be enhanced through the use of **structuring**, a term that refers to various arrangements (e.g., worker–client matching) and symbols (e.g., worker dress and office environment) intended to make the professional more attractive to and trusted by the client. The use of structuring is based on the premise that clients are most likely to be influenced by someone they respect and with whom they feel comfortable. This will often be someone who the client perceives as similar to herself or himself in terms of fundamental beliefs and life experiences. Thus, a social worker might find it useful to mention similarities he or she has in common with the client. For example, the worker might point out that he or she and the client both have children of about the same age or that they share the experience of having grown up on a farm.

Whether the similarities and differences between the client and the worker have a significant impact on the helping relationship is mostly a function of the client's expectations and perceptions. A client who is different from the social worker in terms of age, race, gender, culture, or socioeconomic status may have several concerns and even worries—for example: Can this social worker understand my situation, background, and life experiences? Does he possibly dislike people like me? Does she really care about me and have my best interests at heart? Does this worker have the knowledge, skills, and experience needed to resolve my problems?

Expertness, or the appearance of expertness, can have a positive impact on the initial phases of the helping process. Such things as certificates and diplomas on the wall, a neat and comfortably furnished office, and appropriate professional attire can help to create a positive first impression. To the extent possible, offices and meeting rooms should be inviting, private, and comfortable. If a client must talk with the social worker in a space that lacks privacy and comfort, respect for the worker is diminished. Although the social worker must be alert to the importance of such factors, she or he should remember that clients, like all people, make deliberate decisions about whose influence they accept and whose they reject.

When considering the nature and effectiveness of a helping or therapeutic relationship, it is important to be aware of the phenomena of transference and countertransference. **Transference** occurs when a client projects onto the social worker some motive, intention, or belief that has no basis in reality but rather reflects the client's own desires or expectations rooted in prior experiences such as his or her relationship with a parent or authority figure. The content of the transference might be, for example, feelings of love, romance, resentment, anger, fear, or dependency. Some indicators that a troublesome transference is developing within the worker–client relationship are when the client becomes excessively dependent on the worker; when the client implies that the worker is hostile, rejecting, or manipulative; when the client presumes that the worker desires a romantic relationship; and when the client cannot accept the normal social boundaries inherent in a professional relationship.

The phenomenon of **countertransference** exists when it is the professional's emotional needs, desires, and personal history that cause him or her to misinterpret the client's behavior and intentions. This might happen, for example, when the client reminds the professional of a parent, an ex-spouse, or perhaps his or her own child. A social worker's use of professional supervision, mentoring relationships, and ongoing efforts to expand self-awareness can help to prevent problems of countertransference (see Items 16.3 and 16.8).

Selected Bibliography

Cochran, Jeff, and Nancy Cochran. *The Heart of Counseling: A Guide to Developing a Therapeutic Relationship.* Belmont, CA: Thomson, 2006.

Fox, Raymond. *Elements of the Helping Process*, 3rd ed. New York: Routledge, 2013.

McKenzie, Fred. *Understanding and Managing the Therapeutic Relationship.* Chicago: Lyceum, 2011.

8.2 VERBAL COMMUNICATION SKILLS

Social workers use two broad categories of verbal skills: (1) those intended to facilitate interpersonal helping and (2) those intended to facilitate the exchanges of information within an agency, between agencies, and among professionals. Skills commonly used in direct-practice activities (e.g., face-to-face work with individual clients, families, or therapeutic groups) are described below in Item 8.4. The verbal skills in the second category are presented here.

Communication involves both a message sender and a message receiver. The sender has a responsibility to convey her or his message in a way that is easily received and understood. The receiver has a responsibility to make sure that she or he has accurately received the sender's intended message and has not, in some way, distorted or misinterpreted that message. When **sending a message**, follow these rules:

- Use clear, simple language. Speak distinctly and not too fast.
- Pay attention to your body language; make sure it is congruent with your message. Maintain appropriate eye contact and utilize gestures.
- Do not overwhelm or overload the receiver with information. Break up a lengthy or complex message into several parts so it can be more easily understood.
- Ask the receiver for comments, questions, or feedback so you will know whether your intended message was understood.

When in the position of listening to or **receiving a message**, remember these rules:

- Stop talking. You cannot listen when you are talking.
- Put the message sender at ease and remove distractions.
- Be patient with the message sender and do not interrupt.
- Ask questions if it will help you understand or help the sender clarify his or her message.

The skill of **planning a message** refers to anticipating an upcoming episode of communication and structuring your message around the answers to questions such as the following:

- How much time is available for this exchange?
- When and where am I most likely to have the full attention of the person who is to receive my message?
- What are the essential points of my message?
- What aspects of my message are most likely to be misunderstood?
- How can I organize and present my message so it will be understood and accepted by the receiver?
- Do I have the necessary credibility, position, and status to deliver this message or should someone else present this message?

Because it is the middle portion of a message that is most likely to be misunderstood and distorted by the receiver, the most important points should be placed at the beginning and the end of your message.

The skill of **identifying self** is a concise description of who you are and how your role and responsibilities relate to the conversation. For example:

You may remember me from a previous meeting, but let me begin by introducing myself. My name is Mary Jones. I am a social worker with the Evergreen Family Services Center. Your doctor has asked me to speak with you to find out if . . .

The skill of **explaining the purpose of the communication** refers to the sender's statements that describe the reason for the communication. This helps the receiver place the message in a proper context. For example, a child welfare worker speaking to a prosecuting attorney might say:

As you know, my agency has 10-year-old Ryan Johnson in one of our foster homes. I need to speak with you in order to get a clear idea about when you plan to have Ryan testify in court. This is important to me because I have to inform his school of a planned absence and also arrange Ryan's transportation to the courthouse.

Sometimes, it is important to respond to a receiver's nonverbal communication (e.g., facial expressions) if it suggests confusion. The skill of **following up on nonverbal communication** refers to such efforts. For example:

John, I noticed that you looked a bit puzzled when I was explaining the new agency procedure for scheduling appointments. If you have a question, please ask me at this time.

Such follow-up efforts are especially important when the receiver's nonverbal behavior or communication suggests that he or she disagrees with the message. Here is an example:

When I was explaining the proposed policy change, I could not help but notice that several of you were looking rather distressed. As your supervisor, I want to know how you feel about the proposal. Bob, Anna, and Judy—please voice your thoughts on the proposed policy change.

Sending a message of complaint or constructive criticism is always a challenge because it can so easily put the receiver on the defensive and block further communication. The technique called the **I-statement** or *I-message* refers to a particular way of structuring and wording a message so as to minimize that possibility. To understand the I-message, it is important to recognize that during times of conflict, confrontation, and hurt feelings, we so often use "you-statements"—for example: "You need to study more," "You make me angry," and "You are being selfish and rude." Such you-messages cause the person on the receiving end to feel put down and wanting to strike back.

An I-statement consists of three parts: (1) a brief, clear description of the troublesome behavior, (2) a description of the feeling experienced because of that behavior, and (3) a description of the tangible impact this behavior has had on the message sender. For example:

When you did not show up for our scheduled appointment (troublesome behavior), I felt upset and angry (feeling) because I don't like having to wait around and because I could have spent that time with another client (tangible impact).

The structure of an I-statement allows the sender, the person bothered by the behavior of another, to say, in effect: "This is my concern, this is how your behavior affects me, and this is how I am feeling." Implicitly it says: "I will trust you to decide what change is needed." It gets a point across without sounding accusatory.

The skill of **checking for message reception** refers to the use of questions and probes to determine whether your message has been accurately received. For example:

I am aware that what I have just described is complex and potentially confusing. I want to make sure you understand. Would you please repeat to me what you heard me say?

When on the receiving end of a message, it is desirable to use the skill of **checking one's receipt of a message**. This involves using probes and questions to verify that you have, in fact, accurately received and understood the message. For example:

Before we end this conversation, I want to make sure that I understand what you have told me. Let me take a minute and repeat what I heard you say. If it sounds like I have misunderstood something, please correct me.

It is surprisingly difficult to ask questions. All too often, we attach unnecessary words or extraneous concerns to our basic question, and this can confuse the point of our query. In order to receive a clear answer, your question must be clear. This calls for the skill termed **asking a focused question**. Consider first this example of a very awkward question directed to an agency administrator:

> I am confused about these new agency policies, especially the ones about foster care and, in some ways, about a lot of the policies. This policy manual is organized in an unusual way. What is really expected of us? I mean, what are we supposed to do with new cases and how do we handle the court-ordered evaluations?

It would be difficult for the administrator to give a clear answer because several questions have been asked and all of them are rather vague. The question would be much more focused if phrased like this:

> I have a question about the policy described on page 86 of our agency manual. My question is, do I need my supervisor's written approval before I request a psychological evaluation on a foster child?

The skill of **answering a question** refers to the ability to formulate statements that respond directly to the question asked. This seems simple enough but often people fail to carefully listen to a question. In the following example, a supervisor makes this error but then makes a correct response:

> WORKER: I need some direction on where to send this report. Do I send it to the County Attorney or directly to Judge Smith?
>
> SUPERVISOR: Just remember that Judge Smith is a stickler for details and he wants the report to be concise.
>
> WORKER: Well, yes, I know that but what I need to know is where to send the report.
>
> SUPERVISOR: Oh, I'm sorry. I didn't answer your question. Send it directly to Judge Smith.

Many communication problems arise because people attach different meanings to words or phrases. The skill of **checking for word meaning** refers to inquiries intended to make sure that all parties to a message exchange agree on the meaning of key words. Consider the following example:

> CHAIR OF PLANNING GROUP: I think we need to shift about 20 percent of our budget into child abuse prevention programs.
>
> COMMITTEE MEMBER (checking for meaning of words):   Well, I may or may not agree, depending on what you mean by prevention. Are you thinking of primary or a secondary level of prevention?

Selected Bibliography

McKay, Matthew, Martha Davis, and Patrick Fanning. *Messages: The Communication Skills Book*, 3rd ed. Oakland CA: Harbinger, 2009.
Moss, Bernard. *Communication Skills in Health and Social Care*, 2nd ed. Thousand Oaks, CA: Sage, 2012.
Sidell, Nancy, and Denise Smiley. *Professional Communication Skills in Social Work*. Upper Saddle River, NJ: Pearson, 2008.

8.3 NONVERBAL COMMUNICATION SKILLS

Experts tell us that about 65 percent of the communication occurring during a face-to-face exchange is nonverbal (i.e., conveyed by facial expressions, gestures, etc.). This nonverbal activity is usually beyond our awareness. Consequently, we sometimes say one thing with words and without knowing it communicate something quite different in our nonverbal behavior.

Eye contact is a powerful means of communication. Our eyes reveal much about our emotional state and our reactions. In most Western cultures (e.g., North America, Europe), making eye contact indicates openness and a willingness to engage in communication, whereas avoiding eye contact is viewed as being closed to communication and sometimes suggesting a dishonest intention. In other cultures, such as those of many Native Americans and people from Asia and the Middle East, making direct eye contact is considered to be intimidating, disrespectful, and/or even sexually aggressive. In some cultures, even a private conversation between unmarried men and women may be judged as inappropriate.

Gestures of greeting are important to relationship building. In North America, a firm handshake is the expected gesture among both males and females. However, for many people from countries in Asia and the Middle East, a strong and firm handshake suggests aggression. An embrace or hug is a common greeting among males in Russia, the Middle East, and Latin America. Bowing is the appropriate gesture among the people of Japan, Thailand, and India; the lowest ranking person bows first, and the depth of the bow reflects the status of the person for whom the bow is offered.

Personal space is another important nonverbal element in interpersonal communication. In general, being close to someone communicates trust and interest, but being too close is threatening. People from North America typically prefer to be about an arm's length from one another, whereas those from Asian cultures usually prefer a greater distance. People from the Middle East and Latin America are often toe-to-toe during their conversations. The social worker can avoid invading a client's personal space by reading the client's body language and adjusting accordingly.

Body positioning conveys various attitudes and intentions. It is usually best to face the client at a 90-degree angle, since this suggests both safety and openness. Facing the client directly may communicate aggressiveness. Leaning slightly toward the client communicates attention and interest. When the social worker sits behind a desk, it suggests that the worker is in a superior position and this may cause the client to be more reserved and formal.

Facial expressions—such as smiling, frowning, nodding and shaking the head, lip quivering, and blushing—register our thoughts and emotions. The face is the most expressive part of our body and makes us most vividly present to others. Facial expressions may reveal a worker's disapproval of a client, even when the worker is trying to be nonjudgmental.

Touch is a powerful communication. For example, by touching another's hand, arm, or shoulder or by offering a gentle hug, we can convey reassurance, sympathy, or understanding. However, a social worker must be cautious about touching a client, especially if the client is of the opposite sex or from an unfamiliar cultural background. A social worker's innocent touch can be misinterpreted as a sexual advance or as intimidation by someone who has been physically or sexually abused or by someone with an intense need for attention and affection.

Arm and hand movements frequently communicate strong emotions. Crossed legs, arms folded across the chest, and a rigid posture suggest a defensiveness and resistance, whereas arms and hands in an outreached position or at the body's side suggest openness to others. Clenched fists indicate anger or anxiety. Fidgety movements, finger tapping, and leg bouncing suggest impatience, nervousness, or preoccupation.

Tone of voice will often reveal the emotion we are feeling. A loud and forceful tone suggests anger, aggressiveness, and control. A meek and scarcely audible voice suggests fear and submissiveness. A monotonous or flat voice suggests a lack of interest.

Dress and appearance are also important forms of nonverbal communication. Our choices of clothing and accessories (e.g., jewelry, tattoos) and our hairstyle send a message about who we are or who we want to be and may display our membership in a particular social group or subculture. A social worker must give careful thought to his or her appearance and avoid choices that might distract clients or make them feel uncomfortable. Clothing that is highly unusual or sexually suggestive always should be avoided.

Selected Bibliography

Kavanagh, James. *Worldwide Gestures.* Blaine, WA: Waterford, 2000.

Knapp, Mark, and Judith Hall. *Nonverbal Communication in Human Interaction,* 7th ed. Independence, KY: Cengage, 2010.

Remland, Martin. *Nonverbal Communication in Everyday Life,* 3rd ed. Upper Saddle River, NJ: Pearson, 2009.

8.4 HELPING SKILLS

As used here, the term **helping skill** refers to a message the practitioner presents to the client because the worker believes it will have a beneficial effect. The moment-to-moment decisions concerning what type of message should be sent is guided by the purpose of the interview and by what the social worker knows about the client and her or his situation. Helping skills have both verbal and nonverbal components (see Items 8.2 and 8.3).

We offer here brief descriptions of commonly used helping skills. The terminology applied to some of these skills is borrowed or adapted from Shulman (1981, 2009). The examples used to illustrate a particular skill are drawn from one-on-one interviews, but these skills are also applicable in work with families and groups. Many of the more specialized techniques presented in the remainder of this book are elaborations and special adaptations of the elemental skills described here.

GETTING READY

Prior to the meeting the client face-to-face, the worker should envision what the client might be thinking and feeling as he or she enters the agency expecting to discuss some personal concern and possibly a very painful matter. By trying to anticipate how the client might feel, the worker begins to develop empathy for the client and prepares to address the client's initial reactions and feelings (e.g., anger, fear, confusion). The worker can then plan ways to ease the client into the helping relationship. This has been termed the *tuning-in phase* of the helping process (see Items 10.1, 10.2, and 13.1).

GETTING STARTED

During the intake and engagement phase of the change process and also at the beginning of each session with a client, the social worker must clarify the purpose of the meeting and the worker's role. The helping skill of **explaining purpose** refers to a simple, nonjargonized statement that describes the general purpose of the meeting. It serves to define expectations and reduce client confusion and anxiety. For example:

> WORKER: I am pleased that you were able to meet with me today. As you know, your wife first came to this agency about three weeks ago. She expressed worry about your marriage. I would like to hear your thoughts and find out if you also believe there are problems in the marriage.

When the client initiates the first contact, the worker should encourage the client to begin by describing his or her reason for requesting the interview. If the client has a hard time doing this, the worker might ask some general questions about the circumstances that led up to the request and what the client hopes will come from the meeting.

When the social worker has initiated the first contact, he or she should begin by explaining its purpose in a manner that is clear, direct, and to the point. Consider these two examples of explaining purpose:

GOOD EXPLANATION: I need to talk with you about your son, Max. He has missed 14 of the last 20 school days. I am concerned and I would like to get your thoughts on this problem.

POOR EXPLANATION: Hi there. I know your son Max. I was in the neighborhood so I decided to stop by to chat. How are things going?

The skill of **encouraging the client's feedback on the purpose of the communication** refers to statements that encourage the client to respond to the worker's explanation. This gives the client an opportunity to ask questions or perhaps voice disagreement. Here are two examples:

WORKER EXAMPLE 1:   What are your reactions to what I have said about the purpose of this meeting? Do you perhaps see things differently?

WORKER EXAMPLE 2:   It's quite possible you and I have different thoughts about why we are talking today. I want to know if you were expecting something else.

The skill of **describing the worker's role and method** refers to statements intended to give the client a beginning idea of how the worker might be able to help and the methods to be used. For example:

WORKER: As you get ready to leave this hospital, it is important to anticipate the problems you may face when you get home. That is why I want to meet with you two or three times before you leave. I will ask for your thoughts about what your adjustment will be like and I will share my ideas, as well. Between the two of us, I hope we can come up with a plan that will minimize the difficulties that you will encounter when you return home.

Each session or meeting with a client has three time phases: (1) getting started, (2) the central work of the session, and (3) drawing the session to a close. At the beginning of each session, the social worker should provide an opportunity for **sessional contracting**. Even when there has been a prior agreement on how the session's time will be used, it is important to check once again for a consensus. Quite possibly, some change in the client's situation has altered the client's priorities. The skill of **reaching for between-session data** may be used to initiate the sessional contracting. This form of checking-in entails asking the client to bring the worker up to date and to identify the key topics to be discussed. This effort is an attempt to adhere to the principle of *starting where the client is*. For example:

WORKER: You will recall that at the end of our last meeting we agreed to spend today's session talking about your reluctance to visit your son who is foster care. Do you still think that is how we should spend our time today, or do you now have a more pressing concern?

ASKING QUESTIONS

A social worker uses various types of questions to obtain needed information and to assist the client in expressing his or her thoughts and feelings. A question such as "What are the names of your children?" is termed a *closed-ended question* since it limits how the client can respond. By contrast, a question such as "Tell me about your children" is called an *open-ended question* because it gives the client the latitude to say whatever she or he thinks is important. However, open-ended questions can vary in the amount of freedom they allow. These three questions are all open ended, but some are more open than others:

"Tell me about your job."
"What do you like and what do you dislike about your job?"
"What tasks and responsibilities are parts of your job?"

During counseling sessions, the worker will use mostly open-ended questions. Closed-ended questions are used to gather specific information or when the client is so confused or overwhelmed that some structure is needed to focus the conversation.

The skill of **narrowing the focus** (*or funneling*) refers to a series of questions intended to assist the client in describing his or her concerns or situation with greater specificity. For example:

CLIENT: Things are a real mess at home.

WORKER: What do you mean by a mess; what happened?

CLIENT: Well we were eating supper when Dad came home. He was drunk again and ended up hitting Mom.

WORKER: What did you do when all this was happening?

CLIENT: First, I ran out of the house. Then I came back and yelled at my dad to stop or I would call the cops.

WORKER: What were you thinking and feeling at the time you threatened to call the police?

A worker should never ask questions out of mere curiosity or to fill a silence. Other common errors in questioning include the overuse of closed-ended questions, stacking questions, asking leading questions, and asking too many "why" questions. The term **stacking questions** refers to asking several questions at once. Consider this example of stacking:

WORKER: So, you are interested in adoption. How long have you been thinking about adoption? Have you known others who have adopted? Are you thinking about an infant? Have you thought much about an older child or one who has a disability?

Stacked questions are confusing to clients. It is best to ask questions one at a time.

Leading questions are those that push the client toward giving a certain response. Here are three examples:

"Didn't you think that action was wrong?"
"I assume that you explained to your boss why you missed work?"
"Isn't it true that you were hoping for a fight?"

A leading question may prompt the client to lie rather than openly disagree with the worker. Leading questions can easily offend or insult the client.

Another common error is to ask **why questions**—for example, "Why do you get so angry when Maria spills food?" Essentially, a "why" question asks the client to justify her or his behavior and tends to produce defensiveness. Moreover, most people do not know or cannot articulate the "whys" of their behavior, so, when asked "Why?" they simply guess or give socially acceptable answers. Instead of asking why, use questions that focus on the what, where, when, and how of the client's behavior and situation.

ACTIVE LISTENING

Listening—really listening—is exceedingly difficult. Everyone wants to believe that he or she is a good listener, but few people are. We humans are by nature rather self-centered; we like to be the center of attention. That is why listening to others is so difficult. In order to listen, we must set aside our self-centeredness and make another person the center of our attention.

In active listening, the worker attends to both the client's verbal and nonverbal messages and reflects back to the client what has been heard so that the client will know that his or her message has been received and understood. The skills of active listening are those of using encouragers, clarification, paraphrase, reflection, summarization, and exploring silences.

An **encourager** (also called a *prompt*) refers to a word, short phrase, or nonverbal gesture that encourages the client to continue talking or expand on what he or she has said. Examples of verbal encouragers are "Tell me more," "Please go on," and the repetition of a key word just uttered by the client. Nonverbal encouragers include nods of the head and hand gestures that signal an invitation to continue and say more.

The technique or skill of **clarification** refers to asking a question intended to encourage a client to become more explicit or to verify the worker's understanding of what the client has said. Such questions might begin with "Are you saying that..." or "Do you mean that..." followed by a rephrasing of the client's words. For example:

CLIENT: My life is a disaster. I thought I could get things squared away, but it doesn't look like that will be possible.

WORKER: I am not sure I am following you. Are you saying that things are changing more slowly than you expected or that your situation is now worse than before?

When confused by what a client is saying, it is usually best to acknowledge the confusion and seek clarification. For example:

WORKER: You are talking very fast. I cannot keep up and I am getting a bit confused. Please start over, one point at a time. Also, try to slow down so I will not miss anything.

A skilled social worker focuses on the client's words as well as on the affect or the emotion associated with the words. To do this, the worker will make frequent use of the paraphrase and reflection. The skill known as **paraphrasing** is a rephrasing of the literal meaning of the client's statement, whereas the skill called **reflection of feeling** is an expression of the feeling or emotional component of the message. Examples of paraphrase and reflection are as follow:

CLIENT: That guy down at the employment office is a real jerk. How does he get away with treating people like that? I feel three inches tall when I go down there.

WORKER: I hear you saying that when you go to that office you are treated badly.
        (*a paraphrase*)

Or

WORKER: It sounds like you are angry and feel humiliated at the employment office. (*a reflection of feeling*)

The skill of **summarization** refers to pulling together both the content and affective components of several client messages. For example, a worker might use summarization to draw together the key elements of what was discussed during the previous five minutes. Here is an example of summarization:

WORKER: From what you have been saying, I am hearing a number of things. You are desperate for a job and feel a mix of anger and discouragement because you haven't found one. You have been going to the employment office but that adds to your feelings of shame and frustration. On top of that, you feel regret for having dropped out of high school. Is that an accurate summary of what you have been telling me?

Active listening requires careful attention to times when the client is silent. Silence is a behavior that has meaning. Sometimes it is important to uncover that meaning. The skill of **exploring the client's silence** refers to efforts to gently probe the silence. For example:

CLIENT: (thoughtful silence)

WORKER: You appear to be puzzling over something. Can you tell me what you are thinking about?

An error commonly made by beginning social workers is to respond to silence with a change of topics. This happens because the worker is feeling uncomfortable. A brief silence is best responded to with patience and polite quietness. If the silence is a long one, the worker should explore the silence.

DISPLAYING EMPATHY, GENUINENESS, AND WARMTH

Item 8.1 of this chapter described the importance of empathy, genuineness, and personal warmth in a helping relationship. A number of skills or techniques are used to display these qualities. The skill of **displaying understanding** refers to verbal and nonverbal communication intended to demonstrate to the client that the social worker comprehends what the client is saying and feeling. For example:

CLIENT: Having to place mom in a nursing home is one of the most difficult decisions I have ever made.

WORKER: It must be hard and painful to make a decision that will be upsetting to your mother. It seems like this decision is tearing you apart inside.

It is especially important to acknowledge and display an understanding of a client's negative feelings such as anger and resentment. For example:

CLIENT: I am sick of this place. I don't need to be in this treatment program. I feel like punching the next person who asks me about my drinking.

WORKER: Well, I am a part of this treatment program and you know that I will ask about your drinking. I guess that means you want to hit me. I am not sure how to respond to your threat. What are you expecting me to do?

The skill of **putting the client's feelings into words** refers to the articulation of what the client appears to be feeling but has stopped just short of expressing it in words. For example:

WORKER: How did the visit with your mother go?

CLIENT: OK, I guess, but I don't know if I can take this much longer.

WORKER: Watching your mother die is causing you unbearable distress. It sounds like you hope death will come soon, but I am wondering if such a thought makes you feel guilty. Is that the way you are feeling?

This helping skill gives the client a supportive invitation to express what he or she is reluctant to say aloud. Here is another example:

WORKER: Do you have any other questions about adoption or our agency's adoption program?

CLIENT: No, I don't think so. You explained it pretty well. I guess it's a lot different from what I expected.

WORKER: You sound disappointed. Can you tell me how you are feeling about what I have told you?

It is important to recognize that encouraging a client to express feelings is appropriate only when those feelings are related to the purpose and overall goals of the professional relationship and intervention.

The helping skill of **self-disclosure** refers to a worker's statements that reveal some of his or her own thoughts, feelings, or life experiences. When properly used, self-disclosure can make it easier for the client to talk about a sensitive topic and feel more comfortable in the relationship. Consider these two examples of worker self-disclosure:

WORKER EXAMPLE 1:   I am sorry about how I reacted to you on the phone. I guess you have noticed that I get kind of weepy when we talk about your mother's death. That touches me deeply. I am also struggling with grief since my mother died a year ago.

WORKER EXAMPLE 2:   I can understand how frustrated you feel about your teenaged son. I went through a similar experience when my son was an adolescent. There were times when it seemed like he was from another planet. His self-centeredness and preoccupation with what I felt were superficial fads drove me nuts! But eventually things change. Now, 15 years later, my son is married, has two kids, is a good father, and holds down a responsible job. I once heard grandchildren described as "God's reward for not killing your children."

As a general rule, the use of self-disclosure should be avoided in the early stages of relationship building and used sparingly at other times. The personal information revealed by the worker should always have a clear connection to the client's concern. It is inappropriate for the worker to talk about personal experiences that are unrelated to the client's concerns or the purpose of the interview.

An especially complicated issue for social workers is deciding how to go about **answering personal questions**. Clients might ask a worker a whole range of personal questions, such as: Do you have children? Did you ever go through a divorce? What is your religion? Have you ever used drugs? Have you ever been fired from a job? Whether and how the worker answers such questions will depend on his or her best guess as to why the client is asking and how an answer will affect the professional relationship. There are many reasons why clients might ask personal questions. For example, the client may want to know if the worker is capable of understanding the client's situation. The client may be checking out whether the worker is going to be judgmental. Not infrequently, the client asks personal questions simply because she or he is curious. And in some cases, the client is trying to manipulate the worker (see Item 10.8).

Typically, we feel most comfortable with people whom we perceive are similar to us in terms of values, beliefs, and life experiences. This holds true for the client–worker relationship, as well. Thus, when asked a personal question, the social worker may want to offer a simple, straightforward answer, if doing so will establish some common ground for mutual understanding. On the other hand, the worker should sidestep the question if the answer will underscore or highlight their differences in values, beliefs, and so on. Also, the worker should sidestep any question that seems to be a client's attempt to manipulate the worker or divert the discussion away from the purpose of the meeting.

SUSTAINING CLIENT MOTIVATION

In order for people to make a change, they must be motivated to change. They must feel hopeful about the possibility of change and in addition, feel some discomfort or dissatisfaction with their current situation. Several skills can be used to increase or sustain a client's motivation for change.

Displaying a belief in the potential of work refers to statements intended to convey the worker's confidence that professional intervention will be helpful to the client. For example:

WORKER: The problems you have described are serious. I can understand why you feel overwhelmed. But if we work together and chip away at the problems, one at a time, I believe you will be able to successfully deal with these problems. It won't be easy, but I believe you can make some progress over the next few weeks.

The skill of **recognizing client strengths** refers to expressions of confidence in the client's capacity to accomplish some specific task or cope with a troubling situation (see Items 11.5 and 11.6). For example:

WORKER: I know it is going to be painful for you to visit your kids in their foster home, but your visits are important to the children. You possess the special quality of being honest and upfront with your children. For those reasons, I think you will be able to explain to them why you must now get inpatient treatment for your drug dependency and why you cannot take care of them at this time.

The skill of **pointing out negative consequences** refers to statements by the worker reminding the client that a change is needed in order to avoid undesirable consequences. For example:

WORKER: When you talk about wanting to drop out of the sex offender treatment program, I must warn you of the consequences. If you do not work on your problems and demonstrate a capacity to control your attraction to children, the judge may revoke your probation and you will go to prison.

MAINTAINING PROGRESS TOWARD CHANGE

Effective helping involves some degree of pushing and pulling the client toward change. Tackling a personal problem usually involves having to examine one's assumptions and behavior. This can be difficult, painful, and even embarrassing. Real change requires having to try out new behaviors and perform unfamiliar tasks. That, too, is difficult. Consequently, some degree of fear, ambivalence, and resistance is an expected and are a normal part of the change process. In fact, a lack of hesitation and resistance by the client suggests that what appears to be an effort to change is, in reality, only an illusion.

To keep the process of change on track and moving forward, the worker must, from time to time, make demands that the client face his or her problems and take the steps necessary to achieve a needed change. The skill of **making a demand for work** conveys the message that the worker is serious and she or he expects the client to apply himself or herself to the tasks at hand. This skill must be always coupled with empathy for the client. If the worker is demanding but not empathic, the client will feel misunderstood and rejected. On the other hand, if the worker is empathic but not insistent about doing the work of change, the client is likely to perceive the worker as insincere, weak, and easily put off.

The word *encouragement* means to give courage or to help another surmount a fear. Thus, the skill of **providing encouragement** will often take the form of statements that express confidence in the client's ability to overcome an obstacle or deal with a difficult situation. The worker's words must be genuine and individualized to the client's situation. For example:

WORKER: I know that the recurrence of your cancer is devastating news and that you want to spare your children the pain of knowing the truth. However, they are waiting to hear what you have learned from the doctor. This is one of those times when it is especially difficult to be a mother. This is a time when you must be strong for your children. It will be hard to tell them the truth but it needs to be done.

Statements of **reassurance** are used when the client is experiencing doubt and uncertainty about his or her decisions and actions when they are, in fact, reasonable and realistic. Such worker statements must be based in reality. Trite and thoughtless comments such as "I am sure everything will be OK," and "You can do anything you set your mind to" are inappropriate and insulting to the client. By tying words of reassurance to the facts of the client's situation, the worker can provide support without sounding phony or naïve. For example:

WORKER: Even though you are now feeling scared and unprepared, I think you will be able to handle this new job assignment. I say that because over the past two months you have successfully taken on three new job-related responsibilities. That prior success is a clear demonstration that you possess the skills needed for the new assignment.

The skill of **partialization** refers to the activity of breaking down a large problem or action into several smaller and more manageable components, steps, or phases so the client can more effectively focus his or her attention and energy. For example:

CLIENT: I cannot believe this is happening. Jimmy fell and cut his head and I took him to the hospital. That crazy doctor notified child protective services and accused me of abusing Jimmy. Then my oldest son got into a fight with the landlord, and now the landlord has asked me to find another apartment. I cannot afford a lawyer, my child support check is late, and, on top of everything else, my car won't start.

Things are so screwed up I can't even think straight. The whole world has fallen in on me.

WORKER: I think we better talk about your concerns one at a time. Otherwise, we will feel even more overwhelmed and get confused. Let's first focus on the child abuse report. Later, we will return to the other problems. First, tell me more about Jimmy's injury and the abuse report. For now, let's talk only about that problem, OK?

The skill of **staying on track** involves worker statements intended to keep the client focused on a particular concern or objective. This skill is especially important when a client tends to ramble, go off on tangents, or wants to avoid facing a pertinent issue. For example:

WORKER: Because your boss has now threatened to fire you, I think we better focus on that concern.

CLIENT: Yeah. I guess so. I really wish I could get a transfer. But the company has such old-fashioned policies on things like that. I'm surprised they make any money at all. With the economy the way it is, you would think they would modify the whole operation. They are not prepared for global competition. I read all about that in an article on styles of management.

WORKER: We need to talk about the conflict between you and your supervisor. We need to stay focused on that problem. I know you need this job, so I think we need to figure out a way of dealing with the problem you are having with your supervisor.

The skill of **building a communication link** refers to efforts by the worker to establish a connection or link between the client and those individuals with whom he or she needs to communicate. For example:

WORKER: This is the third time you have told me that you haven't been able to tell your doctor about your concerns. Would you give me permission to call your doctor's office and explain to her that you have a worry and that you need to talk to her about it? That might cause her to spend more time with you when she visits you in the hospital tomorrow. Is that OK with you?

Sometimes, a client will display the outward appearance of having agreed to a certain action but inwardly lacks commitment to the plan. It is also fairly common for a client to decide on an action without fully considering the challenges he or she will encounter. The skill of **checking for acquiescence** is used to flush out a client's hesitation, ambivalence, or disagreement. For example:

WORKER: I certainly agree that you should talk to your math teacher about your failing grade. That needs to be done and I am pleased to hear that you intend to do it. But I also know that you have felt intimidated by that teacher. In what way will talking to him be a difficult or stressful thing to do?

Because facing a personal problem and trying to make a change is inherently difficult, some strong feelings (e.g., frustration, anger, discouragement) and emotionally charged exchanges between the client and worker are to be expected during the helping process. If over a period of several sessions, the client displays little or no emotion and little frustration with the slowness of change, it is likely that the client is not really engaged or invested in the change process. The skill of **challenging the client's avoidance of change** is an effort to point out the client's resistance to taking on the hard work of personal change. The next example illustrates the use of this challenge during a couple's marriage counseling session:

> WORKER: Something concerns me. When you two came to this agency a few weeks ago, you requested help with your marriage. We have met three times. However, both of you have spent most of our time talking about your jobs. You seem to be avoiding any real discussion of your marriage and how you get along. Unless we focus on your marriage we are not going to make progress. What is your response to what I am saying?

A client's progress is sometimes blocked because he or she does not want to grapple with especially painful feelings. The skill of **identifying emotional blocks** refers to messages aimed at increasing the client's awareness of how these feelings are getting in the way of progress. For example:

> WORKER: I have noticed something and we need to talk about it. We started meeting together because you wanted help in learning how to handle your children's behavior. Yet, each time I ask about your daughter Gloria, you become tense and fidgety and start talking about the other children. What is it about your relationship with Gloria that makes you so uncomfortable?

In some cases, the change process is blocked when a client has difficulty talking about an especially embarrassing or perhaps disgraceful situation such as irresponsible sexual behavior, damaging spending habits, or crimes. The skill of **supporting the client in taboo areas** refers to worker communication intended to support or assist the client in discussing an embarrassing or emotionally difficult topic. For example:

> CLIENT: I always feel nervous when I get to the topic of sex. It's hard for me to talk about it because of the way I was raised.
>
> WORKER: You're not alone. Many of us were raised the same way. But it is clear that you and your husband need to discuss your sexual relationship. That area in your marriage is causing some serious problems. It's difficult to discuss, but let's keep at it.

Some clients have had difficulties with authority figures (e.g., parents, employers, police) and view the social worker as one more authority wanting to boss them around and exert control (see Items 10.7 and 10.11). The skill of **addressing the authority issue** refers to a worker's message that invites the client to express concerns or complaints about the worker's real or perceived authority and power in the helping process. Consider this illustration:

> CLIENT: I think things are now a lot better at home. I don't think we need to set up another meeting.
>
> WORKER: I hope things are better, but I think something else is going on here. I have the impression that you think my job is like that of a parole officer and that I am trying to catch you doing something wrong. How about that? Are you possibly afraid that I will make trouble for you?

BRINGING THINGS TO A CLOSE

Not infrequently, clients will wait until the last few minutes of a session before bringing up an important issue. There are several possible motives behind this *doorknob communication*, such as fear of the topic, wanting to inform the worker of a concern but not wanting to discuss it, and so on. The skills of **setting time limits** and **giving a 10-minute warning** are ways of encouraging the client to bring up and remain focused on high-priority concerns. Here are two examples:

> WORKER: Before we begin, I want to remind you that we can talk until 4:00 P.M. I say that because I want to make sure that we use our time to discuss issues that are of greatest importance to you.

> WORKER: I just noticed that we have about 15 minutes left until we need to end this session. Have we gotten to all the topics you wanted to discuss or is there something else that you wanted to bring up?

The skill of **looking ahead to the end** is designed to remind the client of a planned ending for the intervention so the best possible use can be made of the remaining sessions. For example:

> WORKER: When we began meeting a month ago, we agreed to meet for eight times. We have three sessions left. Let's discuss what remains to be done so we will use those three sessions to focus on your high-priority concerns.

The client–social worker relationship may end because their work together is finished, because the social worker must refer or transfer the client to another professional, because insurance benefits have elapsed, or for other reasons. If the relationship has been a meaningful one, the ending may be difficult (see Item 14.8). Also, because many clients have experienced losses during their lives, the ending of a relationship may be painful because it reactivates feelings attached to prior losses. The worker should explore the possible existence of such feelings.

The social worker can help the client best deal with the separation by voicing feelings about termination. This skill is named **sharing feelings about the ending**. For example:

> WORKER: I have been thinking about our relationship. Since you came to this hospital in September, we have gotten to know each other very well. I am glad you are finally able to go home, but I want you to know that I will miss our discussions and miss your positive, upbeat attitude.

It is important to encourage the client to express his or her feelings about termination. These may be positive or negative or a mix of both. The skill of **reaching for ending feelings** refers to worker communication that helps the client articulate these feelings. For example:

> WORKER: I know you are pleased about getting off probation. You are no longer required to see me. But I also sense that you have some mixed feelings about our meetings coming to an end. Am I correct about that?

A review of what the client and worker have done to address the client's concerns is another important element in termination. This skill is referred to as **reviewing progress**. Here is an example:

> WORKER: Altogether, we have been meeting for about four months. A lot has happened since you were reported for child abuse. You have made some positive changes in how you deal with your son, Michael. As you think back over the past four months, what specific changes do you see in your behavior and attitude?

Selected Bibliography

Corchran, Jacqueline. *Helping Skills for Social Work Direct Practice*. New York: Oxford University Press, 2011.

Hill, Clara. *Helping Skills*, 3rd ed. Washington, DC: American Psychological Association, 2009.

Riggall, Sally. *Using Counseling Skills in Social Work*. Thousand Oaks, CA: Sage, 2012.

Shulman, Lawrence. *Identifying, Measuring and Teaching Helping Skills*. Alexandria, VA: CSWE, 1981.

———. *The Skills of Helping: Individuals, Families, Groups, and Communities*, 6th ed. Independence, KY: Cengage, 2009.

8.5 ENHANCING CLIENT MOTIVATION

What can be done when the client lacks motivation to make a needed change or is denying a serious personal problem such as an addiction, a mental illness, or abusive behavior? In such situations, **motivational interviewing** may prove effective. This strategy is built on the premise that one's level of motivation is ever changing. Motivation is not a personality trait; rather, it comes and goes and its strength varies in response to one's perceptions, thoughts, mood, and situation. Motivation is something that arises within a person. Thus, external pressures, by themselves, do not increase motivation. In fact, threats or jarring confrontations often generate additional defensiveness and resistance.

Clients are more committed to a goal or a plan (e.g., treatment, sobriety) when the goal is of their own choosing. Thus, when using motivational interviewing the practitioner does not directly attempt to convince the client that he or she has a problem and needs to make a change. Rather, the worker creates a safe and supportive environment in which the client can lower his or her defenses, examine his or her current situation, and, hopefully, conclude that a change is needed. The techniques of active listening (see Item 8.4) are used to engage the client in a discussion that reveals the discrepancy between the client's behavior (e.g., drug use) and his or her values and personal goals such as, for example, a desire for improved self-esteem, improved health, success on the job, and being a good parent. Gradually, the client will conclude that his or her current behavior (e.g., the substance abuse) is indeed a barrier to achieving what is important and that change is in his or her self-interest. The social worker uses affirmations (recognizing client strengths) to build the client's confidence that change is possible and offers information and suggestions, but always in ways that respect the client's right to self-determination.

The following guidelines will prove useful when a social worker encounters the client who denies the existence of a serious problem or is resistant to the idea of addressing the matter.

- Any attempt by a social worker to increase a client's motivation to effect a change must be based on an appreciation of how difficult it is to alter one's usual and habitual patterns of thought and behavior. After living with a problem or troublesome situation for many years, a person may come to simply accept it, organize her or his life around its existence, and quit trying to change it. When people become accustomed to having a problem, they may have a hard time even imagining a life apart from it. Their adaptations to the problem become intertwined with the other aspects of their lives, such as the choice of friends, job and career, household budgets, leisure-time activities, and dozens of other choices and daily routines. Strange as it seems, some people can reach a point where they are afraid to eliminate a long-standing problem because its absence would disrupt so many of their other habitual and familiar patterns of thought and behavior.

- People naturally resist changes to their patterns, lifestyle, and ways of making sense of life. It is normal for people to be ambivalent about change. It is especially annoying to people when others tell them that they have a problem and need to change. Realize that the resistant client may have some good reasons for not wanting to change; examples include the sheer difficulty of change, a history of prior unsuccessful efforts to change resulting in a pessimism about the possibility of change, a fear that a change will bring with it more disadvantages than benefits, the existence of other concerns requiring time and attention, a disagreement on what constitutes a problem and who might need to change, and so on.

  Demonstrate empathy for and an understanding of your client's reasoning about why change is unnecessary, even when you see things differently. Avoid making any statements that may sound argumentative, fault-finding, or critical, such as "How can you really believe that you do not have a drinking problem?" or "Can't you see that your life would be better if you would change?" If your client is becoming defensive it is probably because you are saying things in ways that are judgmental, confrontational, or insensitive to the client's situation.

- The strategy of motivational interviewing conceptualizes the process of change as unfolding in five stages: precontemplation, contemplation, preparation, action, and maintenance. Individuals are said to be in the *precontemplation stage* when they have no intention of changing, either because they are unaware of their problem or they completely reject the concerns or warnings expressed by others. During the next stage, *contemplation,* individuals are aware that a problem exists and they are at least thinking about and considering the need to do something about it. When in the third stage, *preparation,* individuals have decided that they want to change and are beginning to formulate a plan for making the desired change. During the *action stage* individuals are taking steps to bring about the desired change. And finally, during the *maintenance stage* the individuals are striving to maintain the changes they have made and are working to prevent backsliding or a relapse. A person who is in the process of making changes will cycle through these various stages numerous times. Change does not proceed in a step-by-step or linear fashion. Meaningful change always entails some steps forward and some backward. Setbacks, stumbles, and relapses and are a normal and expected part of the overall change process.

  It is critically important to offer messages and ideas especially relevant and suited to a particular stage or level. Thus, the social worker is always listening and watching for indications of where the client is in the process of change. What the worker says to the client must be tailored to that particular stage of readiness for change. If the client resists the worker's message, it indicates the worker is getting ahead of the client.

  When interacting with a client who is in the stage of *precontemplation,* the social worker seeks to plant some seeds that may germinate later. Explore, listen with empathy, and seek to understand the client's perceptions, rationale, and explanations of why she or he does not have a problem (i.e., a problem or concern reported by or complained about by others). Encourage the client to identify her or his goals and values, and then in a gentle and nonthreatening manner explore how the client's current choices, behavior, or patterns do and do not help the client reach those goals and conform to her or his stated values and ideals. For example, if a man says something like "I want to be a better father to my children than my own father was to me," the worker might then explore and discuss whether the time he spends at the bar with his drinking buddies helps him to be a better father or keeps him from being the father he wants to be.

Call to the clients' attention the obvious discrepancies between what they want for themselves and loved ones and what they are actually doing. It may take weeks, months, or even years for some clients to struggle with and mull over the reality of their situation and finally reach a point or decision and a readiness to work on the problem.

When the client is in the second stage, *contemplation*, it is important to realize that even when the client is acknowledging a problem, it does not necessarily mean that he or she is ready and willing to work toward a change. Many people can accurately describe their problems and wish aloud that things were different, but they never get around to changing anything. Before they make the hard choice to take action, they must believe and feel that change is really possible and that they are capable of doing what will be required. During this contemplation stage, the worker's task is to engage the client in an analysis of the risks and rewards, the advantages and disadvantages, of addressing the problem.

Because the client is likely to be ambivalent, maybe fearful of change, and has doubts about whether change is possible, the worker's messages should be ones that tip the balance in favor of deciding to change. Thus, encourage the client to elaborate on any of his or her statements that sound as if the client is thinking about the disadvantages of the status quo or thinking about the advantages or benefits of a changed situation. Do this no matter how tentative the client might be. Call to the client's attention his or her prior successes with change and facing difficult life challenges. Provide information on the realities and stresses to be faced during a change effort so the client will understand what is required.

When in the stage of *preparation*, the third stage in the change process, the client is ready to change and has made at least a tentative commitment to change, but is still wrestling with ideas about how to go about making a change. The client is unsure of what steps might actually work. For the social worker, the task is to help the client maintain this momentum and to select specific steps or actions that will be realistic and effective. A client's plan for change is more likely to succeed if it identifies and lists the many small but necessary steps needed to bring about the change and includes a method for the ongoing monitoring of progress. Some clients will start to have second thoughts about trying to change as they see more clearly what it will require.

During this preparation stage, the social worker will be asking questions and encouraging discussion that helps the client examine the various ways that change might be achieved and also to anticipate possible barriers and pitfalls. For example, the worker might ask: When will you start? What is the first step? The second? Why is that particular action needed and important? What will your first week of change be like? Who else needs to be involved in making and carrying out this plan of action? Who will encourage you and who might sabotage your plan? How will you know if your plan is working? If it does not work, do you have a back-up plan?

Following the preparation stage, the client enters the fourth stage (action) and then, if all goes well, moves into the final stage of maintenance. Many techniques and guidelines appropriate for use during the action stage and the maintenance stage appear in Chapter 13 of this book.

Selected Bibliography

Arkowitz, Hal, Henry Westra, William Miller, and Stephen Rollnick, eds. *Motivational Interviewing in the Treatment of Psychological Problems*. New York: Guilford, 2008.

Miller, William, and Stephen Rollnick, eds. *Motivational Interviewing*, 3rd ed. New York: Guilford, 2013.

Rosengren, David. *Building Motivational Interviewing Skills*. New York: Guilford, 2009.

8.6 UNDERSTANDING EMOTIONS AND FEELINGS

Many of the clients served by social workers are confused, frightened, or overwhelmed by their emotions, and many have not learned to express their feelings in a healthy manner. A social worker must be able to discuss the nature of emotions in ways that clients can understand and gain greater control over troublesome feelings and emotions.

Although the words *emotion* and *feeling* are often used interchangeably, it is useful to view an emotion as a particular physiological and psychological response and a feeling as one's subjective awareness of that response. **Emotions** are complex, physical, biochemical, and psychological reactions to conscious and unconscious interpretations of an event or an experience. Neuroscience is just beginning to understand how emotions arise within us and how normal emotions can go awry, as when, for example, fear grows into a phobia or sadness turns into a disabling depression.

The root meaning of the word *emotion* is "to move." Emotions move or motivate people to take action. They are a form of primitive survival wisdom that warn us of danger and pull us toward actions that will meet our basic needs. For example, the emotion of fear moves us to withdraw from a dangerous situation, whereas anger moves us to attack those who threaten harm. The emotion of sadness attracts the attention and caring of people. The emotion of remorse or guilt moves us to correct misbehavior, rebuild damaged relationships, and make amends for the harm we have caused. The emotion of anticipation moves us to persist in our efforts to reach a goal.

Emotion is a type of communication that signals a person's state of mind and intentions to others. The facial expressions that reflect emotions such as joy, sadness, fear, and anger are recognizable around the world, regardless of culture.

Emotions vary in intensity. For example, joy can range from serenity to ecstasy. Fear can range from apprehension to terror, and anger from mild annoyance to rage. Although all emotions involve some level of physiological change, the bodily reactions that accompany the primitive fight-flight emotions such as fear, anger, panic, and terror are the strongest of all. Emotional reactions can overpower one's capacity to think clearly and make rational decisions. The power of emotion to affect behavior is most evident in the often impulsive and explosive reactions of children and adolescents. As an individual matures, he or she grows in the ability to maintain self-control.

It is important to understand that emotions are a response to our subjective interpretation of what we have encountered. The usual sequence is as follows: (1) an event or situation occurs; (2) we notice, interpret, and think about this event; (3) depending on our interpretation, we have a particular emotional response; and (4) this emotion may elicit a certain behavior.

Our interpretations may or may not be accurate. Because of past conditioning (learning), we may interpret certain experiences in a habitual (unconscious) manner that involves little or no conscious analysis. The conditioning associated with prior painful life experiences may cause us to misread a situation and thereby elicit emotions and behaviors that others judge to be inappropriate or irrational. An example would be a woman who is fearful of all men because one man abused her. Many emotional reactions are immediate and do not involve conscious thought. For example, little or no thought or deliberation precedes one's emotional reactions to an attacking dog.

People respond emotionally not only to their interpretations of an event but also to their own feelings and behavior. For example, as we experience an emotion, we may think about whether it is right or wrong to be feeling as we do, and, in turn, these thoughts may elicit still other emotions. In other words, we often pass judgment on our own emotional reactions and these judgments or thoughts cause still other emotions to arise within us.

Because of the interplay between thought and emotion, we can, to some degree, alter and control our emotions and feelings by striving to modify the ways we think about and interpret events and experiences. Several steps are involved:

Step 1: *Noticing our feelings.*   Certain bodily sensations inform us that an emotional response is occurring. However, many of us ignore or deny these sensations. Consequently, we may need help in learning to recognize the bodily reactions associated with emotion. One approach is to stop periodically throughout the day and reflect on our body's sensations and ask, for example, "What part of my body is experiencing emotion?" "Does some part of my body feel tense or strange?" "Is my body trying to get my attention?" "What thoughts and interpretations are giving rise to these emotions?"

Step 2: *Naming our feelings.*   Assigning a name to our emotions and feelings helps us to accept them as real and provides a beginning sense of control. But attaching a label to something as nebulous as a feeling is not easy. Many people lack a vocabulary for feelings. A list of feeling words may be of assistance in this naming process (see Item 13.16).

Step 3: *Owning our feelings.*   Before we can gain control over an emotion or feeling, we need to acknowledge its existence and claim it as our own. That can be a challenge if we are in the habit of denying our feelings. Owning a feeling can be made easier if its name is spoken aloud, possibly to another person (e.g., "I am afraid" or "I am feeling sad"). Many people are surprised to discover that this simple acknowledgment and verbalization helps them cope with troublesome feelings.

Step 4: *Looking under and behind our emotions.*   Our emotions are a window through which we can glimpse our underlying and often unconscious interpretations. For example, when feeling anxious or fearful, we might ask ourselves, "Why does this situation seem so frightening or threatening?" "Is it really threatening or am I interpreting it this way because of a prior painful experience?" "Are there alternative ways of viewing this experience?" By looking at things from a different angle, we can often lessen the impact of negative emotions and feelings.

Step 5: *Examining our habits of thought.*   Our ways of interpreting and thinking about our experiences are often learned during childhood. Thus, in order to understand and modify troublesome thoughts and feelings, it may be necessary to examine and reevaluate what we experienced during our childhood. We must decide if what we habitually tell ourselves about ourselves (i.e., our self-talk) is valid in our current situation (see Item 13.7).

Step 6: *Choosing a course of action.*   Even when we cannot change our emotional reaction to a particular situation or event, it is still possible to make choices about how to act and behave. We can make better choices if we ask ourselves the following questions: "When I feel this way, what choices do I have?" "Is my first or instinctive response (e.g., attacking if I am angry) an appropriate one under the circumstances?" "What destructive behaviors must I avoid?" "What responses hurt me or others?" "Which response would be most beneficial to me and others?"

Selected Bibliography

Kelter, Dacher, Keith Oatley, and Jennifer Jenkins. *Understanding Emotions*, 3rd ed. New York: Wiley, 2014.

Lewis, Michael, Jeanette Haviland, and Lisa Barrett, eds. *Handbook of Emotions*, 3rd ed. New York: Guilford, 2008.

Plutchik, Robert. *Emotions and Life*. Washington, DC: American Psychological Association, 2003.

8.7 RESPONDING TO DEFENSIVE COMMUNICATION

A social worker, especially one who is working with mandated clients, will encounter individuals who are defensive and guarded in their communication. Clients may use a number of defensive maneuvers to avoid having to discuss the issues that have brought them into contact with the social worker. These include, for example, *denial* (e.g., I don't have a drinking problem!), *blaming others* (e.g., I wouldn't need to hit her if she didn't make me so mad), *avoidance* (e.g., I just forgot about our appointment), and *pleading helplessness* (e.g., It's no use trying; nothing can ever change). Some clients may seek to *intimidate* (i.e., curse or ridicule) the worker or may use their physical environment (e.g., drawn shades, vicious dogs) or a style of dress as intimidation and ways of keeping people at a distance.

It is likely that the individual who is defensive and hostile within a professional relationship was angry and resentful long before he or she met the social worker. However, a worker's behavior or style can make the situation even worse. For example, the worker is likely to increase a client's defensiveness if the client is kept waiting, if the worker is judgmental or authoritarian, if the worker is brusque, uses a lot of jargon, or dwells on agency rules and regulations. By following these guidelines, the social worker can help to reduce a client's defensiveness:

- View defensiveness as an attempt to protect oneself from some real or imagined danger. Within a context of social service delivery, the threats or danger perceived by clients might be embarrassment, loss of privacy, loss of control over one's life, or the failure to receive a desired service or benefit. The worker can lessen the client's fear by acknowledging the awkwardness of the situation (e.g., "I know that it can be embarrassing to ask for financial assistance"). To the extent possible, give your client opportunities to make choices and thereby maintain some control over what is happening. When appropriate, use words and phrases such as *we, together,* and *this will be your decision*. Such words imply choice and cooperation. Because people become defensive when they experience a loss of individuality, do not label or categorize your client by saying something insensitive like, "All Medicaid recipients have to fill out this form."

- Be aware that for some individuals, defensiveness and wariness is a habitual pattern rooted in their past and not necessarily a reaction to their immediate situation, such as an encounter with a social worker. A pattern of defensive guardedness can develop during childhood in response to abuse, neglect, being bullied, or other forms of maltreatment. After experiencing a few instances of being deceived or exploited, an adult may approach all new relationships with a degree of fear, suspicion, and defensiveness.

- Look for ways to reinforce any movement by the client toward more open communication and a more trusting relationship. One way is to use the technique of **mirroring** that can be described as responding to the client's positive messages in a manner that reflects or mirrors the client's nonverbal behavior. For example, if the client lets down his or her guard to some small degree, follow up with a tone of voice, verbal cadence, posture, and gestures that mirror those just displayed by the client. This can have the effect of helping the client feel accepted and safe. On the other hand, if your client grows more defensive, respond with gestures of openness and a soothing tone of voice. If your client's conversation speeds up because of anxiety or anger, respond with a slower pace, for this may calm the client.

- Use words and phrases that match your client's primary or dominant mode of receiving information. The three basic modes are visual, auditory, and touch. A client reveals her or his dominant mode in the frequent use of certain predicates in phrases such as "I see what you mean" (visual), "I hear what you are saying" (auditory), or "That goal is beyond my reach" (touch). If you can identify your client's dominant mode, try to match your phrases to her or his mode—for example, "Do you have a clear picture of what I am suggesting?" (visual), "Does this plan sound OK to you?" (auditory), or "I think the plan you have suggested is one we can both grab hold of" (touch).

- Display empathy and an understanding of the client's irritation, fears, and anger by using the technique of **joining the resistance**. It involves recognizing and aligning yourself with the client's feelings—for example, "After such a long wait, you deserve to be angry. I would be angry also." Such an alignment tends to remove the client's need to keep up his or her defenses and it gives the client permission to vent.

- If your client uses obscene or abusive language, remain calm. Perhaps say something like, "I know you are upset but it is important that we have a respectful and peaceful conversation." If the client persists in making verbal attacks, consider using the technique of **fogging**. This term comes from the notion that rocks thrown into a fog bank have no effect. If the person under a verbal attack can become like the fog, the verbal "rocks" have no impact and, hopefully, the attacker will soon abandon efforts to inflict discomfort. This technique works because the person under attack does not retaliate in kind and calmly acknowledges that the angry person may indeed have a point and is perhaps justified in her or his criticism. For example:

ANGRY CLIENT: All you ever do is talk!

WORKER: You're right. I do talk a lot.

ANGRY Client: If you would pay attention to what I have been saying, you wouldn't have to ask all these dumb questions!

WORKER: That may be true. I should be very attentive to what you say.

ANGRY Client: You are just like all the other lazy government employees and state social workers! You are always butting into things that are none of your damn business.

WORKER: I am a state employee. It does make sense that state employees would do their job in similar ways.

- In situations where it is critically important to engage the defensive client (e.g., in cases of child abuse), you may need to adopt a very direct and assertive approach. For example, if your client refuses to talk, you might say something like, "I can see that you do not want to talk to me about how your child was injured, but I must remain here until we have discussed this serious matter." If your client behaves in a threatening manner, you will need to say something like, "I will not argue with you. If you are too angry to talk now, I will return this afternoon with a police officer. Would you rather talk now or later?"

  If your client attempts to avoid the central issue by talking about tangential concerns, you will need to take control by saying something like, "I can understand that you have other concerns, but for right now we must discuss how Joey got those bruises." In some cases, clients defend themselves by trying to make the worker feel guilty and intrusive. When that happens, you might say, "I know you are upset and I don't like to see people cry, but your child has been injured. Take a few minutes to compose yourself. Then we must discuss what happened to Joey." (See Items 10.7, 10.8, and 10.9 for more information on defensive, involuntary, and potentially dangerous clients.)

Selected Bibliography

Cormier, Sherry, Paula Nurius, and Cynthia Osborn. *Interviewing and Change Strategies for Helpers*, 7th ed. Independence, KY: Cengage. 2013.

Rooney, Ronald. *Strategies for Work with Involuntary Clients*, 2nd ed. New York: Columbia University Press, 2009.

8.8 APPLYING CULTURAL COMPETENCE TO HELPING

We humans are extremely complex and varied—so, too, are the societies, cultures, and social structures we construct. Each person is like everyone else in so many ways but there are also important differences. Some of the most prevalent aspects this human diversity that may affect social work practice are differences of race, sex, ethnicity, national origin, skin color, gender identity, sexual orientation, age, marital status, political belief, religion, and mental or physical ability and disability. Such human variations should not be viewed as if one is better than another, but rather a display, or maybe a pageant, of beautiful and fascinating diversity.

Attaining a high level of cultural competence is critical for every social worker. A social worker must not only understand her or his cultural background but must also be sensitive to a client's culture, history, and life experiences. Being clear about the similarities and differences in one's own cultural perspectives and the perspectives of clients is central to having the necessary empathy to understand the client situation and avoid inappropriately imposing one's own cultural viewpoint into the practice situation.

A **culture** can be thought of as the totality of what and how a large group or a particular population think, how they behave, and what they create—a totality that is passed on to future generations. That totality is comprised of certain beliefs, values, ideals, customs, standards of right and wrong, symbols and language, and patterns of behavior, all of which are rooted in a people's shared history and experiences. A culture is something like a lens through which a people view life. It shapes how they make sense of their experiences and cope with problems and conflicts, both within their own group and with outsiders. In each cultural variation there will be strengths that should be recognized and, when appropriate, incorporated as part of social work practice (see Item 11.6). Yet, all cultures contain elements that are problematic and these also should be acknowledged and addressed.

A person's culture is often so internalized that he or she does not even recognize its power in shaping thoughts and behavior. All people are somewhat **ethnocentric**, meaning that they assume their own way of life is a reasonable and an appropriate standard for judging all others. To counter this tendency toward ethnocentricity, the social worker must be especially careful to develop and apply cultural competence in understanding and appreciating the different cultural perspectives that clients bring into the practice situation. This cultural sensitivity is important because cultural variations affect such life experiences as patterns of child rearing, the family and work roles of men and women considered appropriate, how one judges the behaviors of others, the place of religion and spirituality in one's life, how one responds to experiences of discrimination and oppression, and so on.

Key to understanding the concept of a culture is the notion that the content and patterns of a culture are transmitted to future generations. Although the word *culture* is sometimes used as a means of grouping people and experiences (e.g., "drug culture," "teen culture"), the term *culture,* as used here, refers to patterns of thinking and behaving that have evolved through generations and are maintained and transmitted by the structures and institutions of society such as family, schools, language, laws, religion, and public policies. Nevertheless, cultures are dynamic; they do change over time. Some cultural shifts are gradual and hardly noticed, whereas others are rapid and disruptive. Cultures are altered by changes in economics, technology, science, and politics, as well as by large-scale societal events such as a war or an economic depression. Typically, the younger generations embrace and absorb changes to their culture, whereas older generations often feel threatened and resist change in their life patterns.

One example of cultural variation is an **ethnic group**, a segment of the larger population that identifies itself and is regarded by outsiders as a distinct group because of its geographical origin, language, religion, ancestry, physical appearance, or some combination of these characteristics. When people define themselves as belonging to a distinct ethnic group, that belief will significantly affect their interactions—including how they interact with social workers.

Whereas culture and ethnicity have to do with differences in a people's values, beliefs, language, and traditions, **race** is a categorization of people primarily on the basis of their physical characteristics such as skin color, body structure, and facial features. **Racism** exists when the members of one group views those of another race as inherently inferior. Racism gives rise to discrimination and oppression, as when, for example, opportunities, protections, liberties, and resources are denied to some on the basis of race. Although the United States has made considerable progress in addressing the problem of racism, it still falls short of being a society free of prejudice and discrimination.

Comparable to the issue of racism are other so-called **isms**, including, for example, ageism, sexism, heterosexism, and classism. The emotions of anger, frustration, and despair are not uncommon among those who are the victims of an "ism" and feel that their educational opportunity, employment, income, and even their access to human services has been restricted because of prejudice and discrimination. Self-aware individuals may detect the existence of prejudice in their own attitudes and may feel guilt and shame. Those who are accused—accurately or inaccurately—of being prejudiced tend to feel defensive. Some in the dominant groups of society may be morally troubled as they come to realize that many of their privileges and benefits exist because devalued groups have been economically oppressed and exploited.

It is likely that everyone, including social workers, when honestly examining their own attitudes and beliefs, recognize the existence of some degree of bias and prejudice toward particular groups or segments of the population. After all, how could one not carry some culturally biased attitudes and beliefs when growing up in a society that treats some groups as valuable, privileged, and preferred while other groups are judged to be less valuable and unworthy?

It is helpful to distinguish between prejudice and discrimination. Whereas *prejudice* is an attitude, *discrimination* is an action that harms the members of a particular group. Prejudice (i.e., to prejudge) refers to attitudes or beliefs that devalue or disparage others simply because they are of a certain race, ethnic group, religion, age, gender, sexual orientation, or physical or mental condition. Prejudice does not always result in acts of discrimination. And discrimination can exist apart from a prejudice as, for example, when an employee thoughtlessly follows an organizational policy that is unfair and discriminatory to a particular group. Social workers must be constantly vigilant to recognize prejudice in themselves and the institutions of society. And they must be prepared to take action to combat discrimination.

Acts of *individual discrimination* may be blatant, such as refusing to hire a qualified individual because of his or her skin color or deliberately causing physical injury to a member of a particular group (hate crimes). Much more subtle and difficult to detect and address is *institutional discrimination*. It exists when prejudice and racism are woven into laws, social structures, organizational policies, and the ordinary patterns of community life. The term *internalized racism* refers to the effects that racism (and this applies to other "isms") can have on its victims when they have absorbed the messages of discrimination and have come to view themselves as inherently inferior.

Central to social work's mission is service to vulnerable populations that are sometimes referred to as disenfranchised groups. A **disenfranchised group** is one whose members, due to historical patterns of oppression that have been institutionalized in society, have significantly less political and economic power than the dominant groups in society. It is helpful to recognize that all members of a disenfranchised group are not of equal status within the group and there will inevitably be status rankings usually based on such factors as income, education, and occupation.

GUIDELINES FOR CULTURALLY SENSITIVE SOCIAL WORK PRACTICE

The National Association of Social Workers' social policy statement (NASW, 2009) calls on all social workers, as well as human services systems, to acquire **cultural competence**, which NASW defines as of a set of behaviors, attitudes, and policies that enable professionals and agencies to work effectively in cross–cultural situations. The NASW Standards for Cultural Competence (2001) further identify several elements that contribute to an agency's or a professional's ability to become more culturally competent. Among these are (1) to value and respect human diversity; (2) diligent self-assessment in regard to one's own or one's agency's cultural perspectives, values, and beliefs; (3) awareness of the special dynamics that are in play whenever people of different cultures interact; and (4) develop programs and services that reflect an appreciation and understanding of diversity. These elements should also be built into a human services organization and reflected in the attitudes and performance of those employed by the agency.

Self-awareness (see Item 16.3) is critical for social workers. Some useful guidelines to follow when examining your own cultural sensitivity are:

- Strive to understand how your own culture, ethnicity, religion, and socio-economic background have shaped your views and opinions.
- Always view the client and her or his situation or problem within the context of the client's social circumstances and culture.
- Be alert to the possibility that you and others may make erroneous and inappropriate judgments based on bias, prejudices, and stereotypes.
- Individualize your approach to a client; never assume that all members of a particular ethnic, racial, or other group should receive the same services and will respond in the same way to a particular practice method or technique.

At the macro level, agencies must also constantly examine their policies and procedures to make sure they are not prejudging or discriminating against certain groups of people. An agency can be helped to develop culturally sensitive and appropriate ways of addressing issues of cultural difference by, for example, including representatives from diverse groups on its governing or advisory boards, soliciting reviews of agency performance by persons from the various segments of the community it serves, and conducting program evaluations.

Here are some guidelines you might keep in mind when reviewing your interactions with clients.

- Strive to learn about the cultural backgrounds of the clients you serve while recognizing that people seldom acquire much more than a cursory knowledge of another culture. This is especially so when language differences are involved. Even so, the social worker can achieve at least a beginning level of understanding by interacting frequently with people from that ethnic or cultural group, consulting with the leaders of the group, attending cultural festivals and religious events, reading group-related newspapers and literature, and so on.
- Never assume that a client's cultural background will predict his or her values, beliefs, or behavior. Rather, always individualize the client. Every attempt to describe a group of people—the white middle-class, people who are blind, African Americans, the able or disabled, the rich or poor—is a generalization and therefore always runs the risk of overgeneralization and stereotyping. Remember that within every minority group there are various subgroups and certainly a wide range of differences among individuals.
- All people must reconcile two sets of beliefs: values and social expectations. One set consists of the somewhat impersonal influences of the dominant culture that are embedded within a society's economic, commercial, political, legal, and educational systems. The second set is very personal and exists within one's family and social network. When these two sets of beliefs, values, and expectations are quite different for an individual, he or she may be confused or uncertain about his or her place in society and about what to expect of self and others. Such a tension is most likely to occur among those who are members of nondominant groups and new immigrants (see Item 15.22).
- Show an interest in your client's name, place of birth, and home community, for these topics are usually good icebreakers and lead naturally to a discussion of the client's cultural and ethnic background. Early in the professional relationship you

**"The Dual Perspective"
a retired item from the
6th edition**

might acknowledge the existence of obvious differences of culture or race as a way of giving the client permission to talk about these matters and perhaps express concerns about not being understood. Encourage the client to identify important cultural values, beliefs, or customs that may need to be considered or accommodated in the professional relationship and service delivery.

A major obstacle in working cross-culturally is that the professional helper and the client may have quite different notions of what constitutes help. Moreover, a particular practice model or approach to professional helping or therapy may strike a client from certain cultures as strange or even offensive. For example, a short-term or task-oriented approach may seem abrasive to a client whose culture believes that extended periods of time spent just getting to know each other is the appropriate way to enter into a new relationship. To some clients, certain helping skills such as reaching for feelings or putting the client's feelings into words may appear intrusive. An individual from an Asian culture may consider it shameful to discuss a personal problem with someone from outside the family. Many Hispanics will expect a helper to offer advice and tangible forms of assistance and may feel confused by a professional using nondirective counseling and the techniques of active listening. Cognitive behavioral or rational emotive techniques that examine and challenge a client's beliefs may offend the client whose culture places a high value on displaying respect and deference. Further, it may be particularly difficult for a client from a minority and oppressed group to discuss a personal problem with a professional who is from the dominant group because this presumes a degree of trust that may not exist.

Overlooking client strengths, misreading nonverbal communication, and misunderstanding family dynamics are among the most common errors made in cross-cultural helping. Also, behaviors motivated by religion, family obligation, and sex roles are often misunderstood or misinterpreted by professional helpers.

• Because members of many minority groups have experienced discrimination, it is to be expected that they will be somewhat distrustful of professionals and the agencies that represent and reflect the beliefs and values of the dominant groups in society. They will enter a helping relationship with caution as they size up the social worker. They may evaluate the worker's trustworthiness by asking, directly or indirectly, about his or her life experiences, family, and children. The worker needs to respond to these probes with honest, nonevasive answers. Since visiting people in their own home is usually an indication of caring and respect, the home visit may help the worker build trust (see Item 10.6).

• Be aware that an extended family structure is common to many cultures and ethnic groups. In these families, the members feel a strong obligation to assist, support and protect other family members. The misbehavior of a family member brings shame to the whole family and an honor bestowed on one member is recognition of the whole family. Typically, the elders are held in high esteem, command deference and respect, and exert much influence on the decisions and actions of other family members. Also, in these families it is fairly common for there to be lines of authority and decision-making structures based on sex. For example, in many Hispanic families, males will possess considerable authority and a wife and even adult children may feel obligated to obtain a male's (husband, father, grandfather) approval before making an important decision, even one involving medical treatment. Within the large extended families common to the American Indian tribal cultures, family members will often delay making an important decision until they have obtained a tribal elder's advice on the matter. Thus, it is always a good idea to ask the client if he or she wants to invite others to the interview or somehow involve them in decision making. Not infrequently, clients will simply bring these respected advisors to important meetings.

- Closely related to the necessity of cultural competence is the need to adapt social work practice to the client's religious beliefs and spirituality. Very often, a client's ethnicity, culture, and religion are interwoven. A professional who ignores a client's spirituality, religious beliefs, and moral code may fail to accurately assess the client's situation and overlook resources that could prove helpful to the client (see Item 15.18).

- Clients who may experience difficulty with the society's common language (e.g., English in the United States) should be asked if an interpreter would be helpful. If you will be working with many people who speak a particular language, strive to learn as much of that language as possible. Make an effort to speak some of the client's language, even if you can master only a few phrases. Doing so will be viewed as a courtesy and as respect for the client's native language and culture.

- Societal or systemic problems (poverty, unemployment, poor housing, lack of access to health care, etc.) bring disenfranchised people to agencies more often than do psychological problems. Thus, the provision of concrete services and the practitioner roles of broker and advocate are of special importance.

In sum, given the wide range of people and communities served by social workers, it is never possible to become completely culturally competent. If the clients served by a social worker or social agency tend to reflect a cultural group based on ethnicity, race, age, gender, handicapping condition, mental health status, and so on, the worker then must become especially knowledgeable about that culture. However, too much dependence on this general knowledge about a population group can lead to stereotyping that fails to capture individual uniqueness and differences, such as a client's resilience regarding negative life experiences. Finding the delicate balance between being cognizant of group tendencies and appreciating individual variations should help the social worker temper her or his assessments and practice approaches.

Selected Bibliography

Hugman, Richard. *Culture, Values, and Ethics in Social Work: Embracing Diversity.* New York: Routledge, 2013.

Lynch, Eleanor W., and Marci J. Hanson. *Developing Cross-Cultural Competence: A Guide for Working with Children and Their Families,* 4th ed. Baltimore, MD: Brookes, 2013.

National Association of Social Workers. Cultural Competence in the Social Work Profession. In *Social Work Speaks: NASW Policy Statements.* Washington, DC: NASW Press, 2009.

_____. *Indicators for the Achievement of the NASW Standards for Cultural Competence in Social Work Practice.* Washington, DC: National Association of Social Workers, 2007. http:// www.socialworkers.org/practice/standards/NASWCulturalStandardsIndicators2006.pdf

_____. *NASW Standards for Cultural Competence in Social Work Practice.* Washington, DC: NASW, 2001. http://www.socialworkers.org/practice/standards/NASWCulturalStandards.pdf

Sisneros, Jose, Catherine Stakeman, Mildred Joyner, and Cathryne Schmitz. *Critical Multicultural Social Work.* Chicago: Lyceum, 2008.

9

Basic Skills for Agency Practice

LEARNING OBJECTIVES

At the conclusion of this chapter, the reader should be prepared to:

- Exhibit the qualities of clear and purposeful writing and skill in telephone use when engaged in professional communication.
- Demonstrate an awareness of the ways in which computers and modern information technology can be utilized within human services agencies.
- Describe the purpose, importance, and characteristics of accurate documentation of client records.
- Demonstrate a familiarity with the *NASW Code of Ethics*.
- Describe the basic principles of time and workload management.
- Identify and contrast several examples of professional behavior, as distinguished from nonprofessional behavior.

Regardless of their practice settings, social workers face the challenge of managing their time and handling the required paperwork. And in every setting they will encounter thorny ethical questions and dilemmas. This chapter offers guidance on how to approach ethical concerns and how social workers might increase their efficiency by incorporating into their daily routines the skills of time management, effective phone use, and information technology. Also included are guidelines on report and letter writing, maintaining client records, and performing as a professional person.

Carefully prepared correspondence and other written communication, as well as accurate record keeping, is essential for demonstrating a social worker's adherence to ethical standards and for documenting the quality of service provision. Professional records must be accurate, complete, concise, useable, and easily retrievable. Ideally, an agency's record-keeping system will create documentation that provides (1) an accurate account of services provided; (2) data that can be used to identify needed changes in policy, service delivery, and staff deployment; (3) data for retrospective and prospective research; (4) data useful in planning staff training; (5) evidence of adherence to relevant legal and policy requirements; and (6) information that will withstand scrutiny by external reviewers (e.g., accreditation bodies, ombudsmen, lawyers, insurance companies, quality control personnel).

In our litigious society, social workers are sometimes named in lawsuits alleging professional negligence, misconduct, or unethical practice. Accurate and complete record keeping is critical to defending oneself against such an allegation. In the absence of proper documentation, there may be no evidence that a social worker's decision or action was appropriate, ethical, and responsible.

9.1 WRITTEN REPORTS AND CORRESPONDENCE

Professional reports and letters must be written with care. Ones that are unclear or inaccurate can create misunderstandings and costly errors. A number of guidelines should be kept in mind.

- Before you begin to write, carefully consider who will be reading this report or letter. Decide what information the readers need and expect. Also, consider whether this document might be sent on to still others such as other agencies, newspapers, or clients. Keep these potential readers in mind as you write and imagine how they are likely to interpret or perhaps misinterpret your words.

- Reports that are to be submitted to courts, doctors, psychologists, lawyers, schools, human services agencies, businesses, and committees need to be formal and tightly organized. Many agencies have a protocol and a prescribed format for such reports. Give careful attention to the accurate use of proper names and titles. A less formal style of writing is usually appropriate, for internal communications (i.e., within one's organization) and in these reports and memos the use of first names, abbreviations, and jargon is usually acceptable. Copies of well-written reports—ones judged by others in the agency to be good examples—can be used as a model to guide your report writing.

- Before writing the first draft of a formal report, organize the content to be presented. Outline the main topics, the various subtopics, and the key points under each. If you present your ideas in an orderly manner and use headings to set sections apart, the reader will be better able to follow your reasoning and understand your message. Two or three drafts or revisions of a formal report may be needed before the final version is produced. Ask peers to review your drafts and offer constructive criticism. However, be clear that you have final responsibility for the content of the report and consider their suggestions as advisory and not dictating what goes into the report.

- A formal letter will have at least the following parts: letterhead, date, inside address, reference line or subject line, salutation, body, complimentary close, typed signature, and written signature. When appropriate, there should also be an enclosure notation (enc.) and a copy notation (cc or pc) that names others receiving a copy of the letter.

    Use proper titles, such as Mr., Mrs., Ms., Dr., Rev., and so on. First names should be used only when addressing children or those adults with whom you have a very close relationship.

As a general rule, all letters to other agencies, professionals, and clients should be typed on letterhead stationery. However, in special instances, a personalized note to a client can be handwritten.

Be cautious about including any information that might violate a client's right to confidentiality if the letter is read by persons other than the intended recipient. Also, be alert to the fact that an agency's name and return address on an envelope reveals the client's involvement with the agency.

A copy of all letters sent should be retained in the agency's physical or electronic files (see Item 9.3). Use certified or registered mail when necessary to document that the letter was delivered.

Due to cost, speed of delivery, and the availability of technology, various forms of written communicating are increasingly transmitted through email (see Item 9.3). The guidelines presented here also apply to electronic communications. Like the hard copies of letters, reports, and other documents, electronic files must also be retained for future reference and maintained in a manner that protects the confidentiality of client information.

"Letter Writing" a retired item from the 8th edition

- Select your words carefully, using only those your reader will understand. Wordiness lessens the force of expression and may distract the reader from the points you want to make. Keep your sentences relatively short, usually 15 to 20 words or less. Most often, the straightforward subject-verb-object sentence is the best structure because it can be read quickly and is seldom misunderstood. Always use complete sentences, proper grammar, and correct spelling. Use the spell check, grammar check, dictionary, and thesaurus available in your computer's word-processing program. The use of shortened phrases and symbols that appear in email and telephone text messages are not appropriate in professional reports and letters.

- Avoid cramming many ideas into a single paragraph. Typically, a page of text should have several paragraph breaks. Ideally, each paragraph should focus on a single idea. In its first sentence, state the central point of the paragraph. Then, if necessary for purposes of clarification, restate the central point in different words. Additional sentences present the evidence, examples, background information, and the logic supporting the central point or idea. Finally, draw the paragraph to a close, summarizing the key point in a single sentence. By reading only the first and last sentence of a paragraph, the reader should be able to grasp the core of what you are trying to communicate.

- Avoid so-called weasel words such as *feel* and *seems*. Instead of saying "I feel placement into foster care is necessary," be direct and state, "I conclude that placement is necessary" or "I recommend placement for this child." Weak and evasive language gives the impression that the writer is uncertain or unwilling to take responsibility for what is being said.

Selected Bibliography

Glicken, Morley. *A Guide to Writing for Human Services Professional.* Lanham, MD: Rowman and Littlefield, 2008.

Geffner, Andrea. *Business English: The Writing Skills You Need for Today's Workplace,* 5th ed. New York: Barron's Educational, 2010.

Healy, Karen, and Joan Mulholland. *Writing Skills for Social Workers,* 2nd ed. Thousand Oaks, CA: Sage, 2012.

9.2 EFFECTIVE TELEPHONE COMMUNICATION

The telephone is used frequently in social work practice. However, a phone is not always the most effective and accurate method of communication because the messages must be delivered entirely by voice and without body language. The telephone can be used when a quick response is needed, when the matter under discussion is easily understood, and when it is not critical to establish a permanent record of the transaction. The use of a letter, memo, or email may be preferred when the message is complex and involves many details. Following these guidelines will help improve telephone use:

- Before placing an important phone call, consider its purpose and jot down the major points you wish to address. Plan to take notes during the phone conversation. Such notes can be placed in the agency file or case record to document the phone call.

- Begin all phone communications by identifying yourself and your organization. In order to protect client confidentiality, it can be important to immediately ask the client if she or he has the privacy needed to carry on a conversation at this time.

- Take time to enunciate clearly. Give complete attention to the person with whom you are speaking; do not "multitask" while on the phone. If the person on the other end is talking at length, interject a brief comment at intervals: "Yes, I see" or "I understand." This lets him or her know that you are paying attention. If the other person gets sidetracked, steer him or her back to the point of the call. Before saying "good-bye," it may be appropriate to summarize the information you intended to convey and the information you received.

- If you must leave a message for a person you did not reach by phone, keep that message short (e.g., your name, phone number, and reason for calling). Repeat the phone number two times, and speak slowly while doing so. Suggest a time for the person to return your call. However, you will probably save time by calling back yourself rather than waiting for your call to be returned.

- Cell phones are a great convenience, but social workers must be careful about when and where they use these phones. Cell phone use, especially in public places, can jeopardize client confidentiality. In addition to that danger, it is difficult for a social worker to give undivided attention to a cell phone conversation while also driving or walking down a busy street. Common courtesy requires that cell phones be turned off during client interviews and agency meetings.

- Master the skills of using your agency's phone system such as transferring calls, using voice mail, or conducting conference calls. When transferring calls to other lines, let callers know what you are doing. Identify the person to whom they will be speaking and why you are transferring their call. If you must leave the phone, say something like "Please hold on while I get that file."

- Be aware that the automated answering and voice-mail systems used in many agencies can be confusing to callers. Many individuals are frustrated and angry after having to listen to a recorded voice, select from a menu of options, and perform numerous dialing maneuvers. Instruct your clients and other frequent callers how to use the system.

Selected Bibliography

Tarbell, Shirley. *Office Basics Made Simple*. New York: Learning Express, 1997.

9.3 USING INFORMATION TECHNOLOGY

Computers are an essential part of social work practice, agency operation, and administration. At a minimum, social workers should be skilled at word processing, the use of a spreadsheet program, inputting client data, accessing online information, and communicating over the Internet. A desktop or laptop computer equipped with a basic software package, and to some degree a smart phone, with a high-speed Internet connection is usually sufficient for performing these activities—although for some specialized applications more sophisticated technology is required.

Next are some applications and information technologies used social work settings.

Online resources

The information technology used most often by social workers is **email**. It is an excellent communication tool for transmitting information, scheduling meetings, obtaining consultation, and providing support for both professionals and clients. At an advanced level, email can be used for client counseling and advice giving, although technology with a visual component (e.g., Skype) is sometimes used by social workers. Electronic messaging improves efficiency as messages can easily be sent and stored, meetings can be efficiently announced and scheduled, clients can be contacted, and reports can be transmitted and received. Participating in Internet or listserv professional discussion groups can also add to social workers' practice knowledge and provide stimulation, especially for workers who live in remote areas. Clients, too, can use email and electronic discussion groups to connect with people experiencing similar concerns as a form of self-help or mutual-aid group experience.

Another widely used online resource is the **Web**, which links Internet information through webpages. Many government agencies, human services organizations, universities, and individuals create and maintain webpages at little or no cost. These pages often provide built-in links to related pages, making it relatively easy for a social worker to access multiple sources of information on a specific topic. Many articles and some professional books are available on the Web and can be downloaded free or at a nominal cost. With the growing emphasis on evidence-based social work practice, it is essential to be able to search for evidence of best practices or the latest information on specific client conditions (see Item 11.22).

Web-based online advocacy continues to be a growing use of this technology. Groups concerned about local, state, national, and even international problems and policies are able to rapidly exchange social and political information and reach large numbers of people to encourage them to take action regarding these issues.

Word processing

An almost universal use of computer technology by social workers is word processing. Much of the necessary correspondence; preparation of case summaries; completion of agency information sheets; preparing memoranda, agendas, reports, and journal articles; as well as other routine agency paperwork now typically bypasses clerical staff and is done entirely by social workers. **Desktop publishing** is used in many agencies to prepare newsletters, bulletins, flyers, and public relations information (see Item 13.35). Finally, **presentation software** packages assist in creating text and graphics for making presentations at professional meetings (see Item 16.10) and for interpreting agency services to other agencies, civic clubs, United Way allocation committees, potential clients, and so on.

Spreadsheets

When the information to be recorded is numerical, **spreadsheet software** is extremely useful. Spreadsheets are used in maintaining data about services provided and clients seen, in accounting and bookkeeping tasks, and in collecting program evaluation and research data. The primary advantage of using a spreadsheet is being able to use formulas so that data summaries can be quickly compiled. In addition, columns can be accurately summed, basic statistical formulas can be applied to data, and professional-looking graphs and charts can be developed. One particularly useful application of spreadsheet software is in making projections; namely, "what-if" questions can be tested by changing one value and then observing how this would modify other values. This application is useful, for example, in estimating the need for financial resources when preparing a grant application (see Item 13.36), in identifying the potential savings from purchasing more efficient office equipment, or in changing the fees charged for services.

Database programs

As the electronic equivalents of filing cabinets and file folders, **database programs** provide an efficient way of maintaining and accessing important information. Regarding a specific client, social workers might include in a database such items as demographic characteristics, a social history, intake information, treatment plans, and progress notes. This data can be readily retrieved to track the progress of the client or merged with data from other clients to prepare a report. Database programs also can be used to schedule appointments, manage "to do" lists, and otherwise reduce paperwork.

Direct client services.

Although the provision of services to individuals, families, and groups by social workers has historically been based on face-to-face interaction, the growth of audio and visual technology is augmenting the social worker's tools for counseling with clients and guiding client groups. Minimizing the cost, time, and inconvenience of clients traveling to social workers—or social workers traveling to clients—increases the availability of services in both congested urban communities and sparsely populated rural areas.

Engaging in family conferencing, caregiver support groups, and other client systems is inevitable as the technology continues to grow. However, social workers are particularly concerned about the so-called *digital divide*. This refers to the fact that not all people have access to technology and those who do not are placed at a distinct disadvantage in, for example, applying for jobs, obtaining education and training, accessing medical information, and obtaining social services. Many who are poor cannot afford the technology and many others do not know how to use technological resources such as Skype or similar technology for social support and intervention activities. Although many younger clients have the skills to make use of such technology if it is available, older clients typically have not developed this ability. Also of concern are issues related to protecting client confidentiality.

Research-related software

Social workers are obligated to assess their practice effectiveness. Tracking the progress of individual clients (see Items 14.4 through 14.7) is made relatively efficient through the use of popular software sold with most computers. Similarly, social workers engaged in program evaluation (see Item 14.9) find it relatively simple to accumulate data from agency records to assess the effectiveness of various programs. In addition, social workers are expected to add to the knowledge base of the social work profession as they become interested in answering questions and testing hypotheses that arise in their practice. Software is available to facilitate such research by selecting a sample size, constructing data-entry forms, calculating the margin of error for a given return rate, suggesting and performing statistical tests, analyzing qualitative data, and presenting the results in graphic format.

Distance learning

Social work practice constantly changes, which means social workers at all levels must learn new theories and techniques. Whenever a worker moves from one practice setting or field to another (e.g., from mental health to corrections), a period of intensive retooling is usually required. In addition, some state licensing boards require licensed social workers to update their credentials periodically by participating in workshops, classes, and other instructional activities. These educational needs often can be met through participation in online academic courses and learning programs, online workshops, as well as webinars and other continuing education offerings by various professional organizations.

Job searches, graduate school applications, and competency exams

Finding and qualifying for social work positions increasingly requires the social worker to be comfortable in using computer technology. Human services agencies regularly post job openings on their websites and the application process typically involves completing an online application form (see Item 16.1). Similarly, master's- and doctoral-level graduate education programs often expect that most of the application process will be conducted electronically. Skills in basic use of word-processing technology for completing forms and writing short essays as part of the application process for jobs and advanced education are required.

The use of paper and pencil competency tests is still required by a few human services agencies, but most large agencies and the national social work licensing exams are now conducted using computerized programs (see Item 16.2). Because these tests are usually time-limited, social workers are can devote more attention to the content of the exams when they are comfortable with the mechanics of computer technology.

As social work practice makes increasing use of information technology, practitioners at all levels must participate in shaping the technology to fit the practice, rather than permitting the technology to shape and drive practice. Social workers also should understand both the benefits and the dangers associated with this technology. For instance, they should be aware of inherent ethical issues, such as the risk when transmitting confidential information electronically, as well as the potential to further distance disenfranchised populations from mainstream society by expecting that people have ready access to this technology. In the end, however, social workers must recognize that electronic technology only provides tools to assist practice. It is the workers themselves who must decide how to use this technology in an appropriate and responsible manner.

Selected Bibliography

Gregor, Claire. *Practical Computer Skills for Social Work.* Thousand Oaks, CA: Sage, 2006.

Hill, Andrew, and Ian Shaw. *Social Work and ICT.* Thousand Oaks, CA: Sage, 2011.

Wang, John (ed.). *Implementation and Integration of Information Systems in the Service Sector.* Hershey, PA: Information Science Reference, 2013.

9.4 CLIENT RECORDS AND DOCUMENTATION

What information should be included in the client's record? How should this information be arranged and organized? The answers will depend on factors such as the agency's mission, the type of service provided, relevant state and federal laws and regulations, and who will have access to the records.

A client record describes the client, his or her situation or problem, and the social work intervention. It shows the rationale underlying the intervention, provides a coherent picture of the services provided, documents the client's involvement in pivotal decisions, and documents compliance with key agency policies. Because these records contain *identifying data* (e.g., names, addresses) and highly personal information, maintaining client confidentiality is an overriding concern in all record keeping and documentation (see Item 10.5).

"Using A Dictating Machine" a retired item from the 3rd edition

Records must be accurate, up-to-date, unbiased, clearly written, and well organized. Depending on agency policy, a client record may be handwritten, dictated, or typed directly into a computerized record. Increasingly, agencies use software programs that aid in the preparation and the management of client records and make the retrieval of information easier (see Item 9.3).

"Process Recording" a retired item from the 6th edition

Given that a court can subpoena client records for use as legal evidence and because a social worker providing court testimony may be asked to read aloud from a client record, a worker must be thoughtful about what information is placed in a record and the words used (see Item 16.7). Pure conjecture, rumors about the client, and information irrelevant to the services provided should never appear in a client record.

The use of *progress notes* or *case notes* is a common method of recording in direct service agencies. After each contact with the client or with persons collateral to client service, the worker writes a few paragraphs (progress notes) that succinctly capture the essence of what happened during the session and, typically, states what the worker plans to do in future sessions.

"Problem Oriented Recording and the Soap Method" a retired item from the 7th edition

In order to prepare progress notes for easier reading and retrieval, the information is often placed within an organizing structure. Examples include the DAP (Data, Assessment, Plan); TIPP (Themes/Topics, Interventions, Progress, Plans); PIG (Problem, Intervention, Goal); and the SOAP or SOAPIER formats. The acronym SOAPIER refers to the following headings or categories of information that reflects one of these approaches to organizing client data:

S   *Subjective data* reports the worker's impressions of the client's mood and feelings and how the client is interpreting his or her situation. This data is derived mostly from a client's self-report. By definition, subjective information does not lend itself to independent or external validation.

O   *Objective data* is that which has been obtained by way a professional's direct observation, clinical examinations, testing, systematic data collection, and the like. This category of information can be independently verified.

A   *Assessment/Analysis* refers to the professional's working hypothesis or tentative conclusions derived from reviewing the subjective and objective information. This action connects the current session to the overall goals of work with the client.

P   The *Plan* focuses on the future and spells out how the professional and/or client intend to address the client's concern or problem.

I *Interventions* describe the steps or actions actually taken to address the client's problem or concerns.

E *Evaluation* presents data that describes the results, outcome, or effectiveness of the interventions.

R *Revision* describes how the intervention plan is being revised or needs to be modified in light of evaluation data.

Figure 9.1 is an illustrative SOAPIER entry related to problems faced by a client, Mrs. Brown.

***Subjective*:** Jane Brown says she is feeling in a "panic" and is "frightened" of losing her children to foster care because she cannot make ends meet. She is "scared and embarrassed" by her financial situation. Since she grew up on welfare, she says she will "never to go on the dole." She expressed a desire to eventually get her GED and maybe some technical training.

***Objective*:** Ms. Brown, age 24, earns about $1,800 per month for her work at a dry cleaning establishment. She rents a one-bedroom apartment from her uncle for $750 per month. She was divorced three years ago but receives no child support. She dropped out of a GED preparation program because its class schedule conflicted with her work.

She appears anxious and jumps from topic to topic. Agency records indicate that she was neglected as a child and spent four years in foster care. Her two children are ages 4 and 7. The 7 year old attends Paxton School. A friend watches the children when Ms. Brown is at work but this friend is not reliable because she drinks.

***Assessment*:** Client does not have sufficient money. She needs to find a different child care arrangement. Ms. Brown is overwhelmed by family and job responsibilities. Her worry, disorganization, and inability to think clearly are due, in part to a fear that she will lose her children to foster care. That fear is, in turn, related to her own experiences of having been in foster care. She believes that accepting any form of welfare will label her as a "bad parent" and for that reason is resistant to the idea of attempting to secure financial assistance.

***Plan*:** Schedule two sessions with Ms. Brown. Help her explore the possibility of securing job training, looking for a higher paying job, and finding a dependable and safe childcare arrangement. Explore options on how she might restart her work toward a GED. Gather information about why she receives no child support from the children's father. Encourage and assist her to apply for SNAP (food stamps). Assure her that such an application is a way for her to be a "good mother" under these difficult circumstances.

***Intervention*:** Active listening. Problem solve her scheduling conflicts. Provide examples and stories of other mothers in her situation that have had to ask for outside assistance. Accompany her to information gathering meetings with representatives from GED program and a job-training program.

***Evaluation*:** After the first two sessions, Ms. Brown says she is less worried. She feels reassured that she will not lose her children if she is being a responsible mother, even if she needs to utilize food stamps or some other welfare assistance. Because her ex-husband is in jail there is no chance that she will be receiving child support. She is making progress on working out a childcare arrangement with a responsible older neighbor who lives on her block. This neighbor will watch the children in exchange for help with shopping, some weekly house cleaning, and doing some home maintenance tasks.

***Revision*:** Schedule two more sessions to teach Ms. Brown about managing self-talk as a way of helping her gain control over her tendency to dwell on negative thoughts and worry excessively. Help her develop a family budget. Follow up on her desire to enroll in GED program that begins in February. Inform Ms. Brown about the MOMS support group and encourage her to attend.

Figure 9.1
Sample SOAPIER Entry

At monthly or quarterly intervals, the information contained in progress notes or case notes may be consolidated into a *narrative summary* and used to update or modify a client's service contract or treatment plan (see item 12.5).

Many agencies utilize various printed forms to collect and organize client information based on the type of client concerns addressed. The headings and checklists built into the forms remind the social worker of the data to be recorded and also facilitate the retrieval of information. Examples of headings that appear on such forms are Client's Presenting Concern or Problem, Client's Family and Social Supports, Client's Health, Client's Employment and Occupation, Client's Cultural Background, Activities and Changes Since Last Contact with Client, and so on.

A consideration in all approaches to record keeping is developing a mode of documentation that helps monitor and measure client progress in order to determine if a given intervention is working. The starting point for all such measurement is clarity and specificity regarding the intervention goals and objectives (see Items 12.1 and 12.4). Chapter 14 describes various scales and techniques used to measure client change. The capacity to document the client's progress is critically important when a client is using a public or private insurance to pay for the service. Numerous books illustrate sample progress notes that are keyed to various client problems and to the *DSM* categories (see Item 11.15).

Selected Bibliography

Jongsma, Arthur. *Adult Psychotherapy Progress Notes Planner*. Hoboken, NJ: Wiley, 2003.
Kagle, Jill, and Sandra Kopels. *Social Work Records*. Long Grove, IL: Waveland, 2008.
Sidell, Nancy. *Social Work Documentation*. Washington, DC: NASW Press, 2011.
Wiger, Donald. *Clinical Documentation Sourcebook*, 3rd ed. Hoboken, NJ: Wiley, 2009.

9.5 DEALING WITH ETHICAL ISSUES

Everyday, social workers encounter complex ethical issues. Sometimes the worker's task is to help clients sort out their notions of right and wrong. And at other times the social worker is struggling to determine if an action he or she is about to take is in keeping with profession's ethical code. Occasionally, the worker is caught up in an **ethical dilemma**, a situation in which all possible options require the social worker to violate one or more ethical principles. A common example is the need to report a client's abuse of her or his child. In that situation it is necessary to take action that can protect the child from injury but doing so violates the worker's obligating to protect the client's privacy (i.e., provide a confidential professional relationship.) Increasingly, the ethical dilemmas faced by social workers involve decisions on how best to allocate scarce resources that may deprive some clients of needed services or force social workers to terminate services before the desired outcomes are fully achieved.

A first step toward resolving ethical dilemmas is to answer several questions that supply important background information and clarify the matter:

- Who is your primary client (i.e., usually the person, group, or organization that requested the social worker's services and expects to benefit from them)?
- What aspects of the agency's or your practice activities give rise to the dilemma (e.g., legal mandates, job requirements, agency policy, questions of efficient use of resources, possible harm caused by an intervention)?

- Who can or should resolve this dilemma? Is it rightfully a decision to be made by the client? Other family members? You? The agency administrator? A combination of people?
- For each decision possible, what are the short-term and long-term consequences for the client, family, agency, community, and so on?
- Who stands to gain and who (if anyone) stands to lose from each possible choice or action? Are the affected people of equal or unequal power (e.g., child vs. adult)? Are some who might be affected particularly vulnerable and thus require special consideration?
- When harm to someone cannot be avoided, what decision will cause the least harm with fewest long-term consequences? Who of those that might be harmed are least able to recover from the harm?
- Will a particular resolution to this dilemma set an undesirable precedent for future decision making concerning other clients?

Once those questions have been answered, the worker must answer three additional questions:

- What ethical principles and obligations apply in this situation?
- Which, if any, ethical principles are in conflict in this situation and therefore create an ethical dilemma?
- In this situation, do certain ethical obligations take priority over others?

To answer these questions, the social worker must be very familiar with the National Association of Social Worker's **Code of Ethics** (1999), which describes basic ethical standards and principles and provides general guidelines for professional conduct. The *NASW Code of Ethics* is organized into six sets of ethical principles:

1. *Ethical responsibilities to clients.* This section addresses such factors as the social worker's primary responsibility to the client, including maximizing client self-determination; securing informed consent; demonstrating cultural competence and competence in any intervention approach used; avoiding conflict of interest; protecting client privacy; and prohibitions regarding sexual involvement, physical contact, sexual harassment, and other boundary matters; as well as appropriate termination of services.

2. *Ethical responsibilities to colleagues.* Section 2 is concerned with treating colleagues with respect; maintaining professional confidentiality; engaging in collaboration and teamwork; proper handling of disputes; making referrals; and reporting colleagues who may be impaired, incompetent, or unethical in their practice.

3. *Ethical responsibilities in practice settings.* The items addressed in this section include competence in providing supervision, consultation, education, and training; the evaluation of the performance of other workers; responsible recording and billing; assuring an appropriate work environment; and so on.

    "Planning for a Temporary Absence or Departure" from the 7th edition

4. *Ethical responsibilities as a professional.* This section addresses items related to accepting assignments only when one is competent to perform the work; addressing any form of discrimination; avoiding private conduct that compromises one's professional responsibilities; engaging in dishonesty, fraud, and deception; addressing personal issues if impaired; and making it clear when acting

as a private citizen and making statements that are not part of professional activities.

5. *Ethical responsibilities to the social work profession.* Section 5 concerns issues related to promoting high standards for social work, contributing to the growth and development of the profession, as well as evaluating the quality of the programs one offers and assessing his or her own practice as a quality control device.

6. *Ethical responsibilities to the broader society.* This section reflects that social workers are charged with promoting the general welfare of the society; the realization of social justice; participating in public debates to shape social policies and institutions; providing services in emergencies; and actively engaging in social and political action to strengthen quality of life for all persons.

A copy of the *Code of Ethics* should be on the desk of every social worker and can be downloaded from NASW at http://www.naswdc.org. It is an important screen that may be used to analyze a practice situation to determine if a specific alternative or action is ethically responsible and to help identify ethical conflicts that may arise in a practice situation. Addressing similar ethical issues, the Canadian *Code of Ethics* (http://www.casw-acts.ca) is organized into 10 areas: (1) primary professional obligation, (2) integrity and objectivity, (3) competence, (4) limits on professional relationships, (5) confidential information, (6) outside interests, (7) limits on private practice, (8) responsibilities to the workplace, (9) responsibilities to the profession, and (10) responsibilities for social change.

A limitation of a professional *Code of Ethics* as a tool for resolving ethical issues is that its standards are listed one after another, giving the impression that all are of equal of equal importance. However, when dealing with an individual case and its special

**"Making Ethical Decisions"
from 8th edition**

circumstances, some standards should be given priority over others. For example, if a social worker learns that a client intends to harm herself or himself, the standard that the social worker should assure confidentiality should be temporarily set aside in order to protect the client's life, a higher good. Sorting out such issues, especially if more than one ethical issue is involved, is difficult.

A second useful screen when addressing ethical issues is provided by Dolgoff, Harrington, and Loewenberg (2012) who provide a useful prioritization of seven fundamental principles. They list these principles in the following order: (1) the protection of life, (2) increasing equality among relevant persons affected by the situation, (3) maximizing clients' autonomy and freedom (including self-determination), (4) following the "least harm" principle, (5) promoting the quality of life, (6) protecting privacy and confidentiality, and (7) practicing with truthfulness and full disclosure of all important information. Thus, in evaluating an ethical dilemma a social worker might seriously consider encouraging clients to make their own decisions about what actions they will take (Principle #3) over protecting confidentiality (Principle #6). Any individual social worker might identify additional principles or order the priorities differently, yet the ranking by Dolgoff and colleagues provides a useful starting point.

It is important to understand that ethical and legal codes are not synonymous. There may be times in social work practice when legal requirements conflict with ethical principles. In fact, social workers can place themselves in legal jeopardy when they do what is ethically correct, if a state and federal law mandates a different course of action (see Item16.6).

It is also important to distinguish between personal morality and the ethics of a profession. The term *morality* (or *personal ethics*) usually refers to an individual's standards of conduct and beliefs as to what is right and wrong. In the case of legal-ethical conflicts, there may be times when the social worker's personal standards are in conflict with either the *Code of Ethics* or legal codes, or both. These are indeed thorny situations that require very careful discernment and probably consultation with trusted peers or experts.

Finally, in addition to serving as a guide for practice decisions, social workers should recognize that their profession's ethical code also serves as a guide for judging if actions they have performed are unethical.* Just as various laws become the standards against which person's actions are judged in a trial, so the profession's ethical standards serve as guidelines by which one's actions are judged if charged with unethical social work practice.

Selected Bibliography

Dolgoff, Ralph, Donna Harrington, and Frank M. Loewenberg. *Ethical Decisions for Social Work Practice*, 9th ed. Independence, KY: Cengage, 2012.

Gambrill, Eileen. *Social Work Ethics*. Burlington, VT: Ashgate, 2009.

National Association of Social Workers. *Code of Ethics*. Washington, DC: NASW, 1999.

Reamer, Frederic G. *Social Work Values and Ethics,* 4th ed. New York: Columbia University Press, 2013.

Rothman, Juliet Cassuto. *From the Front Lines: Student Cases in Social Work Ethics*. Berkeley, CA: University of California, 2013.

9.6 MANAGING TIME AND WORKLOAD

Nearly every social worker is faced with having too much work and too little time. Thus, the worker must use time management skills and, to the extent possible, control his or her workload. However, the measures taken in the name of efficiency must not compromise client services. Consider these guidelines:

- *Understand your agency's mission and your own job description.* Unless you know what needs to be done, you cannot figure out ways to do it more effectively and efficiently. If your assignments and responsibilities are unclear, discuss them with your supervisor or administrative superiors. Find out what tasks and assignments are of highest priority.

- *Plan your work.* At the end of each day, as well as at the end of each week, write down what you must work on or accomplish the next day and the next week. Start each day with a *"to do" list*. Estimate how much time is needed for each item on the list and plan to allocate the time needed. Anticipate deadlines and begin work on those tasks that must be completed within a certain time frame. It is usually best to tackle lengthy tasks before those that can be completed in a shorter time. Work on the most difficult tasks when your energy level is highest (e.g., first thing in the morning). Reserve some time at the end of each day for clearing your desk and taking care of any unfinished tasks.

- *Adopt a system for setting priorities.* One method is the ABC priority system. On your "to do" list, write A's next to those tasks that are most important and have

---

*The National Association of Social Workers maintains a "hotline" a few hours each week (800–638–8799) where members can receive consultation regarding ethical issues in social work practice.

highest priority. Write C's next to tasks that are of least importance and B's next to those in the middle range. Next, prioritize the A tasks in order of importance, labeling them A–1, A–2, A–3, and so on. The B tasks can be labeled in the same way: B–1, B–2, and so on. At the beginning of the working day, start work on task A–1. Then move to A–2 and on down the list.

A less complex approach is to classify all tasks into three categories: (1) tasks that must be completed today, (2) tasks that should be started today, and (3) tasks that can wait a few days. Realize that priorities may change over the course of a day or week. Thus, it is necessary to continually review and revise your "to do" list.

- *Make decisions in a timely manner.* Some people avoid making decisions because they are afraid of making a mistake. Some delay making a decision because they cannot arrive at a perfect solution, although there are few, if any, perfect solutions in the real world of social work practice. One can strive for excellence, but striving for perfection will result only in frustration. If you make a mistake, learn from it, but do not waste time brooding over it. A "good" mistake is one from which you learn and do not repeat. A "bad" mistake is one you will repeat again.

- *Organize your desk and eliminate clutter in your workspace.* Clear your desk of all materials except for those with which you are working. This helps maintain attention on the task at hand. Try to focus on one thing at a time until you either complete the task or reach a preset time limit for that activity. Avoid jumping from task to task. Handle each paper or file only once. If you pick up a letter or report or receive an email communication, take the action required. Do not set it aside; do not let papers pile up on your desk. Keep your agency's policy and procedures manual up-to-date and handy. Much time can be lost searching for misplaced information or following an outdated procedure.

- *Develop a tickler file.* A tickler file will help you keep track of the deadlines for submitting monthly reports and other tasks that must be completed according to a schedule. A tickler file can take several forms: notations on a calendar, a desktop file, a computerized calendar, or an electronic date book. Also, develop a workable system for rapid retrieval of frequently used information such as the names, addresses, and phone numbers of professionals and agencies that you regularly contact. That information might be maintained in a Rolodex, on your cell phone, on your computer, or on your office telephone system.

- *Minimize the time spent in meetings.* Unnecessary and poorly planned meetings waste valuable time. Do not schedule a face-to-face meeting if an alternative is possible, such as a telephone conference call or email exchanges. If you must have a meeting, make sure all those attending know its purpose and agenda so they can properly prepare. Start on time and end on time. Stick to the agenda and stay on task. Consider attending the meeting for only the time necessary to make your contribution. (See Items 13.24 and 13.26 for additional guidelines on meetings.)

- *Structure the schedule.* When possible, structure your day by using scheduled appointments for interviews, collateral contacts (contacts with other service providers), and the like. However, plan also for the unexpected to arise and allow time in your schedule for dealing with surprises and a work-related emergency. When possible, reduce travel time by scheduling all meetings in a given locality for the same day.

- *Reduce interruptions to a minimum.* Drop-in clients are usually less of a problem than staff members who like to chat. Closing your office door or standing up to converse with someone who stopped by can help limit interruptions. Being able to say no or not now to the question "Do you have a minute?" is an important time-management skill. When you cannot avoid an interruption, try to maintain control of the situation by giving the matter your full attention, and, if appropriate, by setting a time limit by saying, for example: "I have only five minutes."

- *Get more training.* If the lack of a skill is slowing you down or causing time-consuming mistakes, obtain the additional training you need. Ask experienced colleagues to help you devise more efficient approaches to your work. For example, secure their suggestions on how to reduce time spent writing client service documentation and agency reports (see Items 9.1 and 9.4). Become proficient in the use of office machines and communications systems (e.g., email, smart phone, computer, printer, copier, fax).

- *Control the workload.* To the extent feasible, exercise control over your workload. If you do not do this, you will be spread too thin and your effectiveness will diminish. When asked to take on additional work, consider the following:

  - Decide if the proposed assignment or request for your time is reasonable, given your job description and current workload. Ask yourself: Is this a matter of high priority? Am I responsible for this task or is someone else? If I take on the extra work, will I soon feel put upon and angry?

  - When unsure if the request is reasonable, obtain more information. If still in doubt, ask for some time to think about the request and set a deadline for making the decision (e.g., "I'll let you know in a half hour").

  - If you must refuse, give a simple and straightforward explanation without making excuses. If you have a good reason for refusing, there is no need to apologize.

"Controlling Workload" from the 7th edition

The preceding discussion of refusing additional work assignments presumes there is opportunity to negotiate. In many practice settings that possibility does not exist. An agency supervisor or an administrator has the authority to make work assignments, even when he or she knows you are already overloaded.

In some work situations you can reduce an excessive workload by assigning or delegating certain tasks to other agency staff such as a secretary, case aide, or paraprofessional. However, do not ask others to perform tasks that are beyond their ability or job description.

Selected Bibliography

Brounstein, Marty, et al., *Thriving in the Work Place*. Hoboken, NJ: Wiley, 2010.
Jones, Lyndon, and Paul Loftus. *Time Well Spent*. Philadelphia: Kogan Page, 2009.
Zeigler, Kenneth. *Getting Organized at Work*. New York: McGraw-Hill, 2005.
Zeller, Dirk. *Successful Time Management for Dummies*, Hoboken, NJ: Wiley, 2009.

9.7 ELEMENTS OF PROFESSIONAL BEHAVIOR

It has been said that a professional is someone who knows what to do and can be counted on to do it, even when he or she does not feel like doing it. That is an insightful description. It suggests that a professional knows what should be done, can be trusted to do it, and does not let matters of personal convenience interfere with her or his performance.

Throughout their career, it is important for social workers to continually examine their performance and make sure their behavior is of a professional nature. Figure 9.2 offers a comparison of professional and nonprofessional behavior.

Selected Bibliography

Lauffer, Armand. *Working in Social Work*. Newbury Park, CA: Sage, 1987.

Payne, Malcolm. *What Is Professional Social Work?* Chicago: Lyceum, 2006.

Sheafor, Bradford W., Armando T. Morales, and Malcolm E. Scott. *Social Work: A Profession of Many Faces*, 12th ed. Upper Saddle River, NJ: Pearson, 2012.

Professional Behavior	*Nonprofessional Behavior*
A deep and abiding committed to the profession's goals, values, and ethics	Views social work as simply a job that can be easily abandoned if something better comes along
Bases practice on a body of knowledge learned through formal education and ongoing training	Bases practice mostly on personal opinions, agency rules, or a political ideology
Makes decision on basis of fact, critical thinking, and scientific research	Makes decisions on basis of feelings, attitudes, or whims
Practice is guided by the profession's *Code of Ethics*	Practice is guided by personal preferences and inclinations
Professional relationships with clients are individualized, purposeful, and goal directed; does not expect to meet own needs within professional relationships	Relationships with clients are routine, perfunctory, and without direction; looks to meet own needs within relationships with clients
Client's well-being is of primary importance;	Own wants and convenience are of highest priority
Adheres to principles of professional practice, regardless of other pressures	Political and organizational pressures easily sway or influence decisions and actions
Continually upgrades knowledge and skills so as to better serve clients	Learns only the minimum required to keep job
Expects and invites peer review and critical evaluations of his or her performance	Avoids having others examine or observe his or her performance
Strives to develop new knowledge and share it within the profession	Does not invest self in search of new knowledge
Assumes responsibility for quality of services provided and for improving own agency's policies, programs, and services	Only concerned with doing a job as assigned by others and does not see self as responsible for improving agency policy and programs
Exercises self-discipline and self-awareness; keeps own emotions in check	Expresses emotions and personal views in thoughtless and hurtful manner
Documents professional decisions and actions, completely and accurately	Avoids recordkeeping, records are incomplete and cursory

Figure 9.2
Comparison of Professional and Nonprofessional Behavior

PART 4

TECHNIQUES AND GUIDELINES FOR PHASES OF THE PLANNED CHANGE PROCESS

Social work supervisors have often heard practicum students and new social workers say something like "I understand the basic theory of working with people, but what should I do when I see Mrs. Jones and her daughter this afternoon?" Obviously, these novice workers have discovered that there is a difference between the knowing and the doing in social work practice. They sense a need for guidance that is more specific than that provided by theories and models.

Part IV of this book addresses this need. As was explained in the Preface, the authors chose to prepare a book focusing mostly on techniques and guidelines. This decision reflects their belief that many textbooks do an excellent job of presenting the theory of practice, yet few provide the concrete guidance so often requested by students and new social workers.

The five chapters of Part IV correspond to the five phases of the planned change process, as was described in Chapter 7. The reader will notice that each chapter has a Section A and a Section B. Techniques and guidelines related to direct social work practice are provided in Section A, whereas techniques and guidelines relevant to indirect practice are provided in Section B. The term **direct practice** refers to those activities that involve frequent face-to-face interaction with a client who has requested a service or is experiencing some difficulty. Direct social work practice might include, for example, individual and family counseling, case management, referral work, group treatment, guiding a support group, advocating for the services needed by a specific individual, and so on. By contrast, the term **indirect practice** refers to activities that benefit those who need various types of services or forms of assistance but does not usually involve direct or frequent contact with the clients or consumers of those services. Examples of indirect practice include administration, staff supervision, program planning, program evaluation, fund-raising, public education, work with community organizations and coalitions of agencies that are concerned about a particular social problem, advocacy on behalf of a whole category of people in need, and efforts to enact legislation and establish social and economic policies that would enhance peoples' lives and well-being.

10

Intake and Engagement

LEARNING OBJECTIVES

At the conclusion of this chapter, the reader should be prepared to:

- Demonstrate familiarity with guidelines regarding preparation for first telephone and face-to-face interaction when initiating a helping relationship with a new client.
- Identify techniques for clarifying a new client's presenting problem and, when appropriate, making effective referrals for additional services.
- Describe the principles that should guide the protection of confidential client information.
- Explain the advantages and disadvantages of conducting in-home interviews and the safety precautions a social worker should take if there are potentially dangerous client interactions.
- Describe guidelines for work with mandated or manipulative clients.
- Identify a process for clarifying the roles and responsibilities of clients and social workers, recognizing the power differentials that are inherent in professional relationships.
- Discuss factors a social worker new to a job should consider regarding the internal functioning of the agency, orientation to the job and agency, and developing knowledge of the community and its resources.

This chapter presents guidelines and techniques for use during the beginning, or start-up phase, of the change process. Although the activities differ somewhat when providing direct services (Section A), as compared to indirect services (Section B), the intent is essentially the same. During this phase, the social worker typically undertakes three sets of activities: preparation, initial engagement, and intake. First, she or he *prepares* for the first contact by reviewing whatever information is available on the client (e.g., agency records), selecting a meeting time and place that will be convenient and comfortable for the client, determining who should be involved in the initial meeting, and remaining alert to any factors that might affect the client's perspective on and investment in the helping process.

Second, the worker will begin the process of *initial engagement* by establishing rapport and helping clients articulate and clarify the nature of their concerns or requests. Typically, clients have tried unsuccessfully to deal with their concerns through friends or other helpers before deciding to seek assistance from a social worker. The client, whether an individual or an organization, is likely to approach the change process with some reluctance, skepticism, and ambivalence.

Third, the social worker must determine if he or she can appropriately address the client's need or request. In short, some form of *intake* or screening decision is necessary. The human services delivery system is complex and people in search of help or assistance may approach an agency or a professional who is unable to address the client's specific concern. Or, at the indirect-service level, the initial group created to address an agency or community issue may not, on more thorough examination of the matter, be the best organization or have the right set of actors to proceed with the change process. The intake decision to be made by the social worker, then, is whether it is appropriate to continue with the client or to refer him or her to another organization or professional better suited to address the client's situation.

SECTION A

TECHNIQUES AND GUIDELINES FOR DIRECT PRACTICE

Since the first contact sets the tone for a helping relationship, the worker should carefully plan this meeting. However, adequate preparation may not be possible if the initial meeting takes place under crisis conditions.

Preparatory activities

Prior to their first meeting, the worker should consider how the client might be feeling. Many clients will be anxious and ambivalent. They may wonder, for example: Will I be treated with respect? Will this person be able to help? Will he or she understand my concerns? Will this worker listen to what I have to say? Can my problem be resolved in a reasonable amount of time? What will I be charged?

A typical client will have had some prior experience with professional helpers and may be skeptical about entering still another professional relationship. If the client is involuntary and has been *mandated* (e.g., court ordered) or somehow pressured to see the worker, she or he may be angry or resentful.

To the extent possible, the social worker should secure a meeting space that offers comfort, privacy, and accommodations for special needs (e.g., access for a wheelchair). The meeting may be in the worker's office, but depending on the client's situation it might be in the client's home, a hospital room, jail, group home, or neighborhood center. If the client cannot leave her or his place of work during usual business hours, an evening appointment may be necessary. If the client has had prior contacts with the worker's agency, the worker should have read the relevant records. The various agency intake forms that might be needed should be readily available. If the contact is to occur through some form of information technology (see Item 9.3), the social worker should make sure that all equipment needed is available and in working order.

If the contact is to take place in an agency, the social worker should be sensitive to how the agency environment or milieu might affect the helping relationship. For instance: Is the receptionist courteous and helpful when a client telephones or stops by the agency? Is the waiting area comfortable? Is childcare available if the client brings young children to the interview? Is the worker's office or the meeting room arranged and furnished in a manner favorable to confidential and undisturbed communication?

Engagement activities

The following worker activities can get the relationship off to a good start and increase the likelihood that clients will invest themselves in a helping process:

- Greet and speak with the client in a way that is nonthreatening and puts him or her at ease.
- Explain any legal or ethical obligations related to confidentiality and the handling of information divulged by the client.
- Help the client articulate his or her requests, concerns, and expectations of the agency and worker.
- Demonstrate genuine interest in the client's situation.
- Encourage the client to ask any questions or express any fears that she or he may have about the social worker and the agency's services.
- Explain pertinent eligibility requirements that may affect service provision.

During this beginning phase, the worker should be alert to people's fear of the unknown and inherent resistance to change. Having to make even a small change can be difficult, especially for clients who tend to be inflexible. When clients are unsure of what is happening or of what is expected, they are likely to become even more anxious, more defensive, and hold tightly to their usual patterns.

Intake activities

One decision the social worker must make during the intake and engagement phase has to do with continuation of service. The worker must determine if there is a proper fit between the client's need or request and the agency's services and eligibility criteria. If so, the next decision is whether the worker should provide continuing services (i.e., guide the remainder of the helping process) or transfer the matter to another worker within the agency. That decision will depend on the nature of the agency's programs, the division of labor in the agency, and the competence of the worker to address the client's specific issues. If it is determined that the worker should continue to provide services to the client, the following actions are important:

- Assess the urgency of the client's needs or presenting problem and attend to the emergency, if one exists.
- Explain the responsibilities that both the client and the worker will assume during the helping process.
- Explain to the client that she or he will need to provide information (in some cases, very personal information) in order to assess the problem or situation.
- Secure the client's signed release of confidential information (if one is needed).
- Reach tentative agreement on the minimum and, if possible, maximum number of meetings that probably will be necessary.

- Explain any fees to be charged. If the needed services or treatment must be authorized by an insurance company, initiate the request for approval.
- Reach agreement on the time, place, and frequency of future meetings.

If the client's request or needs do not match this agency's program and eligibility criteria, the client should be referred to an appropriate source of help. Social workers are expected to know about available human services resources (see Item 10.4).

10.1 MAKING THE FIRST TELEPHONE CONTACT

When clients approach an agency for the first time, many are uncertain about what to expect. Responding to such a client is especially challenging when the first conversation is by telephone. The worker must use this time on the telephone to encourage and reassure the client, obtain a general understanding of the client's concern or request, and, if needed, arrange for the first face-to-face interview. Several guidelines should be kept in mind:

- During a telephone conversation, you cannot observe nonverbal behavior. Thus, miscommunication and misunderstandings are more likely because you will not always know how the client is reacting to what is being said. Minimize this possibility by keeping your messages simple and factual. An explanation of details related to your agency's services should be saved for a face-to-face meeting.

- If speaking with a voluntary client, briefly explore his or her presenting concern or request so you can evaluate the appropriateness of this referral to your agency. However, avoid gathering detailed intake information by phone; that is best done during a face-to-face interview.

- If speaking to a mandated or involuntary client, it is best to confine the phone conversation to simply arranging the first face-to-face interview. The mandated client (e.g., court ordered) often has negative feelings about having to meet with a social worker. Such feelings are much easier to address during a face-to-face interview (see Item 10.7).

- When arranging the first office visit, make sure the client knows your full name and the location of your office. Some clients may need guidance on how to use public transportation to reach the agency or where parking may be available. In some cases, a follow-up letter should be sent to the client, repeating the time and place of the appointment.

- The first telephone contact is an opportune time to ask the caller if other family members or other significant persons are aware of this plan to meet with a social worker. If the call is being kept secret from others, ask why this secrecy is important. Determine if this phone call places the caller in danger, as might be the situation in cases of domestic abuse (see Item 15.6). Also ask if perhaps a significant other should attend the first face-to-face meeting. Explain, for example, that the assessment of a problem will be more accurate and the intervention more effective if everyone affected can share his or her perception of what is happening and voice ideas on what actions or services might prove helpful. If the caller does not want others involved, set up a meeting with the caller alone. Later in the helping process, you might again explore the desirability of involving the client's significant others.

Selected Bibliography

Allen, Gina, and Duncan Lanford. *Effective Interviewing in Social Work and Social Care.* New York: Palgrave, 2006.

Parsons, Richard, and Naijian Zhang. *Becoming a Skilled Counselor.* Thousand Oaks, CA: Sage, 2012.

10.2 CONDUCTING THE FIRST FACE-TO-FACE MEETING

It is not unusual for the social worker to feel a bit uneasy when meeting a client for the first time. It is safe to assume that the client has similar feelings. It is during this first meeting that the worker and client size up each other and form initial impressions. These first impressions can have a powerful effect on what follows. Several guidelines can help the social worker get things off to a good start:

- Prior to the meeting, anticipate what the client might be thinking and feeling. Prepare yourself to respond to the client's possible feelings of fear, hope, confusion, and ambivalence. The client might have unrealistic expectations. Possibly the client perceives the social worker as an intrusion, an unwelcome stranger, and an authority figure. Be prepared to offer a simple but accurate description of your role, responsibility, and usual approach to helping and providing services (see Item 10.10).

- Create a physical arrangement conducive to communication. For a two-person meeting, the client's chair and the worker's chair should be about five feet apart. The chairs for a family interview should be arranged in a circle. Make sure the room is comfortable and offers privacy. If meeting through the use of information technology, be sure the client is in a place free from distractions and can comfortably use any electronic devices needed for the interview.

- If the client has requested the meeting, begin with some introductory remarks and possibly some small talk, but soon move the focus to the concern that brought the client to the agency. On the other hand, if you initiated the interview, begin immediately with an explanation of why you need to speak to the person.

- Explain the rules of *confidentiality* that apply. Inform the client if what she or he says cannot be held in complete confidence. For example, you might say, "Before we begin, I want to make certain you understand that I will be preparing a report for the court. So, what you tell me may end up in my report to the judge. Do you understand that?"

- Begin with whatever topic the client considers important and wants to talk about (i.e., begin where the client is). Realize, however, that many clients will at first test the worker's trustworthiness and competence before deciding whether to reveal their real concerns or the whole story. If you have only limited time to spend with a client, explain this at the beginning of the interview so the topics of highest priority to the client will receive attention.

- Do not rush the client. Rather, convey the message, "I will give you the time necessary to develop your thoughts and decide what you want to say." Do not jump to conclusions about the nature or cause of the client's presenting concern or problem. Do not display surprise or disbelief in response to what the client tells you.

- When you do not know the answer to a service-related question asked by the client, explain this in a non-apologetic manner and offer to find the answer. Be careful not to make promises that you may not be able to keep.

- Some note taking during the intake phase is usually necessary and appropriate. Writing down pertinent client information can demonstrate your desire to understand and remember what the client is saying. Note taking can be distracting, however. If the client is bothered by note taking, show him or her your notes and explain why they are needed. If the client still objects, cease taking notes. If you are completing an agency form, give the client a copy to follow along as you speak.

- If you and the client agree to a second meeting, be sure the client has your business card that it lists your name and phone number. Also, be sure that you obtain the client's full name, address, and phone number.

The social worker will encounter a number of clients who have significant *physical or sensory disabilities*. The place and usual patterns of first meetings may need to be altered in order to accommodate their special needs. A few guidelines should be kept in mind:

- When interviewing a person lying on a hospital bed or using a wheelchair, sit or position yourself at eye level with the client. Do not compel the client to strain his or her neck or body in order to look at you. Do not stand over him or her, for that might place the client in a psychologically inferior position.

- If the client moves about in a wheelchair or with the aid of a walker or crutches, do not offer assistance unless it is requested or clearly needed. Respect the client's desire to remain in control and to decline your offer of assistance. Be patient if it takes the client longer to complete tasks and movements. Avoid fixation on the client's medical equipment or prosthesis.

- When a client is blind or has low vision and is in an unfamiliar space, you may need to provide information he or she needs to move about. For example, you can alert him or her to obstacles or dangers such as overhead obstructions, sharp turns, and steps. When walking with a person who is blind simply stay at his or her side and let the person maneuver. Never grab or move the individual, for this is both insulting and frightening. If the client wants your assistance, he or she will ask or reach out; respond by offering your elbow to hold and then walk about a half-step ahead. If the client has a guide dog, be aware that these dogs are trained to walk down the center of a sidewalk or hallway. Do not touch or speak to a guide dog or a service dog unless you have the owner's permission.

- Individuals with a hearing loss have difficulty accurately interpreting the human voice and separating one sound from another. They may, for example, confuse words that sound similar and they are especially challenged when several people are talking and when there is background noise. Persons using hearing aids will also have some difficulty in a noisy environment. A type of hearing loss caused by long-term exposure to loud noise is fairly common among older people, especially men. Because it involves diminished capacity to hear high-frequency sounds, individuals with this hearing loss may understand a male voice more easily than a female voice.

If your client is struggling to hear, ask what you can do to minimize the problem. You may need to move to a quieter environment, speak louder, or more slowly. Check often to see if the client is able to follow the conversation. Do not make the mistake of interpreting nodding and smiling as a sign of comprehension, for that may be simply the client's response to being embarrassed about not being able to hear.

If your client uses speech reading (lip reading), be sure to position yourself so he or she can see your face. Do not position yourself in front of a window or bright light. Do not look down while speaking. A heavily mustached mouth may impede speech reading. Do not exaggerate your words, since this will make speech reading even more difficult. Realize that even adept lip-readers seldom comprehend more than two thirds of what it said orally. They must guess at the rest.

A person who is functionally deaf is usually prepared to communicate in writing, by sign language, or through adaptive technology. If the individual will be using sign language, find out what system he or she uses and arrange for the services of an interpreter. Some who are deaf use hearing dogs trained to detect certain sounds such as traffic signals and alarms.

• Most governmental offices, hospitals, and other essential services are equipped with devices for use by persons who have difficulty communicating because of low vision, hearing loss, or speech impairments. A social worker likely to encounter clients with these limitations should become familiar with amplifiers, signaling devices, puff-blow devices, electronic artificial larynx devices, telebraille, TDD (telecommunications device for the deaf), TTY (teletypewriter), and other assistive technology.

Selected Bibliography

DeSole, Leah. *Making Contact: The Therapist's Guide to Conducting a Successful First Interview.* Upper Saddle River, NJ: Pearson. 2006.

Kadushin, Alfred, and Goldie Kadushin. *The Social Work Interview*, 5th ed. New York: Columbia University Press, 2013.

Morrison, James, *The First Interview*, 3rd ed. New York: Guilford, 2008.

Murphy, Bianca, and Carolyn Dillon. *Interviewing in Action in a Multicultural World*, 4th ed. Independence, KY: Cengage, 2011.

10.3 CLARIFYING THE CLIENT'S PROBLEM, CONCERN, OR REQUEST

An important activity during intake and engagement is to obtain a description of the concern that brought the client into contact with the social worker or agency. The ways in which clients describe their concerns or problems depends, in part, on whether the client is voluntarily seeking assistance. Mandated or nonvoluntary clients will often minimize the seriousness of their problem, describe them in only a vague and general manner, and withhold significant information. On the other hand, some voluntary clients will overstate the seriousness of their problem and the urgency of their request for service.

Here are examples of questions or statements that a social worker might use to encourage adult clients to more clearly describe their problems or concerns:

- Did someone suggest that you come here and talk to me (or come to this agency)? Who was that? Why did that person think it was important for you to come here?
- Describe the most recent occurrence of the problem.
- Describe the time when this problem was the most serious it has ever been.
- If today's meeting with me accomplishes what you hope it will, what specifically will be different in your life? What will be different in how you behave and feel?
- Do you, your family, and your friends agree or disagree on the nature and cause of this problem?
- Do you know of other people who have a similar problem or concern? What did they do about this problem?
- Who else have you talked to about this concern? What did they have to say about it? What suggestions did they offer?
- How have you managed to cope with this problem up to now? What have you done to keep it from getting worse or even more serious?
- If you could do it, what is the one thing that you would do immediately to make things better for yourself?
- If someone close to you—such as your spouse, child, or parent—were to describe and explain your problem or concern, what would they say about it?
- If someone videotaped your problem and then I watched that recording, what would I especially notice, hear, or see? What would stand out?
- On a scale of 1 to 10—with 1 meaning "of little concern" and 10 meaning "of great concern"—how would you rate the seriousness of your problem today? How would you have rated it two weeks ago? What has changed in the last two weeks? On this scale of 1 to 10, how would your spouse (or child, parent, probation officer, etc.) rate this problem?
- Is there a particular time of day or week when this problem is the most troublesome to you? Is there a time when it is less of a problem?
- In what places or in what situations is this problem most evident or most serious? Less evident and least serious?
- Think of times when you have experienced this problem. Now, tell me what has usually happened just before the problem occurs or turns worse? What usually happens after you have experienced an episode of this problem?
- If your best friend came to you with this same problem or request and asked for your advice, what would you say?
- If, all of a sudden, your problem disappeared, what would be the most noticeable change in your daily routines? How would each day or week of your life be different if you didn't have this problem? If the problem disappeared, what would you be doing instead of trying to cope with this problem?
- What is your theory about your problem or concern? Why has it developed or appeared at this point in your life? How do you explain it? Do you think your problem could have been prevented or avoided?

Selected Bibliography

Cormier, Sherry, Paula Nurius, and Cynthia Osborn. *Interviewing and Change Strategies,* 7th ed. Independence, KY: Cengage, 2013.

DeJong, Peter, and Insoo Kim Berg. *Interviewing for Solutions,* 4th ed. Independence, KY: Cengage, 2013.

Hill, Clara. *Helping Skills,* 3rd ed. Washington, DC: American Psychological Association, 2009.

10.4 MAKING A REFERRAL

A key social work activity is the referral or the linking of individuals to the resources, services, and opportunities they need and can use. Many view referral as a relatively simple task. However, studies indicate that attempted referrals are often unsuccessful in the sense that the referred person does not get to the new service or drops out after the first contact. This high rate of failure, possibly 50 percent, indicates that the referral process is both complex and challenging. By following these guidelines, the social worker can increase the rate of success when making a referral:

- A **referral** is a carefully planned intervention, based on an assessment, and intended to help a client address a specific problem, concern, or request. Thus, a clarification of the client's situation and some level of data gathering and assessment are prerequisite to making a successful referral. That "pre-referral" assessment must determine what the client needs and the type of service or program she or he is willing to utilize.

   If done well, the referral process can be an empowering and therapeutic experience for the referred client. Active involvement in the decisions and tasks of referral can teach the referred person problem-solving and decision-making skills.

- Referral to another agency or program is necessary when you or your agency cannot provide the service needed and wanted by a client. Referral to another professional is appropriate when you do not have the knowledge or skills needed to be effective with a particular client and/or when you have reason to believe your own values, attitudes, religious beliefs, or lack of language skills would be a significant barrier to developing an effective helping relationship. Attempting to shed responsibility for having to deal with a difficult and frustrating client is never an acceptable reason for referral. "Dumping" an especially troublesome client onto another agency or practitioner is both unprofessional and unethical.

- Before attempting to refer a client to another agency, make sure you have considered all the resources available within your own agency. Clients are most likely to utilize the services of an agency with which they are familiar and to which they are already connected or linked. Be realistic about what other agencies and professionals have to offer your client. Recognize that just because a program exists, that does not mean it will be available to your client. And even if a service is available, your client may not be ready and willing to use it. Also, do not overlook sources of assistance that might exist within the client's social support network, consisting of, for example, the client's friends, relatives, and neighbors (see Item 11.7).

- Before considering a referral, make sure you know of all the agencies and professionals already involved with the client. Some client needs and problems are best handled through interagency coordination and improved case management, rather than by a referral that further expands the number of agencies and professionals involved. If possible, those already working with a client should be consulted before attempting to refer the client to yet another program. The client's permission will usually be needed before that discussion can take place. Making a successful referral may involve sharing confidential client information and records with another agency or professional. This will require releases of information signed by the client (see Item 10.5).

- In order to make an effective referral, a social worker must be familiar with the resources in his or her community. You must invest the time necessary to learn about these programs and services and keep up-to-date on changes that occur within a community's network of human services. In most communities, there will be some sort of clearinghouse or database designed to help people identify existing health and social service programs. Many communities operate a 2-1-1 call center that can respond to inquiries and refer the phone caller to an appropriate social services agency. These call centers are often sponsored by the local United Way. However, just knowing that a resource exists is seldom sufficient to make an effective referral. It is most helpful if the referring social worker knows someone employed at the agency or program that might serve as a contact point. Use visits to various agencies, as well as NASW and other professional meetings, as opportunities to meet the staff working in the various agencies to which you may eventually refer your clients.

- Your client's prior experiences with helping professionals and programs will influence her or his willingness to consider a referral. If those experiences were negative, the client may be reluctant to seek assistance from another agency or program. A careful discussion of those experiences may yield clues as to what can be done to facilitate an effective referral.

- The success of a referral will often depend on whether others in the client's family and social network approve of and support the plan. Thus, it is often a good idea to ask the client if he or she would like certain friends or family members to participate in discussing a possible referral. When appropriate and desired by the client, the client's family and significant others should be involved in making these decisions. Their participation will, of course, slow down the process. However, in the long run, their involvement will increase the chances that the referral will be successful. In addition, it will reduce the possibility that they might later sabotage the client's utilization of the service or program.

- When the client is in need of a service for which there is a fee, you must address the issues of cost and the client's ability to pay. Some clients will need guidance and assistance in order to obtain information from insurance companies or managed care organizations, so as to determine whether there is a way of paying for a service. In this era of managed care, you must also consider the question of whether the client's private health insurance or a public medical program (e.g., Medicaid) will cover a specific type of services and whether a particular professional or provider is acceptable to and approved by the managed care company. Helping a client secure the proper preauthorization from the managed care company may be an important step in making a successful referral to a health care provider.

"Dealing with Managed Care" a retired item from the 8th edition

- A person's eligibility to receive certain services and benefits is often tied to questions about whether the applicant fits into a legally defined category and meets specific eligibility criteria. Thus, referral work requires skill in gathering information related to, for example, citizenship, marriage, parent–child relationships, prior employment, income, medical conditions, and so forth. The social worker will need to know how to obtain documents such as citizenship papers, birth certificates, marriage certificates, divorce decrees, death certificates, child custody agreements, tribal enrollment numbers, and military service papers.

- All agencies and private practitioners have their own methods of operation and eligibility criteria. Do not expect them to suspend these procedures as a favor to you or your client. Do not to tell your client that he or she will be eligible for a particular service before that decision is official. Do not second-guess the decisions of another professional or agency.

- If possible, give the client several options from which to choose the program or professional he or she wishes to utilize. If the client asks for your advice or recommendation, you have an obligation to give your honest assessment.

   When assisting a client in the selection of service provider, especially if the service is counseling or psychotherapy, ask yourself this question: Would I refer my own mother or my own child to this professional? Refer clients only to those professionals whom you know to be competent and ethical.

   Ordinarily, when telling your client about services available from another professional or agency, you should be prepared to describe both the advantages and limitations of those services. However, with clients who are confused, fearful, or highly dysfunctional, it is best to avoid focusing on the limitations because doing so may create an added barrier to the client's use of an important and needed service.

- Whenever possible, clients should make their own arrangements for the first contact. However, those who are immature or overwhelmed may need considerable help and guidance in setting up an appointment and actually getting to the new agency or professional. Give special attention to the practical problems that may become barriers to a successful referral (e.g., client's lack of transportation, no phone or Internet access, inability to read, lack of child care during appointments, fear of travel in a high-crime area, inability to take time away from job). Do whatever is needed to establish the linkage. If the client is very confused or fearful, you may need to accompany the client to the first contact or arrange for this to be done by a family member or social service "aide."

- Going to an unfamiliar agency can be upsetting or disappointing to some individuals. They may encounter a harried receptionist, a crowded waiting room, an overwhelmed intake worker, complex application forms, confusing eligibility requirements, and waiting lists. Some may encounter an employee who launches into a detailed explanation of the program and eligibility criteria without first listening carefully to the person's concerns. Certain individuals will need a great deal of emotional support during the referral process, and some will need to be coached on how to approach an agency and apply for services. Instruction may be necessary to prepare some clients to ask the right questions and be assertive when they make their initial visit to a new agency. The referring worker might, for example, prepare the client by role-playing and rehearsing a first contact (see Item 13.4). Without this extra help, they may abandon their effort to obtain the services they need.

- In some cases, the referral of a client to another agency or professional means that the client must end a familiar and positive relationship and face the task of forming a new relationship with a new practitioner. Although the client may agree that she or he needs this new service, she or he may be ambivalent or resentful about having to do so. Explore and address those feelings so they do not block the referral.

- Take steps to ensure that the referred person gets connected or linked to new resource (professional, agency, or program). These **connecting techniques** have proven effective:

  - Write out for the client the name, address, and phone number of the new agency or professional and, if necessary, provide detailed instructions on how to get there (e.g., draw a map or plot the bus route).
  - Compose a letter that the client can present to staff at the new agency or program. The letter should briefly describe the client's concern or request and she or he should be involved in composing this message.
  - In the presence of the client, contact the new practitioner by phone. Then after you have explained the intended referral, hand the phone to the client so he or she can introduce himself or herself and experience some conversation with the new practitioner.

- Even after the referred client has had his or her first interview with the new agency or new practitioner, it is important for the referring social worker to take steps to solidify or cement this connection. Various **cementing techniques** increase the chance that the client will continue using this new resource. For example:

  - Ask the referred client to phone you after making the first contact and discuss hers or his initial impressions and feelings about continuing.
  - With her or his agreement, contact the referred client after the first meeting at the new agency to find out if things went as expected.
  - Plan a few contacts with the client while she or he is using the new program or service in order to provide encouragement and detect possible problems that may be encountered at the new agency.

- Evaluate your referral work. Determine whether the client actually received what he or she wanted from the professional or agency, if the client is making progress, and if your approach to making referrals needs to be modified.

Selected Bibliography

Crimando, William, and T. F. Riggar. *Community Resources: A Guide for Human Service Workers*, 2nd ed. Long Grove, IL: Waveland, 2005.

Frankel, Arthur, and Sheldon Gelman. *Case Management*, 3rd ed. Chicago: Lyceum, 2012.

Moore, Elizabeth. *Case Management for Community Practice*. New York: Oxford University Press, 2009.

Reamer, Frederic. *Pocket Guide to Essential Human Services*, 2nd ed. Washington, DC: NASW, 2010.

10.5 OBTAINING, PROTECTING, AND RELEASING CLIENT INFORMATION

During the engagement and intake phase, the social worker will begin to gather client information and create a client file. This information must be handled in ways that protect the client's privacy. In recent years, the laws and regulations concerning the safeguarding of client information have grown more complex and restrictive. In general, the newer laws provide the consumers of health and social services with greater privacy and make service providers more accountable for how client information is handled.

However, it must be noted that somewhat different federal and state laws apply in different practice settings (e.g., hospitals, schools, substance abuse programs, child protection agencies, correctional programs). In all practice settings, social workers must follow basic and ordinary procedures. For example:

- All client information should be stored in locked files. Only those professionals or agency employees with a legitimate need to know can have access to these materials.

- Computer screens, appointment books, and files containing client information must be kept out of the sight of all other clients, persons in waiting rooms, janitors, and other nonprofessional employees. Access to client computer files should be restricted to those who have approved authorization to view those files.

- Professionals should discuss matters related to clients only when behind closed doors and never in a public place. Phone conversations with clients or about clients should not occur in areas where they might be overheard.

- When a client's file is being used, it should be placed face down on the desk so as not to display the client's name or any other client information.

- The possibility of violating a client's privacy must by evaluated before sending him or her a letter (e.g., an appointment reminder), since even the return address on an envelope and letterhead stationery connects the client to a certain type of professional or organization. This concern also applies to email messages.

- At a fundamental level, the client file or record maintained by a social agency, health care provider or a private practitioner belongs to the client. This means that the client has a right to decide whether and to whom this information will be released. (Parents and legal guardians control the release of information concerning their minor-age children.) Thus, if a social worker wants information contained in a client record maintained by another agency or professional, the worker must first obtain that client's written permission. Similarly, a worker must never release client information to someone outside his or her own agency without first obtaining the client's written permission. There are, however, some exceptions. For example, certain client information may be released if this release if ordered by a court. And in some states, a protective services investigator (i.e., an investigation of child or elder abuse or neglect) can gain access to a certain client records without the client's permission.

  The written permission granted by the client is often called *consent to release confidential information* or simply, a *consent form*. Typically, agencies have a standard legal form for this purpose. Legally and ethically, the client's permission must constitute an *informed consent*. In other words, before signing a release, the client should:

  - Know what information is being requested, by whom, and for what purpose.
  - Have an opportunity to read the material being requested, or have it read and explained in words he or she can understand.
  - Have an opportunity to correct any errors in the record before it is released.
  - Be informed of the possible negative consequences if the information is released and any consequences if the information is not released.
  - Understand that a signed consent form can be revoked at a later date.
  - In most situations, the consent will automatically expire six months after being signed by the client.

The strict rules surrounding the release of client information can make it difficult for professionals and agencies to share information needed for an accurate diagnosis or assessment and, in addition, create barriers to effective case management and the coordination of services when the services used by a client are provided by several different agencies. In addition, laws giving clients easy access to their records can have an effect on what is written into the record. Professionals may be reluctant to include information that would be upsetting to the client or his or her family if they were to read the record. A school social worker, for example, may be reluctant to document what a student has said about his or her parents if the worker knows that the parents are likely to request a review of their child's school record.

When documenting the services provided to a client (i.e., writing an entry into the client record) the social worker should always assume that the client—or the client's parent or guardian—has a right to read this record. Moreover, the client may copy the record, question what is written, and ask that the record be changed to correct any errors.

- Deciding what is and is not part of an agency record or client file is more difficult than it might seem. For example, is a report prepared by a private psychologist part of the agency record just because it has been placed in the client's file? Or, what about a report that the social worker obtained from a school? The social worker must understand agency policy and procedure concerning such questions before responding to a written request to release a client record.

  In the absence of legal guidance to the contrary, the social worker should presume that records and reports prepared by and/or obtained from a third party (e.g., a doctor, another agency) are not a part of the worker's own agency's record. In other words, an agency's client record consists only of those materials that were prepared by or written by the agency's personnel. Thus, the worker should not release letters or reports prepared by persons from outside her or his agency, even if they are contained in the client's file.

- Some professional licensing laws provide for what is termed *privileged communication*, a legal protection that usually applies to doctor–patient, attorney–client, husband–wife, and priest–penitent relationships. However, a state's law might extend the privilege to the social worker–client relationship. This privilege belongs to the client or patient, not to the professional. It is claimed or asserted by the client when she or he learns that personal information covered by the privilege has been subpoenaed and could be disclosed in a legal proceeding. The client has the option of asking the judge to recognize the privilege and prevent the disclosure. The judge must then decide if there is a compelling reason to override the client's request and reveal the information.

- Social workers need to be aware of the client information-related provisions within the federal law known as the Health Insurance Portability and Accountability Act (HIPAA). This law applies to the providers of health and mental health services if they or their organization engages in the electronic exchange of information with health insurance providers, clearinghouses, or other health or mental health care providers. Among the many HIPAA regulations, the following are especially relevant for social workers:

  - At the beginning of the professional relationship, the client or patient must be notified of his or her privacy rights and informed how the provider of services intends to use and possibly share his or her health information.

- The client or patient has a right to see, copy, and supplement (i.e., correct) her or his records. However, the provider may deny a patient access to records in certain circumstances, such as when there is reason to believe that disclosure will cause harm to the patient or some other person or result in the disclosure of other protected information.
- The provider of services is required to have in place various technical and administrative procedures designed to safeguard client information, especially information that is stored in a computer or transferred electronically.
- Providers are barred from disclosing health information to a client's employer.
- Under ordinary circumstances, the provider can release a client's health information only with the client's permission. However, a provider may share client information with others on a need-to-know basis if his or her purpose is to secure a professional consultation; to arrange care, treatment, and other services for the client or patient; to secure payment; and/or to conduct an audit, quality of care assessment, or the like.
- Providers of mental health services can refuse to disclose psychotherapy notes to the client's health insurance company unless this release has been authorized by the client.
- Health insurance companies and health plans may not condition enrollment or the delivery of benefits on obtaining the client's authorization to release information.
- A hospital patient has a right to opt out of having his or her name and health status made available to interested and concerned persons.
- When records and notes are to be discarded, they must be shredded and should not be placed whole in a waste container. Electronic records should be permanently deleted.

Whenever a social worker is uncertain about her or his legal or ethical responsibility regarding the handling of client information, the worker should consult with the agency administrator or an attorney and also review the general legal information offered online by the NASW (www.socialworkers.org/ldf).

Selected Bibliography

Krager, Dan, and Carole Krager. *HIPPA for Health Care Professionals*. Clifton Park, NY: Thomson Delmar, 2008.

National Association of Social Workers. *HIPAA Highlights for Social Workers*. 2004. Available online: www.naswdc.org/hipaa/default.asp.

National Association of Social Workers General Counsel. *Client Confidentiality and Privileged Communication*. Washington, DC: NASW, 2011.

10.6 CONDUCTING AN IN-HOME INTERVIEW

The term **in-home interview** (or home visit) refers to a meeting between the social worker and client in the client's home. In the early days of social work, home visiting was the modus operandi of the worker but it was abandoned by many social workers and agencies because it did not seem professional and did not fit the popular office-based models of therapy and service delivery. Of course, the home visit has always been used by social workers employed by child protection and public health agencies and by those engaged in outreach and the provision of home-based services, and those providing assistance to the frail elderly. Despite its usefulness, the in-home interview is a source of discomfort for many social workers. Following these guidelines can help the worker make proper use of this valuable diagnostic and treatment tool:

- Understand the rationale for meeting with clients in their natural environment. For some clients, a meeting in an agency building or an office is inconvenient and stressful. When in a familiar setting or environment such as their own home, clients are likely to be more comfortable, open, and authentic.

  The home visit or the in-home interview is an especially valuable means of securing an accurate picture of a client's family and neighborhood contexts and for gaining an appreciation of how various forces within the client's environment either support or impinge on his or her social functioning. It is also a window into the client's personality and lifestyle. A person's home is his or her sacred space. It is the place of intimacy and private times spent with family. For some, the home is a source of warmth and security. For others, it is a place of anguish, fear, and loneliness. The way a home is decorated, furnished, and cared for can reflect a person's culture or ethnicity, economic situation, vitality, interests, creativity, and intellectual ability. And it can also reflect lethargy, depression, despair, and disorganization.

- Do not confuse the in-home interview with a purely social call or friendly visit. This technique, like all others, is to be used in a purposeful manner. When the social worker requests an in-home interview, the client should be given a clear explanation as to how and why it can make the service more effective.

- An in-home interview should be scheduled. An unannounced and unscheduled visit should be avoided but this may not be possible if a client does not have a phone, is unable to read a letter, or does not have email access. If you must stop by a client's home unannounced, explain immediately your previous efforts to reach him or her and use the conversation to set up a scheduled visit. (Often, the client will immediately invite you in.)

- When you enter the client's home, extend the same respect and courtesy you expect when someone visits your home. Ask where you are to be seated. Accept an appropriate offer of food or drink. Convey a genuine interest in family pictures and home decorations for they are expression of the client's self-concept and values. The social worker must never show surprise, shock, or disapproval when entering the client's home, no matter what the condition of the home. It may be neat or cluttered, bright or gloomy, hospital clean or teeming with unpleasant odors. The worker must be mentally prepared to encounter unsanitary conditions, dogs and cats, and indications of recent violence, sexual activity, drinking or drug use.

- Obtaining privacy is sometimes a problem during a home visit. Children may run in and out, neighbors may stop by, the telephone may ring, and the TV may be blaring. This will be distracting to you but probably not to your client. On the positive side, it provides a glimpse into the client's daily routine and environment. Significant distractions are best dealt with directly by expressing a need for privacy and giving full attention to the meeting's purpose. When friends or neighbors are in the home, the client should be asked if it is permissible to discuss private matters in their presence. Some clients may invite trusted and supportive friends to sit in on the interview, and this choice should be respected.

- If the client lives in a dangerous neighborhood, it is important to schedule the home visit for the safest time of day. Ask the client for suggestions on how best to minimize the risks. If the client or others in the household are possibly dangerous or if you are concerned that you might be falsely accused of inappropriate behavior, you should bring along a colleague for added protection and to serve as an observer or witness. (For information on personal safety, see Item 10.9.)

Selected Bibliography

Allen, Susan, and Elizabeth Tracy. *Delivering Home-Based Services: A Social Work Perspective.* New York: Columbia University Press, 2009.

Carrilo, Terry. *Home Visiting Strategies.* Columbia, SC: University of South Carolina Press, 2007.

Newton, Nancy, and Kadi Sprengle. *Psychosocial Interventions in the Home.* New York: Springer, 2000.

Wasik, Barbara, and Donna Bryant. *Home Visiting: Procedures for Helping Families,* 2nd ed. Thousand Oaks, CA: Sage, 2000.

10.7 ENGAGING THE MANDATED CLIENT

The term **mandated client** (or *involuntary client*) refers to an individual who is required or mandated to obtain counseling or some other service by a legal authority, such as a judge, probation officer, or child protection agency. Not infrequently, such a client is resentful, angry, and even belligerent. Consider these guidelines when working with a mandated client:

- Prepare yourself for meeting this client by recalling how it feels when you are forced to do something against your will or to do something that seems unfair and unnecessary. Assume that the client will have negative feelings and that you may encounter hostility, anger, shame, fear, embarrassment, and a number of defensive reactions. Do not ignore or sidestep such feelings; rather, acknowledge those feelings and respond with empathy. Maintain self-discipline and do not respond to the client's hostility with anger or threats, for this will generate even more resistance. Use the skills of active listening to help the client articulate his or her perspectives and to tell his or her side of the story (see Items 8.1, 8.4, and 8.6).

- Provide a clear explanation of both your professional role and responsibility, as well as what you or your agency expect of the client. Explain the rules of confidentiality that apply. For example, if you are required to prepare a report to the court, the client has a right to know that what she or he reveals may end up in this report and be discussed by the judge and attorneys in open court.

- Inform the client of any adverse consequences that may occur if she or he does not cooperate. However, respect the client's right to choose the consequences rather than your services. Remind the client who decides not to cooperate that she or he is, in effect, giving up the control she or he now has to influence the outcome.

- During the first meeting, reveal the factual information you have about why the client has been mandated to utilize certain services. If the client denies the accuracy of this information, explain that you will double-check the reports you have been given and, if necessary, seek clarification from the referring source (e.g., probation officer). Strive to resolve any disagreements or misunderstandings so as to minimize the time spent debating why the mandate exists.

- Do not ask questions that could be interpreted as an attempt to test the client's truthfulness. Make it clear to the client that you do not want him or her to lie or fabricate, using an explanation something like this:

  > I am aware that you are angry about having to talk to me. I can understand that. I can also understand that there may be times during our sessions when you will be tempted to lie to me. More than anything, I do not want you to lie. If you lie, you may feel guilty and worry about me catching you in that lie. That would not help you feel better. Rather than lie, I want you to tell me that you simply do not want to answer my question. Is that something you can agree to?

- Within the limits and legal constraints placed on the client, give him or her as much choice as possible. Allowing the client to have some choice and have some control over even minor details will usually lower his or her resistance—for example:

  "Engaging The Hard To Reach Client" a deleted item from the 8th editon

  > We have to meet each Wednesday for the next six weeks. We can meet either at 2:00 p.m. or 4:00 p.m. What is your choice?

- If usual efforts to establish a beginning level of cooperation have not worked and the client remains resistant, consider using the "Let's make a deal" tactic. In this approach, the worker agrees to do something that will lessen the client's distress or help the client get something he or she wants (something legal and legitimate) in exchange for the client's cooperation or the client's completion of certain tasks. An example would be a worker who says something like the following:

  > Well John, it is apparent that you do not want to come here for counseling. But you and I both know that your probation officer, Mr. Roberts, is insisting that you get help with what he calls your anger problem. If you don't do what he wants, then he may make your life even more difficult. How about us making a deal? If you see me for five one-hour sessions, answer my questions, and talk honestly about your relationships with your wife and children, I will, in return, write a letter to Mr. Roberts and say that you have made a good-faith effort to use our counseling sessions to examine what others say is your anger problem.

- Some service providers complain that mandated clients lack motivation. Actually, unmotivated clients do not exist. All clients, all people, are motivated; all have wants, needs, and preferences. When a professional labels a client as "unmotivated," she or he is simply acknowledging that what the client wants is different from what the practitioner wants for the client. Successfully engaging the mandated client requires that the worker tap into the client's needs and wants, and establish intervention goals that are at least partially consistent with the client's desires and preferences. Thus, strive to identify something that both you and the client agree is a legitimate goal or a desirable course of action. Once there is an agreed-on goal, you can more easily engage the client in problem solving. For example, you might say,

  > Well, we both want you to get off probation so you won't have to see me each week. We can agree on that. What ideas or suggestions do you have on how we can work together to achieve that goal?

- In some cases it may be helpful to discuss the client's previous experiences—especially the negative experiences—with professionals or the social services system, along with any preconceived notions he or she may have about social workers, counselors, or other professional helpers. Also, be aware of the client's cultural background or experience with discrimination and how this might add to his or her feeling of being manipulated or alienated from social institutions.

Selected Bibliography

Harris, George. *Overcoming Resistance: Success in Counseling Men*. Laurel, MD: American Correctional Association, 1995.

Rooney, Ronald. *Strategies for Work with Involuntary Clients*, 2nd ed. New York: Columbia University Press, 2009.

Trotter, Chris. *Working with Involuntary Clients*, 2nd ed. Thousand Oaks, CA: Sage, 2006.

Welo, Beverly, ed. *Tough Customers: Counseling Unwilling Clients*. Laurel, MD: American Correctional Association, 2001.

10.8 RESPONDING TO THE MANIPULATIVE CLIENT

Most people, at least occasionally, attempt to manipulate others in order to get what they want. Some individuals, however, rely on manipulation and "conning" as a primary means of coping with life. Social workers who are unable to detect a client's manipulation may quickly find themselves in legal, ethical, and moral difficulties. Here are a few guidelines for dealing with a client who is manipulative:

- People who are skilled manipulators will tell you what they think you want to hear. They will lie and slant what they say to make themselves look good and to blame others. If they do not win you over to their side with charm and deception, they are likely to use subtle forms of intimidation and threat. It is critically important for the social worker to set the conditions and the agenda for their meetings. You must be explicit in outlining your role and your expectations. You must demonstrate firmness and a no-nonsense approach. If the worker is timid, uncertain, or lacks confidence, the client will seize on this weakness and successfully use, manipulate, and exploit the worker. This firmness and control in the professional relationship must exist from the very beginning; if you begin with permisssiveness, the likelihood of ever reestablishing control is lost. This type of client might respect firmness but have little respect for weakness.

- Be reasonable, fair, but unwavering. Hold the client accountable and do not rescue her or him from the consequences of dishonesty. Before deciding to change their behavior, habitual manipulators will usually need to experience the natural and punishing consequences of their actions.

- Do not go along with or overlook the manipulative client's attempts to minimize or sidestep personal responsibility. Many will make frequent use of the word *but* as a way of avoiding responsibility or downplaying the seriousness of a behavior (e.g., "Well yes, I did steal some money *but* only 30 dollars" or "Yeah, I hit him with a baseball bat *but* not very hard").

- With most clients, some degree of self-disclosure by the worker has the effect of decreasing the client defensiveness and resistance. However, when working with persons who are skilled manipulators, you should avoid sharing personal information. The use of worker self-disclosure with these individuals will usually have serious and unwanted consequences because of their ability to spot, exploit, and twist a helper's personal weakness and mistakes.

- Suspect a manipulation whenever your client takes an inordinate interest in your personal life or your feelings about your job. Be especially cautious when your client says things such as "You are the only person who really understands me," "No one else has ever been as helpful as you," "You are the most caring person I have ever met," "I need to tell you something but you must promise not to tell this to anyone else," "If you could just do this one thing for me, I can get my life straightened out," and "I have a wonderful opportunity to pull my life together—I only need a small loan to make it happen."

- Never break or even bend agency rules as a favor or concession to this client. Even a minor concession leads quickly to additional requests or a blackmail situation (e.g., "Look, if you won't do this for me, I'll tell your supervisor that you violated program rules when you allowed me to smoke in the rec room").

- If you suspect that you are being drawn into manipulation, consult with another professional. If you are part of a treatment team, raise your concerns with team members; you may discover that the client is saying very different things to other team members. An elevated level of communication and coordination is necessary to keep team members from being drawn into a situation where one is played against another.

- Not everyone who makes frequent use of manipulation is a sociopath but some of the most practiced, unscrupulous, and dangerous manipulators are termed sociopaths or psychopaths or as having an antisocial personality disorder. Experts believe that about 4 percent of the population fit this description. This is not a rare condition and its cause is not well understood. The existence of an antisocial personality disorder usually becomes evident in childhood. And unfortunately, there is no effective treatment for this disorder.

A hallmark of sociopaths is the complete absence of a conscience and a lack of emotional attachments to people. They do not have the capacity for empathy, remorse, and guilt. They simply do not care about other people and have no hesitation about using and hurting others, even their family, children, and closest friends. For them, truth is whatever serves their purpose at the moment. They are often charming and self-confident. By watching normal people they have learned to imitate or mimic the emotions and sincerity that attract the sympathy and trust of others. For them, all interactions are games of power and attempts to get the upper hand, sometimes just for the fun of it. Additional common characteristics include a glib and superficial manner of relating, egocentric and grandiose thinking, shallow emotions and impulsivity, a strong need for excitement and risk taking, and antisocial behavior.

For sociopaths, their own deception, dishonesty, and manipulation are so much a part of their own lives that they expect everyone else to do the same. Sociopaths are suspicious and distrustful of others because they expect to be lied to and manipulated. Sociopaths distrust social workers and other professional helpers simply because they distrust everyone. The individuals with a sociopathic personality are usually quite content and satisfied with themselves and they see no reason to change. Thus, they are not likely to voluntarily seek counseling.

Many people, including some social workers, cannot imagine and do not want to believe that there can be individuals who lack a conscience, compassion, and empathy. To hold that belief is to put oneself in peril. When dealing with a sociopath, a social worker must be on guard and extremely cautious.

- There is no completely reliable way of detecting a lie, especially when the person who is lying lacks a conscience and is practiced in the art of deception and manipulation. Nevertheless, a few observations and special techniques may help you detect a lie:

  - Engage the person in several minutes of friendly small talk before addressing a topic about which he or she might lie. A deception is suggested by an obvious change in the client's voice, facial expressions, or other body language when you begin to focus on the sensitive area.

  - Most people feel somewhat uncomfortable when they lie. Consequently, when lying, their voices often become higher in pitch, they are more likely to stumble over words, and they are more prone to frequent blinking and fidgeting.

  - Even a clever, confident, and experienced liar cannot completely control her or his facial expressions. Thus, the individual may exhibit a momentary look of panic if she or he begins to fear that she or he has made a mistake and the lie has been detected.

  - When lying, people tend to use fewer descriptive phrases and fewer hand motions than when not engaged in a deception.

  - The experienced liar has prepared and practiced responses to commonly asked questions, but his or her response often sounds emotionally flat. Asking an unusual or unexpected question may catch the experienced liar off guard and uncover a deception.

  - When asked a question, someone telling the truth will respond quickly because he or she has only one thing to say—the truth. By contrast, someone who wants to deceive will hesitate before answering because he or she must first weigh the pros and cons of various answers.

  - A person who is lying tends to decrease the level of intimacy. Thus, she or he will look away and move back slightly from the person to whom she or he is lying. The person who is lying will use words that are less intimate, less personal. For example, she or he will seldom use the pronouns *I, me, my,* and *we* and will instead use more impersonal and emotionally distant words such as *them, that,* and *it.*

  - People who are telling the truth will not hesitate to give detailed and specific answers to questions. Those who are lying will usually answer with generalities because they fear being tripped up by details. However, some who are very skilled at lying may attempt to bolster their credibility by overwhelming the questioner with details. If these skillful liars are told that their answers will be checked for accuracy, they usually back away from what they have said.

  - Individuals who are right-handed typically move their eyes up and to the left when trying to accurately remember an image or set of details. By contrast, when trying to fabricate a deceptive story, their eyes usually move up and to the right. The right and left movements are reversed for a left-handed person.

Selected Bibliography

Lieberman, David. *You Can Read Anyone.* New York: MJF Books, 2009.
Samenow, Stanton. *Inside the Criminal Mind.* New York: Crown, 2004.

Simon, George. *In Sheep's Clothing: Understanding and Dealing with Manipulative People*. Little Rock, AK: A. J. Christopher, 1996.

Stout, Martha. *The Sociopath Next Door*. New York: Broadway Books, 2005.

Waters, Stan. *The Truth About Lying*. Naperville, IL: Sourcebooks, 2000.

10.9 INCREASING PERSONAL SAFETY IN DANGEROUS SITUATIONS

At times social work practice places workers in dangerous situations. The workers most at risk are those who work directly with clients who are angry, stressed, and prone to violence. Such clients are most likely encountered in child protection and correctional programs, hospitals for the criminally insane, and addiction treatment programs. Social workers may find themselves in danger if they inadvertently encounter or witness an illegal activity such as drug dealing. Another potential danger are bio-hazardous materials encountered in health care facilities and possibly during visits to clients' homes, especially if the client's home has been involved in the use or manufacture of illegal drugs. To minimize the risk of being injured, the social worker should adhere to the following guidelines:

- Prior violent behavior is the most reliable predictor of future violence. Individuals who are most likely to become violent will usually have one or more the following characteristics and life experiences:

    - Has a history of being violent
    - Tends to turn violent when under the influence of alcohol or drugs
    - Has been the target of violence and intimidation
    - Has been publicly humiliated, degraded, or disgraced
    - Is part of a violent peer group or gang
    - Is experiencing a high level of stress and conflict
    - Is a male teen or a young adult
    - Has experienced a traumatic brain injury

- Never enter a dangerous situation without first consulting with others about your intentions. Consider the situation to be high risk whenever you are to meet with an individual who has a history of violence and whenever you are to meet an unfamiliar client in a nonpublic or isolated location. Request police assistance if you must enter a very dangerous situation.

- An agency's record keeping system should use some method of flagging the case record of a dangerous client so the social worker meeting with this client can take appropriate precautions. In especially dangerous practice settings, a professional's desk or office should be equipped with an emergency call button. At minimum, agencies should have a telephone code so the staff will recognize a disguised call for help. For example, in a telephone message such as "Hello, Laura. This is Jim. Would you send a copy of our red resource book to my office?" might be code for "I am in danger; send security to my office."

- The office or meeting room where the social worker will encounter a potentially dangerous client should be set up so the worker has easy assess to the door or an escape route. Also, the room should be cleared of items that could be grabbed and used as weapons (e.g., letter openers, staplers, umbrellas, paper weights).

- When making a home visit, keep your office informed of your itinerary and check in by phone according to a prearranged schedule. Before entering a client's home or building, take a few seconds to look around and think about your safety: Am I alone? Where are the escape routes? Is a violent argument in process? Do the people inside sound out of control? If I go in will I be able to get out?

- Never move through a doorway and into a room as a response to an invitation of "come in" unless you can see the person who is speaking and he or she has seen you. Being mistaken for someone else can be dangerous. When entering a room containing a hostile person, move in slowly. Remain on the periphery until you assess the situation. Advance slowly and remain at least two arms length from the person. Rapid or intrusive movements may trigger violent behavior.

   Be alert to anything about the situation that looks or feels unusual, scary, and ominous. We all possess an unconscious danger detector. Thus, trust your gut feelings. If you feel afraid, assume that you are in danger, even if you cannot pinpoint why you are feeling this way.

- Most people who are very angry will vent (e.g., scream, curse, point fingers) for 2 or 3 minutes and then begin to gradually calm down. However, some individuals are further stimulated and agitated by what they are saying and thinking. If an angry individual is not starting to calm down after a few minutes of venting, assume that the situation has become more dangerous.

- Do not touch an angry person and do nothing that could be interpreted as a threat, challenge, or a dare. Encourage the client to sit down, as this will usually have a calming effect. If safe to do so, sit rather than stand, because sitting is a less threating posture. However, avoid sitting in low overstuffed chair because it is difficult to get to your feet quickly from such a chair. Rather, choose a hard and movable chair that could also serve as a protective shield if you are attacked. If you suspect that persons living in the home use injectable drugs, avoid sitting on a cushion or sofa because the cushion might contain a needle left behind after a drug injection.

- Be alert to signs of imminent attack, such as flaring nostrils, rapid breathing, dilated pupils, pulsing veins, grinding teeth, pointing fingers, clenched fists, crouching, and choppy and bobbing (boxer-like) movements of the body. Do not turn your back to an angry or distraught person or let others in the room walk behind you. If the danger level escalates, back away and leave the premises.

- When in the home of a potentially violent person, be aware that guns are usually kept in the bedroom and that a kitchen contains numerous potential weapons. If the person has threatened you and then moves quickly to one of these rooms, leave immediately.

   Do not attempt to disarm a person who has a weapon. Leave that to the police! If your client has a weapon, calmly explain that you intend no harm and then slowly back away or otherwise extricate yourself from the situation.

- An attack on others is often a reaction to being afraid; thus, do what you can to lessen the person's need to be afraid. Remain composed and speak in a gentle and soothing manner. Do not argue or threaten. Demonstrate empathy for the person's situation, frustration, and anger. Use active listening skills to secure an understanding of his or her perceptions. If an inappropriate statement on your part has caused the client to become angry, apologize immediately.

- Aggressiveness and attacks often arise out of a feeling of being trapped or controlled. To the extent possible, increase the client's sense of being in control by offering choices and using words that convey cooperation and respect such as: "Of course, it is up to you to decide what is best" and "Think about what we have discussed and then decide on your course of action."

- Maintain a neat, well-groomed appearance and an attitude of self-confidence so as to indicate that you take your job seriously and can take care of yourself. An angry person is more likely to attack someone who appears weak, afraid, and insecure. Wear clothing and shoes that permit running and a rapid escape from danger. Do not wear long earrings that can be easily grabbed to inflict pain and control.

- If you work with dangerous clients, your phone number, home address, and personal email address should be protected from public disclosure. In rare instances, a social worker's family (e.g., spouse, children) may become the target of a client's anger and violence. A worker's family should be prepared for that possibility.

- If you work in a dangerous neighborhood, secure guidance from experienced peers, local merchants, and the police on how to stay safe. Ask your agency for in-service training on nonviolent self-defense. You must be able to protect yourself without inflicting physical injury on your clients. If you secure training in self-defense be sure to select an instructor who has actually encountered violent persons. Even excellent training does not adequately prepare you for the real thing. Never overestimate your ability to handle a threatening situation or underestimate the paralyzing effect of fear.

- If you work in a hospital or another health care setting, be alert to biological hazards and obtain instruction on how to protect yourself and vulnerable patients against exposure to an infection. That includes knowing how to handle items stained with body fluids, such as bandages, tissues, clothing, and bed sheets. In some instances, the social worker will need to wear a protective mask and gloves when interviewing a hospitalized or seriously ill client.

- Social workers who make home visits should be alert to the possibility of inadvertently encountering a clandestine laboratory where illegal drugs are manufactured. For example, methamphetamine, or "meth," can be cooked using easily obtained chemicals and ordinary kitchen equipment. These labs are extremely dangerous because the chemicals used are highly corrosive and flammable. Also, the person manufacturing drugs may take violent action to prevent the lab from being reported to law enforcement. In some cases, clandestine laboratories are booby-trapped with explosives.

Selected Bibliography

Cambell, Jacquelyn. *Assessing Dangerousness*. New York: Springer, 2007.

Jones, David, ed. *Working with Dangerous People*. San Francisco: Radcliff Medical Press, 2005.

Newhill, Christina. *Client Violence in Social Work Practice*. New York: Guilford, 2004.

Weinger, Susan. *Security Risk: Preventing Client Violence against Social Workers*. Washington, DC: NASW, 2001.

10.10 CLARIFYING ROLES AND RESPONSIBILITIES

Social workers temporarily enter the lives of their clients for a specific purpose. Compared to the long-term relationships with family and friends, the social worker and the client enter into a relationship that is limited in duration. It is also limited in scope and will address only those concerns and those aspects of the client's life that are agreed to by the client. It is important in the early stages of the helping process that the client and the social worker discuss the nature of this special relationship and the expectations for each.

Although one of the principles that guide social workers (see Chapter 5) is to "address all relevant client systems," that principle is not intended to imply that the social worker has authority to pick and choose whatever aspects of a client's life that are of interest or that he or she might like to address. Ethically, the social worker must focus on the area(s) of concern presented by the client and, of course, only those within the worker's areas of competence.

Although the issues that can bring a client and social worker together may vary from the very specific and concrete (e.g., helping a frail older person and his or her family determine the level of care required) to somewhat vague concerns (e.g., building self-esteem), there needs to a clear purpose around which the worker–client relationship is formed. This professional relationship is always intentional, always purposeful. Thus, one of the first steps in working with a client is to engage in a discussion that clarifies for both the client and social worker their purpose for working together (see Item 10.3). Once this purpose is clear, the appropriate roles and responsibilities of both the social worker and the client must be identified and agreed upon.

In every professional helping relationship there are usually implicit or generally understood expectations. For example, the social worker is expected to create a comfortable and confidential setting for their conversations, gather relevant information about the client's concerns or problems, and propose a plan that can help the client improve the situation. The client is expected to attend all agreed-upon meetings, provide truthful information, and actively participate in the efforts and tasks that can help to address the presenting problem. In addition to these general or implied expectations, there will be ones that are specific to their agreed-on intervention or service plan. That agreement or contract can be oral or written (see Item 12.5). The client should come away from this discussion of expectations with a clear idea of what he or she is being asked to do and what the social worker can and cannot do to help the client address a concern or problem.

As indicated in Chapter 4, social workers are usually prepared to perform multiple roles and functions in their practice activities. Clients need to participate in a discussion that clarifies their own roles and responsibilities and those of the social worker. For example, if you are a social worker serving a client as a case manager, you might say something like:

> When working together my primary role will be to serve as your case manager. If there is some problem in obtaining or coordinating the needed services, I will advocate for you to get the services you require from other agencies. Your responsibilities will be to follow up on the connections and arrangements we make to other agencies, as well as to meet with me regularly for a checkup on how our decisions and plans are working out. It needs to be clear that I will not be your counselor related to specific issues such as finding a job, addressing your legal issues, and treating your problem with sleeplessness. However, I will help you connect with the professionals who can help you address those issues. Does that meet with your expectations of what we will be doing together? If so, we can now begin to think about what we need to start doing.

In performing the role of a professional, the social worker cannot—and should not—attempt to intrude into those aspects of the client's life that are not relevant to the agreed-upon purpose of their professional relationship. The purpose of the professional relationship and the nature of an intervention can, of course, shift or change but this is to be done only after the matter has been discussed and the client has agreed to a new or modified purpose and plan.

Other issues and new client concerns may arise and become evident during the course of the work with a client. However, if giving time and attention to these new matters would distract the client and the worker away from their agreed-upon high priority and primary purpose, a referral of those matters to other social workers or agencies should be considered (see Item 10.4).

Selected Bibliography

Hepworth, Dean H., Ronald K. Rooney, Glenda Dewberry Rooney, & Kimberly Strom-Gottfried. *Direct Practice Social Work: Theory and Skills*, 9th ed. Independence, KY: Brooks/Cole Cengage Learning, 2013.

10.11 ADDRESSING POWER DIFFERENTIALS WITH CLIENTS

The very nature of a professional relationship places the social worker in a position of power in relation to the client. Sometimes that power differential has little influence on the helping process as, for example, when the client is completely voluntary and the social worker is in a private practice setting where agency mission and authority are not a significant part of the practice context. However, in many practice settings, the social worker and her or his agency or organization has implicit or assigned legal power or authority. This power *over* the client is most apparent in correctional or child protection settings and when the client is involuntary or mandated to obtain services (see Item 10.7). In these practice situations the social worker has considerable power and must always use it in a thoughtful and cautious manner.

Current thinking regarding the sociology of professions describes the professional–client relationship as one in which the professional is an expert on the issues his or her client is experiencing, competent to guide the change process, and able to select and use appropriate evidence-based interventions. Some practice perspectives view the professional and client as being more or less socially equal (e.g., the feminist perspective reflecting a power *with* the client), but most intervention models view the professional as having some control or authority over how the change process plays out.

The power to control the actions of others can be held by individuals, groups, or institutional structures. In most of social work practice, some degree of power and authority is assigned to the social worker and/or her or his agency. Similar to the teacher having the authority to assign grades in a college class, the social worker can use his or her authority and power in a number of ways, ranging from motivating clients to address an issue, to rewarding clients for their progress or to punishing clients for lapses or missteps.

Bundy-Fazioli, Briar-Lawson, and Hardiman (2008) conceptualize a continuum of power for social work practice. At one end are *hierarchical/imbalanced* power relationships, those that are *negotiated/reciprocal* fall in the middle, and the *shared/balanced* power relationships are at the other end. The traditional conception of professionals based on the medical model views the professional–client relationship at the hierarchical/imbalanced end of this continuum. Given that perspective, the professional studies the problem, makes a diagnosis, and treats the condition with relatively little involvement or guidance by the patient or client. Increasingly, all of the helping professions are moving toward greater decision making and participation by the client throughout the helping process. Even medicine is leaning in this direction. At present, professional–client relationships are more likely to be negotiated and reciprocal. However, various legal mandates, agency restrictions, and concerns over legal liability constrain most social workers and other professionals from creating or achieving a truly shared/balanced professional relationship.

Several social work practice principles identified in Chapter 5 reflect the movement of social work to a mid-ground of meaningful client involvement in decision making. For example:

- The social worker should think of clients as experts on their own lives.
- The social worker should maximize client participation.
- The social worker should maximize client self-determination.
- The social worker should help the client learn self-directed problem-solving skills.
- The social worker should maximize client empowerment.

The concept of client empowerment expands the scope of the professional–client relationship to also address the societal causes of their problems and to expand the client's influence and control within the helping process (see Item 13.18).

The following guidelines related to worker–client power dynamics should be considered by the social worker.

- Be clear about the degree of power/authority the worker legitimately possesses.
- Help the client understand the limits placed on the worker due to the nature of the issues addressed in the case situation, the requirements of the agency or, in some cases, the referring agency, and the demands of the legal system.
- Determine the degree to which the client is capable of assuming or sharing responsible decision-making authority.
- Establish a plan with the client to negotiate shared decision-making power in the relationship where appropriate.

Selected Bibliography

Bundy-Fazioli, Kimberly, Katharine Briar-Lawson, & Eric R. Hardiman. A Qualitative Examination of Power between Child Welfare Workers and Parents. *British Journal of Social Work, 38* (2008): 1–18.

Bundy-Fazioli, Kimberly, Louise M. Quijano, & Roe Bubar. Graduate Students' Perceptions of Professional Power in Social Work Practice. *Journal of Social Work Education, 49* (2013): 108–121.

SECTION B

TECHNIQUES AND GUIDELINES FOR INDIRECT PRACTICE

At the indirect service level, the planned change process usually involves the social worker in activities aimed at making existing programs work better or creating new programs to meet client needs or to prevent problems from developing. For example, the social worker might give formal or behind-the-scenes input or leadership to a change effort by a community task force, or she or he may advocate with agency administrators, legislators, or others to effect a specific change in a policy or law. Usually, indirect service work is done with a committee or some other group that comes together to provide services more effectively and efficiently or develop strategies to accomplish needed change in a policy, program, or budget.

As in most change efforts, it is important for the participants to be invested in the process, committing their time, talent, and (sometimes) financial or other resources. Participants need to be involved early in the process and have opportunities to influence its direction as the change effort evolves.

Preparatory Activities

Social workers attempting to facilitate organizational or community change must know their "turf." Even new social workers must be able to assess the agency where they are employed (see Item 10.12) and the dynamics of their community (see Item 10.14). Attaining that knowledge is prerequisite to any effort to facilitate change in an agency or community.

Typically, the work of the social worker involves bringing together groups of people from within an agency or from a community to address new problems or ones that have not been successfully resolved in the past. Gaining knowledge of past efforts, barriers that existed, and the people or organizations that were involved are a necessary part of one's homework. When providing indirect services, it is rare that the worker faces an emergency or crisis situation that does not allow time for gathering this background information.

When leading a group, the worker should carefully select, invite, and recruit participants; identify a meeting time that accommodates as many potential participants as possible; select a convenient meeting place and arrange the meeting room to facilitate interaction; and have a prepared agenda that includes ample opportunity for participants to discuss the issue at hand.

Engagement activities

A social worker rarely will have the power or authority to individually resolve problematic issues in an agency or community. Support and resources from others will be needed in order to address such matters. It is important, then, that the first meeting of a group or committee is structured to involve the participants in identifying concerns and issues from their own perspectives and to encourage the expression of differing viewpoints. Also, participants should leave the meeting having some responsibility for an action to be reported at the next meeting as a means of maintaining their involvement.

Intake activities

The first meeting of a group or committee must, among other things, reach a decision regarding the desirability of this group continuing to address the matter, deferring to another group that may already be addressing this topic, joining a parallel effort to deal with the matter, or dissolving. The social worker's role, as convener of the group, is to help the group decide which of these options should be followed.

10.12 ORIENTING YOURSELF TO YOUR AGENCY

Social workers are usually employed by either a private or a public agency. **Public agencies** (whether at the city, county, state, or federal level) are established by legislation written by elected officials and are funded primarily by tax dollars. By contrast, most private agencies are **nonprofit organizations** funded primarily by voluntary contributions and possibly by fees, grants, or contracts or they may be **for-profit corporations** designed to yield income for investors and stockholders. Some private agencies enter into the purchase of service contracts with public agencies and are paid to deliver specified services; thus, such private agencies are funded, in part, by tax dollars. The term **membership agency** refers to a private agency that derives a significant portion of its funds from membership fees (e.g., a YMCA or YWCA). **Sectarian agency** describes a private agency that is under the auspices of a specific religious body (e.g., Jewish Community Services, Catholic Social Services).

In order to deliver social services and programs effectively, the social worker must understand the agency's mission, structure, funding, policies, and procedures. The following activities will help the worker learn about her or his agency:

- Ask your supervisor and experienced agency staff for guidance on how best to become familiar with the agency's purpose, policies, and operation. Study the agency's organization chart and determine where and how you fit into the agency structure.

- If your agency is a public agency, read the law(s) that established the agency and those describing the specific programs that the agency is to administer (e.g., state child protection laws) and examine relevant state and federal administrative rules and regulations. If your agency is a private agency, read the bylaws that describe the agency's purpose and the functions of the board of directors and its officers and committees. The bylaws will also describe the responsibilities assigned to the Chief Executive Officer (CEO), who is typically responsible for the organization's day-to-day operation.

- Examine your agency's manual of policies and procedures. Pay special attention to any ethical guidelines that prescribe employee behavior. For example, many agencies will have guidelines for such potential issues as the following:
  - Use of time at work for personal matters
  - Use of agency property (e.g., telephones, fax, automobiles, copy machines, computer, office space) for personal activities
  - Receipt of gifts from clients, other employees, or use of the agency's name or the worker's agency affiliation in outside activities
  - Provision of agency services to friends and family
  - Situations wherein personal or financial interests might conflict, or appear to conflict, with official duties
  - Publication and dissemination of research reports or other information prepared or developed during agency employment
  - Matters related to the confidentiality of client information
  - Persons who are in a position to receive referrals of fee-paying clients from agency employees

- Read documents that describe your agency's history, mission, and philosophy. Find out how the agency has changed during recent years and what community or political forces are having a significant impact on the agency. Seek information about the agency's goals and objectives for the current year and its strategic plan for the next three to five years. Examine the agency's personnel policies and the tools or forms that will be used in the evaluation of your job performance. Read the union contract, if one exists.

- If your agency must conform to standards issued by a national accrediting organization (e.g., Child Welfare League of America, Council on Accreditation of Rehabilitation Facilities), review those portions of the accreditation standards that apply to your areas of service.

- Examine your agency's budget. Pay special attention to the sources of income, because the agency must be responsive and accountable to these sources if it is to continue to attract needed funding. Also review any "purchase of service" arrangements, interagency agreements, or protocol statements that tie the services and operation of your agency to other agencies or funding sources. If you are working on a project funded by a grant or a contract, read the relevant documents so you know what the funding source is expecting of the project.

- Examine annual reports and statistical data compiled by your agency, and determine which of its programs and services are most used and least used by clients and consumers. Also, examine data that describes the people served by your agency in terms of age, gender, socioeconomic status, race, ethnicity, religion, and so on.

- Determine what procedures are used to evaluate agency performance and the quality of services provided. Also determine how the agency's clients and consumers are involved in the evaluation and planning of services and programs.

- Identify the agencies and organizations with which your agency frequently interacts. Determine what community or state agencies have an impact on your agency and how the services and programs provided by your agency are to be coordinated with other agencies in the community.

- Determine what specific roles, tasks, and activities are assigned to the agency's social work staff and those assigned to persons of other disciplines and professions. Also find out what practice frameworks, if any, typically guide service delivery (see Chapter 6).

- Talk to community leaders and professionals outside your agency to ascertain how others perceive your agency and its programs. Identify the public image attached to your agency and how it acquired that reputation.

Selected Bibliography

Hassenfeld, Yeheskel. *Human Services as Complex Organizations,* 2nd ed. Thousand Oaks, CA: Sage, 2010.

Furman, Rich, and Margaret Gibelman. *Navigating Human Services Organizations,* 3rd ed. Thousand Oaks, CA: Sage, 2013.

Lauffer, Armand. *Understanding Your Agency,* 3rd ed. Thousand Oaks, CA: Sage, 2011.

O'Connor, Mary Katherine, & F. Ellen Netting. *Organizational Practice: A Social Worker's Guide to Understanding Human Services,* 2nd ed. Hoboken, NJ: Wiley & Sons, 2009.

10.13 SELECTING AND ORIENTING NEW STAFF AND VOLUNTEERS

The heart and soul of helping rest with the people who deliver needed services. Before any services can be delivered, a human services agency must have a competent professional staff and well-prepared volunteers. Thus, in most human services agencies the helping begins with getting the right personnel in place to provide needed services.

Selecting and training professional staff for an agency is expected of persons in management roles. However, virtually every social worker, whether or not in management, will at some time be part of a search committee involved in selecting other staff members. And once a new employee has been selected, experienced agency social workers may also have a role in helping the new employee develop or sharpen his or her competencies to better fit the needs of the agency.

Securing a group of competent and committed volunteers is also essential to the operation of most social agencies. The U.S. Bureau of Labor Statistics reports that in 2012, 26.5 percent of the U.S. population, or 64.5 million people, volunteered to serve in their communities, many in human services agencies. However, maintaining successful volunteer programs requires a good match between the volunteer and the service needed, work that is carefully planned and rewarding, and volunteers who are properly recognized for their contributions. So, an important staff function that is often part of a social worker's job is to recruit, screen, orient, train, supervise, and evaluate volunteers.

Before staff and volunteers can be used effectively, it is vital to identify the service tasks that are most appropriately performed by volunteers and those that require professional expertise. Assigning appropriate tasks for the person's level of competence is prerequisite to achieving worker or volunteer job satisfaction.

SECURING A COMPETENT PROFESSIONAL STAFF

When serving on a search committee for *professional staff* (i.e., persons with specific professional preparation who are to be employed and compensated for their work), a search committee should carefully match the abilities of each applicant with the requirements of a given job. A beginning point for the specification of competencies usually is found in a job description. Most agencies will have such descriptions from past searches, but it is helpful to review and update the list of tasks and responsibilities and then identify the competencies (i.e., knowledge and skills) required to perform each task.

The position should be advertised widely to attract a diverse and qualified pool of applicants. The advertisement should appear on the agency's website and in local newspapers. It should identify the minimum requirements (e.g., experience in working with older adults, a bachelor's or master's degree in social work, grant-writing skill), the closing date for applications, a description of how to apply, and the expected starting date for the position. If a position requires a professional social worker, advertising in the newsletter of the NASW chapter, sending flyers to other human services agencies, or contacting schools of social work may further stimulate applications from qualified persons.

Typically, the staff-screening process has two phases: a credential review based on information submitted by the applicant and a personal interview with a small number of applicants who appear from their credentials to be the most qualified. The goal of the credential review is to obtain sufficient information for the search committee to rate the applicants on the characteristics established in the job description. In most cases, the candidate will have been asked not only to submit a professional résumé but also to provide a narrative statement regarding his or her interest in and preparation for the position. With this information, the committee will review the completed applications, compare their independent assessments of the candidates and discuss differences in perception, eliminate unacceptable candidates from consideration, and create a priority list of applicants to invite for interviews.

When interviewing a person for a staff position, the process usually involves members of the organization beyond the committee membership. This interview process should (1) provide opportunities to identify the best candidate(s) for recommendation to the person with final hiring authority, (2) provide a chance for the applicant to learn about the agency and job and judge if she or he is a good fit, (3) allow the candidate to ask questions about the job and agency, and (4) provide an opportunity to persuade the applicant to accept the position if it should be offered. The search committee will often prepare a list of questions to be asked of all candidates and/or develop a short case example to be discussed so that comparisons among finalists can be made. Questions such as these might be asked:

- What is it about the population group served by this agency that makes you interested in our position?
- What special skills and experience do you bring to working with these clients?
- Why are you considering leaving your current position, and what about this job seems more attractive to you?
- From a career development perspective, how would taking this job fit into your future plans?
- What can we tell you about this agency (or community) that would assist you in considering this position?
- What support, training, supervision, or professional development opportunities would you see as necessary or valuable in getting started on this job?

All agency personnel engaged in conducting interviews should be warned against asking inappropriate personal questions about a candidate's marital status, plans for having children, child care arrangements, sexual orientation, and so on. It should be assumed that professionals make appropriate provisions for their personal lives. If such questions are asked, the candidate should assure the committee that he or she would be responsible for making certain that personal matters do not negatively affect professional performance.

Before a search committee offers its recommendations, the committee must (1) collect feedback from all persons who were involved in the interview process (a form might be developed to get consistent feedback on key factors), (2) contact the finalists' references (often by telephone) to gain a more detailed and candid appraisal of each candidate than might be included in a reference letter, (3) analyze all the information gathered, and (4) rank the candidates or designate those who would be acceptable or unacceptable. The committee should compile the documentation underpinning its recommendations, and the agency should retain that information for three years in case an unsuccessful applicant should challenge the fairness of the selection process. The final decision maker will then have the responsibility to offer the job, negotiate the conditions, and plan for the entry of the new employee into the agency.

All new staff members will require orientation to the agency. Some of the orientation should relate to the basics of how the agency functions, whom to ask when needing various types of information, where to find supplies, procedures to maintain confidentiality, and so on. Also, new staff members usually require some training to adapt their skills to the unique needs of the agency. This might necessitate in-service training or spending agency funds for professional workshops or training conferences. Bringing new personnel into an agency should not be considered complete until the new employee is given appropriate training.

At least at first, the work of the new hire will be closely monitored. The person who provides this administrative supervision (see Item 16.8) is of critical importance in helping the new staff member get off to a good start. The monitoring function offers both the clients and the agency a level of protection by closely observing the service activities being performed and, if necessary, using administrative authority to protect clients from errors or incompetence until the new person becomes more experienced. It is also useful for another person in the agency to support the new worker as a mentor (i.e., a trusted counselor or guide) to help the new worker develop into a competent staff member (see Item 16.9). A supervisor must be responsible for monitoring the new employee's work and protecting agency interests, whereas a mentor should focus on the new worker's professional development.

DEVELOPING A CADRE OF VOLUNTEERS

The first step in conducting any successful search for volunteers is to determine as precisely as possible the competencies that are needed. For a *volunteer* (i.e., a person who provides services without compensation), this requires clear specification of who the clientele will be, what services he or she will be expected to provide, and how much time will be required to perform the duties. Nothing is more frustrating for a volunteer than being recruited to an agency and then not having his or her time and talents used efficiently.

A second step in securing volunteers is to advertise the agency's need for such help. In general, widely circulated announcements in local newspapers and on the agency website should be the minimum effort at advertising. Speeches on the local circuit of civic clubs and church groups, too, are often productive. These formal announcements should describe the major tasks to be performed, the time demands, and specific skills required. It is important for these recruitment efforts to target specific groups of people in order to reach those most likely to be interested in the position. Word-of-mouth recruiting by experienced volunteers is one of the best ways to secure new volunteers.

Once the application has been received from a potential volunteer, the screening process begins. The initial screening is usually restricted to reviewing information provided on an application form. In general, this information is intended to determine, at a minimum, if anything in the person's background might place the agency's clients at risk and if the person would bring needed skills or strengths to the agency.

Following the paper screening, the face-to-face interviewing process begins. When interviewing persons for volunteer positions, the goal should be to assess each person's motivation, commitment, and capacity for addressing the identified agency or client needs. Questions such as these should be asked:

- Why are you interested in being a volunteer in this agency?
- What type of activity is of greatest interest to you? Here is a list of several tasks or activities you might be asked to perform. Are there any that are of little or no interest to you?
- Are you hoping to have direct contact or involvement with clients? If yes, with what type of clients and what types of interaction?
- What do you expect to gain personally from this volunteer experience?

- Have you been a volunteer for other agencies? If so, what was satisfying about that experience? Not satisfying?
- For how long do you expect to serve as a volunteer? How much time can you contribute each week or month?
- What special skills and experience would you bring? Do you have any physical or emotional limitations that would affect your work at the agency?
- What type of training and supervision do you expect from the agency?
- What is your view of the importance of the confidentiality of client information?

The final selection of volunteers usually rests with a volunteer coordinator or other staff member (often a social worker) assigned to that function. After capable volunteers have been identified, the coordinator will be responsible for matching each volunteer's talents with the agency's needs and initiating the volunteer into the agency. Each volunteer should be given a thorough orientation to the agency and will usually need training to perform the assigned tasks. This training might be conducted on an individual basis, or it might be conducted in a group session for new volunteers. The important point is that the orientation and training should be specific to the tasks to be performed.

Formalizing an ongoing support system for new volunteers is also important. A staff member should have the responsibility for assisting new volunteers in understanding the tasks they are to perform and identifying the best means of carrying out this work.

Selected Bibliography

Connors, Tracy Daniel (ed.). *The Volunteer Management Handbook: Leadership Strategies for Success,* 2nd ed. Hoboken, NJ: Wiley, 2012.

Haski-Leventhal, D., and R. A. Cnaan. Group Processes and Volunteering: Using Groups to Enhance Volunteerism. *Administration in Social Work, 33* (2009): 61–80.

Sherr, Michael E. *Social Work with Volunteers.* Chicago: Lyceum, 2008.

U.S. Bureau of Labor Statistics. Volunteering in the United States, 2012. *Economic News Release.* Available online: http://www.bls.gov/news.release/volun.nr0.htm.

10.14 ORIENTING YOURSELF TO YOUR COMMUNITY

The word **community** is used in a number of ways. For example, it often refers to the people who feel a bond with each other or share an identity and a sense of belonging (e.g., the social work community, the African American community). Another type of community, *a geographic community,* refers to a particular locality such as a neighborhood, city, or county. Such a locality performs certain functions for its people and is also the context or wider environment for many social agencies and programs. As a social worker moves into a new job and locality, he or she needs to examine how well the community is able to serve and support the people who may soon become his or her clients. The basic or typical functions of a geographical community are the following:

- *Provision of goods and essential services.* Water, electricity, heating fuels, food, housing, garbage disposal, medical care, education, transportation, recreation, social services, information, and the like
- *Business activity and employment.* Commerce and jobs from which people earn the money needed to purchase goods and services

- *Public safety.* Protection from criminal behavior and hazards such as fire, floods, and toxic chemicals
- *Socialization.* Opportunities to communicate and interact with others and to develop a sense of identity and belonging beyond those provided by the family system
- *Mutual support.* Tangible assistance and social supports beyond those provided by one's family
- *Social control.* Establishment and enforcement of laws and rules needed to guide and control large numbers of people (e.g., laws, police, courts, traffic control, building codes, pollution control)
- *Political organization and participation.* Governance and decision making related to local matters and public services (e.g., streets, sewer, schools, public welfare, public health, economic development, zoning of housing and businesses).

The characteristics and functioning of a community have a direct bearing on the availability and adequacy of social programs and thus, influence social work practice. A new worker's assessment of the community has three purposes:

1. *To understand the context of one's practice.* The social worker must become knowledgeable about the community's history and demographics, economic base, political structures, and the prevailing values, norms, and myths that affect decision making and intergroup behavior.

2. *To become knowledgeable about the existing human services system.* The social worker needs to know what services are available and to understand community attitudes toward people who have psychosocial problems and utilize the human services. Communities differ in their willingness to collectively respond to human needs and they also vary in how well professionals and agencies work together.

3. *To acquire understanding of the community decision-making structure.* At some point, the social worker's desire for more adequate human services will likely lead to efforts to bring about changes in the community's response to a particular problem or need. To succeed in those efforts, he or she must understand the power structure operating in the community, the beliefs and values of the leaders and key actors who decide what programs and services will be provided and funded, and the formal and informal processes used to reach those decisions (see Item 11.25).

Information that describes a community and its functioning can be gleaned from documents such as census data, economic forecasts, public health reports, prior studies of a community problem, reports related to community planning projects, directories of health and human services agencies, and the like. Helpful documents may be available from the local library, Chamber of Commerce, United Way, and government offices. Supplemental data might be obtained by reading historical accounts of how the community grew and developed and how it has responded to recent problems, by interviewing long-time residents, and by closely following current issues and controversies reported in the local news.

Although the social worker's area of practice will determine the nature and depth of information sought in relation to particular aspects of the community and its service systems, certain general information is essential. The following points will help the social worker develop a profile of the community in which he or she is working:

Demographics

- Total population
- Age distribution, levels of education, occupations
- Minority and ethnic groups; languages spoken by various groups

Geography and environmental influences on community

- Effect of climate, mountains, valleys, rivers, lakes, and so forth on local transportation patterns, economic development, and population distribution
- Effect of transportation routes and other corridors and physical barriers on neighborhood patterns, social interaction, agency location, and service delivery

Beliefs and attitudes

- Dominant values, religious beliefs, and attitudes of the population and its various subgroups
- Types of human services agencies and programs that are valued and respected and that attract community support, favorable publicity, and funding

Local politics

- Form of local government
- Relative power and influence of political parties and various interest groups
- Current political debates, issues, and controversies at local level

Local economy and businesses

- Types of jobs and work available in area (i.e., wages, part time or full time, seasonal or year-round)
- Percentage of labor force unemployed (compared to state and national percentages)

Income distribution

- Median income for women, men, and minority groups
- Number of persons/families below official poverty line
- Number of persons/families experiencing food insecurity or hunger

Housing

- Most common types of housing (e.g., single-family dwellings, apartments, public housing)
- Cost and availability of housing
- Percentage of units overcrowded or substandard

Educational facilities and programs

- Locations and types of schools (i.e., public, private, neighborhood, magnet, charter, etc.)
- School programs for children with special needs
- Dropout rate for all students; for members of various socioeconomic and minority groups

Health and welfare systems

- Names and locations of providers of health care (e.g., emergency services, acute care, home health programs, long-term care, public and private hospitals, public health programs, private clinics)
- Names and locations of agencies providing social and human services (e.g., housing, substance abuse treatment, child welfare, protection from child abuse and domestic abuse, financial assistance)
- Self-help groups and informal helping networks

Sources of information and public opinion

- Influential TV and radio stations and newspapers to which the people look for information and perspectives on current events
- Key leaders and spokespersons for various segments of the community, including racial or ethnic and religious groups

Summary assessment of community issues

- Assessment of major social problems within the community (e.g., inadequate housing, homelessness, inadequate public transportation, insufficient law enforcement, lack of jobs, youth gangs, poverty, substance abuse, teen pregnancy, domestic abuse)
- Major gaps among existing social, health care, and educational services
- Efforts underway to address these issues; leaders in these efforts

Selected Bibliography

Burghardt, Steve. *Macro Practice in Social Work for the 21st Century.* Thousand Oaks, CA: Sage, 2011.
Kirst-Ashman, Karen K., and Grafton H. Hull, Jr. *Generalist Practice with Organizations and Communities,* 5th ed. Belmont, CA: Brooks/Cole Cengage, 2012.

11

Data Collection and Assessment

LEARNING OBJECTIVES

At the conclusion of this chapter, the reader should be prepared to:

- Describe elements of client social functioning a social worker should be prepared to assess, including social role, social supports, personal strengths, self-concept, coping strategies, mental status, and, when appropriate, employment potential.
- Demonstrate knowledge of tools a social worker might use in conducting a social assessment, including various mapping tools, checklists and questionnaires, psychological tests, and the DSM and PIE taxonomies.
- Discuss guidelines for identifying such factors as developmental delays in children or determining various levels of care available for older people or people who are handicapped.
- Demonstrate familiarity with indicators of child or adult abuse and neglect, as well as understanding of the requirements and procedures for reporting suspected maltreatment.
- Explain how the concepts of family dynamics, family functioning, and the changing perceptions of the family can be helpful in conducting an assessment of a family.
- Discuss concepts of group dynamics and group functioning that might be used in assessing the performance of a small group.
- Describe guidelines for assessing the effectiveness of human services organizations, the functioning of a community, and the impacts of social policies and programs.
- Demonstrate ability to access evidence-based information to inform social work assessments and the selection of intervention approaches.

The social worker's focus during the second phase of the planned change process is on collecting information needed to comprehend the client's concern and current situation and determine how it might be addressed. The social worker brings to this activity an expertise not usually possessed by the general public, including skill in determining what data is needed, where it can be obtained, and how it should be interpreted.

Data collection is the activity of securing information directly from the client, from other involved people, and, in some cases, from documents such as medical records, school reports, probation records, community surveys, and so on. The social worker is especially interested in gathering facts but in addition the worker will be alert to subjective perceptions and opinions regarding the situation held by the client, family members, key people in the client's environment and perhaps from the referring agency (e.g., a court, school).

When does data collection end? To some degree, new data is always being collected. Certainly, it is essential that a social worker initially obtain sufficient information to have a clear picture of what is occurring in the client's situation before formulating an intervention plan. However, it is equally important to avoid delaying or stalling the change process by gathering unnecessary or excessive data.

Assessment is the critical thinking process by which a worker reasons from the information or data to arrive at working hypotheses and tentative conclusions. During assessment, the available information is organized and analyzed to make sense of the client's situation and to lay the foundation for a plan of action. An assessment should be *multidimensional*—that is, based on numerous data sources that reflect varying points of view. If the worker, the client, and others involved in the client's situation reach highly divergent conclusions, it will be necessary to collect additional data and do a more in-depth analysis in order to reach a consensus, or at least to reduce the range of opinions.

Social workers must guard against unconsciously or inadvertently making the client's situation or the data collected fit or conform to a particular theoretical orientation, model, or a preconceived diagnostic category. One protection against the worker's own biases having an undue influence on the assessment is to have the client actively involved in identifying the relevant sources of information and in sorting through the information when arriving at an assessment. Further, when a conclusion is reached, the worker should view it as tentative and open to revision as additional information is obtained during other phases of the change process.

SECTION A

TECHNIQUES AND GUIDELINES FOR DIRECT PRACTICE

In direct practice with individuals, families, and small groups, the social worker's data gathering and assessment will be shaped and guided by the *person-in-environment* framework. In other words, attention is given to the client as a unique and whole person as well as the demands and constraints placed on the client by the context or environment in which he or she must function. Ultimately, it is finding, facilitating, or negotiating a workable match between the person and his or her environment that is the focus of a social work intervention (see Chapter 13).

Data-collection activities

A social work assessment should give some attention to all dimensions of the *whole person* and to any factors that impinge on her or his social functioning. For example:

- *Volitional.* The personal choices and decisions, both large and small, that shape one's life; the impact of these decisions on oneself and others

- *Intellectual.* The ability to interpret and give conceptual order to one's experiences; the cognitive processes needed to understand, form judgments, and make decisions; the ideas and knowledge used to understand oneself, others, and the world
- *Spiritual and religious.* One's deepest and core beliefs concerning the meaning and purpose of life; one's relationship with his or her God; the meaning assigned to pain and suffering; one's religious identity, traditions, and practices
- *Moral and ethical.* One's standards of right and wrong; the criteria used to make moral decisions; one's conscience
- *Emotional.* One's feelings and moods, such as joy, love, sadness, anger, fear, shame; the inclination to be drawn toward or to retreat from certain situations and persons
- *Physical.* One's level of energy; capacity for movement; health and nutritional status (e.g., illness, disabilities, pain, care and treatment needed)
- *Sexuality.* One's sexual identity and orientation; libido; the influence of sexual attraction in relationships; the meaning assigned to being male or female; one's sex-role expectations; the capacity for and desire for reproduction
- *Communication.* The ability to express oneself (i.e., verbally, nonverbally, or in writing) in order to make known one's needs, interests, or opinions
- *Familial.* Relationships with one's parents, siblings, spouse, partner, children, and relatives; one's sense of loyalty to and responsibility for family members; one's family history and traditions
- *Social.* Interactions with friends and peers; one's social support network; one's interests and leisure time activities
- *Community.* One's sense of belonging to a group beyond family and friends; one's sense of loyalty to and responsibility for others in the neighborhood and locality; one's place or status in the community; one's use of various formal and informal resources to meet personal and family needs
- *Cultural.* One's beliefs, values, traditions, customs, and creativity as related to one's ethnicity, cultural background, and language
- *Work and occupation.* The nature of one's work and job skills; one's source of income; the meaning of work in one's life; identity with and relationship to employer and occupation
- *Economic.* One's financial resources; adequacy of income to purchase goods and services; capacity to manage and budget one's money
- *Legal.* One's rights, responsibilities, protections, and entitlements as defined in law; desire and commitment to adhere to laws

There are several modes or methods of data collection. Since each has limitations, the social worker should use more than one whenever possible, for this will increase the accuracy of the inferences drawn from the data. A social worker might use the following methods or modes of data collection:

- Direct verbal questioning, such as the face-to-face interview (see Chapter 8)
- Direct written questioning, including the use of questionnaires and problem checklists (see Item 11.12)
- Indirect or projective verbal questioning, such as the story completion or the use of vignettes (see Item 11.12)
- Indirect or projective written questioning, such as sentence completion

- Observation within the client's natural environment, such as home visits (see Item 10.6), observation of children in a classroom, and so forth
- Observations of the client in a simulated situation that is analogous to real life, including such techniques as the role-playing of a job interview
- Client self-monitoring and self-observation with the aid of a recording tool, such as a log, checklist, or journaling
- The use of existing documents, such as agency records, school records, physician reports, newspapers, and so forth

Assessment activities

As mentioned earlier, assessment is the activity of drawing meaning, inferences, and tentative conclusions from the data. During assessment (but hopefully earlier), there must be clarity as to who is the client and who is to be the target of an intervention. In other words, who is asking for and expects to benefit from the social worker's services (*the client system*) and who needs to change (*the target system*). They are not always the same. For example, when a mother requests counseling for a rebellious daughter who is forced to attend the counseling sessions, who is the client? In this situation, we would probably conclude that the mother is the client and the daughter is the target of intervention.

Special effort should be devoted to assessing client strengths. All too often, both client and worker become preoccupied with the presenting problem and all that is going wrong. This can give rise to an inadequate intervention plan. Giving attention to client strengths builds hopefulness and usually uncovers additional resources for dealing with the client's problems and concerns.

Value preferences will of course affect assessments. Both the client and social worker will hold beliefs about the way things could be or ought to be and these views affect the way a problem is defined and the outcomes sought. To the extent possible, these values and beliefs should be made explicit and discussed during assessment and planning.

An *assessment tool* combines data collection with some form of a scoring procedure that will facilitate or guide the interpretation. Typically, these tools provide a way to compare the client's responses to a set of questions, for example, with the answers of a larger collective to whom the instrument has been administered (i.e., a standardized assessment tool; see Item 14.3). Hundreds of such instruments have been published and are available to the social worker. However, sometimes, it is useful for the worker to develop a tool that is tailor-made for use in a particular practice setting or with clients facing a special type of challenge (see Item 14.2). Tools and techniques for organizing data for the ongoing evaluation of a client's progress are described in Chapter 14.

It is in direct social work practice that social workers encounter the concept of diagnosis, which is related to the processes of data gathering and assessment yet are essentially different. In *diagnosis*, the client's problem, condition, or situation is classified and assigned to a particular category within a given taxonomy, such as the person-in-environment (PIE) system or the *Diagnostic and Statistical Manual of Mental Disorders (DSM)* (see Item 11.15). The act of diagnosis applies a standardized terminology to the client's condition or situation in order to facilitate communication among professionals and to aid in the gathering of data needed for research, program administration, and insurance billing. This labeling and categorization may or may not make a useful contribution to the worker's intervention planning, however. In many instances, clients assigned the same diagnostic label require somewhat different approaches to treatment and intervention.

11.1 ASSESSING A CLIENT'S SOCIAL FUNCTIONING

As explained in Chapter 1, the fundamental purpose of the social work profession is to enhance a client's social functioning and capacity to live a satisfying life and to prevent and correct problems in social functioning. It is this focus on a client's social functioning that distinguishes a social worker's assessment from an assessment conducted by, for example, a psychologist, nurse, or school counselor.

The concept of **social functioning**, when applied to an individual, can be thought of as the person's motivation, capacity, and opportunity to meet his or her basic needs and perform his or her major social roles, such as those of parent, spouse, partner, family member, employee, student, citizen, and so on. The word **social** refers to the interactions between and among people and between people and the systems of their social environment (e.g., family, school, employing organization, hospital). Social workers are particularly concerned about the match (or lack thereof) between a client's needs and the resources available in his or her environment to meet those needs.

"The 4 Ps, 4 Rs, and 4 Ms" a deleted item from the 7th edition

The statements listed on the next few pages are intended to remind the social worker of various dimensions of a client's social functioning. Depending on the client's presenting concerns or problem, some aspects of social functioning would need to be examined in more depth than others. If an individual's current functioning or situation departs significantly from the description provided, she or he is probably facing some special challenge or problem. Because most of these statements are written in a positive manner, they constitute a list of possible client strengths (see Item 11.6) and can serve as a starting point when writing the goals and objectives to be included in a service agreement or treatment plan (see Items 12.4 and 12.5).

Independent Living and Self-Care (Adults)

- The client manages basic self-care tasks such eating, food preparation, dressing, bathing, and toileting.
- The client grasps new information, makes logical decisions, and implements plans necessary to execute roles and responsibilities.
- The client possesses physical mobility and has the energy level necessary to care for self and perform ordinary roles and responsibilities.
- The client recognizes dangerous situations (e.g., medical emergencies, criminal activity, gas leak) and knows how to call for help.
- The client initiates interactions with others and can secure their cooperation and assistance in order to care for self.
- The client speaks, reads, and writes the language(s) needed for such activities as shopping, working, attending school, obtaining medical care, and calling for assistance.
- The client has access to and can utilize needed transportation.

Housing and Home Safety

- The client has housing that is safe and provides adequate space and privacy and protection from weather, intruders, and so forth.
- The client has access to clean drinking water, a method of safe food storage, and a sanitary toilet.
- The client keeps food preparation area clean and sanitary.

- The client can safely use the various tools, soaps, and household chemicals needed to keep the home safe from disease-causing microbes, roaches, and rodents.

Nutrition and Health Care

- The client prepares nutritious meals within the food budget.
- The client engages in health-building behaviors (e.g., adequate sleep, proper diet, exercise) and avoids excessive alcohol, street drugs, and the misuse of medicines.
- The client has access to needed health care and the ability to pay for services.
- The client avoids high risk or daredevil activities that could result in injury.

Family Life

- The client's relationship with spouse or partner is mutually satisfying and meets the need for intimacy and companionship; sexual activity is nonexploitative and satisfying to self and partner.
- The client's family members care for and are a source of support, assistance, and encouragement for each other.
- The client provides her or his children with nurturance, guidance, protection, encouragement, and limits.
- The client puts the needs of his or her children before personal desires and is willing to make sacrifices for the good of family and children.
- The client is fair and reasonable in setting limits, discipline, and guidance for her or his children.
- The client encourages family members to participate in activities that further their development and build healthy relationships with people outside the family.

Friendships and Social Supports

- The client builds and maintains wholesome relationships with relatives, friends, and neighbors.
- The client has access to a social support network that can provide encouragement, information, and some forms of tangible assistance.
- The client selects companions who provide acceptance and encouragement and avoids individuals who are manipulative or exploiting.

Spirituality

- The client has values, beliefs, and perspectives that provide meaning, purpose, and direction in life.
- The client possesses and uses a framework of moral and ethical principles for making decisions and choices.
- The client is free to be part of a faith community or religion that provides acceptance, encouragement, support, and guidance.
- The client is able to attend religious services of his or her choice.

Interaction with Community

- The client lives in a community that provides adequate public safety and protection (e.g., police, fire, emergency medical response).
- The client feels accepted by and has a sense of belonging to a supportive and helpful neighborhood and community.

- The client is able to maintain meaningful ethnic, cultural, and language connections and associations.
- The client participates in social, recreational, and political activities of the neighborhood and community.
- The client contributes to activities that benefit and improve the community and the lives of its people.
- The client is unrestricted by and free from discrimination or oppression.

Personal Appearance and Hygiene

- The client maintains the level of personal hygiene needed to prevent illness and infections and maintain social acceptance.
- The client is able to obtain and afford items and services needed to maintain appropriate appearance (e.g., hair care, deodorant, shampoo, washing machine).
- The client selects clothing, accessories, and body decorations that are appropriate to the occasion and that enhance appearance and social acceptance.

Education and Training

- The client is free of cognitive or sensory difficulties that impede learning or is able to effectively compensate for these limitations.
- The client explores new areas of learning in order to challenge self and discover new interests and abilities.
- The client is aware of and has access to types of education and training needed to maintain and develop important job skills.
- The client assesses her or his own learning needs and seeks out instruction needed to perform social roles and fulfill responsibilities at work, home, and school.
- The client has a realistic understanding of his or her capacity to complete various programs of education and training.

Employment and Job Performance

- The client has a satisfying job that is appropriate to his or her level of skill and experience and provides an adequate income.
- The client's working conditions are safe and supportive. If the client is a parent, she or he has access to suitable and affordable day care.
- The client is a responsible employee, is able to perform assigned work, and understands employment-related policies and procedures.
- The client prepares for those job changes and promotions that can increase opportunity, income, benefits, and job satisfaction.
- The client knows about various types of jobs, how to apply and interview for a job, and can determine if a particular job matches his or her skills and income needs.

Income and Money Management

- The client has an income sufficient to meet the basic needs of self and family.
- The client uses budgeting to plan and monitor financial situations.
- The client understands the difference between necessities and wants and has self-discipline to avoid unwise expenditures and debt. He or she recognizes that the purpose of advertising is to encourage spending.

- The client understands basic money concepts such as interest, debt, charge accounts, loans, and late payment penalties.
- The client understands work-related concepts such as payroll deductions, income taxes, FICA, and health insurance.

Citizenship and Law

- The client understands right and wrong and abides by laws and basic moral principles that recognize the rights of others and the common good.
- The client understands basic legal rights and responsibilities and the functions of police, courts, and lawyers.
- The client is aware of laws related to marriage, parent–child relationships, contracts, insurance, leases, loans, taxes, driving an automobile, use of alcohol and drugs, firearms, and so on.
- The client expresses views on public policy and legislation through such activities as voting and participation in advocacy organizations.
- The client avoids situations, associations, and activities that could draw him or her into dangerous or illegal conduct.

Use of Community Resources

- The client knows how to access community resources such as those providing medical care, mental health services, legal counsel, consumer counseling, employment services, recreation, library services, and so on.
- The client knows of organizations/resources that provide services pertinent to her or his concerns, needs, and circumstances.
- The client knows how to use a telephone directory, guides to community services, and the Internet, in order to obtain needed information and resources.

Recreational and Leisure Activity

- The client participates in recreation or leisure activities that provide a respite from ordinary roles and responsibilities.
- The client participates in activities that expand opportunities for physical exercise, new learning, creativity, and new friendships.
- The client selects recreation and leisure activities that are safe and wholesome, and does not expose self to social influences that could prove harmful (e.g., excessive drinking).

Coping with Ordinary Problems of Living

- The client has self-confidence and positive self-worth. She or her does not overlook personal abilities and strengths and does not deny or ignore real limitations.
- The client uses knowledge drawn from past experiences to decide how best to cope with current difficulties and to anticipate challenges.
- The client assumes responsibility for personal behavior and choices. He or she performs roles and responsibilities, even when they are sometimes a source of frustration. The client perseveres in order to complete important tasks.
- The client recovers from anxiety, depression, and emotional turmoil brought on by an upsetting event or life disruption such as a death in the family, loss of job, or breakup of a relationship.
- The client rebuilds alternate intimate relationships following a loss such as one caused by a divorce, separation, or death.

- The client is comfortable with his or her own identity, ethnicity, gender, sexual orientation, economic situation, and life circumstances.
- The client sets reasonable limits on demands by others for her or his time and energy.

Coping with Mental Health Problem or Addiction

- The client recognizes the nature of his or her problems and their consequences and does not deny the existence of significant problems.
- The client makes use of effective therapies, medications, and support groups.
- The client's prior problem behaviors and addictions are controlled and monitored in order to prevent relapse.
- The client avoids relationships and activities that could increase chances of relapse or aggravate mental health problems.

Adjustments to Physical Disability

- The client makes use of rehabilitation programs, medications, and assistive technology (e.g., communication devices, artificial limbs, wheelchair) to minimize the impact of the disability.
- The client is able to discuss the disability and need for assistance without embarrassment or apology. She or he lets others know what she or he can and cannot do.
- The client recognizes disability-related risks and vulnerabilities and plans how to reduce risks and handle possible emergencies or accidents.
- The client's expressions of frustration over his or her disability are reasonable and appropriate and do not shut out or drive away family members, friends, and other helpers.

School Performance of a Child or Adolescent

- The client performs in school at a level consistent with her or his ability, as indicated by observed reasoning ability, problem-solving activities, and standardized tests.
- The client communicates with teachers and school personnel; she or he welcomes and appreciates these exchanges and the guidance of these professionals.
- The client is able to attend school without concern for personal safety.
- The client participates in both planned school-related social activities (e.g., sports, dances, and clubs) and in spontaneous activities involving other students and peer group.
- The client (in keeping with age level) is interested in learning about various career choices and educational opportunities.

Relationship of a Youth to Parents, Siblings, and Family

- The client usually does what parents expect and performs age-appropriate chores and assigned duties (e.g., taking care of clothing, cleaning room, supervision of younger siblings).
- The client frequently joins in the family's recreational, social, or spiritual activities, such as family gatherings, outings, and so on.
- The client interacts with extended family members such as grandparents, aunts, uncles, and cousins.

Child or Adolescent Sexuality

- The client has basic knowledge of sex and expresses comfort with sexuality (consistent with age).
- The client speaks with parents or responsible adults about feelings, thoughts, and questions related to sexual matters.
- The client is respectful of others in dating situations. Sexual activity is kept within the limits of the client's and the partner's own standards of morality. Sexual activity is not compulsive. The client does not coerce or force others to participate.

Ordinary Problems of Childhood and Adolescence

- The client handles feelings and emotions without letting them seriously disrupt relationships at home and school.
- The client (if necessary to adjust to new parent figures) accepts the support and guidance offered by new parent figures, such as stepparents, guardians, or foster parents.
- The client acknowledges and faces up to personal problems and misbehavior. He or she can recognize a problem that is blocking positive interactions and does not underestimate nor exaggerate its effect.
- The client takes steps to avoid a recurrence of prior problem behavior.

Selected Bibliography

Holland, Sally. *Child and Family Assessment in Social Work Practice*, 2nd ed. Thousand Oaks, CA: Sage, 2011.

Martin, Ruben. *Social Work Assessment*. Thousand Oaks, CA: Sage, 2010.

11.2 THE MEANING OF WORK IN SOCIAL FUNCTIONING

Quite often, adult clients have concerns that are intertwined with their job or career, or a lack thereof. Thus, social work assessments and interventions should give attention to the nature and demands of a client's work and how his or her job or occupation might be affecting the other dimensions of the client's life, such as marriage, parent–child interaction, and physical and mental health. Social workers involved in the development of social policy and social programs (see part B of Chapters 10–14) should know about current and projected job markets and the economic conditions and trends that can impact individuals, families, and whole communities. The following are aspects of employment that a social worker should keep in mind as she or he seeks to understand and address a client's concern and problems.

- A paycheck is important, but it is only one of the benefits of having a job. Work is more than an economic necessity; it is a key component of adult psychosocial development. Employment is a major social role, a core aspect of an adult's identity, and a yardstick of perceived personal worth and social status. Adults who have the capacity for gainful employment are expected to have a job. Work provides a sense of purpose and a structure to life. One's workplace is a social environment for meeting basic human needs for interaction, communication, learning, creativity, and a sense of achievement.

- Employment opportunities and jobs that pay a living wage are crucial to people's economic security and to the social stability of their community. In recent decades, economic downturns, globalization, corporate downsizing, mergers, buyouts, and other factors have eroded people's confidence in their economic future. The decline of the manufacturing sector in the U.S. economy has eroded the incomes of many. Also, there is a growing inequality in income distribution. The rich get richer while the majority is falling behind.

- Job markets are constantly changing and highly competitive. Ironically, while many people are searching for a job, many businesses are unable to find the skilled workers they need. Most of the higher-paying jobs now require a solid foundation in mathematics and science, facility in verbal and written communication, the use of information technology, and skills in problem solving. Those who are to be successful in securing a job or advancing within a company must have the capacity to learn quickly and adapt to new technologies.

- Unemployment and underemployment can have a devastating effect on a person's self-confidence and self-esteem. Those who are without a job for long periods often suffer from feelings of inadequacy, hopelessness, shame, and diminished self-respect. Unemployment and the loss of needed income can create tension and conflict within marriages and family relationships, exacerbate medical and mental health problems, and give rise to the abuse of drugs and alcohol. Individual counseling and support groups are critical services for persons who are struggling with the effects of unemployment. Given vicissitudes in job markets and the economy, a society must provide a safety net and effective programs for those who are laid off or injured on the job (e.g., unemployment insurance, worker's compensation, retraining opportunities).

- Principles of social and economic justice recognize that both employer and employee have certain fundamental rights and responsibilities. Employer–employee agreements need to be fair to both parties. However, some tension between employers and employees is inevitable. Company owners need to make a reasonable profit in order to maintain and expand their businesses. Thus, they strive to hold down costs, including wages and benefits. At the same time, employees naturally seek higher wages and additional benefits. Employees have a right to expect a just and reasonable wage, one that makes it possible to meet their basic needs and support their families. Ideally, the employment agreement will include benefits such as health care coverage for the employee and his or her dependents, life and disability insurance, unemployment insurance, a retirement or pension plan, paid vacation, emergency leave time, and reasonable security against dismissal. An employer is expected to provide working conditions that are as safe and satisfying as possible.

- Employees are obligated to always perform the assigned work to the best of their ability and accept instruction and constructive criticism so as to improve their performance. They are to arrive at work on time, treat company equipment and property with care, and not abuse existing benefits such as personal leave and sick leave. While on the job, the employees have a right to occasional rest breaks and refreshments that help to avoid fatigue. They should have a voice in shaping their work environment and, where possible, in decisions on how the work is to be performed. They should be encouraged to offer suggestions on how to improve efficiency, safety, and job satisfaction. Employees are entitled to grievance procedures that can resolve conflicts and they also should have the right to form or join a labor union or similar association.

- Social workers will encounter some clients who dream of starting their own business. Some individuals with exceptional drive, knowledge, and skill can start and grow a business and thereby create jobs for others. The personal and financial rewards of having one's own business can be substantial. Developing a successful business is extremely demanding and involves prudent risk taking. Such initiative is to be applauded and encouraged. However, those individuals who have little or no experience in running a business should be advised and helped to secure an expert review of their business plan. Individuals who are naïve and desperate to earn more money may make unwise decisions and investments and they are susceptible to manipulators, scams, and impractical get-rich-quick schemes.

- For many families and households, two or more incomes are necessary to stay afloat. Needless to say, an extra income helps the bottom line of a family budget. However, when all the adults of a family are working (e.g., both husband and wife, both mother and father) they face some difficult challenges. Obtaining adequate and affordable child care is a major concern. When many hours are spent at work, there is little time available for wholesome parent–child interaction. Similarly, there is a short supply of time and energy for such ordinary tasks as cooking, grocery shopping, laundry, cleaning, home maintenance, and so forth. All too often, a disproportionate share of parenting and home care falls to women. On top of those demands, it is important to recognize that many are also carrying a responsibility for the care of elder relatives. Families provide the preponderance of elder care, the bulk of it by women. Given the inherent difficulty of juggling a job and family responsibilities, social workers should explore the division of labor within a family when the client's presenting concerns have to do with the marriage and children.

- For some individuals, their work or job is all consuming and much like an addiction. They devote nearly all of their time and energy to their job and career. This happens when one's work provides more satisfaction and fulfillment than other aspects of life. For some, a single-minded pursuit of money, power, promotions, and status takes precedence over all other relationships and activities. Such imbalances and distortions have a negative effect on one's marriage, family, and children and on one's overall physical and mental health.

- Sadly, many individuals report a dislike of their jobs. Many hang on to a hated, mind-numbing, exhausting, or dangerous job because they feel they have no other options. Work environments can become psychologically toxic when production, quotas, and the bottom line are valued more than employees. Working in such a setting is often harmful to one's mental health and damaging to family relationships. For most people, job satisfaction is a function of having a sense of challenge, being able to use and develop one's skills and talents, being creative, enjoying one's colleagues, and feeling appreciated. Those who work only for the money are the least likely to enjoy their jobs.

- In our fast-paced society, job-related stress is a common problem that can easily overflow into and affect relationships outside the work environment. Foundational to all other efforts to deal with job-related stress are sufficient sleep, good nutrition, and exercise. Shift work, and especially years of working at night, is a special challenge because such work schedules disrupt biological rhythms, the body's natural clock, and limits participation in normal family, social, and community activities (see Item 16.4).

- For a variety of reasons, some individuals are not able to secure or keep a job that earns enough to pay for basic needs such as food, shelter, and health care. Examples include persons with a severe illness or disability and parents responsible for the full-time care of their small children. Such individuals may need to receive tax-supported welfare benefits. Within the United States, many believe that those who receive a welfare benefit should somehow work for what they receive, simply because "work for welfare" seems to be a fair arrangement and because work is a social good. Thus, a work requirement is often built into a financial aid program's eligibility criteria. All of this makes sense if the recipient is able to work, if a meaningful work experience is available, and if the recipient can be provided with needed child care. Such a work for welfare requirement is neither reasonable nor fair if its purpose is to punish the recipient or discourage poor people from using a needed welfare program.

  Most welfare recipients would prefer a real job rather than financial assistance and would gladly work for their benefits if the work activity would help them learn job skills and lead to a real job. A "work for welfare" program must recognize and address the fact that it often imposes a transportation expense on the client who must travel to and from the "make-work activity." A "work for welfare" program component may not be cost effective if it requires much paid staff to arrange and supervise work activities. Providing appropriate care for the young children of parents who are required to work for a welfare benefit is a perplexing social policy issue and a costly program component (see Item 15.1).

Selected Bibliography

O'Toole, James, and Edward Lawler. *The New American Workplace.* New York: Palgrave/Macmillan, 2006.

Schultz, Duane, and Sidney Schultz. *Psychology and Work Today.* Upper Saddle River, NJ: Prentice-Hall, 2010.

11.3 THE SOCIAL ASSESSMENT REPORT

A **social assessment report** (often called a *social history*) is a particular type of professional report prepared frequently by social workers in direct practice. It describes the client's current functioning and situation and offers selected background information on how the client has adjusted to prior challenges. Because past behavior is the best predictor of future behavior, a well-written social history or social assessment report is especially useful to professionals responsible for making decisions regarding the type of program or service that would be appropriate for a particular client and also to professionals and staff responsible for facilitating a client's adjustment to a new environment such as, for example, a foster home, treatment program, or nursing home.

The report's content will vary somewhat depending on the audience for whom it is prepared (e.g., other social workers, doctors, judges, psychologists, school personnel, interdisciplinary teams). A typical social assessment report has these qualities:

- *Concise and relevant.* Keep the intended reader in mind as you prepare this report. Provide what the reader needs to know. The report should be as brief as possible. Avoid using jargon and diagnostic labels; rather, include descriptions of the client's actual behavior and performance.

- *Objective.* Be as factual as possible. Do not present an opinion or an assumption as if it were a fact. Label your interpretations or hypothesis as such; the best way to do this is to place your conclusions and inferences under a separate heading called "Worker's Impressions and Assessment."

    If possible and appropriate, invite the client to review your draft of the report and offer additions and corrections. Because the report will become part of the client's record, you should assume that the client may want to read it and has a right to do so (see Item 10.5). Avoid using words or phrases that could appear judgmental. When it is necessary to include observations that might offend the client, do so, if possible, by using the client's own words. Note these examples:

    Unacceptable: It is apparent that Jane is a hostile and uncaring individual who is too self-centered and immature to cope with the demands of her elderly father.

    Acceptable: While I was talking with Jane, her father requested a glass of water. She responded in a loud voice and said, "Go to hell, you old fool. I hope you dry up and blow away."

- *Attention to client strengths.* Successful interventions are built on client strengths. Thus, the report should focus on client abilities. Avoid giving undo attention to a client's limitations, deficiencies, and psychopathology (see Item 11.6).

- *Organization.* Use headings to sort the information into categories. Here are some topical headings commonly used in social assessment reports:

    - Identifying Information (name, date of birth, etc.)
    - Reason for Social Workers or Agency Involvement with Client
    - Statement of Client's Concern, Problem, or Need
    - Family Background (data on family of origin, parents, siblings)
    - Current Family/Household Composition
    - Client's Significant Others (e.g., spouse, children, friends)
    - Ethnicity, Religion, and Spirituality
    - Physical Functioning, Health Concerns, Nutrition, Home Safety, Illness, Disabilities, Medications
    - Intellectual Functioning, Education, School Performance
    - Psychological and Behavioral Patterns
    - Strengths, Ways of Coping, and Problem-Solving Capacities
    - Employment, Income, Work Experience, and Skills
    - Housing, Neighborhood, and Transportation
    - Recent Use of Community and Professional Services
    - Social Worker's Impressions and Assessment
    - Descriptions of Proposed Intervention and Service Plan

The sample social assessment report presented in Figure 11.1 illustrates the use of topical headings.

Selected Bibliography

Andrews, Arlene Bowers. *Social History Assessment.* Thousand Oaks, CA: Sage, 2007.

Kagle, Jill, and Sandra Kopels. *Social Work Records,* 3rd ed. Long Grove, IL: Waveland, 2008.

Zuckerman, Edward. *The Clinician's Thesaurus: The Guide for Wording Psychological Reports,* 6th ed. New York: Guilford, 2005.

Greystone Family Service Agency

Identifying Information

Client Name: ___Shirley McCarthy___   Case Record #: ___3456___

D.O.B: ___July 4, 1994___   Age: ___20___   Date of Referral: ___Oct. 8, 2014___

Soc. Security #: ___505–67–8910___   Social Worker: ___Jane Green, BSW___

Address: ___2109 B Street___   Report Prepared: ___Oct. 13, 2014___

___Greystone, MT 09876___

Phone: ___555–0123___

Reason for Report

This report was prepared for use during consultation with Dr. Jones, the agency's psychiatric consultant, and for purposes of peer supervision. (The client is aware that a report is being prepared for this purpose.)

Reason for Social Work Involvement

Shirley was referred to this agency by Dr. Smith, an emergency room physician at City Hospital. Shirley was treated there for having taken an unknown quantity of aspirin in an apparent suicide attempt. She is reacting with anxiety and depression to her unwanted pregnancy. The father is a former boyfriend with whom she has broken off. She does not want him nor her parents to learn that she is pregnant.

She does not want an abortion and does not want to care for a child. She has thought about adoption but knows little about what would be involved. She agreed to come to this agency in order to figure out how she might deal with her dilemma.

Source of Data

This report is based on two one-hour interviews with the client (Oct. 9 and 11) and a phone conversation with Dr. Smith.

Family Background and Situation

Shirley is the youngest of three children. Her brother, John, age 30, is a chemical engineer in Austin, Texas. Her sister, Martha, age 27, is a pharmacist in Seattle. Shirley does not feel close to either sibling and neither knows of her pregnancy.

Her parents have been married for 33 years. They live in Spokane, Washington. Her father, Thomas, is an engineer for a farm equipment company. Her mother, Mary, is a registered nurse.

Shirley describes her parents as hard-working, honest people who have a strong sense of right and wrong and a commitment to family. The family is middle class and of Irish

---

Figure 11.1

Sample Social Assessment Report

heritage. The McCarthy's are life-long Catholics. The three children attended Catholic grade and high schools. Shirley says that if her parents knew of the pregnancy "it would just kill them." Her wish to keep her parents from learning of the pregnancy seems motivated by a desire to protect them from distress.

Physical Functioning and Health

Shirley is 5'7" tall and weighs 115 pounds. She is about three months pregnant. Dr. Smith reports that she is underweight but otherwise healthy. He has concern about her willingness to obtain proper prenatal care; he had referred Shirley to Dr. Johnson (an OB/GYN physician), but she did not keep that appointment.

Shirley says that she is in good health, eats well, exercises minimally, and reports no medical problems. She is not taking any medication.

Intellectual Functioning

Shirley completed two years at the University of Washington and then transferred to the University of Montana where she is currently a junior in computer science. She has an overall GPA of A–. Despite her good grades, Shirley describes herself as a "mediocre student."

She is attracted to subjects where there is a clear right and wrong answer. She does not like courses such as philosophy, which seems "wishy-washy" to her. Although she values the logical and precise thinking that is part of computer science, she explains that she tends to make personal decisions impulsively and "jumps into things without considering the consequences."

Emotional Functioning

Shirley describes herself as "moody." Even before the pregnancy, she had bouts of depression when she would sit alone in her room for hours at a time. She never sought treatment for the depression. In describing herself, Shirley uses the words "childish" and "immature"; she has always felt younger than others her age.

She often feels anger and sadness, but tries to keep her feelings from showing. In this sense, she is like her father, who always keeps things to himself until he finally "blows up."

In spite of her accomplishments, Shirley seems to have poor self-esteem and focuses more on her limitations than her strengths.

Interpersonal and Social Relationships

Shirley has no "close friends." She says it is difficult for her to interact with others and she wishes she had better social skills. She has held various part-time jobs during high school and college, but socialized only minimally with co-workers. In college, Shirley had trouble getting along with her roommates in the dorm, so she moved to an apartment so that she could be alone.

When she drinks alcohol, she feels more outgoing and friendly. However, this fact scares her because several uncles are alcoholic. For the past year, she worked hard at not drinking at all. She was not drinking when she took the aspirin.

Her former boyfriend, Bob (father of her baby), was the first person she ever dated for more than a few months. The relationship ended one month ago. Bob is also a student.

Religion and Spirituality

Shirley was raised as a Catholic and retains many of the beliefs and values she learned as a child. She describes herself as a spiritual person and one who prays quite often. She has clear ideas of right and wrong but also feels she is in a stage of life when she is trying to

Figure 11.1
Continued

decide what she really believes and is in the process of constructing a system of values, morals, and ethical principles.

Strengths and Problem-Solving Capacity

Although Shirley tends to minimize her strengths, she exhibits intelligence, an ability to work hard, a desire to make friends, a loyalty to her family while also wanting to make her own decisions, and a moderate motivation to deal with her situation constructively. She displays a good vocabulary and expresses herself in a clear manner.

She tends to avoid making hard decisions and lets things pile up until she is forced by circumstances to follow the only option still open to her. She usually knows what she "should do" but does not act; she attributes this to a fear of making mistakes. When faced with interpersonal conflict, she is inclined to withdraw.

Economics/Housing/Transportation

Shirley's parents are assisting her with the costs of her education. She also works about 30 hours per week at the Baylor Department Store, earning minimum wage. With this money, she pays rent and keeps her eight-year-old car running.

Aside from her college student health insurance, she has no medical coverage. She does not know if that policy covers pregnancy. Shirley lives alone in a two-room apartment which she says is located in a "rough area" of town. She is afraid to be out alone after dark.

Use of Community Resources

This is the first time Shirley has had contact with a social agency. During our sessions, she asked many questions about the agency and expressed some confusion about why she had been referred here by Dr. Smith. She acknowledged that feelings of embarrassment and shame make it difficult for her to talk to about her concerns.

Impressions and Assessment

This 20-year-old is experiencing inner conflict and depression because of an unwanted pregnancy. This gave rise to a suicide attempt. In keeping with her tendency to avoid conflict, she has not told others of the pregnancy, yet the father (Bob) will need to be involved if she chooses the legal procedure of relinquishment, and her parents' involvement may be needed for financial support. Prenatal care is needed, but it too has been avoided. Abortion is not an acceptable solution to Shirley, and she is ambivalent about adoption and how to manage her life while pregnant.

Goals for Work with Client

In order to help Shirley make the necessary decisions to deal with this pregnancy, I hope to engage her in pregnancy options counseling. Issues to be addressed include making a further assessment of her depression and suicide attempt, obtaining and paying for medical care, and deciding on whether to inform Bob and her own parents. She will need emotional support, some structure, and a gentle demand for work so she can overcome her avoidance, make decisions, and take necessary action.

Note: The names in this report are fictitious.

Figure 11.1
Continued

11.4 MAPPING CLIENT CONDITIONS

Social workers can use several forms of diagramming to present client data in a visual format. By using such diagrams, descriptions that might require several pages of narrative can often be reduced to a single page. Three of the most popular diagrams are the *genogram* (similar to a family tree that depicts family structures and relationships), the *cultural genogram* (a version of the genogram that focuses on a client's cultural background) and the *ecomap* (a depiction of an individual or family within their social context). Client information such as the following can be diagramed:

- Age, sex, marital status, and household composition
- Family structure and relationships (e.g., biological children, stepchildren, parents)
- Job situation, employment, and responsibilities
- Social activities, interests, hobbies, recreation
- Formal associations (e.g., church involvement, membership in service club)
- Sources of support and stress in social interactions (between people and between people and community systems)
- Utilization of professional and community resources
- Informal resources, social supports, and natural helpers (e.g., extended family, relatives, friends, neighbors)

Figure 11.2 presents symbols that are commonly used in the diagrams. In addition, abbreviations and notations—such as "m" for "married," and "div" for "divorced"—can be added for clarification.

GENOGRAMS

Figure 11.3 is a **genogram** that describes a reconstituted family (encircled with a dotted boundary) made up of a man (age 45), his wife (age 33), and three children (ages 3, 1, and 10). The couple was married in 2010. The 10-year-old boy is from his mother's previous marriage; the boy's biological father died in 2008. The 45-year-old husband was divorced from his former wife (age 42) in 2006. Also, we see that he has two daughters (ages 20 and 18) by this former wife and is now a grandfather, since his 20-year-old daughter has a 1-year-old daughter. The former wife is now married to a man who is age 44. Inserting names and other notations could add even more detail. Information on the purchase of software that facilitates making genograms, as well as examples of genograms, may be found at www.genogramanalytics.com.

CULTURAL GENOGRAMS

The purpose of preparing a **cultural genogram** is to help clients better understand their identities by depicting cultural and ethnic groups and influences that shape their identity, life experiences, and family system. The diagram can assist in surfacing cultural conflicts within a family and also reveal an individual's culturally based emotions, assumptions, and stereotypes.

In addition to the mapping provided by a conventional genogram, the cultural genogram incorporates the use of shading or coloring of the person symbols to represent differing racial, ethnic, nationality, and language backgrounds and influences. Completing a cultural genogram with a client can help to flesh out a family's experience with discrimination, a history of intergroup conflict, differences in religious/spiritual perceptions, the value placed on various occupational roles, pride/shame issues, and so on. This form of genogram can also depict generation-to-generation cultural shifts and the merging of different cultures in the offspring in multicultural families.

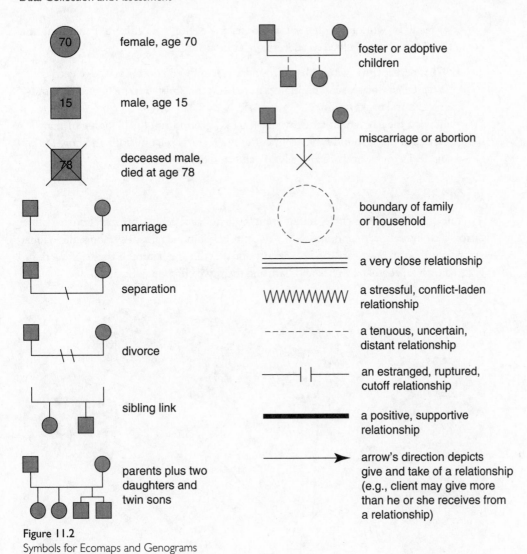

Figure 11.2
Symbols for Ecomaps and Genograms

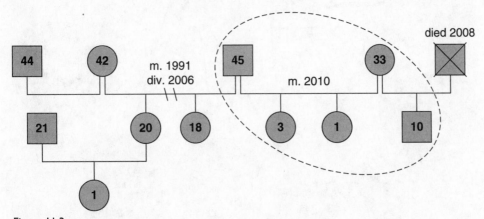

Figure 11.3
Genogram of a Reconstituted Family

As a result of working with a social worker in developing a cultural genogram, the client should have been helped to address such questions as:

- What parts of my cultural background and identity do I embrace or reject?
- What beliefs, biases, and prejudices have been transmitted to me from my family and cultural background?
- How do the examination of my cultural background and the blending of that particular background with other cultures affect my relationships and how I think and feel about who I am and what I value and believe?

ECOMAPS

Typically, an **ecomap** uses circles to represent the significant people, organizations, or other factors that interact with and impact on a client. In addition, various symbols, directional arrows, and short phrases are used to identify and describe the nature of these interactions. Figure 11.4 is an ecomap of Dick and Barb and their two children, John and June.

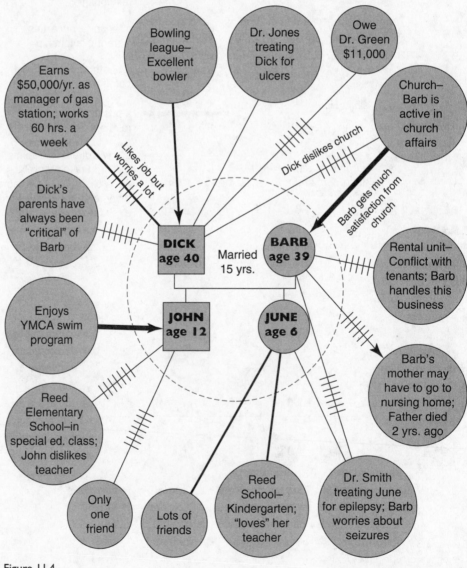

Figure 11.4
Ecomap

Ideally, the development or the drawing of a genogram or ecomap is a joint effort between the social worker and client during a face-to-face interview. The worker's use of these diagrams can help strengthen a professional relationship and demonstrate a desire to better understand the client. The process of drawing these diagrams, and clarifying and discussing the relationships and factors depicted, can help both the social worker and client better understand the client's situation. When practical, it is best for the social worker simply to guide the client in using the mapping tools to construct her or his own ecomap.

Selected Bibliography

DeMaria, Rita, Gerald Weeks, and Larry Hof. *Focused Genograms: Intergenerational Assessment of Individuals, Couples, and Families*. Philadelphia: Brunner/Mazel, 1999.

Hardy, Kenneth V., and Tracey A Laszoffy. "The Cultural Genogram." *Journal of Marital and Family Therapy, 21*, no. 3 (July 1995): 227–237.

McGoldrick, Monica, Randy Gerson, and Sueli Petry. *Genograms*, 3rd ed. New York: Norton, 2008.

McGoldrick, Monica. *The Genogram Journey*. New York: Norton, 2011.

11.5 EXPANDING A CLIENT'S VISION OF CHANGES THAT ARE POSSIBLE

Many traditional and customary approaches to assessment ask the client to provide a detailed description of his or her problem or concern. Although this may be necessary for some purposes, such as making a clinical diagnosis, these descriptions are not necessarily helpful to the process of planning or facilitating change. In fact, giving undo attention to the client's problems, dysfunction, pathology, and all that may be going wrong in a client's life and situation can cause the client to feel rather helpless and hopeless. An alternative approach, one based on the principles of solution-focused therapy (see Chapter 6), is to ask a type of question that will draw the client into viewing her or his situation from new and different angles. Three especially useful techniques—*exploring exceptions*, *scaling questions*, and *using the miracle question*—are shown here as examples.

The technique of **exploring exceptions** refers to questions intended to help the client realize that there are times or situations when the problem is less apparent, less frequent, or less intense. Even when the client feels that the problem exists "all the time" and "everywhere," it is usually possible to find exceptions. When these exceptions are identified and described, the social worker can then encourage the client to consider why these exceptions occur and help figure out what might be done to re-create or prolong these desirable times and situations. Here are examples of questioning intended to uncover and explore exceptions:

This is obviously a very serious problem. How have you managed to keep it from getting even worse?

You have said that you are in trouble with your parents most of the time. Tell me about a time in the last couple of weeks when you and your parents were getting along at least somewhat better than usual. What did you do to make that happen?

You are failing all your school courses except for history. What have you done in order to pass the history course?

Have things been even a little better since you called me to arrange this appointment? [The answer is usually yes.] If things are now a little bit better, tell me what did you do to make things better for yourself?

Are those times when things are going a little bit better usually in the morning? Afternoon? Evening? Are you alone or is someone with you? If someone is with you, what is that person saying and doing to help make things go more smoothly? During the next week and before we meet again, please notice the times when things are going better and write down what is happening each time your problem becomes less troublesome.

The technique of **scaling questions** is designed to help the client realize that the seriousness and the impact of a problem varies over time and that bringing about change is a matter of taking many small steps. The technique consists of asking a core scaling question and several follow-up questions, as in this example:

SOCIAL WORKER: On a scale of 1 to 10—with 1 being the worst your problem has ever been and 10 meaning that the problem had been solved and is no longer of concern to you—how would you rate your situation today?

CLIENT: Oh, probably about a 4 today, but it was a 2 last week.

SOCIAL WORKER: Great! I am glad to hear that things are going better. Given that improvement, I have two questions for you. First, how did you manage to change your situation from a 2 to a 4? And second, what do you think you can do in the next week to move the rating from a 4 to about a 4.5 or a 5?

Here is another scaling question intended to assess the client's motivation:

SOCIAL WORKER: We have talked about some things that you might be able to do in order to address your dilemma. On a scale of 1 to 10—with 1 meaning that you are not willing to do anything to solve the problem and 10 meaning that you are willing to try just about anything to find a solution—how hard are you willing to work on this problem?

CLIENT: Probably about a 9.

SOCIAL WORKER: Wow! That is wonderful! Tell me, why do you feel so strongly motivated today?

A third solution-focused technique, the **miracle question**, encourages the client to visualize what his or her life would be like without the current problem. The client's answers help him or her to identify more clearly what changes he or she needs to make. The miracle question is asked deliberately and rather dramatically. The wording of a miracle question would be something like this:

I am going to ask you a rather weird question. I want you to suppose or imagine that while you are sleeping tonight a genuine miracle takes place. And, as a result of this miracle, the problem that now concerns you has been completely solved. But, because you were asleep when this happened you do not know about the miracle. My question to you is, when you wake up tomorrow morning how would you know that something had changed? What specifically is different? What would tip-off others in your family that the problem had, in fact, disappeared?

The social worker will then ask various follow-up questions to help the client further describe in detail the hoped-for changes. The following examples are from a social worker who is working with a married woman:

What might your husband notice about you that would give him the idea that your problem has miraculously disappeared?

When he notices that positive change in you, what might he do differently in response to how you have changed?

When he behaves differently toward you, what will you do in response to how he is
now behaving toward you?

When you are free of this problem, how will your relationships at home and at work
be different than they are now?

As clients begin to visualize and think seriously about their everyday lives without or
in the absence of their problems, they typically come up with practical ideas about what
they can do to better cope with their problems.

Selected Bibliography

Christensen, Dana, Jeffrey Todahl, and William Barrett. *Solution-Based Casework*.
New Brunswick, NJ: Aldine Transaction, 2007.

DeJong, Peter, and Insoo Kim Berg. *Interviewing for Solutions*, 4th ed. Independence,
KY: Cengage, 2013.

Greene, Gilbert, and Mo Yee Lee. *Solution-Oriented Social Work Practice*. New York:
Oxford University Press, 2011.

**"Multi-Worker Family
Assessment Interviews"
a deleted item from
6th edition**

11.6 IDENTIFYING CLIENT STRENGTHS

An assessment of a client's functioning should always identify a client's strengths.
A **strength** can be defined as something positive and important that the client is doing,
can do, or wants to do. That "something important" may be a behavior, a way of thinking
about a situation, or even an attitude. This is not to suggest a Pollyannaish approach that
ignores or overlooks real problems, but it does ask the social worker to search for strengths
even in the most dysfunctional and chaotic of cases. The reason for this emphasis is
simple: To be successful, an intervention must be built on and around client strengths. If
the worker and client focus only on what is going wrong in the client's life, the client will
likely become even more discouraged and doubt the worker's ability to be of help.

For many in the helping professions, focusing on client strengths requires a *paradigm
shift*—a new way of thinking. It is important to recognize the forces that have encouraged
disproportionate attention on client problems and pathologies. Consider the following:

- *Agency policy and funding.* Most human services agencies are created for the purpose of addressing or correcting some personal or family problem, pathology,
deficiency, or dysfunction. Consequently, those employed by the agency may presume that they should primarily focus on a client's problems.

- *Diagnostic labels.* The frequent use of *DSM* terminology creates a negative mind-
set that produces a tendency to expect, look for, and find problems and pathology
(see Item 11.15).

- *Lack of skill.* Identifying a client's problems is an elementary skill. Most people
can do it with little or no training. On the other hand, identifying strengths is an
advanced or higher-level skill.

- *Personality and temperament.* Many people tend to see the glass as "half empty"
rather than "half full." They just naturally focus on what is missing and on what
is wrong. Some sociobiologists believe that the human ability to zero in on what
is wrong, different, and out of place has survival value for animals and the human
species. Evolution has "wired" our senses and perceptual processes to quickly
notice things that are somehow out of the ordinary because it helps us to detect
and avoid dangers in our environment.

The social worker can identify strengths by carefully observing individual and family behavior. Here are some examples of *individual strengths*:

- Assuming responsibility for one's actions
- Loyalty to and caring for family and friends
- Showing compassion, patience, generosity, and a willingness to forgive others
- Assisting and encouraging others and protecting them from harm
- Seeking employment, holding a job, being a responsible employee, meeting one's financial obligations
- Making constructive use of talents, skills, and abilities
- Exercising self-control and making thoughtful decisions and plans; choosing to avoid irresponsible or self-defeating behavior
- Taking reasonable risks in order to make needed changes
- Being trustworthy, fair, and honest in dealing with others
- Experiencing appropriate sorrow and guilt; making amends or restitution for having harmed others
- Seeking to understand and accept differences among people
- Willingness to keep trying despite hardship and setbacks
- Participating in organizations that improve one's neighborhood and community
- Standing up for one's own rights and the rights of others

Important *family strengths* include the following:

- Family members trust, respect, and enjoy each other.
- Family has traditions, rituals, and stories that provide a sense of history, belonging, and identity.
- Family has clear and reasonable rules that govern behavior and interaction.
- Family members share and make personal sacrifices in order to help each other; members stick together and support each other.
- Members listen to and respect each other's opinions, even when they disagree.
- Each member's ideas, preferences, and needs are considered before making decisions that would affect the whole family.
- Conflicts are acknowledged, negotiated, and resolved.

Strengths can be uncovered by asking questions such as:

- What would you not change about yourself, your situation, and your life?
- What advantages or benefit do others see in your approach to life?
- Despite your current problems, what parts of your life are going fairly well?
- Tell me about times when you successfully handled a serious problem?
- Where did you find the courage to keep going during this difficult time?
- What do other people like about you?

Building on client strengths may require looking at a client's problems from different perspectives. For example, consider the man who has been labeled as uncooperative and resistant. If one views this behavior from a different angle, it may reveal strengths—namely, his ability to assert himself and the courage to resist doing what does not make sense to him. In other words, when viewed from another perspective, he is being logical and assertive. When problems are reframed in this way, one can often discover more effective ways of helping or at least better ways of communicating with the client (see Item 13.10).

Another way of orienting your approach to one that recognizes and builds on client strengths is to assume that within all people, there are innate tendencies toward psychological health and prosocial behavior. Just as there are natural healing processes constantly repairing our body, there are natural forces that, over time, tend to heal and repair psychological damage, ruptured relationships, and the many other hurts that are a part of life and living. If such a belief is a reasonable one, it lends hope to the social worker's efforts and underscores the importance of creating conditions and environments that allow the client's natural healing processes to work.

The more adept a social worker becomes at identifying client strengths, the easier it becomes to build a helping relationship and formulate an individualized intervention plan that will be used by and useful to the client. These guidelines will help the worker maintain a focus on client strengths:

- Assume that the client is honest and trustworthy, unless proven otherwise. Assume that most people, most of the time, are doing the best they can, given their situation and circumstances. At the same time, assume that everyone is capable of making positive change if provided with support, encouragement, guidance, and resources.

- Assume that the client is an expert on his or her own behavior, life, and situation, and probably knows what will and will not work in a treatment plan or change effort. To the extent possible, utilize the client's understanding of his or her situation and his or her suggestions on what can be done to bring about a desired change. View the assessment and the service planning processes as a collaborative activity.

- Anticipate that somewhere within the client's family, social network, neighborhood, and community there is an oasis of potential helping resources who are willing and able to offer assistance to others.

- Avoid discussions of blame and what the client or others could have or should have done. Attempts to find and assign blame usually lead nowhere. Typically, problems of social functioning arise from a combination of many personal and situational factors, and trying to figure out the exact cause of a problem is seldom helpful in addressing the concern.

- Call to the client's attention all indicators, displays, or demonstrations of his or her strengths such as a skill, competence, motivation, or attitude. Often, clients become preoccupied with their problems and forget that they are doing some things that are positive, effective, and working.

Selected Bibliography

Corcoran, Jacqueline. *Mental Health in Social Work: A Casebook on Diagnosis and Strengths-Based Assessment*. Upper Saddle River, NJ: Pearson, 2009.

Glicken, Morley. *Using the Strengths Perspective in Social Work Practice*. Upper Saddle River, NJ: Pearson, 2004.

Jones-Smith, Elsie. *Strengths-Based Therapy*. Thousand Oaks, CA: Sage, 2013.

Saleebey, Dennis, ed. *The Strengths Perspective in Social Work Practice*, 6th ed. Upper Saddle River, NJ: Pearson, 2013.

Simmons, Catherine A., and Lehmann, Peter. *Tools for Strengths-Based Assessment and Evaluation*. New York: Springer, 2013.

11.7 ASSESSING A CLIENT'S SOCIAL SUPPORT

The term **social support** refers to assistance and caring provided by others and perceived by the person on the receiving end as desirable and beneficial. Family, friends, or neighbors are the usual sources of social support but sometimes agency employees or volunteers supply the much-needed support. It can take several forms, such as *tangible* or *concrete assistance* (e.g., a ride to a doctor appointment, a small loan, help with grocery shopping, child care); *guidance and teaching* (e.g., providing information and perspective, helping a friend make a difficult decision, teaching a skill); *care and comfort* (e.g., listening with empathy, reassurance); and *companionship* (e.g., friendship, social activity). The availability of and access to social support can be significant factors in one's physical and mental health and in one's recovery from an illness or injury.

It should be noted that social support is but one component of a person's larger **social network**, which consists of all the individuals and groups with whom the individual interacts on a regular basis. The extent or the size of a person's social network is not necessarily correlated with the availability of social supports. Some people belong to a large family and have many friends but few real social supports. By definition, social support is positive and constructive, whereas some aspects of a client's social network may be harmful, as, for example, the influence exerted by an anti-social peer group or gang.

In order to help a client make appropriate use of her or his social supports, the social worker will need to engage the client in a discussion of current and potential sources of support. A series of questions might guide this assessment process:

- What people are important to you? As you answer that question, consider the people who are in your household or family, your friends and neighbors, people at work or school, and the people who are members of the organizations or religious groups to which you belong.
- Of those you have identified as being important to you, which ones are especially supportive and helpful and a positive influence on your life? And of these individuals, which ones do you see, talk to, write to, or email on a regular basis?
- Are there individuals to whom you often turn to for advice or help in making decisions?
- Are there individuals that you would feel comfortable asking for a ride to work, a ride to the grocery store, or for a small loan?
- Who among those in your network of relatives and friends knows about and understands your situation?
- Do you have individuals in your life that you really trust and could turn to for help or advice concerning a personal problem?
- Who is the one person you can always count on for help, no matter what the circumstances?

After a client has identified individuals who are potential social supports, the worker guides the client in an examination of whether and how the client might reach out to them and enlist their assistance. Whether these individuals actually provide assistance will depend on the client's willingness to ask for and use their help. For some clients, an assessment of social supports can be beneficial even if they never utilize these potential resources. Just knowing that help is available provides reassurance and a sense of being valued and cared for.

Selected Bibliography

Carroll, David W. *Families of Children with Developmental Disabilities: Understanding Stress and Opportunities for Growth.* Washington, DC: American Psychological Association, 2013.

Kemp, Susan, James Whittaker, and Elizabeth Tracy. *Person-Environment Practice.* New York: Aldine de Gruyter, 1997.

Roy, Ranjan. *Social Support, Health, and Illness: A Complicated Relationship.* Toronto, Canada: University of Toronto, 2011.

Schleker, Markus, and Friederike Fleischer, eds. *Ethnographies of Social Support.* New York: Palgrave Macmillan, 2013.

11.8 ASSESSING A CLIENT'S COPING STRATEGIES AND EGO DEFENSES

During the assessment phase, it is often necessary to identify a client's usual ego defenses and methods of coping in order to anticipate how the client will react to an effort to bring about needed change. Some professionals use the terms *coping strategy* and *defense mechanism* interchangeably, but there is a distinction based on the degree to which the response is under conscious and voluntary control and whether self-deception and reality distortion are involved. Thus, we define a **coping strategy** as a deliberate and conscious effort to solve a problem or handle personal distress. By contrast, an **ego defense** is a habitual or unconscious and problem-avoiding maneuver.

Coping strategies have two functions: to solve a problem (*task-focused coping*) and to reduce emotional discomfort (*emotion-focused coping*). These two functions may be in play concurrently. In some very troubling situations, an individual will first need to manage his or her emotional reactions before engaging in effective problem solving.

Individuals vary widely in their emotion-focused coping strategies. For example, given a troublesome situation, some people might elect to go off by themselves, others might visit friends, some perhaps will pray and meditate, and still others might engage in a vigorous physical workout. Other coping strategies—some functional and some not— include ignoring the problem, sleeping more, eating more, and immersion in work. Since an individual will tend to use certain strategies habitually, the social worker can gain a fairly accurate picture of which ones a client uses by asking how he or she responded to or dealt with other disturbing situations.

Regardless of their culture, people react to shocking events and intense distress by using certain **emotion-focused coping strategies**:

- *Crying.* This is a common means of alleviating tension and a common reaction to loss. Crying is a necessary part of successful grief work.
- *Talking it out.* People who have undergone traumatic experiences often need to repeatedly describe and talk about the experience. Over time, this natural desensitization process lessens the intensity of the emotions associated with the traumatic experience.
- *Laughing it off.* Joking and viewing a painful experience with a sense of humor may release tension and put the matter in perspective. In healthy grieving, for example, there is often a good mix of crying and laughter among those adjusting to the death of a loved one.
- *Seeking social support.* It is natural for both children and adults to seek reassurance and comfort from others as a means of regaining a sense of security and emotional equilibrium.

- *Dreaming and nightmares.* These do not fit the earlier definition of a coping strategy (i.e., conscious and voluntary) but they are a common reaction to a traumatic experience. Recurring dreams appear to have the benefit of drawing the individual into consciously grappling with the experience.

If the client is not struggling with intense emotion, the social worker will be mostly focused on helping the client identify and utilize **task-focused coping strategies**. These deliberate choices and actions are likely to bring about changes in his or her functioning, environment, or both. To judge if a client has good task-oriented coping skills and the motivation, capacity, and opportunity to make significant changes, the social worker should determine if the client is able to:

- Ask questions and gather needed information, even when the information may challenge his or her current assumptions and beliefs.
- Recognize that he or she has choices and can, with effort, modify one's behavior and situation.
- Cut any losses and withdraw from relationships or situations that are unhealthy, stressful, and unchangeable.
- Examine the spiritual and religious dimension of life and draw on his or her core beliefs for insight, strength, and direction.
- Identify early indicators of a developing problem so corrective action can be taken before the problem becomes serious.
- Take steps to solve problems, even when such actions are a source of fear and anxiety.
- Release pent-up emotion in ways that do not harm self or others.
- Delay immediate gratification in order to stick with a plan that will attain a desired but more distant goal.
- Use visualizations of future actions or events to mentally rehearse how to handle anticipated difficulties.
- Seek out and use additional skills training and needed professional services.

If the assessment reveals that a client lacks necessary coping abilities, the intervention plan should focus on helping the client learn the needed skills. For example, an abusing parent may need to learn parenting skills, an individual in need of a job will need to focus on job-finding skills, a married couple in conflict may need communication skills, and a youth leaving the foster-care system will need to acquire independent living skills.

A **defense mechanism** is usually defined as a mostly unconscious psychological process that protects the individual against an emotional pain or threat. Everyone uses these mechanisms to some degree when coping with the ordinary problems and stresses of living. However, the excessive or rigid use of defense mechanisms is problematic because they can get in the way of realistic problem solving. Extreme defensiveness and distortions of reality are characteristics of a mental disorder.

An individual who uses the ego defense of *denial* screens out and will not believe or accept some unpleasant and unwanted reality. Some degree of denial is an almost universal response when a person is first told of the unexpected death of a loved one. The ego defense of *rationalization* involves offering arguments that justify one's inappropriate behavior. Behaviors that suggest a rationalization include (1) groping for reasons to justify a behavior or belief, (2) the inability to recognize inconsistencies in one's "story," and (3) an unwillingness to consider alternative explanations and becoming angry when one's reasoning is questioned. Although a rationalization is a distortion of the truth, it is not the same as a lie because its use is usually a matter of unconscious habit and the person is not deliberately trying to fabricate a falsehood. Denial and rationalization are predominant defenses used by people who are addicted to drugs or alcohol.

The defense mechanism of *projection* is in play when one attributes to others one's own unacceptable thoughts or behavior. For example, an individual who has molested a young child may convince himself that he was seduced by the child and is therefore the victim rather than the offender.

The defense of *intellectualization* involves the use of abstractions and ideas as a means of separating oneself emotionally from a troubling situation. For example, the individual who was turned down for a sought-after job may cope with feelings of rejection and disappointment by explaining the inability to get the job as caused by free-trade economics and changing global markets.

Emotional insulation is a maneuver aimed at withholding one's attachment to or investment in a desired but unlikely outcome. It creates a shield that protects the individual from a recurrence of emotional pain. For example, a child who is moved frequently from foster home to foster home may withhold all attachment to the newest foster parents as a defense against experiencing yet another painful separation and loss. Unfortunately, such a child often carries this pattern into adulthood and is then unable to form an emotional bond to a marriage partner or to his or her own children. This defense is closely related to the concept of *learned helplessness*—after a long period of frustration, some individuals may simply give up and quit trying to escape their misery. These are the "broken" individuals who become passive recipients of whatever life brings them. Emotional insulation is commonly observed in persons who have grown up in extreme deprivation.

The person using *fantasy* as a defense spends much time daydreaming and dwells on imaginary situations, either as a way of meeting emotional needs or as a protection against, for example, feelings of loneliness or inadequacy. Serious problems develop when the person prefers fantasy over reality. The inability to distinguish between fantasy and reality is a symptom of serious mental illness.

The defense of *repression* unconsciously excludes an extremely threatening experience from one's awareness. For example, a child may repress the experience of having been sexually abused and not remember this event until years later.

Regression is a retreat from one's present level of maturity and its responsibilities to one that has fewer demands. For example, when a new child is born to a family, the 5-year-old may begin behaving like an infant (e.g., refusing to feed himself, sucking her thumb) as a way of getting more attention and dealing with the fear of being overlooked by his or her parents. Some degree of regression is fairly common among persons who are seriously ill and experiencing much pain and distress.

When using *reaction formation,* a person adopts behaviors that are the opposite of his or her real but unacceptable desires. An example is an individual who comes to realize that he is sexually attracted to children and, in response, works tirelessly to create programs designed to prevent child sexual abuse.

Displacement refers to transferring troublesome emotions (often hostility) and acting-out behaviors (e.g., violence) from the person who arouses the emotion to a less threatening and less powerful person or thing. The classic example is the man who kicks his dog because he is angry with his boss.

Acting out is an attempt to cope with frustration or inner turmoil by taking action, often impulsively, or by striking out physically. For example, a frustrated adolescent girl who is unable to verbally express her feelings may seek a release from this tension by attacking the person she views as the source of her problems. Soldiers in combat who can no longer tolerate the stress and fear of waiting to be attacked have been known to leave the relative safety of their foxhole and blindly charge the enemy.

Several guidelines will assist the social worker in assessing and responding to a client's defense mechanisms:

- When using defense mechanism terminology, certain precautions are necessary. The patterns that we call ego defenses are hypothetical constructs inferred from the way people behave. At best, they are a shorthand language for describing people's behavior and inner struggles. Simply labeling a client's behavior as projection or rationalization, for example, in no way changes or even explains the behavior. You must look behind the surface behavior to identify the need or pain that cause the client to rely on the defense mechanism.

- Because defenses are mostly learned and habitual, an individual tends to repeat those defenses she or he has used in the past. For example, if an individual has a history of frequently using denial and rationalization, you can expect her or him to use those same defenses when again faced with anxiety or conflict.

- People hold tightly to their defensive patterns. The more anxiety or insecurity they experience, the more rigidly they use the defense. It is usually only within a relationship characterized by empathy, warmth, and genuineness that a person can feel safe enough to let down his or her defenses and examine the underlying pain.

Selected Bibliography

Beresford, Thomas. *Psychological Adaptive Mechanisms: Ego Defense Recognition in Practice and Research*. New York: Oxford University Press, 2012.

Blackman, Jerome. *101 Defenses: How the Mind Shields Itself*. New York: Routledge, 2003.

Cramer, Phebe. *Protecting the Self: Defense Mechanisms in Action*. New York: Guilford, 2006.

11.9 ASSESSING A CLIENT'S ROLE PERFORMANCE

As explained in Item 11.1, the social work profession primarily focuses on the social functioning of people. To assess a client's social functioning, one must understand the concept and dynamics of social role. The notion of **social role** derives from the observation that certain behaviors, attitudes, and norms are expected of a person when he or she has been assigned a certain status or occupies a certain position in society. For example, once a person becomes a parent (a social role), she or he is expected to provide his or her young children with food, shelter, protection, guidance, and so on. Within a school setting, the teacher (a social role) is expected to provide instruction, and the student (another social role) is expected to study, learn, and adhere to school rules. The term *role* is borrowed from the world of theater. In a play there is an actor, a script that dictates the actor's role, and the audience that experiences and judges the actor's performance. In real life and within social work's concept of social functioning, there is a person (e.g., the client), the person's role, and those who observe and evaluate the person's role performance (e.g., the person's family, community, and society). Because the idea of role and concepts of role theory bridge both psychological and social perspectives on human behavior, they are helpful in assessing and describing a client's functioning. At a fundamental level, the purpose of most social agencies and social programs is to enhance or improve people's performance of their social roles such as those of parent, spouse, employee, student, neighbor, and citizen.

The concept of **role expectation** suggests that for a given role, there is a cluster of behaviors that are deemed appropriate and acceptable by a reference group or by society as a whole. In other words, the reference group (e.g., peer group, a community, religion, organization) expects the individual to behave in a certain way and will either approve or disapprove of the person, depending on whether he or she conforms to those expectations. Role expectations define the boundaries of acceptable and tolerated behavior.

The term **role conception** refers to an individual's beliefs and assumptions about how he or she is supposed to behave when in a particular role. An individual's role conception may or may not conform to the role expectations, as defined by a community or the wider society.

An individual's actual behavior while performing a role is termed his or her **role performance** (or *role enactment*). In some instances, a person's role performance may be consistent with his or her role conception but not conform to other people's role expectations. For example, a father may be living up to his own beliefs about parenthood, but his behavior may be judged to be child neglect by the community or the court system. In order to successfully perform a given role, an individual must possess certain knowledge, values, attitudes, and skills. These prerequisite abilities are often termed **role demands** (or *role requirements*).

A number of terms are used to describe problems in role performance. **Interrole conflict** refers to an incompatibility or clash between two or more roles. For example, a woman may experience a conflict between her role as the parent to a young child and her role as a corporate executive who is expected to frequently travel and work long hours. **Intrarole conflict** exists when a person is caught up in a situation where two or more sets of expectations are assigned to a single role. For example, a high school student may not be able to reconcile the role of student as defined by his teacher with how being a student is defined by his friends who prefer parties to homework. The problem of **role incapacity** exists when an individual lacks the capacity to perform a certain role; possible reasons include physical or mental illness, lack of the prerequisite skills, drug addiction, mental retardation, and so on. **Role rejection** occurs when an individual refuses to perform a role; an extreme example is when a parent abandons his or her child.

A problem of **role ambiguity** (or *role confusion*) exists when there are few clear expectations associated with a role—a condition most likely to occur in times of rapid societal change. Consequently, the individual is unsure of what is expected and is unable to evaluate his or her own performance. **Self-role incongruence** exists when there is a poor match between the requirements of a role (i.e., role demands) and the individual's personality or self-concept. For example, a person may occupy the role of trial lawyer but not feel comfortable in that role because she or he is, by temperament, rather submissive and passive. Another example is when a person discovers that his or her values, ethics, or lifestyle are at odds with the expectations of a role.

The problem of **role overload** exists when a person occupies more roles than he or she is able to perform adequately. In reality, most people are unable to meet, or choose not to meet, all of the expectations associated with their various roles in life. Thus, most people live with some degree of **role strain**, a situation that necessitates making compromises and trade-offs, setting priorities, and using various coping strategies to reconcile their role conceptions with their limited time and energy.

A number of questions can help the social worker analyze problems of role performance and make decisions concerning the type of intervention needed:

- *What is the nature and degree of discrepancy between the client's actual role performance and role expectation?*
  - How does the client's behavior differ from that considered appropriate or normal for this particular role?
  - What observations, events, or experiences have caused you, the client, or others to conclude that a discrepancy exists?
  - Why are you or the client concerned about or troubled by the client's role performance? Is this role important? What might happen if there is no change in the client's role performance?

- *Is the discrepancy caused by a lack of knowledge, skill, or motivation?*
  - Does the client possess the knowledge or skill needed to perform this role?
  - Could the client satisfactorily perform this role if he or she wanted to?

- *If the discrepancy between performance and expectation is caused by a lack of knowledge and skill, how might this limitation be addressed?*
  - Was there a time when the client could perform this role? If so, what has caused the client to lose this capacity or motivation?
  - Is the client able to learn the prerequisite knowledge and skills?
  - What teaching methods or techniques will help the client acquire the knowledge and skills needed to perform this role?

- *If the discrepancy is caused by a rejection or a lack of interest in this role, how can that be addressed?*
  - Does this role really matter to the client?
  - What roles or activities does the client consider more important?
  - Does the client see any benefits in performing this role?
  - Is the client rewarded or reinforced for performing this role? If not, how can incentives be increased?
  - Is the client being punished by others or by social systems for performing this role? Can this punishment be avoided?

Selected Bibliography

Kimberley, Dennis, and Louise Osmond. "Role Theory and Concepts Applied to Personal and Social Change in Social Work Treatment." In *Social Work Treatment*, 5th ed., edited by Francis Turner. New York: Oxford University Press, 2011.

11.10 ASSESSING A CLIENT'S SELF-CONCEPT

The term **self** refers to that private and inner world of assumptions, perceptions, and thoughts about the "I" or the "me." The self is the center of consciousness, thought, and action. One's sense of self answers the questions: Who am I? What am I really like, regardless of what others may think of me? The term **self-concept** refers to a set of beliefs and images that a person has about himself or herself. These beliefs may or may not be shared by others. Moreover, our self-concept will vary somewhat in response to differing situations, circumstances, and how well we are performing certain roles and tasks. Although the foundation of our self-concept is formed during childhood, experiences throughout life can lead us to modify what we think of ourselves. Self-concept is of critical importance to our social functioning because how we respond to others and to life events and how we perform our social roles is influenced by how we think and feel about ourselves.

Several other concepts help to describe aspects of the self. **Self-identity** is how we define and describe ourselves to ourselves and differentiate ourselves from other people. What we think about ourselves may, of course, be different from the image we try to present or project to other people. Thus, we have a private self and a public self.

Self-worth (or *self-esteem*) refers to our evaluation of our own value as a human being. Self-worth is a highly subjective evaluation. The term **ideal-self** (or *self-expectation*) refers to our deeply personal thoughts about who we could be, should be, or want to be. **Body image** refers to our perceptions and evaluations of our own body and physical appearance. The term **self-acceptance** can be thought of as the degree to which we are satisfied and at peace with what we see as our qualities and attributes, our strengths and limitations. **Self-efficacy** has to do with the beliefs we have about our effectiveness and competence as a human being.

Whether a particular facet of a client's self-concept needs to be discussed during the assessment process depends on the client's presenting concern and the reasons the client and professional are meeting. Some clients are reluctant to share such personal information, whereas others are eager to tell their stories and share innermost thoughts about themselves. To draw out this type of information, the social worker can ask questions that are organized around five common themes in life: love, loss, fear, having been hurt, and having hurt others. Many clients will respond nondefensively to questions like these:

- *Who and what do you really love?* Who and what are of greatest importance to you? For whom do you make personal sacrifices? For what causes do you donate your time and money? Are you, perhaps, unable to care for or love someone, as you would like?

- *Who and what have you lost?* Have you lost parents, children, siblings, and close friends to separation, estrangement, disability, or death? Have you lost purpose and meaning in life or lost your hopes and dreams? Have you lost some physical or mental ability as a result of age, illness, or injury? Have you lost your sense of security and safety as a result of abuse, exploitation, violence, or war? Have you lost contact with your homeland or native language? Have you lost touch with meaningful religious and cultural activity? Have you lost a home or possessions to a fire, flood, or other natural disaster?

- *Who and what do you fear?* Do you live with a fear of hunger, violence, illness, pain, disability, or death? Do you fear that no one really cares for you? Do you fear the loss of respect and status? Do you fear the loss of important relationships, a job, money, or a home?

- *How have you been hurt in life?* How have you been hurt by family and friends (physically, emotionally, financially, etc.)? How do you explain these painful experiences? Have these past hurts given rise to fears of being hurt again or a desire for revenge? How have these painful experiences affected the way you feel about yourself and others?

- *Whom have you hurt?* How and when have you hurt others, either deliberately or unintentionally? How do you explain these experiences? Have those experiences altered the way you feel about yourself? Have you attempted to make amends or restitution for the pain and injury you have caused?

Next are some additional lines of questioning that might be used, in one form or another, to explore a client's sense of self:

- *Family membership.* Who is your family (tribe or clan)? For whom do you feel responsible and obligated to care for, help, or look after? How often do you talk with family members? To which family members do you feel especially close or, perhaps, distant and estranged? Are you comfortable in this family or yours?

- *Identity.* How do you define yourself in terms of the various labels and categories commonly used to describe people, such as, for example: Gender? Marital status? Occupation? Nationality? Ethnicity? Sexual orientation? Religion? Socioeconomic class? Political orientation?

- *Body image.* Are you content with your body and appearance? What do you notice most about your body? What do you think others see when they look at your body?

- *Self-acceptance.* Are you comfortable with your truthful answer to the question: Who am I? Do you enjoy being alone with yourself? When by yourself, are you content or distressed with your inner most thoughts and feelings? Are you at ease or tense when around the people who know you very well? In what ways are you unique? What if anything, would you change about yourself?

- *Self-worth.* What are your strengths, talents, and abilities? What criteria or standards do you use when you judge the worth or importance of another person? How do you measure up on those same criteria? What, if anything, causes you to think you are less valuable or less important than others?

- *Ideal-self.* To what degree are you doing or accomplishing what you expect of yourself? How do you define success? In what areas of life are you successful? In what areas are you falling short of your expectations? What do you want to accomplish or achieve in your lifetime? What special contributions do you want to make to others, your family, or your community? How do you want to be remembered after you die?

- *Self-efficacy.* Do you feel that you are in control of your life? Which has more influence on your life: the decisions that you make or the decisions that other people make? Are you hopeful or pessimistic about your future? Do you usually respond to change with anticipation and enthusiasm or with apprehension and fear?

- *Spirituality.* What experiences or deeply held beliefs provide meaning, purpose, and direction in life? How do you make sense out of the pain, suffering, and disappointments that you and others experience in life? Do you have certain spiritual or religious beliefs, or particular moral standards that I should know about in order to better understand your concerns?

- *Past self and future self.* Do you think you are similar to or different from the person you were five years ago? Ten years ago? Do you have regrets or guilt feelings about the past? Do you expect that you and your life situation will be different in five years? If you expect it to change, will this be a desirable or an undesirable change?

- *Sense of place.* In what physical environment are you most comfortable, content, and happy? Are you satisfied living in your neighborhood or community? Is there another place where you want to live? Where? Why?

Selected Bibliography

Bracken, Bruce, ed. *Handbook of Self-Concept*. Hoboken, NJ: Wiley, 1996.

Elson, Miriam. *Self Psychology in Clinical Social Work*. New York: Norton, 1986.

Mallory, Hershel. *Concept of the Self: Implications of Social Work*. Rochester: New York: MOBIZ Publishers, 2003.

11.11 ASSESSING A CLIENT'S NEEDED LEVEL OF CARE

When serving older people with declining abilities, or other persons with serious illnesses or physical or mental disabilities, social workers often assist them and their families to obtain the care that is needed. Care can range from as much as 24-hour nursing home care to as little as a periodic in-home visit and monitoring by a family member or neighbor.

Prior to helping to arrange for an appropriate level of care and securing the resources to support that service, the social worker must gather relevant information and make a judgment about what type of care is needed. Ideally, decisions related to the level of care needed by an individual are made with input from the client, his or her family, and an interdisciplinary team that includes physicians, nurses, occupational therapists, mental health specialists, and the social worker.

Although many factors should be considered in recommending a level of care, the two most basic guidelines are (1) placement in the least restrictive environment appropriate for the client and (2) maximum preservation of the client's self-determination and dignity. Unfortunately, in a great many cases what the client wants (usually to stay in her or his own home) is not what the client really needs in terms of care, supervision, and safety. Placement recommendations require assessment of the client's physical and mental condition, the capacity of her or his family/social support system, the availability of in-home supportive services provided by community agencies, and the options and costs of the several levels of institutional care resources. For many individuals and families, the cost of care is a major consideration.

All too often these decisions have to be made during a family crisis or emergency and for this reason it is important for the social worker to be prepared well before the crisis arises with the knowledge needed to match the client with the most appropriate available resource. When making such a match, the following factors should be considered.

- *The client's physical condition and home environment.* Personal/environmental physical considerations, such as self-reliance for grooming, hygiene, dressing, toileting, special dietary needs, mobility and exercise ability, medication requirements, projection for ongoing treatment needs, safety of home environment, and housecleaning and home maintenance ability figure into this decision.

- *The client's psychological and intellectual status.* Psychological/intellectual considerations, including reasoning and problem solving, ability, judgment, memory, capacity for communication, worry and anxiety, depression, drug/alcohol dependence, ability to manage finances, and cultural events should be considered.

- *Family/Social support.* Consider the interest and ability of family members, neighbors, or volunteers to provide needed support (e.g., food preparation, personal health/hygiene care, transportation, social interaction).

- *Community support resources.* Communities vary in the in-home services clients might access, but most communities include the following services: case management, homemaker service, home health care or nursing, meal delivery, congregate dining, grocery and other shopping services, transportation, senior companions, adult day care, and so on.

- *The institutional care resources.* Three distinct levels of institutional care typically exist in a community.

  1. *Independent living* involves a residence—usually an apartment—that is part of a larger facility where meals, housekeeping assistance, transportation to appointments and events, a degree of monitoring and supervision, and various recreational and social activities are provided.

  2. A move up in the levels of care is *assisted living,* where the facility and services are more institutional, except the person would have his or her own space and some personal possessions and perhaps furnishings. Staff assistance is immediately available when needed to help with such tasks as dressing, bathing, toileting, getting in and out of bed, and the monitoring of medications. Assisted living provides a safe and secure environment with regular meals and supervision.

  3. *Nursing home care* is designed for persons with severe physical and mental limitations that require 24-hour attention from the facility's staff. Nursing homes are hospital-like and designed to serve a fairly large number of individuals, either as a permanent residence for people who are too frail or sick to live at home or other institutional facilities, or are in need of a temporary facility during a recovery or rehabilitation period.

The judgments involved in matching an appropriate level of care to a particular client is especially complex because of the wide variation in client needs and abilities and the often significant differences in locally available resources. In addition, there can be state-by-state variations in the licensing requirements and standards for the various facilities and in the Medicaid program, a resource utilized by many who are in long-term care. The social worker, then, must draw primarily on information derived from a careful assessment and his or her experience to craft the most appropriate plan for a client.

Selected Bibliography

Altilio, Terry, and Shirley Otis-Green, eds. *Oxford Textbook of Palliative Care: Care Skills and Clinical Competencies,* 2nd ed. New York: Oxford University Press, 2011.

Emanual, Linda L., and S. Lawrence Librach, eds. *Palliative Care: Care Skills and Clinical Competencies,* 2nd ed. St Louis: Elseiver/Saunders, 2011.

Greene, Roberta R. *Social Work with the Aged and Their Families,* 3rd ed. New Brunswick, NJ: Transaction Publishers, 2008.

Miller, Edward A., S. M. Allen, and V. Mor. "Navigating the Labyrinth of Long-Term Care: Shoring-Up Informal Caregiving in a Home-Community-Based World." *Journal of Aging & Social Policy,* 21 (2009): 1–16.

Richardson, Virginia E., and Amanda Smith Barusch. *Gerontological Practice for the 21st Century: A Social Work Perspective.* New York: Columbia University Press, 2006.

11.12 USING QUESTIONNAIRES, CHECKLISTS, AND VIGNETTES

When meeting with a social worker, some clients find it difficult to describe their problems or concerns, either because they feel confused or embarrassed or because they have trouble articulating their thoughts and feelings. In such a situation, certain types of data-gathering tools can prove useful. These tools are also used when an agency needs to collect a set of data from all clients in an efficient manner.

The data-collection tool known as a **problem checklist** is designed to help the client identify his or her concerns. It is essentially a list of the problems and concerns commonly reported by the clients served by a particular agency. A client having difficulty articulating his or her concerns is presented with the problem checklist and asked to identify those statements that come close to describing his or her own concerns.

Consider, for example, the case of a 15-year-old girl who has just given birth to a baby in a hospital and will be dismissed in one day. In such a situation, the hospital social worker would like to meet with this young mother, do a quick assessment, and, if appropriate, refer her to relevant community resources. The worker's goal is challenging because there is so little time to build a relationship. Figure 11.5 is a checklist that could

---

Concerns of Young Mothers: A Checklist

The birth of a baby is a time of happiness and joy. But along with the good feelings are concerns about the changes in lifestyle and responsibility that lie ahead. A new mother often feels uncertain and a bit scared about the responsibility of caring for a baby. If we know about your concerns, we may be able to help you find ways to address them.

Directions: Below is a list of worries and concerns that have been expressed by other new mothers who have had babies in this hospital. Please read through this list and place a check (✓) by all statements that are similar to the concerns you now have. Your responses will be held in strict confidence.

1. _____ Have worries about paying hospital and doctor bills.
2. _____ Have worries about my baby's health and physical condition.
3. _____ Have worries about my own health and physical condition.
4. _____ Uncertain about how to feed and care for an infant.
5. _____ Uncertain where to turn when I have questions about child care.
6. _____ Afraid I may become pregnant before I am ready to have another child.
7. _____ Worried about not having enough money to care for my baby.
8. _____ Concerned about whether I can finish school.
9. _____ Worried about getting or keeping a job when I have a baby to care for.
10. _____ Concerned when I feel resentment or anger toward my baby.
11. _____ Worried about the effects of drugs or alcohol on me and my baby.
12. _____ Worried that my friends will not accept me and my baby.
13. _____ Worried about my relationship with my baby's father.
14. _____ Concerned that I do not feel love toward my baby.
15. _____ Feeling sad and depressed about my situation.
16. _____ Worried that I will be a burden to my own parents.
17. _____ Worried about living alone with my baby.
18. _____ Concerned that my own parents and family will not accept me and my baby.
19. _____ Afraid I am going to lose my independence and freedom.
20. _____ Please describe or list any other concerns not covered by the checklist:

_____

Now, look over all of those items you have checked and draw a circle around the one or two that seem most important. Please feel free to discuss these concerns with a hospital social worker.

Figure 11.5
Sample Problem Checklist

be used with this young mother. In addition to helping her state her concerns, it focuses the communication so that she and the worker can make the best possible use of their very limited time together.

Not infrequently, clients are unaware of the services that can be offered by the social worker. If a worker and a client together examine the items on a problem checklist, the client begins to understand how the worker or agency might be of assistance. In this sense, the checklist can serve as an educational tool. If a client is easily distracted, the checklist can help to structure an interview. In some situations a client could be asked to study the problem checklist as homework prior to the next session (see Item 13.15).

A simple **questionnaire** is another useful tool for gathering information from clients. Figure 11.6 is a questionnaire developed to help clients identify those aspects of their marriage relationship that are satisfactory and those that are troublesome. Because the questionnaire is simple and brief, clients can complete it in only a few minutes. By substituting a different set of items or questions, the basic format illustrated in this example can be easily modified for use with clients with other types of problems.

In some practice situations, the worker needs a type of information that is not easily elicited by direct questions, whether verbal or written. Consider, for example, a child welfare worker faced with the task of deciding whether an individual should be licensed as a foster parent. Among other things, that worker needs to learn about the person's true beliefs and attitudes about discipline. Of course, the worker could ask direct questions such as "Do you believe in spanking a child who misbehaves?" But such a question will likely elicit the answer that the individual thinks the worker wants to hear and not reveal much about underlying attitudes that are so central to parenting.

An alternative to direct questioning is for the worker to prepare a set of vignettes and use them as springboards for discussion and exploration. Basically, a **vignette** is a brief story to which the client is asked to respond. Thus, this technique is an indirect or a projective method of questioning. Figure 11.7 presents two vignettes written for use in the foster home-study process. Needless to say, the social worker using this tool must create vignettes that will engage the client and elicit the type of information needed in the assessment process.

In general, social workers underutilize data-gathering tools such as those just described. However, these tools are useful in many practice situations and not difficult to create. Here are some guidelines that will assist in their preparation:

- As you consider the construction of a data-gathering tool, be clear about its intended purpose, the type of information you seek, and the clients and situation for whom it is being prepared. Rather than developing a single all-purpose tool, it is much better to design several, each with a specific purpose or client group in mind.

- A brief questionnaire is more likely to be accurately completed than a long one. The wording used should be clear and concise and free of jargon, bias, and offensive language. The words should be ones that the client can easily understand. In general, the higher the client's level of education and motivation, the more likely she or he is to deal successfully with a paper-and-pencil, data-gathering tool. Remember, many people lack the basic skills of reading and writing.

- Writing items to be included in a data-gathering tool requires knowledge of possible and probable responses by clients. For example, if a question asks the client to select an answer from a list of five possible answers, the questionnaire designer

Questionnaire on the Husband-Wife Relationship

Explanation: Below are questions about how satisfied you are with what goes on between you and your spouse. Your answers will help us understand and clarify your concerns. To the right of each statement, place a check (✓) to indicate if you are mostly satisfied, or mostly dissatisfied, or perhaps unsure and confused about this aspect of your marriage relationship. If a statement does not apply to your situation, write NA next to the statement.

	Mostly Satisfied	Mostly Dissatisfied	Unsure or Confused
The way we make decisions			
The way we divide up responsibility for child care			
The way we handle and budget money			
The way we divide up housework			
The way we talk to the children			
The amount of money we earn			
The way we resolve conflict			
The way we discipline our children			
The way we get along with in-laws			
The way we use our free time			
The way we talk to each other			
The way we care for our home			
The amount of time we have together			
The way we help and encourage each other			
The amount of privacy we have			
The way alcohol or drugs affect our relationship			
The way we handle birth control			
The sexual part of our relationship			
The way we plan for our future			
The way we get along with the neighbors			
The way we deal with moral or religious concerns			
The way we handle anger and frustration			

Please list here any other concerns you may have about your relationship:

What do you consider to be the major strengths in your marriage?

What do you consider to be the one or two major problems in your marriage?

Figure 11.6
Sample Questionnaire

The Peterson Family: A Situation to Discuss

The Petersons have been foster parents to 15-year-old Sharon for about six years. Religion is very important to Mr. and Mrs. Peterson. They attend church services and participate in several church-related activities on a regular basis. Until about two months ago, Sharon also attended the Petersons' church even though she had been raised in another religious denomination. Sharon now refuses to attend church and tells her foster parents that religion is a bunch of superstition and foolishness. The Petersons are worried and upset by Sharon's attitude because religion is so central to their life and family.

1. What could have caused this situation?
2. How should the Petersons respond to Sharon?

The Allen Family: A Situation to Discuss

Mr. and Mrs. Allen have three children. In order to celebrate Mrs. Allen's birthday, the whole family goes to a restaurant. During the meal, 6-year-old Jimmy throws a tantrum—he cries and throws food at his parents. Others in the restaurant stare at the Allens and obviously disapprove of what they are seeing.

1. What is your evaluation of Jimmy's behavior?
2. How should the parents respond to Jimmy?

Figure 11.7
Sample Vignettes

must know beforehand the answers most likely to be given by clients. When it is difficult to anticipate the range of probable client answers, it will be necessary to ask an open-ended question to which the client writes out his or her answer. However, open-ended questions should be used sparingly because the written responses they garner are often difficult to read and understand. A questionnaire containing numerous open-ended questions offers few advantages over the ordinary verbal questioning during a face-to-face interview.

- Each question or statement should focus on a single idea and should in no way lead or point the client toward a particular answer. When possible, the wording of each question in a series of questions should follow a similar format because this helps the reader move easily from question to question and minimizes the chances that she or he will misinterpret a question.

- A sequence of questions should follow a logical and unfolding order and should usually begin with the general questions and end with the more specific ones. Questions that will be easiest for the client to answer should usually appear at the beginning of a series, whereas the most personal or probing questions should appear toward the end.

- A pretest should be used to determine if clients will understand the wording and questions, whether clients can complete the questionnaire in a reasonable time, and whether the data collected in this way are indeed useful to practitioners.

- To translate a questionnaire into another language, follow the *translate/retranslate procedure*. Once the questionnaire is in satisfactory form in the original language, someone who speaks both languages translates it into the second language. Another person who speaks both languages then translates the questionnaire back into the first language. By comparing the two versions in the original language, the social worker can readily identify any variations in meaning that may occur because of language differences and adjust the questionnaire to avoid those contradictions.

Selected Bibliography

Abell, Neil. *Developing and Validating Rapid Assessment Instruments*. New York: Oxford University Press, 2009.

Horejsi, Charles. *Assessment and Case Planning in Child Protection and Foster Care Services*. Englewood, CO: American Humane Association, 1996.

Millon, Theodore, and Caryl Bloom. *The Millon Inventories: A Practitioner's Guide to Personalized Clinical Assessment*, 2nd ed. New York: Guilford, 2008.

11.13 IDENTIFYING DEVELOPMENTAL DELAYS IN YOUNG CHILDREN

Social workers who have frequent contact with families are often in a strategic position to observe preschool-age children and conduct a cursory assessment of a child's physical and mental development. Children who are malnourished or chronically ill, many who are abused and neglected, and those who have mental retardation or sensory or neurological problems will fall behind developmental norms. However, there can be considerable variation in the growth and development of normal children. Moreover, for a given age, it is not unusual to find some unevenness across the various domains of development as, for example, the child who is early to walk but slow to talk.

Figure 11.8 lists a number of markers for the first five years of life that can be used to judge a child's developmental progress. If it appears that a child cannot perform the motor, mental, language, and social skills and tasks expected at a given age, the child should be referred to a specialist for an in-depth evaluation. An early diagnosis and intervention can limit the negative impact of a developmental problem.

Here are some early warning signs of *sensory problems* and developmental delays in a young child:

Indicators of Hearing Problems

- Exhibits delays in speech and language development
- Does not turn toward source of strange sounds or voices by 6 months of age
- Has frequent earaches or runny ears
- Talks in a very loud or very soft voice
- Does not respond when you call from another room
- Turns the same ear toward a sound he or she wants to hear

Indicators of Delays in Speech Development

- Does not say "Mama" and "Dada" by age 1
- Does not say the names of a few toys and people by age 2
- Cannot repeat common rhymes or jingles by age 3
- Does not talk in sentences by age 4
- Cannot be understood by people outside the family by age 5

Indicators of Delays in Motor Development

- Unable to sit up without support by age 1
- Cannot walk without help by age 2
- Does not walk up and down steps by age 3
- Unable to balance on one foot for a short time by age 4
- Cannot throw a ball overhand or catch a large ball bounced to him or her by age 5

At about 1 month, child will:
- Turn eyes and head toward sound
- Cease crying if picked up and talked to
- Lift head when lying on stomach
- Follow a moving light with eyes
- Stretch limbs and fan out toes and fingers
- Display pupil response when a flashlight is moved in front of eyes

At about 3 months, child will:
- Make cooing sounds
- Respond to loud sounds
- Turn head toward bright colors and lights
- Move eyes and head in same direction together
- Recognize bottle or breast
- Make fists with both hands
- Grasp rattles or hair
- Wiggle and kick with legs and arms
- Lift head and chest while on stomach
- Smile in response to others

At about 6 months, child will:
- Babble
- Recognize familiar faces
- Turn toward source of normal sound
- Follow moving object with eyes when head is held stationary
- Play with toes
- Roll from stomach to back
- Reach for objects and pick them up
- Transfer objects from one hand to other
- Help hold bottle during feeding
- Bang spoon on table repeatedly
- Look for fallen object

At about 12 months, child will:
- Have a 5- to 6-word vocabulary
- Sit without support
- Pull self to standing position
- Crawl on hands and knees
- Drink from cup
- Wave bye-bye
- Enjoy peek-a-boo and patty cake
- Hold out arms and legs while being dressed
- Put objects into container
- Stack two blocks

At about 18 months, child will:
- Use 8 to 10 words that are understood
- Feed self with fingers
- Walk without help
- Pull, push, and dump things
- Pull off shoes, socks, and mittens

- Step off low object and keep balance
- Follow simple directions ("Bring the ball")
- Like to look at pictures
- Make marks on paper with crayons

By age 2 years, child can:
- Use 2- to 3-word sentences
- Say names of favorite toys
- Recognize familiar pictures
- Carry an object while walking
- Feed self with spoon
- Play alone and independently
- Turn 2 or 3 pages at a time
- Imitate parents
- Point to own hair, eyes, ears, and nose upon request
- Build a tower of four blocks
- Show affection toward others

By age 3 years, child can:
- Use 3- to 5-word sentences and repeat common rhymes
- Walk up stairs or steps alternating feet
- Jump, run, climb
- Ride a tricycle
- Put on shoes
- Open door
- Turn one page at a time
- Play with other children for a few minutes
- Name at least one color correctly
- Use toilet with occasional accidents

By age 4 years, child can:
- Ask "what," "where," "who" questions
- Give reasonable answers to simple questions
- Give first and last names
- Show many different emotions
- Say "no" or "I won't" with intensity
- Balance on one foot for 4 to 8 seconds
- Jump from a step and maintain balance
- Dress and undress with little help
- Cut straight with scissors
- Wash hands alone
- Play simple group games

By age 5 years, child can:
- Speak clearly
- Print a few letters
- Count 5 to 10 objects
- Skip, using feet alternately
- Catch a large ball
- Bathe and dress self
- Draw a body with at least five parts
- Copy familiar shapes (e.g., square, circle, triangle)

Figure 11.8

Child Development Markers

Indicators of Vision Problems

- Holds head in strained or awkward position when looking at a person or object
- Is often unable to locate and pick up small objects within reach
- Has one or both eyes crossed

Indicators of Delays in Social and Mental Development

- Does not react when name is called by age 1
- Does not play games such as peek-a-boo, patty cake, and wave bye-bye by age 1
- Unable to identify hair, eyes, ears, nose, and mouth by pointing to them by age 2
- Does not imitate parents doing household chores by age 2 to 3
- Does not understand simple stories told or read by age 3
- Does not enjoy playing alone with toys, pots and pans, sand, and so on by age 3
- Does not play group games such as hide-and-seek, tag-ball, and so on with other children by age 4
- Does not give reasonable answers to such questions as "What do you do when you get sleepy?" or "What do you do when you are hungry?" by age 4
- Does not seem to understand the meanings of the words *today*, *tomorrow*, and *yesterday* by age 5
- Does not share and take turns by age 5

A governmental website designed especially for parents concerned about their child's development is: http://www.cdc.gov/ncbddd/autism/ActEarly/default.htm

Selected Bibliography

Allen, K. Eileen, and Lynn Marotz. *Developmental Profiles: Pre-Birth through Twelve*, 6th ed. Independence, KY: Cengage, 2010.

Berk, Laura. *Child Development*, 9th ed. Upper Saddle River, NJ: Pearson, 2012.

Leach, Penelope. *Your Baby and Child: Birth to Age Five*, 3rd ed. New York: Knopf, 2010.

11.14 ASSESSING A CLIENT'S MENTAL STATUS

When a social worker encounters a client who exhibits highly usual behavior or seems to lack a capacity for organized and rational thought, the social worker needs to do at least a cursory mental status exam to detect symptoms that may signal the existence of a mental illness, neurological disorder, or dementia. When such a condition is suspected, the client should be referred for a medical or psychological exam. A mental status exam consists of careful observation and asking questions that gauge the client's orientation to time and place, accuracy of perceptions, memory, judgment, and appropriateness of affect. To the extent possible, the questions should be worked into the ordinary flow of conversation and not asked one after another in rapid-fire questioning. Engaging the client in a description of his or her typical day—from awakening to bedtime—can provide this context for asking these questions. Following are categories of information typically considered in a mental status exam.

- **Orientation to time and place** refers to whether the client is aware of who she or he is, where she or he is, and what time it is (year, month, date, and day). If present, disorientation and mental confusion is a significant symptom of a mental disorder.

- **General appearance and attitude** considers whether the client's appearance is appropriate to and usual for his or her age and social and economic status. Marked inappropriateness in appearance may be associated with psychological disturbance, particularly if the client's appearance has changed significantly over a short period of time. The client's dress, hygiene, speech, facial expressions, and motor activity provide information about self-perception and self-awareness of others.

- **Perceptual distortions** may occur among some psychologically impaired individuals. Two of the most significant perceptual symptoms are illusions and hallucinations. *Hallucinations* are perceptual experiences in the absence of external stimuli (e.g., hearing voices, seeing things that no one else can see). *Illusions* are misinterpretations of actual stimuli. An illusion may be symptomatic if the misinterpretation is highly unusual, peculiar, or persistent (see Item 15.12).

- **Thought content** refers to the logic and consistency of an individual's attitudes, ideas, and beliefs. Symptoms include *delusional thinking* (false beliefs that cannot be altered by logical arguments) and *obsessions* (fixed or repetitive ideas that the client cannot get out of his or her mind). Speech that is jumbled, incoherent, or unintelligible may indicate a neurological problem.

- **Appropriateness of behavior** considers whether the client's behavior during an interview and as reported by others is reasonable and in keeping with common social norms. Irrational and bizarre behavior, *compulsions* (repeated acts that the client feels compelled to do) and *phobias* (baseless avoidance or fears of certain objects or places) are symptoms of a mental disorder.

- **Memory loss** may be associated with psychiatric, neurological, and other medical problems. Four types of memory can be assessed:

  1. *Immediate recall* refers to the ability to recall things within seconds of their presentation.
  2. *Short-term memory* is generally defined as covering events transpiring within the last 25 minutes.
  3. *Recent memory* refers to the client's recollection of current events and situations occurring within the few weeks preceding the interview.
  4. *Remote memory* refers to the recollection of events occurring months or years ago and of a significant life happening, such as marriage, first job, high school graduation, and so on.

     Immediate and short-term memory can be assessed by asking a question such as "What did you have to eat at your last meal?" Or one might ask the client to remember a word, number, or object and then after the lapse of a few minutes ask the client to recall it. Recent memory can be tested with questions such as "When was the last time it rained?" and "What is the name of the dentist you saw last month?" Remote memory can be tested by asking questions such as "Where were you born?" "Where did you go to grade school?" and "Who was president of the United States when you got married?"

- **Sensorium** refers to an individual's ability to utilize data from her or his sense organs (hearing, vision, touch, smelling, and taste) and more generally, from overall attentiveness and alertness to the surroundings. If a client cannot comprehend visual symbols (and has no visual impairment), ordinary conversation (and has no hearing impairment), or does not respond to other ordinary sensory stimuli, she or he may have a neurological disorder.

- **Intellectual functioning** is screened by evaluating the client's abilities to read, write, and follow simple instructions, do simple arithmetic, think abstractly (e.g., How are an apple and orange alike?), and by testing the client's awareness of common knowledge consistent with his or her level of education. Poor comprehension and deficits in abstract thinking are symptoms of several different psychological disorders. Gauging educational attainment is important because low levels of intellectual performance may be attributable to a lack of education. Poor intellectual performance among educated persons, however, may be indicative of organic disorders. The symptom of intellectual deterioration is most often associated with brain disorders.

- **Mood and affect** refer to the client's prevailing emotional state and the range of emotions displayed during the interview. A problem is suggested if the client's emotions (e.g., sadness, elation, anger, anxiety, apathy) seem unreasonable or unconnected to the situation or the topic being discussed. For example, rapid shifts in mood or smiling and laughter when talking about a sad or tragic situation may suggest a psychiatric disturbance. The symptom of *labile emotions* (i.e., unstable or erratic) is often associated with brain disorders and is fairly common among people who have had a stroke (see Item 15.9).

- **Insight** can be evaluated by asking questions that determine whether the client is aware that he or she is exhibiting unusual behavior or has symptoms that are of concern to family members, the social worker, or a physician, and whether the client can describe reasons why he or she might be having this problem. Paradoxically, the more severe the mental disorder, the more likely it is that the individual will not recognize that his or her thoughts and behavior are unusual and symptomatic.

- **Judgment** refers to the individual's ability to think rationally in regard to an obvious problem. It also refers to a client's mental capability to make ordinary decisions, particularly ones about self-care.

Selected Bibliography

Sadock, Benjamin, and Virginia Sadock. *Kaplan and Sadock Synopsis of Psychiatry*, 10th ed. Philadelphia: Walter Kluwer/Lippincott, 2007.

Sommers-Flanagan, John, and Rita Sommers-Flanagan. *Clinical Interviewing*, 5th ed. Hoboken, NJ: Wiley, 2013.

11.15 USING THE *DIAGNOSTIC AND STATISTICAL MANUAL OF MENTAL DISORDERS (DSM)* AND THE PERSON-IN-ENVIRONMENT (PIE) ASSESSMENT TOOLS

Social workers should be familiar with two classification systems: the *Diagnostic and Statistical Manual of Mental Disorders (DSM)* and the Person-in-Environment (PIE). These taxonomies are intended to refine and systematize the assessment process and facilitate communication among practitioners, administrators, and researchers.

In the widely used ***Diagnostic and Statistical Manual of Mental Disorders (DSM-5)*** more than 300 psychiatric disorders are described in terms of symptoms, diagnostic criteria, usual age of onset, prevalence, level of impairment, and so on. The disorders are grouped into 22 broad categories: Neurodevelopmental Disorders; Schizophrenia Spectrum and Other Psychotic Disorders; Depressive Disorders; Anxiety Disorders; Obsessive-Compulsive and Related Disorders; Trauma and Stressor–Related Disorders; Dissociative Disorders; Somatic Symptom and Related Disorders; Feeding and Eating Disorders; Eliminating Disorders; Sleep-Wake Disorders; Sexual Dysfunction; Gender

Dysphoria; Disruptive, Impulse Control, and Conduct Disorders; Substance-Related and Addictive Disorders; Neurocognitive Disorders; Personality Disorders; Paraphilic Disorders; Other Mental Disorders; Medication–Induced Movement Disorders and Other Effects of Medication; and finally, Other conditions that may be a focus of clinical Intervention.

Knowledge of the *DSM* is important because many clinical social workers and social agencies look to Medicaid, Medicare, and private health insurance companies as sources of payment for the psychotherapy they provide to clients. Prior to submitting an insurance claim, the client must be assigned to a diagnostic category in accord with the *DSM*.

The *DSM* authors warn those using the *DSM-5* of the inherent difficulties of assessing the behavior of a person who is from an ethnic or cultural group different from that of the clinician. A specific behavior that is considered normal or acceptable within one culture may be labeled as a deviance or pathology in a different culture. Moreover, the willingness to tolerate particular types of behavior varies widely across cultures and families. A practitioner who is unfamiliar with the nuances of a client's culture is at risk of misreading a cultural variation as psychopathology.

Those using the *DSM* must always remember that it describes psychiatric disorders and related medical conditions. In short, it is a listing of serious personal problems, anomalies, maladies, and deficiencies. The *DSM* does not focus on or describe strengths. All people, including those who happen to have a mental disorder, have numerous strengths and assets that need to be recognized during an assessment and utilized in any helping effort (see Item11.6). It is also important to recognize that the *DSM* is a classification of mental disorders and not a classification of people. A person is not a diagnostic label. Thus, a term such as *schizophrenic* is to be avoided in favor of an expression such as *an individual with schizophrenia*.

The **Person-in-Environment System (PIE)** was designed for use by social workers and is built around two core social work concepts: social functioning and viewing the person within an environmental context. The PIE system is intended as a supplement to the *DSM*, not a substitute. It classifies client problems or concerns into four classes or *factors*. The terminology used to describe social functioning problems (Factor I) and environmental problems (Factor II) is unique to social work practice. Factor III, mental health problems, utilizes the terminology and taxonomy found in the *DSM*. PIE Factor IV (physical health problems) records a client's diseases and health problems that have been diagnosed by a physician or reported by the client or others. An abbreviated outline of the Factor I and Factor II categories and subcategories is presented here.

PIE Factor I: Social Functioning Problems

- Social role in which problem is defined (four categories and numerous subcategories):
  1. Familial roles (parent, spouse, child, sibling, other family member, and significant other)
  2. Other interpersonal roles (lover, friend, neighbor, member, and other)
  3. Occupational roles (worker-paid, worker-home, worker-volunteer, student, and other)
  4. Special life situation roles (consumer, inpatient/client, outpatient/client, probationer/parolee, prisoner, immigrant-legal, immigrant-undocumented, immigrant-refugee, and other)

- Type of problem in social role (nine types: power, ambivalence, responsibility, dependency, loss, isolation, victimization, mixed, other)
- Severity of problem (rated on a 6-point scale)
- Duration of problem (six categories)
- Ability of client to cope with problem (six levels)

PIE Factor II: Environmental Problems

- Social system where each problem is identified (six major systems and numerous subcategories):
    1. Economic/basic needs system problems
    2. Education and training system problems
    3. Judicial and legal system problems
    4. Health, safety, and social services problems
    5. Voluntary association system problems
    6. Affectional support system problems

- Specific type of problem within each social system (71 subcategories; number varies for each of six social systems). Examples of social system problem subcategories: lack of regular food supply, absence of shelter, lack of culturally relevant education, discrimination, lack of police services, unsafe conditions in home, regulatory barriers to social services, absence of affectional support system, lack of community acceptance of religious values, and so on.
- Severity of problem (rated on a 6-point scale)
- Duration of problem (six categories)

Selected Bibliography

American Psychiatric Association. *Diagnostic and Statistical Manual of Mental Disorders,* 5th ed. Washington, DC: American Psychiatric Association, 2013.

Cocoran, Jacqueline, and Joseph Walsh. *Clinical Assessment and Diagnosis in Social Work Practice,* 2nd ed. New York: Oxford University Press, 2010.

Frances, Allen. *Essentials of Psychiatric Diagnosis.* New York: Guilford, 2013.

_____ . *Saving Normal.* New York: HarperCollins, 2013.

Karls, James, and Maura O'Keefe, eds. *Person-in-Environment System Manual,* 2nd ed. Washington, DC: NASW Press, 2008.

_____ , Compu PIE [computer software]. Washington, DC: NASW Press, 2008.

11.16 ASSESSING A CHILD'S NEED FOR PROTECTION

State laws require social workers to report suspected child abuse or neglect. The following list of physical and behavioral signs suggest the possible existence of physical abuse, neglect, and sexual abuse.

Indicators of Physical Abuse

- Unexplained bruises or welts, especially if on both sides of the child's face or body, or on back, buttocks, or torso
- Bruises in different stages of healing (suggesting repeated injury)
- Multiple bruises clustered in one area and/or bruises with shape of an instrument (e.g., loop marks, lineal or parallel marks, punch marks)

- Bruises that regularly appear after a weekend or a visit with an adult
- Bruises on shoulders or neck in shape of hand or fingers (i.e., grab marks)
- Unexplained burns, such as those caused by cigarettes, and especially if on palms, feet, back, or buttocks
- Hot water immersion or dunking burn on hands or feet (e.g., sock like, glove like) or doughnut-shaped burn on buttocks
- Burns patterned like an electric stove burner, hot plate, curling iron, etc.
- Rope burns or tie marks on wrists, ankles, or mouth
- Unexplained injuries to inner mouth such as frenulum tears or broken teeth (caused by rough feeding)
- Human, adult-size bite marks on child's body
- Unexplained broken bones, head injuries such as a skull fractures, or a subdural hematoma
- Retina detachment or whiplash injuries to neck caused by violent shaking (i.e., shaken baby syndrome)
- Internal injuries caused by a punch to the body
- Poisoning caused by ingestion of street drugs, alcohol, prescription medicines, or household chemicals
- Attempts by child to hide injuries from view, embarrassment or shame over injury, reluctance to talk about injury (nonabused children proudly display accidental injuries)
- Hyper-vigilant, fearful, and guarded when around adults; avoids physical contact with people, including his parents (i.e., seems fearful of human touch)
- Overly adaptive or docile behavior in an attempt to meet parents' needs (i.e., by taking care of and comforting parent, the child seeks to keep things calm and prevent abusive episodes)
- Becomes uneasy when another child cries or acts up (i.e., has learned to associate crying with an adult getting upset and inflicting abuse)
- Serious behavioral problems at young age (e.g., suicide attempts, self-mutilation, runs away, violence, withdrawn)

Indicators of Neglect

- Begging, stealing, or hoarding food; underweight; failure to thrive; bald patches on scalp caused by being left in crib for long periods
- Poor school attendance (sometimes the neglectful parent is so lonely she or he keeps the child home for company; sometimes the child remains home to care for younger siblings)
- Untreated medical and dental problems, even though parent has resources to get medical services
- Primitive and unsocialized eating and toilet behaviors
- Unusual fatigue and listlessness; falling asleep at unusual times
- Stays at school, in public places, or at another's home for extended periods
- Poor hygiene, filthy clothing, clothing is inappropriate for weather
- Child not supervised or protected from dangerous activity

Indicators of Sexual Abuse

- Bruises, scaring, or tissue tears around vagina and anus; bruised or swollen penis (caused by rough fondling and masturbation)
- Blood on child's underwear

- Redness or rash in genital area of child not wearing diaper (caused by frequent rubbing and fondling)
- Redness or abrasions between upper legs (caused by penis placed between child's legs for adult masturbation)
- Recurrent bladder infections (i.e., bacteria from rectum introduced into vagina when there is both anal and vaginal penetration)
- Pregnancy or a sexually transmitted disease in young child
- Semen in vagina, rectum, or mouth
- Frequent masturbation by child that has a driven or compulsive quality
- Unusual sexual play with or exploration of pets or dolls
- Aggressive and forced sexual activity with other children, usually of a younger age
- Sexual touch of adults; sexually provocative and suggestive behavior toward adults
- Unusual level of knowledge about sexual activity (e.g., can describe sexual movement, smells, taste, feelings)
- Preoccupation with sexual matters or, on the other extreme, unusually fearful of anything sexual
- Unusual fear of showers, bathrooms, bedrooms
- Unwilling to change clothes for gym or to expose body (caused by extreme shame of body)
- Frequent and patterned absences from school that are justified by or arranged by one adult (the offender)
- Unusual or bizarre sexual themes in artwork or drawings
- Wearing many layers of clothing (seeking protection of body)
- Frequent use of dissociation as coping mechanism
- Unusually close relationship with an adult that has secretive or sexual overtones
- Extreme protectiveness of child by an adult who keeps child from talking to or establishing relationship with responsible adults

Although certain signs and symptoms can establish that a child has been abused or neglected, these signs do not identify with certainty who is responsible for the maltreatment.

Many parents believe in and utilize corporal punishment as discipline. Thus, the social worker must be able to differentiate an ordinary spanking from physical abuse, as it is defined in a state's legal code. In addition, we offer three criteria for making that distinction:

1. In corporal punishment, the child experiences some pain and discomfort. In abuse, there is actual injury to body tissue.

2. In using corporal punishment, the parent maintains self-control and is aware of where and how hard the child is being spanked. In an abusive situation, the parent typically loses control and strikes the child with excessive force or in places that are vulnerable to injury.

3. Parents who use corporal punishment may, in rare instances, hit too hard but they quickly realize what has happened and are able to make changes in how they discipline the child so this does not happen again. In situations of abuse, there are repeated episodes of excessive, out-of-control punishment and injury.

Although cases of physical abuse and sexual abuse attract media attention, child neglect is actually the most frequent type of child maltreatment. In the United States, about half of the fatalities related to child maltreatment are the result of neglect, and a high percentage of those cases occur in families where the parents are addicted to drugs or alcohol.

Most children who are sexually abused do not tell anyone because they are either afraid or feel overwhelming shame. Most cases of child sexual abuse involve fondling and masturbation, but not penetration. Even if there has been penetration of the mouth, vagina, or rectum, there will be no physical evidence in most cases. It is also important to understand that the majority of sexually abused children will not exhibit unusual sexual behavior. However, sexually abused children are more likely than nonabused children to display adult-like sexual behavior.

The social worker must report suspected cases of child sexual abuse (see Item 11.17). However, the worker must also be alert to the fact that false or mistaken accusations do occur. Both children and adults are suggestible and may misinterpret an experience. Occasionally, an individual will level a false accusation as a means of hurting someone. Although false accusations by a child are relatively rare, the rate increases if the child's accusation is being encouraged or urged by a parent. That rate becomes even higher in cases involving child custody fights between parents.

Once a case of abuse or neglect has been identified, the question of risk must be addressed. In other words, Is the child now at risk of serious harm and in need of immediate protection? Presented here are factors that increase risk to the child and should be considered when conducting an *assessment of risk*.

Child-Related Risk Factors

- The child is vulnerable and unable to protect herself or himself because of young age, illness, disability, health problems, etc.
- The child was previously subjected to abuse or neglect.
- Injuries to the child are at vulnerable body locations (e.g., head, face, genitals) or the injuries required medical attention or hospitalization.
- The alleged perpetrator now has access to the child.
- The child's relationship to others in the household is tenuous or troubled, thus decreasing chances that others would intervene to protect the child.

Parent/Caregiver-Related Risk Factors

- Existing physical or mental illness, mental retardation, or substance abuse limits the caregiver's ability to protect the child.
- The parent or caregiver has a history of domestic violence (e.g., spouse abuse) or other violent criminal activity.
- The parent has a history of having abused or neglected other children.
- The parent of caregiver lacks basic parenting skills and knowledge.
- There are high levels of anger, hostility, or rejection toward the child.
- The child's behavioral problems or special needs (e.g., a disability) place stressful demands on the parent or caregiver.
- Other serious family problems place added stress on the parent or caregiver (e.g., marital conflict, financial, health, chaotic lifestyle)
- Unrealistic and unreasonable expectations have been placed on the child.
- The parent or caregiver denies any problem, is evasive, or refuses to cooperate with child protection workers or other helpers.
- Prior efforts to work with the family were rejected or ineffective.

Environmental Risk Factors

- The condition of the home is a clear danger to the child (e.g., exposed electrical wiring, unprotected household chemicals, lack of sanitation).
- The family is socially or physically isolated; lacks social supports and access to assistance in times of emergency.

An *out-of-home placement* may be necessary if a child is in danger and there is no less drastic means of protecting the child. Such placements can be traumatic to the child and, of course, upsetting to the parents. If a child must be placed into foster care, it is to be done for one reason only: to protect the child from a specific harm. It is unethical to place a child in order to coerce the parent into taking some action. A child should be placed in the least restrictive alternative. To the extent possible, the parent(s) should participate in preparing the child for the separation and placement. During a placement it is important to encourage visits to the child by the parent. It is also important to respect and maintain the child's religious traditions and cultural heritage. Special requirements to maintain the cultural connection of a Native American child are outlined in the Indian Child Welfare Act, a federal law.

Selected Bibliography

Giardino, Angelo, and Randell Alexander. *Child Abuse: Quick Reference for Healthcare, Social Service, and Law Enforcement Professionals*, 2nd ed. St. Louis, MO: G. W. Medical Publications, 2006.

Myers, John, ed. *The APSAC Handbook on Child Maltreatment*, 3rd ed. Thousand Oaks, CA: Sage, 2011.

Tower, Cynthia. *Understanding Child Abuse and Neglect*, 8th ed. Upper Saddle River, NJ: Pearson, 2010.

11.17 MANDATED REPORTING OF ABUSE AND NEGLECT

All states have laws that mandate the reporting of child abuse and neglect by social workers and other professionals. Many states also have laws mandating the reporting of the abuse, neglect, and exploitation of the elderly. Although certain categories of persons are mandated to report, any individual can make a report. However, there are some differences in how a state's statutes define the various types of maltreatment and the procedures for making a report.

Child abuse and neglect

A report can be made to either a protective services agency or to the police. In most states and in most situations, a report of suspected child abuse or neglect will go first to the local or state child protective services agency (CPS). Upon receiving the report, a determination is made on whether the alleged maltreatment fits the relevant legal definitions, whether an investigation is warranted, the current level of risk, how quickly they need to respond, and whether law enforcement needs to be notified.

Child abuse and neglect are usually legally defined as acts (abuse) or omissions (neglect) by the child's parent or caregiver that cause or threaten harm or injury to the child. The harm can be physical, emotional, or sexual. Deliberate and serious injury to a child, or to any person, is also a crime. If the injury is of a serious nature and fits the legal definition of a crime (e.g., physical assault, molestation, rape), CPS will notify law enforcement and the police may initiate a separate investigation. The role of protective services is to protect the victim from further harm by a family member or caretaker. The role of the police is to investigate alleged crimes and gather evidence. That evidence gathered by law enforcement is forwarded to the prosecutor's office that decides if the alleged offender is to be charged with a crime. Thus, in some cases, both the police and a protective services agency will be involved. If the alleged offender is not a parent or caregiver, the matter will be handled entirely by the police and CPS will not be involved.

Typically, a state's statutes define child abuse and neglect as a matter of civil law (e.g., family law) to be handled under civil court procedures. By contrast, a crime is approached using criminal procedures. For example, a police or criminal investigation requires the administration of the *Miranda warning*; usually a CPS investigation does not. In order to convict a person of a crime, the court must have the highest level of evidence, which is *beyond a reasonable doubt*. In a CPS case, a civil matter, the court can arrive at a decision (e.g., to place a child in foster care as protection against further harm) with a lower level of evidence, either a *preponderance of evidence* or *clear and convincing evidence*.

Matters of child abuse and neglect are inherently complex because the victim is a child and the alleged offender is the child's parent or guardian. The child is vulnerable, but unable to escape danger because he or she is dependent on the offender. Moreover, the child has an emotional and family bond with the offender. And it must be recognized that the alleged offender has a set of parental legal rights, such as the right to discipline and control his or her child (see Item 15.4 for list of basic parental rights).

Elder abuse, neglect, and exploitation

Most reports of suspected elder abuse and exploitation will go to the local or state Adult Protective Services (APS) agency. However, if the alleged maltreatment has occurred in a licensed care facility such as a nursing home, the state's Long-Term Care Ombudsman will probably also participate in the investigation. If it appears that a crime has been committed (e.g., forgery, fraud, theft, assault), the police will be notified and they will conduct a separate criminal investigation.

As compared to a CPS agency, an APS agency has considerably less investigative authority and fewer options when it comes to protective actions. Without clear evidence to the contrary, APS must presume that the elderly person, the alleged victim, is legally competent and has a right to make decisions. Thus, how far the investigation can proceed depends largely on the wishes of the alleged victim. And there are a number of reasons why a victim of maltreatment may not want to cooperate with an investigation or volunteer needed information. If the alleged offender is a family member, the elder may want to avoid causing family humiliation or conflict, or perhaps he or she fears retaliation. Elders may fear losing their living arrangement or fear that they will be moved to another care facility.

The elderly who are frail and highly dependent on others for care, and those who are mentally confused, are especially vulnerable to maltreatment and exploitation. In addition to physical and sexual abuse and neglect, the mistreatment can take the form of fraud and financial exploitation, the theft or misappropriation of property, withholding or misapplication of their medications, intimidation, humiliation, and abandonment. One of the more common situations that come to the attention of an APS agency is *self-neglect*. This often occurs when elderly persons are living alone and are no longer able to safely care for themselves because of physical limitations or cognitive problems. When it is apparent that individuals can no longer care for themselves, make medical decisions, or manage their money, the APS agency may petition the court to make a finding of legal incompetence and establish a legal guardianship or conservatorship (see Items 15.5 and 15.8).

Guidelines for reporting abuse and neglect

The following guidelines will apply in many situations. However, it is important to understand that these guidelines are of a general nature and do not constitute legal advice. When a social worker encounters an especially complex situation or is uncertain on how to proceed, she or he should immediately consult with an agency supervisor or an attorney. Most social agencies devote a section of their agency procedure manual to the topic of reporting abuse and neglect.

- Because state laws vary somewhat in how abuse and neglect are defined and in how a report is to be handled, it is critically important for a social worker to read the statutes relevant to his or her jurisdiction. These laws can be accessed on the Internet.

- A social worker must be familiar with the various signs and indicators of abuse, neglect, and exploitation (see Items 11.16 and 15.5). When uncertain about how to interpret a puzzling situation or a suspicious sign or indicator, the social worker should consult with knowledgeable colleagues or, if possible, a specialist.

- A social worker has a legal responsibility to report known or suspected abuse and neglect. A proper report can prevent the death or serious injury to a child or an elderly person. The failure of a mandated reporter to make a report usually constitutes a misdemeanor crime. There is also the remote possibility that a failure to report will give rise to a lawsuit brought by a family member alleging that the social worker, as a mandated reporter, was negligent and that if the worker had made a report, as required by law, the victim's injury or death would have been prevented.

- A social worker needs to know how to report *before* he or she is in a situation that requires making a report. As preparation, we recommend that social workers arrange a meeting with local CPS and APS personnel at which time they seek answers to specific questions such as: When, how, and to whom do I make a report? What kind of information will the protective services agency want from me? What questions will I be asked? What happens after I make a report? Will I be asked to testify in court?

- The protective services personnel need facts. Thus, when a social worker makes a report to a protective services agency, she or he will be asked a number of questions, such as her or his name and address, the victim's name and address, the nature of the victim's injuries or maltreatment, whether the victim needs immediate medical care, the victim's age and current location, whether there are other children or vulnerable persons in the home, the whereabouts of the alleged offender, the level of danger presented by the offender or by others in the home, and the reporter's relationship to the victim and alleged offender. The reporter will be asked to describe specifically what she or he has observed and why she or he suspects a problem of abuse or neglect. The CPS or APS worker taking the report will want enough information to decide if law enforcement should be notified. The reporter may be asked if she or he will provide a signed affidavit that will be used as legal evidence. Depending on a state's law, the protective services agency may need to first establish a *probable cause* level of evidence and obtain a court order before moving forward with an in-depth investigation or protective intervention.

- A social worker or other professional making a report should *not* notify the family or alleged offender. That is the responsibility of CPS or APS and law enforcement personnel. Alerting the alleged offender to the possibility of an investigation can place the child or vulnerable older adult in further danger and possibly result in the destruction of evidence.

- Some social workers, especially those functioning in the role of a therapist, are often hesitant to make a report because they fear that the report will destroy the therapeutic relationship they have with their client and to whom the social worker has a professional and ethical obligation. When making the report this concern should be described to the CPS or APS worker taking the report. In some cases (if the risk of further injury is low), the protective services agency may be able to avoid or defer an investigation or intervention if the agency knows that the situation is being monitored by a professional and that therapeutic efforts are underway to correct the problem of abuse or neglect.

    The potential for a report to protective services to disrupt an existing professional relationship with a client who is the alleged offender is at least minimized when the client knows in advance that this possibility exists. Thus, at the beginning of a professional relationship it is advisable to inform all clients that an assurance of confidentiality has certain limits and that a social worker is legally bound to report known or suspected abuse or neglect.

    When a mandated reporter makes a good faith report of abuse or neglect, state laws typically grant immunity from liability and waive the requirement of confidentiality within a social worker–client, or therapist–client relationship. The life and safety of a child or older adult trumps the importance of privacy in a professional relationship.

- A state reporting law usually prohibits the protective services agency from disclosing the name of the reporter. Nevertheless, a reporter should anticipate that the alleged offender can often figure out who made the report. Protective services agencies do accept reports from anonymous sources, but such a source has less credibility than a person willing to identify herself or himself.

Selected Bibliography

Krause, Kathryn, Ken Lau, and Richard Morse. *Mandated Reporting of Abuse and Neglect: A Practical Guide for Social Workers*. New York: Springer, 2009.

NASW General Counsel. *Social Workers and Child Abuse Reporting*. Washington, DC: NASW Press, 2013.

Payne, Brian K. *Crime and Elder Abuse: An Integrated Perspective*, 3rd ed. Springfield, IL: Charles C. Thomas, 2011.

11.18 REFERRAL FOR PSYCHOLOGICAL TESTING

In some situations, the social worker will want to refer a child or an adult to a psychologist for testing. Testing can provide information about a client's intellectual capacity, level of anxiety or depression, coping behavior, self-concept, patterns of motivation, and general personality integration. In some cases, a psychiatrist will need to be involved if it appears as if a client might have a psychiatric, neurological, or drug-induced disorder. Below are guidelines that should be considered when thinking about or planning a referral.

- List the questions you want a psychological evaluation to answer. The assessment instruments and procedures selected by a psychologist (and sometimes by a psychiatrist) will depend on the type of information sought, client characteristics, and suspected problems. Thus, describe for the psychologist the type of information that would be most helpful in your work with this client and the specific case management decisions you face.

- Provide the psychologist with data concerning the client's age, education, occupation, employment, ethnicity, any unusual fears of testing, and any disabilities, such as problems with vision, hearing, mobility, reading and comprehending written materials, or using the English language. If available, provide the results and reports of any previous testing, including the dates of testing and the names of the tests used.

- After consulting with the psychologist who will do the testing, prepare the client by giving him or her basic information on what to expect, where the testing will be done, and about how long the testing will take.

- Have realistic expectations of psychological testing. In many cases, the test results will simply confirm the impressions already formed by people who have closely observed or worked with the client. Important case management decisions should not be based exclusively on test results. Ask the psychologist to explain the strengths and limitations of the testing procedures and to discuss how the test results might shape the client's treatment or service plan

Selected Bibliography

Hogan, Thomas. *Psychological Testing: A Practical Introduction.* Hoboken, NJ: Wiley, 2006.

Neukrug, Edward. *Essentials of Testing and Assessment: A Practical Guide for Counselors, Social Workers, and Psychologists,* 2nd ed. Independence, KY: Cengage, 2010.

Van Ornum, Bill, Linda Dunlap, and Milton Shore. *Psychological Testing Across the Lifespan.* Upper Saddle River, NJ: Pearson, 2008.

11.19 ASSESSING FAMILY FUNCTIONING

Everyone grows up in a family of one sort or another. From those personal experiences, we know that families take many forms and are inherently complex. Each family is composed of numerous individuals, each of whom is unique. And each family has a rather unique history and faces a particular set of problems and challenges. To be of help to a family, a social worker needs to recognize and understand both its inner dynamics and its social and economic context. The following dimensions of family and family functioning should be kept in mind as the social worker gathers assessment data.

- **Family functions**. For purposes of planning human services programs and maintaining a family-centered approach in the delivery of social and health services, it is useful to define what a family is. A **family** is a group of people related by biological ties, a legal relationship, or expectations of long-term loyalty and commitment, often comprising at least two generations, and usually inhabiting one household. Moreover, at least some of the adults of this group must have the intention and the capacity to carry out all or most of the activities or functions common to a family, such as:

  - *Provide for the rearing and socialization of children* (e.g., prepare children for adulthood; prepare children to function within a particular culture and society; teach and model basic values and morals such as honesty, responsibility, cooperation, compassion, and sharing).

- *Provide family members with intimacy and a sense of belonging* (e.g., acceptance and love).
- *Provide a private and emotionally secure environment for sexual expression by consenting adults.*
- *Provide family members with a place of respite* (e.g., respite from other roles and responsibilities such as those related to occupation, work, and community).
- *Provide family members with a legal and social identity* (e.g., an identity and location for the purposes of legal transactions).
- *Serve as an economic unit* (i.e., manage money, purchase goods and services, budget and plan for future, and care for possessions).
- *Protect and care for vulnerable family members* (e.g., young children, frail elderly, sick, or disabled).
- *Advocate for family members in need of community resources* (e.g., the parent who seeks out medical care for a child, the parent who makes sure each child gets a proper education).

Given these fundamental functions of a family, a key question in the assessment process is: To what degree does the family perform or carry out the functions and activities of a family?

- **Family structure and membership**. The assessment needs to determine a family's basic structure and membership. Who belongs to this family? Who are members of the *biological family* (e.g., bio-parents and their offspring)? Who are members of the *legal family*, as defined by the laws of marriage, divorce, and adoption, civil union, or by court orders affecting child custody? Who belongs to the *perceived family*, those considered to be family, regardless of biological and legal ties? And finally, who belongs to the *family of long-term commitments*, as defined by an expectation of lifelong loyalty, duty, and responsibility.

  The basic structure of a family can take many forms, such as the *nuclear family* (parents and children), the *extended family* (parents, children, and close relatives), the *single-parent family* (one parent plus children), and the *blended family* (two adults, their children from prior marriages or relationships, and children born to them as a couple). A growing number of families take the form of a *functional family* made up of two or more unmarried and unrelated adults (plus their children). Also, there are a growing number of families are headed by *second-time-around parents*, referring to grandparents who have assumed responsibility for rearing grandchildren, often because the biological parents have been incarcerated or impaired by an addiction or illness.

  A social worker's effort to gather information about the family's membership and structure is made easier if the client brings family photo albums and family scrapbooks to an interview devoted to data gathering and assessment. Browsing through these collections can make it easier for the client to describe the various family members and explain relationships.

- **Environmental influences**. A family's functioning is influenced, positively or negatively, by the characteristics of its neighborhood and community. Thus, an assessment should consider such questions as Where does this family live? Do the family members like their neighborhood? Is this a safe place? Do the neighbors care for and look after each other? Do the people have jobs, a decent income, adequate health care, and affordable housing? Do the local schools provide education that includes the special programs needed by exceptional children? Do local grocery stores offer quality foods for a reasonable cost? Are public services adequate, such as police protection, sanitation, transportation, library, parks and recreation?

- **Family boundaries and subsystems**. Over time, the interactions within a family become patterned and organized. In short, a social system is created. As a social system, a family has a *boundary* that delineates the family from its environment. The nature of that boundary will determine whether the family is open or closed to outside influences. The boundary must be sufficiently permeable or open so the family can incorporate information and ideas needed to adapt to an ever-changing social-cultural environment. However, if the boundary is too porous or too weak, the family will be indiscriminately pushed and pulled by outside influences and the family will lose its structure, organization, or "systemness." On the other extreme, if a family's boundary is too rigid and impervious to outside influence, the family will become isolated, estranged, and separated from other people and its community. An extreme example would be parents who prohibit their children from having any exposure to, or contact with neighbors, schools, newspapers, TV, and computers. In that case, the children might be protected from potentially harmful outside influences but they are not being prepared to function in their society.

  Within a family consisting of both adults and children, there are typically four *subsystems*: the *spouse subsystem* (i.e., two adults, usually involved in a sexual relationship); the *parental subsystem* (i.e., the family members—usually adults—responsible for childrearing); one or more *parent–child subsystems* (i.e., special relationships between a particular parent and a particular child); and the *sibling subsystem* (relationship patterns among the siblings). In a healthy family, the boundaries that define these subsystems are clear and in keeping with societal norms. By contrast, for example, in an incestuous family the child is drawn into the spouse subsystem and sexual involvement with a parent. In a similar vein, the child with an alcoholic or drug-addicted parent may enter the parental subsystem, reverse roles, and end up taking care of and protecting her or his parent.

- **Rules and roles**. After family patterns are established, there is a tendency for the members and the family as a whole to maintain the status quo, even when a particular pattern becomes a problem. Various rules and roles and expectations help maintain the familiar and resist change to the status quo. *Family rules* are the explicit and implicit principles that govern member behavior and maintain the family's structure and organization. The existence of such rules is evident in something as simple as the seating arrangement during meals or in who is responsible for putting gas in the car. An explicit family rule might be: "You must clean the bath tub when finished." Although most family rules are practical, innocuous, and sometimes even silly (e.g., "Don't take a trip in the car without first changing your underwear"), others can be dysfunctional. Rules that suppress emotion, cover up irresponsible behavior, encourage dishonesty, or generate feelings of shame are especially harmful. Examples include: "When Dad is drinking, never mention his brother Ed" or "Pretend you don't see Mom and Dad fighting" or "Only an evil child would ever feel anger toward a parent." The children of parents who are alcoholic often grow up with the family rules of *don't talk* (about the drinking or other real issues), *don't feel* (suppress all feelings), and *don't trust* (always be on guard and keep people at a distance). A social worker conducting a family assessment needs to identify troublesome family rules and what happens when rules are broken.

Families also develop a certain role structure. Role expectations guide many of the common tasks of living, such as who cares for the children, who drives the car, who manages the money, who does the laundry. The role structure is often shaped by the family's culture and religion (see Item 8.8).

During childhood, individuals often take on a certain role within their family. Pet expressions for such roles include "mama's boy," "peacemaker," "family worrier," "disciplinarian," "lone wolf," "message carrier," "family banker," and "black sheep." Family therapy literature often makes reference to the roles of "scapegoat," "hero," "mascot," "lost child," and "rescuer."

The boundaries, subsystems, rules, and roles within a family can only be inferred after careful observation. Some family members may be able to describe some rules and roles, but most of these patterns are so ingrained that they feel natural and are never questioned. When adults form a new family, they often repeat or reproduce the patterns they learned within their family of origin. Thus, both family strengths and problems can be transmitted from one generation to another.

- **Separate and together**. Humans have a need for closeness but at the same time have some fear of intimacy. We may avoid getting too close to others because we fear being vulnerable or worry that others will take advantage of an exposed weakness. Within a family, members experience a tension between the need to belong to the family group and their need for autonomy. They want to be connected but not controlled. Within a well-functioning family, members are able to reveal many of their inner thoughts and feelings but also maintain a comfortable level of privacy and independence.

  When personal boundaries are weak and unclear, family members may become intrusive or overly involved in the lives of other members. Such family relationships are termed *enmeshed* or *fused*. The opposite condition is when there is very little meaningful communication and interaction among family members. That type of family is called *disengaged* or *disconnected* and in its extreme form it is little more than a group of people who happen to live under the same roof.

  To understand a troubled family, the social worker must see beyond and behind the most obvious problems and wonder why members behave in ways that create so much distress and disruption. When observing the behavior of a family member, consider: How does this behavior draw members closer together and provide a sense of belonging? How does this behavior provide a protective distance or separation from others?

- **Individual differences**. Although there is value in viewing the family from a systems perspective, it is important to remember that a family is made up of individuals. The members of a family can vary widely in terms of personality, temperament, values, and strengths and limitations. Each is unique in terms of her or his hopes and dreams, interests, and spirituality. Some may be outgoing, whereas others are reserved and introverted; some may be flexible, whereas others prefer stability and predictability; some may be organized and neat, whereas others are disorganized and messy; and some may be calm, whereas others are excitable. When observing the functioning of a family, it is useful to consider whether there is a good match, or a possible mismatch, between the individual member and his or her family.

  A root source of family conflict is the inability of members to accept others as being unique and different from themselves. There are four basic ways of responding to differences and the disagreements they may cause. Three are rather dysfunctional: *suppressing the other* with fault finding, threats, blame, and attack; *eliminating one's self* by being submissive and hiding one's true feelings; and *avoiding conflict* by denying the existence of a conflict and avoiding communication that would reveal differences. The most healthy and functional method of handling conflict and differences is through *open and honest communication* (i.e., acknowledging that a difference exists, discussing it a respectful manner, and negotiating a solution).

Like all social systems, a family will tend to resist change, especially rapid change. Family members use various maneuvers to maintain the status quo or hold on to their usual and habitual patterns. In some extreme cases and when other adaptations have not worked, a family may attempt to preserve itself from a real or perceived threat by *scapegoating* or sacrificing a member for the good of the whole. A request by parents to have their disruptive teenager placed in foster care might be such a maneuver. A related phenomenon, termed *re-peopling,* refers to the family's efforts to regain stability by adding a new member. The decision by a couple with marriage problems to have a child could be a re-peopling maneuver.

- **Family communication**. A pattern of communication develops whenever two or more people interact on a regular basis. Certain unwritten rules and expectations emerge and subtly guide their interaction. To decipher this pattern, the social worker might observe the following: Who usually speaks to whom? Who speaks first? Who responds? Who listens and pays close attention to whom? Who speaks most? Who speaks least? Who speaks last? Who sits next to whom? Are messages directed to one person but meant for someone else? Do the words seem to say one thing but imply something else? Are communications characterized by clarity, respect, and openness or instead by evasiveness, double messages, blaming, threats, hurtful jokes, or interruptions?

- **Decision making**. All families develop a pattern of decision making. In some families, all members participate in decision making; in other families, one member makes all major decisions. A social worker can learn about a family's way of making decisions by meeting with the whole family and asking them to perform a task, such as planning a family outing, while the worker observes the decision-making process.

- **Mood**. Much like an individual, a family is often characterized by a prevailing mood or disposition. For example, is the family warm and caring? Cool and distant? Optimistic? Pessimistic? Playful? Depressed? Excitable? Spontaneous? Controlled? Withdrawn? Content? Hostile?

- **Moral and ethical standards**. Matters of loyalty, fairness, obligation, sacrifice, accountability, and entitlement within a family relate rather directly to moral and ethical standards. Many family conflicts revolve around moral issues and the conduct expected of family members. Some aspects of family behavior can only be understood by first knowing about a family's sense of the sacred—that which is in the sphere of the mysterious, supremely important, and the awesome. This, in turn, will be closely related to their spirituality and religious beliefs and to meanings assigned to life, conflict, suffering, and death.

- **Time and activities**. Family functioning is tied to what the members do with their time and what portion of each day is spent with other family members. Consider, for example, How many hours each day are devoted to job and school?

Travel to and from work? Family meals? Child care? Cooking? Cleaning and laundry? Study and homework? Shopping? Care of a sick or disabled member? Reading? TV? Telephone? Computer? Religious activities? Recreation? Clubs and associations? Sleep?

- **Change**. In most families some members welcome change and want to do things differently, whereas other members oppose change. In order to assess the family's attitudes toward making changes, the social worker might ask the family members to speculate on the effects of a hypothetical change. For example, the worker might ask, "How would a move to another city affect your family as a whole and each of its members?" "Who would be most upset?" "Who would like a change?" "What would each family member do in order to adjust?"

A family's usual patterns of functioning sometimes must change in response to various events that alter its membership, roles, and structure. For example, shifts and modifications will follow the birth of a child, an addition to the family, and when an older child leaves home for a job, college, or the military. And, needless to say, a family's usual functioning can be shaken and stressed by unexpected events such as a member's illness, injury, disability, job loss, or death. Family functioning must also accommodate the developmental stage of each family member (e.g., infancy, adolescence, middle age, old age). It must also adapt to changing circumstances related to the family life cycle (see Item 11.20). A given family may function quite well when the children are young, but will experience serious problems as the children move into the fractious teen years.

"Life History Grid"
a deleted item from the
6th edition

"Life Cycle Matrix"
a deleted item from the
7th edition

Selected Bibliography

Collins, Donald, Catheleen Jordan, and Heather Coleman. *An Introduction to Family Social Work*, 4th ed. Independence, KY: Cengage, 2013.

Manuchin, Salvador, Michael Nichols, and Wai Yung Lee. *Assessing Families and Couples: From Symptom to System*. Boston: Allyn and Bacon, 2007.

Thomlison, Barbara. *Family Assessment Handbook*, 3rd ed. Independence, KY: Cengage, 2010.

Walsh, Froma, ed. *Normal Family Processes*, 4th ed. New York: Guilford, 2011.

11.20 UNDERSTANDING THE FAMILY LIFE CYCLE

For the social worker making an assessment of a family, it is useful to have knowledge of the typical developmental phases and challenges in the family life cycle in order to more clearly understand the family's strengths and problems. As compared to the rather predictable stages of physical, psychological, and social development by an individual, a family's life cycle involves confronting and negotiating a number of tasks, changes, and issues that will vary depending on the type of family being examined. It is apparent that the family as a social institution is undergoing significant change in U.S. society and thus any description of family life must be considered a broad generalization.

In this context we use the term *family* broadly to include (1) households of unmarried persons, usually with intimate relationship patterns; (2) married couples or couples united through civil unions, with or without children; (3) families that are considering or in the process of splitting up; (4) divorced families; and (5) remarried or blended families.

Although federal and state laws vary on the relationships that may be legally recognized, the fundamental tasks and issues for these families are similar.

Households

Increasingly, first marriages and childbearing among young adults begins later in life than was the case for earlier generations, and often after a period of cohabitation. Thus, a significant number of younger adults live for a time (often for many years) in households composed of friends, housemates, and/or a romantic partner. Within these living arrangements, the individual must make a transition from the familiar patterns of his or her family of origin to relationships that are negotiated. Shared living arrangements, whether or not based on romantic ties, involve coming to an agreement on the division of labor for such tasks as cooking, cleaning, and home maintenance; sharing space, bathrooms, and laundry facilities; resolving conflicts over living space and privacy, and establishing workable patterns of communication and interaction. In addition, this is often a time of life when the individual is enrolled in higher education or a training program, adjusting to a new job, starting a career, and learning to manage money.

Married/Civil union couples

Initially, these legally joined couples face many of the same tasks as those learning to live in a household. For the younger couple it is a time of forming a more in-depth commitment and a satisfying sexual relationship. It is a time of forming workable relationships with in-laws, realigning friendships, and striking a balance between family and work. The couple must resolve or learn to live with their differences in expectations, personal habits, and other behaviors and attitudes they learned in their family of origin. Family dysfunction is often passed from generation to generation, so the individual who grew up in a troubled family may struggle with those same problems as he or she settles into a marriage or other committed relationship. Learning to communicate effectively and to manage money is a challenge for a many couples.

If children—and sometimes older adults—also become part of the family household through birth, adoption, foster care, moving in, or whatever else, an additional set of issues arise. The birth of a child draws the couple's attention away from each other and to needs of the child. Family interaction and communication patterns must be adjusted to include the additional members. They must resolve whatever differences they may have about child rearing. Finances may be strained. If both partners are employed there is limited time for family interaction. Established roles, household duties, and decision making must be realigned.

As children grow older and pass through their own developmental stages, the family must adapt its rules and procedures accordingly. At times, grandparents may assume various parenting tasks, again modifying existing family patterns. Finally, as children move on to their own independence and living arrangements, the family must reestablish patterns of living as a couple with continuing emotional ties to the children and, possibly, including grandchildren within the family configuration. As the couple moves into old age, it is increasingly probable that one or both will experience a serious illness or disability. After many years together, the loss of a spouse or partner to death can be a devastating emotional experience that can severely disrupt the survivor's usual manner of coping and living life. The couple's children may need to take on the responsibility of caring of their frail parents. In advanced old age, the need for an assisted living arrangement or nursing home becomes a real possibility.

Separating families

It is not uncommon for social workers to provide services to families that are in the process of separating or contemplating divorcing. Couples believing that they are incompatible for an ongoing family relationship, or that the commitment of one or both partners has been broken, are often referred to social workers or other professionals for counseling. Infidelity, substance abuse, domestic violence, mental illness, and money problems are among the most common factors leading to a divorce. The social worker will help the couple identify the source of their conflict and, if possible, guide the couple in a resolution of the problem. If that fails, social workers might then help to plan for a temporary family break-up or separation with the possibility of divorce as a final outcome. Factors to consider include plans for care and custody of children, visitation arrangements, housing accommodations, financial support, realignment of emotional and parenting relationships, and consideration of ongoing connections with extended family members, such as the children's grandparents. Should divorce be the likely outcome, issues of guilt, remorse, hurt, sense of failure, blaming, and so on are typically addressed.

Divorced families

When a divorce is finalized by court order, the couple comes face-to-face with the painful reality of the break-up. They can no longer deny or avoid the far-reaching impact it will have on their future. If children are involved, the divorce will change to some degree the parent–child relationships as well as the role and responsibilities of each parent. The divorce creates a single-parent family (and frequently two single-parent families) and can easily plunge an individual into poverty. This is especially true for the woman who most often cares for the children after a divorce.

Remarried/Blended families

If one or both partners choose to remarry, another set of issues arises with which the social worker might be helpful. One item that requires discussion is the legal and emotional meaning of marriage and the level of commitment each partner is willing to make to this new relationship. Often, that involves reviewing the factors that led to the break-up of the previous marriages and any continuing emotional attachments, positive or negative, with the previous spouses or partners. New roles and responsibilities must be determined and boundaries established. If children are involved, shared parenting roles and responsibilities must be thoroughly discussed and agreed to by both the parents and children.

In a *blended family*, there may be children from both partners—and possibly children from the parents together—thus sibling relationships must be thoughtfully discussed and procedures identified for resolving the inevitable conflicts in the changed family context. Furthermore, how the members of the blended family will relate to the extended families of the ex-spouses should be considered.

Selected Bibliography

DeGenova, Mary Kay, Nick Stinnett, and Nancy M. Sinnett. *Intimate Relationships, Marriages & Families*, 8th ed. New York: McGraw-Hill, 2011.

Goldberg, Abbie E. *Lesbian and Gay Parents and Their Children: Research on the Family Life Cycle*. Washington, DC: American Psychological Association, 2010.

McGoldrick, Monica, Betty Carter, and Nydia Preto, eds. *The Expanded Life Cycle: Individual, Family, and Social Perspectives*, 4th ed. Upper Saddle River, NJ: Pearson, 2011.

Reisman, Barbara J., ed. *Families as They Really Are*. New York: Norton, 2010.

11.21 ASSESSING SMALL-GROUP FUNCTIONING

Social workers work with and within many small groups, including, for example, committees, interagency planning groups, therapeutic groups, and self-help groups. In general, a *well-functioning group* is one in which the members are clear about the group's purpose and all are working together to achieve that purpose. Such a group energizes its members, brings out their creativity, and usually achieves its purpose. A *dysfunctional group*, on the other hand, seldom achieves its goals and often frustrates its members.

Whenever a social worker is involved in the formation of a new group, he or she should encourage discussions and deliberations that clarify the group's goal or purpose and anticipate the tasks to be performed. The worker should encourage those involved in forming the group to consider how the group should be structured, its ideal size, and the type of leadership and membership necessary to be effective. The worker should assist those who are planning the group to anticipate problems and snags and take steps to minimize these problems. Common group-related problems are poor attendance, lack of leadership, inability to make decisions and resolve conflicts, disruptive or ineffective members, and a lack of resources needed by the group.

When working with or within a group, the social worker should constantly observe and assess its functioning in order to decide what she or he can do to increase the group's effectiveness and efficiency. To do this, the worker must be attentive to both content and process. Basically, *content* refers to the observable actions and activities, whereas the *process* refers to the less visible "how and why" behind what the group does or perhaps avoids doing. It is group content that is described by the formal minutes of a committee meeting. Content is shaped by the group's stated purpose, formal structure, and official agenda. Process is revealed by the emotional mood of meetings, how members interact, who influences whom, how decisions are made, and the degree to which members are invested in the group.

The following sections identify several aspects of small group functioning and provide questions to consider when examining a group's functioning and deciding what might be done to improve its effectiveness.

- **Purpose and goals**. Agreement and clarity on the group's purpose is fundamental. Unless members are working toward the same outcome or goal, the group is likely to drift or get bogged down in conflict. To assess a group's clarity of purpose, answers to the following questions should be informative: What is the group's stated or official purpose? Who selected or framed that purpose? Are all group members in agreement on the purpose? If the members disagree, what is the source of this disagreement?

    When a group lacks agreement on its purpose, the social worker should bring this to the group's attention and encourage a discussion on purpose and goals. Conflict may arise as members voice their differing viewpoints and expectations but that is a necessary step toward achieving clarity.

- **Context**. Small groups exist within organizational and community contexts. These external influences are often the source of hidden agendas and disagreements over the group's purpose and composition. For example, a powerful person in the community may exert pressure on the group's leader or on a member to make a certain decision or move the group in a particular direction.

Answers to the following questions will help reveal external influences: What organization sponsors, hosts, or funds this group (e.g., a committee) or wanted it to be formed? What does that organization expect to gain from the group? In what way is the group impacted by, for example, political pressures, policy and program requirements, and current community controversies? When it is apparent that external influences are having an adverse or inappropriate effect on the group, it is usually best for the group to acknowledge this reality and discuss how it should be handled.

- **Leadership**. Effective leadership is a key to guiding a small group toward its goals. If the designated or official leader lacks leadership skills, the group will flounder and the inevitable conflicts will likely smolder and eventually undermine group functioning. The answers to several questions can help assess the leadership dimension within a group: How and why was the leader selected? Does the leader provide the vision and direction needed to help the group achieve its goals? Does the leader clarify and test out ideas, build consensus, promote needed compromises, and resolve conflicts within the group? Does the leader display the behaviors and commitments that he or she expects from the group's members? Does the leader have credibility and command the respect of members? Do members look to someone other than the official leader for leadership? Do some members undermine or sabotage the leader?

  When the work of a group is being impeded by the lack of effective leadership, a change is usually necessary. Problems of poor leadership can be at least minimized by holding regularly scheduled elections of the group's leader or perhaps an agreed-on rotation of the leadership role. In some cases, an open and critical evaluation of the group's functioning and performance may prompt a change in leadership (see Item 16.12).

- **Membership and participation**. In order for a small group to achieve its purpose, its members must have the motivation, commitment, skills, and authority to achieve that purpose. Having a few highly motivated and skilled members can be pivotal to a group's success. On the other hand, a few negative, unmotivated, or disruptive members can severely limit the group's effectiveness.

  To assess a group's composition and the level of participation, seek answers to the following questions: Given its purpose, is the group about the right size? Is it composed of the individuals needed to achieve its purpose? What skills and attributes does each member bring to the group? Has the membership or level of participation changed significantly since the group was first formed and if so, why? What draws the members to this group and what keeps others from joining? Are the time and place of the meetings convenient to the members? Which members are most active? Least active? Do some dominate the group? Are some members discounted? Are the naturally quiet or hesitant members encouraged to participate? Do members feel free to express disagreement, address conflicts, and take risks? Is open and honest communication expected or perhaps discouraged? Does each member attend the group's meetings because he or she wants to or because attendance is required?

  If a group's effectiveness is hampered because some members do not have the motivation or ability to perform essential tasks, a change in the group's size or composition is necessary. If an individual's poor attendance is a problem, this should be discussed with her or him in private. If a member cannot meet the minimum expectation on attendance, the member should be replaced. If a person is disruptive, the leader or a few influential members should speak to him or her in private and request a change of behavior. In some cases, it may be necessary to find a way of excluding a disruptive member. Whenever the social worker is group member, she or he should strive to display and model behaviors that are important to effective group functioning.

- **Structure, norms, and rules**. Over time, a small group will develop a formal and an informal structure, as well as some norms or rules that shape its activity and how members behave. A particular structure will be more or less effective, depending on the group's size, purpose, and history. The norms and rules are typically a mix of explicit and implicit guidelines.

  The answers to several questions can help assess the appropriateness of the group's structure, norms, and rules: What formal or informal structure and rules govern the group (e.g., seating arrangement, written agendas, *Roberts Rules of Order*)? Does an informal power structure or status hierarchy determine who speaks and who makes decisions? Do the group's rules and norms encourage all members to participate and stay focused on the group's purpose and activities? Is the discussion of certain viewpoints either encouraged or discouraged? Are the frequency and length of meetings suitable to the group's purpose?

  If a group is not achieving its goals because it lacks the structure and rules needed to keep it on course, the group should be encouraged to examine this matter and possibly create an agreed-on set of procedures.

- **Decision making**. An effective group makes thoughtful and timely decisions. Good decisions depend on a membership that is informed and sufficiently diverse so as to provide a variety of perspectives but not so diverse and divided that it gets bogged down in endless debate. A group's decision-making process can be examined by seeking answers to the following questions: Do all members contribute to the group's decisions? Are the decisions deliberate and thoughtful or perhaps rushed, partisan, or ideological? Are poor decisions the result of a subgroup or clique pushing its own agenda? Does the group use a formal procedure to arrive at its decisions (e.g., *Robert's Rules of Order*)? If so, do all members understand this procedure?

- **Resources**. A group's effectiveness depends on having access to essential resources such as a suitable meeting space and money for supplies, photocopying, and communications. This concern can be assessed by these questions: Is the meeting space comfortable and arranged to facilitate participation? Do all members have copies of the agenda, minutes of previous meetings, copies of reports under discussion, handouts, and so forth? If some members have a very limited income, is it possible to cover their expenses for travel, child care, and other fees?

Selected Bibliography

Corey, Marianne, Gerald Corey, and Cindy Corey. *Group Process and Practice*, 8th ed. Independence, KY: Cengage, 2014.

Erich, Stephen, and Heather Kaneberg. *Skills for Group Practice*. Upper Saddle River, NJ: Pearson, 2011.

Toseland, Ronald, and Robert Rivas. *An Introduction to Group Work Practice*, 7th ed. Upper Saddle River, NJ: Pearson, 2012.

11.22 ACCESSING EVIDENCE-BASED INFORMATION

In social work, the call for evidence-based practice is typically met with "OK, but where do I obtain the evidence?" Indeed, there are thousands of studies reported in books, journals, and research papers that can be found in libraries, electronic collections of abstracts, and on the Internet. Many of these resources provide search engines that help social workers cull through considerable data to locate the most relevant information for his or her practice needs, increasing the likelihood of one's practice being evidence-based (see Chapter 7 for a discussion of evidence-based practice).

When it is possible for a social worker to physically gain access to a library with sufficient social work literature to support a good search for evidence, one has the advantage of being able to quickly scan materials, browse through books on related topics, and photocopy materials deemed useful. A specialized type of library is sometimes maintained by large human services agencies that house a small, but highly focused, collection of books and journals related to its practice focus. Usually, however, the most useful local library collections of books and journals are those maintained by universities—especially those schools that include a social work education program. Of course, students and faculty have priority access, but often it is possible to arrange for alumni and field instructors to also have physical and online access to these resources. Not only will university libraries have hard-copy collections but they are also likely to have contracts with search engines that allow one to efficiently screen through massive databases to surface abstracts of published materials that relate to the topic of interest. Some will also have subscriptions to online journals, where it is possible to read and/or download copies of the most relevant materials that will inform one's practice decisions.

Some particularly useful databases are:

- Google Scholar
- Social Work Abstracts
- PsychIINFO
- Social Services Abstracts
- Social Sciences Abstracts

The most complete U.S. book collection resides with the Library of Congress, where searches by book titles, authors, and key words can quickly identify useful resources. To access the Library of Congress collection, use the following steps:

Step 1: Enter www.loc.gov.

Step 2: By selecting "Basic Search," a screen is provided where one might select, among other choices, "Title Keyword," "Subject Keyword," or "Subject Browse." For example, if you want to browse the subject of "evidence-based social work." insert those keywords into the box provided and select the "Begin Search" box.

Step 3: Continuing this example, a list indicating that 33 or more books on the topic appears, and by clicking that line, a list of those books appears.

Step 4: It is then possible to sort those books—for example, if you want to know what's new on the topic—with the most recent books appearing at the top of the list.

Step 5: Upon finding a title that might provide the evidence you seek, click on that title and select "full record" to obtain summary information that can help you decide if you want to seek a copy of that book.

"Best practices" evidence is typically found in databases in which rigorous meta-analysis evaluations of multiple studies of the outcomes of a specific client service yield guidance on the relative success in specific practice situations. These articles are then screened to a small number, analyzing only those that empirically evaluate the effectiveness of a specific intervention. The articles or research reports making the final cut are then subjected to a rigorous protocol by which a panel of experts rates each study on the quality of evidence in relation to factors such as (1) the alignment of the intervention to commonly held ideas regarding this intervention, (2) the replicability of the intervention approach, (3) the adequacy of the outcome measures used, (4) whether the intervention tested statistically significant across important populations that might be served, and (5) the adequacy of controls placed on the manner in which the intervention approach was applied to the clients in the study. Where the studies that stand up to this rigorous assessment agree, best practices are identified.

The National Association of Social Workers' Social Policy Institute maintains a source for identifying current best practices relative to social work at the following web address: (http://www.socialworkers.org/research/naswResearch/0108EvidenceBased/default.asp).

To access these resources, the following steps provide one example.

Step 1: Select the "Research" tab and then "Evidence-Based Practice."
Step 2: Select "Evidence-Based Resources" and then "Evidence-Based Registries and Databases."
Step 3: Among the several choices, for example, is the Campbell Collaboration. Select that option, go to the homepage, and select "systematic reviews."
Step 4: In the search box, insert your key words—for example, "kinship care." You will be referred to an article on kinship care that has used a very sophisticated protocol to summarize studies (meta-analysis) on children removed from their homes due to maltreatment.
Step 5: By selecting "Download Review" you will have immediate access to the full study that you can use to inform your practice.

A parallel selection to "Evidence-Based Practice Resources" is "Online Resources and Research." By selecting that option, the websites of several databases maintained by national organizations can be immediately accessed. Some particularly useful sites on that list for social work practitioners are Child Trends, Child Welfare Information Gateway, Evidence-Based Behavioral Practice, Evidence-Based Group Work, National Alliance of Multi-Ethnic Behavioral Health Associations, National Institute of Mental Health, and the VA Quality Enhancement Research Institute.

Selected Bibliography

Bronson, Denise E., and Tamara S. Davis. *Finding and Evaluating Evidence: Systematic Reviews and Evidence-Based Practice.* New York: Oxford University Press, 2012.

Dunlop, Judy, and Michael J. Holosko, eds. *Information Technology and Evidence-Based Social Work Practice.* New York: Haworth, 2006.

Palionkas, Lawrence A., and Haluk Soydan. *Translation and Implementation of Evidence-Based Practice.* New York: Oxford University Press, 2012.

Wodarski, John S., and Laura M. Hopson. *Research Methods for Evidence-Based Practice.* Thousand Oaks, CA: Sage, 2012.

SECTION B

TECHNIQUES AND GUIDELINES FOR INDIRECT PRACTICE

Large system change is difficult and time consuming. Rarely can one person, or even a few people, decide on changes to be made and easily implement the actions to bring about that change. It takes careful planning, education, negotiation, patience, and the participation of many individuals and groups to achieve meaningful changes in agency policies and programs or affect legislative changes related to the larger community.

Data-collection activities

The first step in preparing for agency or community change is to collect sufficient information to be well informed. For example, change requires working through, or sometimes around, the agency's or community's decision-making structure. To do this, the worker needs to learn about the feasibility of various options, the costs (in dollars and the expenditure of human resources) of changing the current situation, the positive and/or negative implications for associated individuals or systems, and the most effective ways to bring about change.

Data collection requires the worker to accumulate information regarding differing perceptions and accurately summarize the information obtained. Often this data collection occurs in a staff meeting, a board meeting, or from members of a committee appointed to study a particular agency concern. On other occasions, *focus groups* are created wherein intensive verbal interaction is stimulated in order to air various opinions on a topic. Another format for data collection involves creating a questionnaire that invites written responses to a series of questions that can be tabulated and summarized to yield a description of the thoughts and opinions of the respondents. Finally, data collection may mean securing relevant reports and documents and then writing a report that organizes the data so that it might be readily analyzed.

"Focus Groups" from 8th edition

Assessment activities

After the data is collected and summarized, the social worker must have the tools to interpret the meaning of the data and to arrive at conclusions. When working at the organizational level, a social worker is typically concerned with issues such as understanding alternative ways to structure the work to be done in a human services agency or to better understand the needs and problems of the clients served by the agency.

At the community level, a social worker must be able to assess the factors that impinge on decision makers in that particular community. Also, before moving to action, the social worker must accurately assess the social policies that are in place and understand the ramifications of various changes that may be proposed. Having at least a general sense of the elements of a sound policy analysis, then, is important for any social worker, as well as having tools for assessing and building the assets in a community.

11.23 ASSESSING AGENCY STRUCTURE

The organizational structure of an agency has a significant impact on the ability of the social worker to provide effective services. In any type of organization, the structure can be expected to vary according to the complexity of the tasks being performed, the amount of authority reserved for central decision making, and the degree to which policies, rules, and procedures are formalized. For example, many successful industrial organizations are based on the bureaucratic model. That model is most viable when the work requires the performance of relatively simple routine tasks (e.g., putting together parts on an assembly line) that are coordinated through very specific rules of operation. The bureaucratic organizational model, however, is less viable in human services agencies where the work is complex and must be adapted to the unique needs of clients. This work requires individualized judgments by professionals that cannot be readily subjected to centralized control and formalized rules and procedures.

The structures of human services organizations range from highly bureaucratized operations to those that permit considerable worker autonomy. For example, public agencies tend to be bureaucratized, allowing the policymakers and program administrators to maintain a high degree of control over agency functioning. Private nonprofit agencies, by contrast, are usually smaller, offer fewer programs, and tend toward decentralized authority and a minimum of rules and regulations, thus allowing staff members more control over their practice activities and substantial flexibility in how they perform their jobs.

For social workers in all types of human services organizations, it is useful to recognize that various degrees of bureaucratization can exist and that adaptations can be made that create a workable balance between the responsibilities of management to provide oversight and worker discretion in making professional decisions. At times, workers must advocate for structural changes when they find that the agency's structure interferes with service to clients. To inform these advocacy efforts, it is useful to examine several examples of structural formats commonly found in human services agencies.

At one end of the continuum of organizational structure is the **bureaucracy**. In its pure form, a bureaucracy has an elaborate *division of labor* in which work activities are clearly defined and assigned to specialized workers; a *hierarchy* of several of layers of managers, supervisors, and front-line workers is developed; a formalized set of very specific *rules and regulations* is rigidly applied; and the work is carried out in a spirit of *impersonality* that is not adjusted to accommodate individual uniqueness. Bureaucracies are characterized by fairness and equal treatment, but they suffer from lack of flexibility and the ability to individualize. They tend to be stable and consistent yet slow to change.

At the other end of the continuum of organizational structure is the **adhocracy** (i.e., the organization that forms internal structures on an issue-by-issue basis with various collectives of staff members addressing each issue). The ad hoc groups have considerable authority and operate with few rules and regulations that apply to the whole agency. This type of organization has a "flat" administrative structure, in which all staff positions are somewhat equal. Ad hoc agencies are typically weak on both structure and stability, but are able to respond to new issues and undergo change rapidly. They are particularly effective when the nature of the work is dynamic or fluid.

In reality, most human services agencies fall somewhere between a fully developed bureaucracy and a completely ad hoc structure. In smaller agencies, it is possible to have a relatively flat structure with an executive director heading the organization (e.g., representing the staff with the board and the board with the staff) and the professional staff members having somewhat equal status. As agencies become larger and more complex and when the number of staff members for the director to supervise becomes too great for one person to manage, the work must be divided into segments. In this situation, a functional structure is likely to serve the agency well. In the **functional model**, a second-level administrative layer reports to the director and also leads a program unit or supervises a group of workers. A family services agency, for example, might have a counseling unit, a day treatment unit, a social action unit, and an administrative support unit—each with its own unit manager. The executive director would facilitate coordination of these units and oversee the work of the unit managers.

At times, an agency may temporarily supplement one of these structures with a **project-team model**. This model provides for groups of staff to be organized around specific tasks for limited periods of time. In addition to being assigned to a specific unit or supervisor for their primary job, workers may be temporarily assigned on a full- or part-time basis to a team that cuts across units to address a specific problem. An example would be staff members from a family agency's clinical and day treatment units temporarily joining with staff members from the social action unit to plan and carry out a strategy of public education and to reduce the incidence of spouse abuse.

Selected Bibliography

Austin, Michael J., Ralph P. Brody, and Thomas Packard. *Managing the Challenges in Human Services Organizations: A Casebook.* Thousand Oaks, CA: Sage, 2009.

Lauffer, Armand. *Understanding Your Social Agency*, 3rd ed. Thousand Oaks, CA: Sage, 2011.

Patti, J. Rino, ed. *The Handbook of Human Services Management: Purposes, Practice, and Prospects in the 21st Century*, 2nd ed. Thousand Oaks, CA: Sage, 2009.

Schmid, Hillel, ed. *Organizational and Structural Dilemmas in Nonprofit Human Service Organizations.* Binghamton, NY: Haworth, 2004.

11.24 ASSESSING HUMAN SERVICES NEEDS

Human services agencies are set up to address some particular social condition or human need. A critical question that must be asked from time to time is whether the past agency's understanding of this problem or need is accurate and up-to-date. The perspective of the agency board and staff is, of course, a valuable source of information for determining if the agency's goals and services are still needed, appropriate, and relevant. However, it is also important that decisions be informed by a formal evaluation of the need for these services. Thus, agencies should periodically conduct needs assessments. **Needs assessment** refers to the process of identifying the incidence, prevalence, and nature of certain conditions within a community. The ultimate purpose is to assess the adequacy of existing services and resources in addressing those conditions. The extent to which those conditions or problems are not adequately addressed denotes a need for different services or resources.

Before conducting a needs assessment, two decisions must be made by those conducting the analysis and those who will use the findings (e.g., agency board, city council, United Way). First, there should be agreement about what constitutes a need, and second, there must be an honest intent to take action if an unmet need is identified. It is not good use of time or resources to conduct a needs assessment when it is known in advance that there is no intent to take corrective action related to problems identified by the needs assessment.

GUIDELINES FOR CONDUCTING A NEEDS ASSESSMENT

These guidelines should be kept in mind when conducting a needs assessment:

- It is essential to have a clear understanding of the policy issues and administrative concerns that prompted the decision to conduct a needs assessment. In other words, what problems do the decision makers hope to address through the use of a needs assessment? Some possible reasons why situations of unmet need might exist include:

- Insufficient services are available in the community.
- Existing services are not accessible because of transportation problems, eligibility criteria, and the like.
- Persons in need are not aware that services exist.
- Existing services are not integrated or coordinated to provide a continuity of service to individuals and families with multiple problems and needs.
- Existing programs do not have adequate resources to provide quality service.
- Existing services are unacceptable to residents of a particular community. For example, they may be perceived as degrading, threatening, or in conflict with existing ethnic, religious, or cultural norms and values.

- The goals and objectives of the needs assessment must be clear before it is possible to select appropriate methods of data collection and analysis. All too often, those planning a needs assessment jump ahead to the question of what to ask the people being interviewed before they are clear on exactly what kind of data will be useful in the planning of new services or the modification of existing services.

- It is helpful to know how other communities or agencies have approached the task, but it is usually a mistake to borrow someone else's objectives and methodology. Those who are in a position to use the data should decide what approach would be useful and work best in their community. Such decisions should not be made by outside consultants or by persons or agencies that have a vested interest in seeing the assessment yield certain results.

- A needs assessment should not only identify unmet service needs; in addition, it should shed light on the quantity, quality, and direction of existing services. For example:

  Quantity. Does the level of service match the demand? This involves some assessment of the number of persons in need of service compared with the capacity of providers to serve those persons.

  Quality. Are the services effective? Do they accomplish what they are intended to do? Are they efficient and cost-effective?

  Direction, Are the approaches used in service delivery appropriate or possibly out of touch with the real needs of clients? Does the philosophy or beliefs that gave rise to existing programs coincide with ones espoused by experts in the field?

Selected Bibliography

Royse, David, Michele Staton-Tindall, Karen Badger, and J. Matthew Webster. *Needs Assessment.* New York: Oxford University Press, 2009.

Smith, Michael J. *Handbook of Program Evaluation for Social Work and Health Professionals.* New York: Oxford University Press, 2010.

Soriano, Fernando I. *Conducting Needs Assessments: A Multidisciplinary Approach,* 2nd ed. Thousand Oaks, CA: Sage, 2013.

11.25 COMMUNITY DECISION-MAKING ANALYSIS

When social workers seek to influence decisions that affect the quality of human services, they must develop a strategy for convincing the people in authority that a particular course of action is the best choice among the possible options. Ideally, decisions should be made on the merit of the proposal; in reality, however, decision makers usually respond to external pressures and various personal considerations.

Research on community decision making and community power structures does not yield a consistent picture of the forces that lead to these decisions. However, several generalizations can be made regarding variables that partially explain why some communities tend to center the decision making in a small, elite group of people while others are more pluralistic and involve a broader spectrum of the community. Consider the following:

- **Size**. Large cities tend to be pluralistic. They are likely to become more diverse and competitive as they grow, resulting in a broader range of people and interest groups involved in making decisions.

- **Population diversity**. Communities composed of various socioeconomic and ethnic groups develop numerous special-interest groups that compete for power and resources. Consequently, pluralism expands and it is more difficult for an elite group to influence the outcome of community decisions.

- **Economic diversity**. More diversified communities in terms of varied sources of employment, high levels of industrialization, and the presence of absentee-owned industry (as opposed to local people owning the major industries) all tend to make communities more pluralistic in how decisions are made.

- **Local government**. The greater the competition or balance among political groups, the more likely the community will have a pluralistic decision-making structure.

Most communities in the United States have a pluralistic type of decision-making structure, although some small rural communities maintain elite power structures. Influencing decisions requires a careful assessment of the people who are authorized to make the decisions. For example, the critical decision makers regarding an issue of interest to social workers are likely to be an agency board member or an elected official. In most cases, relatively few people are involved in making a decision, and they will tend to be focused on particular issues where they have self-interest (e.g., realtors and bankers focused on housing and economic issues, physicians and other health care professionals focused on health care).

The social worker involved in a community change process must assess three factors that may affect a decision maker's choice. First, *personal characteristics* of the decision maker will potentially affect the decision. For example, the decision maker will be influenced by such considerations such as the repercussions of the decision on his or her personal finances, his or her self-esteem and social status, judgment about the merits of the proposed change, trade-offs linked to other decisions, and so on. Second, some decision makers acquire power due to important *organizational affiliations*. Typically, those associated with financial institutions, large employers, and real estate interests are in critical decision-making positions and, unless persuaded otherwise, will make decisions that support and reward the organizations they represent. Third, the social worker should be aware that some decision makers gain their position from a *communitywide base* and must be responsive to the will of the public if they are to maintain their positions and power. These persons may represent the media, political parties, and various issue-based, special-interest groups. Being clear about the sources of influence for any decision maker is prerequisite for devising strategies to influence her or his decisions.

"Force Field Analysis" from 7th edition

Sorting out the relative power of individuals, organizations, and community groups when concerned with a decision about a social program or a community issue can be complex. Two useful online sources that walk those making a power analysis through the steps of a change process are provided by the National Latino Council on Alcohol and Tobacco Prevention (LCAT) and The Praxis Project (see Selected Bibliography for web address).

Selected Bibliography

Anderson, Donald L., ed. *Cases and Exercises in Organization Development and Change*. Thousand Oaks, CA: Sage, 2012.

Miller, Mike. *A Community Organizer's Tale: People and Power in San Francisco*. Berkeley, CA: Heyday Books, 2009.

National Latino Council on Alcohol and Tobacco Prevention (LCAT). *Take Action; Create Change: A Community Organizing Toolkit*. http://www.healthwellnc.com/TUPCHERITAGETOOLKIT/ September/5General%20Information/LCAT%20Take%20Action%20Create%20Change%20- %20Community%20Organizing%20Toolkit.pdf.

Oatway, Jay. *Mastering Story, Community, and Influence: How to Use Social Media to Become a Social Leader*. Hoboken, NJ: Wiley, 2012.

The Praxis Project. *Health Equity Tool Kit for a Winning Policy Strategy*. http://toolkit.healthjustice .us/power_chart.

11.26 ANALYZING SOCIAL POLICY IMPLICATIONS

When a social worker engages in activity to change an existing social policy, or to introduce a new one, it is important that she or he conduct a careful analysis of that policy. The depth of that analysis will depend somewhat on the social worker's role in making the analysis and the scope of the change envisioned.

It is helpful to recognize that every realistic social policy is a compromise, yet one must be clear about the "best outcome" as a starting point for negotiating a compromise. At a minimum, the social worker should be prepared to analyze the major elements of a policy proposal to assure that compromise does not negate the central goal of the change.

Chambers and Bonk (2013) provide a relatively simple and straightforward guide for analyzing policy proposals. The questions in each of the following categories suggest the kinds of information the worker might seek in order to gain sufficient understanding to engage in a successful policy change process:

- **Social problem analysis**. The first step in the analysis of a social policy or program is to have a clear understanding of what created the situation requiring such a policy. To make this assessment, it is useful to undertake the following activities:

  - Identify the problem or troublesome situation that gave rise to the social policy. How is this problem described or defined? Are there other more appropriate or accurate definitions? How many people experience this problem? What subpopulations are most likely to experience this problem?

  - Determine the causes and consequences of the problem. What forces or factors have caused the problem? Are there multiple causes? Are there multiple consequences from a single cause?

  - Identify the ideological beliefs embedded in the description of the problem. The definition of a problem is influenced by beliefs about what "ought to be," or the values one holds. Is there a difference of opinion about the seriousness or significance of the problem? Do different groups hold varying views about the nature and cause of the problem?

- Identify the gainers and losers in relation to the problem. Who benefits from the existence of the problem? What do they gain and how much? Who loses? What do they lose and how much? How serious are the negative consequences on the lives of the losers?

- **Social policy and program analysis**. Once the problem is understood, the second step is to assess the social policy and/or program being considered as a means of addressing the problem or offering relief to the victims of the problem. The following are useful for this analysis:

  - Search out the relevant program and policy history. Is this a new problem? Have conditions, values, or perceptions changed over time? What is different about the proposed program or policy from past efforts to deal with the problem?

  - Identify the key characteristics of the proposed policy or program. What are the goals and objectives of the proposal? Who would be eligible to benefit from the plan? What benefits or services would be delivered if this proposal gains approval? What administrative structure would be required and how would it work? What staffing would be required to carry out the program? How would the program be financed and how much money would be required? What would be the source of this money?

- **Draw conclusions**. After the preceding information has been collected, it is necessary to judge the merits of the policy or program under analysis. Ultimately, it is the weight of the evidence matched with one's beliefs about what the quality of life should be for members of the society that results in a recommendation favoring or opposing the proposal—or suggesting compromise.

  Answers to the following questions might be considered in arriving at conclusions about this program or policy proposal:

- Does the remedy proposed adequately deal with the causes as well as the consequences of the problem?
- Will it yield an outcome different from policies and programs attempted in the past?
- Would the probable outcomes justify the costs involved?
- Are there better remedies that might be proposed?

  When addressing a social policy, it is particularly important to be conscientious about using accurate data. If challenged by those with competing interests, credibility can be lost by not having sufficient and accurate data to support conclusions and underpin recommendations for change.

  With a solid analysis of the policy or program proposal, the social worker is prepared to influence the decisions that would impact the problem under consideration. At times, the social worker will work through committees or other groups to affect these decisions; on other occasions, it is appropriate to contact a policymaker directly and express a position on the proposal (see Item 13.38).

Selected Bibliography

Chambers, Donald E., and Jane Frances Bonk. *Social Policy and Social Programs: A Method for the Practical Social Policy Analyst*, 6th ed. Upper Saddle River, NJ: Pearson, 2013.

Meenaghan, Thomas M., Keith M. Kilty, and John G. McNutt. *Policy, Politics, and Ethics: A Critical Approach*, 3rd ed. Chicago: Lyceum, 2013.

Ritter, Jessica A. *Social Work Policy Practice: Changing Our Community, Nation, and the World*. Upper Saddle River, NJ: Pearson, 2013.

11.27 CONDUCTING A COMMUNITY ASSETS ASSESSMENT

At the neighborhood and community levels, social workers are, or at least should be, involved in efforts to improve social agencies, social programs, and the community environment to enhance the well-being of all people. Figuring out how to do this first requires careful analysis of the strengths and limitations of the existing resources in the community. Only then can action plans be developed to bring about needed changes.

The **community assets model** of community assessment is focused primarily on identifying community assets. *Assets* are the strengths or the positive factors in a neighborhood or community that already are present and can become the basis of further enhancement of quality of life. Although assets assessment requires an inter-disciplinary approach, it is an approach generally favored by social workers because it parallels the strengths perspective embraced by the social work profession (see Item 11.6).

As opposed to many assessment approaches that will focus on only one aspect of community life (e.g., economic development, workforce deployment, mental health services), an assets assessment is more comprehensive. It recognizes that the various dimensions and aspects of a community are interrelated. For example, opportunities for people to become part of the workforce are affected by the community's economic growth and business climate, and the availability of a competent workforce is partially affected by the quality of the local schools and even by the adequacy of mental health services. Thus, it is essential that an assessment team include knowledgeable people drawn from all the major sectors or community life.

Each community assessment will require a different set of local organizations and institutions to be represented, but typically local government, key businesses and employers, schools, economic and physical space planning groups, hospitals, and human services agencies should be invited to participate. When inviting these organizations to send representatives, it is useful to indicate that the representative will not only be asked to assist in the assets assessment but should be prepared to also carry forward the recommendations derived from the assessment.

In assets assessment the word **capital** is used to describe the available resources with the presumption that investment in these resources will eventually yield positive returns to the community. The following are general descriptions of the forms of community capital an assets assessment might examine and some suggested questions to start the process.

- *Social capital.* Having shared values, relationships, and functioning networks of people and institutions is essential if the effort is to lead to community action. Useful questions to assess this asset might be: To what extent do the people and organizations depend on and take care of each other? Do the community members maintain positive social relationships and experience a sense of community? Do people volunteer their time and talent to improve the community? Do people and organizations collaborate rather than compete to achieve outcomes that are best for the whole community? If a community's social capital is minimal, it may be necessary to first engage in activities to strengthen that asset before addressing other areas.

- *Human capital.* What the people themselves bring to a community is essential to its success. Some beginning questions might be: To what extent are the people educated or trained to meet the community's employment needs? To what degree is the population mentally, physically, and emotionally healthy? Is there opportunity for the expression of the citizens' artistic talents (e.g., theatre, dance, visual arts, and music)? Are the people engaged in healthy recreational activities?

- *Physical capital.* In a community, there must be physical structures that provide a place for people to carry out their lives. An assets assessment might ask: What is the quality, quantity, and affordability of housing for people to live in? Are there adequate buildings in which businesses and other organizations can function? Is there a sufficient infrastructure of streets, bridges, lights, water, and heating/cooling? Is the area aesthetically pleasing with parks and open space present?

- *Financial capital.* Anyone who has experienced a recession knows that the availability of loans and credit is fundamental to a community's ability to adapt to changing conditions. The ability and willingness of financial institutions to invest in the people and community is critical. Thus, a few of the questions an assets assessment might address are: To what extent does the local government offer incentives to attract new businesses? Do the financial institutions offer lines of credit so local businesses can deal with temporary cash flow problems? Are loans for new business/program expansions available? Are the financial institutions flexible in providing home loans and adjusting payment schedules for residents of the community?

- *Environmental capital.* The natural resources of a community provide an important resource if they are properly developed and adequately protected. Some initial questions regarding this asset might include: What is the quality and quantity of the air, energy, and water supply? Are there forests, lakes, streams, or other resources that might be developed for tourist trade or other uses? Are there sufficient foods grown, raised, or produced locally to sustain the community?

- *Cultural capital.* Each community has a history and its inhabitants have brought with them elements of various cultures. Activities that recognize that history and showcase the richness of the cultures that have been blended in the community help to build pride in the community and appreciation of the contributions the different cultures can make. Some sample questions to initiate an assets assessment about cultural capital might include: To what extent do local media sources provide historical information on the community's growth and development? Is there recognition of the contributions made to the community by groups of differing cultural backgrounds? Is there sufficient opportunity for participation in religious/spiritual experiences?

- *Political capital.* A community may have sufficient social, human, financial, environmental, and cultural capital, but without the political will and ability to focus those resources on making the community a better place for its citizens, a community cannot realize its potential. Some questions to ask in an assets assessment might include: What level of voter turnout occurs in local elections? Are voters willing to support bond issues or tax increases for projects that will improve community life? Do public information sources (e.g., newspaper, radio and TV stations) give adequate attention to issues and projects that can enhance the quality of the community?

Selected Bibliography

Green, Gary Paul, and Anna Haines. *Asset Building and Community Development*, 3rd ed. Thousand Oaks, CA: Sage, 2012.

Green, Gary Paul, and Ann Goetting, eds. *Mobilizing Communities: Asset Building as a Community Development Strategy*. Philadelphia: Temple University Press, 2010.

Delgado, Melvin, and Denise Humm-Delgado. *Asset Assessments and Community Social Work Practice*. New York: Oxford University Press, 2013.

12

Planning and Contracting

LEARNING OBJECTIVES

At the conclusion of this chapter, the reader should be prepared to:

- Describe several techniques a social worker might use to help a client focus on a problem(s) that requires an intervention, including a problem search and use of a client needs list.
- Explain the importance of identifying clear objectives for an intervention and discuss the advantages and limits of implied, verbal, and written contracts for service.
- Discuss the merits of engaging informal resources as part of an intervention plan.
- Describe the approach known as family group conferencing and identify concerns that must be addressed when planning such a conference and for forming other small groups.
- Identify strategic planning and other processes that can be used to help a human services agency adapt to change, plan for future changes, and prevent undesirable changes from occurring.
- Demonstrate understanding of factors a social worker should consider when initiating a social change advocacy effort and identify planning tools that can improve the effectiveness of such a social change effort.
- Recognize that a successful long-term social change effort should begin with involving people who are likely to be affected by the change.

After completing an assessment of the client's concern and situation, the social worker and the client focus on planning and contracting, the third phase of the change process. **Planning** is the bridge between assessment and intervention. In some cases of direct practice, the decision on what needs to be done to address the client's concern is fairly obvious, but in other cases, the appropriate action is less apparent and requires careful discernment. In an effort to change complex systems such as organizations and communities, the length of the planning phase will often exceed the time required for the intervention itself.

Effective planning places a special demand on the creativity of the social worker and the willingness of the client to consider alternative courses of action. Each possible option must be evaluated in an effort to predict its probable impact and effectiveness, identify possible unintended consequences, determine the resources required, and estimate the time needed to implement the plan. In addition, the worker must select the most appropriate practice frameworks—perspectives, theories, and models—that can guide the process (see Chapter 6). Recognizing that some methods of facilitating change may be effective but unethical, the *Code of Ethics* should be considered at this point, as it is an important screen or filter when selecting intervention strategies (see Item 9.5). Clients, and sometimes inexperienced workers, may be tempted to rush or shortcut this planning activity. However, action, without a clear plan, is a recipe for confusion and failure. It is said that if you fail to plan, you have, in effect, planned to fail.

Once a tentative plan has been developed, it is important for the worker and client to explicitly agree to this plan. In other words, they enter into an agreement or a **contract**. The issues addressed in a contract are essentially the same whether working at the individual, family, group, organization, or community level. At a minimum, this agreement should delineate the following:

- Problems or concerns to be addressed
- Goals and objectives of the intervention
- Activities the client will undertake
- Activities to be performed by the social worker
- Expected duration of the intervention (in weeks or months)
- Probable location and estimated number of sessions or meetings
- Identification of additional persons, agencies, or organizations expected to participate and their role in the change process

Recognizing that even the most carefully developed plan may need to be modified as the intervention evolves and circumstances change, the social worker and client must be open to such revisions.

SECTION A

TECHNIQUES AND GUIDELINES FOR DIRECT PRACTICE

When working with individuals, families, and small groups during the planning and contracting phase, the social worker must strive to maximize client participation and client self-determination. After all, it is the client who must live with the results of the intervention. The client has certain rights that need to be respected:

- Make decisions and have input concerning the intervention's goals and objectives and the approach to be used.
- Know the likelihood of success and know about any risks or adverse effects associated with the proposed intervention.
- Know about how long it will take to achieve the agreed-on objectives.
- Know about how much time and money will be required of the client.
- Know how progress and effectiveness will be evaluated.
- Know of any consequences for terminating the intervention against the advice of the social worker or agency.

- Know what rules of confidentiality apply and who else (e.g., court, probation officer, school officials, parent) may have access to information about the client's participation and the outcome of the intervention.
- Know about appeals or grievance procedures that could be used to challenge a decision made by the social worker or agency.

Planning activities

Some of the most critical decisions a social worker must make occur during the planning phase. In some cases, a decision can have lifelong consequences for a client—for example, whether to plan the separation of an abused child from his or her parents, whether to recommend probation or incarceration for a youth, and so on.

One possible mistake is to move too quickly toward selecting and implementing an intervention without considering various options and the likelihood of their success. That error may occur because the worker hurries the decision, considers only a narrow range of strategies for change, or interprets agency policy and procedure in an excessively rigid manner, thus stifling creativity and resourcefulness. A related error is to make decisions on the basis of untested assumptions without first weighing information that might contradict the client's or the worker's presumptions about the nature, cause, and solution to the client's problem. Finally, an uncritical application of a particular practice theory or model can lead to bad decisions. A social worker who is overly committed to a particular framework may disregard information that does not fit her or his preferred approach or theory.

Contracting activities

Having a plan is critical. Having agreement on that plan is just as important. The greater the specificity about who will do what, when, where, and how, the more likely it is that everyone involved will understand the intervention plan and the more likely it will be fully implemented. A social worker who has navigated the steps of the change process many times may be tempted to assume that the client, too, knows what lies ahead and already agrees to a particular course of action. That can be a serious mistake. The discipline of carefully developing and discussing a contract is often reassuring to clients, while also encouraging the social worker to rethink steps that may have become routine.

Of the three forms of contracts—implied, oral, and written—*implied contracts* offer the least clarity and are most vulnerable to misunderstanding. *Oral contracts* add an element of clarity, but the details of oral communication can be quickly forgotten. Although more time consuming to develop, *written contracts* (see Item 12.5) are the most beneficial for both the client and worker. A document can be reviewed between sessions to remind the participants of their responsibilities and it provides a solid foundation for evaluation and accountability.

12.1 SELECTING TARGET PROBLEMS AND GOALS

During the planning and contracting phase, the social worker and the client must specify and agree on their goal(s). A **goal** is a desired outcome or the end sought. If the action required to address the client's need is readily apparent, the worker and client can quickly agree on their goals. However, in many cases, the social worker and client will see things differently and must struggle to reach agreement on the nature of the problem and on what can and should be done about it. If the client's situation is unusually complex and both the worker and client are uncertain as to what could or should be done, the agreed-on goal may be to conduct a more in-depth assessment. Sometimes the best plan is to devote more time to assessment and planning.

In direct service helping, the goals of an intervention can take many forms. For example:

- Learn a skill or acquire needed knowledge (e.g., learn how to interview for a job, manage time, make decisions, resolve interpersonal conflict, manage stress).
- Make an important decision (e.g., decide on a college major, whether to get a divorce, whether to relinquish custody of a child, whether to seek help for an emotional problem).
- Change a behavior (e.g., learn a desirable behavior, decrease or eliminate a troublesome behavior or habit).
- Alter attitudes about self or about some other person(s).
- Gather information about availability of certain types of services or programs.
- Become linked to or enrolled in a program or service provided by some agency or professional.
- Rebuild a damaged relationship (e.g., reach out to an estranged parent or child, improve husband–wife relationship).
- Change the way life circumstances are perceived or interpreted (e.g., learn to assign new meaning to events, view things from a different angle).
- Achieve a better adjustment to an unchangeable condition or situation (e.g., strive to adapt to a chronic illness, permanent disability, or the death of a loved one).
- Advocacy to address an injustice.

If the client has numerous problems and concerns, the worker and client must devote considerable time to priority setting in order to decide the primary focus of the intervention and the order in which the problems will be tackled. The value-based principle of *client self-determination* dictates that, to the extent possible, the client has the right to make these decisions. There are also some very practical reasons for expecting the client, rather than the social worker, to select the target problems and goals of the intervention. Namely, it is seldom possible to encourage or motivate a client to do something that he or she does not consider important. Unless the problem to be worked on is a priority to the client and the goal and proposed intervention make sense to the client, the client is unlikely to invest himself or herself in the process of change. Even in work with a mandated client, it is important to give the client as much choice as possible (see Item 10.7).

It is important for the social worker to remember that the client's problems and concerns will almost always affect or involve significant others (e.g., spouse, children, parents, friends, employer). Unless these individuals, who are either part of the problem or part of the solution, are considered in the intervention planning, they may knowingly or unknowingly become an obstacle to the change process.

Both research and practice wisdom suggest that, in order to be effective, the helping process must concentrate available time and energy on just one, two, or possibly three problems at a time. If too many problems are tackled at once, and if priorities are not established, the helping effort flounders and usually ends in frustration for both client and worker. The following procedure will help the client and the worker select targets for change and set priorities:

Step 1: The client identifies and lists what she or he sees as the problems or concerns needing attention (i.e., what the client wants to change).

Step 2: The social worker offers his or her recommendations, if any, and explains why they also need to be considered. The worker makes sure that any mandated problems or goals are included (a mandated problem or goal is one imposed on the client by some legitimate authority such as a court, probation officer, or child protection agency).

Step 3: The problems and concerns are reviewed and sorted into logical groupings so that their interrelatedness is identified. The client examines the list and selects the two or three problems or concerns of highest priority. Then the worker selects the two or three items he or she considers to be of highest priority.

Step 4: Together, the client and worker discuss the concerns identified in Step 3 and examine them against the following criteria:

- Which ones weigh most heavily on the client's situation (e.g., which ones cause the most worry and anxiety)?
- Which ones, if not addressed and corrected, will have the most negative and far-reaching consequences for the client?
- Which ones, if corrected, would have the most positive effects on the client?
- Which ones can be addressed and corrected with only a moderate investment of time, energy, and other resources?
- Which ones are probably unchangeable or would require an extraordinary investment of time, energy, or resources?

Step 5: After considering these criteria, the three problems of highest priority are selected. As mentioned earlier, it is usually counterproductive to address more than three concerns at one time. Task-centered practitioners have termed this principle the *rule of three*.

"Using Checklists in Goal Selection" a deleted item from 8th edition

Selected Bibliography

Epstein, Laura, and Lester Brown. *Brief Treatment and a New Look at the Task-Centered Approach*, 4th ed. Boston: Allyn and Bacon, 2002.

Fortune, Anne. "Task-Centered Practice." In *Social Workers' Desk Reference*, 2nd ed. Edited by Albert Roberts. New York: Oxford University Press, 2008.

12.2 THE PROBLEM SEARCH

The technique termed a **problem search** is essentially a mini-contract or an agreement between the client and the social worker to devote some time to discussing the client's situation in order to determine if the client has a problem and, if so, whether it should be addressed by some type of professional intervention. Most often a problem search is used when (1) the client has been referred by family or an authoritative agency (court) but does not acknowledge the existence of a problem as defined by others or (2) the client has requested a specific service, but in the worker's opinion, it is desirable to help the client to modify that request or redefine the presenting problem. In this later situation, the social worker is concerned that the client's stated problem or need is not accurate or realistic, or that the service requested will not resolve the problem. An example might be the father who requests foster-care placement for his children because he and his wife are having marital problems.

The problem search asks the client to participate in one or two sessions in order to explore her or his situation. The client is asked to withhold judgment about the need for professional intervention until they have explored the question in depth. When using this technique, the social worker moves through these four steps:

Step 1: Explain why you are suggesting this exploration. For example: "I realize that you see no problems that deserve my attention, but what you said about getting fired from a couple of jobs leads me to believe that even though you try to get along at work, you and your supervisors often clash. May I suggest that we meet two times and talk more about your job experiences? If, after the second session, we cannot figure out what might be done to improve your situation, we will stop meeting."

Step 2: Solicit the client's thoughts and feedback on the proposal. For example: "What do you think about my suggestion that we meet two times to discuss your recent experiences at work?" (If the client responds with a no, you might say, for example: "Well, I can understand your reluctance. I will respect your decision, but allow me give you one other reason why it may be a good idea....")

Step 3: Set up a plan for a future meeting. For example: "I'm glad that you agreed to meet with me. As I said, we will meet just two times. If it proves useful, that will be great. But, if after the second session it doesn't seem worthwhile, then we will not continue. How about meeting next Wednesday at 4 P.M.?"

Step 4: Identify two or three topics to be discussed. For example: "When we meet next Wednesday, let's start with a discussion of the jobs you have liked and why. Then I would like to discuss the type of supervision you expect on the job. Does that sound reasonable?"

Selected Bibliography

Fortune, Anne, and William Reid. "Task-Centered Social Work." In *Social Work Treatment: Interlocking Theoretical Approaches*, 5th ed. Edited by Francis Turner. New York: Oxford University Press, 2011.

Marsh, Peter, and Mark Doel. *The Task-Centered Book*. New York: Routledge, 2005.

12.3 THE CLIENT NEEDS LIST

A **needs list** is a tool used to guide the planning of case-management activities related to a certain category of clients. Most often it is used with clients who are highly dependent on human services agencies (e.g., the frail elderly, children in foster care, people with a serious disability). This tool is especially useful when the case-planning activity is being performed by a multiagency or multidisciplinary team because it helps to clarify responsibilities, facilitates interagency coordination, and reduces misunderstandings within the team. A needs list reminds all involved of the concerns that should be addressed in a client's service plan. Those involved in formulating this plan review the list and decide how each of the client's needs can be addressed and which service provider will take on that responsibility.

Figure 12.1 is an example of a needs list used in work with adults who have a developmental disability but are capable of maintaining a semi-independent living arrangement. Also, see Item 11.1 for ideas on specific areas of client functioning that might be included in a needs list.

Selected Bibliography

Frankel, Arthur, and Sheldon Gelman. *Case Management*, 3rd ed. Chicago: Lyceum Books, 2012.

Summers, Nancy. *Fundamentals of Case Management Practice*, 4th ed. Independence, KY: Cengage, 2012.

Needs List for Independent Living

1. Housing suitable for client's level of mobility and physical limitations (consider stairs, wheelchair accessibility, etc.)
2. Safe heating and electrical system and usable toilet facilities
3. Home furnishing (chairs, tables, TV, radio, etc.)
4. Bed, blankets, sheets, etc.
5. Clothing for all seasons of the year
6. Food, food storage, stove
7. Telephone or other means of requesting assistance
8. Items needed for food preparation (e.g., utensils, pots, pans)
9. Items needed to maintain personal hygiene (razor, soap, sanitary napkins, etc.)
10. Financial resources/money management system
11. Transportation
12. Medical and dental care
13. Medication and monitoring of dosage, if needed
14. Social contacts and recreational activities
15. Concern and interest shown by family, friends, and neighbors
16. Protection from harm or exploitation
17. Appropriate level of supervision
18. Training (job-related, community, survival skills, etc.)
19. Employment or work-related activity
20. Adaptive aids (e.g., eyeglasses, hearing aids, leg braces)
21. Therapy and other special treatments (e.g., physical therapy, speech therapy)
22. Maintenance of cultural and ethnic heritage
23. Participation in spiritual or religious activities
24. Legal advice

Figure 12.1
Sample Client Needs List

12.4 FORMULATING INTERVENTION OBJECTIVES

Unless there are agreed-on goals and objectives for an intervention, the helping process will falter and it will be impossible to measure an intervention's effectiveness. Although the terms *goals* and *objectives* are often used interchangeably, they are not the same. A **goal** is a broad and rather global statement (e.g., "to better cope with the demands of my child who has a disability"). Not infrequently, a goal is simply a restatement of a problem in a way that suggests a solution. For example, if the stress felt by a parent erupts in abuse of the children, a logical goal would be to reduce stress.

As compared to a goal, an **objective** is more specific and written in a manner that allows for measurement and evaluation. An objective describes who will do what, by when, and under what conditions. Consider these examples:

Statements Prepared by a Hospital Social Worker

Goal: Improve responsiveness of social work staff to new referrals.

Objective: To conduct at least 80 percent of initial patient or family member interviews within four hours of receiving a referral from a doctor or nurse.

Statements Prepared by the Administrator of a Big Brothers Program

Goal: Obtain more Big Brothers or mentors for our children.

Objective: To recruit, select, train, and match 35 new Big Brothers before August 1.

Statements Prepared by a Child Welfare Worker

Goal: To promote better parent–child relationships.

Objective: To encourage and facilitate parental visitation so that by January 15 at least 70 percent of parents in my caseload are visiting their children in foster care at least once a month.

When examining these sample objectives, notice that an objective makes use of verbs that describe actions to be taken. Examples of verbs that commonly appear in objectives are *attend, visit, learn, practice, discuss, plan, obtain, demonstrate, select, arrange, conduct, decide,* and so on.

A properly developed objective meets the following criteria:

- It usually starts with the word *to,* followed by an action verb.
- It specifies a single outcome to be achieved.
- It specifies a target date for its accomplishment.
- It is as quantitative and measurable as possible.
- It is understandable to the client and others participating in the intervention.
- It is attainable, but still represents a significant challenge and a meaningful change.

When an objective is especially complex and cannot be written in a single sentence, it will be necessary to attach further statements of condition and criteria as clarification. *Conditions* describe the situation or context in which the desired behavior or action is to take place; *criteria* are the rules or the definitions that will be used to decide whether the desired behavior or action has occurred at an acceptable level.

When developing an objective, it is important not to confuse an *input* with an *outcome*. This common error results in statements such as "Mr. Jones is to obtain counseling," which describes an input (counseling) but says nothing about the intended outcome. In this example, counseling is presented as an end, but in reality, it is only a means to an end. What is the counseling to accomplish? A better statement would be "Mr. Jones will obtain counseling focused on his physical abuse of his son, John, and designed to help Mr. Jones learn to use the time-out procedure and positive reinforcement as alternatives to harsh spanking and screaming as discipline." Given that statement, it would be possible to measure whether or not Mr. Jones did in fact learn how to use time-out and positive reinforcement.

It is important to write an objective in behavioral language—words that describe observable actions in terms of their frequency, duration, and intensity. Also, positive language should be used whenever possible. The words should describe what the client will do, not what the client will not do (e.g., "learn and adhere to specified table manners" versus "stop being so messy when eating").

A *timeframe* is an essential part of an objective. In interpersonal helping, for example, an objective usually should not take more than a few weeks or a couple of months to accomplish. Thus, an ambitious objective that might take many months to accomplish should be broken down into several subobjectives, stages, or phases. If the client can perceive he or she is making concrete gains (i.e., achieving an objective), even if the steps are small, he or she will be motivated to continue.

The concept of a task, as used by social workers favoring the task-centered approach, is both similar to and different from the concept of an objective. Basically, a *task* is an observable action or step that can be evaluated in terms of whether it was achieved or completed. A task can be viewed as one of the many steps that must

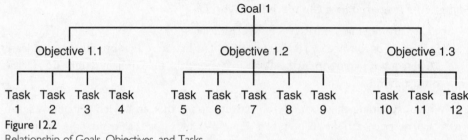

Figure 12.2
Relationship of Goals, Objectives, and Tasks

be completed in order to reach an objective. Whereas an objective is something that might be achieved in a couple of months (e.g., "Learn new methods of discipline with the help of a parent training program"), a task can be completed in a matter of days or a couple of weeks (e.g., "Call a friend to arrange transportation to the parent training program"). Thus, when working toward a single goal, the client may need to achieve several objectives, and in order to reach a given objective, the client may need to complete numerous tasks. The relationship between goals, objectives, and tasks is depicted in Figure 12.2.

An objective is intended to give direction to the helping process and facilitate the evaluation of the intervention's effectiveness. However, the utilization of written objectives should never stifle the humanness and individualization that are essential ingredients in the helping process. A willingness to revise objectives in response to changing circumstances is critical to effective helping.

Selected Bibliography

Gronlund, Norman, and Susan Brookhart. *Gronlund's Writing Instructional Objectives,* 8th ed. Upper Saddle River, NJ: Pearson, 2009.

Mager, Robert. *Goal Analysis,* 3rd ed. Atlanta: Center for Effective Performance, 1997.

_____ . *Preparing Instructional Objectives,* 3rd ed. Atlanta: Center for Effective Performance, 1997.

12.5 WRITTEN SERVICE CONTRACTS

Arriving at an agreement on the services to be provided by the social worker or agency is a fundamental step in social work practice. In most cases and in most settings, a verbal agreement is sufficient. However, many social workers use written service contracts. Depending on the setting, these documents may be termed a *service agreement, case plan, treatment plan, intervention plan,* or *family support plan.* Often these terms are used interchangeably.

A **written service contract** is a document that specifies the desired outcome of the service(s) to be provided, the key actions that will be taken to achieve this outcome, the major roles and responsibilities of those involved in this effort, and the relevant time lines. Typically, the document is signed by the client and service provider(s). Having a written document reduces the chances that some misunderstanding or disagreement will arise at a later date. Consequently, it is also a protection against a malpractice suit. Except in those cases in which the contract is written into a court order, a service contract is usually not considered to be legally binding. However, it is intended to describe and demonstrate commitment to a mutually agreed-on course of action. The core elements of a service contract are depicted in Figure 12.3.

This agreement is between ____(client's name)____ and ____(social worker's name)____, who is employed by the Mountain State Department of Family Services.

The purpose or goal of this agreement is to _____
_____
_____

In order to achieve this purpose or reach this goal, the following objectives must be met:
1. _____ (by date) _____
2. _____ (by date) _____
3. _____ (by date) _____

In order to reach these objectives, ____(client's name)____ is to perform or engage in the following tasks or activities before the dates shown:
1. _____ (by date) _____
2. _____ (by date) _____
3. _____ (by date) _____

In order to reach these objectives, ____(social worker's name)____ is to perform or engage in the following tasks or activities before the dates shown:
1. _____ (by date) _____
2. _____ (by date) _____
3. _____ (by date) _____

Progress toward the objectives will be reviewed and evaluated by means of the following procedures or methods:
_____
_____

The consequences, if any, of not reaching the objectives are the following:
_____
_____

The following steps or actions are required to renegotiate terms of this agreement:
_____
_____

Signed _____ Date _____

Signed _____ Date _____

Figure 12.3
Sample Form for Client-Social Worker Contract

Service contracts should not be confused with behavioral contracts (see Item 13.5). A behavioral contract is much more specific and covers a shorter period of time—often a matter of days or a week or two. The period covered by a service contract may be several months, although it is ordinarily renegotiated and updated every three or six months.

A service contract should address the following questions:

- What is the desired outcome of service to the client?
- What is to be done by the client? By when?

- What, if anything, is to be done by the client's significant others (family, friends, etc.)? By when?
- What is to be done by the social worker and other agency staff? By when?
- What additional services are to be obtained from other agencies or providers? How and when?
- What events will trigger a reassessment of the client's situation and/or a revision of the service contract?
- What fees, if any, will be charged for these services?
- What are the consequences, if any, for not adhering to the plan?

Follow these guidelines for using written service contracts:

- Understand your agency's policy regarding written service contracts and any legal requirements or legal interpretations relevant to their use with the clients you serve. An agency's policies should address both the advantages and disadvantages of using written service contracts. The major advantages are that they clarify purpose, set priorities, delineate roles and responsibilities, increase ownership of the plan, provide a means of measuring progress, and reduce the potential for client–worker misunderstanding. Needless to say, contracts work best with voluntary and motivated clients. They do, however, have a special advantage when working with a reluctant or involuntary client because they facilitate clear and above-board communication and will often lessen the client's fear of being manipulated or set up by some hidden agenda.

    An obvious disadvantage of written service contracts is that considerable time may be needed to prepare a clear and easily understood contract. Also, there is the danger that an unassertive client or one who feels powerless may acquiesce to a contract provision even though he or she disagrees with what the service provider has suggested.

- Develop the contract only after a thorough social assessment during which you and the client study and agree on the problems to be tackled. From the client's perspective, the goals and objectives listed in the contract must be realistic and worth achieving. And, since the purpose of the contract is to facilitate change, it must focus on behaviors or situations that can, in fact, be changed.

    When selecting and formulating objectives, logical sequences must be built into the plan. Some problems must be tackled one step at a time and in a certain order. New behaviors may need to be learned in a particular sequence. For example, the client who wants a job must first learn how to complete a job application.

- By definition, a service contract specifies what the client will do and what the worker/agency will do. A contract must never be one-sided and list only that which is expected of the client. The provisions of a contract must be consistent with the client's capacities, the worker's skill, and the agency's mission.

- The contract should be written in simple, clear language so that the client will know exactly what it means. It will be necessary to prepare the contract in the client's first language (e.g., Spanish) if she or he has a poor understanding of English. In cases where the client cannot read, the worker should consider making an audio recording of the agreement, in addition to preparing a written statement.

- A contract should be developed in a way that makes success probable without sacrificing relevance. It must not focus on trivial outcomes, so as to easily attain success while avoiding objectives that are more important but more challenging.

If the worker believes that the client will be unable to meet the terms of a particular contract, that alone is an indication that its objectives are too ambitious, or the timeframe is too short.

- Provisions of the contract should be modified as necessary to stay in step with changing realities of the situation. This flexibility is important in maintaining the trust of the client.

Selected Bibliography

Rothman, Juliet. *Contracting in Clinical Social Work*. Chicago: Nelson-Hall, 1998.

Wodarski, John, Lisa Rapp-Paglicci, Catherine Dulmus, and Arthur Jongsma. *The Social Work and Human Services Treatment Planner*. New York: Wiley and Sons, 2001.

12.6 MAKING USE OF INFORMAL RESOURCES

When appropriate and acceptable to the client, an intervention plan should consider drawing from the informal resources available within the client's support network, such as family, friends, neighbors, and faith groups. These individuals and groups may be able to provide the client with needed information, encouragement, emotional support, material assistance (e.g., housing, small loan), physical care (e.g., care giving during an illness), and sometimes the mediation of interpersonal conflicts. Some clients may want to prevent others from learning about their troubles, but others may like the ideas of enlisting the help of informal resources. Informal resources may be attractive to a client because this help is available 24 hours a day at no cost; one does not have to be categorized, diagnosed, or otherwise meet agency eligibility requirements in order to secure assistance; and this informal helping involves a relationship among equals or peers—rather than the expert–client relationship that is so often a part of the professional helping process.

A *self-help group* (or *mutual aid group*) is usually considered to be an informal resource, even though some may be affiliated with a state- or national-level organization and some may utilize professionals as advisors. Another important informal resource is the *natural helper*, an individual who has usually resided in the community for a long time and is known for his or her ability to help others. An example would be the "neighborhood Mom" to whom children gravitate for nurturing and advice. Other natural helpers include respected elders, religious leaders, and healers. Another informal resource—one often overlooked by professionals—is other agency clients. Clients can be of help to each other; however, in some cases, they can also exacerbate each other's problems.

Although informal resources are the oldest and most common form of helping activity, some professionals are reluctant to encourage their clients to use them. Possible reasons include the following:

- The professionals assume that formal resources are inherently more effective than nonprofessionals, regardless of the client's problem or situation.
- They have little awareness of the informal helping networks and informal resources available to their clients.
- They assume that the client has already thought about using informal resources and for some reason has rejected the idea.
- They doubt the capacity of informal resources to protect a client's right to confidentiality.

When considering the appropriateness of looking to informal resources as a source of additional help to a client, the social worker should keep the following guidelines in mind:

- The fundamental goal of social work practice is to help clients improve their social functioning. The resources used—whether formal, informal, or a mix of both—are simply the means to that end. Both formal and informal resources are important, and both may be needed. A professional should not feel threatened by a client's use of or preference for informal resources. Although invaluable in many situations, informal resources are neither a panacea nor an inexpensive alternative to professional services needed by a client.

- The client's social support network should always be viewed as a potential reservoir of helping resources. If a source is identified, the advantages and disadvantages of attempting to use it should be discussed. However, in the final analysis, it is the client who decides whether to contact others and involve them in the helping process. Some clients may need guidance on how to reach out to an informal resource and also handle the expectation of reciprocity (see Item 11.7).

- The ethical and legal codes concerning client confidentiality need not be a barrier to the use of informal resources. In almost all situations it will be the client who first approaches the informal resources. Thus, the client is in control of what he or she chooses to reveal. In cases where the social worker needs to talk with an informal resource, the worker must, of course, first secure the client's permission.

- Some clients are reluctant to approach or join a self-help group or support group because they do not want to admit that they have a problem. They may find a group more attractive if they come to view their own participation as a means of helping others. Thus, a worker attempting to connect a client with such a group might emphasize that because of the client's life experiences, he or she will be able to offer valuable guidance to the group's members.

- A worker should not attempt to "professionalize," train, or direct the actions of an informal helping resource. Generally, these people are most effective when they follow their judgments and respond spontaneously.

Selected Bibliography

Gitterman, Alex, and Lawrence Shulman, eds. *Mutual Aid Groups, Vulnerable Populations and the Life Cycle*, 3rd ed. New York: Columbia University Press, 2005.

Kurtz, Linda. *Self-Help and Support Groups*. Thousand Oaks, CA: Sage, 1997.

Norcross, John, John Santrock, Linda Campbell, Thomas Smith, Robert Sommer, and Edward Zuckerman. *Authoritative Guide to Self-Help Resources in Mental Health*, rev. ed. New York: Guilford, 2003.

Steinberg, Dominique. *The Mutual Aid Approach to Working with Groups*. New York: Haworth, 2004.

12.7 FAMILY GROUP CONFERENCING

The technique of **family group conferencing** (also known as *family group decision making* and *family unity meetings*) was developed during the 1980s by child welfare personnel in New Zealand. It was designed to engage the large extended families and kinship groups (common to indigenous peoples) in decision making and planning for a child who has been abused or neglected by a parent. In recent years the basic format of the family group conference (FGC) has been applied in many countries and in additional practice settings such as mental health, juvenile probation, care of the elderly, and education. The description presented here illustrates its use in child welfare.

A family group conference brings together all who are concerned about the situation and asks this group to come up with a plan for keeping the child safe. In many cases, making plans for the child also involves making decisions and a plan that will help the parent make the changes needed to resume the parenting role.

In addition to the parent and his or her family and relatives, those attending the FGC might include some of the parent's close friends, the parent's clergyperson, the child's school personnel or day-care providers, attorneys, foster parents, social and mental health service providers, and others who are somehow involved with and concerned about the child and the child's parent. However, the professionals or service providers who attend the family group conference are there only to provide information; they do not propose solutions or make decisions.

A typical FGC session lasts from two to three hours, but some go on for an entire day. Young children do not attend but an adolescent might be invited to participate. The FGC technique is based on the following assumptions, values, and beliefs:

- The individuals who are most deeply concerned about and committed to the long-term well-being of the child are, most likely, his or her blood relatives and close friends of the family.
- Family members know one another's histories and their strengths, limitations, and problems.
- A plan that is developed by family, relatives, and trusted family friends is more likely to be accepted and successfully implemented than is a plan developed by a social worker, a social agency, or a court.

The FGC approach is attractive to many social workers because it is inherently culturally sensitive and family-centered, and it builds on family strengths. The family group conference demonstrates to the abusive or neglectful parent that many people care and want to help. As the parent comes to this realization, his or her denial and resistance will often fall away. Many who are experienced in the use of the FGC express amazement at the creativity and resourcefulness displayed by the people attending a family group conference, as they strive to come up with feasible solutions to the problem(s). Not infrequently, individuals from the parent's family or kinship group will step forward and offer invaluable resources to address the parent's problems. A side benefit of the FGC process is that it often initiates reconciliation and the healing of ruptured family relationships.

The FGC can be used with most families. The families most likely to benefit are ones in which family members (and others) can focus on the needs of a specific child, can communicate honestly, and will strive for a consensus in decision making. Here are several guidelines for using family group conferencing that is focused on the well-being of a child:

- The FGC is to be used only when the parent(s) has agreed. All of those invited to attend the meeting must first be "nominated" by the parent. The parent is encouraged, however, by her or his social worker to invite all family members, relatives, and friends who are genuinely concerned about the situation, even if the parent does not like them. If the parent wants his or her attorney present, the attorney can be invited but only if the attorney agrees to allow a free-flowing discussion and takes a nonadversarial approach to the problem-solving effort. (In some states, the child protection agency is required to invite the parent's attorney to a family group conference.)

When making decisions about whom to invite to the conference, the FGC coordinator and the parent also must consider safety issues. An individual who is intimidating, violent, or under the influence of drugs or alcohol should usually be excluded.

- A family group conference is usually attempted in these situations: (1) when the agency and the parent have reached an impasse; (2) when the out-of-home placement of a child is under consideration by a child protection agency or court; and (3) when the parent's change effort is "stuck" and his or her family and friends are needed to encourage the parent to get back on track and work on current problems. (In some states, the use of a FGC can be court ordered in an effort to arrive at a plan for a child in need of care.)

- The FGC coordinator or facilitator of the meeting should possess a neutral attitude toward the parent and not have an ongoing or prior relationship with the parent or the family. Thus, the parent's current social worker, case manager, therapist, or service provider should not assume the role of coordinator.

- For a family group conference to be successful, the coordinator or facilitator must carefully prepare the potential participants. During this preparation phase, the coordinator meets with each potential participant (i.e., someone nominated by the parent) to explain the purpose and process of the FGC, to answer questions, to encourage attendance, and, if necessary, to arrange for transportation, child care, and so on. Typically, a coordinator will invest 30 to 40 hours in preparing for a single FGC meeting.

- At the beginning of a FGC session, certain ground rules must be explained and displayed for all to see. For example:

  ▪ The coordinator will guide the process without imposing her or his views or ideas on the group.
  ▪ Focus on finding solutions. Keep the focus on the needs of the child and on making decisions and plans that are in the child's best interests.
  ▪ Focus on what can be done in the future, not on what happened in the past.
  ▪ Be respectful of each other. No name calling, blaming, shaming, or threatening. No one will be allowed to intimidate another person or prevent another from speaking.
  ▪ It is important for everyone to voice his or her ideas and suggestions. It is OK to disagree, but do so in a respectful manner.
  ▪ Only one person is to speak at a time.
  ▪ After this meeting, be sure to maintain confidentiality about what was discussed.

- A typical FGC session related to possibly removing children from their parents might unfold as follows:

  ▪ The coordinator welcomes the participants and explains the purpose of the meeting. For example: "We are here to see how we can help Margaret and her children and make it possible for the family to stay together."
  ▪ The coordinator explains the ground rules for the meeting (see above). At the beginning of the meeting, a ritual that is meaningful to the family may be used

to set the tone for the discussion. This ritual might be, for example, a prayer, recalling the family's traditions, or recalling some special time in the family's history.

- All who are present introduce themselves and briefly explain their relationship to the parent(s) and children.
- The parent is asked and helped, if necessary, to describe his or her goals for the meeting and the hoped-for outcome.
- The coordinator guides a discussion of the parent's and the family's strengths.
- The coordinator guides presentations by selected child protection personnel, professionals, and family members. This serves to describe and explain the current problems, the special needs of the child, and the possible legal ramifications or court action if the problem is not resolved. The professionals in attendance answer all questions asked by those in attendance. After their presentations, the professionals may be asked to leave the group.
- Family and friends are asked to propose their ideas on how the child can be protected from further maltreatment and how the parent might be helped to make needed changes. In cases in which the child must be separated from the parent, the group decides where the child might live. (These discussions may take place with or without the coordinator being present.)
- The coordinator reviews the group's recommendations and decisions and a follow-up plan is formulated.
- Meeting is adjourned and perhaps followed by a celebration ritual and sharing of food.

- The use of family group conferencing does not abrogate the responsibilities of the social worker, agency, or the court in protecting the child. They can, if absolutely necessary, veto the plan. However, if the plan generated by the family conference will keep the child safe, it should be approved by the child welfare agency or court.

- Following the meeting, the coordinator compiles notes on the meeting and puts the agreed-on plan into written form and sends this report to all participants and the child protection agency.

Selected Bibliography

Burford, Gale, and Joe Hudson, eds. *Family Group Conferencing*. Elison, NJ: Transaction Publishers, 2000.

Okamura, Amy, and Elizabeth Quinnett. *Family Group Decision-Making Models for Social Workers in Child Welfare Settings*. Berkeley, CA: University of California, California Social Work Education Center, 2000.

Pennell, Joan, and Gray Anderson, eds. *Widening the Circle: The Practice and Evaluation of Family Group Conferencing*. Washington, DC: National Association of Social Workers, 2005.

12.8 THE SMALL GROUP AS A RESOURCE

Small groups can be an invaluable helping resource to clients and their utilization should be considered during the service planning process. A group provides its members with acceptance, encouragement, and opportunities to acquire new skills, develop self-awareness, and help others. For many individuals, what they experience in a group proves more beneficial, more helpful, than one-on-one counseling. Clients are often more open to the suggestions voiced by other group members than to ones offered by a professional. For example, an adolescent is more likely to listen to another adolescent than to a 50-year-old social worker. Moreover, group members are often more willing than a professional to confront a member. For example, a social worker might be reluctant to confront a client who seems to be lying but another group member may quickly voice this suspicion. Small-group approaches are essential for working with clients who are defensive and manipulative, as is frequently the case with clients whose problems revolve around substance abuse, sexual offenses, and domestic abuse.

For the most part, the groups utilized in direct practice are *formed groups*, meaning that they are purposefully planned and created by a social work practitioner. By contrast, a *natural group* is one that develops naturally among friends, peers, and neighbors. There are occasions when a social worker can work with the naturally occurring groups in neighborhoods, schools, and institutional settings.

When a number of people meet on a regular basis, this group will typically move through five **stages of group development**: (1) preaffiliation, (2) power and control, (3) intimacy, (4) differentiation, and (5) separation. During the first stage, *preaffiliation,* the members size each other up, consider what they might have in common, and decide whether they want to be a part of the group. Unless individuals feel comfortable and see that belonging is beneficial, they are likely to avoid meaningful involvement, even if they remain physically present. During this first stage, members tend to look to and depend on the designated leader for direction and structure.

During the *power and control stage*, members test each other and come to a decision of where they fit in the group. They may challenge each other for position, rank, and leadership. Some members may challenge the designated leader. At this time, informal rules emerge as to what is and is not acceptable behavior within the group. As the members get to know each other, they gradually let down their defenses and the group enters the third stage, *intimacy,* during which the members recognize and come to value what they have in common.

Next, the group moves to the *stage of differentiation*, wherein differences are exhibited but accepted and respected. Members begin to learn more about each other's roles and responsibilities outside the group. As the life of the group approaches its ending, it enters the *separation stage* and each member must struggle with the loss of meaningful relationships.

For those who want to make a group experience available to their clients, these guidelines are suggested:

- Before attempting to plan or design a group, be clear as to its purpose and why the group experience might benefit your clients. A group's purpose might be education, recreation, socialization, therapy or behavior change, mutual aid, or self-help. Answers to most questions about how best to structure and guide a group will relate directly back to the group's purpose or desired outcome. As a general rule, the more specialized the purpose, the better it serves the members. If all the members have similar concerns and similar reasons for being in the group, they are more likely to invest themselves and actively participate.

- Decide which clients are to be offered the group experience. Some social group workers hold definite beliefs about the mix of personalities they want in the group (e.g., having outgoing members to balance those who are reserved). Also, some group workers may want to eliminate from consideration those who tend to be resistant or uncooperative. However, in many practice settings, the worker does not have the luxury of using detailed selection criteria and must include in the group those who have a need for a group experience and have at least a minimal capacity to form relationships and tolerate differences. A voluntary member should be free to drop out if the group is not meeting his or her needs or expectations.

When screening or selecting potential members, the group worker must balance the needs of the individual with the needs and safety of other group members. People exhibiting dangerous behavior should be eliminated from membership unless the meetings occur within an institutional setting that can provide monitoring and safety. Individuals who are at high risk of suicide or actively using or selling illegal drugs also may not be appropriate for inclusion.

When extending an invitation to join a group, be prepared to explain how the group may be of benefit, what will usually occur during the meetings, and the atmosphere you hope to create (e.g., informal, fun, learning, sharing). Also, offer information that might spark interest and reduce fears about participating.

- It is seldom possible to predict with accuracy how an individual will behave and function in a group. As a general rule, however, people will behave in a formed group about like they do in other situations. For example, if an individual does not express feelings to family and friends, he or she will usually carry this same pattern into the group. Likewise, the person who controls and dominates others at home and at work will most likely try to dominate and control the group.

- Decide on an appropriate group size. Size depends on such factors as the age of the clients, the concerns to be addressed, and the leader/facilitator's professional experience. The group should be small enough so all members have a sense of belonging and a chance to actively participate but large enough to yield a variety of opinions and minimize pressure on those who are shy or fearful. For preadolescents, a group of only three or four is often workable. For adolescents, a group of six to eight is about right. For adults, a group of eight to ten is a comfortable size. You must also anticipate the inevitable problem of nonattendance and dropouts. The group must be large enough to continue functioning when some members miss a meeting and after a member or two decides to drop out.

- Decide on the frequency of meetings and the length of each session. For adults, a meeting lasting 1½ to 2 hours is about right. Because children and adolescents have a shorter attention span, it is usually best to have shorter but more frequent sessions. The practice setting will also dictate the frequency of meetings. In an institutional setting, daily meetings are often possible and desirable. When members are drawn from the larger community and must travel long distances, it may not be feasible to meet more often than biweekly or monthly.

- Decide when and where the group will meet. A meeting space should be quiet, private, comfortable, and large enough for people to move around and to accommodate a circle of chairs. The decision of when to meet must consider each member's work schedule, family responsibilities, personal convenience, travel required, and, of course, the availability of a meeting room.

- Decide on the approximate number of times the group will meet. This is, of course, tied to purpose. An information sharing or training group might meet only once or twice, whereas a support or therapy group might meet weekly for several months or much longer. Consider setting a limit (e.g., three, five, or ten meetings) with the understanding that at the end of that period, the group will decide whether the meetings should continue. This can help to keep members involved because they will know there is a planned ending and it can also prevent a group from continuing to meet even when there is no longer a need to do so.

- Decide whether the group will be open or closed to additional members. This is sometimes a decision for the group to make. If the group is to decide, this decision needs to be made during the first or second meeting. Incorporating new members into an already functioning group has the advantage of maintaining group size if some members drop out. Also, new members may bring fresh perspectives. However, the introduction of new members can interfere with the development of group cohesion and prevent the group from entering the intimacy stage.

- Decide if the group is for voluntary clients, involuntary clients, or both. Obviously, there are advantages to limiting membership to persons who want to attend. Although individuals can be mandated by court order to attend a therapeutic group, they cannot be made to interact in a meaningful and productive manner. However, the use of group approaches in correctional settings, chemical dependency, and domestic abuse treatment programs demonstrates that groups composed of involuntary clients are both feasible and effective (see Items 10.7 and 10.8).

  The addition of involuntary or mandated members to a mostly voluntary group will usually work if the group has been functioning well for a time and the new involuntary member is cooperative to at least a minimal degree. On the other hand, it is usually problematic to bring a mandated and resistant member into a newly formed group or into one that is not functioning very well. Before adding such a member, it is best to wait until the group has reached the intimacy stage. The addition of new members, especially ones who are manipulative or domineering, should definitely be avoided during the power and control stage. Whenever a group member is resistant and manipulative, the group leader must be strong and highly skilled.

- Be prepared to establish rules to govern the behavior of group members. Possible rules include the following:

  - Members are expected to attend all meetings.
  - Members are expected to maintain confidentiality.
  - Members cannot smoke or do drugs during the meeting.
  - Members cannot remain at the meeting if they are under the influence of alcohol or drugs.
  - Minor-aged members must have parents' written consent to participate.
  - Members are to avoid romantic involvement with other members.
  - Members who bring weapons, threaten violence, or engage in sexual harassment will be excluded.

- As the group moves through the usual stages of development, it is important to monitor the functioning and behavior of each group member and, when necessary, use various techniques to deal with problems (see Items 8.4, 11.21, and 13.26). A fairly common problem in small groups (and in family counseling) is that a few members dominate the discussion. The *talking stick* technique, which is commonly used in Native American cultures, addresses that problem. An object, the talking stick, is passed around the group, from person to person. Whoever is holding it has permission to speak while all others are silent and give the speaker their undivided attention. It is passed around the group as many times as necessary to assure that everyone has the opportunity to speak, to clarify their message, and be heard. In a session with a family, the talking stick might be an object that commands the family's respect (e.g., family photo, religious symbol).

"The Talking Stick"
a deleted item from the
8th edition

- Select activities (programs) for each meeting (e.g., introductions, icebreakers, refreshments, structured discussion, role-play, guest speaker). These activities should be consistent with the group's purpose and encourage the type of activity relevant to the group's stage of development (see Item 13.22).

- Anticipate how you can handle the numerous practical problems associated with a meeting, such as the room is too hot, too cold, or too small; members arrive late; members bring uninvited guests; conflict between smokers and nonsmokers; deciding if there will be refreshments and, if so, who will bring them or pay for them; the leader must miss a meeting; and so on.

Selected Bibliography

Garvin, Charles, Maeda Galinsky, and Lorraine Gutierrez. *Handbook of Social Work with Groups*. New York: Guilford, 2006.

Gitterman, Alex, and Robert Salmon, eds. *Encyclopedia of Social Work with Groups*. New York: Routledge, 2009.

Shulman, Lawrence. *The Dynamics and Skills of Group Counseling*. Independence, KY: Cengage, 2011.

Toseland, Ronald W., and Robert Rivas. *Introduction to Group Work Practice*, 7th ed. Upper Saddle River, NJ: Pearson, 2012.

Zastrow, Charles. *Social Work with Groups*, 8th ed. Independence, KY: Cengage, 2012.

SECTION B

TECHNIQUES AND GUIDELINES FOR INDIRECT PRACTICE

Social workers engaged in indirect service activities must give careful attention to the planning and contracting phase of the change process. As systems become more complex, it is increasingly difficult and time consuming to promote meaningful change in their ways of operating. When working with organizations and communities, one should also be aware that change in one system or one part of a system will reverberate not only through that system but through related systems, as well. Therefore, change efforts must be carefully planned and the responsibilities of each actor in the process should be clearly identified.

Planning activities

Organization and community planning are forms of social work practice typically performed by social workers with advanced education and training. We do not intend to address these more complex processes; rather, we will provide some guidelines that are useful for the front-line social worker (i.e., the direct-practice worker whose job sometimes involves indirect-practice activities). Much of the front-line worker's planning activity related to organizations and communities involves the ability to assess various alternatives for remedying a problem, selecting the best alternative for achieving a positive outcome, and plotting the schedule of tasks and activities to make the change process as efficient and effective as possible.

Contracting activities

After plans for organizational and community change have been developed, there must be explicit agreements among the participating parties about the responsibilities and timetable for carrying out the associated activities. In a community change effort, for example, once an assessment is made and a plan is developed, individual or committee assignments for implementing the plan must be agreed on. Typically, someone must prepare a position statement, someone must organize the people concerned with the issue to take action, someone must provide relevant information to the media, someone must lobby the decision makers, and so on. These actions must be orchestrated to be sure that they are done in a timely manner, as subsequent actions may depend on those tasks having already been completed.

12.9 ESTABLISHING AND CHANGING ORGANIZATIONS

In a sense, every social agency must stake out a claim regarding the particular need or problem it will address in the community. To do so, they must clearly state their mission, the goals they intend to achieve, the services they will provide, and the policies and procedures they will follow. Only then can the public be accurately informed about the nature of the agency, can clients know what services to expect, can unplanned duplication and overlap of services among agencies be minimized, and can staff members plan and coordinate their work.

An effective social agency is dynamic; it must constantly adapt to community and societal changes, to new knowledge about the nature of personal and social problems, to changes in public attitudes, and to ever-changing fiscal and political realities. Thus, a social worker can expect to participate, to some degree and at some level, in efforts to modify agency goals, structure, and operations.

Public agencies are particularly reactive to any change in the state and federal laws and budget modifications relevant to their areas of service. In response to such changes, the agency's policies and procedures may need to undergo significant change within a short period of time.

Private agencies, too, must be capable of responding to a variety of forces. When a private agency is created, the bylaws spell out its mission and decision-making structure. Although the original bylaws may capture the intent of the founders, such agencies must change over time to keep pace with changing community needs and new concepts of service. Leadership for needed change by a private agency often falls first to the CEO and the staff, with the board and/or a broader membership group subsequently amending the bylaws or revising the agency's policies to reflect the needed changes.

Although change is inevitable, an agency, like all social systems, will resist change; in fact, it may take considerable effort to make needed change. The following guidelines suggest what to consider when planning and initiating organizational change:

- Begin by describing as precisely as possible the change that is needed and why. Then secure and study all documents that may pertain to the desired change. These may include, for example, federal and state laws and regulations, administrative and personnel manuals, union contracts, accreditation standards, agreements and contracts involving other agencies, and so on. The information drawn from these sources will determine, to some degree, what changes are possible, how the change process must proceed, and who must support or approve the change.
- Assess the organization's readiness for change. Review its prior experience in initiating and accepting change. People are likely to resist change if prior

change efforts have been misguided, ineffective, or frustrating. On the other hand, they will tend to accept change if they trust those promoting or leading the change effort, when they believe the proposed change is needed and feasible, and when the proposal has addressed their questions, concerns, and fears about the change.

- Determine if the desire for change is shared across the various levels, departments, and units of the organization. Pay special attention to the views of those who will be affected most directly by the proposed change. A common error is to overlook or disregard the opinions of line workers and clerical staff—those who often know most about how the proposed change will affect day-to-day agency operations and agency clients.

- Assess the degree to which the change is compatible with the agency's mission, traditions, current goals, and fiscal resources. Determine the degree to which the change is desired and likely to be supported by top management and the board of directors.

- Identify and assess the relative strength of the organizational subsystems and individuals who are likely to favor the change and those who will oppose it. Determine who stands to gain and who stands to be hurt by the proposed change. A strategy most likely to overcome resistance is one that either (1) increases the power of those within the agency that favor the change or (2) introduces innovative programs or brings new resources into the organization that will minimize the impact of the change on those who are resistant.

- The agency, or a unit of the agency, will most likely adopt a proposed change if it can be shown that the change will result in an increase in scope, authority, autonomy, funding, and other resources. A change that decreases power and resources will be resisted. People will favor a change that makes their work easier or more successful; they will resist a change that makes their work more complex or demands more of their time.

- The members of an organization will strongly resist a change that they perceive as a threat to their jobs, advancement, or opportunities within the organization. Also, they will be resistant whenever they suspect others are withholding information about the true intentions of the change.

- An organization will be more open to a proposed change if it can be demonstrated that other similar organizations have successfully made this change.

- A change is most likely to be accepted by the organization after its advantages have been demonstrated in a trial run or implemented within only a part of the organization. Thus, it is desirable that the initial phase of a more far-reaching change effort begin by focusing first on a specific program or activity of limited scope.

- Whenever possible, changes should be integrated into current structures and procedures so as to minimize the disruption of existing relationships and patterns.

Selected Bibliography

Anderson, Donald L. *Organization Development: The Process of Leading Organizational Change.* Thousand Oaks, CA: Sage, 2010.

Lewis, Judith A., Thomas R. Packard, and Michael D. Lewis. *Management of Human Services Programs,* 5th ed. Independence, KY: Cengage, 2012.

12.10 AGENCY PLANNING PROCESSES

To operate in an effective and efficient manner and to grow and develop as an organization, a social agency must formulate both short-range and long-range plans that guide its ongoing activity and decision making. All too often, agencies neglect long-term planning and then find that they must make hasty decisions and rapid changes in response to a situation or crisis they did not anticipate and for which they were unprepared.

Ideally, an agency's planning process is proactive and forward looking. The plan should include a description of how it will utilize its resources (i.e., staff time, money, knowledge, skills, etc.), how it can capitalize on its strengths and opportunities, how it will correct its weaknesses, and how it can respond to certain unwanted but possible future events such as overwhelming demand for service, loss of staff, or a reduction in funding.

A fruitful planning process is complex and time consuming. It can be especially difficult because all planning decisions rest on a set of predictions as to what will happen in future months and years. Unfortunately, it is difficult to predict accurately the ever-changing political, economic, and public opinion forces that may affect an agency's operation. Given these uncertainties, even the best of plans must be constantly reviewed and revised.

Broadly speaking, there are three types of planning processes: (1) problem-solving planning, (2) operational planning, and (3) strategic planning. They differ primarily in terms of the time period covered.

Problem-solving planning has a lifespan of 60 to 90 days. It focuses on some specific problem that is having an adverse effect on the agency's usual activity. The process involves (1) identifying and examining the problem, (2) selecting a set of corrective actions or measures, (3) planning the implementation of these measures, and (4) monitoring their effectiveness. If the agency is successful in its operational and strategic planning, the need for problem-solving planning will be minimized.

"Decision Trees" a deleted item from 4th edition

Operational planning refers to short-range planning covering a period of 3 to 12 months or perhaps one budget cycle. This planning process formulates objectives, details performance standards, and prepares an action plan to reach the stated objectives.

Strategic planning may cover a period of 3 to 10 years. Basically, the strategic planning process strives to develop a plan for achieving the agency's mission or long-term goals. This type of planning calls for the identification and analysis of broad social and economic trends, for speculation on what challenges and opportunities the agency will face in the next few years, and for forward-looking decisions about how best to use agency resources. Strategic planning is based on the belief that it is important to have a plan that considers all identifiable and significant conditions and factors that may impact the agency, regardless of how uncertain the future must be. Because it is so speculative and based on so many presumptions and uncertain variables, a strategic plan must be continually reviewed and revised.

Following these guidelines will enhance the planning process:

- Make certain that adequate and accurate data is available to those engaged in the planning process. Such data should describe these factors:
  - The agency's mission and goals
  - Current and projected budgets and a history of the agency's fiscal condition
  - Programs and services provided and the number of clients/consumers participating in each program or service area

- Characteristics of the persons served by the agency (e.g., age, income, ethnicity, religion)
- Agency staff (e.g., education, training, interests, skills)
- The agency's relationship with other local, state, or national agencies
- Requests and concerns voiced by staff/clients/consumers and other agencies and community groups
- Trends and projections (i.e., demand for services, capacity to raise funds, demographic changes in the community)
- Special problems faced by the agency

- Keep the planning process as simple as possible so that all those who should participate can do so despite their other responsibilities and day-to-day pressures. Do not demand more of their time than is absolutely necessary. Keep the number of meetings and the paperwork to a minimum.

- Make sure that all who might be affected by a decision or proposed change are invited to participate in the discussion and encouraged to voice their thoughts and concerns. Avoid the top-down approach (i.e., decision making and planning by only the upper-level administrative personnel). Facilitate the flow of information between the decision makers and those who might be affected by the decision.

- Gather and organize ideas and promote creativity by performing a SWOPA analysis of the agency. The acronym **SWOPA** stands for Strengths, Weaknesses, Opportunities, Problems, and Action.

  - *Strengths.* Identify the services, programs, and activities currently provided at a level of quality that meets or exceeds professional standards.
  - *Weaknesses.* Identify the services, programs, and activities that fall below acceptable levels of quality or needed levels of quantity.
  - *Opportunities.* Identify the services, programs, and activities that are promising for future development or expansion because of growing demand, available funding, staff interest, and so on.
  - *Problems.* Identify the areas of agency performance that are especially troublesome.
  - *Actions.* Identify activities or changes that would build on agency strengths, exploit opportunities, address areas of weakness, or better manage the problems faced by the agency.

- Perform a *competition analysis.* This asks those participating in the planning process to examine the activities of other agencies, organizations, or professional groups to determine how they compete with the agency's current programs and services. For example, are other organizations developing services that would attract your agency's clients or staff or are other agencies making requests for the funds now utilized by your agency? Are there opportunities for collaboration or formal contracts with other agencies regarding the provision of services?

"Developing Protocol Statements" from 5th edition and "Establishing Formal Interagency Collaboration" from 7th edition

- Perform a *stakeholder's analysis.* Stakeholders are those individuals, groups, or organizations that have a special or vested interest in the agency. Their beliefs, values, and possible reactions to changes in the agency must be given serious consideration. Examples of internal stakeholders are clients/consumers, agency staff, unions representing staff, members of the board of directors, and so on. Examples of external stakeholders include professional associations, politicians, other agencies, businesses and corporations, local newspapers, citizen groups, taxpayers, contributors, former clients, and the like.

- Perform a *threat analysis*. A threat is some possible future circumstance or action by others that could harm the agency. Examples might include a lawsuit against the agency, an employee strike, loss of funding, loss of key staff, rapid change in community demographics, significant changes in the laws, regulations, and accreditation standards that affect the agency, damaging news stories, and so forth.

- Make sure that the many facets of the planning process are coordinated and well integrated. For example, decisions concerning budget, staffing patterns, performance standards, and programs and services to be offered are all interrelated. In particular, financial planning must be incorporated into all other areas of planning. If the many components of the process are not properly coordinated and integrated, much time will be wasted, confusion will occur, and the planning process will flounder.

Selected Bibliography

Bryson, John. *Strategic Planning for Public and Non-profit Organizations.* 4th ed. San Francisco: Jossey-Bass, 2011.

Fallon, L. Fleming, James Begun, and William Riley. *Managing Health Organizations for Quality and Performance.* Burlington, MA: Jones and Bartlett Learning, 2013.

Kettner, Peter M., Robert M. Moroney, and Lawrence L. Martin. *Designing and Managing Programs: An Effectiveness-Based Approach,* 4th ed. Thousand Oaks, CA: Sage, 2013.

12.11 SELECTING CHANGE ISSUES FOR ADVOCACY

Social workers encounter many people who are experiencing a problem or social injustice caused by the policies, actions, or the inactions of a business, large corporation, or governmental agency. Not infrequently, the problem is one of discrimination based on social-economic class, race, ethnicity, gender, age, sexual orientation, or disabling conditions. When such a problem is affecting large numbers of people, perhaps even a whole neighborhood or community, it may be necessary to engage in political or social action in order to rectify the situation. The social worker can help the people impacted by these sorts of problems to clarify and express their concerns, to decide what kind of change is needed, and to mobilize and build coalitions to effect the desired change.

Since the outcome of an advocacy action (e.g., a petition drive or protest demonstration) directed at a powerful organization or special-interest group is always somewhat unpredictable and can have unwanted consequences, the issue to be tackled and the tactics to be used must be selected with great care. In general, a favorable outcome is most likely when the issue or the desired change is one that touches the lives and the emotions of many people, the concern and the desired change is relatively easy for people to understand, the issue mobilizes and unites many people, and when the people involved have reason to believe that success is possible.

Another important part of planning advocacy to address an issue is the readiness of the community to change. These questions might prove helpful in examining the capacity of a community to engage in a change effort:

- Are efforts, programs, or policies already in place that attempt to address this issue?
- To what extent do community members know about these efforts and their effectiveness?

- How much do members of the community know about the extent of the problem and the consequences for the persons affected, as well as its impact on the community at large?
- Do elected officials and other influential members of the community support addressing this issue? If not, why?
- Is the prevailing attitude in the community toward this issue one of resignation or one of willingness to assume responsibility for addressing the matter?
- To what extent are people likely to commit time and other resources to bring about change in this situation?

As suggested by these questions, those people who select and define the issue to be addressed must grapple with the fundamental question of whether a particular change effort is feasible, realistic, and likely to succeed. The issue selected must be one that will motivate people and attract their involvement in the change process.

After an issue has been selected and it has been determined that the community is ready to address it, the next critical step is to build a membership base. Typically, the effort to seek change is initiated by a few highly committed people, but unless the membership can build to a more substantial number, there is little hope for success. Politically, economically, and socially powerful people can best be influenced when the advocacy group's power comes, for example, from having a large number of members who might boycott a company or product, form a voting block, or conduct a public demonstration. The advocacy group must be able to convince the general public that those in power can be influenced and persuaded to change.

Because the outcomes of aggressive and confrontational tactics are usually unpredictable and may result in an unfavorable backlash against the advocacy group, it is best to first attempt less polarizing approaches such as negotiating, collecting and analyzing data for a position paper, conducting a public education campaign, or using other techniques described in the following chapter of this book. However, knowing that an advocacy organization has the capacity to mobilize a large group of people for action will help get the attention of powerful people and encourage them to consider solutions (perhaps requiring compromise from both sides) before a more conflicted and bitter situation develops. (For additional information on social change and advocacy, see Items 13.32 and 13.37.)

Selected Bibliography

Kahn, Si. *Organizing: A Guide for Grassroots Leaders*, rev. ed. Washington, DC: NASW, 1991.

Kapin, Allyson, and Amy Sample Ward. *Social Change Anytime Everywhere: How to Implement Online Multichannel Strategies to Spark Advocacy, Raise Money, and Engage Your Community*. San Francisco: Jossey-Bass, 2013.

Lipsky, Michael. *Street-level Bureaucracy: Dilemmas of the Individual Public Services*, 30th anniversary expanded edition. New York: Russell Sage Foundation, 2010.

McNeil, Lori. *Street Practice: Changing the Lens on Poverty and Public Assistance*. Burlington, VT: Ashgate, 2013.

12.12 PROJECT PLANNING AND EVALUATION

Human services agencies are dynamic. They must constantly respond to changing needs and circumstances with new services, programs, and projects for accomplishing their organization's goals. The challenge is how to introduce such change with a minimum of disruption to the staff and the organization's day-to-day operations. This is possible only if those advocating for the innovation have carefully considered whether and why the proposed change is needed and how its introduction is to be orchestrated.

PLANNING FOR CHANGE

Planning to strengthen a social agency calls for selecting the best changes in goals or programs from among the possible alternatives. Those responsible for making these decisions should ask the following questions in relation to each alternative being considered:

- Would this change be consistent with the agency's overall mission and goals?
- Would making this change raise any legal or ethical concerns?
- To what extent is it likely this change will be successful in reducing or eliminating the problem or concern?
- Would making this change be an efficient use of agency or community resources?
- Would the change be likely to have a lasting positive impact?
- Are there negative side effects that could result from this change?

SCHEDULING

A variety of techniques have been developed to help schedule a program change or introduce a new type of service into an agency. One scheduling tool called a **Gantt chart** provides a visual grid depicting the relationship between the activities required for a project and the timeframe for completing each. The activities are listed down the left column, and the periods of work on each activity, charted by month or week, are shown across the top of the page (see Figure 12.4). A Gantt chart is useful because it helps identify the sequencing required for the entire project and helps keep track of the completion dates for specific activities.

The Program Evaluation and Review Technique (**PERT chart**) is another useful scheduling tool. This chart is especially helpful for sorting out the proper sequencing of events and estimating the amount of time required to complete each activity or event. When developing a PERT chart, recognize that each *activity* will require staff time to complete. Thus, by adding up the days or hours devoted to the various activities, it is possible to estimate the cost in staff time to carry out the project. An *event* is an action taken by someone other than staff on a target date that affects the time line of the project. By first identifying the dates on which various events are likely to be completed and then charting the activities that must occur to prepare for each event, it is possible to start with the intended completion date for the project and work backward to build the PERT chart. Figure 12.5 illustrates a section of a PERT chart developed for a client survey regarding the effectiveness of an agency's services.

TASK PLANNING

The final step in completing a special project is to identify and carry out the activities required for its implementation. This involves identifying the *tasks* to be completed, specifying the rationale for engaging in this activity, noting when it must be completed, who should be involved, and estimating the time required for completing the task.

It is noteworthy that if seeking funding to support a project (see Item 13.36), evidence of the careful planning represented by Figures 12.4 and 12.5 can demonstrate to funding sources that you have a thoughtful and feasible plan for implementing the proposed project.

Activity	J	F	M	A	M	J	J	A	S	O	N	D
1. Collect literature on parent-effectiveness training.	▓	▓										
2. Secure permission to initiate parent-effectiveness training group from supervisor.			▓									
3. Interpret parent-effectiveness training in staff meeting.				▓								
4. Request all workers in unit to nominate families for parent-effectiveness training.					▓							
5. Send letters to nominated families, inviting them to participate and asking for preference on which night to meet.						▓						
6. Set meeting times, reserve room, and notify families of first meeting.							▓					
7. Make day-care plans for children of the participants.								▓				
8. Prepare presentations and materials for parent-effectiveness training sessions.								▓	▓			
9. Hold 12 weekly meetings with participants.								▓	▓			
10. Assess the value of the sessions to the participants.											▓	
11. Report results to supervisor and other staff members.												▓

Figure 12.4

Sample Gantt Chart for Parent-Effectiveness Training

Selected Bibliography

Bender, Michael B. *A Manager's Guide to Project Management: Learn How to Apply Best Practices.* Upper Saddle River, NJ: FT Press, 2010.

Horine, Greg. *Absolute Beginner's Guide to Project Management.* Indianapolis, IN: Que, 2005.

Shore, Arnold S., and John M. Carfora. *A Guide to Proposal Development and Project Management: The Art of Funding Ideas.* Thousand Oaks, CA: Sage, 2011.

12.13 PLANNING A PRIMARY PREVENTION PROGRAM

Most social programs are initially created as a reaction to an existing problem and are designed to offer treatment or assistance to the people who experience that problem. Equally important are programs designed to prevent the problem from developing in the first place. Prevention efforts make sense, but the design of an effective prevention program is complex and difficult.

Although many view prevention as essentially different from intervention, it is useful to consider prevention as a type of intervention. **Primary prevention** consists of

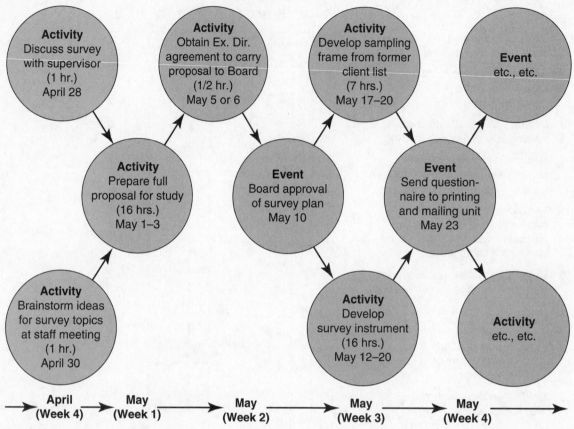

Figure 12.5
Sample PERT Chart for Client Survey Proposal

a set of actions intended to intervene and modify those conditions or situations that will, if not changed, lead to or result in a problem. Thus, those engaged in planning a prevention effort must be able to identify the factors that cause the problem and then engage in a set of actions and activities that will control or eliminate those factors. Increasingly, primary prevention programs are built around ideas of risk and resiliency. In relation to children and youth, for example, considerable research identifies a high correlation between certain negative family, neighborhood, and community influences (risk factors) and the development of social problems such as delinquency, drug and alcohol abuse, school dropout, emotional disturbance, gang activity, and teen pregnancy. Among the corrosive influences that give rise to these problems are poverty, discrimination, lack of opportunity, family breakdown and dysfunction, feelings of low self-worth, easy access to drugs and alcohol, and poor schools. For reasons not well understood, some young people are more "resistant" to these negative influences than others. They have within their personalities, environment, and life experiences certain protective factors that shield them from the full force of negative influences. They are said to possess *resiliency* in that even when exposed to stress, trauma, and adversity, they do not develop serious problems.

Human growth and development includes many self-righting or "healing" mechanisms that can counteract or compensate for trauma and life stressors. These *protective factors* include self-confidence, self-esteem, problem-solving skills, warm and supportive relationships with family members, the presence of caring people in the school or work environment, and/or supportive factors in one's ethnic, neighborhood, or community interactions. This is not meant to suggest that what happens at one point in a person's development has no impact on what follows. Rather, it suggests that the impact of significant negative events is more elastic than often assumed and it is possible for these resilient people to more easily overcome the problems that do arise in their lives.

Efforts by social workers to prevent problems from occurring are helpful for both the resilient and not-so-resilient people. Following these general guidelines will help those involved in the design and implementation of primary prevention programs.

- Enter the initial planning stage with caution and thoughtfulness. Early in the planning process, consult with those people who have experience in designing prevention programs and review the literature that reports efforts to address these target problems. Know from the start that most problems have multiple causes, that it is always difficult to gain control over those causative factors, and that it is difficult to precisely measure the impact of a prevention effort.
- Clearly define and describe the problem or condition you are attempting to prevent. Without an operational definition of your target problem, you cannot design an effective program of prevention.
- Identify the signs or indicators of the problem's existence so that you can later measure the impact of your prevention effort. Without a way of measuring success, your program is not likely to attract funding and support for more than a brief demonstration period. Make sure that these indicators are understandable, measurable, and clear reflections of the problem(s) addressed by this prevention program. Consult the literature and people skilled at program evaluation (see Item 14.9) early in the planning process.
- Recognize that any plan for prevention rests on the knowledge, beliefs, and assumptions made about when, why, and how this problem develops, as well as judgments about which individuals or groups are most likely to experience this problem. Thus, a critical step in planning is to formulate and articulate one's beliefs about the nature and causes of the problem to be prevented. This is a challenge because the social and behavioral sciences are seldom able to identify clear cause and effect relationships. Social problems are complex and a whole host of interrelated factors usually contribute to their development.
- When the factors that cause the problem have been identified, it is necessary to decide which contributing factors, if any, can be influenced and changed. Identify the specific risk and protective factors related to the problem you want to prevent. A *risk factor* is a condition, situation, or set of circumstances that increases the likelihood that a problem will occur. A *protective factor* is a condition or circumstance that reduces the chance that the problem will develop. The prevention program should be designed to weaken or reduce risk factors and, at the same time, strengthen or expand protective factors. As a general rule, a prevention program is most likely to be effective if it targets those at greatest risk of experiencing the problem.
- Finally, determine how the necessary changes can best be accomplished. In many cases, important contributing causes (e.g., large-scale economic and societal forces) are beyond the reach of community-based prevention programs. A social

worker may choose instead to advocate for change at the state or national levels. In other cases, the action plan would require intervention at the local level or at both the local and national levels.

Selected Bibliography

Cohen, Larry, Vivian Chavez, and Sana Chehimi, eds. *Prevention Is Primary: Strategies for Community Well-Being*, 2nd ed. San Francisco: Jossey-Bass, 2010.

Gullotta, Thomas P., Gary M. Blau, and Jessica M. Ramos, eds. *Handbook of Child Behavioral Issues: Evidence-Based Approaches to Prevention and Treatment*. New York: Routledge/Taylor & Francis, 2008.

12.14 PARTICIPATORY ACTION PLANNING

On occasion a human services agency or a community will hurriedly launch a planning effort intended to come up with a set of recommendations for dealing with some particular issue or problem that has suddenly attracted the public's attention, such as, for example, a media exposé or a feature story about human trafficking or a murder resulting from failed treatment at a mental health clinic, the prevalence homelessness in the community, increased gang activity and drug use by teens, or a case of child abuse resulting in death. Not infrequently, with such public attention to an issue there is sudden demand to do something about the problem.

All too often the approach taken is the traditional one that views this planning process as a top-down activity in which leaders drawn from professional associations, city planning personnel, health care providers, educators, economic development specialists, human services agencies, law enforcement officials, and representatives from business and industry come together to discuss the problem and formulate plans for corrective action. One option available to those responsible for the change being demanded (usually political and civic leaders) is to hire a consultant to gather information, collect data about the situation, write a report describing the problem, and make recommendations about what can be done about it. Another option might be to schedule public meetings to give interested persons an opportunity to present their ideas and opinions to the community leaders who then decide if there is a need to plan programs to address the matter and, if so, design and implement those programs.

In many cases the plans generated by these well-intentioned efforts fall short of the desired outcome and are not successfully implemented because they do not gain acceptance and support from those affected by the problem—that is, the *stakeholders*. This failure often happens because the recommendations reflect either an incomplete understanding the problem or fail to collect and seriously consider the viewpoints of the stakeholders.

Rarely do the community leaders spearheading the planning effort invest much time seeking out the viewpoints of people who have not attended public meetings nor submitted written testimony. Thus, for example, the voices often not heard from are those who are fearful of speaking in public, those unable to take time off from work, those who cannot attend the public meeting because they lack transportation or child care, those who have physical and mobility limitations, those who are uncomfortable with their ability to speak English, or those are unable to read or write. In order to secure a true cross-section of stakeholder opinions and ideas, it is necessary to actively reach out to those who have experienced, or are at risk of experiencing, the problem. To obtain their valuable insights and recommendations for dealing with a particular issue, it is often necessary to proactively contact them and facilitate their input.

Given the limitations of the usual approach to formulating plans to address such problems, social workers who become part of the planning process are in a position to propose a more participatory process. By securing participation by persons affected by the issue, the social worker reinforces some core principles of social work (see Chapter 5), such as "maximize client participation," "maximize self-determination," and "maximize client empowerment." A downside of this approach is that it takes time to seek out and patiently listen to the voices of those who are most affected by the issue, but do not make themselves heard individually or through a special-interest or advocacy group. Such an inclusive process is perhaps less efficient, but likely to be more effective in the long-run.

As an approach to address issues within an organization, participatory action planning has evolved in the field of health care. Known in that field as *action research*, this approach has focused on bringing together professionals who are providing health services and asking them to engage their clients or patients in evaluating the service outcomes. By then reflecting on these and other perceptions of the issues and their causes, it is possible to generate ideas for improvements and take action to strengthen the services delivered by these providers. In effect, action research is a type of program planning developed *with, for,* and *by* those giving and receiving the services.

At the community level, *community-based participatory research* (also known as *community-based collaborative action research*) applies many of the principles of action research to plans for addressing community issues. It also follows the planned change model described in Chapter 7 of this book in that it begins with engaging stakeholders as partners in addressing an issue. It then moves to the collection of data to inform decisions, then proceeds to engaging in thoughtful reflection on the data to evolve a plan about how to address the issue. The research then continues by involving community members in taking corrective action, and anticipates continuous monitoring and evaluation of what does and doesn't work.

In sum, community-based participatory planning is dynamic in the sense that key participants are the people who will be affected by the outcome and their perceptions become the starting point of the change process. After considerable thoughtful give and take among the participants to be sure they fully comprehend the meaning of the data, this information is shared with other stakeholders, as well as those who will determine the outcome. Only then is a plan for addressing the issue(s) negotiated and implemented. Finally, the outcome of the changes is fed back to the various participants and the cycle is repeated as long as the issues are not adequately resolved.

Professionals and civic leaders who typically control a community change process are busy people and anxious to complete the process as soon as possible—often lacking the patience to allow all stakeholders and other members of a community to say their piece and to really be listened to. A critically important role for a social worker, then, is to convince these decision makers of the merits of stakeholder input and to offer to perform the role of encouraging and assisting community members to make their views known. This may involve assisting those affected, or potentially affected, by the outcome to prepare and present their viewpoints in writing or by making oral presentations in sessions facilitated by the social worker. Securing community participation might also involve engaging those who are reluctant to participate or hesitant to voice their ideas. From a social work perspective, reaching out to the poor and disenfranchised of a community is reinforced by the social work values of serving the most vulnerable and striving for social justice.

Selected Bibliography

Gamble, Dorothy N. "Participatory Methods in Community Practice." In *The Handbook of Community Practice*, 2nd ed. Edited by Marie Weil, Michael Reisch, and Mary L. Ohmer. Thousand Oaks, CA: Sage, 2013, pp. 327–343.

Israel, Barbara A., Eugenia Eng, Amy J. Schultz, and Edith A. Parker, eds. *Methods for Community-Based Participatory Research for Health*, 2nd ed. San Francisco: Jossey-Bass, 2013.

Johnson, Michael P. *Community-Based Operations Research: Decision Modeling for Local Impact and Diverse Populations*. New York: Springer, 2012.

Pavish, Carol Pillsbury, and Margaret Dexheimer Pharris. *Community-Based Collaborative Action Research: A Nursing Approach*. Sudbury, MA: Jones and Bartlett Learning, 2012.

13

Intervention and Monitoring

LEARNING OBJECTIVES

At the conclusion of this chapter, the reader should be prepared to:

- Discuss several techniques a social worker might use to help a client modify a specific behavior.
- Identify several techniques a social worker might employ to help a client address issues in role performance, poor self-concept, and low self-esteem.
- Identify specific considerations and tools a social worker might use to help a client deal with troubling decisions, a personal crisis, a financial crisis, conflict resolution, and supporting caregivers.
- Recognize the purpose of programming and its use in group work.
- Describe skills a social worker needs for leading groups, such as ability to plan effective meetings, knowledge of parliamentary procedures, and tools to help groups identify concerns and reach consensus about actions to be taken.
- Discuss guidelines for special projects a social worker might offer an agency such as training volunteers, building a budget, engaging in marketing and fund-raising, and grant writing.
- Describe a process for bringing people in a community together to address a concern and identify cautions to observe when attempting to influence community decision makers.

The most visible phase in the change process is termed *intervention and monitoring*. Sometimes called the *action phase*, it is the time when the client, the social worker, and possibly others implement the plan they believe will bring about the desired outcome. Since each phase of the change process builds on the prior ones, the success of the intervention depends on the validity of the conclusions reached during the prior phases, such as engaging with the client, data collection and assessment, and planning.

Because the intervention phase typically takes up most of the time and energy expended during a change process and because concrete actions by the social worker are a central part of an intervention, many intervention techniques have been developed for use in both direct and indirect practice. Often, the greatest challenge for the social worker—whether serving individuals, families, groups, organizations, or communities—is to select an approach and the techniques that will facilitate change.

As the intervention proceeds, the social worker will **monitor** what is happening and, depending on what is or is not working, the social worker must decide if the intervention should be continued, modified, or possibly aborted, and a new plan negotiated. Monitoring differs from the evaluation phase, although both are discussed in Chapter 14, in that *monitoring* occurs while the intervention is underway, whereas *evaluation* takes place at the end of the change process, looking back to assess and measure overall progress.

A frequently overlooked element of monitoring is continuing to examine the client's situation for a period of time before completely terminating the professional relationship. This is important because whenever change occurs, various systems are disrupted and there is a tendency toward relapse or slipping back into a prior pattern. Thus, the social worker should determine if the observed change is more than a temporary accommodation to the intervention activities and, if so, to ensure that the changes and improvements are indeed firmly rooted and maintained as part of the client's ongoing functioning.

SECTION A

TECHNIQUES AND GUIDELINES FOR DIRECT PRACTICE

When working directly with individuals, families, and small groups, the social worker must adapt the intervention approach to the uniqueness of the situation and the people involved and to support the clients as they strive to make needed changes. The worker, too, must constantly monitor the client's response to the change process and regularly assess progress toward the agreed-on objectives.

Intervention activities

As the social worker engages a client in a helping relationship and introduces the client to the process of change, he or she must select an appropriate practice framework to guide this process (see Chapter 6). In addition, the worker must choose a number of specific techniques and guidelines that are likely to facilitate and encourage the desired change. In this Section A, an array of direct-service techniques and guidelines are presented. These are but a sampling. Social work literature, supervisors, colleagues, and workshops are sources of still others. None, however, is likely to be effective unless it is used by a caring and competent social worker.

Monitoring activities

Monitoring involves keeping watch over the change process. To do this, the social worker must regularly interact in person or through another means of communication with the clients. The worker must be sensitive to how the change activities are affecting the client and also how other people or related social systems are being affected. If progress toward the agreed-on objectives is lacking, the worker should suggest needed modifications in the intervention plan and possibly even cycle back to earlier phases of the process to reexamine problems or issues being addressed and perhaps look for other solutions.

Whenever possible, the social worker should share the results of this monitoring with the clients. When clients are aware of the changes that are occurring, whether positive or negative, they are more likely to involve themselves more deeply in the change process and possibly come up with useful modifications to the intervention plan. Most often, the monitoring results are fed back to the client in an informal manner. Increasingly, however, social workers are collecting empirical data about client change and feeding that information back to clients to assist them in understanding the effects of the services being utilized. Some of the commonly used tools for organizing this data can be found in Chapter 14.

As explained in Chapter 7 and elsewhere in this book, the process of making change happen is often difficult and slow. When clients do not find a quick solution to their problems or when they slip back into an old and troubling pattern or habit, they may become discouraged and be tempted to give up. Change can also be scary because it usually requires that clients do things differently, learn new skills, make difficult decisions, view their situation from a different angle, or place themselves in an unfamiliar social environment. When clients are hesitant about moving ahead, it can be helpful to remind them that when nothing changes, nothing changes. In other words, making a change requires a change and doing something new and different. Without that effort, nothing can possibly change.

13.1 PREPARING FOR AN INTERVIEW

One of the most common errors made by new workers is to go into a meeting with a client without a clear purpose and plan. However, this plan must be tentative and flexible in order to respond to new client concerns or unexpected developments. The answers to the following questions will help a social worker prepare for the interview.

- What are the overall goals and objectives of the intervention with this client? How will my next session or contact relate to these goals and objectives?
- What needs to be accomplished during the interview or meeting? What decisions need to be made during the session?
- Should the next contact be a face-to-face or a telephone interview? Should it be a one-on-one, family, or group session? Who needs to be present?
- Will other professionals and/or concerned individuals participate in this session (e.g., a family conference in a medical setting)? If so, what do they expect from the session?
- How much time do I have to devote to the interview or meeting? How much time can the client and others devote to the session?
- Where and when will the interview take place? What arrangements are necessary prior to the interview (e.g., scheduling a room, transportation, care for client's children)?
- What techniques might be used during the session to complete important tasks and work toward intervention goals and objectives?
- What factors related to the client's current physical functioning (e.g., mobility, pain, discomfort, hearing problems, effects of medication) need to be considered when preparing for the interview or meeting?
- Does the client's emotional state (e.g., anger, fear, confusion, depression) need to be considered in preparing for the session?

- What factors related to the client's culture, values or religious beliefs, and social and family network need to be considered?
- What documentation of this contact is necessary for the agency record?

In every session some time should be devoted to talking about client experiences that are positive and that help the client feel good about himself or herself. This is important because so often counseling, case management, and problem-solving sessions focus mostly on what is going wrong and what needs to be "fixed." To counterbalance this attention to the negative, a social worker should create opportunities for clients to recognize and verbalize their successes and strengths.

Selected Bibliography

Corcoran, Jacqueline. *Helping Skills for Social Work Direct Practice*, New York: Oxford University Press, 2011.

Murphy, Bianca, and Carolyn Dillon. *Interviewing in Action*, 4th ed. Independence, KY: Cengage, 2011.

O'Hare, Thomas. *Essential Skills of Social Work Practice*. Chicago: Lyceum, 2009.

13.2 INFORMATION, ADVICE, AND PERSUASION

Change is difficult. Not infrequently, clients are ambivalent or fearful of taking the necessary steps toward change. For example, a client may resist the idea of using a critically important service or program simply because it will be a new experience. In order to encourage action by the client, the worker may need to provide the client with information and possibly explicit advice, and, in some cases, persuade the client to move ahead.

As used here, *providing information* refers to offering the client certain facts, observations, and descriptions so she or he can make an informed decision or perform a task. The term *advice giving* refers to worker statements that recommend and encourage a certain decision or action. When using the skill of *persuasion*, the worker uses logical arguments in an effort to convince a client that a particular action is important and in his or her best interests.

When **providing information** to a client, the social worker should keep these guidelines in mind:

- Adapt your message to the client's educational background, intelligence, command of the language, and the like. Also, consider the client's state of mind. If, for example, the client is feeling anxious or overwhelmed, he or she may not comprehend or remember what you provide. If the client is unable to grasp or comprehend your message, seek her or his permission to convey this information to family members or trusted friends so they might help the client make use of the information.

- Appreciate how easily a message can be misunderstood. For example, the statement, "Fill out the form and take it to the person at the desk over there" could be confusing to someone who is not sure what the words *form, it, person,* or *over there* are referring to. Always provide sufficient detail and description so there will be no mistake. Provide information or directions in a logical, step-by-step fashion. Complicated instructions (e.g., how to get to another agency), names, addresses, and phone numbers should be written out for the client.

- Give the client time to think about what you are saying, and invite him or her to ask questions. Check to see that your message was understood. Say something like, "Now I want to make sure that I was clear in what I have been telling you. Would you please repeat back to me what you heard me say?" Do not simply ask, "Do you understand?" All too often, people will answer that question in the affirmative, even when unsure or confused.

One of the common errors made by inexperienced social workers is to give advice when the client has not asked for it. This is an understandable error because often the worker knows how other individuals dealt with a certain problem and wants his or her client to benefit from those experiences. However, there are many pitfalls in **advice giving**, and the worker needs to be cautious. Follow these guidelines:

- Before offering advice to a client, reflect on how you feel when someone gives you advice. Often we feel annoyed or irritated, regardless of their good intentions. And very often, we do not follow others' advice, even when we have requested it. When we do follow advice, it has usually been offered by someone we know well and trust completely.

- Whether it is appropriate to offer advice depends largely on the purpose and nature of the worker–client interaction. If the purpose has to do with securing a needed service, making a referral, or advocating for a client, advice giving may be important and necessary. When the worker is providing counseling or therapy, giving advice is only rarely appropriate.

- Do not offer advice until you have determined that the client genuinely wants your opinions and suggestions. Test the client's receptivity by asking questions such as "Have you asked others for suggestions?" and "Would it help if I tell you what other people usually do in that situation?"

- When you do give advice, present it in a way that says, in effect, "This is what I would do" or "This is what others have done." Explain the reasoning or logic behind the guidance you offer. Leave the responsibility for accepting or rejecting the advice with the client. And never give advice on a topic outside your area of training and expertise.

- Consider the issue of legal liability if you advise a client and he or she later experiences a negative personal or financial consequence because of your recommendation. For example, beware of advising a client who asks questions such as, "Do you think I should get a divorce?" "Do you think I should quit my job and look for another?" "Do you think I should I cut back on my medicine?"

- Be alert to the dangers of giving advice to a manipulative client, who may then hold you responsible if things do not turn out well (e.g., "I did what you said and it didn't work, so now you need to fix this problem"). Also, be alert to the danger of encouraging dependency in clients who can and should take responsibility for their decisions and actions.

In some situations, it is necessary to use the skill of **persuasion** to encourage a fearful or hesitant client to take an important step. The worker should follow these guidelines:

- Present your suggested course of action through the use of personal stories that will engage and touch the client's feelings and emotions. Use stories and examples that the client can easily understand, given her or his age, background, and life experiences. When people do change their minds, it is usually in response to such stories and experiences, rather than in response to rational arguments or statistics.

- Present the suggested course of action after first identifying other options or positions that may appeal to the client. This demonstrates to the client that you understand the client's dilemma, hesitation, or ambivalence.

- Explain how the suggested action is compatible with the client's core values and goals and how not taking this particular action would be inconsistent with his or her stated goals and values.

- Describe the advantages and risks of following the suggested action while also pointing out the negative consequences of not doing so.

- Offer an approach or plan that will allow the client to move ahead cautiously in small steps or phases so he or she can gradually try out or test the suggested course of action.

- Enlist the assistance of persons whom the client trusts and respects and ask them to encourage the client toward the suggested course of action.

Selected Bibliography

Cialdini, Robert. *Influence: Science and Practice*, 5th ed. Upper Saddle River, NJ: Pearson, 2009.

Kotter, Jeffery. *A Brief Primer of Helping Skills*. Thousand Oaks, CA: Sage, 2008.

Shulman, Lawrence. *The Skills of Helping Individuals, Families, Groups, and Communities*, 6th ed. Independence, KY: Cengage, 2009.

13.3 REINFORCEMENT AND RELATED BEHAVIORAL TECHNIQUES

The various behavioral techniques, drawn from learning theory, are some of the most powerful available to the social worker if the purpose of an intervention is to help a client learn a new behavior or modify an existing one. They are used to either strengthen (increase) or weaken (decrease) a target behavior. The term **target behavior** refers to an observable and operationally defined behavior that is the focus of the intervention.

Reinforcement is any action that increases or strengthens a target behavior. There are two forms of reinforcement: positive and negative. In this context, *positive* refers to adding and *negative* refers to removing or subtracting. Both positive and negative reinforcement increase the frequency, intensity, or duration of a target behavior. **Positive reinforcement** involves giving or adding something to the client (such as attention, objects of value, or privileges). A positive reinforcer is usually something that most people would consider to be desirable or pleasurable but for some individuals, even a painful event can become a positive reinforcer (e.g., self-mutilation, head banging). Thus, only by carefully observing its effects, can one determine for sure what is and is not a reinforcer for a particular individual. To do this, it is necessary to first establish a **baseline measurement** of the target behavior prior to beginning the intervention or reinforcement.

There are two kinds of positive reinforcement: primary and secondary. **Primary reinforcers** are inherently rewarding and almost universally reinforcing. Examples include food, safety, and so on. **Secondary reinforcers** are learned, usually as a result of having been associated with primary reinforcers. Examples include money and special privileges. Praise and attention are usually considered to be a form of secondary reinforcement but there is some evidence that they are universally reinforcing. As a general rule, a reinforcer will be what a person chooses to do when he or she does not have to do something else (e.g., how a person spends extra time and money).

Negative reinforcement involves subtracting or removing some object or condition that is aversive or unpleasant, which then has the effect of increasing or strengthening the target behavior. An example might be lifting or revoking the requirement that a person complete some unpleasant or onerous task. Negative reinforcement is often confused with punishment, but they are not the same. Punishment weakens the target behavior, whereas negative reinforcement strengthens the target behavior.

As a technique of behavior change, **punishment** involves the presentation of an unwanted or unpleasant stimulus (an event or action) that has the effect of suppressing a target behavior or reducing its strength. For ethical and legal reasons, the social worker must usually avoid the use of punishment. Most agencies and treatment programs prohibit the use of punishment for one or more of the following reasons:

- Often the results of punishment are short-term. When the threat of punishment ends, the target behavior often returns.
- A professional's use of punishment displays a poor model of behavior and might be imitated by the client.
- Punishment can become excessive when administered by a person who is angry or frustrated.
- Punishment may also suppress desirable behavior and make the client afraid to respond even in normal and functional ways.
- The use of physical punishment may make the worker vulnerable to a civil lawsuit or criminal charges (e.g., malpractice, abuse, assault).

A behavior that is not reinforced will, over time, tend to decrease in frequency, duration, or intensity. The term *extinction* describes the planned withdrawal of reinforcements so as to eliminate or weaken an unwanted behavior.

There are two basic **reinforcement schedules**: continuous and intermittent. *Continuous reinforcement* presents the client with a reinforcer each time the desired target behavior occurs. In *intermittent reinforcement*, the target behavior is only periodically or occasionally rewarded. Continuous reinforcement is often used in the first stages of a program designed to teach a new behavior because it promotes faster learning than intermittent reinforcement. However, a behavior that has been continuously reinforced will often weaken or disappear if no longer reinforced. To make the newly learned behavior resistant to extinction, the initial continuous reinforcement should be replaced by intermittent reinforcement. A behavior that is maintained by *random reinforcement* (e.g., slot machine, bingo, fishing) or learned during a time of intense emotion is highly resistant to change and difficult to extinguish.

A useful behavioral technique is to ignore an unwanted target behavior while at the same time, reinforcing an incompatible desired behavior. This is called **differential reinforcement**. When one behavior is described as incompatible with another, it means that a person cannot perform both behaviors concurrently. For example, a child cannot play basketball and watch TV at the same time.

"ABC Model and the "Behavior Matrix" a deleted item from 8th edition

The techniques of chaining, prompting, fading, and shaping are useful when the objective is to help a client learn a new behavior. These techniques are frequently used in training programs for people who have an intellectual disability, in speech therapy, and in certain aspects of physical rehabilitation. **Chaining** refers to a procedure that breaks down a complex behavior (e.g., dressing) into many separate steps and then teaches each step, one at a time. As a step is learned, it is "chained," or linked, to the ones already learned. The number of steps needed to teach a particular behavior will depend on the complexity of the behavior and the capacity of the client. There are two types of chaining: forward and backward. In *forward chaining*, the first step in a chain is taught first. For example, in teaching a man to put on his trousers, he would first be taught how to pick up and hold his pants. A second step might be to put his left leg into the left pant leg. All subsequent steps are taught in the order of a usual or natural sequence as determined by having observed how people usually perform the behavior (i.e., putting on pants).

In *backward chaining*, the last step in the chain is taught first. Thus, all the prior steps in the sequence would be done for the client except the one being taught. For example, when teaching a man to put on his pants, the first step to be taught would be to button the pants around his waist. The advantage of backward chaining is that the last step in the chain is always the one that is reinforced. Thus, the client is always reinforced at the very end of the behavior chain (e.g., when he has finished putting on his pants) and this prevents the client from getting stuck on a step before reaching the rewarding success of the entire sequence.

The term **prompting** describes any form of assistance given by the trainer to guide the client in performing the target behavior. A prompt may be a verbal cue or instruction, a gesture or other nonverbal cue, or physically moving the client through the behavior. Prompting should be used only when necessary.

Fading is the process of gradually withdrawing prompts and decreasing the frequency of reinforcement as the client begins to learn the desired behavior. In the first steps of a training program, the trainer will use continuous reinforcement and frequent prompting to help establish the new behavior. Later, when the client regularly performs the behavior, the trainer will gradually fade out or decrease the frequency of reinforcement and prompting.

Shaping is a technique of building up a new behavior by reinforcing closer and closer approximations of the desired response. For example, a speech therapist teaching a child to say "cookie" may reward the child when he says "gowk." Perhaps later, the child is reinforced for saying "gook-koo" and still later, "ookie." Finally, after many weeks of reinforcing the child for closer and closer approximations of the desired sound, the child has learned to say "cookie."

Much of what people learn, especially social behavior, is learned by observing others and subsequently imitating that behavior. This learning process is called **modeling**. Both functional and dysfunctional behaviors are learned through modeling. Thus, it is always important for a young person to have positive role models—people she or he can observe and as a result learn positive and prosocial behavior. A social worker can enhance a client's learning of functional behaviors by keeping in mind several principles of modeling:

- Individual A is most likely to imitate the behavior of individual B (the model) if he or she views B as having a valued status (e.g., power, prestige, attractiveness) and if he or she observes B being rewarded for the behavior.
- In addition, individual A must in some way identify with B and feel similar. If A views B as being significantly different (e.g., in age, education, social economic class, race), individual A may conclude there is no chance he or she could actually perform the behavior and/or that there is little chance that the behavior would be rewarded.

- Individual A is most likely to learn B's behavior if he or she has an opportunity to perform or practice the behavior soon after observing it and the behavior is rewarded.

Under ordinary conditions, licensed foster parents and child care staff working in hospitals, treatment centers, and group homes are prohibited from using any form of physical punishment. The procedure called **time out** is an alternative to physical discipline. Consider this set of instructions given to a foster parent who is learning the technique of time out for use with a 7-year-old boy named Tyler:

- Find an area in your home that can be used for time out. Choose an area that has no breakable or dangerous objects, in case Tyler kicks or throws things when he has tantrums. You might use his bedroom or other quiet area that is well lighted and ventilated.

- Identify the undesirable or unacceptable behaviors that will result in time out (i.e., clearly define the target behavior). For example, you may decide to use time out whenever Tyler hits you or another child.

- Each time a target behavior occurs, use the time-out procedure immediately. Walk up to Tyler, explain what rule he has broken, and tell him what must now happen—for example, "Tyler, whenever you hit your sister, you must go to time out." Accompany the child to the time-out area; do not look at or talk to him on the way. If he resists, carry him there as quickly as possible.

- Leave Tyler in the time-out area for a predetermined period of time. As a rule of thumb, use the formula of one minute per year of the child's age. At the end of the time-out period or when Tyler is quiet and behaving well, go to the door and ask if he is ready to come out and behave correctly. For example, if he had thrown toys, say, "Tyler, are you ready to come out and put your toys away?"

    If he answers yes, have Tyler come out and correct the earlier behavior. Reinforce the correct behavior with praise. For example, say, "I like the way you are picking up your toys."

    If Tyler does not answer yes or he screams, cries, throws a tantrum, or displays other undesirable behavior, walk away from the door and wait until he is again quiet and behaving appropriately. Then go back and repeat the question.

- At first, you may have to question Tyler several times before he is ready to come out and correct the bad behavior. Do not be discouraged—just continue to follow these rules.

- Arrange a special activity, privilege, or treat at the end of each day or half-day that Tyler did not have to be taken to the time-out area and tell him that it is a reward for his good behavior.

Selected Bibliography

Hersen, Michel, ed. *Encyclopedia of Behavior Modification and Cognitive Behavior Therapy* (three volumes). Thousand Oaks, CA: Sage, 2005.

Martin, Gary, and Joseph Pear. *Behavior Modification*, 9th ed. Upper Saddle River, NJ: Pearson, 2011.

Miltenberger, Raymond. *Behavior Modification: Principles and Procedures*, 4th ed. Belmont, CA: Thomson Wadsworth, 2008.

Watson, David, and Ronald Tharp. *Self-Directed Behavior: Self Modification for Personal Adjustment*, 10th ed. Independence, KY: Cengage, 2007.

13.4 BEHAVIORAL REHEARSAL

The technique of **behavioral rehearsal** is designed to teach a client how to handle a specific interpersonal exchange or situation. Essentially, it is a form of role-playing that makes use of modeling and coaching as teaching tools. Like other forms of role-play, behavioral rehearsal provides the client with an opportunity to try out and practice a new behavior in a safe and accepting environment. The technique can be used, for example, to prepare a client for a job interview (e.g., the social worker takes the role of the employer and conducts a simulated job interview). Whether used during a one-to-one interview or during a group session, the steps are basically the same:

Step 1: The client identifies the problem situation with which she or he wants help. The client is asked to demonstrate how she or he would usually behave in that situation.

Step 2: The worker (and/or group members) makes suggestions on how the client might handle the situation more effectively.

Step 3: The client is given an opportunity to provide additional information about the problem or concern and to ask the worker (or group members) to further explain or describe their suggestions.

Step 4: A role-play is used to demonstrate for the client the behavioral changes being suggested. In this demonstration, the worker (or group member) will usually take the role of the client.

Step 5: After this demonstration, the worker (or members) identifies the positive aspects of the performance and possibly offers additional suggestions. The role-play may be repeated to further illustrate the recommended way of behaving.

Step 6: When the client understands how she or he ought to behave and is ready to do a role-play, she or he rehearses the behavior until satisfied with her or his performance. Homework outside the session can be used to practice the new behavior.

A possible limitation of behavioral rehearsal is that the client may perform well in the presence of the social worker but may not be able to generalize this behavior to a real-world situation. Sometimes the real situation poses problems that cannot be anticipated during a practice session.

Selected Bibliography

Spiegler, Michael, and David Guevremont. *Contemporary Behavior Therapy*, 5th ed. Independence, KY: Cengage, 2010.

Sundel, Martin, and Sandra Sundel. *Behavior Change in the Human Services*, 5th ed. Thousand Oaks, CA: Sage, 2005.

13.5 BEHAVIORAL CONTRACTING

Essentially, a **behavioral contract** is an agreement, usually written, that is designed to encourage a specific behavior change. It usually involves an exchange of rewards or positive reinforcements between two or more persons. There are two forms of behavioral contracting. In a **contingency contract**, one person (often a professional) arranges for a positive consequence to follow the performance of a desired target behavior by another person (such as a client). For example, a group home manager may agree to take a resident to a movie if the resident cleans his room five days in a row. By contrast, a **reciprocal**

behavior contract is an agreement between the members of a dyad (e.g., husband–wife), in which each agrees to reward the other for the performance of a desired behavior. For example, the husband agrees to take his wife to a movie of her choice if she will take the car to the repair shop, and she agrees to cook his favorite meal if he will clean the house.

Thus, we see that a behavioral contract might be negotiated between the social worker and the client or the worker may help two or more clients (e.g., a parent and adolescent) negotiate a contract. Any behavior can become the focus of a behavioral contract so long as it is observable and can be described clearly. When helping to formulate a reciprocal behavioral contract to be used by a couple or family, the following guidelines are important:

- Assist all parties to select a change (or target behavior) that provides each person with some immediate reward, relief, or desired payoff for participating and completing the assigned tasks.
- Select tasks or behaviors that everyone agrees are worthwhile and possible, given the current circumstances.
- Allow for approximations. It should be possible to recognize and reward even a partial success and a person's genuine effort to complete the task.
- Set up a simple plan for recording performance and the exchange of rewards.
- Before the participants leave the negotiation session, ask each one to describe and explain the contract and the tasks he or she has agreed to carry out. Make sure there is no misunderstanding.

Variations of contingency behavioral contracting, often called *point systems* or *token economies*, are frequently used in special educational settings and residential treatment facilities. Under such systems, a client earns points or tokens for performing desired behaviors (e.g., completing homework, cleaning one's room) and can then use the tokens to "purchase" privileges or valued objects such as snacks, movie tickets, and similar items.

When using a contingency contract, the reinforcement (rewards) for compliance, along with any adverse consequences for noncompliance, should be clearly described and understood by all. Whenever noncompliance could have serious repercussions for a client, the contract should be in writing. In other situations, a verbal agreement may suffice.

Selected Bibliography

Cooper, John, Timothy Heron, and William Howard. *Applied Behavioral Analysis*, 2nd ed. Upper Saddle River, NJ: Pearson, 2007.

Gambrill, Eileen. *Social Work Practice*, 3rd ed. New York: Oxford University Press, 2012.

13.6 ROLE REVERSAL

When applying the technique known as **role reversal**, the social worker asks a client to temporarily adopt and act out the point of view or perspective of another person in order to better understand how that person is feeling or what that person is thinking. This technique also allows an individual to observe and hear his or her own words and attitudes, as interpreted and dramatized by another. The technique is especially useful during marriage and family counseling.

The social worker might initiate the role reversal by saying something like, "Joe and Keiko, I want you to try something. I would like you to switch roles in order to see how it feels being the other person in your relationship." The two people are then asked to switch chairs (if the clients do not change chairs, they often become confused as to which role they are playing). The worker might explain, "Joe, when you are in this chair, you are yourself. In that chair, you are Keiko."

The social worker might get the role-reversed discussion going by focusing attention on a particular line of repetitious or contentious dialogue, for example: "Joe, I want you to start playing Keiko's part in this conflict and begin with the line, "Joe, you don't realize or care about how much work I have to do." And Keiko, in the role of Joe, I want you to respond by saying how those words make you feel. As their discussion unfolds, the worker uses various interviewing techniques to encourage each to express the thoughts and feelings of the other, as they imagine it. Given the nature of this technique, the clients should be instructed to approach their effort at role reversal with a spirit of light-heartedness and humor so they can, hopefully, laugh at themselves and their situation.

After a few minutes of role reversal, the worker asks each person to return to his or her own chair. The content of what was said during the reversal is then discussed so each will better understand the other's perspectives and feelings regarding the issue causing the conflict. The role-reversal technique may be assigned as homework, asking, for example, the couple or family members to take time to experiment with role reversals prior to the next session.

"Family Sculpting"
a deleted item from the
5th edition

Selected Bibliography

Erford, Bradley, Susan Eaves, Emily Bryant, and Katherine Young. *Thirty-Five Techniques Every Counselor Should Know.* Upper Saddle River, NJ: Pearson, 2010.

Brock, Gregory, and Charles Barnard. *Procedures in Marriage and Family Therapy*, 4th ed. Upper Saddle River, NJ: Pearson, 2009.

McGinnis, Ellen. *Skill Streaming the Adolescent.* Champaign, IL: Research Press, 2012.

13.7 MANAGING SELF-TALK

The term **self-talk** refers to what we mentally tell ourselves about ourselves and about our situation. The thoughts we dwell on, our self-talk, reflects our unique interpretations of what we have experienced. Consider, for example, how you might feel about yourself if you really believed the following statements: "I will be alone and rejected by everyone unless I meet all of their expectations." "Worthwhile people always give a 110 percent effort to everything they do." "I cannot be happy until I have lost 50 pounds."

If a person habitually thinks about her or his life experiences in irrational and self-limiting ways, she or he generates inner turmoil and also creates problems in interpersonal relationships. Negative self-talk evokes emotional reactions, which can, in turn, draw us into self-defeating behaviors. Here are some common types of distortions:

All or nothing. Thinking in the extremes of being entirely right or entirely wrong, all bad or all good; there is no middle ground (e.g., we conclude that a single mistake proves we are a complete failure).

Jumping to conclusions. Drawing conclusions on the basis of little or no evidence (e.g., we form a judgment before we have gathered information).

Selective attention. Paying attention to only those facts that support what we already believe or expect.

Catastrophizing. Interpreting a situation as far worse than it actually is (e.g., experiencing a socially awkward situation as unbearable and horrendous).

Magnification of failure. Exaggerating the importance of a setback or mistake (e.g., we may have ten successes and one failure, but we focus only on the one failure).

Minimization of success. Downplaying or rejecting a positive experience or success (e.g., we attribute a desirable outcome to dumb luck).

Negative beliefs about self, others, and the world. Holding tightly to the belief that everything and everybody is bad, hopeless, and getting worse.

Personalization. Assuming that every problem is caused by our own inadequacy or mistakes.

External locus of control. Believing that whatever happens to us is caused by external factors and beyond our influence.

By helping a client learn to think more critically, the social worker can help him or her control troublesome emotions and behave more effectively. This is, of course, much more difficult than it sounds. Patterns of thinking are habits; they are not easily changed and are themselves a barrier to change. A five-step approach can help a client modify distortions and control a tendency toward negative self-talk. Ask the client to do the following:

Step 1: Identify what you are feeling and thinking right now about the matter we are discussing.

Step 2: Get in touch with your self-talk. Pay attention to extremes in your thinking as suggested by your use of words, such as *never, always, everybody, completely,* and so on.

Step 3: Examine the facts and objective reality of your situation. Once the facts have been identified, relax, take a deep breath, and repeat them out loud three times.

Step 4: Notice that when you hold to the facts and avoid using inaccurate and extreme words, you begin to feel differently and more hopeful.

Step 5: Keeping the facts of your problem situation in mind, identify what you can do about it.

This five-step method is illustrated here in the dialogue between a social worker and a college student who has just learned that he failed a math exam:

CLIENT: I cannot believe I am so stupid. I had a B average in math and I got an F on the last test. I might as well leave school and get a job as a dishwasher. I am a complete failure. I don't deserve to be in school.

WORKER: Wait a minute! You have said before that you wanted to learn how to stop putting yourself down. Let's try something. Start by telling me again what you are feeling and thinking right now.

CLIENT: Well, I just can't pass math tests. I'm stupid. I am embarrassed. I hate myself. I am never going to get through college. My parents are going to kill me. This is the worst possible thing that could have happened. My future is down the drain. Everything is just awful and ruined.

WORKER: Let's take a look at that kind of negative self-talk. Try to recognize what you are saying to yourself; notice your extreme language. Let's talk about the way things are in reality. Is it true you cannot pass math tests?

CLIENT: Well, not really. I passed all of them before this one and I still have a B average in college.

WORKER: Are your parents really going to kill you?

CLIENT: Well, of course not, but they will be disappointed.

WORKER: Is failing a test really the worst possible thing that could happen to you?

CLIENT: Well, no, but it seems awful right now.

WORKER: Does failing this test really mean you have no future?

CLIENT: Well, I still have a future. I know what you are saying and I agree that I am overreacting. But I don't know how to put a lid on those negative thoughts and feelings.

WORKER: Do this for me. Repeat the truth—the reality, the facts—of your situation, which is as follows: I flunked one math test. My parents will be unhappy. I have a B average in college. I can remain in college. My life is not over.

CLIENT: (repeats above)

WORKER: Now take a couple of deep breaths and relax. Now say that again, three times.

CLIENT: (client follows instruction)

WORKER: How do you feel when you change your self-talk?

CLIENT: Well, I guess it isn't as bad as I thought. I feel less upset than before.

WORKER: Our emotions react to what we tell ourselves. If your self-talk is distorted, your emotions are going to be more extreme and more negative than they need to be. You can use this technique yourself when your mind starts to race and your feelings start to get out of control. Certainly, your situation is not as bad as it seemed when you were telling yourself those awful things. But you still have to make plans on how to prepare for your next math test. Now let's talk about that.

**"The Empty Chair"
a deleted item from the
7th edition**

When a client is able to describe his or her pattern of maladaptive self-talk, the cognitive restructuring techniques of self-instruction, visualization, and journaling may prove helpful. **Self-instruction** (also called *positive self-talk, covert speech,* and *countering*) refers to a set of statements that are repeated by the client on a regular basis, perhaps three times a day, and especially in times of distress. Often, the statements are said aloud in front of a mirror. These messages are to be factual and incompatible with the client's habitual negative self-talk. They are meant to counteract the dysfunctional pattern and foster self-acceptance and self-confidence. The use of this technique rests on the observation that when an individual actively argues against her or his own irrational thoughts, those thoughts are weakened.

This technique should not be confused with positive thinking, which is blindly optimistic and may gloss over important realities and allow self-deception. Rather, self-instruction requires that the messages be truthful and realistic, given the client's abilities and situation. The messages should be as specific as possible and tied directly to the client's concerns. Self-instruction works but it works slowly. Consistent practice for a year or more may be needed to make a significant and lasting change. Consider, for example, the woman who avoids taking a better job because her dysfunctional self-talk tells her: "If I make a mistake on the job, people will think I am stupid and will criticize me." This woman might be taught to repeat the following message: "Each time I make a mistake on the job, I have an opportunity to learn something very important. If someone criticizes me, he or she is either right or wrong. If the person is right, I have learned something. If he or she is wrong, I can ignore it."

In using the technique of **visualization**, the client is taught to prepare for a future worry-causing event by repeatedly imagining this event and mentally rehearsing the steps necessary to handle it successfully. It is important that the images are ones of vivid and detailed activity. For many individuals, visualization reduces their fear of the event and builds confidence in their ability to do what they know they must do. For example, a client might prepare for a frightening job interview by visualizing being asked difficult questions and giving clear and appropriate answers. This might need to be practiced dozens of times before the interview.

The technique of **journaling** asks the client to keep a daily log of significant thoughts and feelings. It is especially useful for clients who like to write. It helps them recognize recurring themes and patterns in the meaning they assign to their experiences. As a way of structuring this homework, the client might be instructed to respond in writing to specific questions, such as: What have I learned about myself today? What feelings and moods did I experience? What thoughts gave rise to these feelings? What were the two most significant events of the day? What thoughts and feelings did I have in relation to these events? What personal strengths did I observe in myself today? What troublesome thoughts do I need to work on and what is my plan for doing so? How will my plan build on my personal strengths?

Selected Bibliography

Berlin, Sharon. *Clinical Social Work Practice: A Cognitive-Integrative Perspective*. New York: Oxford University Press, 2001.

Corcoran, Jacqueline. *Cognitive Behavioral Methods: A Workbook for Social Workers*. Boston: Allyn and Bacon, 2006.

Erford, Bradley, Susan Eaves, Emily Bryant, and Katherine Young. *Thirty-Five Techniques Every Counselor Should Know*. Upper Saddle River, NJ: Pearson, 2010.

13.8 BUILDING SELF-ESTEEM

What we think of ourselves has a far-reaching effect on how we feel and behave. Food, water, and shelter are critical to our physical survival, but our psychological and spiritual survival depends largely on whether we feel worthwhile.—in other words, our **self-esteem**. Individuals who do not value or respect themselves will struggle with a multitude of self-imposed limitations and are especially vulnerable to exploitation and abuse by others. Individuals with low self-esteem lack self-confidence and often engage in self-defeating and self-destructive behaviors. Because they are often preoccupied with how they are feeling, they may appear self-centered and aloof. Low self-esteem can manifest itself in shyness, social isolation, and excessive fantasy and wishful thinking. Some individuals with low self-esteem may bully, dominate, and control others in an attempt to bolster their own sense of importance. By following these guidelines, the social worker can help the client build self-esteem:

- Help clients understand that their feelings of self-worth are rooted in how they judge themselves and how they compare themselves to others. These self-evaluations are highly subjective, not always accurate, and not necessarily consistent with the judgments and evaluations of people who know us. Consequently, person "A," who is violent, narcissistic, and dishonest, may have high self-esteem, whereas person "B," who others view as a genuinely good and admirable human being, may have low self-esteem.

- Self-esteem cannot be taught but it can be learned from one's experiences. Certain types of experiences can provide learning opportunities that can cause the client to reevaluate her or his beliefs about self. Seek to place or draw the client into social situations or environments that create some cognitive dissonance and induce the client to examine and reconcile a positive outcome or experience with her or his negative opinions and expectations of self. For example, if an individual participates in a support group, personal growth group, or faith community, that person will usually have the experience of being accepted and respected by others. When that occurs, the individual may begin to reexamine his or her beliefs about self and hopefully conclude that he or she is indeed appreciated and worthwhile. In a similar vein, taking a new job, changing occupations, returning to school, becoming a volunteer, or forming new friendships can set in motion such self-examinations. Needless to say, persons with low self-esteem are often fearful of new experiences. They will need encouragement and help to understand that to get something you have never had, you must do things that you have never done.

- People with low self-esteem often have a habit of comparing themselves with the best in the field (e.g., with the best musician, the best student, the most attractive person). Given that mode of thinking, they will always suffer by comparison, and this reinforces their beliefs that they are not as good or as worthwhile as other people. Help clients recognize this self-defeating pattern of thinking. Help them see that another person may indeed be outstanding in a particular area but will not be outstanding in all areas because all people have both strengths and limitations. Self-awareness and self-acceptance are the building blocks of self-esteem.

- As a way of helping clients examine their beliefs and assumptions about themselves, encourage them to imagine specific conditions or circumstances that—if they existed—would elevate their feelings of self-worth. Then engage them in an examination of the values implicit in those conditions and whether these particular values are suitable criteria for measuring the worth of a person. For example, many people believe they would be happy and feel good about themselves if only they were attractive, popular, rich, or famous. A critical look at those assumptions reveals that these are the shallow values of a society obsessed with physical appearance, possessions, and self-aggrandizement. There are numerous examples of individuals who have all these things and still lack happiness, contentment, self-worth, and a sense of purpose in life. Other values such as generosity, compassion, honesty, and kindness are more authentic measures of personal worth. Help clients understand that their own value is not dependent on what others may think is important.

- Self-esteem grows from experiences of success and achievement. Thus, encourage clients to establish realistic and achievable objectives for themselves. Assist them in working toward those objectives and call to their attention their successes.

- Encourage and assist clients to develop a sense of purpose and meaning and a healthy spirituality. Self-worth grows from knowing that you are living your life in accord with your ideals and moral and ethical standards. For this reason, when clients are facing difficult decisions, they should be encouraged to do what they know is right so they can maintain a sense of personal integrity (see Item 15.18).

- For some clients, low self-esteem is tied to one or more significant separation and loss experiences (e.g., separation from bio-family, loss of one's childhood through sexual abuse, loss of respect from valued others). Help these clients recognize and grieve for what they have lost (see Item 15.17).

Selected Bibliography

De Wais, Stefan, and Katerina Meszaros. *Handbook of Psychology of Self-Esteem*. Hauppauge, NY: Nova Science Publications, 2011.

Kernis, Michael. *Self-Esteem: A Sourcebook on Current Perspectives*. New York: Psychology Press, 2006.

McKay, Matthew. *Self-Esteem Companion*. Oakland, CA: New Harbinger, 2005.

Mruk, Christopher. *Self-Esteem and Positive Psychology: Research, Theory, and Practice*, 4th ed. New York: Springer, 2013.

13.9 CONFRONTATION AND CHALLENGE

A *challenge* or a *confrontation* refers to a gentle and respectful effort to help the client recognize that he or she is utilizing a deception, rationalization, or evasion that is a barrier to more effective functioning. This technique invites the client to take a careful look at a self-defeating attitude or behavior, such as the client's refusal to acknowledge and address an obvious problem. Or it may point out a discrepancy between the client's stated moral principles and how the client is actually behaving. Here is an example:

CLIENT: I should be more involved with, my son Jason. His mother, my ex-wife, says that Jason feels like I don't care about him. I feel bad about that but I just don't have the time. I have a new wife and my job is very demanding.

SOCIAL WORKER: What do you mean by the word *involved?*

CLIENT: Oh, you know, I should spend time with Jason—take him to a ballgame, that sort of stuff.

SOCIAL WORKER: I recall you saying this same thing several times over the past few weeks. You say that you should be more involved with Jason, but you are not doing what you think you should be doing. I am aware that you are striving to make your new marriage work and that you are a very responsible employee. But judging from your behavior, it appears as if you have decided to set aside your role of father and devote your time to other things. What is your honest reaction to what I am saying to you?

There is always some risk in using a confrontation. Clients who are highly defensive will usually reject the message by further rationalizing or verbally attacking the worker. If used with a client who is depressed or has low self-esteem, the client may feel criticized and withdraw from the relationship. Several guidelines need to be considered in the use of this technique:

- For a challenge to be effective, it must come from someone the client trusts and respects. Moreover, it must be offered at a point when the client appears some-what open to hear and consider the message. When a challenge or confrontation is offered, it is the responsibility of the worker to help the client understand it accurately and consider the validity of the message.

- Do not confront or challenge a client when you are feeling angry or exasperated with her or him. Unless you have a genuine concern and empathy for the client, a confrontation will be little more than an expression of your own frustration with a difficult client.

- Your message must be presented in a nonjudgmental manner. Use an I-statement format throughout the challenge (see Item 8.2). Couple the confrontational message with positive observations about the client. In other words, present the message within a context of recognizing and supporting the client's strengths.

- Present the facts or observations on which your message is based and make sure the client understands the distinction between facts and the inferences you have drawn from those facts. A fact or observation can be stated directly: "I observed you hitting..." or "Last Friday you specifically told me that..." or "I have received four reports that describe your fights in school." An inference should be stated tentatively: "Because of what I have been told, I am inclined to conclude that..." or "Unless you can offer another explanation, I have to assume that...."

Selected Bibliography

Cormier, Sherry, Paula Nurius, and Cynthia Osborn. *Interviewing and Change Strategies for Helpers*, 7th ed. Independence KY: Cengage, 2011.

Egan, Gerard. *The Skilled Helper*, 8th ed. Belmont, CA: Brooks-Cole, 2007.

Hepworth, Dean, Ronald Rooney, Glenda Dewberry Rooney, and Kim Strom-Gottfried. *Direct Social Work Practice*, 9th ed. Independence KY: Cengage, 2013.

McClan, Tricia, and Marianne Woodside. *Initial Interviewing*. Independence. KY: Cengage, 2010.

13.10 REFRAMING

The technique known as **reframing** (also called *relabeling*) is used to help a client modify the meaning he or she has assigned to a particular event, behavior, or life experience. As a general rule, how a person interprets a particular event or situation has a greater impact on the person's thoughts, feelings, and behavior than does the event itself. The following example illustrates a social worker's use of reframing:

FOSTER PARENT: I get so upset with Anna [foster child]. So often, she blows up and gets angry with me. But I haven't done anything to make her angry!

SOCIAL WORKER: I can understand how frustrating and disappointing that must feel. As you know, Anna is an angry child because of the severe abuse she experienced long before she met you. But, in one way of looking at it, Anna is paying you a big compliment. When she expresses her anger in your presence she is demonstrating that she feels safe with you and trusts that you will not retaliate and hurt her as others have done in the past. If she did not feel safe with you, she would be too afraid to express her anger.

Another example of reframing is illustrated in the following statement to a 35-year-old client who has experienced a lifetime of physical and emotional pain related to a car accident and also having been physically and sexually abused as a child.

SOCIAL WORKER: I have been thinking about your life experiences. Despite all you have been through, here you are at age 35 still alive and still struggling to do the best you can. In the school of life, you have received a very expensive and a good education—much better than what a Harvard or a Yale could provide. What I am saying is that because of your painful experiences you have learned things about people and about life that most people never learn, no matter how long they go to school. Your tuition has been paid in the form of personal pain and suffering, but in return, you have acquired great wisdom.

An alternative to the social worker providing the new or a reframed perspective is to encourage the client to brainstorm several new and different interpretations. A client will usually agree that five people will most likely tell five somewhat different stories about the same experience. Using that agreement as a foundation, the worker can encourage the client to come up with additional stories (interpretations) about the life experience being discussed. After thinking up several alternative perceptions, the client will usually soften her or his original position and acknowledge that there may indeed be a different and more positive way to interpret the situation.

Still another use of reframing is to help a client redefine and view his or her troublesome behavior as a basically positive motive taken to an extreme. In other words, a problem is viewed as a client strength spinning out of control. For example, consider the young mother who has injured her 3-year-old child as a result of harsh spanking. The discussion of her abusive behavior might be approached by first recognizing that the mother wants to teach the child proper behavior but in this situation her motive to be a good mother jumped off the track or went spinning out of control. When the worker redefines the client's problem as a good intention gone wild, the client feels less defensive, less accused, and more hopeful. From the client's perspective, it seems easier to try to tone down or get control of a personal strength than to get rid of a problem behavior. The words that a helper uses do make a difference.

Selected Bibliography

Erford, Bradley, Susan Eaves, Emily Bryant, and Katherine Young. *Thirty-Five Techniques Every Counselor Should Know.* Upper Saddle River, NJ: Pearson, 2010.

De Jong, Peter, and Insoo Kim Berg. *Interviewing for Solutions*, 4th ed. Independence, KY: Cengage, 2013.

Ronen, Tammie, and Arthur Freeman, eds. *Cognitive Behavior Therapy in Clinical Social Work Practice.* New York: Springer, 2006.

13.11 HELPING CLIENTS MAKE DIFFICULT DECISIONS

Decision making is the process of choosing among possible options or alternatives. This can be especially difficult for clients who are feeling overwhelmed or pulled in many directions by multiple problems and conflicting advice from family and friends. All too often, people either avoid making decisions or make them impulsively without considering all the options or the possible ramifications of each choice. To facilitate decision making by clients, the social worker can utilize several principles and techniques.

- The critically important first step in the decision-making process is to be as clear and as specific as possible about what one wants to achieve or accomplish with the decision he or she is about to make. In other words, as you make this decision what goal are you trying to reach? Identifying that goal can be difficult for some people but it is essential. With that goal in mind, each of the possible options is evaluated in terms of whether and to what degree it will help the person reach this goal.

- Help your clients describe their usual approach to decision making. Encourage them to think about significant decisions they have made previously and to describe how they went about making the decision. Do they make decisions mostly on the basis of feelings or mostly on the basis of logic and reasoning? Do they tend to act impulsively? Do they procrastinate? Do they consult with others? Do they follow or resist advice offered by others? Do they often regret the decisions they have made? Do they avoid making a decision until forced to do so by circumstances or a deadline? Also, encourage clients to think about personality factors that may influence their decisions. Examples might be an intense fear of making a mistake, a lack of self-confidence, or a strong desire to please others. When clients have gained some awareness of the factors that may influence their decisions, encourage them to consider how they can capitalize on the strengths and avoid being pushed and pulled by negative factors.

"Priorities Weighting Grid"
a deleted item from the
4th edition

- Feelings and emotions can exert a strong influence on a person's decisions. One's feelings as to what is the right decision may or may not point to a wise and satisfying decision. Many individuals mistake their feelings for reasoning and logic and some are unduly swayed by what others want or expect. Help the client identify the feelings and emotions elicited by each of the options he or she is considering. Also, help the client identify the possible source of these feelings. For example, does the feeling have its origin in the beliefs and values of the client's family of origin? Are the feelings possibly related to one's religious background, culture, or ethnic group? Are the feelings connected to the bad outcome of a prior decision? As the client becomes more aware of why he or she may feel a certain way about a particular option, the client is better able to decide what importance or weight should be given to the feeling or to what he or she may label as intuition.

- When faced with a difficult decision, many individuals fail to differentiate their goal from the various ways of reaching that goal. In other words, they do not **distinguish the means from the end**. Consider, for example, the client who is trying to figure out how the obtain sufficient money to buy a car because he needs to get to and from a new job. In this case, the client's problem is a lack of transportation, not the lack of a car. Having a car is only one means of transportation. Others might be public transportation, walking, bicycling, or paying another employee for a ride to work.

- Creating a simple listing of the various means of reaching a desired end may help the client keep these ideas separate. For example, consider a young, single mother who had approached a family services agency and requested a foster-care placement for her child because she cannot care for the child while holding a job. With some guidance, she was able to list five other possible solutions: licensed day care, paid babysitter, informal exchange of babysitting with friend, change jobs, and change hours of work. Once the client's presenting problem was redefined as the need for child care, rather than a need for placement, several new options emerged.

- Another tool, the **decision-making matrix**, can help a client think through the pros and cons of various options and arrive at a decision. The matrix has three columns: (1) Alternative, (2) Cost, and (3) Benefit. In the Alternative column, the client lists the options being considered. Then, to the right of each alternative, in the other columns, the client describes both the drawbacks (costs) and the advantages (benefits) associated with each option. After studying all the pros and cons, the client is better able to select the best option. Figure 13.1 is an example of a matrix completed by a social worker and a battered wife during an interview focusing on the question of whether she should return to her husband or leave him and end her marriage.

Alternative	Cost	Benefit
1. Return to John	a. Abuse would probably continue b. Children are fearful c. Would have to face same hard decisions in future d. I could get seriously hurt or killed e. Medical expenses	a. Preserve family b. Hard decision is delayed until later c. Would have place to live and money d. John says he cares for me
2. Leave John and end the marriage	a. Fear of the unknown (I need to be with somebody) b. Trauma of divorce for me and kids c. Would have less money to live on d. Legal costs e. Custody battle over children	a. Abuse would end b. Decision would have been made and I could try to put my life together c. Children would be less nervous and upset d. I could find out if I can function on my own e. Opportunity for fresh start

Figure 13.1
Decision Making Matrix

- A social worker familiar with the key issues and common client thoughts and feelings surrounding a particular type of decision can facilitate a client's decision making by constructing a **decision-making worksheet**. It serves to focus the client's attention on the important questions, factors, and possible consequences that need be considered. Figure 13.2 contains excerpts from a decision-making worksheet designed for use with pregnant teenagers who are considering whether to relinquish their babies for adoption. As can be seen from this sample, a worksheet is simply a format for raising questions and helping clients analyze their situation. Obviously, skilled interviewing could accomplish the same thing, but the worksheet can provide added structure and can also be used as homework between sessions.

Selected Bibliography

Hammond, John, and Howard Raiffa. *Smart Choices: Practical Guide to Making Better Decisions.* New York: Random House, 2002.
Iyengar, Sheena. *The Art of Choosing.* New York: Hachette Book Group, 2010.
Kaheman. Daniel. *Thinking Fast and Slow.* New York: Farrar, Straus, and Giroux, 2011.
O'Connor, Annette, and Dawn Stacey. *Ottawa Personal Decision Guide.* University of Ottawa Hospital and Research Institute, Ottawa, Canada, 2011.

13.12 HELPING CLIENTS WITH HARMFUL HABITS

Basically, a *habit* is a learned and deeply ingrained behavior. Habits are a natural part of living. In fact, we could not function at all if not for our capacity to develop habits that allow us to perform many important tasks (e.g., keyboarding, playing a musical instrument, driving a car, reading) with little conscious thought and effort. Both good and bad habits develop slowly over many months and years. Many are learned during childhood.

Planning for My Baby

I. Questions about my relationship with my baby's father.
   A. Can I count on him for financial support?
   B. Can I count on him for emotional support?
   C. Has my relationship with him changed since I got pregnant?
   (and so on)

II. Questions about my relationship with my parents.
   A. What do my parents want me to do?
   B. Can I go against their wishes?
   C. If my mother helps take care of my baby, is it possible the baby will become "her baby"?
   (and so on)

III. Questions about my life after having the baby.
   A. If I keep the baby, how will this affect future dating, marriage, and children?
   B. If I give my baby up for adoption, how will this affect my future dating, marriage, and children?
   (and so on)

IV. A daydream exercise.
   A. If I could pick the ideal time for having a baby, when would it be? Where would I be? What would the baby's father be like?
   B. How does the above ideal situation compare with my real situation?
   (and so on)

V. Picturing myself.
   A. Draw a picture of yourself one year ago. Around your picture, indicate in words or pictures the things that were important to you then. What were your activities, how did you use your time? What were your goals and aspirations one year ago?
   B. Think about yourself now. Change the above picture of yourself one year ago to fit things today. Cross out those activities in which you are no longer involved. Have your goals and aspirations changed?
   C. Draw a picture of yourself one year from now. Again, around your picture, write in those things that you will be involved in one year from now. How will you spend your time? In one year, what will be your goals and aspirations?
   (and so on)

Source: Lutheran Social Services, mimeographed item (no date), pp. 1–2, 4–5. Used with permission.
Figure 13.2
Decision Making Worksheet

The process by which habits are formed is fairly well explained by learning theory. A behavior that elicits some sort of reward or reinforcement is likely to be repeated. After many repetitions, the behavior is so ingrained that we are easily drawn to perform the behavior, often without even noticing what we are doing.

The ancient philosophers were very aware of how good habits could help a person find happiness and success, whereas bad habits were a source of frustration, misery, and failure. Throughout much of history, good habits were termed *virtues* and bad habits were called *vices*. Many of the spiritual practices and techniques taught by the major religions help people cultivate and develop good habits such as compassion, patience, self-awareness, and honesty. For example, if we respond to others with compassion and do that over and over again, we gradually become compassionate. In a sense, we become what we choose to do.

Bad habits have been described as the barnacles we accumulate throughout life that keep us from doing what we would like to do and from being the kind of person we want to be. Bad habits can adversely affect one's health, relationships, career, and financial situation. Examples of bad habits are gambling, overeating, spending too many hours on the Internet or watching TV, yelling at one's children, procrastinating, excessive shopping, knuckle cracking, nail biting, spitting, annoying table manners, and so on. For some individuals, shoplifting, viewing pornography, and promiscuity are habits.

In some respects a bad habit is like a nonchemical addiction. However, habits do not involve the physiological phenomena of tolerance, withdrawal, and craving associated with an addiction to a chemical substance (see Item 15.11). Determination and willpower can exert some control over a habit whereas a complete loss of control is a defining feature of an addiction or a psychological compulsion. However, a habit can be the beginning stage of an addiction. For example, smoking is initially a habit but then gradually develops into an addiction as the body becomes accustomed to and starts to crave the nicotine. An addiction to pornography may start out as mostly curiosity or seeking stimulation, but over time develop into a compulsion.

Breaking a bad habit is no easy matter. Most of us know that from personal experience. Many of us start each New Year with a resolution to break one or more of our habits, but we seldom succeed. Here are some suggestions and information that a social worker might share with a client who is wanting to break a harmful habit.

- Accept the reality that you cannot break a bad habit unless you truly believe that its elimination will require the application of special techniques. Breaking a habit requires motivation, persistence, a plan, and hard work.

- Analyze the habit. Write down your answers to the following questions: How long have I had this habit? What rewards or reinforcements (e.g., pleasure, relief from tension, stimulation, attention) do I get from this behavior? In what situation is it most likely to occur? What moods and feelings precede, accompany, and follow this behavior? If I get rid of this bad habit, what else will I be losing or giving up? If I break this habit, what will I gain? Given what I have to gain and what I have to lose, do I want to get rid of this bad habit?

- Identify the reinforcers or rewards that maintain its existence (see Item 13.3). A study of the habit should also reveal the existence of *triggers* that precede or set up its occurrence. Triggers may take the form of certain environments, thoughts, moods, or rituals that increase the likelihood that the habitual behavior will follow. For example, many who have a habit of excessive eating do so when feeling bored, worried, or lonely. Or perhaps, they start to think of food whenever they sit down to watch TV. Being alert to and avoiding such triggers can help control a habit.

- Prepare a written plan for eliminating the bad habit. Keep the plan simple and make sure it fits with your other normal routines and responsibilities. For example, a simple plan to exercise at least 30 minutes, three times a week is more likely to be followed and successful than a more complex one that requires exercising on Monday, Wednesday, and Friday from 4 to 5 P.M. using walking on Monday, biking on Wednesday, and weights on Friday. Obviously, the second example is too specific and rigid and easily disrupted by the ebb and flow of daily life.

- For at least one week prior to starting work on the habit make a detailed written record of how often you engage in this habit. This frequency count will serve as a baseline from which you can measure progress (see Item 14.1). In some instances, the act of carefully monitoring a habit will, by itself, decrease its frequency. Maintain a record of your progress and find ways to reward yourself for success.

- Make a list of both the disadvantages and the advantages of having this bad habit. The point of this exercise is to heighten your awareness that each time you feel the urge to engage in the habit, you are about to choose between a set of disadvantages and a set of advantages.

- Create an environment that will strengthen your commitment to change. For example, announce to your friends that you are embarking on a plan to eliminate a habit and ask them to call this habit to your attention whenever they observe it. Perhaps, give a friend a hundred dollars and explain that he or she is to return the money if you succeed in breaking the habit but he or she may keep it if you fail. Consider wearing a rubber band on your wrist and snapping it whenever you are about to engage in the habit. If for example, your bad habit is spending too much time on the Internet, set a kitchen timer to remind you that your allotted time is up. If you snack too much, make an entry into your log as soon as you feel the desire to eat and keep a list of everything that you do eat.

- One of the most effective methods of breaking a bad habit is to develop a replacement habit that is incompatible with the habit you want to eliminate. For example, if you snack while watching TV, it may be because you usually eat meals in front of the TV and have been conditioned to associate food with TV. As a correction, cultivate the habit of eating only at a table and without TV.

- As people struggle with a habit, it is not uncommon for them to construct rationalizations as to why their bad habit is not so bad after all, why it cannot be changed, and why it is futile to even try. In order to make progress you will need to honestly confront and carefully examine this type of self-defeating self-talk (see Item 13.7).

- The first month or so of trying to either extinguish a habit is especially difficult because you must rely heavily on choice and willpower to bring about this change. After a couple of months of success, the new pattern will begin to feel more natural. After a year, it will be fairly firmly established. However, as you make progress, guard against complacency because it is easy to slip back into old patterns.

Selected Bibliography

Baumeister, Roy, and John Tierney. *Will Power*. New York: Penguin, 2011.

Clarborn, James. *The Habit Change Workbook*. Oakland, CA: New Harbinger, 2001.

Huebner, Dawn. *What to Do When Bad Habits Take Hold*. Washington, DC: Magination Press, 2009.

Ladouceur, Robert, and Stella Lachance. *Overcoming Pathological Gambling*, New York: Oxford University Press, 2006.

13.13 HELPING CLIENTS WITH FINANCIAL PROBLEMS

A job loss, a large medical expense, a divorce, and a variety of other factors can rather quickly plunge an otherwise fiscally responsible individual into a serious financial bind. Some individuals gradually slip into a serious problem because their income is inadequate or because they lack the self-discipline necessary to monitor their expenditures and control overspending. The power of advertising, peer-group influences, and feelings of low self-esteem can draw people into buying on credit and purchasing things they do not need. Regardless of cause, individuals in financial difficulty face the daunting task of working their way out of a hole. (See Item 15.1 for information on the client living in poverty.) The following information and suggestions may apply when working with clients struggling with a financial problem.

- Every individual and family needs a budget, but more importantly, they need the discipline and motivation to adhere to that budget. A *budget* anticipates and plans to cover the costs for food, housing, utilities, insurance, transportation, debt related to credit cards and loans, health care, clothing, recreation, charitable contributions, communications, taxes, and so on. A budget should also include provisions for regular savings and handling emergencies. It can be as simple as a few columns and entries in 3-ring notebook or as complex as a software package on a home computer. Whatever its form, the budget needs to be monitored on a daily or weekly basis, for this will reveal problems that need to be addressed and items that can be trimmed.

  A special challenge arises when the client cannot do arithmetic. The method known as **envelope budgeting** can be taught to clients who need a very simple method for keeping track of their money. If the client can count, he or she can usually use this approach. The first step in setting up an envelope budgeting system is for the client to identify the key categories of expenditure (e.g., food, rent). The next step is to determine how many dollars need to be spent on each category during a spending cycle, such as a two-week period. An envelope is labeled for each category. In the "food envelope," for example, the client places the cash allotted for food. All of the envelopes are kept together in a shoebox or folder. As cash is removed from an envelope and spent, the client has an observable measure of cash flow and can view the balance that remains. The client is encouraged to resist the temptation to shift money from one category to another, but this may sometimes be necessary. As the client secures income, cash is again distributed across the envelopes for the new spending cycle.

- Help the client analyze his or her debt situation. To do so, make four columns on a piece of paper. In column 1, list all of the items that are billed on a regular basis (e.g., loan payment, credit card, utilities, rent, insurance). In column 2, list the expected payment due for each item in column 1. In column 3, list the amount that the client can actually afford to pay each month toward each item. In column 4, total the amount owed for all items. Next, have the client mark all the Column 1 items for which interest is charged; these should then become high-priority targets for payment. If the client must skip a payment or reduce the amount paid toward a bill, it should be on an item that does not involve interest or late payment charges. Also, prioritize the interest-related items according to the amount still owed. The client should concentrate on paying off those on which the least amount is owed, for this will eliminate all credit charges associated with that bill and free up money for other bills. Completely paying off a bill also helps the client see progress. Moreover, this record of progress in paying off debt can be used to argue for a payment extension from a business or lender because it demonstrates the client's ability and resolve to pay what is owed.

- Paying some bills while deferring payment on others is sometimes necessary, but this will damage a credit rating and possibly have legal ramifications. If a client cannot pay a bill or must miss a payment, he or she should immediately contact the creditor or business and explain the problem. If the client demonstrates a genuine desire to pay, the creditor or business may be willing to temporarily adjust the bill or negotiate a less burdensome payment plan.

If a business concludes that an individual is ignoring a bill, it may eventually turn the matter over to a collection agency or seek legal action such as the garnishment of wages. A collection agency does not want to repossess property or do anything that will decrease the individual's ability to pay in the future. What it wants is payment. If the individual avoids the bill collectors and shows no effort to make payments, the collection agency will do whatever is legal to obtain the money owed or repossess the items not yet paid for. Those being pursued by a collection agency need to be aware that some collections personnel make statements and threats that are untrue and illegal. If a collections agent is saying things that seem unfair, unreasonable, or abusive, an attorney or the police should be consulted.

- When a client's bills exceed her or his income, the client must find a way to trim spending, increase income, or both. Obtaining a loan or buying on credit is a short-term emergency fix but this makes the problem even worse in the long run. Credit cards are convenient but for many individuals they are the cause of serious money problems. No one should enter into a credit card contract without reading the fine print and understanding the amount of interest, service fees, and late charges. Paying a high rate of interest can set in motion a spiral of ever-growing debt. If the overuse of credit cards is a problem, the client will need to destroy the cards and close the account. If paying by cash is not practical and the use of credit cards is necessary, the client should strive to pay each credit card bill before incurring an interest payment or other fees.

  When excessive spending is driven by emotional needs and a lack of self-discipline, it is important to help the client address this issue and modify these harmful habits (see Item 13.12). Many who spend more than they should need help to distinguish between what they want and what they need. Someone wise observed that we have two choices in life, we can strive to have what we want, or we can strive to want what we have. A self-help group like Debtors Anonymous may prove helpful to persons who are prone to impulsive and indiscriminate spending.

  In some situations, the client may need to sell nonessential possessions and use the proceeds to pay off debt. For example, the client might consider selling a car, unless it is essential for work-related transportation. A car loan creates a cycle of debt because by the time it is paid off, the car must often be replaced.

- Consider referring the client for **credit counseling**. A consumer credit-counseling program can help a client prepare a budget, develop self-discipline, and possibly avoid bankruptcy. However, do not confuse the credit-counseling services that are available for little or no cost from nonprofit agencies with the various for-profit businesses that offer financial counseling, including debt adjustment, but provide this service for a higher fee and interest. Before referring a client to a credit-counseling type program, find out who sponsors the program, what fees are involved, and the program's reputation for honesty and effectiveness. Unfortunately, there are unscrupulous and unethical businesses that prey on desperate people by promising a quick and easy method of getting out of debt.

- When less drastic methods fail to reduce the client's debt, *loan consolidation* might be considered. In this approach, one takes out a new loan (a new legal contract) that is sufficient to pay off all other loans and overdue accounts. The single payment on this new loan is designed to be smaller than the combined total for the current loan payments. However, a consolidation loan stretches one's payments over a longer period of time. The client must still pay all that is owed before becoming debt free and that requires paying interest throughout the life of the new loan. Another disadvantage of consolidation is that the new payment may seem small in comparison to previous bills and it is easy to forget how much is actually owed, making it tempting to make unneeded purchases.

When a client is overwhelmed with debt and has no practical way of paying it off, the client may need to consult an attorney and consider seeking the legal protections offered by a court declaration of bankruptcy. For individuals and married couples, the Federal Bankruptcy Act provides two types of **bankruptcy**: Chapter 7 (called a *straight bankruptcy* or *liquidation proceeding*) and Chapter 13 (called a *wage-earner plan*). A means test is used to assess the petitioner's ability to pay off his or her debts and determines which type of bankruptcy can be used. As a general rule, if the individual earns more than the median income for his or her state, that individual must file for a Chapter 13 proceeding. People seeking bankruptcy protection must avail themselves of credit-counseling services.

A Chapter 13 bankruptcy requires payment of some or all debt. This proceeding allows the individual to keep personal possessions while she or he pays the debt under an installment plan monitored by a court-appointed trustee. The plan provides for the repaying of debts over a designated period, usually three to five years. If the judge approves this plan, creditors must stop all collection efforts and cease charging interest and late fees on most types of debt. Each payday, a fixed amount of the client's wages or other income is turned over to the court trustee who then pays the creditors.

In the case of a Chapter 7 bankruptcy proceeding, the bankruptcy judge notifies the creditors of their right to file claims for their losses and to question the individual filing for bankruptcy on the witness stand. The creditors are given the opportunity to object to the individual not having to pay what is owed. If there are no compelling objections, the bankruptcy judge grants a discharge in bankruptcy that relieves the individual from legal liability for all debts at the time of this bankruptcy. All the person's possessions, except those exempted by law, are then turned over to a trustee to be sold and the proceeds are distributed to the creditors who filed claims. The remaining debt is then legally erased. Certain debts such as child support, alimony, taxes, fines, and/or debts obtained under false pretenses cannot be discharged.

Bankruptcy has a number of significant negative consequences. Because it is a matter of public record, it can never be hidden from those who take the time to find this information. Also, a bankruptcy remains on one's credit rating report for many years and affects one's ability to secure loans and other credit. If a client reaches a point of needing to consider bankruptcy, he or she should consult with an attorney and carefully weigh the pros and cons of this legal procedure.

Selected Bibliography

Lawrence, Judy. *The Budget Kit*, 6th ed. New York: Kaplan, 2011.

Leonard, Robin, and Margaret Reiter. *Credit Repair*, 10th ed. Berkeley, CA: Nolo, 2011.

Schollander, Wendell, and Wes Schollander. *The Personal Bankruptcy Answer Book*. Naperville, IL: Sphinx, 2009.

Stouffer, Tere. *The Only Budgeting Book You'll Ever Need*. Avon, MA: Adams Media, 2012.

13.14 HELPING CLIENTS IN CRISIS

Although the word *crisis* is widely used, it has a specific meaning within the field of mental health. Essentially, a **crisis** is a sudden but temporary breakdown in a person's capacity to cope and function that is brought on by some overwhelming and threatening event. Situations that might precipitate a crisis include the death of a loved one, a diagnosis of a life-threatening illness, loss of a job, a house fire, rape, witnessing a violent death, or some other traumatic event. For the individual, this experience is so disturbing that she or he reacts with anxiety, panic, despair, confusion, and disorganization.

By definition, a crisis is *time limited*. Within a matter of about 4 to 6 weeks, the person will begin to reestablish a plateau or equilibrium of adjustment and functioning. However, that plateau may be either better or worse than the person's level of functioning prior to the onset of the crisis. Thus, a crisis is a time of both danger and opportunity. It is dangerous in that if the crisis is not resolved constructively, it can set in motion a downward spiral that results in a deterioration of functioning and chronic emotional problems. However, if the crisis is managed well it can turn out to be an opportunity to learn new coping skills, reevaluate one's perspectives on life, and actually elevate the person's overall social functioning. The outcome is dependent, in large part, on how others respond to the person during the crisis.

It is important to distinguish between a genuine personal crisis (i.e., a time-limited period of distress and readjustment) from a lifestyle in which there is one emergency after another, year after year, but no real change in how the person behaves, copes, or functions. For individuals immersed in this crisis-ridden mode, life is a roller-coaster ride. For some individuals, the ever-present emergencies are energizing and almost addicting.

The concept of crisis overlaps, to a degree, with two mental disorders: acute stress disorder and posttraumatic stress disorder (PTSD). The essential feature of an **acute distress disorder** is the appearance of certain symptoms within one month after exposure to a traumatic event. Symptoms include anxiety, "numbing" (or an absence of emotional responsiveness), reduced awareness of one's surroundings, a feeling that life is unreal, a feeling of being detached from one's body, an inability to concentrate, and an inability to remember important details about the traumatic event. If this condition goes untreated and/or if the person experiences additional traumatic events, the second condition, PTSD, may develop.

A **posttraumatic stress disorder** is characterized by the same symptoms as acute stress disorder plus flashbacks, recurring frightening dreams about the event, and reactions of distress when reminded of the event. Posttraumatic stress disorder may arise three or more months after exposure to an intensely emotional and/or life-threatening experience, such as rape, kidnapping, torture, an auto accident, combat, and witnessing the traumatic death or injury of another person. If an individual is not making progress in working his or her way through the crisis period (a matter of weeks) and if symptoms of an acute stress disorder or PTSD become evident, he or she should be referred for appropriate psychiatric treatment.

The following guidelines will be useful when dealing with a person in crisis:

- Individuals who are in crisis are preoccupied with the precipitating event and their own fears and anxiety. They often feel a sense of failure because they are unable to cope and perform even the ordinary tasks of everyday life. They are unable to stay focused and to think clearly. Before the client can consider alternatives, make good decisions, or plan ways of addressing their situation, they need to feel safe,

"Crisis Cards" a deleted item from the 6th edition

accepted, and understood. They need time to sort things out and comprehend what has happened. Thus, do not rush or push the client to take action before she or he is ready. A client in crisis should be advised to delay, if possible, making important decisions that will have a far-reaching impact on her or his future (e.g., selling a house, moving to another city). Listen attentively and guide the discussion in ways that will help the client assess her or his situation realistically. Offer support that may range from simply acknowledging the existence of the upsetting experience to offering reassurance (e.g., "You did the right thing in leaving that violent situation and coming to our shelter").

- Involve others in the helping process. People in crisis are usually most receptive to the assistance, advice, and support offered by persons they know and trust (e.g., family, friends, employer, minister, neighbors). Encourage the client to reach out to others, or, with his or her permission, contact these significant others and enlist their help on behalf of the client.

- The person in crisis often feels as if he or she is confronting a giant, insolvable problem. Thus, a social worker might use the technique of *partialization* to break this frightening situation into numerous components and into small steps and decisions so they seem more manageable to the client and can be addressed one at a time. As the client starts to take even very small steps, the client will begin to regain confidence in his or her own capabilities.

- Emotional reactions can make a situation feel worse than it is. Misunderstandings and misinterpretations can exacerbate the crisis and intensify emotional reactions. Thus, provide factual information, a realistic perspective and give honest feedback to correct misunderstandings. Help the client weigh the pros and cons of various options and anticipate the consequences of his or her decisions and actions. It may be necessary to provide very specific directions and instructions as to what the client needs to do in order to address a concern.

- A hopeful attitude is an essential element in responding to a person in crisis. Convey confidence in the client's ability regain control and deal with his or her challenges. If you communicate belief in the client's ability to cope, she or he will be less frightened and insecure. Help the individual recall times when she or he effectively dealt with other serious problems. Consider using a behavioral contract (see Item 13.5) as a means of providing the client with structure and a clear plan of action. This can help the client maintain a focus and mobilize inner resources.

- When several individuals or a whole family is in crisis because they have experienced the same traumatic or distressing event, a group meeting or a family therapy approach may prove useful. In such a meeting, all are encouraged to talk about their experiences and feelings and offer to others their perspectives, support, and mutual aid (see Item 15.23 and trauma-related interventions in Chapter 6).

Selected Bibliography

Jackson-Cherry, Lisa, and Bradley Erford. *Crisis Assessment, Intervention, and Prevention*, 2nd ed. Upper Saddle River, NJ: Pearson, 2014.

James, Richard, and Burt Gilliland. *Crisis Intervention Strategies*, 7th ed. Independence, KY: Cengage, 2013.

Kanel, Kristi. *A Guide to Crisis Intervention*, 4th ed. Independence, KY: Cengage, 2012.

Roberts, Albert, and Kenneth Yeager. *Pocket Guide to Crisis Intervention*. New York: Oxford University Press, 2009.

13.15 HOMEWORK ASSIGNMENTS

The technique known as **homework** refers to various types of activities that the client is asked by the social worker to perform between sessions. Homework is often used when the objectives of the intervention involve teaching the client new skills that need to be practiced within the client's natural environment. For example, given a client whose problems revolve on low self-esteem and an inability to interact comfortably with others, a homework assignment might be for the client to strike up at least two conversations per day while riding on the bus to and from work.

The use of this technique presumes that the client is willing to accept direction from the worker. The homework assignment must seem possible and make sense to the client, given his or her concerns or problems. They are to be given with clear, precise, and often written instructions. These instructions might include, for example, one or more of the following types of statements:

- *"Do" statements* that begin with action words such as *talk, read, write, observe, count, obtain,* and *give.*
- *Quantity statements* such as "Observe three people who are doing..." and "Spend 30 minutes talking to...."
- *Recording statements* such as "Write down the number of times that you..." and "Mark on your chart...."
- *Bring statements* such as "Bring your list of ...to our next session."
- *Contingency statements* such as "If you succeed, then reward yourself with..." and "Each time you get angry and curse others, you are to donate $2 to an organization that you dislike."

The client needs to understand that although the social worker gives the assignment with the hope that it will be completed, the homework is optional and if it is not completed, the worker will in no way judge or chastise the client. If the client cannot complete an assignment, it can be helpful to discuss why it was especially difficult and what blocked its completion.

Selected Bibliography

Jongsma, Arthur, L. Mark Peterson, and Timothy Bruce. *Complete Adult Psychotherapy Homework Planner,* 4th ed. Hoboken, NJ: Wiley, 2006.

Jongsma, Arthur, L. Mark Peterson, and William McInnis. *Adolescent Psychotherapy Homework Planner,* 5th ed. Hoboken, NJ: Wiley, 2013.

Knapp, Sara. *School Counseling and School Social Work Homework Planner,* 2nd ed. Hoboken, NJ: Wiley, 2013.

Rosenthal, Howard. *Favorite Counseling and Therapy Homework Assignments,* 2nd ed. Philadelphia: Brunner-Routledge, 2010.

Schultheis, Gary. *Couples Therapy Homework Planner,* 2nd ed. Hoboken, NJ: Wiley, 2010.

13.16 THE FEELINGS LIST

Many of the clients known to social workers grew up in dysfunctional families (e.g., alcoholic, abusive) where they learned to deny and suppress their feelings. Often, they were punished for expressing emotion or for asking the "wrong" questions or saying the "wrong" thing. Many were exposed to a child-rearing pattern that invalidated or discounted the feelings they did express, such as when a mother tells her angry child: "You're not really angry; you're just tired." As these individuals grow older, they carry with them a tendency to mistrust and misinterpret their emotions and feelings. Many cannot distinguish one from another and can speak of feelings in only broad words such as *sad, upset,* or *OK.*

Simplistic as it sounds, a written list of perhaps 25 to 50 feeling words can help a client find a word to express his or her feelings and in the process become more self-aware. For example, as the client struggles to describe what he or she is feeling, the social worker presents the feelings list and asks the client to review it in search of a descriptive word.

A feelings list can prove useful in work with individuals, families, and groups. If you believe such a list might help your clients, prepare one consisting of words that will be especially meaningful to individuals served by your agency. A client's age, life experience, culture, and educational level need to be considered when compiling this list. It should be a mix of both positive and negative feelings. Examples of words reflective of positive feelings might be *safe, relieved, freedom, valued, dependable, confident, hopeful, rescued, content, grateful, courageous, compassion, reassured, forgiven, reconciled, elation, excitement, responsible, anticipation, proud,* and others. Words reflective of negative feelings could be *betrayed, trapped, bewildered, abandoned, hateful, desperate, heart-broken, disgusted, disloyal, misunderstood, controlled, rejected, embarrassed, ashamed, guilty, manipulated, lost, vulnerable, lonely, suicidal,* and so on. (Many feelings lists can be accessed through an online search.)

It is often helpful to remind clients that feelings and emotions are natural and normal parts of living. Although some feelings are pleasant and some unpleasant, they are neither good nor bad. How one chooses to behave in response to feelings may be appropriate or inappropriate, but the feelings themselves are neither right nor wrong in a moral sense (see Item 8.6).

Selected Bibliography

Black, Claudia. *Deceived: Facing Sexual Betrayal, Lies, and Secrets.* Center City, MN: Hazelden, 2009.
Porter, Eugene. *Treating the Young Male Victim of Sexual Assault.* Syracuse, NY: Safer Society Press, 1986.
Rosenberg, Marshall. *Nonviolent Communication: A Language of Life,* 2nd ed. Albuquerque, NM: Center for Nonviolent Communication, 2009.

13.17 CLIENT ADVOCACY

When a social worker assumes the role of an advocate, he or she speaks for, argues and bargains for, and negotiates on behalf of another. In **client advocacy** (or case advocacy) the worker represents the interest of an individual. In *class advocacy,* the worker represents the interests of a whole group of people (see Item 13.32). Client advocacy may be necessary when an individual has been unable to obtain services to which she or he is entitled or has been subjected to unfair treatment by an agency or business and is unable to respond effectively to this situation without the social worker's help. When a worker is considering the need for advocacy on behalf of a particular client, she or he should remember these guidelines:

- Make sure your client wants you to become his or her advocate. Do not engage in advocacy unless you have an explicit agreement with your client and he or she understands both the potential benefits and the possible drawbacks of this action. To the extent possible, involve your client in all decisions concerning the actions that you will take on his or her behalf.

- Because client advocacy usually involves challenge and confrontation, there are some risks in using this tactic. For example, your advocacy can strain or damage your relationship with the other agencies, service programs, or professionals. Such a damaged relationship may create problems in the future when you need their cooperation and goodwill in order to serve other clients. A decision to assume the role of client advocate should arise out of a genuine desire to be of service to your client and never from a desire to rebuke or embarrass another agency or professional.

- Before you decide to use this tactic be sure that you understand the facts of the matter. Do not base your decisions on hearsay or on a one-sided description of what has occurred. Realize that clients sometimes misunderstand, misinterpret, and even misrepresent events and explanations. Secure and review copies of all letters sent and received, as well as other documents relevant to the issue. If an individual has been denied a service, seek information on the various eligibility criteria. For example, it is often possible to use the Internet to access a public agency's policy manual, eligibility criteria, etc. A review of these criteria can clarify the client's concern or complaint and help determine if case advocacy is indeed appropriate.

- Once you decide that the tactic of advocacy is required, arrange a meeting with the appropriate agency or program representative. Face-to-face meetings are almost always more effective than phone calls, emails, and letters. However, a letter outlining your client's situation and your own concern and questions may be helpful as preparation for a face-to-face meeting.

    Respect an agency's chain of command. For example, do not ask to speak with a supervisor until you have spoken to the employee who was in contact with your client. Do not ask to speak with the agency administrator until you have spoken with the supervisor.

- Before you speak with the agency representative, prepare an outline of what you intend to say and the questions you will ask. Begin your conversation with a courteous request for an explanation of why your client was denied service or treated in a certain way. Communicate your concerns in a factual and respectful manner, but in a tone that conveys your resolve. Maintain a detailed written record of the people you have talked to, the questions asked, and their responses.

- If the agency or program in question wanted to provide the service requested by your client but could not because of a technicality or an unreasonable procedural requirement, request information on how the denial of service decision can be appealed. Ask if administrators, board members, or legislators should be informed of the difficulty faced by your client or consulted on how this matter can be addressed for your client and future clients.

- If further action is required, you will need to secure information on how to file a formal complaint or initiate an official appeal. In some cases, you will need legal advice before proceeding. As preparation for an appeal you will need detailed documentation of what happened and what was attempted, step by step, to resolve the matter. You will need names, dates, and copies of all relevant documents.

Selected Bibliography

Ezell, Mark. *Advocacy in the Human Services*. Independence, KY: Cengage, 2001.

Hoefer, Richard. *Advocacy Practice for Social Justice,* 2nd ed. Chicago: Lyceum, 2012.

Katz, Marsha. *Don't Look for Logic: An Advocate's Manual for Negotiating the SSI and SSDI Programs.* Missoula: University of Montana Rural Institute on Disabilities, 2005.

Schneider, Robert, and Lori Lester. *Social Work Advocacy*. Independence, KY: Cengage, 2001.

Wilks, Tom. *Advocacy and Social Work Practice*. New York: McGraw-Hill International, 2012.

13.18 CLIENT EMPOWERMENT

Many of the clients seen by social workers in direct practice settings have been beaten down by oppression, poverty, abuse, and other adverse life experiences. They want their situation to improve but feel powerless and helpless. Some have a pervasive sense of failure and feel rejected and ignored. In order to counter or modify these negative and self-limiting perceptions, social workers and social agencies need to emphasize empowerment.

The word **empowerment** literally means to invest another with power or to authorize or permit another to exercise a certain power. As a social work strategy, empowerment is a way of working with clients that assists them in acquiring and exercising the competencies and power they need for improving their own functioning and changing the public policies and societal attitudes that are adversely impacting their lives. To apply this approach, the social worker should adhere to these guidelines:

- Social workers and agencies that want to embrace the empowerment strategy must realize what it asks of them. Fundamentally, they must be willing and able to share power and responsibility. It asks workers and agencies to recognize and implement the principle of client self-determination and to create true partnerships with their clients. The client is viewed as an expert on his or her life and situation. Thus, the worker must seek out and be willing to accept the suggestions and ideas proposed by clients. The social worker's role is primarily that of a teacher-trainer or consultant, and not an authority, expert, nor therapist. The worker looks for and seizes all opportunities to teach clients how to solve problems and access and utilize resources. The worker refrains from doing things for clients if they can be taught to do it for themselves.

- In selecting the empowerment strategy, the social worker is assuming that a client (individual or group) already has or can learn the prerequisite competencies needed to effect changes and also that her or his current difficulties are caused primarily by social barriers and a lack of needed resources. If these are not valid assumptions for a given client, the empowerment approach, by itself, will not be effective or sufficient.

- Fundamental to empowerment is the conviction that each individual is an important resource to others and a potential participant in social and political action. As people cooperate, share responsibility, teach others, and learn from others, they come to understand the social, economic, and political context of their current situation. When they work with others, they no longer feel alone and realize that others share in their struggles and ideals. By working together, people can effect needed changes in their neighborhood and community. As they work toward change they learn the skills of communication, problem solving, leadership, critical thinking, persuasion, assertiveness, and negotiation. As they grow in confidence, they are motivated to take additional steps that can improve their lives.

- The term *power* refers to an individual's or a group's capacity to influence the behavior of others, such as the decisions of a politician, government official, agency administrator, or organization's board of directors. The social worker should assist clients in making an inventory of the types of power they already possess, such as knowledge gained from life experience, motivation, time, energy, knowledge of their neighborhood or community, understanding of a particular problem, sense of humor, willingness to take risks, right to vote, solidarity with others, and the like. As the clients become aware that they do, in fact, have certain types of power, the worker helps them exercise that power by allowing and encouraging them to make decisions, individually and as part of a group. It is also important to allow clients to experience the consequences of those choices, whether positive and negative. One does not learn to make good decisions unless given the opportunity to make decisions and observe their effects.

- Encourage and assist your clients to arrange, host, and attend meetings and events that will help them understand the people, organizations, and systems they hope to influence and change. An example would be for clients to arrange a meeting with members of the city council or the state legislature. When clients meet face-to-face with politicians, program administrators, and other decision makers, they often come away with a better understanding of what change is possible and a greater sense that they can make a difference.

- Once your clients understand that they are not helpless and do possess some power, assist them in using this power in a planned and disciplined manner to bring about some desired and feasible change. However, keep in mind that there are some pitfalls at this stage. When oppressed individuals realize that they have some power to influence others, they may not exercise that power in the most appropriate manner. Built-up anger and a sense of injustice cause people to become aggressive or combative and that may alienate potential supporters or attract added opposition to their goals. While encouraging clients to use their power, also help them understand that making social change can be frustratingly slow and that various realities may limit whether and how quickly decision makers can respond to their requests. For example, an agency may not be able to make immediate or far-reaching changes in its policies or programs because of budget limitations, existing laws, and the needs of others that they serve.

- As people examine how they have been held back in life by public attitudes, policies, and the powers that be, they are sometimes engulfed by resentment. Some may get stuck at this point and become prisoners of their anger. Help these clients express and understand their feelings, and then encourage them to let these feeling go and move beyond this bitterness. Make frequent use of reframing (see Item 13.10) to help clients view their prior experiences of mistreatment or injustice from a different angle. For example, help them view the past as a painful but invaluable source of wisdom about what is really important in life and how and why people behave as they do. Help the clients see that if they choose to be taught new behaviors rather than continue to hurt, they will uncover many opportunities to grow as people. Even personal distress can be beneficial if it pushes clients to carefully reexamine their situation and take action to change those things that are causing pain or discomfort.

- As an overall philosophy, empowerment is applicable in work with most clients and in most settings. However, what a social worker can do to empower others will vary widely depending on the setting and the types of clients served. For example, an empowerment strategy is highly applicable in work with women who have been abused and with persons with physical disabilities. It would have less applicability in direct practice with frail nursing home residents who are mentally confused. In working with inmates in a correctional facility, the legal context and security concerns would not allow a professional to relinquish some decision making to his or her clients.

Selected Bibliography

Adams, Robert. *Empowerment, Participation, and Social Work*, 4th ed. New York: Palgrave Macmillan, 2008.

Eamon, Mary. *Empowering Vulnerable Populations: Cognitive Behavioral Interventions*. Chicago: Lyceum, 2008.

Lee, Judith. *The Empowerment Approach to Social Work Practice*, 2nd ed. New York: Columbia University Press, 2001.

Linhorst, Donald. *Empowering People with Severe Mental Illness*. New York: Oxford University Press, 2006.

Wise, Judith. *Empowerment Practice with Families in Distress*. New York: Columbia University Press, 2005.

13.19 RESOLVING CONFLICT THROUGH COUNSELING AND MEDIATION

Social workers are frequently involved in helping clients resolve or minimize conflicts. For example, conflicts might arise between spouses or partners, perhaps over divorce and child custody; between a parent and child; between landlords and tenants; and even between social workers. Interpersonal conflicts can arise as a result of differences in beliefs and values, inaccurate or incomplete information, or differences in how an event is perceived and interpreted. A social worker can help people resolve some types of conflict by fostering better communication and mutual understanding. However, resolving a fundamental disagreement may require a more structured means of intervention known as *mediation*. And it must be recognized that not all conflicts can be resolved.

For some social workers, conflict resolution has become a practice specialty. Organizations such as the American Arbitration Association (AAA), the Association for Conflict Resolution (ACR), and the Institute for Advanced Dispute Resolution offer training programs and certifications to social workers and other professionals who have the knowledge and skill needed to resolve conflicts. In addition, the AAA and ARC, along with the American Bar Association, have created a "model of conduct" for mediators (2005) that, like the *NASW Code of Ethics,* offer guidelines for professionals engaged in conflict resolution interventions.

COUNSELING STRATEGIES

Conflict resolution requires an application of basic social work counseling and facilitation skills. However, compared to many social work interventions that involve advocating on behalf of one's client, the conflict resolution approach involves taking a neutral position while helping the affected parties examine their situation, identifying and clarifying the factors that contributed to the conflict, and considering alternative solutions. Some guidelines to keep in mind when counseling clients and others in relation to a conflict include:

- As part of planning and scheduling a meeting to address the conflict, urge the parties to consider these questions: Do I really want to resolve this conflict, or do I have another motive or agenda? Is what I have stated regarding this matter true, or have I exaggerated or provided only partial truth? What relevant information can I add to the discussion? What can I offer as a constructive step toward resolving this matter?

- When beginning the session, appeal to the parties to demonstrate mutual respect while discussing the issue, to reflect a willingness to listen to one another, and to make an honest effort to understand their different perceptions. Invite the parties to designate you as the person in the discussion who will enforce basic rules of fairness so that each can speak his or her mind without interruption.

- To the extent possible, encourage the parties to identify the source of the conflict. For example, is it possibly caused by a lack of information? Do both parties have the same facts and information? Are there differences in how the facts are interpreted? Is there agreement on the facts, but a difference of opinion on what would be the most reasonable and desirable outcome or action?

- Use basic helping skills (e.g., clarifying, paraphrasing, reframing, summarizing) to assist each party to express and explain her or his viewpoint. It may be useful, at times, to ask each party to repeat what she or he heard the other party say in order to help each clarify points and develop some level of empathy for the other person's perspectives.

- When there appears to be sufficient understanding of the issues, use brainstorming to identify potential solutions to the conflict (see Item 13.31). During this process, look for opportunities to remind the parties of their shared interests and what they have already agreed on (e.g., values, compromises, concern for a third party who is potentially affected by the outcome) and to build possible solutions that do not violate those areas of agreement.

MEDIATION

A more structured alternative to counseling is *facilitative mediation*, a method where a neutral third party, who has no authority or decision-making power in the situation, works with both sides to help them agree to terms for settling the dispute. As opposed to *arbitration*, where the participants are bound by the decisions of the third party, mediation does not impose a resolution but rather engages the disputing persons as active participants arriving at a mutually agreed-on solution, which leads to a win-win situation. **Mediation**, then, is essentially a dialogue between parties who are in conflict over such things as values, power, status, or access to resources, in which a social worker or other third party facilitates a balanced and even-handed search for a solution.

Moore (2003, pp. 64–65) has developed a typology that distinguishes five forms of conflict often addressed by mediation:

- *Relationship conflicts* are caused by experiences such as strong emotions, poor communication, misperceptions, and negative or antagonistic behaviors. In addressing this type of conflict, interventions should include helping participants to control emotions, to promote expression and clarity feelings, and to encourage positive problem-solving approaches.

- *Data conflicts* are created by a lack of information or misinformation, competing views on what is relevant information, or different interpretations of data. Addressing these conflicts requires determining which data is important and accurate, how additional data might be collected, and resolving issues about the interpretation of the data.

- *Interest conflicts* are caused by competition over substantive interests or resources. Thus, helping parties resolve these conflicts requires minimizing entrenched positions, looking for objective criteria for developing possible solutions, and developing trade-offs to arrive at a mutually agreeable solution.

- *Structural conflicts* are created by destructive patterns of behavior, imbalance of power or resources, and time or geographical constraints that hinder cooperation. Structural conflicts are often the most difficult conflicts to mediate because it requires the parties to modify behavioral patterns, establish a mutually agreeable decision-making process, and/or modify or disregard the influence of external pressures on the parties.

- *Value conflicts* develop when the parties come from very different family or cultural backgrounds, have different goals, or operate from different religious perspectives, worldviews, or ideologies. In working with the parties to such a conflict, the mediator might help them search for agreement on a broader or more important goal, agree to disagree on some issues, or seek a way to define the problem in some way other than a value conflict.

Because the mediator does not operate from a position of power or authority, her or his primary strengths must be the ability to quickly build a trusting relationship with both parties and to effectively use basic social work helping skills (see Chapter 8). Especially important is the ability of the social worker to guide the change process (see Chapter 7) in order to assure that the parties are indeed equal and active participants.

Selected Bibliography

American Arbitration Association, American Bar Association, and Association of Conflict Resolution. "Model Standards of Conduct for Mediators," 2005. http://www.adr.org/aaa/ShowProperty?nodeId=%2FUCM%2FADRSTG_010409&revision=latestreleased.

Emery, Robert E. *Renegotiating Family Relationships: Divorce, Child Custody, and Mediation*, 2nd ed. New York: Guilford, 2012.

Hansen, Toran. *The Generalist Approach to Conflict Resolution: A Guidebook.* Lanham, MD: Lexington Books, 2013.

Mayer, Bernard S. *The Dynamics of Conflict Resolution: A Guide to Engagement and Interaction*, 2nd ed. San Francisco: Jossey-Bass, 2012.

Moore, Christopher W. *The Mediation Process: Practical Strategies for Resolving Conflict*, 3rd ed. rev. San Francisco: Jossey-Bass, 2003.

13.20 PROVIDING SUPPORT FOR CAREGIVERS

When clients are recovering from a trauma, experiencing gradual decline in the ability to care for themselves, or facing a terminal condition, social workers are often in the position of recommending a level of care appropriate for the person's needs (see Item 11.11).

Frequently, the best option for the client is to reside in one's own home or the home of a relative or friend where care is provided. It is the social worker's responsibility to assure that the environment is safe and warm, sufficient nutritious food is provided, and the client is well cared for physically and emotionally. It is also the social worker's responsibility to assure that the caregiver is competent and physically and emotionally able to perform the necessary tasks.

In most cases, the **caregiver** is a spouse or an adult child, but occasionally this may be a friend or neighbor. Caregiving can be a rewarding activity because one can have the satisfaction of carrying out the moral duty of simply making someone's difficult situation more tolerable or, perhaps, giving back to a friend or loved one who has been important in her or his life. However, for many caregivers this activity is stressful, exhausting, and burdensome. It is an added responsibility to an already full plate that typically involves continuing to perform one's job, raising a family, and maintaining some semblance of a normal lifestyle. In addition, the caregivers' spouse and children may resent the intrusion of another person into the household, as well as the expenditure of scarce financial resources and/or the diversion of the caregiver's time and attention to the person needing care. Too often, the caregiver experiences overload, frustration, and a strong sense of guilt in not being able to give adequate attention to these competing responsibilities.

When supporting a caregiver, some questions the social worker should periodically consider might be:

- To what extent is the caregiver educating himself or herself about the loved one's condition?
- Is the caregiver developing the necessary skills to be of maximum help to the client?
- Is the caregiver experiencing the sense of feeling completely overwhelmed and unrewarded for performing this demanding role?
- Is the caregiver able to balance the responsibilities as a caregiver with the rest of her or his life?
- Are there other family members, friends, or neighbors the caregiver can enlist to temporarily do the caregiving if he or she cannot be present or simply needs a break?
- Is the caregiver aware of community services, such as respite care or adult day care that can provide some of the person's care?
- Is the caregiver involved in a "caregiver's support group" (if one is available in the community)?
- Will the caregiver recognize when in-home care is no longer viable and placement in a higher level of care facility is the better choice for the client?

Selected Bibliography

Carter, Rosalynn, with Susan K. Golant. *Helping Yourself Help Others: A Book for Caregivers*, rev. ed. New York: Public Affairs Press, 2013.

Goldberg, Stan. *Leaning Into Sharp Points: Practical Guidance and Nurturing Support for Caregivers.* Novato, CA: New World Library, 2012.

Jacobs, Barry. *The Emotional Survival Guide for Caregivers.* New York: Guilford, 2006.

Zucker, Elana. *Being a Caregiver in a Home Setting.* Upper Saddle River, NJ: Pearson, 2013.

13.21 INDIRECT DISCUSSION OF SELF IN SMALL GROUPS

This small-group technique is designed to stimulate group members to discuss their own problems without having to acknowledge the problem as their own and to discuss it with a bit of emotional distance. It is also effective in drawing reluctant or quiet group members into the discussion.

To begin the process, each participant is given three blank 3" × 5" cards. Each participant labels the cards A, B, and C. On each card the participant will complete or finish a stem sentence or respond to a specific question. The questions are labeled question A, question B, and question C. Before they write, the social worker tells the group that the cards will be collected, shuffled, and redistributed randomly for discussion. The participants are warned against writing a response that might reveal their identity. The participants can be completely honest in answering these questions, since the identity of the person writing the card will be protected.

The social worker using this technique selects the three questions beforehand. The questions are, of course, ones that the worker wants the group to discuss and ponder because he or she knows or suspects these are three important or troublesome issues. The following is a set of stem sentences used in a session with a group for parents who have abused their children.

> *On Card A:* (complete the statement) "Before a hitting episode, I feel..."
> *On Card B:* (complete the statement) "The thing I feel most after hitting my child is..."
> *On Card C:* (complete the statement) "One thing I could do to prevent a hitting episode is..."

The technique is also useful in training sessions. The next example is a set of stem sentences used in a training session for foster parents who are struggling to get along with the biological parents of children in foster care:

> *On Card A* (complete the statement) "In my contacts with biological parents, I find it most difficult to..."
> *On Card B:* (complete the statement) "I know I shouldn't have this negative feeling toward biological parents, but I sometimes feel..."
> *On Card C:* (complete the statement) "The thing that would help me to improve my interactions with biological parents is..."

After all of the participants have finished writing their responses to the three stem statements, collect the cards in sequence: First, collect all the A cards, then all the B's, and then all the C's. Shuffle each stack separately. Then randomly distribute the A cards, then the B cards, and then the C's. This ensures that each participant will receive a card holding a response to each of the three-stem questions. At this point each participant should hold three cards.

The next step is to have groups of three or four members (if part of a larger group) study and discuss the cards they have been given. The social worker might ask each small group to summarize what the cards seem to be saying or to find the common themes.

The foster parents, for example, might be asked to study all their cards and answer the following:

- Identify the difficulties experienced in contacts with biological parents.
- Identify the possible causes of the difficulties when in contact with the biological parents.
- Identify methods of improving relationships with biological parents.

Typically, what the participants find on these cards are thoughts, observations, and feelings quite similar to their own. This can be enlightening and reassuring. After a subgroup has studied its cards, participants are encouraged to trade their cards with other subgroups in order to obtain even more data.

The technique works best in groups larger than about 15, but it can be adapted for use in smaller groups and even with families. When used with a group smaller than 10, the social worker should also submit a set of cards. Sometimes, the worker can move things along or "prime the pump" by writing responses that are sure to provoke discussion.

Selected Bibliography

Furman, Rich, Diana Rowan, and Kimberly Bender. *An Experiential Approach to Group Work.* Chicago: Lyceum, 2009.

Gitterman, Alex, and Robert Salmon, eds. *Encyclopedia of Social Work with Groups.* New York: Routledge, 2009.

Zastrow, Charles. *Social Work with Groups*, 8th ed. Independence, KY: Cengage, 2012.

13.22 PROGRAMMING IN GROUP WORK

As used in social group work, the term **programming** refers to the purposeful use of various activities and group exercises to move the group process in a desired direction and to create opportunities for group members to learn specific social skills and behaviors. A broad range of activities can be used in programming—for example, drama, dance, games, camping, puppet shows, storytelling, care of animals, art, crafts, sports, community service projects, and the like.

Consider, for example, how playing a game might affect people's behavior and attitudes. Games are fun and engaging. They often allow for creativity and fantasy and teach the importance of obeying rules and maintaining boundaries. They often challenge the players to test themselves against others. Complex games and those involving teams may teach a variety of important skills such as self-control, problem solving, communication, decision making, planning, cooperation, leadership, and how to handle feelings related to success, failure, and authority. An individual's behavior during an activity can provide important assessment and diagnostic information. For example, the observation of a child's interaction during a game or an animal-assisted activity may yield insights into the child's behavior that could not be obtained from a battery of psychological tests.

"Animal Assisted Intervention" a deleted item from the 8th edition

The type of programming selected will depend on the social worker's assessment of individual members, their needs and strengths, the group's purpose, and the level of group functioning. Guidelines include the following:

- The selection of a particular activity is always tied to the question: What behaviors, attitudes, and skills do I want to encourage within the group? The activity should elicit and reinforce prosocial and functional behaviors by members and also help the group achieve its purpose. The chosen activity should not encourage or reward troublesome behavior such as bullying, ridicule, teasing, and dishonesty.

- When selecting an activity, carefully consider such factors as the members' ages, intellectual abilities, physical capacities, motor skills, endurance, attention span, need for control and protection, social skills, and so forth. Carefully consider whether the members possess the prerequisite skills or knowledge required by the activity. For example, does the activity require writing, reading, oral communication, cooperation, competition, initiative, memory, quick judgment, self-control, or the ability to follow detailed instructions? An activity should offer some challenge to the members but not generate excessive frustration.

- A group activity should be attractive and interesting. For example, young adults are often attracted to activities such as car maintenance, cooking, dance, music, basketball, and woodworking because such activities are age appropriate and combine the learning of useful skills with social interaction. Those who are physically fit might enjoy hiking, volleyball, or swimming. Older people might prefer more sedentary activities such as bingo, cards, and sewing; they might enjoy dancing if the music is familiar.

- Carefully consider what the activity will require of the social worker. For example, does the activity require the worker to function as a teacher, leader, rule enforcer, advisor, planner, referee, timekeeper, or a provider of transportation or food? Also critical in this consideration is the group's size. Obviously a large and diverse group presents the worker with more challenges than will a smaller group that is easier to manage and supervise.

- Consider how the rules of the activity will affect individual members. For example, does a game or activity involve the selection or ranking of participants, the choosing of sides, or the elimination of a "loser" from further competition? Can the members—such as those with low self-esteem, impulsivity, or a short attention span—cope with whatever frustration and disappointments the rules may generate?

- The appropriateness of a particular activity will depend on the group's stage of development. For example, in the get-acquainted or *preaffiliation stage*, you would select an activity that encourages communication and friendly interaction and would avoid activities that involve competition or requires a member to assume a leadership role (see Item 12.8).

- Consider how the activity fits with scheduling constraints and the physical environment. How much time is required? How much space? Is it safe? Is it noisy?

Selected Bibliography

Benson, Jarlath. *Working More Creatively with Groups*, 3rd ed. Clifton, NJ: Routledge, 2010.

Carrell, Susan. *Group Exercises for Adolescents*, 3rd ed. Thousand Oaks, CA: Sage, 2010.

Cheung, Monit. *Therapeutic Games and Guided Imagery*. Chicago: Lyceum, 2006.

Ciardiello, Susan. *Activities for Group Work with School Aged Children*. Warminster, PA: Marco Products, 2003.

Haslett, Diane. *Group Work Activities in Generalist Practice*. Independence, KY: Cengage, 2005.

SECTION B

TECHNIQUES AND GUIDELINES FOR INDIRECT PRACTICE

Due to the complexity and multiple layers of decision making in organizations and communities, facilitating change in these large systems is usually a time-consuming and labor-intensive process. The social worker engaged in these change activities should recognize that complex social organizations were built by people and can be changed by people, but the process of changing them is often difficult. Typically, large system change efforts must be sustained over a long period of time, although occasionally intensive work on a project during a shorter period is effective. Successful outcomes depend on such factors as timing, knowledge of alternative programs that have succeeded, and involvement of key people in the organization or community.

Intervention activities

When working to change organizations and communities, like in all social work practice, the success of the activity is partially based on relationships. As compared to direct-service practice where the central relationship is with clients, these relationships take the form of interactions with administrators, board members, media representatives, elected officials, and others who are in a position to make or influence decisions.

Most interventions to change organizations and communities involve incremental change activities. Much of that work is geared toward facilitating teamwork, resolving disputes within an agency or between agencies, generating ideas for new or innovative services, raising funds for programs, or developing grant applications. These interventions are central to improving the services to clients or future clients.

The more dramatic change activities are those that attempt to solve immediate and stressful problems. Those interventions include activities such as promoting changes in agency programs, organizing staff to address issues, chairing a committee or leading a problem-solving group, designing new programs, helping the media interpret social problems to the public, advocating for vulnerable groups, and lobbying key decision makers.

Monitoring activities

Similar to the direct services, the monitoring of indirect-service activities uses techniques either to inform actions while the change effort is in process (i.e., *formative evaluation*) or to sum up the results of an action after it is completed (i.e., *summative evaluation*). Some tools for both monitoring and evaluating practice are presented in Chapter 14.

13.23 WORKING WITH A GOVERNING OR ADVISORY BOARD

With the exception of for-profit human services agencies, social agencies operate at the will of the people. Governing or advisory boards made up of community representatives play a critical role in establishing the policies and programs that these agencies provide. Boards also serve as the interface between the community and staff and thus their actions and decisions affect the resources (e.g., funds, volunteers) available to support the services provided by the agency. It is essential that the social worker understand the authority and responsibilities of the agency's board because, for example, if the programs fail to adequately meet the needs of clients, the social worker must be prepared to advocate for change with that board.

In a private agency the **governing board** has final authority for the functioning of the agency. The board should be representative of the community but also attract and provide expertise or resources that are needed. Some agencies, but not all, select members with the expectation that they will be major fund-raisers or donors. However, the responsibilities are far greater than addressing the agency's finances. The board's communication to the public regarding the agency's mission and services, the assurance of responsible allocation of funds, and the ongoing evaluation of services are essential for building public trust in the organization.

In nonprofit social agencies, the governing board is legally responsible for the total operation of the organization. However, board members cannot and should not be present on a day-to-day basis to manage the operation of the agency. That is the job of the chief executive officer (CEO), sometimes called an *executive director* or *manager*. A governing board shares its authority with the CEO, who then employs staff members to provide the services. In this arrangement, the lines of authority must be clearly drawn so there is no confusion that interferes with the provision of client services by the professional staff.

In sum, the governing board of an agency is responsible for policymaking to establish the agency's goals, methods of operating, and programs; planning to link the agency with the needs of the community; fund-raising to assure the resources needed to operate the organization are available; securing a competent CEO; providing facilities in which to deliver the programs; communicating with the public regarding the agency's successes; and conducting evaluations to assure accountability for the trust placed in them to govern the organization.

In a public agency, by contrast, the **advisory board** (also called an *advisory council* or *advisory committee*) has no legal authority or responsibility for the operation of the organization. An advisory board is established either because the public officials responsible for the operation of the organization desire citizen input and/or because a legal code or agency regulation requires an advisory body as a channel for citizen participation. As the name implies, it offers advice but cannot require compliance with that advice. Advisory boards typically are created for these purposes:

- To help identify the needs of the community and recommend new or revised programs
- To evaluate agency programs and propose new procedures for conducting the agency's business
- To assist in fund-raising, public education regarding the agency's work, and advocate for support of the agency

Typically, the members of both governing and advisory boards volunteer their time and talents to the agency. The motivations of board members may vary from a desire to help others, to a desire to use their special knowledge to benefit the community, to seeking personal recognition and social status. It is important to understand these motivations and use this resource in a manner that both serves the agency and satisfies the board member's need.

Selected Bibliography

BoardSource. *The Nonprofit Board Answer Book: A Practical Guide for Board Members and Chief Executives*, 3rd ed. San Francisco: Jossey-Bass, 2012.

Eadie, Douglas C. *Extraordinary Board Leadership: The Keys to High-Impact Governing,* 2nd ed. Sudbury, MA: Jones and Bartlett, 2009.

Trower, Cathy A. *Govern More, Manage Less: Harnessing the Power of Your Nonprofit,* 2nd ed. Washington, DC: BoardSource, 2010.

13.24 CONDUCTING EFFECTIVE STAFF MEETINGS

An important factor in the successful operation of a social agency is the quality of staff communication, making the staff meeting a critically important tool in agency management. Properly used, the staff meeting enhances communication and can prevent organizational problems caused by staff members who might otherwise act on inaccurate or incomplete information. Ineffective or poorly run staff meetings can be both costly for the agency and frustrating for the staff. A one-hour meeting involving a staff of eight, for example, is the equivalent of a day's salary for one person. The cost of the meeting should be justified by its benefits for achieving the agency's purpose, as compared to the staff providing service to clients during that time.

It is important to distinguish between a staff meeting and other types of meetings, such as case staffings and consultations and the meetings used for case assignments or by special committees and project teams. The distinction between staff meetings and team meetings can be made in terms of purpose (e.g., exchange of information regarding the agency versus a discussion of practice techniques related to specific cases); content (e.g., discussion of policies, procedures, organizational maintenance, and professional practice issues versus a specific issue of practice activity regarding a case situation); formality (e.g., a formal decision-making structure), membership (e.g., inclusive of practitioners and support staff); and size (e.g., typically larger than a team meeting).

Staff meeting time should not be spent on routine or easily understood information that can be disseminated by other means, such as memos and email. Staff meeting time is best spent only on matters that require verbal clarification, feedback from staff, or a staff decision. Also, staff meetings should be held at the same time each week or month, have a set starting and ending time, and last not more than one hour. Attendance should be mandatory, and the leader should prepare and circulate an agenda in advance of the meeting and take responsibility to keep the discussion moving. However, staff meetings are not solely a management responsibility. All staff members should be expected to contribute agenda items, be prepared for discussion of those items, and assume responsibility for following through on items that require their attention. If an issue requires extensive discussion, a separate meeting should be scheduled. In many settings, the preparation of minutes is useful to disseminate information and properly record staff decisions.

Barretta-Herman's (1990, p. 145) analysis of staff meetings in human services organizations identifies three elements of successful meetings:

1. They should fulfill their objectives by jointly involving management and practitioners.

2. They should provide a forum for active discussion, creative problem solving, and participation of staff members.

3. The conclusion of discussion on a topic should clarify responsibility to follow through with action.

Selected Bibliography

Barretta-Herman, Angeline. "The Effective Social Service Staff Meeting." In *Business Communication: New Zealand Perspectives,* edited by Frank Slegio. Auckland, New Zealand: Software Technology, 1990, pp. 136–147.

Gallop, Les, and Trish Hafford-Letchfield. *How to Become a Better Manager in Social Work and Social Care: Essential Skills for Managing Care.* Philadelphia: Jessica Kingsley, 2012.

13.25 BUILDING INTERPROFESSIONAL TEAMWORK AND COOPERATION

Given the complexity of human services, often involving both multiagency and multidisciplinary interaction in the workplace, the social worker must be skilled at working as a team member and encouraging teamwork and cooperation from others. The following guidelines are useful for strengthening this interaction:

- In general, individuals and organizations cooperate with each other when it is of benefit to do so. Those benefits may be personal, professional, organizational, political, or financial. Cooperation is fostered by emphasizing what the parties have in common and how they and clients will benefit from working together.

- Genuine teamwork and interagency cooperation does not occur by accident; they must be encouraged and nurtured. Statements of thanks, recognition, praise, and taking a personal interest in other team members will help reinforce cooperative behavior. Avoid or halt any discussions that are disrespectful of other professionals and agencies because an atmosphere of negativity tends to diminish cooperative behavior.

- Teamwork and cooperation are built on the common purpose of combining resources to serve clients. If self-interest appears to be guiding decisions, suggest the team members or agency representatives revisit the question: "What are we trying to achieve for our clients?"

- Encourage the selection of a leader or chairperson who is nondefensive, supportive of others, and respected by the group. Be proactive and willing to plan and prepare carefully for team meetings and assume a leadership role when appropriate.

- Concern for client confidentiality is a reason sometimes given for not working closely with other agencies and professionals. Often, this issue is more imagined than real. If professionals or agencies want to work together but are hesitant to do so because of confidentiality, they should ask their agency's legal counsel to recommend a workable procedure.

- Be alert to the fact that many interagency conflicts center on questions of which agency has primary fiscal responsibility for providing a particular service. In other words, many disagreements boil down to the question of whose budget is to be used to pay the cost of services. Work out a policy for addressing these issues rather than attempting to resolve them on a case-by-case basis.

- Understand your role and responsibility and those of the people with whom you are working. Make sure everyone knows what she or he can and cannot expect of each other. Clarify interagency expectations by developing documents such as contracts, letters of agreement, protocol statements, and purchase of service agreements.

- Teamwork can be especially challenging when the team is attempting to make difficult, value-laden decisions. Members should be encouraged to address directly and openly any conflicts or hidden agendas that may disrupt team efforts. Conflict that arises from thoughtful differences of opinion is healthy. However, conflict that stems from bias or thoughtless loyalty to actions of the past is disruptive. Attempts to suppress or avoid conflicts or significant differences of opinion by denial, capitulation, or domination often make the problem even worse. If it is necessary to express a difference of opinion, use I-statements and other communication skills that convey your message in a clear, straightforward, and nonthreatening manner and use negotiating skills to reach consensus agreements.

"Developing Professional Cooperation" from item 12.23 in 1st edition

- Realize that some of those with whom you must work may not be committed to teamwork. When this is evident, be firm but diplomatic in expressing the need for cooperation and for putting the benefit to clients before other considerations.

Selected Bibliography

Davis, John M. and Mary Smith. *Working in Multi-Professional Contexts: A Practical Guide for Professionals in Children's Services.* Thousand Oaks, CA: Sage, 2012.

Mosser, Gordon, and James W. Begun. *Understanding Teamwork in Healthcare.* New York: McGraw-Hill, 2013.

Thistlethwaite, Jill E. *Values-Based Interprofessional Collaborative Practice: Working Together in Health Care.* Cambridge: Cambridge University Press, 2012.

13.26 LEADING SMALL-GROUP MEETINGS

Group decision making has become increasingly popular in the human services. Therefore, social workers spend considerable time participating in groups, agency staff meetings, interagency team meetings, and various community committees. Although group consideration of issues potentially leads to better decisions, group meetings without proper planning and direction can waste much valuable time and interfere with the opportunity for making real change. As the leader of a small group, the social worker is responsible for making the meeting as productive and efficient as possible. The following principles and guidelines should be followed by the worker when in a leadership position:

1. *Prepare for the meeting by engaging in the following activities:*
   - Clearly identify the purpose of the meeting.
   - Decide who should participate.
   - Identify objectives for the meeting and anticipate what the participants will and should expect, when possible by involving participants in the planning.
   - Decide the best time and place for the meeting, and determine how participants will be notified of the purpose, agenda, starting time, and location of the meeting.
   - Decide how much time will be required for the meeting and construct a realistic agenda, addressing high-priority items first.
   - Decide what physical arrangements are necessary (e.g., room reservations, seating arrangements, audiovisual equipment, refreshments).
   - Decide if a written report of what occurred in the meeting will be needed and, if so, who will prepare it and how it will be distributed.
   - Decide if a follow-up meeting will be needed.

2. *Get the discussion off to a good start.*

- Make sure that all members are introduced to each other and supply name tags if members do not already know each other.
- Explain the purpose of the discussion and its relevance to the participants.
- Distribute materials needed for the discussion (e.g., fact sheets, outlines, case examples).
- Create an atmosphere that helps the participants feel valued, appreciated, and responsible for contributing to the discussion.

3. *Give all members an opportunity to participate.*

- Explain in your opening remarks that the role of the group leader primarily will be that of coordinator to ensure that all members have an opportunity to be heard.
- Address your comments and questions to the group as a whole, unless specific information is needed from a particular person.
- Scan the entire group every minute or two. If you notice a member who appears unusually quiet or disturbed by the discussion, draw that person into the discussion by asking if he or she would like to add something to the discussion.
- If the group contains members who dominate the discussion, try to control them for the benefit of the group. A number of techniques can be used; begin with a more subtle approach and become directive only if necessary. Here are some possible ways to deal with such members:
  - Seat the talkative members where they are more easily overlooked by other members.
  - When a question is asked of the group, meet the eyes of those members who have spoken infrequently and avoid eye contact with the dominant talkers.
  - When a frequent talker has made a point, cut in with something like "How do the rest of you feel about that idea?"
  - Propose a rule that each person can make but one statement per topic.
  - In private, ask the excessive talkers for assistance in getting the quiet members to speak more often.
  - Point out the problem and ask others to contribute more—for instance: "We have heard a lot from John and Mary, but what do the rest of you think about...?"
- If asked by a member to express a personal opinion about a controversial issue, try to bounce the question back to the group, unless members already have expressed their opinions. Say, "Well, let's see how others feel about this first." If you must express a personal opinion, do so in a manner that will not inhibit others from speaking on the topic.
- Avoid making a comment after each member has spoken. Doing so tends to create a wheel's "hub and spokes" pattern of communication, with the leader becoming the hub and the focal point of all communication.
- React to what members say without judgment, showing only that a point is understood or that it needs clarification. If evaluation seems necessary, invite it from others with a question such as "Does that fit with your perception on the matter?"
- Use nonverbal communication to promote discussion. Nods and gestures can be used to encourage participation, especially from the quiet members.

4. *Promote cooperation and harmony in a small group.*

- Be alert to the possibility of counterproductive hidden agendas, and, if necessary, call them to the attention of the group. The group usually can solve a problem of conflicting purposes if it is brought into the open for discussion.
- Emphasize the importance of the mutual sharing of ideas and experiences and the need for clear communication.
- Use the word *we* often to stress the group's unity of purpose.
- Keep conflicts focused on facts and issues. Stop any personal attacks.
- Do not let the discussion become so serious that the members do not have some fun. Humor can reduce tension. Effective discussion is characterized by shifting between the serious and the playful.

5. *Use questioning techniques to maintain attention on a topic and encourage analytical thinking.*

- When possible, use open-ended questions that will encourage group members to express their thoughts and feelings. For example, "What do you see as the merits of . . . ?" Avoid questions that can be answered with only a word or two.
- Questions should be understandable to all. Vague or obtuse questions frustrate the members.
- Questions should be asked in a natural and conversational tone of voice.
- Questions should usually be addressed to the group as a whole, rather than to a particular individual. This motivates everyone to think and respond.
- Questions occasionally should be asked of persons who are not giving their attention to the discussion. This usually stimulates the individual and the whole group to redirect its attention to the topic.
- Questions should be asked in a manner that indicates the leader's confidence in the person's ability to respond.
- Questions should be selected to maintain the focus on the topic under discussion. Avoid questions that would cause the group to leave its task and go off on a tangent.
- Ask for more detail and specification. Dig for the rationale and assumptions behind an opinion or a belief. Help those offering opinions to furnish evidence for their positions without making them defensive.
- See that the evidence offered for a position is tested and not accepted at face value.
- Assign one or two members of the group to challenge ideas and play devil's advocate so that differences are aired openly.

6. *Keep the discussion orderly, efficient, and productive.*

- Keep the participants focused on the meeting's goals and purpose. For example, occasionally ask, "Are we still on target for reaching our objectives?"
- Be alert to extended departures from the topic. If the group is drifting away from the topic, call this to everyone's attention. Ask if the digression means that there is disagreement on the goal or if it is an indication that the group is ready to move on to another topic.
- If there is much repetition in the discussion, ask if the group has exhausted the subject at hand. If so, help them get started on a new topic.
- Be the group's timekeeper. Keep the group informed of the time limits so high-priority topics will get the attention they deserve.

- Bring the discussion to a conclusion, which might include any of the following:
  - A summary of progress made by the group
  - Comments about planning and preparation for another meeting
  - Assignments for follow-up and implementation
  - Commendations when appropriate
  - A request for an evaluation of the meeting in order to improve future meetings

Selected Bibliography

Galanes, Gloria J., and Katherine Adams. *Effective Group Discussion: Theory and Practice*, 14th ed. New York: McGraw-Hill, 2013.

Kemp, Jana M. *Moving Out of the Box: Tools for Team Decision Making.* Westport, CN: Praeger, 2008.

Kraybill, Ron, and Evelyn Wright. *Group Tools to Facilitate Meetings.* Intercourse, PA: Good Books, 2006.

Larson, James R., Jr. *In Search of Synergy in Small Group Performance.* New York: Psychology Press, 2010.

Wheelen, Susan A. *Creating Effective Teams: A Guide for Members and Leaders*, 4th ed. Thousand Oaks, CA: Sage, 2013.

13.27 THE RISK TECHNIQUE

At times, committees (and especially staff committees) need to address fears and concerns related to some perceived risk or threat. For example, when controversial policies are adopted by a board, when new legislation is passed that affects a social program and/or the resources available, or when administrators establish a change in routine, it becomes important to identify and clarify the facts and issues in the situation and set aside rumors and fantasized outcomes. In these situations, a process using the RISK technique can be useful.

To use this technique, the leader must take a nondefensive posture and communicate interest in having the group members express their fears, issues, concerns, complaints, and anticipated problems. Using this approach, the leader encourages members of the group to express their views and to listen and understand other's fears.

As an illustration, assume that a change is proposed in an agency that would double the number of days that social workers are on 24-hour call. To address concerns about this proposal, the supervisor might use the RISK technique by taking the following steps:

Step 1: The leader schedules a meeting with all agency workers and presents a detailed description of the proposed change in the on-call section of the agency's personnel policy.

Step 2: The leader explains that he or she will utilize the RISK technique to help workers identify their concerns about this proposed change.

Step 3: The leader begins by asking workers to voice any and all fears, concerns, and worries they have in relation to the proposed change. These "risks" are written on newsprint for all to see, with the wording of the statement acceptable to the person raising the concern. Discussion of the items is not permitted at this time. (Note that up to this point, the RISK technique is similar to brainstorming, Item 13.31.)

Step 4: The leader continues to encourage workers to voice additional concerns about the proposed change. It is important to allow adequate time for this session because the most disturbing and threatening concerns often will not surface until late in the discussion.

Step 5: At this point, the initial session ends and the leader schedules a second meeting to occur in the next three to seven days. Meanwhile, all workers receive a written listing of the risks identified during the meeting.

Step 6: At the second meeting, the leader encourages workers to voice any additional risks they may have thought of since the initial meeting or to change the wording of any risk statements. The group is then asked to discuss and react to each risk item and decide if it is, indeed, a serious and substantive concern or issue. The risks considered to be minor or of little concern are dropped from the list. Those remaining are further discussed and clarified. The second meeting is then ended with the understanding that the identified risks are now defined as those of the group as a whole, and not the person who first identified any risk.

Step 7: The leader places the group's identified risks (i.e., the final list from the second meeting) on an agenda for a meeting between the workers and administrators.

Selected Bibliography

Erich, Stephen, and Heather Kaneberg. *Skills for Group Practice.* Upper Saddle River, NJ: Pearson, 2011.

Galanes, Gloria J., and Katherine Adams. *Effective Group Discussion: Theory and Practice*, 14th ed. New York: McGraw-Hill, 2013.

13.28 THE NOMINAL GROUP TECHNIQUE (NGT)

Committees that depend on a consensus approach sometimes get stuck when trying to reach a decision. One technique that helps bring issues into the open and moves the group toward consensus is the nominal group technique (NGT). It is particularly suited for groups of six to nine people; if used with a larger group, the committee should be divided into smaller groups. Depending on the scope and complexity of the matter being addressed, it might take from little as an hour and a half to a much longer period to complete the process.

There are four main elements in the NGT process:

1. The participants generate ideas in writing.
2. Each group member is provided an opportunity to record an idea in a terse phrase on a flipchart.
3. Group discussion of each recorded idea is held for clarification and evaluation.
4. Voting on the most important ideas establishes priorities with the group's decision being mathematically derived through rank ordering or rating.

The following process is suggested to help structure a NGT session:

1. The chair acts as facilitator and does not vote.
2. A brief description of the issue or concern is written on a flipchart.
3. The pros and cons are freely discussed for 10 minutes.
4. Each person is asked to spend 5 to 15 minutes working silently, writing down ideas or solutions on a piece of paper.

5. Each idea or solution is listed on the chart and numbered. The chair then polls each member for a second idea or solution and repeats this process until the lists have been exhausted.

6. An additional 10 more minutes are allowed for clarification of the ideas or solutions presented—not for defense of the position.

7. All members vote on a secret ballot, ranking their top five choices 1, 2, 3, 4, 5. By adding the scores for each idea or solution, the lower scores will reflect the most favored positions.

8. Discuss the several items with the lowest sores. Encourage critical thinking, invite disagreement, and seek careful analysis of the items.

9. If a clear consensus is not reached, revote and then discuss the items again. This can be repeated until a synthesis of ideas is developed or there is clear support for one idea.

The NGT process encourages active involvement by all participants as they consider and write down their ideas. Too often, in a group process, a few members carry the discussion and others do not actively and creatively think about the issues from their own perspectives. The interactive presentation of the issues allows all committee members an opportunity to express themselves and respond to the ideas from both the verbal and less-verbal members.

Selected Bibliography

Tague, Nancy. *The Quality Toolbox*, 2nd ed. Milwaukee, WI: ASQ Quality Press, 2005.
Toseland, Ronald W., and Robert F. Rivas. *An Introduction to Group Work Practice,* 7th ed. Upper Saddle River, NJ: Pearson, 2012.

13.29 CHAIRING A FORMAL COMMITTEE

The committee is a particular type of small group for which the social worker might assume leadership. Unlike some groups where the effect of the group process on the members is the most important outcome, the committee's outcome is focused on a decision or recommendation. One type of committee is the *standing committee* that is charged with the ongoing responsibility for studying and recommending changes in a specific area. For example, an agency may have a standing committee responsible for a process of peer evaluation. Another type of committee is the *ad hoc committee* that has a charge to complete an assignment and then be disbanded. An example of this type of assignment might be to develop a job description for a new agency staff position. For both types of committee, the end result is a decision that represents the committee's judgment about a matter. Thus, the chair's guidance and the group's process must facilitate the committee arriving at a conclusion that reflects the thinking of the group.

The social worker chairing a committee should make use of the guidelines for working with small groups (see Item 13.26) and must believe in the worth and wisdom of group decision making. That belief recognizes that the decisions made by a small group, as compared to those made by a single individual, are more likely to be based on complete information and on a wider range of considerations; thus, the decisions are more likely to be sound. That is not to say that committees do not make bad decisions. They do. But a group is less likely to make a bad decision or a serious error in judgment than is an individual acting alone.

The leader must also recognize the danger of *groupthink*, a situation of false agreement or false consensus that arises when a powerful committee member (or members) takes a strong stand on an issue and other members simply acquiesce rather than argue an opposing point of view. Thus, the decision reached is not adequately considered. This incomplete consideration of the matter can be avoided if the chair makes sure all points of view are expressed and debated before a decision is made.

Committee membership is usually voluntary and most people are willing to serve on a committee if they believe their time will be used efficiently and the committee's work will result in a real and positive change. On the other hand, many people have reasons for disliking and avoiding committee work, especially when:

- There is a lack of clear purpose (e.g., members are not sure why they are meeting or what they are to accomplish).
- There is a lack of leadership and direction by the chairperson (e.g., the chair does not keep the group moving and focused; real issues are not addressed or difficult decisions are avoided).
- Committee discussion is controlled or dominated by one individual or subgroup.
- There is a lack of preparation for the meetings (e.g., no agenda, needed information is not made available).
- There is a lack of follow-through (e.g., members or the chair promises to do something but fails to do so).
- The chair or members have a hidden agenda (e.g., some members have an ax to grind or will accept only one outcome, regardless of majority opinion).

One means of helping a committee avoid pitfalls that can lead to unproductive meetings is to engage the members in setting goals and operating procedures for the committee and to periodically review and renegotiate the objectives and methods of operation so that members can express their views about problems, make adjustments to their thinking, and renew their investment in the work. Dyer, Dyer, and Dyer (2013) identify several steps that should be followed in building a productive committee:

Step 1: *Give the work realistic priority.* It is important to give members a chance to discuss why they are serving on the committee, clarify the relative importance of this work in the context of their total responsibilities, and indicate the amount of time they are able to commit to this activity. Sharing these matters helps establish the pace at which the committee can operate and allows the chair to identify persons who have the time and interest to carry major responsibilities.

Step 2: *Share expectations.* Each person should be asked to identify his or her greatest concerns about working on this committee, how he or she sees it functioning, and what actions are necessary to ensure positive outcomes.

Step 3: *Clarify goals.* The committee members should collectively discuss and write down a statement that represents the group's core mission. Subgoals can then be developed to reflect the intermediate or short-range objectives necessary to accomplish this mission. During subsequent committee work, each decision and action should be examined for its contribution to the mission or subgoals that have been established.

Step 4: *Formulate operating guidelines.* The committee members should then establish procedures for their operation. Answers to the following questions will provide guidance for the chair and allow members to know how to proceed:

- How will we make decisions?
- What will be our basic method of working as a group?
- How do we make sure everyone gets a chance to discuss issues or raise concerns?
- How will we resolve differences?
- How will we ensure that we complete our work and meet deadlines?
- How will we change methods that are not producing results?

The formality with which a committee operates often depends on its size, the existing relationships among the members, and the speed with which it needs to complete its work. However, in most cases *Robert's Rules of Order* is the accepted set of procedures to be followed when making final decisions. *Robert's Rules* can be intimidating because they were designed for parliamentary decision making ranging from very simple committee work to very complex legislative actions. For most situations in which a social worker would be chairing a meeting, knowing just the following simple procedures is usually all that is necessary.

- Discussion of the item begins when its place on the committee's agenda is reached.
- At some point in the discussion an individual or committee introduces a "motion" to propose specific language for action in relation to the matter. Another member of the committee must "second" the motion and then debate is limited to the motion.
- If, during the debate, a member wants to change the language of the motion, she or he can move to "amend" the original motion. If there is a "second" to the motion to amend, the chair then limits discussion to the amendment and it is voted up or down. Other amendments can then be presented—one at a time. At any point there can be a motion to "table" or discontinue discussion of the item until a later meeting.
- When the matter has been thoroughly discussed, the chair calls for a vote on the motion. Unless the committee has agreed otherwise, a "majority" of one vote more than one-half of those voting determines the committee's decision. If amendments to the original motion have been adopted, the amended motion is then voted up or down, the matter is settled, and the chair moves the group on to the next agenda item.

The website http://www.robertsrules.org provides an orientation to *Robert's Rules* and includes a helpful downloadable chart to use when chairing a meeting.

Selected Bibliography

Dyer, W. Gibb, Jr., Jeffrey H. Dyer, and William G. Dyer. *Team Building: Proven Strategies for Improving Team Performance,* 5th ed. San Francisco: Jossey-Bass, 2013.

Jennings, C. Alan, Plamen Hristov, and Simon Whitbread. *Robert's Rules for Dummies,* 2nd ed. Indianapolis, IN: Wiley, 2012.

Petz, Jon. *Boring Meetings Suck: Get More Out of Your Meetings, or Get Out of More Meetings.* Hoboken, NJ: Wiley, 2011.

13.30 PROBLEM SOLVING BY A LARGE GROUP

At times, it is necessary for a social worker to initiate problem-solving activity within a large group. The technique described here is intended to elicit ideas from all members and provide an opportunity for participation, even when as many as 30 or more people are involved.

The technique begins with the group leader explaining the purpose of the meeting—for example: "We need to come up with a method of collecting information from the agencies in town on trends in the number of homeless people applying for help." These steps should then be followed:

Step 1: *Each individual is asked to think privately about the problem and possible solutions.* Members are asked to make written notes on their thoughts.

Step 2: *Dyads are formed.* Each person in the dyad is instructed to interview her or his partner and to try to understand that person's perspective on the problem and proposed solutions. The dyads work for 10 minutes.

Step 3: *Quartets are formed.* For 15 minutes, each group of four people discusses the problem and possible solutions. Each quartet records the key points of its deliberation on a large piece of paper, which is hung on the wall for all to see.

Step 4: *Each individual studies the papers for 10 minutes.*

Step 5: *The whole group reassembles and shares its analysis of the problem and proposed solutions.* This final step sets the stage for the prioritizing of proposed solutions to be explored in more depth.

Selected Bibliography

Brody, Ralph. *Effectively Managing Human Service Organizations,* 3rd ed. Thousand Oaks, CA: Sage, 2005.

Tropman, John E. *Making Meetings Work: Achieving High-Quality Group Decisions,* 2nd ed. Thousand Oaks, CA: Sage, 2003.

13.31 BRAINSTORMING

Problem solving includes the important step of identifying all possible alternatives or solutions. Too often, some potential solutions are overlooked because they do not fit preconceived notions or expectations. Rigidity and following old patterns of thought can limit creativity during the problem-solving process. The technique of **brainstorming** is designed to overcome this limitation and encourage thinking "outside the box." It can be applied to any problem for which there may be a range of solutions. The objective of brainstorming is to free persons temporarily from self-criticism and from the criticism of others in order to generate imaginative solutions to a specific problem. Brainstorming is most often used in work with groups or committees, but many workers adapt its principles for use in one-on-one counseling sessions.

For the social worker leading a brainstorming session, the first step is to clearly define the problem and be sure all participants are aware of the problem. Next, the session focuses on the spontaneous and unrestrained generation of possible solutions that can be expressed in a few words. Many ideas may be unrealistic, but it is only after all alternatives have been identified that the participants are permitted to evaluate the proposed solutions in search of those that are feasible. A social worker setting up a brainstorming session should give several instructions:

- Encourage participants to develop a large number of solutions. The goal is to generate a quantity of solutions—quality will be determined later.
- Encourage participants to be freewheeling in their thinking. Even wild ideas are welcomed and accepted without judgment.
- Recommend that participants combine and elaborate on the solutions that are offered.
- Do not allow participants to criticize or evaluate one another's proposed solutions.

During the brainstorming session, a recorder writes down all the ideas as fast as they come up. Do this on a whiteboard or flipchart so the visual record stimulates additional ideas. The leader of the session should quickly stop any criticism of these ideas, whether verbal or implied by tone of voice or nonverbal gesture. Also, the group leader needs to keep the participants focused on the problem under consideration.

When all of the proposed solutions or ideas have been heard and recorded, the session moves to a second stage: the critical examination of each idea. De Bono (1999) suggests a useful technique for ensuring that six types of questioning and thinking are applied during the evaluation stage. Each of these six categories of thinking is called a "hat," and each hat has a color. Thus, for example, when the group is asked by the group leader to "put on your red hats," the group is being asked to evaluate the proposed solutions in terms of hunches, intuition, and gut feelings. If asked to put on the "black hat," the group is to view the solutions in a highly critical and skeptical manner.

The six thinking hats to apply to each idea are as follows:

- *White hat* (focus on objectivity and data): What information do we have? How reliable is this information? What additional information do we need?
- *Red hat* (focus on hunches and intuition): What are our gut feelings about this proposed solution? Does it "feel" right? Let's trust our instincts!
- *Black hat* (focus on caution and risk): What are the legal, policy, political, and funding problems we will encounter? This cannot be done and will not work because....
- *Yellow hat* (focus on optimism): It needs to be done, so let's try! Who cares if it has never been done before? Let's try something different! It will work if we really want it to work!
- *Green hat* (focus on creativity and other combinations of ideas): Are there still other ways of thinking about this? Can we combine the best parts of several different proposals?
- *Blue hat* (focus on the big picture and holistic thinking): How does this idea fit with other things we know about this issue? Are we missing something important? Let's summarize the conclusions we have reached and the decisions we have made so far. Is our way of discussing and approaching this issue working for us? Are we making progress toward a decision or solution?

Be sure to provide sufficient time for a brainstorming session. Considering that many ideas might be generated in a single session and that time will be needed to evaluate each proposed solution, a brainstorming session could easily take more than an hour.

Selected Bibliography

Adair, John. *Decision Making and Problem Solving Strategies*, 2nd ed. Philadelphia, PA: Kogan Page, 2010.

de Bono, Edward. *Six Thinking Hats*, rev. ed. Boston: Back Bay Books, 1999.

Scannell, Mary, and Mike Mulvihill. *The Big Book of Brainstorming Games: Quick, Effective Activities that Encourage Out-of-the-Box Thinking, Improve Collaboration, and Spark Great Ideas!* New York: McGraw-Hill, 2012.

13.32 CLASS ADVOCACY

The term **class advocacy** refers to actions on behalf of a whole group or class of people. This is in contrast to client advocacy (see Item 13.17), in which the advocacy is on behalf of a specific individual or family. Because class advocacy seeks change in law and public policy at either the local, state, or national level, it is essentially a political process aimed at influencing the decisions of elected officials and high-level administrators. It entails building coalitions with other groups and organizations that share similar concerns about a social issue. The social worker typically (but not always) participates as a representative of an organization, rather than as an independent practitioner.

Since the goal is to bring about a change in the status quo, some degree of opposition or "push back" is to be expected. Not everyone is comfortable with the interpersonal and interorganizational conflicts that can arise in this type of advocacy. Further, each organization must examine the pros and cons of taking on an advocacy role and decide whether having its representatives perform this role fits with the purpose of the organization.

For those who choose to become engaged in class advocacy, following these guidelines may increase the chance of success:

- Realize that advocacy intends to help bring about needed changes in laws, policies, and programs. Bringing about such change is slow and difficult—but not impossible.

- You cannot do it alone. Individual social workers will need to join with others. A group has more power than an individual, and several organizations working together have more power than a single organization working alone. Working with other organizations will mean that your own organization will have to share some resources, make some compromises, and perhaps do some things differently. In the long run, however, you will accomplish more as part of a coalition than by working alone.

- Many improvements are needed in our human services systems. Since you cannot do everything that needs to be done, you must decide which concern has the highest priority. If you, or your organization, take on several causes at one time, you may be spread too thin. It is better to make real gains in just one area than to make minimal or no gains in several.

- It is also important to choose a cause where success is possible. Be realistic! Do not waste your time and energy on a lost cause. A successful experience generates hope and a feeling that other successes are possible. If participants can see even small successes, they will be more willing to invest themselves in future advocacy efforts.

- Successful advocacy is built on a foundation of careful analysis and planning. It is important to clearly define and carefully study the problem before you make a decision on what to do about it. Do not launch an effort to change something until you know exactly what has to be changed, why it needs to be changed, and what will be involved in bringing about the change.

- Before you take action, carefully assess what achieving your goal will require in the way of time, energy, money, and other resources. Do you have the resources? If not, it is best to scale down your goals or wait until later when you are better organized and more capable of reaching your goal.

- Try to understand those who will oppose you. There is always resistance to change, and analysis of the situation should include understanding why there is resistance. The advocate needs to be able to put himself or herself in the opponent's shoes (i.e., have empathy). People always have reasons for opposing change. You may not agree with their reasons, but you must understand them if you are to figure out a way to successfully overcome that resistance.

- Successful advocacy requires self-discipline. One of the most serious errors one can make in advocacy is to act impulsively. If that happens, the other organizations in the coalition may pull back or be reluctant to cooperate because they fear that your recklessness will cause damage to their organization or to the coalition. Also, if you act impulsively, those who oppose you can more easily discredit you.

- Advocacy involves the use of *power*. Essentially, power is the ability to make others behave the way you want them to behave. Think of power as a resource that can be used or "spent" for a particular purpose. There are different kinds of power (see Item 11.25). It is important to study your own organization and its membership in order to discover the type of power that you possess.

Among the types of power possessed by social workers is the power that comes from knowledge and expertise. For example, if you are advocating on behalf of children, you should have detailed information about the everyday lives and concerns of children and troubled families, and you should know how the system works or does not work. Information, if carefully assembled and presented, can have a powerful impact on legislators, agency administrators, and the public.

Perhaps some members of your organization are highly respected in the community and have credibility that gives them a type of power. Individuals who are esteemed and respected can have a significant influence on legislators and administrators. You need to encourage and help those individuals to advocate actively in behalf of the issue.

Do not forget that personal commitment, time, and energy are also types of power. Much can be accomplished just by sticking with a task and seeing it through to the end. Organizational solidarity is also a type of power. If legislators and decision makers can see that members are solidly behind their organization, they will pay attention to what the organization's leaders have to say.

Within your organization are members who are natural leaders. Others may be charismatic and articulate with the ability to excite people and get them to work together on a cause. Charisma is a rare quality, but it is definitely a type of power. Identify charismatic individuals in your organization and let them speak for your cause. There are times when class advocacy must take the form of a lawsuit. Many societal changes and reforms would never have happened without lawsuits and court decisions. For example, many of the reforms in the areas of mental health and mental retardation have grown out of legal actions. An organization committed to advocacy will, at times, need to encourage and finance lawsuits that have potential for bringing about a needed change.

Most people in the United States depend on television, newspapers, and the Internet for information. If one wants the public to understand and support a cause, it is important to know how to present the message in a way that will command public attention and sway and mobilize public opinion. Reach out to individuals who work in advertising or the media and ask them to support the cause by donating their skills. Or perhaps approach an advertising agency or a school of journalism and ask for their assistance in designing a public information campaign.

Selected Bibliography

Jansson, Bruce. *Becoming an Effective Policy Advocate*, 7th ed. Independence, KY: Cengage, 2014.

Lustig, Stuart L., ed. *Advocacy Strategies for Health and Mental Health Professionals: From Patients to Policies*. New York: Springer, 2012.

Rice, Ronald E., and Charles K. Atkin, eds. *Public Communication Campaigns*, 4th ed. Thousand Oaks, CA: Sage, 2013.

13.33 TEACHING AND TRAINING

Social workers do a lot of teaching. They frequently teach skills related to parenting, interpersonal communication, stress management, job seeking, independent living, and so on. Their teaching may be directed to clients, volunteers, colleagues, or concerned citizens. It may occur within the context of a one-to-one relationship, a workshop, or a formal classroom situation. Several guidelines can help the social worker increase her or his effectiveness as a teacher:

- The adage "It hasn't been taught until it has been learned" underscores the difference between teaching and learning. Teaching activities are planned and controlled by the teacher, but learning is not. Learning occurs within the learner and is tied to such factors as motivation, ability, and readiness. The teacher's job is to find a way of engaging and motivating the learner to examine and consider the ideas and information being taught.

- That which we teach and learn falls into three broad categories: knowledge, beliefs and values, and skills. Of these three, knowledge is the easiest to teach because there is an agreed-on language to explain facts, concepts, and theories. This is not so when we focus on values and attitudes. Values and attitudes can be described and modeled by the teacher, but it is the learner who must decide whether to adopt or adapt them to his or her own belief system. Skills, such as values and attitudes, are best taught and learned through the use of modeling and demonstration.

- It is said that the truly educated person is one who has learned how to learn. How we learn varies with such factors as our sensory preferences (hearing, seeing, kinesthetic, etc.), our need for or resistance to structure and direction, our desire for either competition or cooperation, our tendency to move from the specific (parts) to the general (whole) or vice versa, our tendency to either break apart or build concepts, our need to read and write in order to learn, our preferences for either solitary or group learning, and so forth. An important first step in teaching, then, is to plan for differences in how people learn. An effective teacher must be prepared to use several different methods when teaching a single topic.

- When teaching, begin by identifying and teaching only essential terminology and concepts. The acquisition of specialized vocabulary is a fundamental step in the acquisition of new learning. However, too much information too soon can overload a learner. For example, before someone can learn to do the work of the social worker, she or he must first master the terminology and basic concepts related to the profession's values, roles, principles, and practice theories. The teacher, however, should carefully pace the introduction of new concepts in order to avoid having the learner shut down because of "information overload."

- Because skills and techniques have a behavioral component, they must be taught by way of demonstration and modeling. The learner must observe the skill and then perform and rehearse this skill in a real or simulated situation with supervision and coaching from the teacher. When teaching a skill, utilize the teaching model known as "watch one, do one, teach one." First, have the learners observe someone performing the skill activity, then have them do it, and, finally, have them teach it to someone else.

- When planning a class or training session, begin with an analysis of learner characteristics (e.g., developmental stage, formal education, prior experience) and the identification of the knowledge, values, and skills they are expecting (and will be expected) to learn. Then select the methods that are most likely to engage the learners and push and pull them toward the learning objectives.

- Review and consider using existing curricula and teaching materials, but realize that such materials nearly always need to be modified. Materials and methods that worked well with one group of learners may not work for others.

- To the extent possible, use teaching techniques that actively engage both the learner's mind and body (e.g., role-plays, simulation exercises, debates, and discussions). Reduce to a minimum the time spent in formal presentations. Lectures are among the least effective methods. In order to teach, we must attend to the learner's thinking, feelings, and behavior.

- Place emphasis on helping the learner immediately use the information, knowledge, or skill being taught. In the human services, the primary reason for learning is to do something with whatever has been learned. Thus, encourage the learner to ask "Why am I interested in this topic?" "What can I do with it?" "How can I apply it?" "How will it help me answer some other question or solve a problem?"

- Critically evaluate your teaching. We can assess our effectiveness as teachers on four levels:

    Level 1: Simply ask the learners if they liked it. This is the most commonly used method of evaluating teaching. The problem is that one can enjoy a class or a workshop, but learn little. Moreover, learning is not always an enjoyable experience.

    Level 2: Determine if the learners actually learned something new. Did they leave the session with knowledge or skills that they did not have when they began? To assess training at this second level, some type of pre-session and post-session testing is necessary.

    Level 3: Assuming that new learning occurred, then ask if the new knowledge and skills were used after the session. To assess training at this level, we need a follow-up system for monitoring the learner's behavior subsequent to the training session.

    Level 4: Finally, determine whether the learners' application of the new knowledge and skills had a positive impact on their lives or work. Unless what is learned has a real and a positive impact, the session was of little value no matter how enjoyable or how much was learned.

Selected Bibliography

Beebe, Steven, Timothy Mottet, and K. David Roach. *Training and Development.* Upper Saddle River, NJ: Pearson, 2013.

Heacox, Diane. *Differentiating Instruction in the Regular Classroom: How to Reach and Teach All Learners,* updated ed. Minneapolis, MN: Free Spirit, 2012.

Mulholland, Joan, and Chris Turnock. *Learning in the Workplace: A Toolkit for Facilitating Learning and Assessment in Health and Social Care Settings,* 2nd ed. New York: Routledge, 2013.

13.34 PREPARING A BUDGET

A budget is an important planning tool that lists an agency's anticipated income and expenditures during a designated period, usually one or two years. Typically, a budget will be revised several times during the period it is in use. A *preliminary budget* is often used to estimate expenses and serve as the basis for securing funding. That budget will be revised when firm commitments have been made by the funding sources. An *operating budget,* when approved by a legislative body (in the case of a public agency) or by a board of directors (in the case of a private agency), becomes the authorization for the agency's CEO or executive director to spend the amounts listed for each budget category. However, in the course of the budget period, there may be a shortfall in one or more income categories, unanticipated costs in expenditure categories, or emergent reasons to shift funds from one category to another. Given the relative fluidity of demand for services, agencies need the capacity to make changes in programming or staffing during budget periods.

When building a budget, several questions should be asked and answered:

- What agency goals and objectives are to be emphasized during the budget period?
- What types and how many employees are needed to carry out the agency's programs? What salaries and benefits are needed to attract and retain a competent staff? What liability or malpractice insurance is needed to protect the employees and the agency if problems arise? What ongoing training will be required for staff and volunteers—and what is the cost of that training?
- How might changes in program activities affect budget items such as numbers of staff with various competencies, training expenses, travel, supplies and equipment, consultation, and so on?
- What central office space and outreach locations are needed? What is required to keep the space clean, well-maintained, and safe? What will be the cost of rent, utilities, insurance, security, and so forth?
- What is required to develop and maintain community support for the agency such as printing and publications, postage, marketing materials, audits, and the like?
- What are the sources of income (e.g., agency fund-raising efforts, United Way, government appropriations, fees for service, grants, contracts, bequests) and how reliable is each as a base of support?
- If the budget must be cut at some later time, what reductions could be made that will do the least damage to the agency's capacity to carry out its mission?

In a stable organization, the budget should be built on past experience with allowance for anticipated changes in income or expenditures or to accommodate new programming. Since most human services agencies are highly labor intensive, the personnel aspects of the budget become the most critical to consider if any substantial change is anticipated. In addition, the constant tug between *efficiency* (cost per unit of service) and *effectiveness* (ability to achieve service objectives) should be addressed as part of the budgeting process.

Three types of budgeting are commonly found in human services agencies. Each yields different information about the cost of doing business.

1. LINE-ITEM BUDGETING

This type of budget is the most commonly used in social agencies. It requires that the various income and spending categories be identified and that the amount of money allocated to each category be stated. The accounting system of the agency is organized around these categories, making it possible to obtain a historical picture of the income and expenditures that will serve as the basis for projecting the future. Since a preliminary budget is a planning device, it must be prepared in advance of the year it will be in effect. In other words, next year's budget must be based on incomplete information about how well this year's budget estimated income and expenses. Thus, a preliminary line-item budget will reflect educated guesses about how each budget line will play out during the remainder of the current year and how it will change during the subsequent year.

Typically, the *income items* (revenue) included in a line-item budget would include any carryover funds (positive or negative) from the previous year, contract or grant funds, fees from services provided, and, if a private nonprofit agency, membership dues and contributions/gifts/bequests. The revenue for a public agency is essentially the allocation approved by elected officials such as a state's legislature and governor. The *personnel expenses* are usually the largest part of the budget and include salaries; employee benefits, such as insurance, retirement funds, and Social Security taxes; and fees for consultation and staff development. The ope*rating expenses* are related renting or maintaining office space, office supplies and equipment, telephone service, information technology support, any tangible goods (e.g., food, clothing) provided to clients, and travel required by staff.

The line-item budget must then be backed up by an audit report verifying the last year's actual income and expenditures and listing the amounts of any other assets, endowments, or building fund reserves that are excluded from the operating budget.

2. INCREMENTAL BUDGETING

Based on estimates of increases or decreases in revenue, a series of budget projections might be built on the basis of the current line-item budget. That is, using a "what-if?" approach, the expense items of a budget might be developed to reflect the impact of 2 and 5 percent income reductions, no change in revenue, or 2 and 5 percent revenue increases. An incremental budget is particularly helpful in reflecting the impact of gradual increases in salaries and utilities, as well as the implications of increases and decreases in revenue. Such a budget is also useful in assessing the cost of adjusting an organization's current program to provide new services.

3. PROGRAM OR FUNCTIONAL BUDGETING

A final type of budget used by social agencies is the program or functional budget. Again, this is built from a line-item budget and adds the feature of attributing portions of the total cost in each income and expense category to the various components or functions of agency operation. This approach makes it possible to estimate income and expenditures related to any function of the agency, thus providing a picture of the cost-effectiveness of that function.

Preparing a program budget involves estimating the distribution of income (e.g., fees, contributions) and expense items (e.g., salaries, operating expenses) according to their contribution to each of the various agency programs (e.g., adoption, foster care, family counseling).

Selected Bibliography

Finkler, Steven A. *Financial Management for Public, Health, and Not-for-Profit Organizations*, 4th ed. Upper Saddle River, NJ: Pearson, 2013.

Weikart, Lynne A., Greg G. Chen, and Ed Sermier. *Budgeting and Financial Management for Nonprofit Organizations: Using Money to Drive Mission Success*. Thousand Oaks, CA: Sage, 2013.

13.35 MARKETING AND FUND-RAISING FOR HUMAN SERVICES

Most social workers are not accustomed to thinking about their services as a product to be advertised, displayed, and sold. However, marketing increasingly is required of social agencies. Once the reputation of the agency or service is well known, it is then possible to convert the reputation into attracting clients, recruiting new staff and volunteers (see Item 10.13), and fund-raising to expand the financial base to further develop agency's services.

"The 5 Ps for Marketing Services" from 7th edition

MARKETING

Marketing, in this context, is a planned approach to informing both targeted audiences (stakeholders) and the general public of the accomplishments and capabilities of a human services agency—or the private practice of a social worker. When developing a marketing plan, consider the following important aspects of a marketing strategy.

- *Have confidence in the quality of services.* Successful salespeople are enthusiastic about their product. The most essential first step when marketing human services, then, is to truly believe that clients' lives are enhanced by the services the agency or social worker offers.

- *Make an analysis of the strengths and limitations of the services.* At a minimum, those marketing the services must be able to explain their merits in simple language and be prepared to back up these beliefs with data drawn from independent evaluations.

- *Make an analysis of reasons for interest in the services.* It is necessary to understand what attracts both clients and supporters to the agency and its services. The following are some questions that might be asked.

  What are the characteristics of those who use this service?
  Who are the community members most interested in having the agency succeed?
  How committed to the agency are the professional and support services staff members?

- *Identify the stakeholders.* In addition to marketing to the general public, it is useful to determine which subgroups are most likely to be interested in a particular program and target part of your marketing to them. For human services agencies, there are typically several stakeholders that a marketing strategy might address: board or advisory committee members; legislators; volunteers; clients, former clients, the family of clients; community influencers; and other supporters and contributors to the agency.

- *Create a brand.* Develop a symbol or image (e.g., photo, drawing, logo) that will visually represent the agency and create a positive feel about what the agency does. This might also include a *tag line* that captures the essence of the agency's mission, such as: "Changing the Lives of Homeless People."

- *Be explicit about the payoff for stakeholders.* The most important indication of success in human services is what people gain by supporting or using the services. When contributors or volunteers give their money and time, they are not able to give those dollars or hours to some other worthy cause. Thus, they need to know that their gifts are appreciated and will make a real difference in someone's life. For clients, the payoff is that they are treated with respect by all staff members and receive high-quality services to justify expending their time, money, and emotional investment with this agency.

- *Get out the message.* The final part of a marketing strategy is to be sure your message gets out to both stakeholders and the general public. Your goal is to keep people informed of the agency's services, which might be accomplished through speaking to various community civic, social, and religious groups, and becoming the subject of stories in newspapers and on TV.

"Dealing with the Media" from 7th edition

- *Keep your message current.* Today, most people wanting to learn about an agency or program first visit that agency's webpage or learn about it through social media such as Twitter or Facebook sites maintained by the agency. Central to your marketing strategy should be a high-quality **webpage** that is regularly maintained and is referenced in all printed materials. The following content might be included in a web page: a description of each program and service provided; how a potential client should request service; how someone could donate money or volunteer time; short case summaries of successful services; and an "about us" tab where information about the board and staff, as well as the most recent annual report, may be found. Periodically test the webpage with clients and other stakeholders, asking them to review and critique the page, and then revise and place the material on the Web.

FUND-RAISING

Closely associated with marketing is the development of a fund-raising plan. If a not-for-profit human services agency is to survive and develop its programs, it must have a secure and diversified funding base. In the final analysis, that depends on the willingness of people to contribute their money to the agency because the fees generated from vulnerable populations simply cannot cover the costs of delivering high-quality services. One aspect of **fund-raising**, or what some prefer to call *friend-raising*, refers to the identification and nurturance of those supporters who genuinely believe in the value of the agency and can be counted on to make a financial contribution to support its services year after year or possibly to provide for the agency through a bequest or inclusion in someone's will.

Agencies also supplement their programs through relatively small events for which a social worker might provide leadership. These local events include such activities as garage sales, silent auctions, dinners hosted by local restaurants, online fund-raisers, races on bicycles or by runners, cookie sales or cake auctions, a special performance by a local musical or theatre group, and so on. To be done well, these events take considerable planning and require support for volunteers committed to the agency's purpose.

On occasion, a major **fund-raising campaign** is planned in which funds to start a new program or build a facility are solicited. This requires a very different approach to fund-raising, and inexperienced agency personnel are seldom prepared for the demands and complexity of such a campaign. It takes time, energy, and know-how to successfully mount such a campaign. Moreover, such a campaign must compete with well-known, experienced, and sophisticated fund-raising agencies such as United Way or the American Red Cross.

Before attempting a major fund-raising campaign, the following questions should be considered.

- Is it possible to devote sufficient staff time to oversee this fund-raising activity without significantly compromising services to clients?
- Have the agency's marketing effort and other fund-raising activities provided a solid foundation for a capital campaign?
- Has sufficient time and expertise been devoted to the careful planning of the campaign? The creation of a feasible plan takes from many months to a year or more.
- Are key leaders in the community not only willing to make a contribution but also to personally ask others to contribute to the campaign?
- Is there the likelihood of sufficient initial financial commitments from a few selected donors and enough funds included in the agency's budget to cover the costs of the campaign?
- If indicated, will the agency seriously consider hiring professional fund-raising consultation to guide the campaign activities?

"Fund-Raising for a Human Services Agency" from 9th edition

To initiate a successful a campaign, the agency must begin by setting a realistic goal in terms of people involved and amount of dollars to be raised; selecting a respected community leader to head the campaign; spelling out an overall plan and timetable for accomplishing the many tasks of recruiting and training campaign workers, preparing materials, and asking for contributions; maintaining accurate records; and so on.

When planning a campaign, remember, too, that many people are hesitant to ask others for money, but that is what fund-raising is all about. It is best if people have already given their fair share before they ask others for money. Small amounts of money can be raised by mail, email, and telephone campaigns, but big money is raised through face-to-face contact with the donor. People are more likely to donate money if asked by a friend or a respected individual. As a general rule, big donors are mostly giving to the person who has asked, rather than to a cause or a program. It is critically important that the right person ask another for money and that the request be made in the right way, for the right reason, and at the right time.

Selected Bibliography

Andreasen, Alan R., and Philip Kotler. *Strategic Marketing for Nonprofit Organizations,* 7th ed. Upper Saddle River, NJ: Pearson/Prentice-Hall, 2008.

Bray, Ilona. *Effective Fund-Raising for Nonprofits: Real-World Strategies that Work,* 4th ed. Berkeley, CA: Nolo, 2013.

Dunham, Sarah. *Brandraising: How Nonprofits Raise Visibility and Money through Smart Communications.* San Francisco: Jossey-Bass, 2010.

Klein, Kim. *Reliable Fundraising in Unreliable Times: What Good Causes Need to Know to Survive and Thrive.* San Francisco: Jossey-Bass, 2010.

Madia, Sherrie A. *The Social Media Survival Guide for Nonprofits and Charitable Organizations: How to Build Your Base of Support and Fast-Track Your Fund-raising Efforts Using Social Media.* Voorhees, NJ: Full Court Press, 2011.

Rosen, Rudolph A. *Money for the Cause: A Complete Guide to Event Fund-Raising.* College Station: TX: Texas A&M University Press, 2012.

Warwick, Mal, with Eric Overman. *How to Write Successful Fund-Raising Appeals*, 3rd ed. San Francisco: Jossey-Bass, 2013.

13.36 DEVELOPING GRANT APPLICATIONS

The resources available to a social agency are usually fully committed for operating existing programs, and any incremental increases in funds obtained each year are often consumed by normal salary increases and inflation. The opportunity to demonstrate or test program innovations or conduct research on some aspect of the agency's program frequently cannot be done without the infusion of grant funds. A social worker who is knowledgeable about locating potential grant funds, able to facilitate the work of key staff members to identify ideas and information to include in a grant application, and skilled at preparing such applications is a valuable asset to his or her agency.

Before beginning the grant-writing process, three prerequisites must be met. First, the idea or program innovation to be demonstrated or studied must be sound and clearly thought out. Second, the agency's administrators and governing body must be committed to the idea. Finally, an assessment of the competence and capacity of the staff members and the agency to carry out the proposed activity must indicate it is likely that this work can be successfully completed. The person or team involved in grant development should be prepared to invest considerable up-front time and effort into preparing a grant application, which frequently must be done in addition to ongoing work assignments. Yet, obtaining grant funding is often the only way to significantly improve services.

SOURCES OF GRANT FUNDING

A variety of funding sources might be considered. Sometimes, a local business will underwrite a project that is of interest to it. A computer company, for example, might donate equipment to demonstrate the potential effectiveness of a computerized interagency referral network. Other times, a group of persons interested in a project might undertake a fund-raising effort to provide funds to help support this activity. However, the primary sources for a project are grants from government agencies or private foundations.

Government grant

The largest amount of grant money is available through agencies of the federal government, although states may also allocate such funds. Most government grants relate to areas that the sponsoring agency has defined to reflect its priorities. The public is notified of available funding through a *Request for Proposals (RFP)* or *Request for Applications (RFA)*. Grant applications are then reviewed by a panel of experts and awarded on a competitive basis. Some discretionary funds may also be available to allow for innovative program ideas that are not currently among the granting agency's established priorities. Before investing much time and energy in developing a proposal, it is helpful to discuss your ideas with staff members of the government agencies who administer the funds in your area of interest (e.g., aging, child welfare, AIDS). These individuals can help you assess the fit between your proposal and the agency's interest and provide other helpful information about the application process.

If applying to the federal government, two published sources of information are particularly useful regarding grant possibilities. The *Catalog of Federal Domestic Assistance* contains a comprehensive listing and description of federal programs. Programs are cross-referenced by function (e.g., housing, health, welfare), by subject (e.g., drug abuse, economic development), and by the federal agency that administers the program. The description of each program includes information such as restrictions on the use of funds, eligibility requirements for applying, and the application and award process. A second source is the *Federal Register*. It is published every government working day and contains notices, rules and regulations, guidelines, and proposed rules and regulations for every federal grant-giving agency. Both the *Catalog of Federal Domestic Assistance* and the *Federal Register* are available through many libraries and on the Internet.

Private foundations

A more likely source for the small grants is a private foundation. Most foundations develop specialized areas of interest, and some make monies available only for programs located in a specific geographic region. Perhaps the most helpful source is *The Foundation Directory*. Part 1 of that directory includes those foundations that give away more than $200,000 per year, and Part 2 contains those that give smaller amounts. The Foundation Center periodically publishes a series of specialized directories of grant sources that are focused on areas such as children, youth, and families; aging; the economically disadvantaged; health; and women and girls. Another directory, The *Directory of Corporate and Foundation Givers*, provides background information about potential funding sources in the private sector. Many local libraries and universities will have copies of these publications. Once a foundation is identified that appears to be a good match with your interest, go to that foundation's website where considerable information on their selection criteria and application process is listed.

GUIDELINES FOR DEVELOPING A PROPOSAL

The planning and preparation of a proposal is a labor-intensive process. Make sure you have the necessary time and motivation. A hastily written proposal, or the so-called *all-purpose proposal* that is indiscriminately sent to a number of funding sources, has little chance of success. Several guidelines are important to your application for a specific grant:

- *Do your homework.* Make a thorough study of the potential funding source (foundation or government agency) before deciding to submit a proposal. Pay special attention to the published funding priorities, history of prior awards, eligibility requirements, geographical limitations, type and size of grants available, funding cycle, process for selection, and so on. Secure the name, address, and phone number for the contact person should you have questions.

- *Make informal inquiries.* Save time for yourself and for the funding agency by informally inquiring about its possible interest in your ideas. However, assume that the recipient of your inquiry is busy, skeptical, not especially interested in your problems, and faced with many more requests than he or she can evaluate thoroughly, let alone fund. Be very businesslike in your approach and be prepared to describe your proposal clearly and concisely in one or two pages or in five minutes on the phone. If you think you will be making an application, request an application packet and all relevant instructions.

- *Write the proposal.* Study the instructions in the funding agency's guidelines and follow them to the letter, addressing every section or question. You should anticipate answering at least the following questions:

  ▪ What do you want to do, how much will it cost, and how long will it take?

  ▪ How does the proposed project relate to the funding agency's interests and priorities?

  ▪ Are you aware of other projects like the one you are proposing and how is yours similar or different? (You will need a good literature search.)

  ▪ How do you plan to carry out the project? Does your staff have the necessary training and experience? Why are you particularly well-prepared to conduct this project, rather than someone else?

  ▪ Who stands to benefit from the proposed project? What impact will it have on your agency, clients, community, state, or nation? How will you measure, evaluate, and report the impact?

  ▪ If successful, how will you continue the work after the grant support has ended?

  ▪ The written proposal must be very clear and well organized, with justification for the various expenditures described in detail. Often, the proposal cannot exceed a certain number of pages and has a firm closing date. Usually the closing date is a designated postmark, but sometimes the proposal must be in the hands of the granting agency either physically or electronically by that date. Also, if a team is writing a proposal, designate one person who will have final authority to edit the materials into a coherent document.

- *Be a good salesperson for your project.* Your written proposal and/or oral presentation should reflect knowledge, enthusiasm, and commitment. Focus your proposal on its alignment with the funder's goals and how you can contribute to clients or improve the provision of human services beyond your existing program if you are funded. Coming across as helpless and needy (e.g., "We really, really need the money") will pretty much assure that you will not be funded. However, if those selecting proposals to be funded become convinced that the people associated with the program are capable and responsible, they may work especially hard on finding a way to fund the proposal. Obtaining letters of support from related agencies and key people in your community might help sell your proposal. Ask these supporters to address specific areas of the proposal (e.g., the need, the agency's history of sound management, the staff's ability to carry out the project, community support for the program).

- *Be accountable.* If you receive the grant requested, be prepared to carry out the project according to your written plan and within the proposed budget. The acceptance of a grant carries with it the responsibility for managing the money properly, submitting regular progress reports, reporting project results, and giving appropriate credit to the funding source. Good stewardship of the grant funds is very important and is essential if future grant requests from that source are to be funded.

Proposal contents

Stress the quality of what you can do with grant support, as opposed to stressing why you have not done it before. Remember that your proposal is in competition for scarce grant resources and that it will be evaluated against the criteria set out in guidelines. In general, the following components will be expected:

- *Cover page.* Include the project title, principal investigators, name of agency, dates for project activity, total budget request, and signatures of authorized agency personnel approving the application.
- *Abstract.* Prepare a short statement of the objectives and procedures to be used, methods of evaluation, and plan for disseminating results.
- *Statement of problem and objectives.* Indicate the rationale for this project and prepare a clear statement of the objectives in measurable terms.
- *Methodology, procedures, and activities.* Describe the design and approach of the project, identify who will be served, and discuss the administrative structure for the project. Lay out a clear plan of action with phases and dates for each activity. The use of Gantt and PERT charts (see Item 12.12) can help make processes and timelines clear to reviewers.
- *Evaluation methods.* Describe how the results or outcomes of the activity will be assessed. Your application will be strengthened if the evaluators are not directly associated with your agency or personally invested in the outcome of your project.
- *Dissemination of results.* Indicate how the results of the project will be disseminated so that others can benefit from the knowledge gained from this activity.
- *Personnel and facilities.* Describe the staff required to carry out the project, include short resumés of key personnel who will be assigned to this activity, and indicate how any new staff will be selected. Also, describe any special equipment required, and indicate how the agency will make space available to accommodate project activities.
- *Budget justification.* Provide a detailed budget of the anticipated costs of the project and an explanation or justification for those expenditures. Indicate what will be required from the funding source and what will be contributed by the agency or other sources. Many funding sources require that matching funds from local sources be identified as a requirement for funding. In some instances, a cash match is required, but in others, in-kind contributions (e.g., staff time or office space) are acceptable. A budget will usually include personnel costs (including fringe benefits), outside consultants or evaluators for the project, consumable materials (supplies, printing, postage, etc.), equipment, travel, and indirect costs. The latter includes the real costs to an agency (space, heat, light, etc.) consumed by the project staff that cannot readily be documented. Some public agencies limit indirect cost to as little as 8 to 15 percent of the project expenses and some foundations do not allow charging for any indirect costs. Also, be prepared to describe what will happen to the project after the grant funding has ended.

Selected Bibliography

Catalog of Federal Domestic Assistance. Available online: www.cfda.gov.

Coley, Soraya, and Cynthia Scheinberg. *Proposal Writing: Effective Grantsmanship,* 4th ed. New York: Springer, 2013.

Directory of Corporate and Foundation Givers. Washington, DC: Taft Group, most recent edition.

Farqui, Saadia. *Best Practices in Grant Seeking: Beyond the Proposal.* Sudbury, MA: Jones and Bartlett, 2011.

Federal Register. Available online: www.gpoaccess.gov/fr/index.html.

Greever, Jane C. *The Foundation Center's Guide to Proposal Writing*, 6th ed. New York: The Foundation Center, 2012.

O'Neal-McElrath, Tori. *Winning Grants Step-by-Step: The Complete Workbook for Planning, Developing, and Writing Successful Proposals*, 4th ed. San Francisco: Jossey-Bass, 2013.

13.37 ORGANIZING NEIGHBORHOODS AND COMMUNITIES

In recent years right-wing politics has tried to brand social activism and community organizing as somehow anti-American and a threat to the proper order of society. In reality, such activity is democracy at its very best. Neighborhood and community organizing brings people together so their voices can be heard and so they can bring about needed change. Community organizing is especially important in efforts to assist the poor, marginalized, and disenfranchised to make their concerns known to elected official and other decision makers.

Facilitating progressive change in the social structures of our neighborhoods and communities requires the social worker to become an **activist**—in other words, have skill in organizing people to identify and address the sources or causes of a particular problem or concern, and then to mount strategic change efforts to address and rectify the problem. Changing the status quo is sure to find opposition. Thus, the activist must be skilled in dealing with and resolving conflict.

Issues and problems that are deeply imbedded in societal structures and culture can be addressed only through very broad social change efforts best described as **movements**. These efforts require skills in national or statewide organization that attempt to change the public's basic thinking and understanding of the issues at stake. Some examples that have been of special concern to social workers include the Civil Rights Movement, the Women's Movement, the Community Mental Health Movement, and the Gay Rights Movement. Some social workers may be a part of local organizing efforts affiliated with a movement, but few would be in the role of orchestrating the movement's overall actions.

More typically, social workers are involved in neighborhood and community efforts to bring about social change locally. Unlike some other parts of the world, in the United States relatively few social workers have jobs that focus primarily on neighborhoods or communities. Rather, U.S. social workers are largely concerned with individuals, families, groups, and sometimes organizations. However, when social workers provide services to a number of people experiencing similar issues, it becomes clear that something more than an individual's characteristics or choices are at the root of the issue. For example: "Why are so many African American males in jails and prisons?" "What is behind the violence against people who are gay or lesbian?" "Why is the suicide rate so high for older males?" "Why are so many people homeless?" "What are the reasons so many Hispanic high school graduates cannot secure resources to attend college?"

Two forms of organizing characterize social workers' efforts to affect community and neighborhood change. One form has been labeled **community organization**. This is largely interagency work or efforts to strengthen the service delivery system in the neighborhood or community at large. Due to social workers' unique focus among the professions to aid people in using the resources in their communities, social workers become keenly aware of the difficulties clients have in accessing services, as well as recognizing the gaps in services where there simply are not sufficient resources. This change effort, then, is largely interagency work. The skills required for this work include leading small-group meetings (see Item 13.26), sometimes chairing committees (see Item 13.29), helping groups of interested people problem-solve about the issue (see Item 13.30), and engaging in community advocacy (see Item 13.32).

At a more grassroots level, social workers help facilitate the efforts of people who experience an issue to come together to better understand the causes and plan strategies to remedy, or at least decrease, the impact of the issue. This form of organization is known as **neighborhood** or **community development** with the goal of increasing *social justice* for local people. Depending on the issue, this might involve energizing people living in a neighborhood (e.g., trailer park, ghetto, or barrio) or it might require engaging people from throughout a community concerned with a specific social problem (e.g., various expressions of discrimination, restricted access to public resources, or poverty). This approach to social work practice leans heavily on the principle of *empowerment* (see Chapter 5), where the social worker facilitates the change-oriented activities of the people most affected by the issue.

Two goals are dominant in this neighborhood/community development work: (1) helping individuals from the community recognize and develop their own skills of leadership and (2) helping those from the community address the issues and problems that concern them. For the social worker, this is essentially behind-the-scenes activity where she or he is mostly involved in gathering information and providing guidance to those in the leadership roles, but only if and when advice is requested. The skills critical to this role are critical thinking, building up people's strengths and talents, and the basic communication skills discussed in Chapter 8. Typically, this type of social work practice begins with the formation of a group that will likely disband after the issue is resolved. In some cases, an initial success gives rise to the formation of a formal organization that will address still other issues of importance to the local community.

Selected Bibliography

DeFilippis, James, Robert Fisher, and Eric Shragge. *Contesting Community: The Limits and Potential of Local Organizing.* New Brunswick, NJ: Rutgers University Press, 2010.

Homan, Mark. *Promoting Community Change*, 5th ed. Independence, KY: Cengage, 2011.

Kahn, Si. *Creative Community Organizing: A Guide for Rabble-Rousers, Activists, and Quiet Lovers of Justice.* San Francisco: Berrett Koehler, 2012.

Netting, F. Ellen, Peter M. Kettner, and Steven L. McMurtry. *Social Work Macro Practice*, 5th ed. Upper Saddle River, NJ: Pearson, 2012.

Weil, Marie, Michael S. Reisch, and Mary L. Ohmer, eds. *The Handbook of Community* Practice, 2nd ed. Thousand Oaks, CA: Sage, 2013.

13.38 INFLUENCING LEGISLATORS AND OTHER DECISION MAKERS

Decisions made at the local, state, and national levels by elected representatives and other public officials have substantial impact on the human services. Because social workers are in a unique position to observe how public social policy helps or hinders the most vulnerable members of society, their perspective should be articulated to legislators and other community decision makers so that client needs and concerns are not overlooked.

When planning an effort to influence a decision maker, the worker should keep several guidelines in mind. First, a social worker is more likely to influence a decision when he or she has an established relationship with the decision maker. Although it takes time and considerable effort to build these relationships, the worker should make a point to cultivate such relationships before attempting to influence a particular decision. Second, the decision maker is more likely to be influenced by the worker if she or he presents information that can be trusted. The social worker should make a careful analysis of the issue before attempting to influence the decision makers (see Item 11.26). Never distort the facts or give information that cannot be substantiated, nor should you initiate contact before you are thoroughly prepared to discuss the matter. Finally, the worker should be selective about the issues presented to decision makers. One's credibility with decision makers can be diminished if too many issues are addressed. In short, when formulating an approach, the worker should remember that decision makers are most likely to be persuaded by persons they perceive as well-informed, competent, engaging, and genuinely committed to the issue.

Sometimes social workers must work through others who are in a better position to exercise influence over decision makers. At other times, however, the worker should directly communicate with the decision maker through personal contact, in writing, or both.

VISITING WITH A POLICYMAKER

Many legislators and other key decision makers spend their time in a somewhat restricted environment; they speak primarily with their staff, lobbyists, and colleagues. Hence, they often welcome the opportunity to hear the positions of people who have firsthand knowledge of issues they must decide. This communication might occur by attending a legislator's open forum or town meeting or by talking individually with the decision maker. Sometimes, when it is difficult to schedule a face-to-face meeting with a decision maker, communication with her or his aide or advisor can be almost as effective.

The following guidelines can help to make visits with decision makers (or their advisors) productive:

- *Use time efficiently.* The decision maker's time is valuable. If you are to get that person's full attention and have a favorable climate for communicating your information, you must be efficient. When planning an individual meeting, schedule an appointment in advance and ask that a specific amount of time be reserved for the meeting. Be on time, even though you may have to wait for the legislator to complete other responsibilities before meeting with you. Also, get to the point quickly. Have your presentation planned so that you can pack a lot of information into a short time period.

- *Be positive.* Begin on a friendly note. Find a reason to praise the decision maker for some action taken in relation to prior contacts (if appropriate) and thank him or her for being willing to take time to hear your position on this matter.

- *Express your conviction.* Let the legislator know that, as a social worker, you are in a unique position to recognize the implications of this decision. Leave no doubt in the legislator's mind that you believe in what you are proposing. Back up your view with facts and examples. If the information is at all detailed, prepare a handout that can be left with the decision maker and others who may be present.

- *Be specific.* Be very sure that the person knows what you want her or him to do. For example, do you simply want the person to understand the situation better? Do you want her or him to propose an amendment to a piece of legislation? Do you want her or him to vote for or against a particular bill?

- *Follow up in writing.* Send or leave a statement that reflects your position and provides the facts that you presented. The purpose of this document is to supply material that will be placed in the legislator's file on the topic and to serve as a reminder of your position when it is time to take action. Be sure that your name, street address, email address, and telephone number are on the materials so you can be contacted to clarify points or provide information on related matters.

WRITING OR EMAILING A POLICYMAKER

Although face-to-face contact is probably the most effective way to influence a legislator or other decision maker, many times that is not possible because of constraints of time, distance, resources, or the availability of the decision maker. Letters, fax messages, emails, and telephone calls, when properly timed, can also be effective in influencing decisions. The mailing address, email address, and telephone numbers of public officials will usually be listed in newspapers or are readily available through an Internet search. Locating other officials may require more research.

Observe these guidelines when writing to a decision maker:

- *Be accurate.* Be sure that you use the correct spelling of the person's name, the proper title, and the accurate address. Be sure that the decision maker has correct information about you in case he or she wants to respond to your communication.

- *Be brief and to the point.* Limit your communication to one page. Focus only on one issue or piece of legislation in each communication. If you are interested in several matters, send separate correspondence so each can be filed with materials about those matters.

- *Clearly identify the issue or bill that concerns you.* Provide identifying details (e.g., the bill's number, name, and dates) so there can be no misunderstanding of what you are writing about.

- *Write simply and clearly.* Remember that those who will read your material are very busy and may receive hundreds of letters and emails each day. Make it easy for them to understand the points you wish to make.

- *Begin in a positive manner.* Address the legislator in a respectful manner and use titles appropriate to the office. If possible, relate the preferred action on this matter to other positions he or she has supported.

- *Provide facts and figures that support your position.* Explain the impact of the decision and how many people will be affected. Short case examples are often effective in helping the legislator understand how the issue affects individuals.

- *Clearly identify the action you desire.* Make sure the reader knows what you want to happen (e.g., vote for HR 254, oppose the filibuster of SB 1543).

- *Pay attention to timing.* Be sure to time communicating your opinion to just precede the debate on the topic. Typically, a legislator will make up his or her mind early in the hearing process and long before time for a final vote.

- *Follow up the action.* After the decision or vote is completed, write again, thanking the legislator for considering your viewpoint if she or he took the action you requested. If not, express regret about that action. Such follow-up reminds the person that you are truly concerned about the issue and will continue to observe his or her actions on this matter.

Selected Bibliography

Hardina, Donna. *Interpersonal Social Work Skills for Community Practice.* New York: Springer, 2013.

Haynes, Karen, and James Mickelson. *Affecting Change: Social Workers in the Political Arena,* 7th ed. Upper Saddle River, NJ: Pearson, 2010.

Richan, Willard C. *Lobbying for Social Change*, 3rd ed. New York: Haworth, 2006.

14

Evaluation and Termination

LEARNING OBJECTIVES

At the conclusion of this chapter, the reader should be prepared to:

- Demonstrate the ability to select valid numerical data, create rating scales, and/or use established (standardized) scales to measure client change during an intervention.
- Discuss the merits and issues involved when assessing a social work intervention when using the following assessment tools: Service Plan Outcome Checklist, Task Achievement Scaling, Goal Attainment Scaling, or Single Subject Designs.
- Recognize the importance of carefully terminating professional relationships and give attention to the possible effects of the termination on the client and other affected persons.
- Identify the need for agencies to utilize tools of program evaluation to update their programs and respond to the continually changing demand for services.
- Express commitment to obtaining regular evaluation information from current and former clients of the social worker's and agency's services.

Every helping relationship must end. Services to individuals and families must be concluded and groups or committees must eventually be disbanded. Furthermore, responsible social work practice ends with a final evaluation of the successes and failures of the intervention.

Termination is that important final phase in helping clients—the time when the worker guides the concluding activities in a manner that is sensitive to issues surrounding the ending of a relationship. If a meaningful relationship has been formed between client and worker (a key to successful helping), it is not surprising that this ending phase is often experienced with mixed emotions—for both the client and the social worker. One common reaction is that the client and worker are pleased that their work together has been concluded. Consequently, the client will no longer need to invest time, resources, and emotional energy in the change process and the worker can move on to new responsibilities. A competing emotion is the sense of loss. Clients sometimes feel anger, rejection, sadness, and anxiousness when the relationship ends. Thus, the worker must provide an opportunity for the client to express his or her feelings and concerns and the worker must lay the groundwork for a resumption of service in the future, should that be needed.

Occasionally, service will unexpectedly end at a time other than that originally planned or expected by the worker and client. For example, an abrupt termination may occur in these circumstances:

- The client, for personal or financial reasons, decides to stop participating.
- The worker accepts employment elsewhere or transfers to a different position in the agency.
- The helping process is blocked by a problem or conflict in the worker–client relationship necessitating transfer to another worker.
- The client requires specialized services that are best provided by another social worker, professional, or agency.

If the termination is prompted by the worker or agency, the worker should clearly explain what is happening and why. If the client simply stops participating, the worker should attempt to make a final contact to bring their relationship to an amicable closure.

Also, a final **evaluation** should occur at the conclusion of the change process. At this time, the degree of client change is measured and the social worker assesses the success of the intervention. The growing impact of various funding sources on the practice of social work today, coupled with an already important obligation for accountability to clients, agencies, and the community, makes it imperative that social workers are skilled at evaluating their practice. As compared to the ongoing monitoring that occurs throughout the helping process, the final evaluation occurs during or after termination.

Two forms of evaluation are of primary concern to the social worker. **Direct-practice evaluation** is the assessment of the interventions and their impact on a specific client (e.g., an individual, family, or small group). This evaluation can serve two purposes. It can be *formative evaluation*, which is used to inform and guide the ongoing practice decisions related to the intervention and, as such, is a tool for monitoring and changing the planned intervention when necessary. Direct-practice evaluation can also be a *summative evaluation*, in which one assesses the final outcome, identifies the factors that contributed to the relative success or failure of the intervention, and many times serves as the basis of a final report to a referring agency or funding source.

The second form, **program evaluation**, attempts to evaluate the effectiveness and efficiency of a program that serves many clients or perhaps even a whole community. Program evaluation, too, can be both formative and summative. It is formative if it is used for assessing a program and changing aspects of its functioning to better serve the agency's clients or community. It is summative when, for example, it is used to report the results of a demonstration program to an agency's board or a funding source.

The planning of an evaluation should begin at the point when the intervention's goals and approach are selected. Unless the desired outcomes are specified and measured in the early phases of the change process, the worker will not be able to adequately judge any change that may have occurred. Additionally, the worker must specify the criteria by which to measure the variables (e.g., improvement in client behaviors, cost of additional agency services) that are expected to change during the intervention.

The perception reflected here is that social work practice is all about change—helping clients change, helping their environments change, and helping agencies or communities change. The philosophy behind the evaluation of social work practice, then, is that the change that occurs during a practice intervention can be measured based on the following logic:

- If a social problem or negative social condition does not exist, then there is no need for intervention.
- If a problem or negative situation does exist, then it exists in some quantity (e.g., frequency, intensity, or duration) and can, therefore, be described and measured.
- If it can be measured, then it is possible to measure or document the degree to which it changes over time.

In short, the outcomes of all social work practice can be evaluated. The challenge is to figure out how to measure the client condition(s) and determine the amount of change that occurred.

When deciding how to measure change in client functioning, the social worker should consider the following factors and questions:

- *Validity.* Does the measurement procedure actually measure what it is assumed or believed to measure?
- *Reliability.* Does the procedure yield similar results when the measurement is repeated under similar circumstances?
- *Ease of application.* Is the procedure sufficiently brief, easy to use, and understandable to the nonspecialist?
- *Sensitivity.* Is the measurement procedure able to detect relatively small levels of change and degrees of difference?
- *Nonreactivity.* Can the procedure detect differences without modifying or influencing the phenomena being measured?

When selecting standardized measurement tools, the social worker should review the manuals that accompany the instrument or published articles about the tool's development to obtain descriptions of how it is appropriately used, its strengths and limitations, and its psychometric properties. If this information is not available and no comparable instrument can be found, the social worker should make only tentative and cautious judgments based on the measurement.

The measurement techniques included in this chapter can be used for both monitoring practice and making a comprehensive or final assessment of the intervention activity. Thus, these techniques could be placed in either Chapter 13 or Chapter 14 of this book. Due to the large number of intervention techniques reported in Chapter 13, these measurement techniques are located in this chapter to give them more visibility.

SECTION A

TECHNIQUES AND GUIDELINES FOR DIRECT PRACTICE

The social worker is ethically obliged to be accountable for the quality of services provided. The *NASW Code of Ethics* recognizes that social workers should monitor and evaluate their practice activities (Section 5.02.a). In addition, it is important, when possible, to engage clients in the review of the intervention, to encourage them to judge the success and usefulness of the experience from their vantage point, and to express their thoughts on the worker's performance. From this information, the worker can more accurately assess his or her practice successes and failures and, where appropriate, seek consultation or training to enhance the quality of future practice.

Evaluation activities

There is a growing emphasis on the need for data-based or *empirical evaluation* of social work practice, suggesting that social workers should become *practitioners/scientists*. This development is not without controversy. Five primary themes are reflected in this debate:

1. It is argued that social work intervention is primarily an act of human caring and that the whole person cannot be broken down into discrete components and measured in any meaningful way, as those components are interdependent. Proponents of direct-practice evaluation, however, argue that people come to social workers for help with specific problems and conditions, and that change in the client's situation is what determines if the intervention was effective.

2. Opponents of empirical evaluation contend that it is time consuming to select or design measurement scales, collect and analyze data, and then interpret the results—all of which take valuable time away from interactions with clients. Those on the other side of the debate contend that much of the data needed for evaluation will usually have already been gathered for purposes of assessment and monitoring. The only additional time needed is to organize the data in a way that allows systematic analysis. Once the worker develops the skill, it takes little additional time to empirically evaluate an intervention. Moreover, because the evaluation process can often actively engage the client, it can help increase the client's motivation and involvement in the change process.

3. Some who object to empirical practice evaluation suggest that only a relatively few social workers and agency administrators have the skills needed to implement this type of evaluation. Proponents, however, contend that the profession cannot wait around for some future generation of social workers to be trained in the use of these evaluation techniques. Given the demands from managed-care companies and the general public for evidence that social work interventions are effective, the profession must move quickly to adopt systematic evaluation as a regular component of practice.

4. Opponents of evaluation also contend that because systematic data collection and evaluation is not yet a common activity or what clients usually expect, the clients will resist this practice. However, those supporting such evaluation contend that it is usually the social workers, not the clients, who resist collecting the data. Most clients are accustomed to physicians measuring and recording changes in their body temperature, blood pressure, and weight—or even asking for a patient's judgment on a 1 to 10 scale regarding less quantifiable factors, such as how much pain is being experienced. For the clients there is little difference between being asked by a social worker to record, for example, the number of anger outbursts experienced in a week or completing a questionnaire that measures the level of marital conflict, and keeping a record of changes in one's temperature or blood pressure for a physician.

5. Some social scientists contend that it is not possible to arrive at clear cause-and-effect conclusions from the methodologies available for the evaluation of a social work intervention. These scientists suggest that (a) there is too little control over extraneous variables, (b) the evaluation designs and procedures must be adapted to unique client situations (thus minimizing one's ability to generalize the results to other cases), (c) the range of designs is too limited to accommodate the breadth of social work practice, and (d) the conclusions are suspect because the social worker, as a practitioner/scientist, cannot remain sufficiently objective. Proponents don't disagree, but counter that this form of evaluation is not intended to yield the same kind of information as traditional research, and the results should not be generalized to other clients. Rather, these methods are primarily intended to help assess one social worker's intervention with one client (or group of clients). Also, proponents call for caution in concluding that the measures alone provide sufficient evidence to prove that an intervention by itself *caused* a change in a client's attitudes, behaviors, or actions. Additional information would be needed to arrive at a genuine cause-and-effect conclusion. Even so, those supporting empirical evaluation conclude that it is valuable for what it can measure—for example, to substantiate that the client or situation did change, that the change occurred following introduction of a specific intervention, or that the client's condition improved and that the improvement was sustained over time.

These basic criticisms of the empirical evaluation of social work practice should signal the worker to be cautious not to overestimate the power of the data to predict outcomes. The data should supplement, rather than replace, other indicators of effectiveness. The worker can feel most confident about client change when the empirical data is consistent with her or his own practice observations, the client's self-reports and perceptions, and the views of collateral resources or observers, such as family members or other professionals. If at least three perceptions are comparable (i.e., *triangulation*), the social worker can feel relatively confident about the results.

When collecting data to be used in the evaluation of a direct-services intervention, the social worker should follow these guidelines:

- *The informed consent of the client should be sought.* The client should be fully informed about how the data will be collected and used, and should give his or her consent for participation in the evaluation process (*NASW Code of Ethics,* Section 5.02.e). Clients may fear that the data collected could potentially be used against them—for example, by a court, school, or family member—and should have the right to refuse to supply this information. In addition to the obvious ethical matter of collecting and maintaining such information without client permission, it is also unlikely that useful data will be obtained if the client is not a willing and active participant in the process.

- *Practice requirements should take precedence over data collection.* It is sometimes tempting to structure and manipulate service delivery in a way that makes it easier to collect the data needed for evaluation. But compromising client services for the purpose of evaluation (e.g., delaying needed intervention to obtain baseline scores, continuing services beyond the client's needs to obtain additional data) is not in the best interest of the client and thus should be avoided.

- *The research questions to be answered through the practice evaluation should be viewed as fluid.* The traditional research process begins with identifying the research questions or hypotheses, selecting the methods for data collection, determining the sampling process for selecting the respondents to provide data, and so on. There is little flexibility once the process is begun. By contrast, direct-practice evaluation begins with developing a service plan for an individual, family, or group and only after that is established are the research questions generated, the measurement tools selected, and the evaluation design adopted. The range of questions one might attempt to answer could relate to measuring change concerning:

  - *The client.* A fundamental purpose of monitoring and evaluating practice is to determine if the client was, in fact, helped to make the needed or desired change. For example: If change occurred, was the change in the desired direction? If a family or a group showed positive change, did each member also experience positive change? Did the client accomplish the agreed-upon tasks? To what extent did the client achieve his or her goals? If more than one client condition was being addressed, was their similar change in all conditions? Was the change sustained after termination?

  - *The intervention.* We sometimes want to study the effectiveness of the particular interventions we use. We might ask questions such as these: To what extent did the intervention approach yield the desired change? If the client participated in several interventions or services, was one more effective than another? Was an intervention more effective when used alone or in combination with other interventions? With what types of clients or under what circumstances is a particular intervention effective or ineffective?

  - *The worker.* We also may want to use practice evaluation as a means of answering questions about ourselves and the success of our service provision—for instance, to what extent do my clients achieve their goals? Do I provide some services more successfully than others? In what components of my practice do I need to seek improvement?

  Also, unlike traditional research, the questions one attempts to answer may change as the practice situation unfolds. For example, a client's service plan may begin with the premise that a particular intervention approach will be the best means of serving a client, but as the worker monitors the client's progress it may become apparent that a different approach should be tried. As the collection of measurement data continues, the questions asked of a direct-service evaluation may need to be altered as the service plan is adjusted.

- *The evaluation design should be viewed as changeable.* Once the questions to be answered by the evaluation have been framed, the worker can select the most appropriate ways to measure change in the dependent variables (i.e., the client's actions, emotions, behaviors) and establish the process by which measurements will be taken, organized, and analyzed.

A critical feature of any evaluation is to identify and accurately measure the variables or factors in the client's life that the intervention is intended to change. One form of measurement is to count and record *numerical data*, such as school attendance, acts of violent behavior, number of family arguments, and so on (see Item 14.1). A second form of measurement is to develop a tool specifically tailored to the issues or problems faced by the particular client or an *individualized scale* (see Item 14.2). Finally, in some cases, scales may already exist that will accurately measure the factors being considered (see Item 14.3). These *standardized scales* might be utilized both to initially assess the client and periodically measure changes in the client's condition.

As a guideline for selecting any of these tools for measuring client change, consider the following questions.

- Will I get accurate data?
- Will the data be at least at the ordinal (or ranked data) level so that progression or regression can be identified?
- Can the measurement process meaningfully involve the client?
- Is using this tool feasible (e.g., cost, time, agency approval, language)?
- Is this measurement tool applicable to this client or population group (e.g., sensitive to culture, age, developmental level, reading competence)?
- Are there ethical issues in using this measure?
- Will the measure yield valid and reliable information?

With measurement data in hand, the social worker can then organize the information in a manner that will allow her or him to answer the practice evaluation questions and reach conclusions about the degree of success. Items 14.4 through 14.7 provide examples of tools one can use to conduct these evaluations.

Termination activities

Although termination is recognized as a key element in planned change, it has been given surprisingly little attention in the social work literature. With the increased limits placed by managed care and other funding sources on the number of sessions a social worker can have with a client, this ending point increasingly is arbitrary and often premature. However, termination should be discussed at appropriate times throughout the helping process, and concluded in a manner that leaves the client with positive feelings and improved capacity to sustain gains made during the period of service. Item 14.8 provides some guidelines for the worker closing a case and terminating a professional relationship.

Social workers should remember, too, that the *NASW Code of Ethics* (Section 1.16) states that termination should be planned with the needs of the client as the primary consideration. If termination is necessary before the change process is completed, there should be an appropriate referral to other helping sources.

Selected Bibliography

Bloom, Martin, and Preston A. Britner. *Client-Centered Evaluation: New Models for Helping Professionals.* Upper Saddle River, NJ: Pearson, 2012.

Krysik, Judy L., and Jerry Finn. *Research for Effective Social Work Practice*, 3rd ed. New York: Routledge, 2013.

National Association of Social Workers. *NASW Code of Ethics.* Washington, DC: NASW, 1999.

Thyer, Bruce, and Laura Myers. *A Social Worker's Guide to Evaluating Practice Outcomes.* Alexandria, VA: Council on Social Work Education, 2007.

14.1 MEASURING CHANGE WITH FREQUENCY COUNTS

There are numerous reasons why social workers need to measure various aspects of a client's condition or situation. For example, knowing about the duration, intensity, frequency, severity, and so on, of a client's problem is prerequisite to determining if an emergency exists, if the client or someone else is at risk, or if a referral should be made (see Items 11.16 and 11.17). Such measurements also allow the worker and the client to track the amount and the direction of change occurring during the helping process and to decide if the current service plan or approach should be modified. A comparison of the measurements taken at the beginning and end of a service period or an intervention can determine if the desired change actually occurred. Also, a close examination of evaluation data drawn from work with a number of clients can inform a social worker about his or her strengths and weakness as a helper and lead to a professional development plan to strengthen his or her competence. Such data, if drawn from a number of social workers, can help an agency design its overall staff development plan.

In short, accurate measurement can benefit clients, workers, and agencies alike. It must be acknowledged, however, that measurements of human behaviors, attitudes, feelings, and interactions are rarely completely accurate. Yet, with careful selection of appropriate indicators and a rigorous process of data collection, usually a good approximation of a factor being measured can be achieved.

A useful, but often overlooked source of information regarding client change is a simple recording of the number of times an event occurs (i.e., a *frequency count*). Oftentimes such data is already recorded but not organized in a form that change can be assessed. For example, schools keep records of absences and disciplinary referrals to the principal's office, and hospitals monitor and record many factors about the patient's condition. Other times it is relatively simple for the social worker to record events (e.g., negative self-talk during an interview or an older person's examples forgetfulness) or to establish a plan for the client(s) to keep a tally on a calendar of an event occurring (e.g., arguments between spouses or a child's failure to complete household chores). Additionally, some other person might record these events, such as a teacher recording a student's disruptions in the classroom or failure to turn in homework, and report them to the social worker for analysis.

The data tends to be based on clearly identified, tangible, and concrete incidents or behaviors and many times offers an advantage of being compiled retrospectively from existing records. So long as the data is consistently recorded, these frequency counts can provide an accurate representation of change or serve as a proxy for change in a related aspect of client functioning. One example is a social worker who recognized that a nursing home patient's frequent shouts and yelling were indications of agitation. By recording the number of such shouts in a five-minute period with various types of background music playing near the client (e.g., classical, country, musicals, 1950s pop), the social worker discovered that classical music was associated with a decrease in this patient's feelings of agitation.

A caution in using numerical counts to represent client conditions is that such data may not be consistently recorded, may not be an adequate proxy for the client condition being addressed, or the client may attempt to manipulate the data to gain some desired outcome. In the latter case, it is essential that the social worker develop a trusting working relationship with the client and that the client be fully informed of the importance of recording accurate information.

Selected Bibliography

Bloom, Martin, Joel Fischer, and John G. Orme. *Evaluating Practice: Guidelines for the Accountable Professional,* 6th ed. Boston: Allyn and Bacon, 2009.

14.2 MEASURING CHANGE WITH INDIVIDUALIZED RATING SCALES

In addition to frequency counts, another approach to measurement is to construct an **individualized rating scale** that is developed or adapted to fit the client's unique situation. This "homemade" scale is particularly useful if the client can be involved in the process of creating the scale. Often, clients become clearer about their situations and what it might take to bring about a desired change when they work on designing a scale to measure the change they want to make. In this process, vague thoughts and feelings are translated into concrete descriptions of what it is that they hope to change. Thus, the development of an individualized rating scale can become a valuable part of the helping process. Furthermore, when scales reflect the respondent's own descriptions of the variables, the *face validity* of the scale is high and repeated measurements can be relatively accurate indicators of the client's experience. Finally, an individualized scale is able to address some concerns that defy standardized descriptors. For example, how does one standardize a person's feeling of grief, or a spouse's level of listening, or someone's motivation to change? With individualized scales, it is possible to "start where the client is" and construct measures of differing degrees of change from the perspective of that client.

"Homemade Data Gathering Tools" from 4th edition

Follow these steps when constructing an individualized rating scale:

Step 1: *Help the client recognize the value in measuring behaviors, attitudes, and feelings.* Unless the client is invested in measuring her or his condition, the results are unlikely to be very helpful. This measurement, however, should be a familiar experience for most clients. Just as other professionals routinely utilize indices of a patient's physical health, social workers require indices of a client's psychosocial health or social functioning. Many clients will welcome a close look at such indicators and find the results confirming of their own observations.

Step 2: *Carefully identify what is to be measured.* Many times, the problem or concern being addressed cannot directly be measured. If measured indirectly, it is critical that the items selected for measurement are valid or logical indicators of the problem being addressed. For example, just as an elevated body temperature might be an indicator of infection, the number of arguments a couple has might be an indicator of marital discord. It is also important that each scale is designed to measure only one dimension of client functioning. If more than one dimension is involved, a separate scale for each dimension should be created. Further, if there are multiple indicators for a single dimension, the use of several indicators can help to confirm or raise caution about the results from any one indicator.

Step 3: *Develop a scale in which the client's status on a continuum from negative to positive functioning can be designated.* When developing a scale, one task is to determine how many points on a continuum—that is, from least to most or worst to best—will be identified. There can be as few as 2 points (e.g., yes or no, more or less), although this allows for very little variability and should be avoided if possible. More informative scales typically range anywhere between 3 and 10 points. A general guideline is to have only as many points as the client can clearly distinguish—usually 5 to 7 points. Whether to have an odd or even number of points depends somewhat on the item being scaled. For some items, it is appropriate to have a midpoint, but often that creates a situation in which the respondent simply takes a noncommittal middle-ground that provides little useful information. An even-numbered scale, by contrast, compels the respondent to at least lean toward one direction or the other.

After the number of points on the scale is determined, anchoring statements or **anchor points** should be developed that describe each number on the scale. One method is to describe the most negative point on the scale (e.g., "I lost my temper at least once each day") and then define the most positive anchor point (e.g., "I did not lose my temper at all during the week"). With the two ends of the continuum identified, some or all of the points between them can be defined. Care should be taken that the client can identify differences in the increments between points. Another method for developing anchor points is to begin describing the client's functioning at the current time and making that description the midpoint. A description of what it would be like if things should get worse (a worst-case scenario) would become the negative end of the continuum and progressive levels to the midpoint on the negative side identified. Then the process is repeated on the positive side of the continuum.

When the anchor points use the client's own words (e.g., "I feel encouraged," "I am furious," "My thoughts are fuzzy," "I flew off the handle"), the scale is referred to as a *self-anchored scale* and the **face validity** of the scale is enhanced. At other times, it is helpful to use anchor points that have been utilized in other scales and are generally accepted as reflecting progressive scale values. When numerical categories are placed on a scale, be sure there are no gaps or overlaps in the numbers (i.e., *mutually exclusive categories*). It must be possible to place every potential response on the scale and impossible for any response to fall into more than one category. Usually, the negative end of the continuum is placed on the left side of a page and the progressive steps (i.e., identified by the anchor points) flow from left to right. For young children or persons with limited cognitive ability, progression can be represented by something as simple as smiley, neutral, and frowny faces. Some frequently used response categories include the following:

Frequency

- rarely > seldom > occasionally > frequently > almost always
- none > 1 or 2 times > 3–5 times > 6–7 times > more than 7 times
- never > rarely > sometimes > often > very often > always

Duration

- 0–20% of the time > 21–40% > 41–60% > 61–80% > 81–100% of the time
- never > some of the time > most of the time > almost always

Intensity

- strongly disagree > disagree > agree > strongly agree

- not at all > slightly > moderately > very much > extremely

Change in Amount

- substantial decrease > some decrease > no change > some increase > substantial increase

Step 4: *Determine how the data will be collected.* Determining a process for completing the scales is the next step. Who should do the rating (e.g., the client, the worker, a teacher, a relative)? When should the rating be made? For example, the rating scale might be completed just before each counseling session, first thing each morning, Sunday evenings, and so forth. Where can the client provide thoughtfully considered responses (e.g., at home? in the agency's waiting room? in the worker's office with the worker participating?)? Perhaps the most important general guideline is to attempt to achieve consistency regarding the conditions under which the ratings are made.

Step 5: *Present the data in a form that allows clear interpretation.* Charting scores, possibly in different colors, on a graph is often sufficient visual evidence of change. However, if a series of measurements are taken to reflect change over time or to compare changes in two or more variables, it is useful to create simple line graphs to track the progression. Such organization of the data can provide a useful basis for discussion of change or lack of change with clients.

Selected Bibliography

Abell, Neil, David W. Springer, and Akihito Kamata. *Developing and Validating Rapid Assessment Instruments.* New York: Oxford University Press, 2009.

Bloom, Martin, and Preston A. Britner. *Client-Centered Evaluation: New Models for Helping Professionals.* Upper Saddle River, NJ: Pearson, 2012.

Jordan, Catheleen, and Cynthia Franklin. *Clinical Assessment for Social Workers: Qualitative and Quantitative Methods*, 3rd ed. Chicago: Lyceum, 2011.

14.3 MEASURING CHANGE WITH STANDARDIZED RATING SCALES

In many instances, the social worker can measure a client's social functioning by using one of the several hundred previously developed instruments. **Standardized rating scales** are indices of behaviors, attitudes, feelings, and so on. They consist of a set of questions that measure a clearly defined construct such as, for example, depression, self-esteem, or satisfaction with one's marriage. As opposed to individualized rating scales that are designed for a specific individual client or client group (see Item 14.2), standardized indexes can be used to measure the experiences of many different clients. Typically, they are copyrighted and often they must be purchased.

A well-established research methodology, known as **psychometrics**, underpins the development of standardized instruments. During their development, the scales are examined to assure that they not only represent the meaning of the construct being measured (*validity*) but that the scale would also yield approximately the same result each time it is administered (*reliability*). In the development phase, the scales are administered to a large number of respondents and the responses are statistically analyzed. For example, the results might be compared to other indicators of that condition. The scale is then revised and adjusted until it meets the criteria for a valid measure.

"Rapid Assessment Instruments" from 4th edition.

Using standardized scales has three main benefits. First, because they have been tested, they are ready for immediate use. Thus, they can be used for diagnostic purposes where it is necessary to quickly assess the severity of a client's problem or condition. Second, periodic application of standardized assessment scales when working with a client can track changes over time to inform practice decisions regarding the desirability of continuing or changing the intervention plan. These scales can also be used to help a social worker sum up the results or the outcome of the intervention with a client (i.e., comparing the client's score on the scale before the intervention begins and at the conclusion of service). In addition, empirical analyses of practice outcomes as reflected by standardized measurement tools are increasingly requested by funding agencies.

Although standardized self-report scales vary in length, most contain between 15 and 30 one-sentence statements that a client is asked to rate on a 3- to 7-point scale. Therefore, these scales can be completed in a short period of time. One set of scales, known as the *WALMYR Assessment Scales*, illustrates a typical format used to measure constructs applicable to social work practice. For example, one of the WALMYR scales is designed to measure the extent of a client's problems with self-esteem. Here are 5 of the 25 items on the *Index of Self-Esteem:*

Item 1: I feel that people would not like me if they knew me really well.
Item 4: When I am with others I feel they are glad I am with them.
Item 14: I think my friends find me interesting.
Item 16: I feel very self-conscious when I am with strangers.
Item 24: I am afraid I will appear foolish to others.

The client rates each item on a 7-point scale with (1) none of the time, (2) very rarely, (3) a little of the time, (4) some of the time, (5) a good part of the time, (6) most of the time, and (7) all of the time. To ensure that the respondent carefully reads and considers each item, some of the items are written as a positive statement and others as negative. In these cases, the responses must be **reverse scored**. To illustrate, an answer of "most of the time" on the preceding Item 1 would be a negative statement about the client's self-esteem, whereas on Item 4, a response of "most of the time" would reflect a positive attitude. Clear instructions are provided with the scales to guide the worker in reverse scoring.

The descriptions and user instructions that accompany a standardized scale inform the social worker about its proper application, and in many cases published data is available on the instrument's validity and reliability. Although there are no strict guidelines, generally when judging a scale's *validity* for use in the human services area, a correlation coefficient of +.60 or greater when compared to other indicators is acceptable. For *reliability*, an Alpha score of +.80 or greater is sufficient. Some scale descriptions will also specify the respondent's age and reading level for which the measure is acceptable. Finally, the worker must decide if it is feasible to use the instrument in the particular practice situation. For example, the worker should determine if the measure has been normed with the cultural or age group that includes the client, is of appropriate length to use in the practice situation, is sensitive to the issues on which the practice is focused, and does not take an inordinate amount of money to secure or time to score.

Another feature of some scales is that cutting scores have been established. **Cutting scores** indicate the point on a scale where a client's score reflects a very serious problem or, at the other end of the continuum, indicates the absence of a serious problem that would typically require professional intervention. Many of the WALMYR scales, for example, measure the severity of problems with scores ranging from 0 (low severity or intensity) to 100 (extremely high level). For some scales, a cutting score of 70 has been standardized to indicate the level of severity at which the client begins to be at high risk to self or others. Similarly, a score below 30 is an indication that clinical intervention is probably not required.

> - Corcoran, Kevin, and Joel Fischer. *Measures for Clinical Practice: A Sourcebook*, 4th ed. New York: Oxford University Press, 2009. (This two-volume handbook of measures was developed specifically for social work practice and describes more than 300 different standardized instruments for use with children, couples, families, and problematic adult characteristics. For each scale, a short description is provided, its psychometric properties presented, and sources for obtaining permission to use the scale (with or without a fee) are included.)
> - Hudson, Walter W. *WALMYR Assessment Scales Scoring Manual*. Available online: www.walmyr.com. WALMYR Publishing Co., P.O. Box 12217, Tallahassee, FL 32317–2217. Email: walmyr@walmyr.com. (This collection of nearly 30 short self-report scales includes personal adjustment measures, problems with spouse or partner, family relationship problems, and measures of organizational outcomes. The psychometric properties and a description of the construct being measured by each scale are also included with the set of scales.)
> - Rush, A. John, et al., eds. *Handbook of Psychiatric Measures,* 2nd ed. Washington, DC: American Psychiatric Association, 2008. (This sourcebook contains 230 carefully selected measures of various psychiatric conditions. For each measure, the authors identify the goal of the measurement tool; describe what it measures; identify practical issues of test administration, availability, and cost of instruments; report the psychometric properties; and discuss its clinical utility.)
> - Sajatovic, Martha, and Luis Ramirez. *Rating Scales in Mental Health*, 3rd ed. Baltimore: Johns Hopkins University Press, 2012. (Primarily written for psychiatrists, this sourcebook provides information on more than100 scales. Especially useful for social workers are scales measuring anxiety, depression, social/ family functioning, client satisfaction, substance abuse, suicide risk, eating disorders, geriatric issues, and others.)

Figure 14.1
Sources of Standardized Scales for the Social Worker

Finally, it must be recognized that even a well-designed standardized scale cannot yield a valid measure with great precision. Known as the **standard error of measurement (SEM)**, SEM represents the amount of change that must occur in either direction that can be considered meaningful. For example, the WALMYR Index of Self-Esteem has an SEM of 3.70, meaning that any change in a client's score of less than 3.70 on repeated tests could just be the inability of the test to measure self-esteem and should not be considered real change in the client condition.

Reports on standardized scales are scattered throughout the social work and psychology literature and are often difficult to locate. Several sources that contain collections of standardized rating scales are identified in Figure 14.1.

Selected Bibliography

Abell, Neil, David W. Springer, and Akihito Kamata. *Developing and Validating Rapid Assessment Instruments.* New York: Oxford University Press, 2009.

Bloom, Martin, Joel Fischer, and John G. Orme. *Evaluating Practice: Guidelines for the Accountable Professional,* 6th ed. Boston: Allyn and Bacon, 2009.

14.4 A SERVICE PLAN OUTCOME CHECKLIST (SPOC)

A **Service Plan Outcome Checklist (SPOC)** is a tool for collecting data on client preferences for service outcomes and then measuring client perception of progress in achieving those identified outcomes. Unlike most other monitoring tools, a SPOC can be developed and used with multiple clients (e.g., a group or a worker's caseload), as well as with an individual client.

A SPOC is relatively easy to construct and is in some ways an elaboration of a client problem checklist (see Item 11.12). The central feature of a SPOC is a menu of outcome goals the agency or worker typically helps the clients address. A SPOC need not focus only on the outcome of a service plan. It may be adapted to focus on how much was learned, how well skills were developed, how satisfied the client was with the intervention, and so on. It would be important to also adapt the language of the achievement rating scale (see Figure 14.2) to be consistent with the change being assessed. A SPOC is also useful for identifying the content that group members hope to address during group sessions, information that can help in planning the group experience, as well as in assessing what was achieved during the group sessions. Although the format of a SPOC is standardized, the list of outcomes included in the menu will be unique for each type of service offered. Such a list can be derived from interviews with clients, analysis of client records, a review of the agency's manual, and interviews with experienced workers. The menu of outcomes in Figure 14.2 was created for clients in an Area Agency on Aging (AAA) caregiver support group.

The first step in using a service plan outcome checklist is to ask the client(s) during the initiation of service to review the list of desired outcomes (left-hand column of Figure 14.2) and to place a check (✓) by each goal he or she wants to achieve. This selection might be done independently by the client or with the assistance of the worker. Workers often find that discussion of these items yields helpful information and provides a way to focus an initial interview or adapt plans for a group's content or activities in response to client interest. To assist in prioritizing services, the two or three items the respondent considers most important should also be identified (circled).

If used with a client over an extended period, the client's perception of achievement might be obtained at interim points in the change process to assess the progress of the intervention effort. At a minimum, all items on the menu of possible outcomes should be rated at the point of termination (shaded section of Figure 14.2). A by-product of this final evaluation is that clients often find it helpful to revisit their initial selection of outcome goals, as well as the other outcomes addressed, and reflect on what was actually achieved. When applied to an individual client, examination of the client's view of the level of outcome achievement is one indicator of the success of the intervention.

When a SPOC is applied to a group of clients, it yields information that can help the worker identify both the importance and level of achievement for the various menu items. The menu in Figure 14.2 was developed in relation to the items the worker anticipated addressing when planning and conducting a group experience for caregivers of older clients.*

Before the group sessions began, the worker constructed the list of items in the menu (left column) by scanning literature on caregiver stress and including items that typically concern caregivers, interviewing staff members who provided service to caregivers, and discussing a draft menu with persons who had been participants in previous caregiver support groups (see Item 13.20). The members of the current group were subsequently given a copy of the SPOC with 14 potential items for group discussion identified and

---

*Prior editions of this book contained outcome menus from a child and family services agency (4th edition), community mental health center (5th edition), hospice bereavement group (6th edition), medical trauma center (7th edition), pain management group (8th edition), and an addictions recovery group (9th edition).

Instructions: *Complete steps 1 and 2 within two weeks of initiation of program.*

Step 1: In the far left column, (✓) check all desired outcomes. If a desired outcome does not appear on the menu below, add items in the space provided at the end of the questionnaire.

Step 2: Review the items checked in Step 1 and circle the two or three outcomes that you consider of highest priority to address in this group.

At the end of the program, complete Step 3 (i.e., the shaded area).

Step 3:   Rate each checked item from "no progress" to "fully achieved" by circling the number from 1 to 5 that best represents your judgment about progress made to date.

	Circle Your Assessment of Progress (*at completion of program*)		
	No Progress	About Half Achieved	Fully Achieved
____ 1. Get support for handling my stress	1 2 3 (4) 5		
____ 2. Find time for my family and friends	1 (2) 3 4 5		
✓ 3. Find time for my own needs	1 2 (3) 4 5		
____ 4. Get rid of guilt as a caregiver	1 (2) 3 4 5		
✓ 5. Get rid of anger at my loved one for being ill	1 (2) 3 4 5		
✓ (6.)Understand my loved one more	1 2 3 4 (5)		
✓ (7.)Learn better caregiving skills	1 2 3 4 (5)		
✓ 8. Gain a sense of capability as caregiver	1 2 (3) 4 5		
____ 9. Learn how to balance caregiving with rest of my life	1 2 3 (4) 5		
✓ (10.)Learn about resources in the community	1 2 (3) 4 5		
____ 11. Become better at asking for help	1 2 3 (4) 5		
✓ 12. Become better at setting and maintaining boundaries	1 2 (3) 4 5		
✓ 13. Learn to develop long-term plan for end of caregiving	1 2 3 (4) 5		
____ 14. Be able to plan for life after caregiving Additional outcomes I would like to address:	1 2 (3) 4 5		
15. Not losing serenity-due to experiencing loss	1 2 3 4 5		

Source: Adapted and modified from evaluation conducted by Michelle Embroski, Colorado State University.

Figure 14.2
Service Plan Outcome Checklist (SPOC) for Area Agency on Aging Caregiver Support Group

asked to place a checkmark by every item they would like to address while in the group and then to circle the two or three items that would be their highest priority. In addition, a final item was an open-ended question allowing group members the opportunity to identify topics that may have been omitted from the menu. At the last group session, the worker returned the SPOCs to the group members and asked them to rate their achievement for each item on a 5-point scale, whether or not the member had selected the item in the beginning.

To determine the importance of each item to the group members, the social worker summarized the group members' responses as reflected in Columns 2 through 5 in Figure 14.3. The steps followed were as follows:

Step 1: In Column 2, the worker recorded the number of group members who had selected that item and computed a percentage of the total (i.e., 7 of the 7 participants, or 100.0 percent selected Issue #12, I want to "Become better at setting and maintaining boundaries" as an issue they wanted to address).

Step 2: In Column 3, the worker followed the same procedure and arrived at the number and percentage for each item selected as one of the two or three priority issues to address by the group members. For Issue #12, 5 of 7 caregivers (71.4 percent) indicated "setting and maintaining boundaries" was a priority item.

Step 3: Given that both the expression of interest and the priority given an item are valid indicators about how important an item is for each member, an *Importance Index* (Column 4) was compiled by adding the two percentages from Columns 2 and 3. Thus Item #12 had an importance index of 171.4. Note that this is an index number, not a percentage.

Step 4: At the time of termination, each group member rated her or his achievement on the 5-point scale in the shaded section of the SPOC form (see Figure 14.2). The social worker then recorded each client's rating, computed a mean achievement score for each item, and entered that in Column 5.

Step 5: Finally, the worker used a spreadsheet program to **sort** the items, using Column 5 (in descending order) as the first sort. (Note that in making this calculation in a spreadsheet program it is necessary to select all columns on the chart and all items that have been rated so that the data stays with each item description.) Doing so produced a list of the items in order of the Importance Index score, with the most important items at the top of the chart. The mean or average achievement score for the group members was parallel to the importance score for each item.

Having completed these calculations, the worker could then interpret the group members' perceptions of success by visually comparing Columns 4 and 5. For example, in Figure 14.3, Item #12 had a 171.4 importance index and an achievement score (3.14 of a possible 5.00), suggesting the group believed they had been moderately successful in addressing this issue. However, Item #7 also had a moderately high importance index (114.3), but only a 2.00 mean achievement. According to this data, the group was not successful in helping members "Learn better caregiver skills," which the participants considered a tie for the second most important item on the list. This would suggest that the worker should seek additional knowledge or training about how to help group participants develop their skills in caring for their loved one. The "other" item added by a group member, Item #15, "Not losing serenity due to experiencing loss" might suggest that this item should be added to the menu the next time this SPOC is used. Also, it should be noted that the "other" items were not scored and not included in the summary data since all members did not have the opportunity to rate them.

Item #	Column 1 Outcome Selected	Column 2 # and % Selected		Column 3 # and % Priority		Column 4 Importance Index	Column 5 Mean Achievement
12	Become better at setting and maintaining boundaries	7	100.0	5	71.4	171.4	3.14
9	Learn how to balance caregiving with rest of my life	5	71.4	3	42.9	114.3	3.43
7	Learn better caregiving skills	6	85.7	2	28.6	114.3	2.00
6	Understand my loved one more	6	85.7	2	28.6	114.3	4.64
10	Learn about resources in the community	5	71.4	1	14.3	85.7	2.86
1	Get support for handling my stress	5	71.4	1	14.3	85.7	3.71
11	Become better at asking for help	6	85.7	0	0.0	85.7	3.57
13	Learn to develop long term plan for end of caregiving	3	42.9	2	28.6	71.4	3.57
5	Get rid of anger at my loved one for being ill	4	57.1	1	14.3	71.4	2.74
3	Find time for my own needs	3	42.9	2	28.6	71.4	3.29
8	Gain a sense of capability as caregiver	3	42.9	1	14.3	57.1	3.00
4	Get rid of guilt as a caregiver	4	57.1	0	0.0	57.1	3.14
14	Be able to plan for life after caregiving	3	42.9	0	0.0	42.9	3.00
2	Find time for my family and friends	3	42.9	0	0.0	42.9	2.86
15	Other: Not losing serenity due to continued loss	Not Scored		Not Scored		Not Scored	Not Scored
		N = 7 clients				Group Mean	3.17
						Possible Range = 1.00 to 5.00	

Source: Adapted and modified from evaluation conducted by Michelle Embroski, Colorado State University.

Figure 14.3
Service Plan Outcome Checklist (SPOC) Summary for Area Agency on Aging Caregiver Support Group

Two additional applications of a service plan outcome checklist can be used to strengthen social work practice. First, a social worker might administer a SPOC to all or a sample of his or her clients and compute the scores, as in Figure 14.3, in order to identify areas where clients could benefit from the worker gaining additional knowledge and skill. Second, a supervisor on a unit of an agency might give a SPOC with a menu of the unit's services to a sample of clients in order to judge overall unit performance and to identify workers who are particularly strong in addressing specific outcomes so that the most competent workers could be assigned to clients with these specific needs.

Selected Bibliography

Horejsi, Charles. *Assessment and Case Planning in Child Protection and Foster Care Services.* Englewood, CO: American Humane Association, 1996.

Sheafor, Bradford W. "Measuring Effectiveness in Direct Social Work Practice." *Social Work Review,* X (2011): 25–33.

14.5 TASK ACHIEVEMENT SCALING (TAS)

Task achievement scaling (TAS) was developed for use with the task-centered practice approach (see Chapter 6) wherein work toward the client's goals and objectives is broken down into many small specific tasks or steps and then worked on sequentially. A **task** is an action by the client or worker that is necessary in order to reach a desired outcome and is usually something that can be accomplished in a matter of days or, at most, in a few weeks. For many clients, this process of breaking down the work toward an objective into steps or tasks makes the work seem more manageable and elevates their confidence that it can be achieved. Usually, not more than three or four tasks are worked on at a time. Each session with the client begins with a review of the progress on tasks selected for attention during the previous session and ends with identifying tasks to be undertaken before the next session. Because the TAS reports the percent of achievement for each attempted task, some tasks may be judged as completed, as no longer required, or as tasks to be continued. New tasks can be added at any point. A percent of achievement on the combined tasks yields a representation of overall movement toward the practice objectives.

For purposes of illustrating the use of task achievement scaling, consider a social worker's services in a co-parenting case involving a divorced couple having issues regarding joint custody of their child. In contrast to mediation where the mediator makes a decision when the parents can't resolve issues (see Item 13.19), in co-parenting the effort is to assist the parents to cooperate and reach an amicable agreement. To begin the co-parenting intervention, the social worker met individually with each parent wherein both parents expressed uncertainty about the process and feelings that the other would not comply with agreements reached in the sessions. However, both indicted they cared deeply for their three children and agreed to "give it a try" for four weekly sessions.

The history of the family was that the couple (John and Karla) had been divorced for two years. At the time of the divorce there had been a custody agreement established in family court, but the agreement had begun to unravel as Karla's boyfriend was accused of abusing the children while in his care. John remarried (to Karla's best friend), creating strained communication between the parents. John argued that his new wife should be part of any co-parenting plan, but Karla felt betrayed by her former best friend and wanted no interaction with her. The decision was reached that only the biological parents would participate in the co-parenting sessions.

Using a combination of the solution-focused and the task-centered models as her intervention approach, the social worker helped the parents identify three initial tasks to accomplish prior to the deadline for presenting a co-parenting plan to the family court judge. These tasks involved reaching agreement regarding (1) how, when, and by whom discipline will be used with the children; (2) what will be the schedule for the times each parent will be responsible for the children; and (3) who will be responsible for paying for the children's medical and dental needs and getting them to related medical appointments. At their first session, the social worker and parents discussed each of the three tasks and agreed-upon four incremental steps that would reflect progress related to each task. Each step was assigned a numerical value of 0 to 4 that represented five distinct levels of achievement reflecting no progress, minimally achieved, partially achieved, substantially achieved, and completely achieved. Following the task achievement scale (TAS) format, Figure 14.4 displays the agreement reached between the parents on what would represent progress in developing a co-parenting plan to present to the judge.

Overall Goal : *Develop Co-Parenting plan for Family Court*
Clients: *Karla and John K.Family* (*divorced*)
Worker: *Nikole Ordman*
Week #1, May 20

Achievement	Task #1: Develop Discipline Plan	Task #2: Develop Child Care Time-Schedule	Task #3: Plan Responsibility for Children's Health Care
No Progress (0)	Parents did not address the task	Parents did not address the task	Parents did not address the task (✓)
Minimally Achieved (1)	Parents began general discussion of discipline issues (✓)	Discussion of differences between prior court plan and current preferred plans (✓)	General discussion of issues related responsibilities for appointments and payment
Partially Achieved (2)	Each parent prepared a written statement of points of agreement/disagreement	Identification of issues for each parent related to preferred plans	Each parent presents a proposal for appointment/ payment responsibility
Substantially Achieved (3)	Identification of possible compromises to address disagreements	Discussion of possible compromises and implications for the children	Discussion of possible compromises/solutions
Completely Achieved (4)	Agreement on a plan to present to Family Court	Agreement on a plan to present to Family Court	Agreement on a plan to present to Family Court
Change Score	1	1	0
Possible Change	4	4	4
% of Possible Change Achieved	25	25	0
Percent of Change for all Three Tasks: (2 change steps of possible 12) = 16.7%			

Source: Adapted and modified from evaluation conducted by Nikole Ordway, Colorado State University.

Figure 14.4

Task Achievement Scale (TAS) for K. Family Co-Parenting Plan

Figure 14.4 also reflects the beginning progress made on the three tasks during the first session. The percentage of accomplishment is computed by dividing the actual change in level by the possible change in level. For example, for Task #1 the change in level (minimally achieved) was 1 and the possible change (completely achieved) is 4. Thus, 1 divided by 4 = .25, or 25 percent. For Task #2 there was also 25 percent achievement, and for Task #3, which was not addressed in this session, there was "0" achievement. By combining the accomplishment for the three tasks (i.e., change of 2 points with possible change of 12 points), the overall task achievement score for that week was computed (i.e., 2 divided by 12 = 16.7 %). At the end of the session, the parents were encouraged that they had clearly laid out what they needed to accomplish, the responsibilities for each parent were identified, and already they were making some progress. In three subsequent sessions the overall achievement scores increased to 33.3 percent, 58.3 percent, and 83.3 percent. At that time it was concluded that there was sufficient agreement to take the plan to the Family Court where the four weekly TAS charts were presented to the judge. Note that in this case the tasks did not change, although it would have been possible to replace one or more task if they are completed or if the need for work on new tasks had become evident.

Another useful means of tracking a client's level of task achievement is to cast the weekly scores into *a time-series chart* as described in Item 14.6. Such graphing of the percent of task achievement from day-to-day or week-to-week can be useful in recognizing and reinforcing positive change by the client, whereas a downward trend can signal a client's decline in interest or motivation. Using the time-series format also makes it possible to graphically compare the percent of task completion with some other variable to answer a practice question such as, "To what extent is the level of task achievement associated with the client's level of personal stress?"

Selected Bibliography

Coady, Nick, and Peter Lehmann, eds. *Theoretical Perspectives for Direct Social Work Practice: A Generalist-Eclectic Approach*, 2nd ed. New York: Springer, 2008.

Fortune, Anne E., Philip McCallion, and Katharine Briar-Lawson, eds. *Social Work Practice Research for the 21st Century.* New York: Columbia University Press, 2010.

14.6 GOAL ATTAINMENT SCALING (GAS)

Goal attainment scaling (GAS) is a procedure that provides an estimate of the degree of movement toward goals that accrues from an intervention. As opposed to short-term tasks, **goals** are the desired outcomes for the social worker's interventions with the client (an individual or family). The basic format for a GAS is the same for all clients, although adjustments are made to accommodate the number of goals selected. It consists of several 5-point scales (usually two to four scales) that are individualized for the specific client to represent the agreed-upon goals. Measurement of progress toward these goals could take the form of frequency counts, various levels of performance on individualized scales, scores on a standardized assessment instrument, or a combination of these. Here are the steps in constructing a GAS:

Step 1: *Identify two to four goals, and develop a 5-point scale for each.* To establish a GAS, the worker and client describe in a few words the client's condition or situation prior to the intervention. This is done for each identified goal. Ideally, this description indicates the second-lowest point on a 5-point scale where a score of 2 (less than expected success) is assigned. The lowest point (assigned a score of 1) on the scale is then described, indicating what a step backward would represent. Next, the best outcome that could reasonably be expected should be described; a value of 5 is assigned. Then, two levels of improvement between the current situation and the best possible scenario can be identified and assigned scores of 3 and 4. The result should be a 5-point ordinal scale for each goal where the worker and client have created explicit descriptions (anchor points) for each of the five levels.

The goal attainment scaling in Figure 14.5 was created by a social worker in a mental health center. The client, Stanley B., was a self-referred, single, 47-year-old male who expressed feelings of depression, isolation, and a poor self-image due to being overweight. He has been in and out of therapy at the mental health center for a number of years and displayed Asperger-type symptoms with very flat affect, difficulty maintaining eye contact, and problems in engaging is socially appropriate behavior. When the intervention began, Stanley was unemployed and had difficulty finding employment because he had a felony conviction for bringing a small bomb to work in an effort to "be funny."

Stanley immediately indicated that he was not interested in the usual deficit-centered treatment approaches he had experienced in the past. The social worker suggested a strengths-based approach coupled with motivational interviewing (see Chapter 6). This would require Stanley and the worker to identify a few goals and develop a plan for Stanley to achieve these goals. Stanley identified his strengths and resources as his intelligence to critically examine and understand his problems, the emotional and monetary support received from his family, and his access to sufficient transportation, housing, food, and clothing. In the first two sessions the following goals were selected: Goal #1, Reduce Stanley's depression to a level not needing clinical intervention; Goal #2, Reduce Stanley's weight from 222 pounds to under 200 pounds; and Goal #3, Assist Stanley to obtain full-time permanent employment. As reflected in Figure 14.5, the social worker and Stanley developed three 5-point scales to measure steps in his success (or lack of success) in attaining each of the three goals. Five levels of change ranging from "Most unfavorable" to "Most favorable" were identified for each goal.

Step 2: *Assign a weight to each goal to indicate its importance in relation to the other goals.* Assigning a percentage of 100 points to each goal reflects the relative importance of that particular goal. In Figure 14.5, the social worker and Stanley decided that Stanley's inability to secure employment contributed to his lack of independence and his subsequent depression; it also contributed to his weight problem because he overate when he was not busy. Therefore, they gave Goal #3 the highest weight of 50, Goal #2 a weight of 25, and Goal #1 a 25 weighting. By assigning a weight to each goal, not only could the progress on each goal be identified, but an indicator of overall goal achievement (due to the fact that the goals were interrelated) also could be computed.

Step 3: *Place a checkmark (✓) in the cell that best describes the client's condition for each goal at the point that intervention begins.* Usually this checkmark will appear in the number 2 cell, "Less than expected success," since remaining at that level would not represent progress. Sometimes, however, the checkmark will appear at a different attainment level due to the difficulty in identifying five levels of change. The checkmarks, then, become the baseline or "before" measurement for the GAS.

Step 4: *When the service or intervention is terminated, place an (✗) in the cell that best describes the client's condition for each goal at that time.* This mark (✗) represents the "after" measurement, and the difference in measurement from the initial checkmark

Client: Stanley B.
Worker: Ryan Douglas

(✓) = Beginning Level (✗) = Terminating Level	Goal 1: Reduce depression to a nonclinical level on Generalized Contentment Scale (GCS)	Goal 2: Decrease weight to less than 200 pounds	Goal 3: Attain permanent full-time employment
Attainment Level	Weight: 25%	Weight: 25%	Weight: 50%
(1) Most unfavorable outcome thought likely	GCS score = 70 or above	Weight = 230 lbs. or more	Remain unemployed and have parents' financial assistance discontinued
(2) Less than expected success	GCS score = 57-69 (Score of 61) (✓)	Weight = 220 to 229 lbs. (Weight = 222) (✓)	Remain unemployed and have parents' continue financial assistance (✓)
(3) Expected success	GCS score = 44-56 (Score 48 on GCS) (✗)	Weight = 210 to 219	Secure part-time employment (✗)
(4) More than expected success	GCS score = 31-43	Weight = 200 to 209 (Weight = 207) (✗)	Secure temporary full-time employment
(5) Best anticipated success	GCS score = 30 or less	Weight = 200 or less	Secure permanent full-time employment
Summary	Goal 1:	Goal 2:	Goal 3:
Weight	25	25	50
Change Score	1	2	1
Weighted Change Score	25	50	50
Possible Weighted Change	75	75	150
Percentage Attainment	33.3	66.7	33.3
Total Weighted Change (125) / Total Possible Weighted Change 300) = 41.7%			

Source: Adapted and modified from evaluation conducted by Ryan Douglas, Colorado State University.

Figure 14.5

Goal Attainment Scale (GAS) for Stanley B., 9/27/20__ to 12/15/20__

reflects the steps of change that occurred during the time of service. Note that in some long-term cases it may be useful to identify an interim attainment level for each goal as a means of monitoring the change process.

Step 5: *Determine the weighted change score for each goal.* Computing the change score involves subtracting the steps of change from the beginning score (✓) to the ending score (✗) and multiplying by the weight assigned to that goal. In Goal #2 of Figure 14.5, for example, the client's weight decreased and thus Stanley's goal attainment increased from the level 2 attainment to the level 4 attainment—a positive change of two steps. The change score is then multiplied by 25 (the weight for Goal #2), and a weighted change score of 50 was recorded.

Step 6: *Compute the percentage of possible change for each scale.* Determine the highest score a client might generate for each scale by identifying the change that would have occurred from the beginning point (✓) if the client had fully reached the goal (i.e., the 5 level) and record that score. Note that all scales do not start at the same level, thus it is necessary to count the levels of progress from the starting point. Then divide the actual weighted change score by this possible change score. For Goal #2 in Figure 14.5, this would involve dividing 50 by 75, yielding a change score of 66.7 percent for that goal.

Step 7: *Compute an overall goal attainment score.* Perhaps the most valuable information derived from a GAS is the combined score, which gives a comprehensive indication of the client's overall level of goal attainment. To derive that score, the possible weighted change scores for all the goals are summed and then divided into the sum of the actual weighted change scores. In Figure 14.5, the percentage of overall change is reflected at the bottom of the chart (i.e., total weighted change [125] divided by possible weighted change [300], which yields a percentage change of 41.7 percent). In sum, this intervention resulted in some progress related to losing weight, but more time was needed to secure full-time employment and address the depression.

If goal attainment scaling is used widely in an agency, data can be gleaned from GAS charts that will also be useful in program evaluation. For example, data might be accumulated regarding the following:

- The types of goals chosen as targets for intervention, their frequency, and the percent of goal achievement on each
- The amount of progress made on particular goals by the clients served by a specific worker
- The relative success in goal achievement with particular groups of clients (e.g., age, ethnicity, gender)

Selected Bibliography

Dudley, James R. *Social Work Evaluation: Enhancing What We Do.* Chicago: Lyceum, 2009.
Kiresuk, Thomas J., Aaron Smith, and Joseph E. Cardillo. *Goal Attainment Scaling: Applications, Theory, and Measurement.* Hillsdale, NJ: Erlbaum, 1994.

14.7 SINGLE-SUBJECT DESIGNS (SSDs)

The most well-known method for direct-practice evaluation is single-subject research design—also known as *single-system, single-case, N = 1,* and *time-series design.* As compared to more traditional forms of research that accumulate data from multiple respondents, either before and after an intervention or with experimental and control groups, **single-subject designs** (SSDs) involve comparing repeated measurements from a single subject (e.g., individual, couple, family, or group) over time.

Two fundamental assumptions underpin SSD. First, it is assumed that if left unattended, the client's condition or problem will stay about the same or worsen. Second, it is assumed that barring evidence to the contrary, one can cautiously conclude that if change occurs after the introduction of an intervention, the intervention is an important contributor to that change. Thus, by clearly specifying the client's behavior, attitude, or functioning *before* the intervention begins (i.e., a baseline measurement), any change that occurs during the period of service is assumed to be influenced by the intervention. However, it is not possible to conclude that the intervention *caused* the change, but it can be said that there is (or is not) an *association* between the social worker's intervention and change in the client condition.

There is no uniform format for a single-subject design. In fact, one of the strengths of this methodology is its flexibility. Because the SSD monitors what occurs in practice, the design must be adaptable to changing practice situations. Unlike traditional social science research, it is acceptable to modify a single-subject design during work with the client. For example, if a decision is made to alter the intervention approach, the evaluation design should also be adjusted.

The following steps reflect a process for conducting a single-subject evaluation:

Step 1: *Select a case situation in which it will be possible to take several measurements over time.* Because data that reveals trends in a client's actions or feelings provides the basis of this design, repeated measurements must be taken. These measurements might occur before the intervention is begun, during the intervention, and even after the intervention is completed. The frequency of measurement will depend on the case situation and could be daily, weekly, or even monthly.

Step 2: *Select the target behaviors/attitudes/beliefs, and determine how each is to be measured.* During the assessment and planning phases of the change process, the factors, conditions, or patterns targeted for change will have been identified and, in order to monitor change, a valid and relevant numerical measure must be selected. This may be a frequency count (how often something happens) or a score on an individualized or standardized scale (see Items 14.1, 14.2, and 14.3). The worker and client should establish a plan for consistently taking the measurements under similar conditions. If measuring more than one variable, it might be useful to alternate when the scales are administered—for example, using one scale every other session and another at the alternate sessions.

Step 3: *Select a single-subject design, and designate the phases of the process on a chart.* The characteristic way of organizing SSD data is a graph that depicts the independent variable (e.g., client's behavior, attitude) on the left axis (*y*-axis) and a time line in days or weeks along the bottom (*x*-axis).

With a little practice with Microsoft Excel or a similar program, charting the data is not difficult. As reflected in Figure 14.6, the different phases of the process (e.g., baseline phase, intervention phase) are identified across the top of the graph with dashed vertical lines separating each phase. *A* is always used to represent a *baseline period* or the condition of the variable before the intervention was initiated. Usually this measurement is made as a part of the assessment and planning phases of the change process, but in some circumstances data previously collected in client records (i.e., *retrospective data*) might also be used as part of the baseline. The letters *B, C, D*, and so forth (except for *M* and *F-U*) denote the use of different intervention approaches when serving the client. If multiple interventions are used simultaneously, a slash is placed between the letters representing those interventions (e.g., *B/C*). Should there be a modification in frequency or intensity of an intervention (e.g., shorter sessions, increased medication), that modification should be noted with a superscript designation (e.g., B^1). *M* is reserved to designate a period in which a minimum level of service is maintained before a case is closed (the maintenance phase) and *F-U* denotes a follow-up measurement after service has been terminated. By including a descriptor (e.g., *B* = family therapy, *C* = participation in

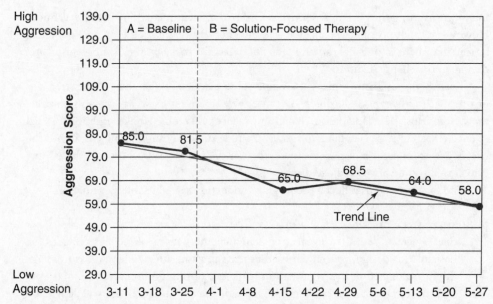

Source: Adapted and modified from evaluation conducted by Aaron Shea, Colorado State University.

Figure 14.6

Single Subject Design (SSD) Aggression Questionnaire Scores for Chris B

a parenting group) in a textbox at the top of the chart, there is clear identification of the intervention(s) being used at any phase of the process.

The variations in the design used will depend on the practice situation, the worker's creativity, and the questions the worker intends to answer. The most elementary SSD is a *B* design or a case study in which there are no baseline or follow-up data and the worker simply tracks what happens in regard to the variable(s) while the services is being provided. This format allows the worker to record what is changing during the intervention in order to adjust the practice approach, if necessary, or to inform future practice decisions. If the intervention is changed, this would become a *B C* design.

The most commonly used form of a single-subject design, the *A B* design, allows the worker and client to compare measurements from the baseline period through the intervention phase. This type of study might also allow the worker to examine any change in the key client variable(s) associated with introducing a different intervention (an *A B C* design) or adding a second intervention, such as group therapy, to the individual counseling already in process (an *A B B/C* design) to assess the relative effectiveness of each approach or combination of approaches.

The case example reflected in Figure 14.6 was conducted by a social worker in a day treatment program for children ages 9 to 18 who suffer from significant emotional and behavioral problems. The goal of the program was to address each child's issues and help him or her return to the public schools and/or prepare for responsible living in the adult world. The client in this case was Chris B., a 17-year-old male who had been experiencing delusional thought patterns, problems associated with drug and alcohol use, and criminal assault charges due to attacking another male about his age. Chris identified his central concerns as anger and frustration at events experienced outside the day treatment center, including altercations with his sister and heated arguments with his mother. His primary goal for the work with the social worker was to learn to control his aggression. Following a search for evidence-based interventions appropriate for this situation (see Item 11.22), solution-focused therapy was adopted.

To assess change in this situation, the social worker selected a standardized scale, the Aggression Questionnaire (AQ), developed by Buss and Perry (1992). This 29-question instrument measures four aspects of aggression: physical aggression, verbal aggression, anger, and hostility—with each aspect representing a characteristic through which one's aggression is manifested. A summary score indicating overall aggression is considered the primary predictor of the client's aggressive behavior. For each question, the respondent rates herself or himself from a score of 1 (extremely uncharacteristic of me) to 5 (extremely characteristic of me), with a possible range from 29 (low aggression) to 145 (high aggression).

Step 4: *Collect and record baseline, intervention, maintenance, and/or follow-up data on each factor.* Ideally, baseline measures should be repeatedly taken until a stable score on the variable is established. However, the realities of social work practice rarely permit many measurements. If possible, two or three baseline measurements (before the intervention is begun) should be collected, but as in the Chris B. case, only two baseline scores could be obtained before the intervention was started.

When scores are obtained on each variable, the score should be plotted on the client's graph. Because the chart reflects the sequence of related scores through time, a *line chart* as depicted in Figure 14.6 is the preferred format. The known data points should be connected with solid lines. If there is missing data at an interval when data regularly would have been collected, the two known points should be connected by a dashed line, which represents the assumption that the missing data would have fallen along the line between the two known points. It is also important to note on the *y*-axis if a high score represents a positive or negative outcome on each factor.

Returning to the case example, Chris B. completed the Aggression Questionnaire every other week and the results were cast into a time-series chart (Figure 14.6). His first baseline (A) score was 85.0 and the second 81.5. Both are relatively high aggression scores, yielding an average baseline score of 83.25. Measurements were initiated two weeks after the solution-focused intervention was begun and Chris's total aggression score had dropped to 65.0. At two-week intervals it increased to 68.5, declined to 64.0, and ended at 58.0—an overall improvement of 25.25 points from the average baseline score to the ending score.

Step 5: *Interpret the data and compare empirical evidence with other practice observations.* When data points have been entered on a chart, it is then possible to examine the data and make judgments about the success of the intervention. Several cautions should be considered when interpreting SSD data. First, if there is a sequence of interventions being evaluated, such as in the A B B/C design, there could be a *carry-over* effect in which the change made in one phase affects the next. Withdrawing all interventions (i.e., returning to a second baseline) can help to reveal if there has been a cumulative influence from the series of interventions. The *order of presentation* of various intervention strategies can also affect the impact of a specific intervention. This problem can be addressed in subsequent practice situations by changing the order of introducing the various intervention strategies. If one strategy appears most effective regardless of order, a worker can feel more confident about using that strategy in similar practice situations. Finally, SSDs often suffer from *incomplete and inaccurate data*. The realities of practice are that clients may miss sessions, data-collection instruments may not be fully completed, clients might provide incorrect information, and so on. These problems do not weaken the rationale for conducting direct-practice evaluation; rather, they argue for cautious interpretation of the results and reinforce the importance of *triangulation*.

Visual examination of the pattern of change, positive or negative, will often produce a clear picture of the client's situation. However, when data is erratic, it may be difficult to detect trends. When this happens, it is helpful to compute a *mean* or *median* score to identify the most typical responses. For each phase of the process, then, horizontal lines can be drawn to represent the central tendency. Other more sophisticated analyses of data can be conducted, in which *trend lines* or *celeration lines* project the future direction of client performance on the factor being measured. Computer programs such as Excel can readily compute trend lines (see Figure 14.6). Moreover, if there is sufficient data, it is possible to determine if a change is *statistically significant*. Tables have been developed that identify levels of statistical significance based on the proportion and frequency of observations above and below a trend line both before and after the intervention is begun. However, one should be cautious about using elaborate statistical manipulation, as it can imply more rigorously controlled data collection than the SSD methodology permits. The effort devoted to determining statistical significance might be better spent on examining the *practical significance* of the information (i.e., the importance of the change to the client).

In addition to measuring change in a key client characteristic, some standardized scales also provide scores for discrete elements that are included within the characteristic. For example, in the case of Chris B., each element of aggression was also measured by the Aggression Questionnaire and could be individually charted just as the total aggression scores appear in Figure 14.6. An alternative is the following simple table that helped the client and social worker assess the aspects of aggression that were contributing to Chris's overall improvement in his total aggression score.

	Total Aggression	Physical Aggression	Verbal Aggression	Anger	Hostility
Baseline	83.25	28.50	16.75	20.50	17.50
Final Score	58.00	22.50	9.50	15.00	11.00

Using this data, discussion during the termination phase of the intervention focused on the social worker congratulating Chris for substantial improvement and facilitated discussion of things he might do to further decrease his physical aggression and anger.

In a different practice situation involving work with a group of clients, a mean score for the group derived from measurements taken periodically might be informative about the change experienced by the group as a whole. However, the possibility that a group approach might be helpful for most members, yet damaging to others, should be considered. To address this possibility, the scores for each member could be charted, along with the mean score for the group, to compare both individual and group change.

In sum, once the rudiments of single-subject designs are mastered, the opportunities for developing a wide variety of designs to inform one's practice are limited only by the worker's creativity. For example, a variation of an SSD to help clients visualize change is a client self-rating scale (CSRS) that can be used to track changes from session to session.

"Client Self-Rating Scale" from 4th edition

Selected Bibliography

Bloom, Martin, Joel Fischer, and John G. Orme. *Evaluating Practice: Guidelines for the Accountable Professional*, 6th ed. Boston: Allyn and Bacon, 2009.

Buss, Arnold H., and Mark Perry. "The Aggression Questionnaire." *Journal of Personality and Social Psychology, 63* (1992): 452–459.

Weinbach, Robert W., and Richard M. Grinnell, Jr. *Statistics for Social Workers*, 8th ed. Boston: Allyn and Bacon, 2010.

14.8 TERMINATION OF SERVICE

Termination, the process of formally ending the relationship between the worker and the client, should be viewed as a planned component of the helping process. Ideally, termination is a mutual decision that occurs when the service objectives have been reached and both client and worker are satisfied with the outcome of their work together. In many cases, the social worker and client know from the start that the service will be time limited. In other cases, the worker and client must decide when termination is appropriate. The following factors should be considered:

- Is the problem or situation that brought the client to the agency sufficiently resolved so the client can now function at an acceptable level? If so, is there a plan to maintain the goals that were achieved?
- Has the client and/or worker reached a point where one or both do not anticipate significant benefit from future contacts?
- Has the worker and/or agency made a reasonable investment of time, energy, and skill without sufficient results? If so, have alternative services provided by another agency or professional been identified that might be helpful to the client?
- Has the client become inappropriately dependent on the worker or agency? If so, is there an appropriate referral that can be made (see Item 10.4)?

In some situations, a transfer of the client to another worker within the agency is necessary. This type of termination or intraagency transfer may be necessary when any of the following occurs:

- The worker will no longer be available to serve the client (e.g., worker moving to another job, a student internship is completed).
- The client will be better served by another agency staff member.
- A conflict between the worker and client cannot be resolved and is interfering with client progress.
- For some reason, the worker cannot develop necessary empathy and warmth for the client.
- There is a serious and insurmountable gap in mutual understanding and communication caused by difference in values, religious beliefs, language, or cultural background.

Unfortunately, there are unplanned terminations when the client decides to end the relationship before reaching the objectives, and sometimes circumstances dictate that the worker decides unilaterally to terminate. Examples of the latter include the following:

- The client is a physical danger to the worker or continually harasses the worker.
- The client files a lawsuit or an official complaint against the worker and/or agency.
- The client violates, without good cause, a financial agreement regarding the payment of fees for service.
- The client is no longer invested in the intervention.

The social worker should be aware that in some instances legal issues could arise around the timing of a termination and how it was handled. For example, if a former client commits suicide soon after the termination of a counseling or therapy relationship, the client's family may file a lawsuit alleging professional negligence and the worker's abandonment of a client needing service. The social worker should always maintain careful records of any circumstances or events that might contribute to an eventual termination of service, as these may be needed as evidence to explain or justify the termination.

In the case of an intraagency transfer or a unilateral termination by the worker, the client should be notified in writing, and, if possible, during a face-to-face meeting. The reasons and circumstances surrounding the transfer or termination should be clearly documented in the case record.

The social worker has an obligation to make a termination or transfer as positive an experience as possible. Several guidelines can aid in this process:

- The worker should do everything possible to keep termination from being abrupt or unexpected. Termination should be discussed during the planning and contracting phase of the helping process and the client should be reminded from the beginning that intervention is goal oriented and time limited. The client should be gradually prepared for termination if the intervention includes ongoing monitoring of progress.

- In a case where an adult client wants to terminate but the social worker thinks he or she should continue, the worker should explain to the client the possible consequences of terminating. If the client still wishes to terminate, his or her decision should be respected. Usually, a child or adolescent client does not have the authority to decide the termination of services and the child's parent or guardian must make the decision.

- Special attention should be given to any termination prompted by an agency's administrative decision to cut back on services provided or modify client services due to either a change in the worker's status with the agency or the end of financial reimbursement from a third-party payer (e.g., an insurance company, Medicaid). When a client continues to need services, the worker is obliged to advocate on behalf of the client to receive such services (see Item 13.17). Additional care must be observed if services were being provided under court order to be sure that all terms of the order have been met. When making decisions about termination, the worker should be guided by Section 1.16 of the *NASW Code of Ethics* (1999).

- The social worker should anticipate how the termination might affect other people in the client's family and social network. In situations where a termination may place the client or others at risk of harm, it may be appropriate to notify others of the termination. This notification must, of course, be done in ways consistent with the law and ethics concerning confidentiality.

- In some cases, termination can be difficult because of a social worker's own psychological needs. A worker may want to be needed and appreciated so strongly that she or he maintains regular contact with a client even when there is no professional reason for doing so. If the need to be needed by one's clients is a recurring problem, the worker and/or his or her supervisor must address it (see Item 16.3).

- As termination approaches, it is desirable to gradually decrease the frequency of contact. If the client is quite dependent on the worker, this weaning process should be accompanied by efforts to connect the client with natural helpers and informal resources within her or his neighborhood or social network.

- The feelings of loss or abandonment that may accompany the ending should be broached by the worker, even if not mentioned by the client. The scheduling of a follow-up interview or telephone contact (i.e., a booster session) several weeks after official termination may be reassuring to the client who fears separation. Also, the client should be informed that he or she can return to the agency if the need arises.

- The ending of a meaningful professional relationship should utilize some type of ritual to mark this transition. Fortune (2009) notes that such markers include culturally appropriate good-byes such as hugging and shaking hands and, in the case of terminations within a support group or treatment group, they might involve the exchange of token gifts, potluck meals, and celebrations at which the participants recall highlights in the group's experience. Such ending rituals are especially important in work with children.

Selected Bibliography

Fortune, Anne E. "Terminating with Clients." In *Social Workers' Desk Reference,* 2nd ed. Edited by Albert R. Roberts. New York: Oxford University Press, 2009, pp. 627–631.

National Association of Social Workers. *NASW Code of Ethics.* Washington, DC: NASW, 1999.

Reamer, Frederic G. *Social Work Malpractice and Liability: Strategies for Prevention,* 2nd ed. New York: Columbia University Press, 2003.

Walsh, Joseph. *Endings in Clinical Practice,* 2nd ed. Chicago: Lyceum, 2007.

SECTION B

TECHNIQUES AND GUIDELINES FOR INDIRECT PRACTICE

Many of the guidelines for termination and evaluation identified in the introduction to Section A of this chapter also apply to indirect practice (work with organizations and communities). However, modifications are necessary because individual clients are not the focus of the evaluations, professional relationship terminations are usually less intense, and/or a large number of participants or stakeholders are typically involved.

Termination activities

Organization and community change does not come easily. For social workers employed in administrative positions or with agencies focused on community or social policy change, projects are terminated and new projects are subsequently initiated. For most social workers, however, large system change is usually not part of their job description. Rather, the typical social worker contributes personal time or squeezes indirect service work into an already packed schedule. This effort might be as a team of staff members or a special committee from the community that works on bringing about the desired change. The conclusion of a successful organization or community change effort becomes a time for celebration, or, if unsuccessful, a time for critique and recognition of the significance of making the effort. Refreshments in a conference room, dinner out together, a gathering at someone's home, or some other symbolic recognition can be important concluding activities that terminate the process.

Evaluation activities

A number of techniques are available to social workers serving as administrators or specialists in community or policy change positions. However, for most social workers the indirect service evaluation activities involve securing client feedback regarding the quality of services they received, engaging in program evaluation, occasionally evaluating the full range of agency services, or assessing the results of a community change activity.

"Worker Performance Evaluation" from 4th edition

Serving as an administrator or supervisor in a human services agency inevitably involves assessing the skills of the staff and providing feedback to improve that person's knowledge and skills, as well as to serve as information on which salary and promotion decisions are made. Thus, skills in personnel assessment are needed. Two examples of approaches that might be used are *worker performance evaluation* and *peer review.* Worker performance assessments are designed to measure the extent to which the worker is achieving the requirements of his or her position. Peer review is a format sometimes used in agencies where one's colleagues, on a rotational basis, provide critique of each other's work and the supervisor periodically examines these reviews to identify strengths and limitations in staff competence.

"Peer Review" from 4th edition

14.9 PROGRAM EVALUATION

Because an agency program is a set of activities designed to achieve desired client and/or social change, its success in achieving that change is partially determined by its ability to respond to changing needs, concerns, and circumstances. Unless programs are regularly evaluated, they can rapidly become out-of-touch with client needs and lose the support of the community. **Program evaluation**, then, is the systematic examination of a program to determine the degree to which it is achieving its goals and objectives. Sound program evaluation and the correction of any identified deficiencies are essential if the program is to effectively serve its purpose and is likely to be supported by funding sources.

The following guidelines should be followed when considering a program evaluation:

- *Identify the users of the evaluation data and report* (e.g., administrators, practitioners, grant sources, legislators, fund-raisers). What do they really want and need from this evaluation? What type of information can they understand and use? Is it reasonable to believe that evaluation results will affect the continuation, modification, or termination of the program? It is not a good use of time and resources to begin a program evaluation effort unless the results can make a real difference in terms of the program's operation and the services provided.

- *Decide if an evaluation is feasible.* Do you have the necessary time, money, and skill available? If not, do you have access to experts in program evaluation for consultation? Is the data you need readily available? Are key staff members committed to the idea of evaluation and making constructive use of the results? Is the program stable enough to make an evaluation meaningful?

- *State the goals and objectives of the program.* Are there clear statements of the program goals and objectives? You cannot evaluate a program until you know precisely what it is trying to accomplish. Often, *goal clarification* is the first step in engaging the stakeholders in a program evaluation.

- *Describe the program's activities that are to be evaluated.* The activities must be logically connected to the program's goals and objectives and must focus on factors or forces over which it has control. Another initial step is to clearly describe the program's units of intervention or services. For example, to describe when an intervention activity is happening, you might ask: When does it begin and end? Who can best describe the intervention—worker, client, and/or someone else? Can you clearly distinguish an intervention from other client–staff interactions? Can you decide when a service has been used to determine if the client or consumer has sufficiently received the intervention? (For example, if a client attended only two of five scheduled sessions of a parenting class, has she or he received parent training?)

- *Select measurable indicators of change.* Once you are clear as to the specific attitudes, behaviors, or conditions your program is trying to change and you are clear as to the interventions used to help bring about those changes, you need to select indicators of change that can be detected and measured. Make sure these indicators are ones that can be reasonably attributed to your program's intervention. Also, decide if it is reasonable to believe that the desired effects of the intervention will occur within the time frame you are using. If you cannot wait to measure long-term benefits, you must choose indicators that reflect more immediate changes.

- *Select appropriate and feasible data collection and measurement tools and/or instruments.* Developing a valid and reliable instrument is a complex, time-consuming, and expensive process, so try to use available instruments. Look online for evaluations done on similar programs and use or adapt instruments that others have found useful.

- *Plan how you will collect, tabulate, and analyze the data.* Do not collect more data than you can manage and use. Make sure the data you want is actually available. For example, if you plan to gather data from case files, be sure the files contain the information you need. If your data is stored in the computer system, can you retrieve it? Can the information you seek be obtained without a release from the client? If your evaluation design involves contacting former service consumers, will you be able to locate them?

- *Interpret the results of your evaluation.* The final product of your effort is to report the results to the various stakeholders who are invested in this evaluation. Caution should be used in interpreting the data because factors other than those reflected in the data may account for a program's success or failure. For example, low staff morale may produce poor outcomes despite a well-conceived program. An effort should be made to *triangulate* the results—that is, to look for other indicators of program success that support or contradict the results of the program evaluation.

One useful tool for guiding program evaluation is known as the **logic model**. The essence of this model is to create a structure appropriate for the evaluation and to ensure a rigorous and logical assessment of each aspect of a program. According to the logic model, the following items should be considered in conducting a program evaluation:

- *Priorities established for the program.* The fundamental criteria for evaluating a program are first expressed in the "broad strokes" of the agency's mission, vision statement, specification of whom to serve and how to serve them, mandates from the public, and so on. Thus, the first step in program evaluation is to review these statements as expressed when the program was created and then to update them to reflect any changes in emphasis that may have occurred.

- *Inputs into the program. Inputs* are the resources the agency invests in the program—for instance, staff, volunteers, money, equipment, information technology, and other elements necessary to carry out the day-to-day program activities. How much of each resource is needed? How much is being used? What does each cost?

- *Outputs from the program. Outputs* are what a program actually does or accomplishes. An evaluation must identify these outputs in order to develop appropriate measures of a program's functioning. Some human services programs can be evaluated by focusing on the individual / family / group sessions conducted, others in terms of the training provided to volunteers, and yet others in public education provided or the number of research studies conducted. Outputs, too, might be reflected in the number of clients served, groups facilitated, days of care provided, or participants in community education meetings.

- *Outcomes, impacts, and results.* The impact or effect of an agency's activities might take several forms—for instance, people gaining awareness or knowledge of a social issue, client success in addressing personal problems, or workers developing skills to better serve their clients.

The logic model provides a tool for specifying the factors that should be considered when engaging in program evaluation and summarizing the results. A number of formats for applying the logic model can be found at http://www.bing.com/images/search?q=logic+model&qpvt=logic+model&FORM=IGRE.

Selected Bibliography

Grinnell, Richard M., Jr., Peter A. Gabor, and Yvonne A. Unrau. *Program Evaluation for Social Workers: Foundations of Evidence-Based Programs*, 6th ed. New York: Oxford University Press, 2012.

Knowlton, Lisa Wyatt, and Cynthia C. Phillips. *The Logic Model Guidebook: Better Strategies for Great Results*, 2nd ed. Thousand Oaks, CA: Sage, 2013.

Mertens, Donna M., and Amy T. Wilson. *Program Evaluation Theory and Practice: A Comprehensive Guide.* New York, Guilford, 2012.

14.10 A CLIENT SATISFACTION QUESTIONNAIRE (CSQ)

Client or former client input should be an element in both program evaluation (see Item 14.9) and agency evaluation (see Item 14.11). A **client satisfaction questionnaire (CSQ)** solicits information from clients about the services they have received. It asks clients to rate their experience with aspects of the helping process, such as the atmosphere of the agency and its efficiency when providing services, the success of the intervention, the competence of the staff, and so on. Typically, a questionnaire or other format for data collection is administered at the point of termination or shortly thereafter, although some agencies administer a CSQ after three to five interviews and periodically thereafter to identify issues that should be immediately addressed.

Figure 14.7 is an example of a typical CSQ. Although CSQs vary in length, they should be easy for a client to complete; therefore, they should be relatively brief and not request too much detailed information. If the CSQ uncovers a concern that needs to be explored in more detail, the questionnaire might be followed up with an in-depth interview or perhaps a focus group composed of current or former clients.

A limitation of the CSQ format is that it records only the client's perceptions of what happened as a result of the intervention at the point of termination, although that perception may change over time. Also, there is a tendency for satisfied clients to return a greater portion of the questionnaires (particularly if a mailed questionnaire) than those who are dissatisfied— skewing the data toward positive responses.

The process for implementing a CSQ is as follows:

Step 1: *Decide what population of clients to sample.* The sample could be representative of agency clientele in general, of clients who have received a particular type of service, or of clients who make up a particular demographic group (e.g., clients over age 60). Unless all members of the target group are to be included in the study, a basic knowledge of sampling methods is required in order to draw a representative sample. Criteria for CSQ distribution should relate to the purpose of the evaluation, statistical requirements, and administrative convenience.

Step 2: *Design the questionnaire.* Keep it simple and brief and avoid professional jargon. The agency may want to gather certain client and demographic information in order to determine if satisfaction with or complaints about services are related to factors such as the client's ethnicity, age, socioeconomic status, and the like. However, asking for such information tends to weaken assurances of anonymity.

Step 3: *Administer the questionnaire.* This step can be carried out by clerical staff, volunteers, or social service aides; however, those administering the questionnaire must be trained in its use in order to increase reliability and protect confidentiality. A mailed CSQ, too, can provide the client with anonymity but does presume that the client can read and understand the language used. If the agency has contact information on file, the questionnaire can be mailed, emailed, or administered by phone. If it includes clients who are still in regular contact with the agency, the questionnaire can usually be administered by a receptionist. The greatest amount of work in administering the questionnaire will probably be in following up on those clients who fail to return the questionnaire, as these clients will have to be called individually or sent a letter to obtain a reasonable return rate. If the responses are to

Evaluating Your Experience at ABC Agency

Thank you for taking a few minutes to evaluate the services you have received at our agency. Your answers to this brief questionnaire will help us improve our services. Feel free to offer additional comments in the space provided or on the back of this page.

Instructions: For each question below, check (✓) your answer.

A. How do you feel about the way you were treated by the receptionist?
—— (1) dissatisfied
—— (3) no feelings either way
—— (5) satisfied
Comments:

B. How do you feel about the length of time you had to wait before our agency provided you with service?
—— (1) unhappy or dissatisfied
—— (3) no feelings either way
—— (5) pleased or satisfied
Comments:

C. Did you accomplish what you expected to achieve when you came to this agency?
—— (5) yes, completely
—— (4) mostly accomplished
—— (3) some accomplishment
—— (2) no real progress
—— (1) worse off than before
Comments:

D. Did you feel your situation/problem(s) changed when you became involved with this agency?
—— (1) things became much worse
—— (2) things somewhat worse
—— (3) no change
—— (4) things somewhat better
—— (5) things became much better
Comments:

E. Which of the following statements comes closest to your feelings about the impact of this agency's services on your situation or problem?
—— (1) made things much worse
—— (2) made things somewhat worse
—— (3) no change
—— (4) made things somewhat better
—— (5) made things much better
Comments:

F. How competent do you feel the social worker was to deal with your situation or problem?
—— (5) very competent
—— (4) moderately competent
—— (2) somewhat incompetent
—— (1) very incompetent
Comments:

G. If a friend needed services from an agency like ours, would you recommend our agency?
—— (1) never
—— (2) probably not
—— (4) probably yes
—— (5) definitely yes
Comments:

H. Overall, how do you feel about your experience with our agency?
—— (1) very dissatisfied
—— (2) dissatisfied
—— (4) satisfied
—— (5) very satisfied
Comments:

It is helpful to know something about the person completing this questionnaire: Are you:

—— Client
—— Parent of agency client
—— Spouse of agency client

—— Male
—— Female

Client's age:
—— under 21　　—— 51–65
—— 21–50　　　—— over 65

Figure 14.7
Sample Client Satisfaction Questionnaire

be anonymous, there will be problems in follow-up; therefore, a guarantee of confidentiality without the added assurance of anonymity may be preferable. Statistical techniques can determine whether there are significant differences between those who return the questionnaire and those who require urging.

Step 4: *Tabulate and analyze the questionnaire data.* Manual tabulation may be possible for short questionnaires. Computer processing is desirable for lengthy questionnaires and when a large number of questionnaires must be tabulated.

Step 5: *Use the results.* Obvious as it may seem, too often data will be collected and not used or taken seriously. From the beginning, a plan should be in place to assure that the clients' views are carefully considered by staff and, when needed, adjustments in the services are made to address client concerns.

Selected Bibliography

Martin, Lawrence L., and Peter M. Kettner. *Measuring the Performance of Human Service Programs.* Thousand Oaks, CA: Sage, 1996.
Sue, Valerie, and Lois A. Ritter. *Conducting Online Surveys.* Thousand Oaks, CA: Sage, 2007.

14.11 AGENCY EVALUATION

Social agencies are expected to demonstrate that they are efficient and effective in the provision of services. Agency boards, legislative bodies, and other funding sources regularly demand that agencies review their functioning and report the results of that evaluation. Individual workers, too, are often interested in performance indicators that might stimulate organizational changes necessary to improve the quality of services. Thus, social workers should be familiar with some of the indicators used in agency performance reviews.

An evaluation must be preceded by a clear statement of goals. Often, the first task in agency evaluation is for the governing board or other policymakers to explicate the current goals and objectives for the organization. It is only with this information that appropriate performance indicators can be selected and methods of data collection identified.

An agency's evaluation should address the degree to which its programs respond to community need, the quality of services offered, the satisfaction of clients (see Item 14.10), efficiency in use of resources, and so on. Here are some of the areas that should be considered:

- *Responsiveness.* To what extent do the agency and the agency's programs respond to community needs and concerns? Does its purpose and programs reflect and support the community's values?
- *Relevance.* Do sponsors, constituents, and consumers find the agency's programs appropriate to the needs or problems they seek to address?
- *Availability.* Are the amount and type of services provided sufficient to meet the needs of the community?
- *Accessibility.* Are the location, cost, times, and days that services are offered appropriate for the clientele of the agency? Are there groups that do not receive services due to accessibility issues?
- *Quality.* Do the services meet expected standards of quality as judged by client satisfaction, expert opinion, or accreditation organizations?

- *Awareness.* Is the general population, as well as other human services providers, sufficiently aware of the services offered to assure that persons who need the services know how to obtain them?
- *Productivity.* Does the program efficiently use its resources to accomplish the agency's goals?

With clarity about the questions to be answered when collecting data, it is then possible to select a set of *performance indicators* that can measure the agency's level of success and, if indicated, lead to improvements. Selecting appropriate indicators and finding accurate data regarding them is a complex task. The following indicators illustrate a few essential areas to include in measures of agency success:

- *Personnel-related factors.* Rate of turnover, absenteeism, staff vacancies, number of hours contributed by volunteers, frequency of in-service training, and so forth
- *The intake process.* Data on the number and sources of referrals, number of telephone or email contacts, number of people on the waiting list, average length of time between first contact and initiation of service, and so on
- *Service-related factors.* Number of new cases opened each month, average length of service per case, number of clients served, number and type of cases referred elsewhere, number of former clients returning for service, average cost per client, client satisfaction with services, and so on
- *Staff productivity.* Size and type of caseload per worker, number of counseling sessions provided each day, number of hours spent per case, amount of inter-agency contacts per month, number of miles of work-related travel each week, and the like
- *Cost of providing services.* Average cost of staff time per case, number of clients paying a fee for service, source of fee payment (e.g., private pay, insurance, other third party), average travel cost per case, average time spent in case recording and other indirect service, estimated value of volunteer hours per week, and so on

This data, once collected, must be carefully analyzed. Data collected over time will allow for the examination of trends within the agency and response to adjustments to improve the efficiency and effectiveness of the agency. Also, the data can be compared to data from similar agencies, making it possible to gain a relative picture of the agency's functioning.

Selected Bibliography

Knapp, Stephen A., and Gary R. Anderson. *Agency-Based Program Evaluation: Lessons from Practice.* Thousand Oaks, CA: Sage, 2010.

Posavac, Emil J., and Raymond G. Carey. *Program Evaluation: Methods and Case Studies.* Upper Saddle River, NJ: R. G. Carey and Associates, 2007.

PART 5

SPECIALIZED TECHNIQUES AND GUIDELINES FOR SOCIAL WORK PRACTICE

The techniques and guidelines described in prior sections of this book could be used by almost all social workers, regardless of their practice setting. In addition to these generic tools of the social worker's trade, specialized knowledge and skills are required for some practice situations and activities. Part V concludes the book with two chapters on these specialized aspects of social work.

Some client groups require a special sensitivity and understanding by the social worker. For example, unique insight is required to help a client deal with the devastating impact of poverty, to provide services to a woman who has been battered, or to intervene when an individual is at risk of committing suicide. Clients of different sexual orientations and those of different age groups call for special sensitivity, too. Working with a child or adolescent requires knowledge of developmental factors and communication skills that connect with young people. And at the other end of the age spectrum, older people have unique needs that must be recognized. Specialized knowledge and skills are also required when clients have a physical disability, brain injury, intellectual disability, chemical dependence, mental illness, eating disorder, or is an immigrant. Chapter 15 identifies guidelines for working with these clients.

Another set of specialized guidelines can help the social worker have a satisfying and productive career. Chapter 16 presents guidelines that will assist the worker in obtaining employment, preparing for licensing and certification exams, dealing with job-related stress, testifying in court, avoiding malpractice suits, and addressing issues of sexual misconduct. Finally, to support the social worker in carrying out her or his professional obligations, this chapter also provides guidance on how to provide and utilize supervision, consume and contribute to social work knowledge, improve the social work image, and assume a leadership role within the human services.

15

Guidelines for Working with Vulnerable Client Groups

LEARNING OBJECTIVES

At the conclusion of this chapter, the reader should be prepared to:

- Explain the special challenges experienced by individuals and families who live in poverty.
- Describe special practice considerations when a social worker's client is in a particular age group, such as: a young child, an adolescent, a person parenting a child, or an older person.
- Discuss guidelines for responding to a potentially violent practice situation such as domestic violence or a possible suicide.
- Identify guidelines for social work practice when working with a client who experiences an intellectual disability, a brain injury, or a serious physical disability.
- Describe guidelines for social work practice when working with clients experiencing a chemical dependency, serious mental illness, personality disorder, or taking psychotropic medication.
- Summarize basic principles that should guide the delivery of services to clients who are gay, lesbian, bisexual, or transgender.
- Describe guidelines for serving clients experiencing grief or problems associated with her or his religion and/or spirituality.
- Identify special considerations a social worker should address when working with clients experiencing issues related to the criminal justice system, the effects of war, the adoption of a child, immigration, or a widespread disaster such as a flood, wildfire, or tornado.

Social workers practice within a wide variety of settings, and consequently, they encounter a wide variety of clients with many different types of concerns, problems, and requests. Even though the clients served by a particular program may have presenting problems that are quite similar, each client will react to his or her situation and to the social worker in a unique way. Thus, social workers must always adapt their approaches and techniques to a client's unique needs, characteristics, and circumstances.

The items selected for this chapter illustrate how a social worker might adapt her or his approach to a client by providing information and guidelines on several different client groups. By comparing the approaches recommended for these diverse client groups, you will come to a deeper appreciation of why direct-service practitioners, as well as those who design and administer programs, must always consider the uniqueness of the clients they serve. In addition, you will understand more clearly why an approach that works well for one group may not be appropriate for another.

15.1 THE CLIENT WHO IS EXPERIENCING POVERTY

Many of the individuals and families encountered in social work practice are living in poverty, meaning that their income is insufficient to purchase adequate food, suitable and safe housing, and basic health care. No matter what the cause of a person's poverty, no one should have to live in poverty in a wealthy society such as the United States. No one should have to live in conditions that are dehumanizing, unsafe, and unhealthy. Social workers, regardless of their practice settings and job titles, have a responsibility to collaborate with others in order to advance social and economic policies and programs that will prevent or reduce the incidence of poverty.

Poverty has devastating effects on individuals, families, and communities. It is a contributing factor to numerous other problems such as the breakup of families, violence, crime, substance abuse, suicide, and disease. Children experiencing poverty are especially vulnerable to the effects of poor nutrition, disease, family insecurity, and social instability.

Although the characteristics and degree of poverty will vary depending on whether one is examining poverty in a modern and developed or a developing country, the root causes of widespread and persistent poverty are to be found in a society's economic system and in its political and economic decisions regarding what it will produce, how it is produced, by whom, and for whom. In short, poverty is fundamentally an issue of social and economic justice. Regrettably, when it comes to a question of justice, there are no completely fair economic systems. None of the systems—whether free market economies, planned economies, or mixed economies—is able to deliver all that its theory promises.

An economic recession or depression, or a war can quickly push large numbers of people into poverty. Regional and localized pockets of poverty can result from natural disasters such as floods and earthquakes and from the loss of an industry such as steel, textiles, or lumber. The more immediate or situational causes of poverty among the individuals and families encountered in social work practice are usually job layoffs, the inability to secure a job that pays a living wage, and an illness or injury that precludes employment.

Even in good economic times, some groups are at high risk of slipping into poverty. This is especially true of those lacking in education and marketable job skills and also those with an intellectual limitation, mental illness, addiction, or debilitating health problem. Individuals and families can quickly slide into poverty after loss to the family's breadwinner because of death or imprisonment, a house fire, a serious health problem, and the like. People on a fixed income, such as the elderly, are at risk when faced with a high rate of inflation and rapid increases in the cost of food, housing, utilities, and health care. Racism, sexism, and other forms or discrimination restrict the economic opportunities available to various segments of a population.

In the United States, many of those who are poor are the so-called working poor—those who may be working two or three part-time jobs but still not earning an adequate income and not receiving benefits such as health insurance or a retirement plan. Many of those living in poverty are single mothers and their children. Families headed by young mothers are at high risk of being poor. After a divorce, many mothers who are raising their children are unable to make ends meet because many fathers do not or cannot pay adequate child support. Women with limited education face special challenges since many of the jobs available to them (e.g., waitress, maid, personal care aide) pay low wages, do not provide benefits, and their working hours are often at night or on weekends when child care is especially expensive and transportation is difficult to arrange.

Direct service social workers responding to individuals and families who are poor will find this additional information and guidance useful:

- When designing or selecting an approach to working with clients who are poor, recognize that when people become poor, they encounter a multitude of forces and barriers that keep them in poverty. For example, in order to get a job, an individual must have appropriate clothing, transportation, recent job experiences, a permanent address, a telephone, email, and access to a computer, printer, and the Internet—things that many poor people do not have. A parent who wants to work may discover that the cost of child care will consume much of the pay received from a minimum-wage job. Working one's way out of poverty requires not only motivation and capacity but also the opportunity to do so. It is a slow process that requires planning and methodically executing a multitude of small steps (see Item 13.13). Changing one's life circumstances is difficult for anyone, but doing so when poor is especially difficult, given the demoralizing and exhausting effects of poverty.

- Social workers must possess a working knowledge of the various government programs and private agencies that provide financial assistance and job training. The most effective programs are those designed to address an array of personal and family needs and concerns in addition to financial problems. Providing access to education and technical training is one of the most cost-effective approaches to addressing poverty among people who are healthy and capable. However, education and job-training programs are usually not, by themselves, sufficient. Completing a program of education or training can be especially difficult for those who are overwhelmed by other personal problems and family responsibilities and by persons who suffer the psychological effects of domestic violence, child abuse and neglect, death of a loved one, and other traumatic life events. Thus, counseling, child care, transportation, and other supportive services are essential components of successful adult education, job training, and employment programs.

  Securing a job and financial independence is a feasible goal for many who are poor. For some individuals of working age, however, this is not a realistic goal because their capacity for gainful employment is severely limited by serious and chronic conditions such as mental illness, mental retardation, brain injury, and substance abuse.

- Disparities in how complex welfare policies, rules, and eligibility criteria are interpreted can become an obstacle for people who desperately need government assistance and services. Client or *case advocacy* by the social worker may be needed to help individuals secure the welfare assistance for which they are eligible. *Class advocacy* is necessary to make these systems more responsive to the needs of people (see Items 13.17 and 13.32).

- A client's views and beliefs about being poor are of importance because they can influence his or her response to current circumstances. Among those who are poor there are a variety of beliefs, attitudes, and feelings about being poor. For example, an individual who has always been poor may view living in poverty quite differently than an individual who for many years had an adequate income before becoming poor. Moreover, a person who lives in a community made up of mostly poor people will view her or his situation differently than the person who lives in a community where few others are poor. Some who are in poverty, as officially measured by government standards or other objective criteria, may not define themselves as being poor. To better understand the client's responses to the current situation, consider the following questions:

  - What personal and family characteristics, situational factors, and economic forces are contributing to the client's economic problems?
  - Did the client grow up in a community where most others were poor? If yes, what meaning did he or she assign to being poor?
  - Are the client's family and relatives also poor or is he or she economically different from family and relatives?
  - Has the client been abandoned or rejected by family, relatives, and friends who are better off economically? If yes, did a problem such as mental illness, substance abuse, or criminal activity contribute to this ostracism?
  - Who are the client's sources of social support and everyday assistance? Are these persons also poor?
  - What strengths or resiliency factors has the client relied on to cope with the challenges of living in poverty?

- Living in poverty is extraordinarily stressful because so many aspects of the individual's life are worrisome and unpredictable. This commonly gives rise to anxiety, fear, and frustration. Consequently, some who are poor are quick to anger and resentful toward anyone who might somehow make their lives even more difficult. Still others feel hopeless and respond to their circumstances and to service providers with passivity and emotional dependency.

  Because the dominant American culture values work, money, material possessions, and independence, persons who are poor are prone to feelings of inferiority and shame. They may feel inadequate, rejected, and shunned. They may feel guilty about being poor, especially if they are the parents of young children and see that their children are being harmed by their life circumstances. Some cope with these painful feelings by withdrawing from ordinary social relationships. Some express their embarrassment and resentment by criticizing and tearing down the work and performance of other people, including those working in programs that address the problems faced by the poor.

  Some of the people who live on the streets or in shelters for the homeless are especially challenging clients. Their economic situation may be complicated by substance abuse, mental illness, inadequate nutrition, and disabling and untreated health problems. Some of these individuals are so immersed in a lifestyle of day-to-day survival that they approach all relationships in a suspicious and calculating manner. Some are belligerent and aggressive; others are passive and dependent. A client's frustration, sense of hopelessness, and unpredictable lifestyle can be barriers to her or his effective utilization of professionals and human service programs that expect their clients to be cooperative, adhere to schedules, and follow through on plans.

- Strive to reduce the social distance and power differential between yourself and the client. Do this by looking for opportunities to talk with clients about the very ordinary aspects of life, such as their interests, hobbies, and special times in their lives. Invite your clients to share their music, art, and other creative skills. When possible, utilize in-home interviews and when appropriate to the practice setting, share meals with clients (see Items 10.6 and 10.11). Above all, recognize their humanness, their uniqueness, their worth, and their dignity.

- Identify and arrange opportunities for clients to share their knowledge and skills for dealing with poverty. For example, many who are poor have learned to be frugal and thrifty in shopping and stretching their very limited resources. Many have located and learned to use community resources that are overlooked by others. And many are very creative in working out arrangements that permit several individuals or families to share what little they have and to help each other cope. Still others have arrived at profound insights into the human condition and developed a truly inspiring spirituality. These are all important strengths that need to be recognized and, if the client is willing, shared with others who struggle with many of the same issues.

- In keeping with the empowerment strategy, offer clients opportunities to shape the programs they utilize by serving on agency boards or advisory groups, or by testifying at a legislative hearing. Many clients have a need to express appreciation and reciprocate in some way for the help they receive. If this is important to a client, arrange for him or her to make an in-kind contribution to the relevant program or agency. For example, a client might want to do volunteer work or somehow assist the agency to serve other clients. Unfortunately, issues of insurance and concerns over legal liability may be barriers to arranging suitable opportunities for reciprocity by clients (see Items 13.17, 13.18, 13.32, and 13.38).

- Social workers should look for opportunities to join with others in the formation of organizations that help people reduce their expenditures or increase their earnings. Two examples are local cooperatives and micro-loan programs. A *co-op (cooperative)* is a membership organization that pools the purchasing powers of a large group and passes the savings on to its members. The members typically pay a small membership fee and/or volunteer their time to work in the organization. For example, a food co-op buys wholesale groceries in a large quality and then sells them to the co-op members at prices lower than retail stores. A co-op might focus on sharing and cultivating a garden space to grow vegetables. Still others might focus on sharing the rent for shop space and equipment needed for auto repair and maintenance. Child-care co-ops can reduce the cost of child care for working parents. Close neighbors might share in the ownership and use of a car, lawnmower, snow blower, or the tools and ladders needed for home repair and maintenance.

    A *micro-loan program* is essentially a community-oriented bank that specializes in making small, unsecured, and short-term loans to responsible individuals who need a small amount of money to launch an income-producing enterprise. An example would be an individual who has plans to operate a window-washing service but needs $450 to purchase tools and supplies.

- Desperation and hopelessness can push a person into making decisions that others judge to be unwise and imprudent. For example, a mother with very little money may splurge and buy her child a pair of expensive shoes. Fear and worry over a lack of money can also draw a person into activities that are illegal or that violate his or her conscience. For example, in an effort to secure money, a desperate individual might sell drugs, steal, or engage in prostitution. As a professional, you will probably feel disappointed and irritated because such choices by your client make things even worse. Although you cannot condone illegal behavior, try to see the world through your client's eyes and understand why individuals make these choices. Do not allow yourself to become judgmental or moralistic, for that would only create a barrier to further work with the client.

- Many professionals (e.g., social workers, physicians, nurses, psychologists) admit to feeling somewhat uncomfortable when working directly with persons who live in truly desperate economic circumstances. This discomfort stems, in part, from the obvious fact that the client has so little and, by comparison, the professional has so much. In addition, the professional realizes that she or he does, in fact, have the ability (i.e., the money) to alleviate this client's immediate financial distress, at least for a few hours or a few days. It is this awareness that tugs on the professional's conscience and sense of fundamental justice. In working with clients who have other types of problems, the professional knows that he or she does not have the ability to bring about such an immediate change. In work with the economically poor, the professional must struggle with the question, If I have the ability, do I have the responsibility? (See Chapter 2, "Personal Responses to Clients in Need")

Selected Bibliography

Albert, Raymond, and Louise Skolnik. *Social Welfare Programs: Narratives from Hard Times*. Independence, KY: Cengage, 2006.

Eitzen, D. Stanley, and Kelly Smith. *Experiencing Poverty: Voices from the Bottom*, 2nd ed. Upper Saddle River, NJ: Pearson, 2009.

Iceland, John. *Poverty in America: A Handbook*, 3rd ed. Berkeley: University of California Press, 2013.

Midgley, James, and Amy Conley, eds. *Social Work and Social Development*. New York: Oxford University Press, 2010.

Payne, Ruby, Philip De Vol, and Terie Smith. *Bridges Out of Poverty: Strategies for Professionals and Communities*. Highland TX: aha! Process Inc., 2006.

Minuchin, Patricia, Jorge Colapinto, and Salvador Minuchin. *Working with Families of the Poor*, 2nd ed. New York: Guilford, 2007.

Shipler, David. *The Working Poor*. New York: Vintage Press, 2005.

Yunus, Muhammad. *Banker to the Poor: Micro-Lending and the Battle against World Poverty*. New York: Public Affairs Press, 2007.

_____ . *Building Social Businesses*. New York: Public Affairs Press, 2011.

15.2 THE CLIENT WHO IS A CHILD

Because children are not miniature adults, many of the techniques that are effective with adult clients do not work with children. When their clients are children, social workers must add some new skills to their repertoire, such as the use of play. The sections that follow provide guidelines for a range of tasks involved in working with a child under the age of about 12.

Planning the Interview

- Be clear about why you are meeting with the child and what it is that you hope to accomplish. Plan several alternative methods to accomplish your goal. Anticipate what could go wrong (e.g., the child will not talk, the child cries, the child will not leave parent) and consider how you might handle such awkward situations. Conduct the interview in a room that is familiar and comfortable to the child. If that is not possible, consider an open space such as a park or playground. Be cognizant that only limited confidentiality can be provided to a child. Parents will usually have access to records kept on their child.

- Consider using some form of play to put a young child at ease and facilitate communication. Prior to the interview, assemble play materials that may be helpful. For younger children, provide art materials (e.g., finger paints, clay, building blocks), as well as objects that can be used to portray family members and situations (e.g., dolls, hand puppets, doll house, toy animals). For older children, consider simple board games, toy telephones, puzzles, and electronic games.

Introducing Yourself and Getting Started

- Place yourself at the child's level physically; sit or squat so you do not tower over the child. When introducing yourself, inform the child how you want to be addressed and give a simple description of your role (e.g., "My name is Ron Hoffman. Please call me Ron. My job is to help children who have problems at home"). Be prepared to offer a simple and truthful explanation as to why you need to speak with the child. It may be necessary to assure the child that she or he is not in trouble and that the interview is not a punishment. If the child is at least 6 or 7 years of age, ask what he or she has been told about the purpose of the interview. This may reveal what the child is expecting. You might ask if someone (e.g., a parent) has told the child what he or she should say or do during the interview.

- Perhaps you will begin with some friendly conversation and showing an interest in what the child is wearing or carrying or asking about the child's school or favorite activities or TV shows. If the child is frightened, attempt to normalize the situation by saying something like, "When I was your age, I was always afraid to talk to new people." If the child appears reluctant to talk for fear of retaliation by others, you might need to describe what you are prepared to do to keep him or her safe. But do not make promises you cannot keep.

  If the child refuses to talk or interact, try engaging her or him in a parallel activity and then gradually initiate conversation about the activity. For example, if the child does not talk but begins to play with a doll, then you might pick up another doll and engage in similar play. This will often lead to some interaction and opportunity for verbal exchanges.

  Young children who are frightened and withdrawn will sometimes relax and let down their guard in response to a bit of clowning. However, this clowning or joking around must be done in a way so the child knows for sure that you are trying to be silly. For example, if you put on a clown's red plastic nose, the child will understand your intentions. Another technique is to do something rather unexpected, such as, "Brian, while we are talking, we may get thirsty. Should we go get some juice now or should we wait until later?"

Gathering Information from Children

- Because young children have limited verbal ability, much of the information you gather will come from observing the child's nonverbal behavior during play and social interactions. However, in order to draw valid inferences about a child's personality or behavioral patterns, you must observe the child in several different situations. Do not base a conclusion or assessment on a single observation.

- Young children act out their concerns in play and often project their concerns and feelings into the stories they make up and into their play, drawings, and art. Thus, consider using these activities to set up imaginary or pretend situations that are relevant to the topics you wish to explore. For example, present the child with a set of dolls and ask the child to make up a story about what makes the dolls happy or afraid. Or, you might ask the child to draw a picture of a family or children at school and then tell a story about the people in the picture. If the child is hesitant, you may need to initiate the storytelling about the dolls or pictures, but once the child is attentive, ask the child to continue the story.

  Although it is true that young children incorporate their thoughts, feelings, and experiences into their play, stories, and drawings, they will also incorporate themes drawn from TV programs, books, and incidents described by their friends. Thus, you must be cautious about interpreting what you observe because it may be difficult to pinpoint the source of the themes that appear in a child's play or stories. It is important to remember that themes of violence are quite common in the play of normal children. Thus, violence-related talk and play, especially by boys, is not by itself an indicator that a child has experienced or observed violence.

- Children between the ages of about 3 and 6 are usually eager to please adults. They are also suggestible, especially if asked leading questions. Children of this age may modify what they have to say in order to make it fit with what they believe the adult wants to hear. Young children are easily distracted and jump quickly from one topic or activity to another. Consequently, they may express only once what they think or feel about a particular concern. Asking a child to remain focused on a topic is seldom successful. If pressured to stay focused on a painful or sensitive topic, the child may become noncommittal or silent. Children who sense disapproval from adults will often cease talking.

- Most children older than about 6 years are able to answer simple, age-appropriate questions. However, they may need assistance to fully describe a situation or event. For example, you may use prompts such as: What happened next? Then what did you do? Where were you when this happened? Who was with you? As a general rule, avoid asking "why" questions, because children find it difficult to explain their motivations.

- Special techniques like story completions, doll play, and drawings may still be necessary and useful when interviewing children between about ages 7 and 9, but many children who are older than this will give a thoughtful response to an uncomplicated question. By age 9 or 10, children pay attention to the meaning and implications of words and can often detect phony or insincere messages. They will become suspicious when they observe incongruence between a person's words and actions.

  Many children of this age group find it easier to talk about personal matters if they can do so while engaged in some nondemanding activity such as a simple card game or a board game like checkers that does not require much concentration. Talking back and forth on a toy telephone or between hand puppets can facilitate communication. Sentence completions may work with older children (e.g., "When at home, I am afraid of _____" and "When I grow up and have children I will always _____").

• The game of "Hot or Cold" may prove useful when exploring a particular topic. For example, if the child is reluctant to describe a concern, you might say something like the following:

> Michael, I am going to make some guesses about what is bothering you. If my guesses are getting closer to what is troubling you, tell me that I am getting warmer. If my guesses are wrong, tell me that I am getting colder.

How Children Think

• Children between the ages of about 3 to 6 are concrete and egocentric in their thinking. For example, they believe an event or activity that makes them happy will have the same effect on all people. Their way of understanding is characterized by an all-or-nothing viewpoint; the child is unable to understand mixed feelings or ambivalence. The child may describe a person as mean and then just minutes later describe the same person as nice or fun. Such thinking in extremes and absolutes leads them to categorize both themselves and others as, for example, good or bad, smart or dumb, and so on. Children of this age typically describe themselves and others in terms of external characteristics (e.g., size, hair color, grade in school); they seldom mention personality traits except in global terms such as "She is happy" or "He is a bad person."

• At about age 6, the child's thinking starts to become more objective and logical. Gradually, the child acquires the ability to imagine being in another person's situation (empathy) and understand that different people have different feelings and experiences. However, even a 7-year-old may still believe that he or she is the total cause for how others, especially parents, feel and behave. It is not until about age 9 or 10 that children understand that they are not the cause of the behaviors and emotions they observe in others.

• By around age 10, children can view themselves as an individual with a mixture of characteristics and abilities (e.g., skilled at some things but not in others, sometimes good and sometimes bad). At this age, the child realizes that it is possible to have conflicting thoughts and feelings and opposing emotions simultaneously (e.g., to be angry at someone you love). The child can now anticipate how others will probably behave in a particular situation or react to certain information. Thus, the child can now manipulate words and information in order to influence how others will respond.

Assessing the Truthfulness of a Child's Statements

• A social worker responsible for investigating reports of abuse and neglect or conducting child custody evaluations will often need to form an opinion about whether a child is telling the truth. As a general rule, the younger the child, the less able and the less likely he or she is to fabricate a falsehood. However, children, like adults, may misunderstand and misinterpret their experiences and they may lie to escape punishment or get what they want.

• Sometimes, a parent or another adult will pressure a child to lie to a social worker in order to avoid the disclosure of some problem or criminal activity or as a way of hurting another person, such as an ex-spouse. If an adult has coached a child on what to tell a social worker, the child will often use adult-like language, use few gestures, display few facial expressions, and speak without genuine and appropriate emotions. Moreover, the child will be either inconsistent regarding the major elements of the story or, on the other hand, extremely consistent on certain points but unable to describe supporting or connecting details.

- Assessing the truth of a child's statement is a special challenge in the case of alleged child sexual abuse. As a general rule, sexually abused children are reluctant to report the abuse and do not want to talk about it. When children do self-report sexual abuse, they seldom lie about such matters. Deliberate false reports (i.e., actual lying by the child) are rare among children below about age 12 and infrequent among teenagers. Nonetheless, the possibility that the child is lying, misinterpreting a situation, or has named and accused the wrong person must always be kept in mind. The probability of a deception and false report increases whenever the child is the focus of a custody or visitation dispute. In these situations, one parent may instruct the child to accuse the other parent of some wrongdoing. Indicators of a possible deception by a child or duplicity by a parent include the following:

    - Disclosing of and talking about the incident seems too easy for the child (i.e., the child is not afraid or reluctant to tell others what happened).
    - The child does not show expected or authentic emotion when describing what happened (e.g., she or he does not cry or display distress, embarrassment, fear, anger).
    - The child uses adult-like words to describe sexual activity (as if coached or rehearsed by an adult).
    - The child describes the sexual activity using only visual images and not information drawn from the other senses (i.e., smell, taste, touch, sound).
    - The child does not seem to be afraid of the alleged offender (e.g., the child does not seem hesitant to meet with the alleged offender when that possibility is mentioned).
    - The child is not hesitant to talk about the sexual abuse in the presence of a nonoffending parent. (Most children try to shield the parent from the details of what happened.)
    - The child talks about having been sexually abused but does not display any of the other behavioral signs and symptoms associated with child sexual abuse (see Item 11.16).
    - The child's parent, while encouraging the child to report the sexual abuse, does not display the expected emotions such as being shocked, alarmed, angry, anxious, worried, or fearful. The parent may express anger at the alleged offender but does not display genuine distress over what has supposedly happened to the child.

- Children from about age 4 to 6 will often exaggerate or embellish, but when asked, "Is that pretend or real?" or "Is that really, really true?" they will usually acknowledge the difference between a truth and a make-believe story. In trying to describe something that happened, they will usually recall key actors or central events but not the connecting details, such as what happened before and after the event and how one thing led to another. They can remember special times and rituals such as a mealtime or a birthday party but they do not accurately remember things that are unrelated to their routines and familiar activities. They may tell a simple lie in order to avoid punishment but they do not have the cognitive abilities necessary to fabricate a story having several interrelated elements, actions, or actors.

- Preschool-age children do not grasp the concept of time and can seldom accurately describe when something happened. They do not use clocks or calendars to measure time. Children in the first and second grades will still use events such as nap-time, lunch time, Christmas, start of school, and other events as markers of time. Reference to such markers can help establish timeframes.

- Children between about 7 and 11 years old place a high value on fairness and honesty. They are quick to notice cheating or rule-breaking in a game. They may, however, embellish the truth in order to tell an exciting story. At this age, they possess the cognitive ability necessary to deliberately mislead others by selectively withholding information and using other simple deceptions. Children in the age range of about 9 to 11 are usually eager to please adults and tend to say what they believe adults want to hear. They have good memories of central actors and events and can usually recall relevant specifics with a little probing by an interviewer.

Additional Suggestions

- Children will behave differently in various situations and when with different people. Thus, you get only a sample of the child's behavior during an interview. The farther removed the child is from his or her usual social and family context, the more cautious you must be in drawing conclusions about the child's behavior. The child who is anxious or withdrawn during an office interview may be reacting to an unfamiliar environment. Multiple interviews with the child and in-home interviews are needed to secure a truly reliable assessment of a child's functioning.

- Be cautious about offering gifts or treats to a child. Although they are an extension of normal adult–child interaction and may be helpful in building a relationship, children and parents can easily misinterpret them. Make sure that your gift to a child is not viewed as competition with the child's parents.

- Because young children are attentive to nonverbal communication by adults, it may be helpful to make deliberate use of facial expressions and gestures when sending an important message. Light physical touch may be appropriate, but do not hug or caress a child, because this makes many children uncomfortable and, in addition, this could be misinterpreted as inappropriate sexual contact. Touch can be especially confusing and even threatening to a child who has been physically or sexually abused.

- During an interview, give the child as much choice as possible. But be sure to offer choices that you can accept. This point is illustrated in the following statements:

MISLEADING: "Well, Ellen, what would you like to do? We can do whatever you like."

BETTER: "Ellen, today you can use either the finger paints or the crayons. Which one do you want to use?"

- When behavior-control rules are necessary during an interview, explain the rules, along with any consequences for breaking them (e.g., "You are not permitted to hit me; if you hit me, I will put away the toys").

- Children are protective of their parents. They will usually defend their parents, even abusive parents. Be objective and nonjudgmental when talking about the parents' behavior (e.g., "Your dad has a problem with alcohol. When he is drinking he says and does bad things. That is why your parents are getting a divorce"). Avoid statements that the child could construe as a criticism of her or his parents.

- Answer a child's question honestly and directly (e.g., "I believe you will be in foster care until the school term ends"). Do not use euphemisms. Avoid explanations that are elaborate or complex. When giving important information to a child, present it as simply as possible and in small doses.

Children In- and Out-of-Home Placements

- Many of the children known professionally to social workers are in an out-of-home placement (i.e., foster family care, group homes, institutional care) and many were exposed to severe abuse or neglect. Regardless of the reason for the placement, a separation from parents and family is usually a disruptive and emotionally traumatic experience for children. The children may be confused about why they are in an out-of-home placement. Children often blame themselves for the family problems that led up to the placement and view their separation from family as a punishment for some real or imagined wrongdoing. Once separated from family, many children worry about the well-being and safety of their parents and any siblings still at home. Assume that the child has many questions about his or her current situation and future. Make it as easy as possible for the child to ask questions.

  Do everything possible to maintain frequent contacts and visits between the child in placement and his or her parents, siblings, and other relatives. In the long run, visitation is helpful to the child, even if the visits are upsetting. If, for example, the child's mother is addicted to drugs and acting irresponsibly, it is important for the child to see this behavior and recognize that the parent is in no shape to provide care. If a child in foster care has little or no contact with family, she or he will usually create an imaginary story or live out a fantasy that helps her or him cope with feelings of abandonment. It is better for the child to struggle with an unpleasant reality than to live within a pleasant but untrue fantasy.

- To a child, relationship losses, especially a series of losses, have long-lasting, negative effects. It is critically important to minimize the number of separations and placements experienced by a child. If a child must be separated from someone to whom he or she is emotionally attached, the move should be as gradual as possible, thus giving the child an opportunity to adjust. A ritual such as a going-away party helps the child make this transition by symbolically ending one relationship and beginning another. Without such a ritual, the child might feel as if he or she was given away or rejected. A transition ritual gives the child permission to let go of one relationship and embrace a new one. After the physical separation, it is important that the child be able to return to his or her former home for occasional visits.

- Because foster children experience so much change and uncertainty, the child's social worker must be prepared to become a dependable and stable figure in the child's life. The foster child is especially sensitive to any hint of rejection. Contacts with the child should be regular and predictable. If you must miss an appointment, explain this directly to the child.

- Children often feel shame and embarrassment about being in foster care, and consequently they may fabricate a story to explain their situation. When a teacher or school classmates discover this fabrication, the child may acquire a reputation as being a spinner of tall tales or a liar. Thus, it is important to help these children develop a truthful but abbreviated explanation of why they are in an out-of-home placement so they can more comfortably describe their current living situation to teachers, friends, and others.

- When speaking with a child's foster parents, adoptive parents, or group care staff, be truthful about the child's behavior, situation, and history. An effort to conceal or disguise a child's background because you fear others will not understand or accept the child almost always backfires.

Selected Bibliography

Camilleri, Vanessa, ed. *Healing the Inner City Child: Creative Arts Therapies with At-Risk Youth.* Philadelphia: Jessica Kingsley, 2007.

Poole, Debra, and Michael Lamb. *Investigative Interviews of Children.* Washington, DC: American Psychological Association, 1998.

Schaeffer, Charles, and Athena Drewes. *Therapeutic Powers of Play.* Hoboken, NJ: Wiley, 2014

Timberlake, Elizabeth, and Marika Cutler. *Developmental Play Therapy in Clinical Social Work.* Boston: Allyn and Bacon, 2001.

Webb, Nancy. *Social Work Practice with Children.* New York: Guilford, 2011.

Wilson, Claire, and Martine Powell, eds. *A Guide to Interviewing Children.* New York: Brunner-Routledge, 2001.

15.3 THE CLIENT WHO IS AN ADOLESCENT

The developmental period known as adolescence—between about ages 12 and 18—is a time of rapid physical and psychological change and awakening sexual desire. It is often a time of conflict and tension between adolescents and their parents regarding issues of authority and control. Parents typically worry that their adolescent children will become involved with drugs, have irresponsible sexual involvements, or are injured by recklessness.

The problems most likely to bring adolescents to the attention of a social worker include family conflict, alcohol and drug use, running away, behavior problems in school, violence, delinquency, pregnancy, threat of suicide, and the need for foster care or residential treatment. The following background information and guidelines are useful when working with adolescents:

- Adolescents are typically idealistic, painfully self-conscious, struggling with authority issues, preoccupied with their appearance and sexuality, seeking popularity and conformity within their peer group, and desperately trying to develop an identity apart from their family. Adolescents want and need positive adult role models and mentors who can prepare them for adulthood, but they will often resist the influence of their own parents. They need opportunities to learn skills—whether athletic, academic, musical, or vocational—that provide a sense of accomplishment and competence.

- Many of the adolescents encountered in social work practice are involuntary or mandated clients who are sent to a social worker or a social agency by parents, school officials, a juvenile court judge, or a probation officer. This is, of course, a very uncomfortable and awkward situation for the adolescent because of the authority struggles common to this developmental period. The adolescent may respond with silence, noncooperation, rudeness, or abusive language. In such a situation, a social worker's patience and self-control can be severely tested. In addition, the worker's own unresolved parent–child and authority issues may surface and intrude into the professional relationship.

Despite the challenges they present, adolescents are usually resilient and have a great capacity to grow and change. Effective social work intervention during this developmental period can have lifelong positive effects. Because they are usually lively and inquisitive, work with adolescents can be stimulating, fun, and truly rewarding.

- Adolescents need an environment that is predictable and provides structure, boundaries, and limits. In many practice settings, such as group homes and treatment centers, social workers have the responsibility for creating this environment and deciding what rules are necessary. Adolescents will typically test the rules put in place by adults. Thus, before you create a new rule, make sure it is really necessary, can be enforced, and worth fighting over. Once you have decided that a particular rule is necessary, inform the adolescent of the rule and the consequences for violating it. When enforcing rules, it is critically important to be fair and consistent. Behavioral contracting works fairly well with adolescents (see Item 13.5).

- Because the peer group is so important during adolescence, group approaches (e.g., group discussion, psychodrama, and group counseling) can be especially useful. Most adolescents are more accepting of a group-related intervention than to one-to-one counseling. Adolescents in need of out-of-home placement usually do better in a group home setting than in foster family care.

- Because of adolescents' high energy level, a meeting or interview should be planned around movement and physical activity. If possible, avoid office interviews; rather, try talking with an adolescent while walking, shooting baskets, working out in a gym, or riding in a car. Movement seems to make it easier for adolescents to interact, talk, and express feelings.

- Adolescents are sensitive to any hint of artificiality in others, even though they themselves may pretend to be someone they are not. Thus, it is important for the social worker to be genuine. Do not try to speak or act like an adolescent. It is nearly impossible to keep up with the latest adolescent fads, music, and slang. Imitating adolescent talk is likely to make you appear phony.

- Most adolescents are focused on the here and now. They tend to be somewhat impulsive in their decision making and may not anticipate the consequences of their choices. This, of course, can lead to bad choices that are potentially harmful to themselves and others. When counseling adolescents who are struggling to make a decision, gently encourage them to examine their options in light of their goals and hopes for the future. When their thinking is clearly unrealistic, it is usually best to tell them so, along with the reasoning behind your conclusion.

- Adolescents have an intense need to be heard. They want others to pay attention and take them seriously. Listen carefully and be alert to the underlying meaning in what they are saying. Encourage them to share their perspectives and experiences. Ask about their hopes, dreams, values, significant life experiences, the times when they learned something important, and what adults do not understand about their life, interests, and challenges.

- When an adolescent is sullen and refuses to speak, the technique of "passing a note" might break the impasse. The social worker simply stops talking, pulls out a pencil and paper and, in silence and in a deliberate manner, writes a note to the client. In the worker's own words, this note might say the following:

  - There are times when people do not want to talk. That is OK.
  - Being asked personal questions can be irritating.
  - Sometimes being quiet just feels better.
  - I apologize if I have said something that was offensive.
  - If you would like to do so, please write back.

  When finished writing, the worker announces, "I've written you a note. Here it is." Most likely the client expects the message to be some kind of criticism. Receiving a personalized note, especially one that is positive and displays empathy may cause enough of a surprise that it alters the client's mood and prompts an interaction with the worker.

- Because of estrangement and conflict between the divorced parents, and high rates of single motherhood, many children and adolescents do not have a meaningful relationship with their biological fathers. In the United States, for example, about 40 percent of boys are "fatherless" in the sense that they are being raised apart from their biological fathers and have little or no contact with their fathers. The absence of an interested and caring father has negative effects that are especially noticeable among boys. These effects include poor school performance, school dropout, delinquency, drug use, violence, and gang membership. One of the most reliable predictors of whether a boy will succeed or fail in high school is whether he has in his life a responsible and positive adult male model and mentor. Both girls and boys need healthy adult role models. Ideally, the parent will be this positive model but when that is not the case, modeling and mentoring by other adults (e.g., concerned relatives, family friends, Big Brothers, Big Sisters) is critically important.

- Some adolescents are drawn into gang activity. They join gangs for a variety of reasons, but often because the gang meets their needs for a sense of identity and belonging, self-esteem and pride, recognition, and camaraderie. In some instances, they might join a gang because membership offers protection in a dangerous neighborhood. For many adolescents, the tribal nature of a gang serves as a substitute family. In the past, the illegal activity of youth gangs was mostly theft. At present, many youth gangs have adult leaders, have grown more violent, and are involved in very serious criminal activity such as drug dealing, extortion, and murder.

Selected Bibliography

Alexander, James, Holy Waldron, Michael Robbins, and Andrea Neeb. *Functional Family Therapy for Adolescent Behavior Problems*. Washington, DC: American Psychological Association, 2013.

Geldard, Kathryn, and David Geldard. *Counseling Adolescents*, 3rd ed. Thousand Oaks, CA: Sage, 2010.

Laser Julie, and Nicole Nicotera. *Working with Adolescents*. New York: Guilford, 2011.

McWhirter, J. Jefferies, Benedict McWhirter, Ellen McWhirter, and Robert McWhirter. *At Risk Youth*, 5th ed. Independence, KY: Cengage, 2013.

Steele, Ric, David Elkin, and Michael Roberts, eds. *Handbook of Evidence-Based Therapies for Children and Adolescents*. New York: Springer, 2008.

15.4 THE CLIENT WHO IS A PARENT OR GRANDPARENT

Parenting is a difficult and demanding undertaking—one that is a mix of joy and worry. Even when the parent is skillful and conscientious, the outcome is uncertain. Many influences besides the parent's actions will shape a child's behavior, values, and choices. Many of the factors important to child development such as the child's temperament, genetic makeup, physiology, and sociocultural environment are beyond a parent's influence. Even with good parenting and a supportive environment, a child will grow into an individual who has some self-doubt, some anxieties, some feelings of inadequacy and will, on occasion, make bad judgments or cause harm to self and others. Such is the human condition.

Many social work clients are parents, and many of the organizations that employ social workers provide services that focus on the role of parent and problems in the parent–child relationship. Also, a significant number of grandparents provide full-time care for their grandchildren when the child's parents are incapacitated, called for military duty, or otherwise absent or unavailable. Following are some factors that social workers should keep in mind as they work directly with parents or grandparents or work on behalf of them when administering or designing programs that impact children and families.

- A social worker must be always cognizant of a **parent's legal rights and responsibilities**. Certain basic parental rights are well established by legal precedent. Parents have the right to guide the care and upbringing of their minor-age child, to select their child's school and religion, and to decide what medical care their child will receive. They have a right to discipline and punish their child but they may not injure the child, for that would constitute abuse. Parents also have the right to control and manage the earnings and property of their minor-age child and to receive proper legal notice of any action instituted on behalf of or against the child. It is only in very unusual situations or when the child's life is at risk that a court will override these basic parental rights and decisions. Parents also have the right to consent to marriage and military service by their minor-age child and the right to consent to medical procedures and surgery needed by the child. It must be noted, however, that specific statutes may allow a mature minor to obtain certain forms of health care (e.g., mental health counseling, birth control, treatment for venereal disease, abortion) without parental permission; such statues vary from state to state.

    Parents also have certain legal responsibilities. These include the responsibility to provide the child with maintenance (e.g., food, shelter, clothing), provide the child with basic health care, supervise and protect the child from harm, and provide the child with a basic education. A failure to meet these responsibilities may constitute child neglect (see Item 11.16).

- Research has identified a number of parenting behaviors that contribute to the development of healthy and wholesome children. These include listening to the child so as to understand the child's thoughts, feelings, and motives; sensitivity to and respect for the child; providing comfort, affection, and nurturance; providing encouragement and using praise to reward the child's effort and accomplishments; providing structure with clear and reasonable rules and expectations; using consistent, reasonable, and nonviolent consequences for misbehavior; spending time playing, reading to, and working with the child; engaging in activities that promote attachment and bonding between parent and child; and anticipating problems and being proactive to minimize their effect.

- The parent–child relationship is always a two-way interaction; the parent's behavior affects the child and the child's behavior affects the parent. This relationship is an interaction of two unique personalities. Moreover, the siblings within a family can be quite different in personality and temperament and, consequently, a particular approach to discipline or guidance that works well with one child in the family may have quite different results with another. Some special challenges and conflicts can arise if the parent and child are very different in terms of their temperaments, intellectual abilities, or interests. For example, a gregarious and outgoing parent may feel inept and frustrated if his or her child is by temperament shy and introverted. Or an athletic father may secretly resent a son who shows no interest in sports.

  A parent may do an adequate job with a child at a certain stage of development but have problems when the child moves into another stage. For example, most parents are severely tested when their child enters adolescence. A parent may do well with a normal child but become distraught and overwhelmed when caring for a child with a mental or physical disability.

- Parents tend to raise children the way they were raised. This tendency is an asset if they were lucky enough to have experienced a loving and caring relationship with their parents. On the other hand, this tendency can be a source of serious problems if their parenting models were troubled or dysfunctional. An individual may enter parenthood resolving never to repeat the mistakes of his or her parents but later discover (or worse, be unaware) that he or she is visiting those same patterns on the next generation. This is most likely to happen when the parents are stressed and overwhelmed. Many parents have been jolted when they heard themselves saying things to their children that they hated hearing from their own parents. Needless to say, not all parents repeat the mistakes or the dysfunctions of their own parents, but breaking this cycle requires self-awareness, conscious efforts, and often parent training and counseling.

- When parents do not have easy access to persons experienced in parenting, they can feel alone, unsure, and overwhelmed. A parent who has little contact with other parents and children may form unrealistic expectations of his or her own child. Stress and social isolation are contributing factors to the problems of child abuse and neglect. Social workers should look for opportunities to promote friendships and to build social support networks among parents so the parents gain knowledge and perspectives on how to be a parent.

  Parents must have the emotional and psychological maturity to give of themselves and manage their emotions. Parents who are fearful, overwhelmed, or self-absorbed will have difficulty being attentive and responsive to their children and are likely to act impulsively and make bad parenting decisions. Those with serious personal problems (e.g., addiction, mental illness, domestic violence) and those who grew up in families that experienced such problems will, almost always, face some special challenges in the parenting role. The young and immature parent and the parent with cognitive delays will find the demands of parenting especially difficult. Parents who are busy, distracted, or disorganized may overlook a child's need for adequate sleep, good nutrition, and a predictable daily routine—the lack of which contributes to behavioral problems, irritability, and poor school performance. In order to help a parent become more effective in the parent role, the parent's other personal concerns and problems must be addressed.

Parents cannot give what they do not have. For example, if a mother does not feel physically safe, it will be difficult for her to help her child feel safe and secure. If a father does not possess a sense of personal worth, it will be difficult for him to help his child develop healthy self-esteem.

- Most parents struggle in their efforts to create and enforce rules. To be effective in the area of discipline, the parent must, first of all, have a truly caring, trusting, and loving relationship with his or her child. Within the context of that positive relationship, the parent must be able to distinguish between behavior that arises from the child's immaturity and inexperience and behavior that is truly defiant and a deliberate violation of known and reasonable rules. Boundaries and protections should be the response to immature behavior. To truly defiant behavior, the parent needs to respond firmly with nonviolent but real and realistic consequences.

- Some of the grandparents who are raising their grandchildren are ambivalent about assuming this responsibility. On one hand, they want to provide this care out of their love for the children but, on the other hand, caring for grandchildren may strain their finances and disrupt a hoped-for retirement. Some find this responsibility burdensome because it often comes at a time when they are experiencing health problems and lack the energy needed to look after a young child or teen. It is important for social agencies to develop programs that will address the concerns of these grandparents.

- Most parents can benefit from parent training, parent support groups, and counseling focused on the parent–child relationship. The most effective programs strive to reach out to parents during difficult times, such as after the arrival of a first child or when the child enters the teen years. Successful programs also recognize the unique challenges faced by certain groups of parents. For example, a foster parent, an adoptive parent, and the parent of a child with disabilities will usually have a unique set of concerns and questions about being a parent. Being a single parent is inherently stressful because all the responsibilities fall to one person. Because of societal attitudes and prejudices, parents in same-sex relationships and those in interracial marriages sometimes face special challenges, too.

Successful parenting programs build on the parents' strengths. Such programs operate on the assumptions that most parents do the best they know how but often have difficulties because they lack knowledge and skills or are overwhelmed by other personal, family, or economic problems. These programs are prepared to address the concerns or problems that are of high priority to the parent, even when those concerns are not directly related to the parent role. They address the situational and contextual factors that are adversely affecting the parent. Effective parent training programs collaborate with other agencies and connect parents to other needed resources (e.g., health care, financial assistance, housing, counseling, job training).

As a general rule, fathers are less involved than mothers in the care of children and less likely to avail themselves of opportunities to learn parenting skills. Thus, the professionals and agencies must actively reach out to fathers and design programs that connect with the ways men think and feel. Whenever possible, parenting classes for men should be taught by a man.

Most parent training programs presume that the parent can read and write and will make use of written materials, workbook assignments, and the like. Unfortunately, there are many parents who are not literate. Special efforts should be made to identify those parents so alternative modes of teaching can be utilized.

Ironically, the parents most likely to utilize parent training and other parenting resources are parents who are already doing an adequate job. The parents who are most in need of these services seldom seek them out. In order to attract those parents, programs must be welcoming and have a vigorous outreach component.

- Most agencies deliver parent training within the context of a small group because that environment provides the participants with opportunities to learn from each other and receive assurance that they are not alone in having worries, frustrations, self-doubts, and questions. A fairly typical parent education group meets once a week for about eight weeks. A session should last about one and one-half hours. The optimal size is between 8 and 16 parents. The group can be larger if the teaching format is mostly didactic but smaller if it utilizes techniques of role-play and discussion. It is usually preferable to have both members of the parenting couple participate (e.g., both mother and father). Parents are expected to attend all sessions. Members should not be added after the group is formed and underway. Ideally, groups for parents will have two leaders or trainers, a male and a female. It is best to have separate groups for the parents of adolescents since their concerns are significantly different from the parents of younger children.

  When feasible, each potential participant should be interviewed before being admitted to the group in order to determine if what the group has to offer is appropriate for the parent. The parents who have been referred to the group by a child protection agency or mandated to attend by court order should be carefully assessed because they are often angry and resistant and sometimes disruptive to the group process. However, a skilled facilitator can usually successfully integrate them into the group (see Item 12.8).

  For parents who will not or cannot attend a group, the use of home visitation and a parent-to-parent approach is a helpful alternative. In a home visitation program, a parent trainer or a "resource mom" meets the parent in the parent's own home. This highly individualized approach is tutorial in nature and their discussions focus on the parent's child and unique concerns and circumstances.

- Social workers must sometimes evaluate a parent's capacity to provide his or her child with safe and appropriate care. For example, a social worker employed by a child protection agency might be asked to prepare a report and recommendation to the court concerning whether a mother who had neglected her child is now able to resume the care of her child who is in foster care. When conducting such evaluations the social worker must remember that there is no one, always right, way of raising a child and that every parent makes some mistakes. Children do not need perfect parents but they need and deserve parents who can provide at least a minimally acceptable level of care.

  In order to assess a parent's capacity and performance in the parent role, it is essential to observe the parent interacting with her or his child in several different situations and contexts. It is important to gather information on parent-related values, attitudes, and knowledge, as well as how the parent has come to terms with her or his own parents and possible troublesome experiences. And of course, it is important to determine if the parent's capacity is diminished by problems of addiction, mental illness, and the like.

Within the context of a nonthreatening interview, a social worker can initiate a discussion about parenting by asking a number of simple questions, such as: Tell me about Martina? In what ways is Martina like other kids her age? In what ways is she different from other children? Does Martina have a personality and temperament similar to yours or different from yours? In what ways are Martina's experiences as a child similar to or different from what you experienced as a child? What have you liked most about being a parent? Is being a parent fun for you? What is most difficult about being a parent? Has being a parent gotten more or less demanding as Martina has grown older? How would you rate the parenting abilities of your own parents? Many people say they want to be a better parent than their own parent; have you ever had that thought? If you could start over, is there anything you would do differently as a parent? Have you ever made a big mistake in how you dealt with your child? What do you think it is like for Martina to have you as a parent?

A social worker must guard against the possibility of favoring the child to the detriment of the parent. Since a child is more vulnerable than an adult, it is natural to be attentive to the child and possibly value the child over the parent, especially when the parent has been irresponsible or has harmed the child. This very human inclination can, however, give rise to an unfair and biased assessment and treatment of the parent.

Selected Bibliography

American Bar Association. *Complete Personal Legal Guide*, 4th ed. New York: Random House, 2008.

Bigner, Jerry, and Clara Gerhardt. *Parent-Child Relations: An Introduction to Parenting*, 9th ed. Upper Saddle River, NJ: Pearson, 2014.

Brooks, Jane. *The Process of Parenting*, 9th ed. New York: McGraw-Hill, 2013.

Briesmeister, James, and Charles Schaefer, eds. *Handbook of Parent Training*, 3rd ed. Hoboken, NJ: Wiley, 2007.

Hilarski, Carolyn. "Best Practices in Parenting Techniques." In *Social Worker's Desk Reference*, 2nd ed. Edited by Albert Roberts. New York: Oxford University Press, 2008.

Priwer Shana, and Cynthia Phillips. *Gay Parenting: Complete Guide for Same Sex Families*. Far Hills, NJ: New Horizon, 2006.

15.5 THE CLIENT WHO IS AN OLDER PERSON

In most developed countries, a growing percentage of the population is in the older age range. Given this trend, social workers and human services programs must give increased attention to the concerns of persons in their seventies, eighties, and nineties. The background information and guidelines presented here will assist the social worker serving these clients.

- As people grow older, they experience numerous losses (e.g., the death of loved ones and friends, loss of health and mobility). They often feel more vulnerable and begin to worry about their ability to care of themselves and possibly becoming a burden to their children or other family members. In response to these fears, they may hold rigidly to whatever independence they still possess. They may resist any offer of help or service that they view as limiting their freedom and choice. Thus, when working with older clients, allow them to make choices and retain control over their lives to the greatest extent possible.

- Most older persons will prefer a social worker who is friendly and outgoing, but some will react negatively to a professional who seems too casual or informal. When addressing older clients, use the title Mr., Mrs., or Miss until you have their permission to use a first name. Some older persons may be offended by what they judge to be immodest clothing, unusual hairstyles, or strange jewelry, tattoos, or piercings if worn by a professional or other service provider.

- For both physical and psychological reasons, older clients often prefer to have professional interviews and meetings in their homes rather than in an office setting. When in a client's home or room, a good way to break the ice and start a conversation is to show an interest in family pictures, homemade items, or decorations. Begin building a professional relationship by focusing first on the client's most obvious and concrete concerns and needs such as transportation, medical care, and social activity. Only after a trusting and positive relationship has been formed is the older client likely to feel comfortable discussing more personal concerns such as family conflicts, money problems, grief, feelings of isolation, and so on.

    Many older clients are concerned about the cost of services and their ability to pay. Some find using public programs and "taking charity" to be humiliating and embarrassing. Some will simply reject a service rather than reveal their inability to pay.

- Most older people will experience some degree of diminished vision, hearing, energy, and mobility. It is important to speak clearly and repeat your message if necessary. Nonverbal communication is important as a means of helping the client with an auditory deficit to grasp your message. The pace of an interview may need to be slower and the client's lack of stamina may limit the length of an interview or meeting.

- As people grow older, many will think more about death and dying and their spirituality. Often they will value more deeply their relationships with children and grandchildren. Contacts with family and longtime friends take on added importance. Some may want to reach out to others in order to make amends for harm they have caused. Many will not fear death itself but most will fear the disease, disability, dependency, and suffering that so often precedes death.

    As an individual approaches death, it is important for him or her and for family members to express the thoughts and feelings that might heal past hurts and conflicts. Professionals who work with the dying identify these special words as: "Please forgive me," "I forgive you," "Thank you," and "I love you." To the extent possible, a social worker should facilitate intergenerational family communication and reconciliation.

- Allow and encourage the older client to reminisce. Thinking and talking about the past is a normal activity—it is not a sign of deteriorating mental abilities. Listen carefully to the reminiscences, for they may reveal much about the client's values, feelings, and concerns. A few open-ended questions will often encourage an older client to speak about meaningful life experiences, such as: What was the world like when you grew up? What was the most significant event of your childhood? How did you meet your spouse? What was the happiest time of your life? What do you consider to be your greatest accomplishment? What was your greatest disappointment or regret in life? What are you most thankful for? What has your life taught you about what is really important and worthwhile? What do you most want the younger generations to know about life? What were your biggest surprises in life?

- Given that racism, discrimination, and prejudice can inflict so much pain on people, strive to be especially sensitive when interacting with older people who are members of racial or ethnic minorities. As a general rule, they will be somewhat wary of social agencies and hesitant to ask for and utilize social services. The values common to a particular ethnic group can make life more or less difficult for the aging person. For example, in certain ethnic groups (e.g., Chinese American, Native American), older people occupy a position of respect and influence within families. On the other hand, the importance of hard work and productivity within an ethnic group (e.g., Slavic American) may make the nonworking elderly person feel useless and unworthy.

- Be alert to indicators of **elder abuse and neglect** (especially self-neglect), such as unusual bruises, cuts, and burns; untreated injuries that are explained in a vague or defensive manner; improper clothing for the weather; wandering outside at odd hours; mail and newspapers that have not been picked up; many unpaid bills or facing a utility shut-off even though the person has sufficient money. Also, highly unusual or strange behavior; unpleasant odors associated with poor hygiene or unsanitary housekeeping; inability to recognize familiar people; and being confused or disoriented may be indicators of maltreatment, self-neglect, or mental deterioration. An elderly person is especially at risk if she or he is dependent on a caregiver who is under great stress, chemically dependent, or mentally ill.

- Elderly persons who are frail or confused are vulnerable to exploitation and theft by an individual who can gain access to their money, bank accounts, possessions, or medications. Some older persons can be manipulated into changing his or her will; buying products, home repair, or insurance that they do not need; signing away ownership of home or property; and making other decisions that are opposed to their self-interest. In some instances, vulnerable individuals are made to feel that they are a severe financial or emotional burden on family and are manipulated into taking their own lives.

- Those who work with older persons should be alert to indicators or **symptoms of dementia**, a term that refers to an irreversible loss of mental abilities such as memory, judgment, and the capacity for self-care. Dementia is different from depression or delirium in that it comes on insidiously over months and years. The four major types of dementia are Alzheimer's disease, Lewy Body Dementia, Frontal Temporal Dementia, and Vascular Dementia. In the United States, Alzheimer's disease accounts for about 65 percent of all dementia cases.

    In the beginning stages of dementia, a person's family and caregivers notice that the individual is gradually becoming more and more forgetful and confused. She or he may, for example, forget frequently called phone numbers, lose the ability to balance a check book or pay a bill, and have unusual difficulty in making decisions or solving rather ordinary problems. Over time, other symptoms become apparent. For example, the person may engage in repetitive activities and statements, exhibit poor judgment, become disoriented as to time and place, withdraw from normal activities, neglect personal appearance and hygiene, have trouble understanding visual images and spatial relationships, have new problems with words in speaking or writing, and exhibit personality changes. When such symptoms appear, a medical evaluation is needed.

When a dementia such as Alzheimer's has progressed to an advanced stage, it is obvious that something is terribly wrong and the individual now needs full-time supervision. In later stages, the individual cannot read, add or subtract, or recognize family members. They may lose their ability to speak, wander about, become combative, and engage in other inappropriate behaviors.

Needless to say, family members experience a gut-wrenching sadness as they watch the deterioration of a loved one. A medical social worker can often provide guidance to the family on caring for and planning for a family member with a dementia and also connect the family to resources such as specialized nursing home care, legal advice, and relevant family support groups.

- Older people and their families will typically face a number of legal issues and decisions. These include preparing a will, estate planning, advance directives related to end-of-life choices, legal guardianship, power of attorney, long-term care insurance, and the like. When such matters are encountered, the social worker should refer the client and family to competent legal counsel.

Selected Bibliography

Crawford, Karin, and Janet Walker. *Social Work with Older People,* 2nd ed. Thousand Oaks, CA: Sage, 2008.

McInnis–Dittrich, Kathleen. *Social Work with Older Adults*, 4th ed. Upper Saddle River, NJ: Pearson, 2014.

Moore, David, and Kirsty Jones. *Social Work and Dementia*. Thousand Oaks, CA: Sage, 2012.

Soniat, Barbara, and Monica Mickios. *Empowering Social Workers for Practice with Vulnerable Older Adults*. Washington, DC: NASW Press, 2010.

Wacker, Robbyn, and Karen Roberto. *Community Resources for Older Adults*, 4th ed. Thousand Oaks, CA: Sage, 2013.

15.6 THE CLIENT WHO IS EXPERIENCING DOMESTIC VIOLENCE

As used here, the term *domestic violence* (or *domestic abuse*) refers to a situation in which an adult is being physically, sexually, and/or emotionally abused by a spouse or intimate partner. In the United States, a woman is more likely to be assaulted, injured, raped, or killed by a her male partner than by a stranger or any other type of assailant. The vast majority of the abusers are men and the abuse occurs most often within a heterosexual relationship. However, it may also occur within gay and lesbian relationships. (For ease of discussion, the authors will refer to the offender or abuser as male and the victim as female, although females sometimes perpetrate domestic violence.)

The abuse can take several forms, but all are intended to control the woman—for example:

- *Physical injury or threats of injury* (e.g., choking, punching, beating, forced sex, threatening to hurt her or the children)

- *Emotional abuse* (e.g., humiliation, making her the object of demeaning jokes, blaming, undermining her confidence, saying she is crazy, insisting that she deserves to be punished, denying her opportunity to make decisions)
- *Isolation* (e.g., monitoring and limiting who she talks to and where she goes)
- *Economic manipulation* (e.g., controlling her access to money, giving her only an allowance, preventing her from having a job, threatening to take all possessions and leave her with nothing)
- *Intimidation* (e.g., displaying weapons, abusing pets, destroying her property, threatening to commit suicide if she does not do what he wants)
- *Using the children* (e.g., threatening to take the children, threatening to report the woman for child abuse)

Typically, there is an observable cycle in domestic or spousal abuse. The cycle can be as short as a few days or unfold over several months. The three major phases of the cycle are as follows:

Phase 1: Tension building. Tensions between the two people begin to rise. Some outbursts may occur but these are minimized and rationalized away often by both parties. The woman tries to protect herself and maintain control over the situation by being submissive and compliant and not showing anger.

Phase 2: Explosion. The abuser finally explodes. Anger is expressed in extreme verbal abuse, physical violence, and/or rape.

Phase 3: Repairing the damage (Honeymoon). Fairly soon after the explosion the abuser expresses sorrow for what he has done. He becomes very attentive, loving, and thoughtful. Since this loving behavior is incongruent with his abusive behavior, the woman is confused and may even doubt her own perceptions and sanity. She may want to believe that the episode of abuse was a fluke and will not occur again. She may conclude that she is responsible for the abuse and think: "If only I would have done things right, he would not have gotten angry." This period of good behavior by the abuser eventually runs its course and the cycle begins once again.

The men who abuse women typically have several of the following characteristics:

- Extreme and irrational jealousy and possessiveness toward the woman, often coupled with an unwarranted belief that she is interested in other men.
- Desire to control the woman and isolate her from friends and family by saying such things as: "All we need is each other—no one else."
- Quick to anger and an explosive temper.
- Moods and behavior fluctuate from being kind and gentle to being mean spirited and violent.
- Denies or rationalizes his outbursts and abusive behavior; blames others, especially the woman, for whatever goes wrong in his life.
- History of being abused as a child or a witness to family violence.
- A history of legal violations related to violence.

There are a number of reasons why battered women are reluctant to leave an abusive relationship or will return to it after only a brief separation:

- Fear of retaliation and even more serious violence.
- Lack of money, transportation, and a suitable place to live.
- Fear of losing her children, home, and economic security.

- Self-doubt, low self-esteem, shame, or a distrust of others.
- Fear of not being believed or blamed for causing the abuse.
- Religious beliefs that emphasize maintaining a marriage.
- Desire to preserve the family for benefit of the children.
- Wanting to believe that the abuse will stop and a tendency to deny or minimize the seriousness of the abuse.
- Equating love to submission and dependency.

An abusive situation should be considered especially dangerous if there is a pattern of frequent and/or severe violence, the abuser and/or the abused woman use drugs or alcohol, the woman or her children have been threatened with death, the abuser has access to deadly weapons, either the abuser or victim has a psychiatric impairment, the abuser has a history of criminal activity, the abuse has taken the form of forced sexual acts, the abuser has threatened suicide, the abuser has tortured or killed animals as a display of his willingness to take extreme action, and the woman has made suicide threats or attempts.

Social workers and programs offering services to battered women must strive toward the following goals:

- Make sure that the woman and her children are safe and protected.
- Help the woman understand the nature and cycle of abuse and that she has options that can keep her and her children safe.
- Help her make decisions, formulate plans, and obtain the services she will need in order to be safe.
- Help her and her children heal from the psychological effects of abuse and reestablish a sense of personal boundaries.

Those working directly with abused women should keep the following guidelines in mind:

- Give immediate attention to the issue of her physical safety and her basic needs such as the need for food, housing, medical care, transportation, child care, legal counsel, and so on. If meeting this client for the first time, do not immediately assume that the battered woman is in a heterosexual relationship; refer to the abuser as "partner" until you learn the gender of the offender.
- Focus on the woman's strengths and call them to the woman's attention. Her strengths may be her decision to reach out for help, her efforts to protect her children, and the decisions and behaviors that have kept her alive. Help her to identify and name her survival skills as a way of counteracting her feelings of self-doubt and helplessness.
- If she decides to remain with or return to the abuser, assist the woman in developing an escape plan (safety plan) that she can immediately implement if she is again threatened. The plan should include preparing and then hiding from the abuser a bag that contains money, clothing, personal items, and copies of legal documents that she (and her children) would need to live apart from the abuser.
- Anticipate that the woman's emotions will fluctuate widely and that she will experience great ambivalence about ending the relationship. Discourage her from speaking with the abuser when she is feeling especially insecure and confused. At such times she is vulnerable to his manipulation and is likely to return to him without considering the danger.

- Do not assume that the abused woman has some underlying psychological need or problem that caused her to enter or remain in an abusive relationship. However, as a response to ongoing abuse, the woman may indeed develop problems such as alcohol or drug abuse, depression, anxiety and posttraumatic stress disorder.

- Understand that the woman may have to leave and return to the abuser several times before she is finally convinced that the abuse will not end unless the abuser is motivated to enter a program of therapy and training. Couples counseling (i.e., both partners attend same session) is usually not an appropriate mode of intervention because the abused woman may be afraid to speak honestly in the presence of the abuser and the abuser will typically accuse her of exaggeration or lying.

- After leaving an abusive relationship and even with counseling, it may take from two to four years before the battered woman recovers emotionally and becomes significantly less fearful, anxious, and depressed. The same can be said for the children who have experienced the terror of seeing their mother beaten and threatened.

Selected Bibliography

Bent-Goodley, Tricia. *The Ultimate Betrayal: A Renewed Look and Intimate Partner Violence.* Washington, DC: NASW Press, 2011.

McClennen, Joan. *Social Work and Family Violence.* New York: Springer, 2010.

Roberts, Albert, ed. *Battered Women and Their Families*, 3rd ed. New York: Springer, 2007.

Walker, Lenore. *The Battered Woman Syndrome*, 3rd ed. New York: Springer, 2009.

Wexler, David. *Stop Domestic Violence: Innovative Skills Techniques, Options,* 3rd ed. New York: Norton, 2013.

15.7 THE CLIENT WHO IS AT RISK OF SUICIDE

Given the high rate of suicide among teenagers, young adults, and older adults, the social worker will encounter clients who are at risk of taking their own lives. The **warning signs of suicide** include intense depression and hopelessness, preoccupation with death and pain, giving away prized possessions, unexplained changes in behavior, sudden increase in the use of drugs and alcohol, and impulsive or reckless behavior. Although not all people who end their lives are clinically depressed, studies reveal that depression is often present. The **symptoms of depression** include pervasive sadness, feelings of hopelessness, lack of interest in activities once enjoyed, inability to concentrate, thoughts of suicide, unexplained aches and pains, fatigue and restlessness, changes in appetite, withdrawal from others, early waking from sleep or erratic sleep patterns, irritability, and unexplained crying. Whereas depression in adults usually results in a reduction of activity, depression in children and youth is often expressed in agitation.

Legally and ethically, the social worker must make every reasonable effort to prevent a client's suicide. This includes providing or trying to provide counseling, staying with the person during times of high risk, and, if necessary, calling the police. State laws dictate when police can detain a suicidal person and also when involuntary hospitalization is permitted. However, it must be noted that it may not be possible to prevent the suicide of a person who is firmly committed to taking his or her own life. If the person really wants to die, he or she will probably find the opportunity and the means.

The following guidelines will help the social worker in assessing a client's suicide potential and responding to the client who is at risk of suicide:

- Take every message about suicide seriously. It is always significant that the person is talking about harm to self rather than expressing unhappiness and frustration in other ways. It is a myth that people who talk about suicide will not kill themselves. Unfortunately, their message may be veiled and, in some cases, it is not until after the death that its meaning becomes clear. In 10 to 20 percent of suicides, there are no noticeable warnings prior to the death.

- Listen for subtle and indirect statements of suicidal intent, such as "I won't be around much longer," "There is nothing worth living for anymore," or "I just can't stand the pain any longer." Be especially concerned about such statements if the person has recently experienced the loss of an important relationship, a loss of status, an episode of family violence, or is in the throes of dealing with chronic pain, a life-threatening illness, or a serious physical limitation.

- If you believe that a client is at risk of suicide, always consult with other professionals on how best to proceed. Do not allow yourself to be "hooked" by the suicidal client into a promise of complete confidentiality. Ordinary rules of confidentiality must be broken in order to prevent a death.

- The person thinking about suicide is usually experiencing intense **ambivalence**—the desire to live and, at the same time, the desire to escape pain, even if by death. At a fundamental level the person does not want to die but sees no other way to deal with his or her distress. Encourage and support that part of the person holding on to life.

    Most suicidal people have "tunnel vision"—they can think only about their pain and helplessness. It is important to help them identify and consider alternative methods for dealing with the situation. Ask how the individual managed stressful situations in the past? Will any of these methods work in the present situation?

- Do not be afraid to ask if the individual is thinking about suicide. Speaking openly will not increase the likelihood of suicide. Direct questioning tells the suicidal person that you are concerned and not afraid to talk straight. Examples of questions include the following: Are you thinking of killing yourself? Can you tell me why suicide seems like the answer? Who else knows that you are thinking about suicide? What has happened recently that caused you to think more and more about suicide? Why do you believe your situation will not improve or change? How might your situation be different in a few weeks or a couple of months from now? Have you attempted suicide in the past? If you thought about suicide in the past, what caused you to change your mind?

- Determine whether the person has worked out a suicide plan. Ask questions such as: Do you have a plan for killing yourself? How do you plan to get the gun you intend to use? Where do you plan to kill yourself? What time of day do you plan to kill yourself? The more detailed and specific the person's plan the higher the risk of suicide. Many suicidal people have thought about a suicide plan but most have not thought about an alternative plan or a "plan B." Thus, if you can interfere with a key element of their plan, you can often thwart their suicide.

- The person who has chosen a method of suicide and has access to that method is at high risk. The more lethal the chosen method, the higher the risk and the more likely a suicide attempt will result in death. Highly lethal methods include shooting, jumping from a height, hanging, drowning, carbon monoxide poisoning, car crash, or taking high doses of barbiturates, sleeping pills, or aspirin. Less lethal methods include wrist cutting, gas fumes, or tranquilizers and nonprescription drugs (excluding aspirin and Tylenol). Advise the family and friends of a suicidal person to lock up medications, remove guns from the home, and take other actions that will deny the suicidal person access to a method of suicide.

- Many who commit suicide feel alone, ignored, or isolated from people. The risk of suicide increases when a person is widowed, divorced, or separated. Encourage significant others come to the support of the suicidal person.

- Help the person see that suicide is a permanent solution to a temporary problem. Identify other possible solutions to dealing with the pain the individual is experiencing. If necessary, ask her or him to agree not to commit suicide for a specific period (e.g., two weeks) or to promise not to commit suicide before talking to you one more time. Urge the person to call the toll-free suicide prevention lifeline at 1-800-273-TALK (8255). Urge the person to immediately enter counseling. If a referral for counseling is made, you or someone else should possibly accompany the client to the initial interview. Follow-up is necessary to ensure that the client is making use of the service.

- In extreme situations and when no other approach has had the desired effect, attempt to engage the person in a discussion of what will happen when he or she is found dead. Sometimes this will jar the person into thinking more clearly about the real consequences of a suicide. For example, you might ask the following questions: Who is likely to find your body? Who should be notified of your death? Should some of the individuals to be notified be approached or talked to in a certain way? Who will be most upset when they learn that you are dead? Are some of them children? What should the children be told about your death? What questions might they ask about you? Can we make a list of all the people who should be notified of your death so they can attend your funeral? What kind of a funeral service do you want? Would you want a burial or cremation? What do you want your obituary to say?

- When dealing with persons who are actively suicidal, it is important to remember that some individuals may have no hesitation about also killing you or someone else in the process of taking their own life. For example, a suicidal person with a gun might shoot you if you attempt to take away the gun.

Selected Bibliography

Bonger, Bruce, and Glen Sullivan. *The Suicidal Patient*, 3rd ed. Washington, DC: American Psychological Association, 2013.

Granello, Darch, and Paul Granello. *Suicide: An Essential Guide for Helping Professionals and Educators*. Upper Saddle River, NJ: Pearson, 2007.

Quinett, Paul. *Suicide: The Forever Decision*. New York: Crossroad, 2004.

Worchel, Dana, and Robin Gearing. *Suicide Assessment and Treatment: Empirical and Evidence-Based Practices*. New York: Springer, 2010.

15.8 THE CLIENT WITH AN INTELLECTUAL DISABILITY

The terms intellectual disability and *mental retardation* are synonymous. Because of the stigma attached to the word *retardation*, parents and professionals have sought an alternative terminology. Gradually, the term *intellectual disability* has gained acceptance and is used in the newest edition of the *DSM* (see Item 11.15). However, the term *mental retardation* often appears in medical literature and is still commonly used by medical and education professionals.

Three features define an **intellectual disability**: (1) an IQ below about 70; (2) significant limitations in adaptive behaviors such as communication, self-care, memory, problem solving, social interaction, and academic skills; and (3) these impairments or limitations existed prior to age 18. Experts speak of four levels of severity: *mild* (IQ between about 50 and 70), *moderate* (IQ between about 35 and 55), *severe* (IQ between about 20 and 40), and *profound* (IQ below 20). It is important to note that an IQ score of below 70, by itself, is not a sufficient criterion for diagnosing an intellectual disability; additional factors must also be considered. And intellectual disability can be caused by dozens of conditions and events, such as inborn errors in metabolism, chromosomal aberrations, head trauma, malnutrition, infections, and the ingestion of toxic chemicals.

Roughly 3 percent of the population have an intellectual disability. Of those, about 80 percent have a mild level of impairment and about 10 percent are in the moderate range. Those with a mild and moderate level of disability can usually achieve at least an upper–grade-school level of education and as adults hold unskilled or semi-skilled jobs. Many will marry and have children. Persons with a severe level of impairment can learn simple counting and some written word recognition. They require much assistance and close supervision. The 1 to 2 percent with a profound impairment will usually have serious neurological disorders and other complex medical problems. Most of those individuals will need around-the-clock nursing care.

The term *developmental disability* is a legal and programmatic category. Although definitions vary slightly from state to state, a **developmental disability** is often defined as a severe disability caused by a physical or mental impairment that limits a person's development, appears before the age 18 (or 22), is likely to be lifelong, and affects the person's functioning in self-care, learning, self-direction, language, independent living, mobility, and/or economic self-sufficiency. The developmental disabilities include mental retardation, cerebral palsy, autism, severe dyslexia, and epilepsy. Of these, mental retardation (intellectual disability) is the one most frequently diagnosed. All persons with an intellectual disability have a developmental disability, but not all persons with a developmental disability have subnormal intellectual ability. Early diagnosis and medical and educational intervention are of critical importance to minimize the effects of these conditions (see Items 11.13 and 11.18).

The following guidelines and information will aid the social worker serving an adult client with a significant intellectual disability:

- Throughout history and in most societies, individuals with intellectual disabilities have been disparaged and often their parents suffered feelings of guilt, shame, and embarrassment. In more recent times this situation has improved significantly but remnants of those negative attitudes remain. Social workers and other professionals must examine their own attitudes and shed any negative preconceptions or stereotypes they may have absorbed from the wider society. Most of all, they must recognize the worth and dignity of every person, regardless of mental capacity, and understand that an individual with an intellectual disability has the same basic human needs (physical, emotional, social, sexual, and spiritual) as everyone else.

- Certain medical disorders and particular behavioral patterns are associated with some types of mental retardation. Among them are neurological problems and diminished functioning in the areas of vision, hearing, coordination, mobility, and physical strength. A familiarity with such medical conditions is of critical importance in assessment and case planning and when working as part of a team with other disciplines, such as medicine, psychology, physical therapy, occupational therapy, speech therapy, special education, and vocational rehabilitation.

- Many persons with an intellectual disability will have limited verbal ability and at best, only rudimentary skills in the areas of reading and writing. Consequently, the verbal counseling and helping skills commonly used by social workers will have but limited applicability with this client. Alternative skills and techniques are needed. These include behavioral techniques, modeling and demonstration, special teaching methodologies, nonverbal group work, and the creative arts.

   Because the client's attention span may be short, the length of a meeting with a client needs to be adjusted accordingly. And because the client's memory may be limited, each contact should be planned as a discrete event rather than assuming it will be a continuation of previous conversations. Your communications and vocabulary must be adjusted to the client's level of comprehension. Communication needs to be clear-cut and simple, but never patronizing.

- When formulating an intervention or a helping strategy, focus on and build on the client's abilities—on what he or she can do rather than on limitations. To the extent possible, the client should participate in making decisions that will affect his or her life circumstances. However, such participation may be quite limited if the client is severely disabled. Because the client's situation is typically influenced, supervised, or controlled by others (e.g., family, legal guardian, group home manager), the social worker must always involve those individuals in the formulation of a service plan. The practice roles of client advocate, case manager, and broker are especially important in work with this client group (see Chapter 4 and Item 13.17). The skills of teamwork are essential in planning and providing services to persons with a severe disability.

- People with an intellectual disability tend to be friendly, trusting, and naïve. Consequently, they are vulnerable to manipulation, exploitation, and abuse by unscrupulous individuals. Because they often experience frustration and social rejection, they are at risk of developing emotional problems and patterns of unusual and inappropriate behavior. Avoid doing anything that might reinforce or reward inappropriate social behaviors or mannerisms that attract negative attention. For example, hugging is not a conventional greeting among adults who are not close friends. Thus, the social worker should model the use of a handshake rather than allowing one's self to be inappropriately hugged by the client.

- In order to facilitate appropriate learning and socialization by persons with an intellectual disability and also reduce the chances that they will be stigmatized, the principles of normalization and social integration should guide the design and delivery of social services and the formulation of case plans or habilitation plans. **Integration** exists when persons with a disability participate, to the greatest extent possible, in the ordinary and usual activities of family, community, and society. **Normalization** is a philosophy of service planning and delivery that emphasizes the utilization of helping approaches and services that are culturally normative. The phrase *culturally normative* refers to that which is typical, ordinary, or conventional within the community. The following example may illustrate the notion of what is culturally normative. Where does a man get a haircut? The answer is a barbershop. Thus, a man with a disability should also obtain his haircut at a barbershop. It would be a violation of the normalization principle for a case manager to arrange for a barber to visit a group home in order to give haircuts to all the residents.

    The term *normalization* should not be misunderstood as being or becoming "normal." Rather, it is an effort to decrease separation and the perception of deviance (i.e., socially created differences). Moreover, the principle of normalization does not dictate that a person with a disability be placed in situations that would generate unusual frustration or impossible competition just because those situations are typical for the average person. However, normalization does call for the removal of unnecessary overprotection and recognizes that learning and living involves some degree of risk taking and possible failure.

- It is in relation to clients with severe disabilities that a social worker is likely to encounter the legal procedures known as guardianship and conservatorship. In a **guardianship** arrangement, a court finds a person to be legally incompetent because of young age or mental or physical incapacity and invests a responsible person (the guardian) with the power to manage the incapacitated person's money and property and to make certain other decisions such as those related to health care. In a **conservatorship**, the court appoints another person (the conservator) for the more limited purpose of managing the legally incompetent person's estate. Neither of these legal procedures should be confused with **power of attorney**, which does not involve a court finding of legal incompetence, but simply involves the use of a notarized document in which one legally competent person voluntarily gives to another the legal power to take certain actions such as selling a property, depositing or withdrawing funds from a bank, or paying bills.

Selected Bibliography

Belrne-Smith, Mary, James Patton, and Shannon Kim. *Mental Retardation: An Introduction to Intellectual Disability,* 7th ed. Upper Saddle River, NJ: Pearson, 2006.

Drew, Clifford, and Michael Hardman. *Intellectual Disabilities*, 9th ed. Upper Saddle River, NJ: Pearson, 2007.

Odom, Samuel, Robert Horner, Martha Snell, and Jan Blacher. *Handbook of Developmental Disabilities*. New York: Guilford, 2007.

Schalock, Robert, et al. *Intellectual Disability: Definition, Classification, and Systems of Support,* 12th ed. Washington, DC: American Association of Intellectual and Developmental Disabilities, 2012.

15.9 THE CLIENT WITH BRAIN INJURY

The human brain is incredibly complex. Our brain controls all bodily, sensory, and mental activity. It is composed of possibly 100 billion nerve cells (*neurons*). Each neuron is connected to and communicates with thousands of others by way of minute structures (*synapsis*), electrical impulses, and a variety of chemicals known as *neurotransmitters*. In a single second, the brain performs billions of actions. Much of the brain has a physical consistency similar to Jell-O—very soft and very fragile. Any injury to the brain can have significant and often devastating consequences.

Just below the skull bone and to the front of the head is the largest and most complex part of the brain known as the *cerebral cortex*. Because of its size and location it is especially vulnerable to trauma such as a blow to the head. The cerebral cortex is divided into two halves (*hemispheres*). Although separate, the hemispheres communicate and work together. The left side controls the right side of the body and the right side controls the left side of the body.

The most common causes of damage to the brain are strokes, trauma, poisoning, infections, and degenerative diseases (e.g., dementia). Advances in medical treatment can often save the lives of people who have sustained such damage but all of these individuals will have some residual effects, ranging from the mild to the very severe. The aftereffects of brain injury may arise in the areas of alertness, concentration, self and bodily awareness, perception, memory, learning, reasoning, planning, decision making, problem solving, speech and language, emotions, mobility, balance and coordination, fatigue, dizziness, seizures, bowel and bladder control, or spasticity.

The type of impairment resulting from a brain injury depends on what parts of the brain are damaged and the extent of that damage. For example, the effects of stroke (cerebral vascular accident, or CVA) can be quite circumscribed because a blocked blood vessel may cause damage to just one area of the brain. For this reason, once the location of stroke-caused damage is known, the aftereffects can be predicted with some accuracy. By contrast, the consequences of a traumatic brain injury, such as one acquired in an auto accident, are rather unpredictable because there is usually a tearing and shearing of tissue in several different parts of the brain.

Coping with and adjusting to the aftereffects of a brain injury is an extreme challenge both to the individual who suffered the injury and to his or her family, loved ones, and friends. For example, individuals with significant brain injury, especially if caused by trauma, will often develop a pattern of rigid thinking. They tend to hold tightly to their ideas and beliefs because they have difficulty interpreting subtle differences among ideas and nuances in meaning and are easily frustrated by complexity and ambiguity. They are inclined to view an issue or opinion as either entirely right or entirely wrong. These individuals have difficulty accepting a middle ground and find it hard to examine and consider both the advantages and disadvantages of a proposal. This black-or-white type of thinking can make it difficult for them to make good decisions and may cause others to perceive them as rigid, abrasive, opinionated, and narrow-minded.

Stroke

Typically, the most visible sign of a stroke (CVA) is a paralysis on one side of the body. Damage to the left side of the brain results in right-sided paralysis and problems with speech and language (termed *aphasia*). In addition, the person tends to be slow, hesitant, and disorganized when faced with an unfamiliar situation.

Stroke-caused damage to the right half of the brain results in left side paralysis and causes difficulties in perception. The person who has suffered a significant stroke tends to be impulsive, have poor judgment, and overlook his or her limitations. This individual can often describe tasks that are to be performed but is not able to do them. He or she has trouble both expressing emotions and accurately perceiving the emotional signals of others.

Many who have suffered a stroke have what is termed *one-sided neglect,* meaning that they have lost sections of their visual field or have lost sensory signals to parts of their bodies. For example, a man with a paralyzed arm may be unaware that his arm is dangling near a hot stove. Another illustrative example is the woman who sees her own leg while lying in bed and becomes upset because she thinks someone is lying beside her. Persons with such perceptual problems are easily confused while traveling or moving about.

Other problems commonly associated with a stroke include (1) the person becomes careless and neglectful of personal grooming and appearance; (2) loss of memory retention span (i.e., a decrease in the number of things that can be retained and attended to at one time); (3) decreased capacity for short-term memory, which makes new learning difficult; (4) difficulty in generalization (i.e., applying what was learned in one situation to another); (5) emotional lability (i.e., erratic emotions such as laughing or crying for no apparent reason); (6) sensory deprivation (i.e., loss in the ability to taste, hear, see, perceive touch, etc.); and (7) fatigue.

Traumatic brain injury

Trauma to the brain may result in paralysis or other physical symptoms such as seizures and a decrease in strength and coordination. However, it is quite common for the person with trauma-caused brain injury to appear physically normal but have a number of significant cognitive, behavioral, and emotional problems. Difficulties in memory, judgment, attention, perception, and impulse control can cause major problems in social interaction and job performance. About 50 percent of all cases of traumatic brain injury are caused by auto accidents.

For the social work practitioner who may encounter a client who has had a stroke or a traumatic brain injury, several guidelines are important:

- Be alert to the possibility of brain injury effects whenever a client has symptoms that involve personality changes, memory problems, poor judgment, and impulsiveness. Inquire if there is a history of a concussion, coma, stroke, skull fracture, or other injuries to the head caused by, for example, car accidents, sports injuries, or violence. If there is reason to suspect the existence of a brain injury, consult with a rehabilitation specialist, neurologist, or neuropsychologist to determine if a referral for an in-depth evaluation is indicated. A medical doctor who specializes in physical rehabilitation and in treating the aftereffects of stroke and head injury is called a *physiatrist.* This medical specialty is known as *physiatry,* not to be confused with *psychiatry.*

- Rehabilitation programs can be successful in teaching patients how to compensate for some of the deficits caused by brain injury. These programs are most effective and beneficial when started as soon as possible after the injury has occurred. Because an individual with a brain injury may have impaired judgment and decision-making ability, her or his family or a social worker may need to continually encourage the individual to stick with an often demanding and exhausting rehabilitation program. In addition to their usual role in case management, arranging for support services, and participation in psychoeducation (see Chapter 6), a social worker might also be involved in teaching the patient various methods of coping with and compensating for a mental or physical impairment. An example might be teaching various techniques that can help a person with difficulties in the areas of memory, planning, and decision making.

- Individuals with a significant brain injury may not be a reliable source of information about their problems, abilities, and current functioning. They may, for example, try to conceal their problems of poor memory, learning difficulties, and their loss of reading and writing skills. They may hold tightly to a false belief because the belief helps them make sense out of unorganized bits of information and the confusion they experience. The family may be distressed and frustrated when the person with brain injury insists on the truthfulness of an obviously false assertion.

- The family of a person who has a brain injury will need information, guidance, and support in learning to cope with the many stressful changes they face. Their loved one may now seem like a very different person. The personality changes often associated with brain injury can put a severe strain on a marriage and on relationships with children. If the individual with the brain injury tends to make illogical decisions, the family or spouse should be encouraged to review relevant legal documents, contracts, wills, financial agreements, and the like and to develop legal protections against impulsive decisions and poor judgments by the brain-injured family member. Organizations such as the Brain Injury Association of America and the American Stroke Association provide information as well as support to the survivors of head injury and stroke and their families.

- State departments of vocational rehabilitation may have special employment programs for persons with cognitive deficits caused by head injury. Such services may include job coaching and extended or supported employment programs. Severe cognitive deficits that preclude competitive employment may qualify a person for Social Security Disability Income benefits (see Item 15.10).

Selected Bibliography

Applegate, Jeffery, and Janet Shapiro. *Neurobiology for Clinical Social Work*. New York: Norton, 2005.

Farmer, Rosemary. *Neuroscience and Social Work Practice*. Thousand Oaks, CA: Sage, 2009.

Parker, Jackie. *Good Practice in Brain Injury Case Management*. Philadelphia: J. Kingsley, 2006.

Senelick, Richard. *Living with Stroke: A Guide for Families*, 4th ed. Birmingham, AL: Health South Press, 2009.

Stoler, Diane, and Barbara Hill. *Coping with Concussion and Mild Traumatic Brain Injury*. New York: Avery, 2013.

15.10 THE CLIENT WITH A SERIOUS PHYSICAL DISABILITY

Many people live with physical impairments of one sort or another. As used here, the term **impairment** refers to a long-standing or permanent bodily or sensory limitation caused by disease, injury, or advanced age. If this limitation significantly hampers a person's capacity to perform his or her major social roles and the ordinary activities of living (e.g., self-care, mobility, employment), it is termed a **disability**. Whether a particular impairment is a disability depends on its severity, on whether assistive technology can help compensate for the limitation, and on the physical and social barriers that exist within the person's immediate environment. An example of a physical barrier would be a set of stairs for a person using a wheelchair. An example of a social barrier for that same person would be a bias or prejudice that keeps her or him from being hired for a job for which she or he is qualified and for which the ability to walk about is not a requirement. Eliminating physical and social barriers and using adaptive technology and equipment can go a long way in keeping an impairment from turning into a disabling condition.

The following information and guidelines will prove helpful when working with persons who have a physically disability:

- A core principle in work with persons who have a serious disability is to focus primarily on the individual's abilities, and not primarily on the disability. People are more than their bodies; they are also mind and spirit. Despite their malfunctioning nerves and muscles and despite an often painful and tiring daily routine of self-care, those with a serious disability hold demanding and responsible jobs, they are active in the community, and they are engaged in the creative and expressive arts. Those who have faced squarely their own limitations often develop a deep self-awareness, true compassion, and an authentic spirituality. By contrast, many who are "normal" often remain rather superficial and in denial of their own limitations and imperfections.

- In a society obsessed with youth, physical appearance, and celebrity, persons with a serious physical disability are often ignored and marginalized. In working with this client group, the strengths perspective, maximizing client self-determination, empowerment, and advocacy are especially important. Thus, the social worker should strive to normalize as much of the client's life as possible and prevent social isolation. Help and encourage the client to meet people, build friendships, pursue interests, explore new opportunities, and participate in community activities. Securing or retaining employment will be priority for many clients. However, employment may not be a possibility for persons with complex medical conditions and needs.

- In recent decades, federal laws such as the 1973 Rehabilitation Act, the 1975 Education for All Handicapped Children Act, and the 1990 **Americans with Disabilities Act (ADA)** have been extremely helpful to persons with disabling conditions. Schools, primary and higher education, are required to provide educational services and make reasonable accommodations for students with a disability. The ADA provides a national mandate and the legal mechanisms to remove barriers for and eliminate discrimination against persons with disabilities, especially in the areas of employment, access to public services and public transportation, access to goods and services offered by businesses, and access to telecommunications. The ADA is a solid basis for social work advocacy with and in behalf of persons with disabilities.

- A social worker must be familiar with the programs and services relevant to a client with a disability. The two most significant federal programs are worker's compensation, which provides financial assistance to a persons recovering from a work-related injury, and programs under the Social Security Act, including

Supplemental Security Income (SSI) and Social Security Disability Insurance (SSDI). In most communities, there will be state programs (e.g., vocational rehabilitation) and numerous organizations and private agencies that focus on specific disabling conditions (e.g., cerebral palsy, arthritis, multiple sclerosis, spinal cord injury, blindness). Support and informational groups are invaluable resources to persons with a disability and their families.

- Encourage and assist the client to secure the medical evaluations and treatments, rehabilitative services, training, and assistive technology that can maximize his or her independence and functioning. Such services and equipment are expensive and may be difficult to access, depending on where the client lives. Thus, a social worker must build bridges with and cultivate working relationships with the various programs and service organizations that might be able to provide financial assistance, transportation, and other services. The worker must be prepared to engage in case advocacy when the client is not receiving needed services.

  In some situations, a social worker might help organize a fundraising effort in order to secure money needed to cover expenses not covered by insurances or human services programs. It is important to note that how a fundraiser or a benefit is set up legally can affect the individual's eligibility for certain government programs. If not set up properly, the money raised can disqualify the client from receiving means tested services and benefits. Before initiating a fundraising effort, be sure to consult with someone familiar with this potential problem.

- Occupational therapists, physical therapists, and other rehabilitation specialists can provide guidance on the selection of the assistive technology that will be helpful to a particular client. Be alert to the fact that this technology needs to be maintained and adjusted on a regular basis. For example, if a brace or a wheelchair is not properly fitted to a person's body, it can cause discomfort and exacerbate medical problems. A child's growth, weight gain, or changes in a person's medical condition are just a few of the factors that should prompt adjustments in such equipment.

- A home or workplace assessment by an occupational therapist can identify physical barriers and offer specific recommendations for remodeling that can make a bathroom, kitchen, or bedroom more useable to a person with a disability that limits mobility and self-care. In the absence of such recommendations by an experienced professional, a well-intentioned remodeling project by family or friend can be a waste of money and effort. For example, it is not uncommon for a well-meaning friend to build a wheel chair ramp that is too steep and therefore unsafe and unusable.

- Because an individual with a serious disability may be dependent on care provided by family or a paid caregiver, these direct-care personnel should be involved in formulating a service plan for the client. Caregiving is demanding and at times exhausting. It is important to ensure that the caregivers have adequate social and emotional social support and sufficient rest and respite (see Item 13.20).

Selected Bibliography

Mackelprang, Romel, and Richard Salsgiver. *Disability,* 2nd ed. Chicago: Lyceum, 2009.

May, Gary, and Martha Raske. *Ending Disability Discrimination: Strategies for Social Workers.* Upper Saddle River, NJ: Pearson, 2005.

Oliver, Michael, Bob Sapey, and Pam Thomas. *Social Work with Disabled People*, 4th ed. New York: Palgrave Macmillan, 2012.

Yuen, Francis, Carol Cohen, and Kristine Tower. *Disability and Social Work Education*. Binghamton, NY: Haworth, 2007.

15.11 THE CLIENT WHO IS CHEMICALLY DEPENDENT

Many of the individuals and families receiving services from social workers and social agencies are affected, directly or indirectly, by alcohol and drug-related problems. The use and abuse of drugs and alcohol is a contributing factor to a wide range of individual, family, and social problems, such as marital discord, domestic violence, child maltreatment, poor job performance, financial difficulties, and criminal activity. Drunk driving is the cause of many auto accidents. Substance abuse also contributes to the spread of AIDS by way of intravenous injections and indiscriminate sexual behavior related to the disinhibiting effects of drugs and alcohol. The use of alcohol and drugs by a pregnant woman can damage the fetus and result in various birth defects and neurological and developmental problems. Heavy and longtime use of alcohol and certain drugs can cause or aggravate various health conditions, including brain damage (see Item 15.9).

Individuals who have an alcohol or drug problem are usually difficult and challenging clients because denial, rationalization, and self-delusion are core characteristics of a dependency or addiction. Typically, they will seek professional help or join a 12-step program only after they find themselves in the midst of a very serious personal crisis or when court ordered or coerced into treatment by family or friends. The social worker's response to these clients must be based on an understanding of how alcohol and drugs affect the mind and body and on the realization that it is seldom possible for an individual to overcome an addiction without persistent effort and specialized treatment.

Many of the abused chemicals alter the body's neurochemistry and physiology, resulting in the development of tolerance, craving, and withdrawal. *Tolerance* refers to a need for an ever-increasing amount of the chemical in order for it to produce the desired mood-altering effect. The term *craving* describes an intense, almost painful, desire for the chemical. An individual experiencing craving is preoccupied with getting the chemical and can think of little else. When an individual is deprived of the chemical to which he or she is addicted, the person will often experience symptoms of *withdrawal* (i.e., the individual becomes anxious, panicky, or physically ill when unable to take in the chemical). An individual may engage in reckless and extreme behaviors (e.g., stealing, violence, deceit) in order to secure the chemical and escape distressing withdrawal symptoms. The existence of tolerance, craving, and withdrawal are key indicators of a chemical addiction.

In their beginning stages chemical dependencies and addictions are rooted in a learning process. Each time a mood-altering substance provides the user with a desired effect (e.g., relaxation, self-confidence, euphoria), usage is thereby rewarded or reinforced, thus increasing the likelihood that the substance will be used again. Individuals who suffer from a mood disorder (e.g., depression, bipolar disorder, anxiety) are particularly vulnerable to developing a dependency. Individuals with low self-esteem, feelings of powerlessness, loneliness, and other types of emotion pain are also drawn to the mood-changing or numbing effects of certain chemicals.

An individual with an alcohol or drug problem will typically exhibit several of the following behaviors and patterns:

- Continues to use the chemical or substance even though it causes personal, family, health, and work-related problems
- Displays an increased tolerance to the chemical
- Experiences withdrawal symptoms and often uses the chemical to relieve those uncomfortable experiences
- Uses more of the chemical, uses it more often, and uses it over longer periods than intended and as a result is often late for or misses work-related appointments and family events
- Abandons previously important activities and relationships in favor or drinking and/or drug use
- Voices a desire to cut back on use but is unsuccessful in efforts to control use
- Neglects appearance, grooming, and hygiene
- Experiences a decrease in physical and intellectual capacities, such as physical stamina and ability to concentrate and think logically
- Participates in reckless and/or illegal activities in order to obtain the chemical

It is important to note that the information presented here is of a basic and general nature. The reader should consult the *DSM-5* for descriptions and criteria used in the diagnosis of various types of substance-related disorders and in identifying the existence of tolerance and withdrawal (see Item 11.15).

Generally speaking, the substances most sought after are those with a rapid onset of effects. *Onset of effect* is related to chemical properties, dose, method of intake, and the user's personality characteristics. The psychosocial setting can also influence a person's response to a chemical.

There are local and regional differences in the popularity of various substances and the preferred methods of intake. Moreover, the street lingo applied to illegal substances continually changes and new chemical combinations appear frequently. Presented next are brief descriptions of the legal and illegal chemicals that are most often abused and involved in dependency problems.

Nicotine

The nicotine found in tobacco is a stimulant and highly addictive. The use of tobacco is widespread and a contributing cause in the development of certain cancers as well as heart and lung disease. Tobacco use causes more illness and death than all the illegal street drugs combined. Tobacco is usually smoked but some individuals prefer the smokeless tobacco products that are inhaled into the nasal cavity (i.e., "snuff"), chewed, or placed next to the gums. The cessation of tobacco use brings on a physical withdrawal syndrome and a craving. These uncomfortable effects can be alleviated almost immediately by returning to the nicotine. This makes quitting exceedingly difficult.

Alcohol

If one considers the number of individuals and families affected, the number of injuries and deaths caused by drunken driving, and the number of health problems either caused or exacerbated by drinking, then the number-one drug problem in the United States is the abuse of alcohol (a legal drug). The American Medical Association, the National Council on Alcoholism, and the American Society of Addiction Medicine define *alcoholism* as a chronic disease that is progressive and fatal. Because alcohol depresses the central nervous system (CNS), it can be very dangerous when used in conjunction with other drugs or prescription medications that also depress the CNS. Genetic, psychosocial, and cultural factors influence the development and manifestations of this disease. There is no cure; at best, it can be controlled through complete abstinence from alcohol. Treatment experts generally agree that once a person has the disease of alcoholism, she or he can never again become only a casual user of alcohol (i.e., a social drinker). If an alcoholic tries to drink in moderation, he or she will almost always resume a pattern of uncontrolled drinking.

In its early stage, alcoholism is difficult to recognize because the symptoms are subtle and the person's drinking behavior may be indistinguishable from someone who occasionally drinks too much but is not addicted to the chemical. Often, the emerging alcoholic can consume a large amount of alcohol without showing the effects and may be described by friends as "someone who can really hold his [or her] liquor." This physiological or metabolic phenomenon may be genetic in origin. The person who is becoming dependent will drink more and more often than others do and gradually the consumption of alcohol is a part of all his or her social and recreational activities. Yet, during this early stage, the use of alcohol may not significantly interfere with work or family functioning.

In the middle stage, the alcohol-dependent person is physically addicted. When her or his blood-alcohol level is lowered, she or he will experience withdrawal symptoms, including anxiety, agitation, tremors, and sweating as well as fluctuations in blood pressure and blood sugar levels. Increasingly, the individual will have trouble remembering what occurred while drinking, a phenomenon called a *blackout*. He or she will drink more and for longer periods. Family relationships and job functioning will be adversely affected. Family and friends will usually ask the individual to please cut back. The individual may quit drinking for a few weeks at a time but will eventually start again. Experiencing these short periods of abstinence will convince the alcohol-dependent person that it is possible to quit whenever he or she really wants to and therefore drinking is not a problem. Concerned family members may reach out for professional help, but typically, the alcoholic will deny that there is a problem.

In the late stage, the seriousness of the problem is apparent to everyone but the alcoholic. By this point in the disease process, the individual may have lost her or his family and job and may have several alcohol-related health problems. However, the denial and self-delusion will continue, and possibly only a major personal or health crisis will force the alcoholic to face reality.

A client's answers to the four so-called CAGE questions will help to identify an alcohol problem:

- Have you ever felt you ought to **C**ut *down* on your drinking?
- Have people **A**nnoyed you by criticizing your drinking?
- Have you ever felt **G**uilty about your drinking?
- Have you ever had a drink first thing in the morning (an **E**ye *opener*) to steady your nerves or get rid of a hangover?

If one or more answers are positive, the social worker should further explore the possible existence of an alcohol dependency problem.

Amphetamines

All amphetamines are CNS stimulants. Some, such as Dexedrine, are prescription medications used in the treatment of narcolepsy, brain dysfunction, and obesity, whereas others, such as Adderall and Ritalin, are used to treat attention deficit. Other forms (i.e., the methamphetamines) are illegally manufactured and widely abused because of their strong effects and low cost. Among the chemicals used in making methamphetamine in a "meth lab" are cold and allergy medicines that contain pseudoephedrine, acetone, ether, sulfuric acid, rubbing alcohol, brake cleaner, rock salt, farm fertilizer, iodine, red phosphorus from matches or road flares, and lithium. Several of these chemicals are extremely toxic and flammable, especially when heated. Exposure to the chemicals can produce illness. Meth labs have been found in basements, bathrooms, kitchens, garages, and hotel rooms.

Small batches of a methamphetamine can be made in a soda bottle by mixing crushed cold medication tablets containing pseudephedine with certain other chemicals. This method does not use a flame to heat the chemical mix but it leaves a toxic waste and may explode.

Among the forms of methamphetamine are methamphetamine sulfate (i.e., "crank"), methamphetamine hydrochloride (i.e., "crystal meth"), and dextrometh-amphetamine (i.e., "ice"). These highly addictive chemicals produce feelings of self-confidence and an intense and long-lasting euphoria. Depending on their form, they may be snorted, swallowed, smoked, or injected.

The user of these stimulants is seeking the intensely pleasurable or euphoric sensations that they can produce. The abuse of these stimulants is indicated by symptoms such as hyperactivity, nervousness and anxiety, dilated pupils, irritability, and going for long periods without sleep or food. Some users experience a dry mouth, sweating, headache, blurred vision, dizziness, and sleeplessness. High doses can cause rapid or irregular heartbeat, tremors, loss of coordination, and physical collapse. Long-time use can lead to malnutrition, skin disorders, ulcers, weight loss, kidney damage, dental problems, depression, and speech and thought disturbances. A methamphetamine injection causes a sudden increase in blood pressure that can precipitate a stroke or heart failure.

Heavy use of amphetamines can result in a psychosis involving hallucinations (seeing, hearing, and feeling things that do not exist), delusions (having irrational thoughts or beliefs), and paranoia (extreme unfounded fear and distrust of others). In such a state, the person may exhibit bizarre and violent behavior. Methamphetamine use is often a contributing factor in child abuse and neglect, domestic abuse, and other forms of violence. Withdrawal (often referred to as "crashing") is extremely distressing and characterized by fatigue, nightmares, insomnia, depression, and a wildly fluctuating appetite.

Cocaine

This central nervous system stimulant is derived from the coca plant native to the mountain regions of South America. It is smuggled into a country as a fine, white, crystalline powder (cocaine hydrochloride) and then diluted, or "cut," to increase its bulk and stretch the supply for selling.

A common method of intake is intranasal or "snorting" the powder. When snorted, the euphoric effects begin within a few minutes, peak within 15 to 20 minutes, and disappear within about 45 minutes. During this brief period, the user often feels confident, energetic, talkative, and omnipotent.

Chemical procedures can be used to separate or free the pure cocaine from the other usual additives in powdered cocaine. The process of "freebasing" involves the dangerous procedure of adding ammonia and ethyl ether to powdered cocaine and burning it to free up the "base" cocaine. This yields "freebase" that can be smoked as a more direct and rapid way to transmit the chemical to the brain. Since freebase cocaine is water soluble, it can also be injected. Because injection produces an immediate and intense euphoria, intravenous use is highly addictive.

Smokeable "crack" or "rock cocaine" is made by mixing powdered cocaine with baking soda and water and then burning off the liquid to form tiny "rocks." It came to be called "crack" for the crackling sound of the cooking process. Smoking crack cocaine produces a short but very intense "high."

Regular users of cocaine often report feelings of restlessness, irritability, anxiety, and sleeplessness. Cocaine causes physical and mental damage similar to that caused by the amphetamines. High doses over a long period may precipitate a psychosis with hallucinations of touch, sight, taste, or smell. Because cocaine stimulates the body and its nervous system, it is not uncommon to experience a physical "crash" and a mental depression following a period of use. These depressions and mood swings can be debilitating and last from a few hours to several weeks. The uncomfortable psychological and physiological effects of withdrawal are a source of worry for many who use cocaine.

Marijuana

Marijuana is the common name for a dried leafy material derived from the cannabis sativa plant. The main psychoactive ingredient in marijuana is THC (delta-9-tetrahydrocannabinol). The amount of THC in the marijuana determines its strength and effects on the user. Concentrating the resin found in the plant's leaves and flowers makes *hashish*, which contains more THC. Marijuana and hash are usually smoked but can be prepared for oral consumption. The user of marijuana seeks a state of care-free and euphoric relaxation.

Because marijuana is not physically addictive and relatively harmless and because it can provide relief from the discomforts of chemotherapy, chronic pain, and certain other ailments, there is some public support for decriminalizing its use. Several states have legalized marijuana use but at the time of this writing federal law classifies marijuana as an illegal substance.

Research and the experiences of drug treatment programs identify several potentially adverse effects. Some users become psychologically dependent and some heavy users report feeling unusually passive and sluggish. Marijuana users do not experience the physiological withdrawal syndrome, but it is not uncommon for them to report a degree of psychological withdrawal that includes cravings. An individual "high" on marijuana or hashish will have dilated pupils and may speak rapidly and louder than usual. Some individuals experience sensory distortions. Longtime and heavy use can impair short-term memory and reduce the ability to perform tasks that require concentration and quick reactions such as in driving a car or operating machinery.

Plant-based marijuana should not be confused with *synthetic marijuana*, a designer drug called "spice," which mimics the relaxing effects of ordinary marijuana but has a different chemical composition. Its physical and psychological effects have not been extensively studied but there are indications that the heavy and prolonged uses of synthetic marijuana has some adverse effects not usually associated with ordinary marijuana, such as the possibility of agitation, withdrawal symptoms, convulsions, and heart problems.

PCP

Phencyclidine (PCP) was developed as an anesthetic but later taken off the market for human use because it often caused hallucinations. It continues to have use in veterinary medicine. PCP is easily manufactured and available in a several forms (i.e., white crystal-like powder, tablet, or capsule). It can be swallowed, smoked, sniffed, or injected. PCP powder, sometimes referred to as "angel dust" or "dust," may be sprinkled on marijuana and smoked.

The sought-after effect of PCP is euphoria. For some users, small amounts act as a stimulant. For many, it changes how they perceive their own bodies and objects. Movements and time feel as if they have slowed down. The effects of PCP are unpredictable, and for this reason many "experimenters" abandon its use. Others, unfortunately, become dependent.

Negative effects of PCP include increased heart rate and blood pressure, flushing, sweating, dizziness, and numbness. Users may show signs of paranoia, fear, and anxiety. Frequent use negatively affects memory, perception, concentration, and judgment. The effects of large doses include drowsiness, convulsions, coma, and sometimes death. Its use can produce violent or bizarre behavior. When under the drug's influence, some individuals become aggressive; others withdraw and have difficulty communicating. A PCP-induced psychosis may last for days or weeks.

Hallucinogens

The hallucinogens or psychedelics are chemicals that affect a person's perceptions, sensations, thinking, self-awareness, and emotions. This category includes LSD, mescaline, and psilocybin. *LSD* is manufactured from lysergic acid found in a fungus that grows on grains. It is sold on the street in tablets, capsules, or occasionally in liquid form. LSD is usually taken by mouth. *Mescaline* comes from the peyote cactus and, although it is not as strong as LSD, its effects are similar. Mescaline is usually smoked or swallowed in the form of capsules or tablets. *Psilocybin* comes from certain mushrooms. It is sold in tablet or capsule form or the mushrooms themselves may be eaten.

The effects of psychedelics are unpredictable and depend on dosage as well as the user's personality, mood, expectations, and surroundings. Several different emotions may be felt at once or swing from one to another. Sensations become mixed and seem to "cross over," giving the user the feeling of hearing colors and seeing sounds. A person feels a change in one's sense of self and time. For some, these odd sensations are an interesting and enjoyable experience. For other users, these strange sensations are alarming and frightening and give rise to a "bad trip" that may last a few minutes or several hours and involve confusion, suspiciousness, anxiety, feelings of helplessness, and loss of control. Physical effects include dilated pupils, higher body temperature, increased heart rate and blood pressure, and often sweating, irregular breathing, and tremors. Some users sit in a stupor, whereas others become agitated.

A manufactured hallucinogenic known as MDMA, or "Ecstasy," is usually taken by capsule or tablet. Its use brings on mild distortions of perceptions, has a calming effect, and, for many, creates a feeling of empathy with others. It does not cause the visual illusions often associated with the psychedelics. Physical dependency is not a major problem, but psychological dependence develops in many users. Growing evidence indicates that frequent and heavy use of MDMA causes some damage to the brain.

The use of hallucinogens can unmask underlying mental or emotional problems. Some users experience *flashbacks* (i.e., intense and intrusive memories and emotions that can occur days and even weeks after having taken the drug). Heavy users sometimes suffer impaired memory, loss of attention span, confusion, and difficulty with abstract thinking.

Inhalants

These chemicals produce semi-toxic vapors that are inhaled in a practice sometimes called "huffing." The inhalants are grouped into four classes: (1) volatile solvents (e.g., certain glues, gasoline, paint thinner, nail polish remover, lighter fluid); (2) aerosols (e.g., spray paints); (3) anesthetics (e.g., ether, chloroform, nitrous oxide); and (4) amyl and butyl nitrates. Nearly all of the inhalants depress the body's functions. At low doses, users may feel slightly stimulated and some, such as butyl nitrite, produce a "rush" or "high" lasting for a few seconds or a couple of minutes. Young people are likely to abuse inhalants, in part because they are available and inexpensive.

Possible negative effects include nausea, sneezing, coughing, nosebleeds, fatigue, bad breath, lack of coordination, and a loss of appetite. Solvents and aerosols decrease the heart and breathing rates and affect judgment. Deep breathing of the vapors may result in a loss of self-control, violent behavior, and unconsciousness. Inhalants can cause death from suffocation by displacing oxygen in the lungs and by depressing the central nervous system to a point that breathing stops. Moderate to long-term use can damage the brain, liver, kidneys, blood, and bone marrow.

Opiates

The chemicals known as opiates or narcotics are used medically to relieve pain. They are potentially addictive and habit forming. Some opiates (opium, morphine, heroin, and codeine) are derived from the Asian poppy plant. Others, such as meperidine (Demerol), are manufactured.

Opiates are ingested, snorted, smoked, or injected intravenously. After causing an initial rush, they relax the user. Indicators of opiate abuse include needle scars on the arms and the backs of hands, drowsiness, frequent scratching, red and watering eyes, sniffles, and a loss of appetite overall but an attraction to sugar and candies. In contrast to the effects of most other abused drugs that dilate the eye's pupils, the opiates constrict the pupils. When an opiate-dependent person stops taking the drug, withdrawal symptoms begin within 4 to 6 hours. These symptoms include anxiety, diarrhea, abdominal cramps, chills, sweating, nausea, and runny nose and eyes. The intensity of the symptoms depends on how much was taken, how often, and for how long. Withdrawal symptoms for most opiates are stronger approximately 24 to 72 hours after they begin but subside within 7 to 10 days.

Most of the physical dangers associated with opiate abuse result from overdoses, the use of nonsterile needles, contamination of the drug by other chemicals, or combining the drug with other substances. Long-time opiate users may develop infections of the heart, skin abscesses, and congested lungs.

Sedative hypnotics and other prescription medications

The misuse or overuse of certain prescribed medications can lead to a chemical dependency and even to death. These drugs are available only by a physician's prescription but unused pills can be found in many family medicine cabinets. In some cases, an individual can obtain a doctor's prescription by falsely reporting symptoms of pain, anxiety, or insomnia or by forging a prescription document. Some of these medications are obtained by home break-ins or the robbery of a pharmacy. Those who have the pills may exchange them with friends or sell them on the street.

Contributing to the problem of addiction to prescription medications is an uninformed attitude that "it's just a pill" and "it must be safe" because it was prescribed by a doctor. Trading pills, ingesting several different medications at the same time, and taking them with alcohol adds to the danger they present. The abuse of medications is a growing problem.

The most commonly abused prescription drugs are the pain medications such as OxyContin, Lortab, Lorcet, Darvon, Percodan, Percocette, Vicodin, Codeine, Methadone, and Morphine. The effect sought by users is a deeply relaxed state of tranquility. These pain medications are addictive and very dangerous if taken in high dosage. Also commonly abused, especially by teens and college students, are the stimulants used to treat attention deficit such as Adderall. Those using a stimulant hope to feel energized and attentive.

A group of medications known as *sedative hypnotics* are the sleeping pills, sedatives, and tranquilizers. Two major categories are the barbiturates and the benzodiazepines, which include Valium, Librium, Ambien, and Ativan. These medications depress the central nervous system, have a calming effect, and promote sleep. If an individual takes a higher than prescribed dosage, he or she may appear drunk (e.g., staggering, slurred speech, sleepiness) but will not smell of alcohol. When taken with alcohol (also a depressant), these drugs can cause unconsciousness and death.

The prolonged use of a sedative-hypnotic drug can result in both physical and psychological dependence. When a user stops taking the drug, she or he may experience withdrawal symptoms, ranging from restlessness, insomnia, and anxiety to convulsions and even death.

GUIDELINES FOR DEALING WITH A CHEMICALLY DEPENDENT CLIENT

Throughout their professional relationships and interventions with a chemically dependent client and his or her family, social workers should carefully consider the following guidelines:

- Because the abuse of and dependence on alcohol and other drugs is so pervasive in society, the social worker should be alert to the possible existence of this problem even when neither the client nor the client's family has mentioned it. In all individual and family assessments, some questions should be asked about the client's use of alcohol and drugs. However, it must be recognized that chemically dependent persons are seldom willing to accurately describe their use of chemicals and are often adamant in denying any connection between their personal problems and the use of drugs and alcohol. In many cases, the social worker's application of *motivational interviewing* will increase a client's willingness to acknowledge and address a dependency or addictions (see Items 8.5 and 11.5).

- Never underestimate the psychological power of alcohol and drugs. A dependency or addiction is a pathological relationship with a mood-altering substance. The dynamics of this relationship resemble those of a neurotic love affair, but in this case, the love object is a chemical. A chemical dependency or addiction can turn a kind and honest person into a self-centered individual who is willing to lie, cheat, and even injure loved ones in order to continue using a chemical.

- When, in the course of your professional activity and/or when within your agency setting, you encounter an intoxicated individual you must be alert to the potentially life-threatening danger of delirium tremens or a drug overdose and also to the issue of public safety. A consideration of legal and ethical duties would suggest that a professional must make a reasonable effort to prevent a foreseeable injury, death, or tragic occurrence. For example, if you know that an intoxicated person intends to drive a car, you have a duty to attempt to prevent it and, if necessary, to notify law enforcement in order to prevent an auto accident.

- If your client is intoxicated when he or she arrives for a scheduled interview or meeting, explain in a polite but firm manner that you need accurate information and his or her full attention to do your work so you must reschedule the session for a time when he or she is sober. The client may argue and become angry but remain calm and hold firm to your decision.

- Do not allow yourself to become part of an enabling system. For example, do not lend the client money and do not write letters or make phone calls that provide excuses or "cover" for his or her irresponsible behavior. Do not shield or protect him or her from the real-life consequences of substance abuse.

- Learn about the behavioral pattern of *codependency* that develops as a result of living for many years with someone who is chemically dependent. Those who are codependent typically protect and provide excuses for the person who is using and abusing chemicals. They tend to assume responsibility for the behavior of others (e.g., the alcoholic) while neglecting their own needs. They are often hostile and angry because they have been mistreated by someone they love, controlling because their own situation is so out of control, manipulative because manipulation is the only way to get things done, and vague in their communication because they live in a family system or a relationship that cannot tolerate truthfulness.

- Because a person who is chemically dependent is seldom able to stop using without the help of a treatment program, a referral for treatment likely will be necessary. However, before attempting a referral, it is best to consult with a treatment specialist on how best to approach the client and how you might handle his or her denial and resistance to the idea of entering treatment. The available options for securing treatment will need to be examined and planned in conjunction with the client's health insurance program or perhaps an applicable tax-supported program.

    In some cases, inpatient medical care will be needed to manage physiological withdrawal (detoxification). After undergoing medically supervised detoxification, if needed, the individual will enter a treatment program that will take one of several forms (e.g., inpatient, outpatient, day treatment). Ongoing weekly or twice-weekly outpatient counseling sessions (both individual and group) may continue for six months to one year or longer.

    Many recovering addicts will be involved in a *12-step program* (e.g., Alcoholics Anonymous, Cocaine Anonymous, Narcotics Anonymous), which provides encouragement and teaches methods of day-to-day coping. Through the use of story telling, sharing, and mutual support, these programs help an individual develop a life-style free of alcohol and drugs and emphasize the importance of spirituality—a spiritualty often called "The Spirituality of Imperfection" (see Item 15.18).

- The assistance and support of the client's family and friends will usually be needed to effect a referral to a treatment program. Thus, it may be necessary to reach out to these individuals and engage them in the assessment, planning, and helping process. However, be alert to the possibility that some of these individuals may also have a substance abuse problem and/or may be contributing to your client's problem through enabling and codependency behaviors.

- Encourage family members to make use of Al-Anon and Alateen groups, along with other resources such as COA (Children of Alcoholics), ACOA or ACA (Adult Children of Alcoholics), and programs that address the problem of codependency. Learn about these 12-step recovery programs by attending open meetings. Members of these groups are usually eager to consult with professionals who want to learn about the recovery process and effective ways of dealing with the many challenges presented by clients who have substance abuse problems.

- Once the individual stops using chemicals, special attention must be given to relapse prevention. This involves helping the individual develop a plan for coping with those times and situations when he or she will be at highest risk of resuming the use of alcohol and drugs. Once an addicted individual has stopped using his or her chemical of choice, he or she remains vulnerable to becoming addicted to another substance. A recovering addict must be especially vigilant with regard to use of both prescription and over-the-counter medications. Recovering addicts should always inform their physicians about their prior problems with chemical dependency and addiction.

Selected Bibliography

Abbott, Ann, ed. *Alcohol, Tobacco and Other Drugs*, 2nd ed. Washington, DC: NASW Press, 2012.

Fisher, Gary, and Thomas Harrison. *Substance Abuse*, 5th ed. Upper Saddle River, NJ: Pearson, 2013.

Hart, Carl, and Charles Ksir. *Drugs, Society, and Human Behavior*, 15th ed. New York: McGraw-Hill, 2013.

Kurtz, Ernest, and Katherine Ketcham. *The Spirituality of Imperfection*. New York: Bantam Books, 2002.

McNeece, C. Aaron, and Diana DiNitto. *Chemical Dependency*, 4th ed. Upper Saddle River, NJ: Pearson, 2012.

Miller, William, Alyssa Forehimes, and Allen Zweben. *Treating Addictions: A Guide for Professionals*. New York: Guilford, 2011.

Smith, Ellen, and Robert Meyers. *Motivating Substance Abusers to Enter Treatment*. New York: Guilford, 2007.

Van Wormer, Katherine, and Diane Davis. *Addiction Treatment: A Strengths Perspective*, 3rd ed. Independence, KY: Cengage, 2013.

15.12 THE CLIENT WITH SERIOUS MENTAL ILLNESS

The three foremost mental illnesses are schizophrenia, bipolar disorder, and major depression. All three are caused primarily by biochemical abnormalities within the brain. Each may be episodic and vary in intensity and in the degree to which it impairs a person's functioning. A persistent illness is especially disruptive to family relationships and occupational roles. Some of those who experience these illnesses become psychotic and lose touch with reality.

Schizophrenia is a baffling and debilitating illness. About 1 percent of the population is afflicted with this disorder. The usual age of onset is between 15 and 25 years old, when the frontal lobes of the brain are maturing. Many experts believe that a stressful environment, infections, and other physiological conditions may trigger the onset of this illness in those who are predisposed by heredity. An individual with schizophrenia will exhibit several of these symptoms:

- *Delusions* (e.g., holds to false beliefs that have no factual basis)
- *Hallucinations* (hearing voices is the most common hallucination; visual hallucination [seeing nonexistent things] is relatively rare but is more likely if the individual is also abusing drugs; olfactory and tactile hallucinations are less common, but possible)
- *Disordered thinking* (e.g., loose or illogical connections among thoughts; reaches conclusions unrelated to facts or logic; makes up words or uses sounds or rhythms that are meaningless to others, shifts rapidly from one topic to another)
- *Blunted or inappropriate affect* (e.g., narrow range of emotional responses; emotions or feelings do not fit the situation; speaks in a flat monotone)
- *Extreme withdrawal* (e.g., withdrawal from ordinary life and social interactions; deterioration in work or school performance; apathy in regard to appearance and self-care)

About one-fourth of those who have a schizophrenic episode will recover and never have another episode. Some will have occasional relapses. Between 20 to 30 percent have symptoms that persist throughout life.

The other two types of serious mental illness—major depression and bipolar disorder—are often termed *mood disorders or affective disorders*. Individuals with a **major depression** experience persistent feelings of sadness and melancholy. They often become tearful, irritable, or hostile for no apparent reason. Other symptoms common to depression include:

- Intense feelings of worthlessness, hopelessness, or guilt
- Anxiety and rumination over problems and situation
- Diminished ability to think, concentrate, or make decisions
- Loss of interest in friends, family, and usual activities
- Recurrent thoughts of death and suicide
- Poor appetite and weight loss or increased eating and weight gain
- Change in sleep pattern (sleeping too much or too little)
- Excessive fatigue; loss of energy, decreased sexual drive
- Change in usual activity level (either increased or decreased)

About 1 percent of the population suffers from **bipolar disorder**, which is characterized by swings between periods of depression and mania. Mania, a state of hyperactivity, is often characterized by these qualities:

- Exaggerated, intense, or irritable moods
- Decreased need for sleep
- Inflated self-confidence and grandiose ideas
- Increased energy and activity; unusually high levels of involvement in work, pleasurable activities, and sex
- Unrealistic optimism, poor judgment, impulsive decision making
- Rapid and pressured speech and racing thoughts
- Distractibility

Most often, the depressive phase follows a manic phase. Sometimes, the two phases are separated by periods of near normal functioning. These episodes may come and go and last from several days to several months. Without treatment, there is usually an increase in the frequency of the episodes and the severity of the symptoms.

Some individuals experience the bipolar disorder as mostly depressive episodes or mostly manic episodes. Often, a person's mental health history will predict how the bipolar disorder will manifest itself in the future. For example, a person who historically experiences depression in the autumn may continue to experience more severe symptoms during these months of the year. There is evidence that this disorder has a basis in heredity.

When working with a client who has a serious mental illness, the social worker should consider these guidelines:

- Whenever a social worker suspects that his or her client is experiencing a mental illness, the client should be referred to a competent physician, preferably a psychiatrist, for a proper diagnosis and treatment. In many cases, an evaluation by a clinical psychologist will supplement the diagnostic process. For most individuals with a serious mental illness, some combination of medication and psychotherapy is the preferred treatment. An individual taking a medication should be under the care of a physician who can monitor the effectiveness of the medication and its effect on bodily functions and other medical conditions (see Item 15.14).

- Because depression gives rise to feelings of hopelessness, the risk of suicide must always be considered. Of those with schizophrenia, about one in four attempts suicide and about one in ten dies of suicide. Thoughts of suicide or self-mutilation by someone with schizophrenia place her or him at high risk (see Item 15.7).

- Delusions are a common symptom in schizophrenia. A *delusion* is a set of ideas and beliefs that remain fixed, even in the face of clear evidence to the contrary. The individual holds to these delusional beliefs because they help make some sense out of his or her mental or perceptual confusion. Be very cautious about how you respond to a person's delusions. Listen carefully and try to understand the assumptions on which the delusion is built, but do not criticize, challenge, or confront the delusional thoughts for that will probably destroy the relationship you have with the individual. Also, confronting a delusion increases the risk that you will become part of the individual's delusional system of thought and defined as an enemy or involved in a plot or conspiracy.

- A small percentage of persons who become psychotic will experience *command hallucinations,* which are voices that tell these individuals to hurt themselves or hurt others (e.g., a voice telling them to jump off a bridge or kill the mayor). These command hallucinations, although rare, are very dangerous. If this symptom cannot be controlled by medication, the individual should be hospitalized.

- An individual with a serious and persistent mental illness will usually have difficulty managing and coping with the ordinary demands of every day life. For this reason he or she may need of the assistance provided by a social worker functioning in the role of a case manager. A case manger's encouragement, challenge, counseling, and guidance can assist this client to secure and coordinate psychotherapeutic and medical services; monitor the effects of medications; secure suitable housing and employment; and deal with other tasks such as constructing a budget, paying bills, handling insurances, and the like. The

"The Clubhouse Model"
a deleted item from the
7th edition

case manager will also strive to keep the client connected to family, friends, and a support group.

The *clubhouse model*—which provides peer support, acceptance, meaningful work, social activity, and other services—is especially helpful and important to persons with a persistent mental illness.

- An individual's mental illness has a profound and painful impact on her or his family and close friends. The social worker should address the concerns of the family by doing the following:

  - Provide practical information about the mental illness and its usual treatment. Ask about the family's possible fear of physical assault and worry over irresponsible financial decisions by the individual who is mentally ill.
  - Encourage family members to join a self-help or support group such as the National Alliance for the Mentally Ill.
  - Help the parents and siblings recognize their need for and a life apart from the anguish and worry they feel toward the family member who is mentally ill.
  - Assist family members in securing services such as case management and respite care that can provide opportunities for rest and renewal and help soften the stress and responsibility of caregiving (see Item 13.20).
  - Encourage the family to secure legal guidance on how to address the questions and concerns they may have about, for example, involuntary hospitalization, dealing with their loved one's finances, dangerous behavior, misuse of medications, and the rejection of medical treatment.
  - Help family members grieve the loss of their loved one who, because of mental illness, may now seem changed and like a stranger.
  - Remain accessible to the families, especially during family crises that can be precipitated by episodes of especially disruptive behavior.
  - If appropriate, encourage the client to authorize the release of confidential medical and therapy-related information to trusted family members so they will understand the client's condition and can help him or her utilize needed services.

- The treatment and management of a mental illness can be further complicated by the presence of an additional serious condition(s) such as substance abuse, a personality disorder, brain injury, or a developmental disability (see Items 15.8.15.9,15.11, and 15.13). The term **dual diagnosis** is applied to such a situation.

Selected Bibliography

Beck, Aaron, and Brad Alford. *Depression: Causes and Treatment*, 2nd ed. Philadelphia: University of Pennsylvania, 2009.

Gray, Susan, and Marilyn Zide. *Psychopathology: A Competency-Based Treatment Model for Social Workers*, 3rd ed. Independence, KY: Cengage, 2013.

Lefley, Harriet. *Family Psychoeducation for Serious Mental Illness*. New York: Oxford University Press, 2009.

Linhorst, Donald. *Empowering People with Severe Mental Illness*. New York: Oxford University Press, 2005.

Longhoffer, Jeffery, Paul Kubek, and Jeffery Floerch. *On Being and Having a Case Manager: A Relational Approach to Recovery in Mental Health*. New York: Columbia University Press, 2010.

Rubin, Allen, David Springer, and Kathie Trawver, eds. *Psychosocial Treatment of Schizophrenia*, Hoboken, NJ: Wiley, 2010.

15.13 THE CLIENT WITH A PERSONALITY DISORDER

In most practice settings, social workers will encounter individuals who display a pattern of thinking and behaving known to mental health professionals as a personality disorder. A **personality disorder (PD)**, of which there are several types, is characterized by a long-standing, inflexible, and maladaptive way of perceiving, thinking about, and relating to other people and to life itself. This deeply ingrained pattern shapes all of the person's interactions and roles and results in a significant level of impaired functioning. This pattern typically becomes evident during adolescence.

As a general rule, individuals with a personality disorder seldom see anything unusual about their own behavior and will typically blame others for whatever difficulties they encounter in life. Thus, they seldom seek treatment or feel a need to change how they are functioning.

The *DSM-5* (see Item 11.15) describes 10 specific personality disorders (PD) in three clusters or subgroups. In Cluster A, there are the Paranoid, Schizoid, and the Schizotypal PD. An individual with one of these three disorders will often be described by acquaintances as aloof, strange, odd, or eccentric. In Cluster B, there are four personality disorders: Antisocial, Borderline, Histrionic, and the Narcissistic PD. Individuals in that cluster are often described as being overly dramatic, highly emotional, erratic, unpredictable, or untrustworthy. The third cluster, Cluster C, consists of the Avoidant, Dependent, and the Obsessive-Compulsive PD. Individuals in this cluster usually appear fearful, anxious, and rigid.

In order to understand the nature of a PD it is useful to recall that the term *personality* refers to a relatively consistent and stable pattern of behavior, thinking, and feeling. It is important to distinguish between a *personality trait* and a *personality disorder*. A *trait* is a behavior or an attitude that is fairly typical of an individual but it does not necessarily impair one's functioning. If, however, a trait or a cluster of traits exists in an extreme form and impairs functioning significantly, it can be described as a *personality disorder*. For example, consider the fact that we are all inclined to avoid situations that cause us to feel awkward or ill-at-ease. If that avoidance behavior exists in an extreme form and interferes with normal functioning, it might properly be termed an Avoidant PD. As another illustration, consider that it is natural for people to desire attention from others. However, if this desire is extreme and the individual is constantly engaged in unusual and inappropriate behaviors so as to become the center of attention, this may suggest a Histrionic PD.

It is critically important to understand that a diagnosis of personality disorder requires that the individual's pattern of behavior, thinking, and feeling is persistent and pervasive throughout his or her life's activities and that it is a source of significant impairment in functioning. A personality disorder is something very different from the various quirks and peculiarities that we all have. Most of the people that we might describe as "difficult" or "a little strange" do not have a personally disorder and most of the people we dislike or find annoying probably does not experience this disorder. The patterns and traits that constitute a personality disorder stand at the extreme end of a continuum.

Here we offer guidance on how best to interact with and approach clients who have a personally disorder and provide brief descriptions of four personality disorders. This information will provide beginning-level social workers with a heightened awareness of the special challenges they may face when their client has a personality disorder.

- The diagnosis of a PD depends heavily on an examination of the client's behavioral history over many years. Thus, a social history or social assessment report compiled by a social worker can be invaluable to the diagnostic process (see Item 11.3). For example, a client's social history can help to answer the key question of whether a client's troublesome behavior and problems are indeed long-standing, entrenched, and impacting all relationships or, by contrast, of recent origin and evident in only certain relationships and in only some situations.

- If experienced clinicians have a detailed description of a client's past and current behavior, they can usually come to an agreement on the existence of a PD. However, clinicians will often disagree on which type of PD best describes the client. This is because some of personality disorders have similar or overlapping characteristics.

- Personality disorders, especially borderline personality disorders, are diagnosed with increasing frequency. The reason is unclear. It may be that professionals are now more aware of these disorders. However, some experts believe the growing incidence of this type of mental disorder reflects the effects of societal and cultural changes on family functioning and child-rearing patterns.

- Because a PD is a deeply engrained pattern, change is extremely difficult. Conventional forms of counseling and psychotherapy are seldom effective. Moreover, individuals with a PD seldom seek professional help and when they do, they are not likely to remain in therapy long enough to effect change. They are difficult to engage in a helping relationship and the slightest misstep or misunderstanding by a therapist can alienate, anger, or scare off the client.

    Because treating and changing a PD is so difficult, it is usually more practical and efficient to focus on creating a better fit between the client and her or his social environment and situation. Thus, a social worker should assist these clients in finding an occupation, job, workplace, and living arrangement that can minimize the negative impact of the personality disorder on self and others.

- A key characteristic of a personality disorder is a long history of conflicted and disrupted relationships within families, on the job, and in the community. The parents and siblings of someone who has a PD will usually feel frustrated, baffled, worried, manipulated, and angry. They want to help but nothing seems to work. Family members will usually benefit from participation in a support group and a psychoeducation program (see Chapter 6) that explain the nature of personality disorders and offer practical advice on ways of interacting with the troublesome family member.

- Of the 10 personality disorders descried in the *DSM-5*, **Borderline personality disorder (BPD)** is the one most commonly diagnosed. Possibly 5 to 6 percent of the population have BPD. Individuals with this disorder often feel empty and dissatisfied with life and they experience frequent and rapid shifts in mood. For example, one day they can feel confident and on top of the world and the next day feel depressed, anxious, irritable, and even suicidal. Deep within they have an intense fear of being abandoned by others. They have little awareness of personal boundaries and have difficulty distinguishing between their own feelings and the feelings of other people. They will form emotionally intense, demanding, and romantic relationships with people they have just met or hardly know. Typically, these relationships last only a short time. When other people do not respond the way they "should," an individual with BPD may feel anger, rage, depression, or anxiety. On one day an acquaintance is their best friend and the next day that same person is perceived as their worst enemy. The individual with this disorder leaves a trail of broken and conflicted relationships. An inner sense of boredom and dissatisfaction can cause the person to impulsively seek excitement and stimulation in such activities as promiscuity, reckless spending, substance abuse, shoplifting, and self-mutilation. Whenever this individual has a problem, he or she presumes that others have caused it.

It is believed that the disorder is caused by a combination of biological and social-environmental factors. The biological component is an emotional makeup or a temperament that is highly reactive. Emotions are felt with great intensity and once aroused they are slow to return to a calm or composed state. In addition, many who have a BPD were raised in a social and family environment that was invalidating and emotionally chaotic. For example, they were punished or ignored when they expressed their feelings and consequently grew up confused about what they were actually feeling, and never learned how to interpret or manage their emotions.

Working with a client who has the Borderline personality disorder can be a frustrating, unpredictable, exhausting, and sometimes scary experience. The helping relationship is fraught with challenges and pitfalls. Because of their tendency to form emotionally intense and unstable relationships, these clients easily distort the nature and purpose of the helping relationship. At one point they may be inappropriately dependent and clinging and at another become furiously angry at and deeply disappointed with the professional. Not infrequently, they presume a sexual attraction on the part of the professional. Critically important in any counseling or therapeutic effort is the formulation of a very clear and detailed treatment plan or service agreement that spells out the goals, what is expected of the client, and the role of the practitioner. In addition, this agreement should detail when and how the professional can and cannot be contacted and the specific times and place for treatment sessions.

The use of therapeutic services and making change is very difficult for these clients, but an approach known as *dialectical behavioral therapy (DBT)* shows more promise than other methods. This treatment combines techniques drawn from cognitive behavior therapy with client training in the practice of mindfulness that provides the client with a new way of understanding human relationships. It teaches the client to experience feelings and emotions without either shutting down completely or overreacting. (See the description of DBT in Chapter 6.)

• Persons with an **Antisocial personality disorder** are also described as *psychopaths* or *sociopaths*. A number of characteristics or traits describe these individuals: a lack of guilt, remorse, or shame for having hurt others; a lack of empathy; failure to learn from experience; unwillingness to accept responsibility for one's actions; glibness and superficiality; a grandiose sense of self-worth; an inclination to lie, deceive, and manipulate; poor judgment; and impulsivity. They tend not to anticipate or consider the consequences of their actions. Many with this very serious disorder will have a reputation for being a "smooth talker" and for being both charming and dishonest. Inexperienced social workers and counselors can be easily deceived and manipulated by persons with this disorder (see Item 10.8).

Experts believe that about 2 percent of the population has an Antisocial personality disorder. Not surprisingly, many of those with this disorder get in trouble with the law. However, not all who commit crimes have this Antisocial PD and not all who have this disorder will commit crimes. It is estimated that from 60 to 80 percent of those in prison have Antisocial personality disorder. In extreme cases, individuals with this disorder can murder, rape, or abuse children without hesitation or guilt.

Those with this disorder will not attempt to change their behavior unless and until they truly believe and understand that they are hurting themselves as well as others. Work with this client must include a strong educational component that emphasizes client accountability and responsibility. Because this client is usually a skilled manipulator, group therapy is especially important because he or she is seldom able to deceive or manipulate everyone in the group. Consequently some in the group, especially other manipulators, will detect the lies and see through attempted deceptions. Also, feedback and confrontations coming from peers usually carries more weight than statements by a professional.

- The key characteristic of individuals with a **Dependent personality disorder** is their extreme need to be taken care of by others. Whereas a person with the Avoidant personality disorder stays away from people, an individual with a Dependent personality disorder desperately pursues relationships, clings to others, is submissive and passive, and fears greatly any type of separation or criticism. These individuals feel helpless and are convinced that they cannot make decisions. They want others (e.g., the social worker) to provide specific directions, even on such matters as to what clothes to wear and what to eat. Because of their extreme lack of self-confidence and intense need to be guided and cared for, they are vulnerable to exploitation by manipulators.

  A client with this condition can usually be helped to become more independent and confident. A cognitive behavioral approach works best. It is important to provide the client with a structure and training on how to trust her or his judgments, make decisions, and take independent action. Because this client cannot tolerate rejection, he or she is usually motivated to follow the practitioner's directions and is more likely to stay in treatment than are those with other types of personality disorder. However, the social worker must avoid becoming an authority figure and should not allow the client to become inappropriately dependent.

- When the social worker is in the role of case manager, case advocate, or a broker of services for the client, it is sometimes necessary to find ways of explaining the client's behavior to those with whom he or she must interact and offer some suggestions on how best to approach and communicate with the individual who has a personality disorder. Consider, for example, a client who has a **Paranoid personality disorder**. This individual is a valued and skilled employee in a technical job but his or her supervisor and fellow employees find him or her to be hypersensitive, rigid, always expecting to be tricked or manipulated, always suspicious and on guard, and unusually conscious of power, rank, and authority within the organization. Given that situation, a case manager might look of opportunities to help the client's colleagues at work to appreciate the client's skill, understand and accept his or her rather odd and irritating behavior, and strive to avoid communications that contain criticism and confrontation.

Selected Bibliography

Babiak, Paul, and Robert Hare. *Snakes in Suits: When Psychopaths Go to Work*. New York: HarperCollins, 2006.

Beck, Aaron, Arthur Freeman, and Denise Davis. *Cognitive Therapy of Personality Disorders*, 2nd ed. New York: Guilford, 2004.

Gunderson, John. *Borderline Personality Disorder: A Clinical Guide.* Washington, DC: American Psychiatric Association, 2008.

Kreger, Randi. *The Essential Family Guide to Borderline Personality Disorder.* Center City, MN: Hazelden, 2008.

Porr, Valerie. *Overcoming Borderline Disorder: A Family Guide for Healing and Change.* New York: Oxford University Press, 2010.

Schouten, Ronald, and James Silver. *Almost a Psychopath.* Center City, MN: Hazelden, 2012.

Simon, George. *Character Disturbance.* Little Rock, AK: Parkhurst Brothers, 2011.

Van Dijk, Sheri. *Dialectical Behavioral Therapy Made Simple.* Oakland, CA: New Harbinger, 2012.

15.14 THE CLIENT ON PSYCHOTROPIC MEDICATION

A social worker will encounter many clients who take or are in need of medications that control psychiatric symptoms. These medications fall into several major groups: drugs for depression, anxiety, bipolar disorder, psychotic disorders, and drugs for insomnia. Each medicine has a chemical name, a generic name, and sometimes a brand name. Each will differ somewhat in its purpose or target symptom, effectiveness, possible side effects, recommended dosage, and cost. The selection of a medication for a particular patient is based on the patient's medical history, physical exam, laboratory tests, potential drug interactions with other chemicals such as other prescribed medications, alcohol and street drugs, and, of course, the symptom or disorder being treated. In especially complex cases, the doctor may consult with a clinical pharmacist to better assess the pros and cons of using a particular medication and determining how it may interact with other medications taken by the patient.

A psychotropic medication can exacerbate other medical conditions such as hypertension, liver disease, epilepsy, and glaucoma. Among the side effects associated with certain psychotropic medications are dry mouth; weight gain; drowsiness; oversensitivity to the sun; menstrual cycle disturbance; muscles spasms of the eye, face, neck, and back; blurred vision; shuffling gait; and tremors. Children and the elderly are most likely to experience adverse side effects. A medication that is effective in adults may not work the same way in children and may produce different and unexpected reactions. Because a child's brain is still developing and because an adolescent is going through significant biological changes, doctors must be knowledgeable and cautious when prescribing these drugs for young people. The effects and risks of psychotropic medications in children are not well understood.

Despite the possibility of side effects, symptom control is critically important to persons suffering from a mental illness. In general, a physician will reduce side effects by prescribing the lowest dosage that produces the desired effects, discontinuing a problematic medication and trying another, avoiding the simultaneous use of two medications that have a similar effect, and, whenever possible, treating only one symptom at a time.

Some prescription medications can cause psychiatric symptoms, but the causal link is often difficult to establish. The appearance of unexpected symptoms during a course of drug therapy could be due to an underlying medical condition, a previously unrecognized psychopathology, a unique reaction to the medication or some psychosocial factor. In some instances, a rapid withdrawal from a prescription medication can cause symptoms such as anxiety, psychosis, delirium, agitation, or depression.

When an individual is hospitalized and/or is experiencing disabling symptoms, the patient may be started on a quick-acting medication or given a fairly large dose. Most patients will not need to take the same dosage after leaving the hospital. After the symptoms subside, the physician may reduce the dosage or switch to a medication that is slower acting but has other advantages. A physician will usually reduce the dosage to the minimum effective level. This reduction is best done gradually—a process that may take several weeks or months. Even when on a maintenance dose, some patients find that their symptoms worsen from time to time. This may be due to stress, biochemical changes, or other factors.

Some patients are frightened when a doctor suggests that they take less medication because the patient fears a return of symptoms. On the other hand, some patients are reluctant take medications because they fear side effects or because it is perceived as a loss of control or a blow to their self-esteem.

When working with a client who is taking psychotropic medications, keep several guidelines in mind:

- The decision to prescribe a medication is a complex and technical medical judgment to be made only by a physician, preferably a psychiatrist. A social worker must never give medication-related instructions unless directed to do so by the physician.

- Encourage your client to maintain regular contact with a medical professional so the effects of the drug can be monitored. If you observe what appears to be an unusual or unexpected side effect, refer the client for a medical exam. If your client is unwilling to see a physician, get the name and dosage of the medication and consult with a physician about what might be the best course of action.

- Alert your client to the dangers of using alcohol or street drugs while taking a medication and the dangers of modifying the prescribed dosage and exchanging medications with others. If your client takes more than one medication, an adverse drug interaction could occur. This happens when two or more drugs mixed together have an effect very different from when each is taken alone. Side effects can also occur when the client mixes a psychotropic medication with nonprescription drugs such as a cold medicine. Some foods (e.g., aged cheese) may cause adverse reactions when eaten by a person on certain medications.

- As in the case of other forms of medical treatment, an adult has a right to refuse psychotropic medications. Exceptions are when a court has declared that the individual is not legally competent to make that decision and/or when his or her behavior constitutes an imminent threat to self or others. Because the decision to reject a needed medication can have tragic results when symptoms recur, you should do everything possible to inform the patient and the patient's family of the possible consequences. In the final analysis, however, the decision of a legally competent adult must be respected.

Selected Bibliography

Bentley, Kia, and Joseph Walsh. *The Social Worker and Psychotropic Medication*, 4th ed. Independence, KY: Cengage, 2014.

Dziegielewski, Sophia. *Social Work Practice and Psychopharmacology*, 2nd ed. New York: Springer, 2010.

Preston, John, John O'Neal, and Mary Talaga. *Handbook of Clinical Psychopharmacology for Therapists*, 7th ed. Oakland, CA: New Harbinger, 2013.

15.15 THE CLIENT WHO IS LESBIAN, GAY, BISEXUAL, OR TRANSGENDER

In most practice settings, social workers will encounter clients who are lesbian, gay, bisexual, or transgender (LGBT). We humans are classified and labeled at birth as being either a male or a female on the basis of anatomy and genitalia. However, our sexual orientation and sexual identity is not be so clear-cut. In reality, human sexuality exists as a range of orientations and identities.

The term **sexual orientation** refers to the nature of a person's romantic and sexual attractions. Sexual orientation exists as a continuum: from very straight to the very gay and from an occasional to an exclusive sexual attraction. Researchers are not able to fully explain why some individuals are sexually attracted to the opposite sex, some to their own sex, and some to both sexes. However, there is growing evidence that sexual orientation is primarily a function of in-utero development and, for most individuals, firmly fixed by adolescence. Thus, it is inaccurate to speak of either heterosexuality or homosexuality as simply a "choice" or a "preference." It is possible that environment plays a small role in shaping one's sexual orientation but, thus far, research indicates that growing up with homosexual parents has no effect on a child's sexual orientation.

The vast majority of people identify themselves are heterosexual or "straight." Homosexuality is something like left-handedness; it is a departure from the statistical majority or mainstream but is an otherwise normal condition.

Several surveys find that around 5 percent of the U.S. population identify themselves as lesbian, gay, bisexual, or transgender. About 1.7 percent say they are gay, about 1.7 percent say they are lesbian, about 1.8 percent (mostly women) say they are bisexual, and about 0.3 percent identify themselves as transgender. It is difficult to determine with precision the number of people who are LGBT because such statistics rely on self-report and some individuals may wish to conceal their true sexual orientation. Adding to the uncertainty in these figures is the fact that those self-reporting their sexual orientation or identity may have somewhat different definitions in mind as they answer a survey questions. (For additional information on the concepts of sex and gender see the *Feminist Perspective* presented in Chapter 6.)

The poorly understood phenomenon of **transgender** (gender dysphoria) is usually described as a matter of gender identity, rather than sexual orientation. Gender is more subtle and complex than sexual attraction and orientation. It has to do with one's inner sense of being a male or being a female. At a fundamental level, persons who are transgender do not feel comfortable or at ease with their physical or "assigned sex." Basically, they identify with the other sex. For example, a transgender male may feel that he would be more real and authentic if he had a female body. Transgender individuals may feel awkward or out of place wearing the clothing typically worn by their physical sex and may prefer to take part in activities traditionally associated with the other sex. A small percentage of transgender persons pursue sex change or sex reassignment surgery in order to have a body more like the other sex. About 0.3 percent (less than one-half of 1 percent) of the adult population identify themselves as transgender. They may heterosexual, homosexual, or bisexual.

About one in every 2,000 babies is born with ambiguous and abnormally developed reproductive organs and genitalia. This is often an amalgam or fusion of both male and female genitalia. In such cases, it is not possible to determine the baby's sex with certainty by examining the child's genitals. This condition is often related to abnormal chromosomal patterns. The birth of a child with this **intersex** condition requires a gut wrenching decision by parents and physicians. Should surgery be performed to "make" the baby a male or a female? (Constructing female genitalia is usually an easier surgery than is the construction of male genitalia.) In the past, a sexual assignment surgery was often performed in infancy but most doctors and child development experts now recommend delaying a possible surgery until later childhood when it is apparent that a particular sexual orientation has emerged. An individual with an intersex condition is vulnerable to developing various psychosocial problems, especially ones related to self-concept and body image (see Item 11.10).

Within the United States and in most countries around the world, people who are LGBT are often maligned. The term **homophobia** refers to an irrational fear and hatred of homosexuality and sexual diversity. It can lead to discrimination in employment, housing, health care, social services, and other areas. Sometimes homophobia foments violence directed against persons who are known to be or suspected of being LGBT.

A fear of rejection, discrimination, and violence, as well as a desire to protect their families from embarrassment and worry, causes some who are LGBT to hide or deny their sexual orientation or gender identity. The inability to acknowledge and be at peace with something so basic as one's sexuality can be a source of emotional turmoil. Increasingly, gay and lesbian persons are "coming out," and demanding equal rights, justice, and societal acceptance.

The following guidelines will be useful in working with clients who are LGBT:

- Carefully examine your own attitudes and moral standards for signs of possible bias, prejudice, and discrimination toward people who are LGBT, and perhaps toward people who are straight. Consider, for example:
  - Your beliefs on whether differences in sexual orientation and gender identity are pathological conditions or a normal variation of human sexuality
  - Your level of comfort in hearing of affection and sexual activity within a same sex relationship
  - Your beliefs and attitudes regarding same-sex marriage and the parenting of children by persons who are gay, lesbian, bisexual, or transgender

- Do not be afraid to acknowledge your lack of understanding and to face up to your own prejudices. Also, realize that an ignorance of variations in sexual orientation and gender identifications can exist among those in the helping professions, among clients who are straight, and even among some who are themselves lesbian, gay, bisexual, or transgender. Work hard to learn about the concerns of persons who are LGBT. Get to know leaders and professionals within the LGBT community and seek their consultation when unsure about how best to work with clients who are LGBT.

  Leaders of LGBT-related organizations and advocacy groups should be consulted regarding the design and delivery of health and social services. Such consultations will help make these services more accessible and acceptable to persons who are LGBT. And, of course, the professional staff working in health and human services programs must be alert to how well their practices and approaches accommodate differences of sexual orientation and sexual identity.

- It is fairly common for persons who are homosexual, bisexual, or transgender to go through many years of confusion and uncertainty before finally recognizing and accepting their true sexual orientation or gender identity. For example, they may suppress their sexual attractions. They may become sexually active with the opposite sex and even enter into a marriage in order to reassure themselves and demonstrate to their families that they are "normal" and heterosexual. Such confusion and turmoil is especially difficult for the adolescent and may lead some to consider suicide.

- In recent years, we have witnessed a remarkable change in societal attitudes toward those who are LGBT. Homophobia and prejudice has diminished. A slight majority of the population now favors same-sex marriage and a growing number of states recognize same sex marriage. Nevertheless, ignorance and prejudice still exists and for that reason, some who are LGBT may be cautious when seeking services from a professional they do not know. Some who are LGBT speak openly about their sexual orientation or gender identity; others do not.

- When LGBT individuals seek health care, social services, or counseling, their sexual orientation or sexual identity, per se, will seldom be a relevant issue. Thus, as a general rule, it is not necessary for social workers or other professionals to ask about or discuss a client's sexuality unless it is clearly related to the client's presenting concern or request.

    In those practice settings where the professional may need to know about the client's sexuality and sexual activity (e.g., public health, counseling), a social worker might approach this topic by saying something like: "In order for us to provide an individualized and appropriate service, I need to ask some questions about your sexuality. Would you be comfortable discussing this topic?"

    Clients who are LGBT may hide their sexuality until they are sure the social worker is free of prejudices. When the social worker is LGBT, he or she may elect to self-disclose in order to lessen the client's concerns. Or, a social worker might use some personal stories to reveal that she or he understands the insidious effect of stereotypes and prejudice and thereby demonstrate to the client a capacity for acceptance and understanding.

- When working with a same-sex couple, expect that their relationship problems will be similar to those of heterosexual couples. For example, their conflicts will most likely revolve around matters such as money management, unfaithfulness, domestic abuse, substance abuse, balancing home and work responsibilities, child care, and an unsatisfactory sexual relationship. In most states their relationship will lack the legal status and protections that come with a marriage. In the absence of a legally recognized marriage or civil union, ordinary concerns such as securing health insurance for one's partner, arranging survivor benefits, inheritance, child custody, adoption, and hospital visitation can be especially complex and troublesome. Thus, it is important to help these couples find the legal guidance they may need to address such matters and construct special legal arrangements.

- If your adult LGBT client is considering the decision to "come out," help him or her to thoughtfully weigh both the pros and cons of doing so. On the surface, disclosing one's true sexual orientation and identity may seem to be simple honesty and a liberating and therapeutic action. However, some who do this can pay a high price. Unfortunately, ignorance, hostility, and discrimination still exist and this is more of a problem in some communities and occupations than in others. As an individual ponders this decision, he or she should not ignore or minimize the possible negative ramifications of coming out, which may include alienation from family and the loss of housing or a job.

- As a group, gay men have been especially hard hit by *Acquired Immune Deficiency Syndrome (AIDS)*, a potentially life-threatening disease caused by a virus known as *Human Immunodeficiency Virus*, or HIV. Many gay men have suffered the loss of friends or lovers to the disease, and others live in fear of contracting the disease. Typically, the symptoms of AIDS do not develop until several years after being infected. The virus is spread by way of vaginal, anal, or oral sex with an infected person (whether male or female) and also by sharing drug-injecting needles with someone who is infected. The virus can be passed from an infected mother to her baby during pregnancy or childbirth and in rare instances through breastfeeding. Promiscuity, whether heterosexual or homosexual, increases the risk of contracting the infection. Because there are now drugs that can control the disease, some individuals become complacent and careless in their sexual behavior. The use of condoms, other safe-sex techniques, and HIV testing can reduce the spread of this disease.

Selected Bibliography

Anderson, Kevin. *Counseling LGBTI*. Thousand Oaks, CA: Sage, 2012.

Bieschke, Kathleen, Ruperto Perez, and Kurt DeBord. *Handbook of Counseling and Psychotherapy with Lesbian, Gay, Bisexual, and Transgender Clients*, 2nd ed. Washington, DC: American Psychological Association, 2007.

Mallon, Gerald, ed. *Social Work Practice with Lesbian, Gay, Bisexual, and Transgender People*, 2nd ed. New York: Haworth, 2008.

Morrow, Deana, and Lori Messinger, eds. *Sexual Orientation and Gender Expression in Social Work Practice*. New York: Columbia University, 2006.

Petrocelli, Ann. *Prejudice to Pride: Moving from Homophobia to Acceptance*. Washington, DC: NASW Press, 2012.

15.16 THE CLIENT WITH AN EATING DISORDER

Social workers sometimes serve clients with eating disorders. The term *eating disorder* is an umbrella term that describes any of several problems linked to a person's relationship to food. The three most prevalent eating disorders are anorexia nervosa, bulimia nervosa, and obesity. At one extreme is the person who self-starves; at the other extreme is the person who eats to excess.

There are many other examples of actual or potentially harmful behaviors related to food and nutrition. For example, it is not uncommon for male athletes to intentionally overeat to gain weight (e.g., offensive linesmen in football) or lose weight (e.g., wrestlers seeking to compete in a certain weight class). Nor is it uncommon for older people to experience food-related problems when, for example, their food intake is insufficient because they are lonely and "cooking for one" seems like too much trouble or when the food served in a nursing home lacks a preferred taste. Fad diets and misguided fasting can disturb body chemistry and give rise to health problems.

Anorexia nervosa

The condition known as *anorexia nervosa* is characterized by intentionally maintaining a body weight substantially below normal (i.e., 15 to 25 percent below normal). This disorder is most commonly found in middle- and upper-class female adolescents, with symptoms typically beginning between ages 12 and 18. The exact causes of anorexia are not known, but it is often associated with high stress, pressure from one's cultural group, and the presence of an eating disorder among other members of the person's family. A biological predisposition may play a role in this disorder.

Some psychological *indicators of anorexia* are a distorted perception of one's own body size, weight, and shape; an intense fear of gaining weight; and high self-expectations or perfectionism. Some physical symptoms are excessively low weight, the absence of or irregularity in the menstrual cycle, dry skin, loss of hair, refusal to eat normal amounts of food, anxiety about eating, and episodes of spontaneous or induced vomiting.

An intervention begins with a focus on assisting the client in restoring her or his physical health and regaining a medically safe body weight, and then implementing various psychological interventions to prevent the recurrence of this condition. When a person is literally starving to death, his or her physical condition must be addressed before the social and psychological factors. Treatment may involve a period of hospitalization and possibly the use of various medications.

When intervening with a person who is anorexic (or bulimic), it is important to be very direct about the person's destructive behaviors and the consequences of those behaviors, as well as to gain the person's trust as a foundation for helping her or him reestablish a sense of self-worth. Specific psychosocial interventions may include individual and family therapy, ongoing supportive treatment of the individual, cognitive therapy, behavior modification techniques, and participation in self-help groups. Recovery from anorexia nervosa requires actions on many fronts, including a team of professionals, family, and other significant people in the client's lives. Eating a sufficient amount of nutritious food is difficult for the anorexic to accomplish without considerable encouragement and reinforcement from others. It is thought that about one-half of the diagnosed and treated anorexics recover within two to five years. Yet, about 18 percent never recover and, for them, the possibility of death from suicide or health problems resulting from the person's depleted physical condition is quite high.

Bulimia nervosa

This condition is characterized by a morbid fear of becoming fat. With this disorder, a person usually stays within 10 percent of normal body weight but experiences a lack of control over eating behaviors. As opposed to the person with anorexia who avoids food when under stress, the bulimic deals with stress by turning toward food. Periodically (i.e., three times or more a month), the person experiences a severe craving for food and binges, followed by induced vomiting, use of laxatives, severe dieting, excessive exercise, or fasting as a means of preventing weight gain. This bulimic cycle can be understood as the fear of becoming overweight leading to self-starvation, with a periodic eating frenzy followed by guilt and efforts to void the weight produced by the food, thus reinforcing the fear of becoming fat—and the cycle continues.

The causes of bulimia are not known. Symptoms usually begin in adolescence or early adulthood. The typical bulimic is thought to be a successful white woman in her mid- to late-twenties. Because of this stereotype, bulimia is considered a "woman's disease" and men tend to deny or hide the fact that they also experience this disorder. Estimates of the number of young women experiencing bulimia are as high as 15 to 20 percent; however, young men, too, experience bulimia at the rate of about 5 to 10 percent. The binge-and-purge cycle can have disastrous physical effects, causing fatigue, seizures, and muscle cramps, as well as having long-term damaging effects on the person's esophagus, teeth, and bone density.

It is often difficult to determine if a client might be experiencing bulimia because there are no obvious physical symptoms such as the weight loss or emaciation that occur in cases of anorexia. However, some clues are periodic consumption of large amounts of food, usually eaten alone or secretly; preoccupation with food or one's weight; excessive exercise or fasting; frequent trips to the bathroom following meals; diminished sexual interest (sometimes); and depression or self-loathing.

As compared to persons who are anorexic, bulimics are more likely to seek and accept treatment, but their strong need for perfection leads to frustration when there are no immediate cures. Some interventions focus on helping them become more accepting of failure and imperfections in life, improving nutrition, and using medication to deal with depression, if it exists. Cognitive-behavioral therapy is often used to assist the client in interrupting the binging, establishing normal eating patterns, and modifying distorted view of foods and body image. The client is helped to reveal the problem to family and other significant people and to seek their help in maintaining a balanced diet. Finally, group approaches have been successful in helping bulimics disclose and discuss their problem, reduce their guilt, learn to self-monitor their eating behaviors, gain nutrition information, learn relaxation techniques as an alternative to dealing with stress by binging, and address cultural pressures they experience regarding body weight.

Overeating and obesity

Overeating and excessive weight gain is a problem for many people. They are aware that they eat too much or eat the wrong types of food but are drawn into a pattern of overeating by the pleasure of eating, by the way foods are engineered by the food industry, by their social surroundings, and by advertising. Weight gain occurs when an individual takes in more energy (as measured in calories) than he or she expends in activity. About 3,500 excess or unburned calories result in a gain of one pound.

Weight gain over a long period leads to the condition known as **obesity**. The term *moderate obesity* applies to a person who is 20 to 100 percent above recommended weight for his or her age, gender, and height, whereas a person experiencing *morbid obesity* would exceed the 100 percent level. Obesity is an epidemic in the United States and a growing problem in other developed countries. Those who are excessively overweight are at higher risk of developing numerous health problems such as high blood pressure, heart disease, stroke, diabetes, joint problems, and complications of pregnancy.

A variety of biological, psychological, and social factors are associated with the growing problem of excessive weight gain and obesity among the people living in the more prosperous societies where food is abundant. Psychological factors include overeating as a compensation for boredom, unhappiness, depression, and painful life events. Research points to connections between being overweight and one's genetic makeup and also to the effects of hormonal imbalances, especially those related to insulin production. The eating patterns and types of meals common to one's family and culture also contribute to weight gain and to the social acceptance of being overweight. Many processed and refined food products and store-bought snack or pleasure foods are loaded with sugar, starches, fat, and salt, and are deliberately designed or blended by the manufacturer to make the food tantalizing and difficult to resist. People with low incomes are susceptible to weight gain because they must often purchase the less expensive processed foods that are high in calories. Healthy foods such as fruits and vegetables tend to cost significantly more.

Achieving weight loss requires a significant decrease in daily calorie intake (e.g., to 1,200 or 1,500 calories) and an increase in physical activity. Although many individuals lose weight when adhering to a prescribed diet, once they end a structured diet most will regain the weight. As weight is being lost, the body reacts as if starvation has occurred and one's appetite actually increases. Permanent changes in eating habits and life style are essential to maintaining a weight loss.

A social worker's interventions will typically include helping the client learn to self-monitor food intake, create a social environment (e.g., family and friends) that has a positive influence on eating patterns, participate in an appropriate exercise programs, connect to support groups wherein feelings of isolation and embarrassment are diminished, and provide the client with individual and group therapeutic services as warranted.

Social workers are sometimes in a position to assist with nutrition education and to offer guidance on identifying foods that can achieve a balanced diet at a reasonable cost. Most clients will benefit from learning to apply behavior self-modification techniques designed to change eating habits and reward their commitment to a weight loss plan. Individual counseling or therapy may be helpful for those clients who are exceedingly self-conscious and embarrassed by their appearance. Group counseling and support groups are helpful to adults willing to speak about their problems. Group approaches can be especially useful in work with overweight children. Purely medical or drug interventions have not proven successful in most cases of obesity. The *bariatric surgeries* designed to restrict food intake will result in weight loss but they carry some risks and are usually recommended only for persons who are morbidly obese and suffering from other serious health problems related to the obesity.

Selected Bibliography

Judd, Sandra, ed. *Eating Disorders Sourcebook*, 3rd ed. Detroit, MI: Omnigraphics, 2012.

Kessler, David. *The End of Overeating*. New York: Rodale, 2009.

Lask, Bryan, and Rachel Bryant-Waugh, eds. *Eating Disorders in Childhood and Adolescence,* 4th ed. New York: Routledge, 2012.

Natenshon, Abigail. *Doing What Works: An Integrative System for Treating Eating Disorders*. Washington, DC: NASW Press, 2009.

Yager, Joel, and Pauline Powers, eds. *Clinical Manual of Eating Disorders*. Arlington, VA: American Psychiatric Association, 2007.

15.17 THE CLIENT EXPERIENCING GRIEF OR LOSS

The experience of grief is as old as humanity itself. **Grief** is the intense emotional suffering brought on by the loss of or separation from someone or something deeply loved. The sudden and unexpected death of a loved one is probably the most common precipitator of intense grief. However, other types of loss can also precipitate grief reactions—for example, a divorce, losing a job, a planned or spontaneous abortion, placing one's child in foster care, the termination or relinquishment of one's parental rights, loss of physical mobility, loss of a house to bankruptcy, loss of a beloved pet, and the destruction of possessions in a house fire or natural disaster.

A grief reaction to the death of a loved one, and the mourning of this loss, typically moves through four phases:

1. *Numbness.* The person is shocked, dazed, confused, and overwhelmed. Physical symptoms might include nausea, tightness in the chest and throat, shortness of breath, disturbed sleep, loss of appetite, and headaches. This phase lasts from several days to several weeks.

2. *Yearning.* The grieving person is preoccupied and withdrawn and may wander about as if in search of the deceased person; he or she may report seeing and being with the deceased individual. Intense crying and feelings of anger, guilt, anxiety, and frustration are common.

3. *Despair and disorganization.* As the reality of the loss settles in, the person experiences feelings of helplessness, despair, depression, and fatigue.

4. *Recovery and reorganization.* Over a period of many months or even years, the person gradually resumes her or his usual routines at home and at work and feels less depressed, sleeps better, has more energy, and establishes a more normal pattern of social activity. However, to some degree, a feeling of loss remains for the rest of her or his life.

The term **acute grief** describes the reaction that occurs at the time of the loss, such as a parent's immediate reaction to his or her child being killed in an auto accident. It is a response to a sudden and unexpected loss. Another pattern, **anticipatory grief**, is set in motion by the realization that a serious loss will occur in the near future. The diagnosis of a terminal illness might prompt that type of grieving. The term **anniversary reaction** describes a recurrence of grief precipitated by remembering a prior loss, such as the sadness that occurs each year around the date when one's child or spouse died.

When a client is in the throes of grief, a social worker should keep several guidelines in mind:

- The intensity of a person's grief is affected by the nature of his or her relationship to the person or object that has been lost, prior experiences with loss, cultural and ethnic background, gender, age, circumstances surrounding the death or loss, access to social supports, the person's usual coping patterns, and so on. Everyone grieves in his or her own unique way.

- In order to grieve successfully, an individual must work through certain tasks or phases such as accepting the reality that the person or object is gone forever; confronting, experiencing, and coming to terms with the emotions and conflicts associated with the loss; constructing a life without the loved person or object; reinvesting emotional energy in other relationships and activities; and honoring the memory of the lost person or object. These tasks are, of course, overlapping and the grieving individual will revisit each one many times before achieving a satisfactory adjustment.

- The initial and most intense feelings of grief will slowly diminish in six months to a year, but some level of grieving may continue for three to five years (or even longer). Time is the great healer. With time and the support of family and friends, most people are able deal with their loss without professional assistance.

    Not infrequently, significant personal growth occurs as a person deals successfully with grief. An individual may, for example, uncover previously unknown strengths, grow in self-confidence and competence, discover new areas of interest, and form new and rewarding relationships. People can and do learn valuable lessons about life and living from their misfortunes. It is said that experience is the best teacher. Although experience is an effective teacher, experience is not necessarily a *good* teacher. A good teacher would never give the test before providing the lesson.

- Support groups can be helpful to many who are struggling with a loss. These groups can offer advice about day-to-day tasks, such as handling finances or taking on new household tasks, and provide emotional support and a safe place where the grieving person can talk about the loss and learn that her or his painful emotions are a normal part of the grieving process. Also, many who are grieving find comfort and strength in their spirituality, religion, and faith community.

- Sometimes the normal grieving and healing process stalls and the grieving person develops dysfunctional behavior or sinks into depression. In these situations, clinical interventions are appropriate. This usually begins with *supportive counseling,* which would consist of active listening, encouraging the client to talk about his or her feelings, providing information about the grieving process, helping the person think through and complete important tasks of living (e.g., handling legal matters, filing insurance claims), and guiding and encouraging the client to resume the roles and responsibilities of managing the home, returning to a job, budgeting, paying bills, and so on.

  As the client makes some progress in accepting the loss and resuming usual activities, the social worker might then help him or her remember positive experiences from before the loss occurred. For example, if a woman is grieving the loss of her husband, the worker might help her recall and appreciate their good times together by viewing and talking about photos or by visiting places that were special to her husband. Some clients use art, stories, poems, and music as a means of getting in touch with their feelings and honoring the person they have lost. *Guided mourning* is a cognitive-behavioral approach in which the grieving client is encouraged to recall the details of the loss experience and to find appropriate ways to say good-bye through ritual and journaling.

- When very intense and complicated grief reactions are giving rise to serious psychological problems or affecting a person's marriage or family, some form of individual, couple, or family therapy and/or medical intervention is needed. Some individuals suppress or hide their grief or deny the pain of a loss. If they do not work their way through the grieving process, their mental health may be adversely affected for years after the loss. In such situations an approach termed *regrief therapy* may be used to activate or restart the grieving process and help the individual to relive, confront, and resolve the loss experience.

Selected Bibliography

Holland, Debra. *The Essential Guide to Grief and Grieving.* New York: Penguin, 2011.

Hooyman, Nancy, and Betty Kramer. *Living Through Loss: Interventions across the Life Span.* New York: Columbia University Press, 2008.

Pomeroy, Elizabeth. *The Grief Assessment and Intervention Workbook.* Independence, KY: Cengage, 2009.

Walsh-Burke, Katherine. *Grief and Loss,* 2nd ed. Upper Saddle River, NJ: Pearson, 2012.

Worden, J. William. *Grief Counseling and Grief Therapy,* 4th ed. New York: Springer, 2008.

15.18 THE CLIENT WITH CONCERNS RELATED TO SPIRITUALITY AND RELIGION

Various surveys suggest that about 90 percent of the adults in the United States believe in a God and for a majority of these, spirituality and or religion are important to how they live their lives. Many of those who are not drawn to organized religion and many of those who do not believe in a God nevertheless strive to nurture their spirituality. Thus, if a social worker serves a cross-section of the population, religion and/or spirituality will be of some significance to most of her or his clients. Yet, many social workers and other professional helpers often feel poorly prepared to discuss these matters with clients.

Social workers, psychologists, and other professional helpers are often taught to side-step a discussion of religion with their clients. Folk wisdom also warns against discussing religion (and politics) with friends because these discussions often turn into arguments that strain the relationship. So, how should a social worker respond to client concerns that are intertwined with her or his religion, spirituality, and faith? On the one hand, spirituality and religion will be of importance to many clients and possibly also a valuable resource to the helping process. On the other hand, discussing these aspects of a client's life carries some risk of alienating the client or perhaps giving the appearance of proselytizing. Handling this dilemma practice requires sensitivity and knowledge.

Most people in the world probably could not speak of their spirituality as being separate from their religion. However, making such a distinction is fairly common in the United States and often useful because some individuals have an active spiritual life but engage in few religious practices. And some individuals regularly participate in religious activities without seeming to possess a deep spirituality.

Spirituality is difficult to define or describe because it is deeply personal and unique to each individual. Even if two people practice the same religion, their spirituality will differ. The word *spirituality* has its origin in images of the invisible wind, or the "breath of God." For many, **spirituality** is their connection to a higher power or ineffable presence that many name God. It involves an awareness or mindfulness of the mystery, beauty, and awesomeness inherent in human life and the universe. Spirituality has been variously described as an inward journey, a holy longing, a yearning for meaning, one's enduring and core values, the essence of one's character, the way one lives his or her life, how a person directs or orders his or her inner unrest and desires, one's lived experience with the mystery of life, and that which puts life in one's life. The idea of mystery is a common theme in people's attempt to describe their spirituality. In this context, *mystery* refers to a dimension of experience and awareness that the person knows to be real but is beyond description and understanding.

Spirituality is the ultimate source of all religion. A **religion** is a set of beliefs, traditions, stories, rituals, and practices that bind people into a community. A religion supports and sustains spiritual growth and offers answers to the persistent questions of life, such as: Who am I? What is the purpose of my life? How should I live my life? Is the universe a friendly place? Why does evil exist? Why does goodness exist? What happens when we die? How am I to pray or communicate with my God?

To better appreciate the place of religious faith in people's lives it is helpful to recognize that most people have a faith of some type and live by that faith. In other words, we place our trust or our confidence in "something" that we believe or hope will provide happiness, fulfillment, and security. For many people that something is a religion or a type of spirituality, but others may place their trust in, for example, money, social status, academic or business success, public recognition, beauty, sex, physical fitness, a political ideology, and the like.

We are drawn to spirituality, religion, and faith because deep within we have a sense that we are somehow adrift, incomplete, or lacking wholeness. We seek an anchor or a foundation that provides stability in the midst of uncertainty. For many people, religion and/or spirituality provide a sense of meaning, direction, hope, and a moral compass. A religion can help people cope with troublesome realities such as death, pain, grief, despair, and outrage at the injustice and cruelty of life. For others, however, their experiences with religion and their spiritual struggles are a source of inner turmoil, family conflicts, shame, and guilt. At its best, a religion creates a sense of community and transforms people's lives for the better. At its worst, religion impedes human advancement and spawns narrow-mindedness, intolerance, and even war. Generally speaking, discussions that focus on spirituality uncover similarities among people, whereas a focus on religion reveals differences that divide or separate.

Following is some background information and guidelines for the beginning-level practitioner who has clients for whom spirituality and/or religion is related to their presenting concerns or problems:

- Examine your own experiences with and attitudes toward religion and spirituality. Be alert to any presumptions or prejudices that may limit your ability to serve clients who have beliefs that are quite different from your own. An effective social worker has the capacity to accept and respect persons with strong religious beliefs as well as those with none at all. Addressing issues and concerns related to a client's religion and spirituality requires of the social worker a high degree of self-understanding and self-discipline (see Item 16.3).

- Approach these concerns much as you would approach matters related to a client's culture (see Item 8.8). A person's religion is like a culture in that it is a "lens" through which the client will view, understand, and interpret life's experiences. It will shape his or her moral standards and definitions of right and wrong. Moreover, a client's religion or spirituality can influence what the client defines to be a problem, its cause, and its solution. A religion, much like a culture, will seem reasonable and "common sense" to the person immersed in that religion.

- It is important for social workers and human services programs to build working relationships with local clergy, leaders of faith communities, and trained spiritual directors so that these individuals can be consulted on how best to approach unusual or especially complex issues related to a client's religion or spirituality. When a client's concern is primarily within the realm of religion, faith, and spiritually, and therefore outside the domain of professional social work, the social worker should refer that client to the appropriate religious or spiritual counselor or clergy person.

- If the client wishes to discuss spiritual and religious matters related to his or her concerns or problems, the social worker must demonstrate a readiness to do so and be at ease with the topic. If that openness is not apparent, clients may withhold important information because they fear that their beliefs and practices will be misunderstood or dismissed as irrelevant. The social worker must display an accepting and nonjudgmental attitude but this can be a challenge if the client's beliefs seem highly unusual or harmful. The worker must avoid defining a client's genuine spiritual or religious concerns and struggles as only a psychological issue or problem.

- During the data-gathering and assessment phase, the social worker should do at least a cursory exploration of the client's spiritual and religious beliefs and practices. This will allow the worker to determine whether the client's presenting concern is tied to her or his spirituality and/or religion and to identify possible client strengths and helping resources. Simple and straightforward inquiries will usually work—for example: What do I need to know about your values and beliefs to better understand what is important to you? How do you find encouragement and strength during difficult times? Is religion and spirituality a part of your life? Are you a member of a church, synagogue, mosque, temple, or a faith community? The nature of the client's responses to such exploratory questions will dictate if a more in-depth assessment is necessary and appropriate.

In some situations it may be necessary to probe more deeply. For example, a practitioner in direct practice (e.g., counseling, case management) might ask specific questions about the client's spirituality and/or religious beliefs and background when the client is experiencing troublesome thoughts and feelings, such as guilt, regret, grief, despair, and meaninglessness, and when the client is struggling with a moral dilemma. Client statements such as the following illustrate these situations: "I feel like a failure as a parent because none of my children goes to church," "I have hurt so many people; I need to make amends for the harm I have caused," "My life is empty and meaningless," "I wish I had some type of faith, but I don't know how to develop one," "The people in my 12-step program talk about their Higher Power, but I'm not sure I even have one," "So often, I pray that my illness will be cured, but my medical condition is getting worse," "As I approach my death, I wonder if there is an afterlife," "My daughter is under the influence of evil spirits," "I want to forgive my father for what he did, but I am consumed by bitterness and festering with anger."

The social worker in indirect practice (e.g., community organization, administration, program management) must understand the religious beliefs, traditions, and practices common to or prevalent in a neighborhood or a community. This knowledge is needed in order to develop programs and policies that will be respectful and relevant to the people who are to utilize an agency's programs.

- The numinous mystery or power that is named God (or another sacred name) cannot be described in words and is, by definition, beyond the grasp of the human mind. Nevertheless, people use words and form mental images as they think about and speak of God. Even those who do not believe in a god will hold a concept of god that they have rejected as fiction. People's images and ideas about God vary widely.

  When a client voices confusion about what she or he really believes about God, it may be prove helpful to encourage her or him to examine her or his image of God and consider how and when these images were formed. This can be important because it is through a particular image that the client relates to God, and depending on how God is conceived or imagined, it can cause that client to feel loved or rejected, secure or fearful, accepting or intolerant. In general, people's various images and notions of God will tend to emphasize either immanence or transcendence. *Immanence* refers to God as within and all around us, whereas *transcendence* views God as apart from and beyond the world as we know it. Some individuals imagine God in very personal terms much like a loving parent, whereas others conceive of God as an impersonal and remote power or energy. Thus, people's images of God range from, for example, God as a father, mother, or grandparent to more abstract ideas such as a divine presence, ultimate reality, primordial mind, and the ground of being.

- It is often during a personal crisis or a time of painful self-examination that people decide that they need to cultivate a deeper spirituality and find a better way of living their lives. If a social worker's client has joined a 12-step program in an effort to deal with a substance abuse problem or some other addiction, this client will hear other group members speak of their spirituality. That new experience may prompt the client to ask his or her social worker about the nature of spirituality and how one develops spirituality.

When working with a client who wants a more meaningful spiritual life, it may be helpful to discuss the difference between a spiritual search and a spiritual journey. A person on a search is always looking and always exploring new possibilities. By contrast, a person on a journey has chosen a particular path and strives to follow that path. A search is necessary and important but constant searching gives rise to restlessness and dissatisfaction. Spiritual growth can begin only after one has a sense of direction or commits to a particular path. For most people, there comes a time when, despite many unanswered questions and doubts, he or she must step off the diving board and say, in effect, "This is my choice, this is my path, this is how I choose to live my life." The philosopher Kierkegaard called this choice the "leap of faith."

The metaphor of a spiritual journey is not meant to suggest that spiritual growth is linear. Rather, it is like a spiral in that the core struggles and life's questions must be revisited and confronted again and again. The path chosen by a client must fit his or her authentic self. And regardless of the path taken, the person will need to set aside regular time for quiet reflection, solitude, prayer, or meditation. Spiritual growth also requires service to others. A spirituality that does not include service and caring for others soon becomes self-absorption and egoism. Spiritual growth involves going deeper within one's self and being truthful and honest with what one finds there. Many resist this self-examination because they fear what they will learn about themselves. Indeed, the self-understanding that comes from prayer and meditation can be a source of discomfort. Still other individuals are ambivalent about pursuing spiritual growth because they fear that a deeper spirituality will demand changes in their lifestyle and priorities that they are not prepared to make. In many ways, spiritual growth is a process of changing one's perspectives, of seeing things in a different way, and letting go of the desire for control, power, possessions, and prestige. The fear of letting go is the greatest barrier to spiritual growth.

A social worker should help her or his client understand that spirituality has to do with one's choices and with distinguishing the important from the unimportant, the lasting from the fleeting, and the ends from the means. Different choices have different consequences. The importance of one's choices is captured in a Native American parable:

> A grandfather sought to teach his grandson an important lesson about how to live his life. The grandfather told his eager young listener that every person has two wolves inside and the two wolves are engaged in an ongoing fight for dominance. One is the wolf of generosity, honesty, compassion, contentment, and justice. The other is the wolf of selfishness, deceitfulness, hatred, and greed. "Which one will win?" asked the grandson? The grandfather replied, "Whichever wolf we feed."

This story teaches us that even the small choices that we make every day will have consequences and a cumulative effect that will orient our life in one direction or another. If, for example, we "feed" our tendency to be self-centered, we gradually become a selfish person. If, on the other hand, we "feed" our desire to be honest and compassionate, that is the sort of person we will become. Our spirituality is displayed in our choices and in how we live out our life.

Striving for intellectual honesty and for moral integrity are also prerequisites to developing an authentic spirituality. Clients should be encouraged to be true to their conscience and adhere to what they believe to be true and right. Violating one's moral code precludes achieving a sense of contentment and wholeness and will often result in a loss of self-respect and generate feelings of guilt, shame, and remorse.

Clients should also be helped to understand that developing a spirituality is a life-long process and never a quick fix for personal problems. Neither is it a solitary activity. Rather, it is mostly communal in the sense that one's deepest questions and personal struggles can only be honestly examined when in dialogue with others. Self-scrutiny requires support and guidance from others and especially from persons who are experienced in living a spiritual life, for they can help the beginner avoid discouragement, self-absorption, self-deception, and spiritual arrogance.

Spiritual growth involves cultivating a sense of gratitude and thankfulness for whatever life offers us. Ironically, it is often the people who face great challenges or suffering who develop this sense of gratitude, because gratitude involves understanding and accepting our weakness and limitations. Contrary to the assumptions of our can-do culture and the teachings of some self-help gurus, not everything is possible if only we will think positive and work hard. We have real limitations such as those set by age, intelligence, temperament, physical abilities, and the like. We need to be honest with ourselves, recognize both our strengths and our weaknesses, and then strive to be all that we can be within the circumstances and conditions that are beyond our control.

The various religious institutions exist to cultivate spiritual growth. Although they are composed of and led by persons who are very human and flawed, religious organizations are invaluable resources, for they are the primary means of transmitting spiritual wisdom from generation to generation, and should be considered as appropriate referral sources when matters of spirituality and religion are deeply troubling to clients. If the social worker's client is open to approaching a representative of a religion and speaking with a clergy person or spiritual director, he or she should be encouraged to do so.

• Much like those who belong to an ethnic or cultural minority group, many who follow a religion must struggle to live in "two worlds" and negotiate socially and economically within an environment that may be unsympathetic or even hostile to their way of life. When people feel that their cherished values, beliefs, and practices are being threatened, they may strike out at the perceived threat. Or they may refuse to participate in the social, school, and community activities they view as threatening. Parents, especially, will take action to protect their children from societal influences they perceive as destructive to their children's spiritual well-being.

Thus, it is important for a social worker to recognize the dilemmas faced by deeply religious and/or spiritually oriented individuals as they try to live, work, and raise a family within an environment that seems to undermine their cherished beliefs and values. The dominant values of U.S. society are materialism, consumerism, greed, competition, and individualism. By contrast, authentic religion and spirituality emphasize a very different set of values and virtues, such as honesty, justice, humility, modesty, compassion, forgiveness, and service to others.

- The usual challenges of direct social work practice are compounded when the client's presenting problem involves a clash between his or her conscience or moral code and a government's criminal code. Consider, for example, that for one person a particular action can be legal but immoral (e.g., war, abortion, blood transfusion), whereas for another individual an action can be morally correct but illegal (e.g., refusing to pay taxes that support a war). Helping a client think through and deal with a conflict between one's moral principles and the law of the land may call for consultation with religious or spiritual leaders who have an in-depth understanding of the client's moral reasoning and in some cases, the advice of an attorney.

- A social worker faces a challenging situation when a client's religious and/or spiritual beliefs and practices are unhealthy and harmful to the client or to others. In such cases, the social worker can at least try to help the client examine the observable effects and consequences of these beliefs and practices. It must be recognized, however, that people hold tightly to their core beliefs and values and are not easily swayed by what others (and sometimes even themselves) may view as reason and logic.

  A healthy religion or spirituality recognizes that humans are complex with many interrelated dimensions (i.e., physical, spiritual, psychological, emotional, intellectual, sexual, social). All human dimensions are valued, not just the spiritual. There is an emphasis in social work, too, on being fully human and on the qualities of wholeness, integration, and connectedness.

  By contrast, an unhealthy spirituality or religion is unbalanced, fragmented, or one-sided. It can cause harm to one's body, mental health, social relationships, and community. It can fracture families and friendships and sow the seeds of intolerance, violence, or oppression. When helping a client attempting to decide whether a particular spirituality or a religion is healthy or unhealthy, consider these questions: Does it make for contentment or fear, hope or despair, self-worth or shame, openness or rigidity, freedom or control, peace or conflict, intellectual honesty or deception? Does it encourage, lift up, and support the person or does it drag the person down? Is the person helped or haunted by his or her beliefs?

- When a client is an active member of a faith community (e.g., a church, synagogue, mosque), that community may be a potential resource and support to the helping process. Depending on the client's concern or need, the possible use of this resource might be explored. However, it is important to understand that some individuals will describe themselves as belonging to a certain religion or faith community when, in fact, they have only a tenuous connection to it. Thus, a client's self-identification with a particular religion does not necessarily signify that she or he will have access to the informal social support network or other resources usually associated with active membership (see Item 12.6).

  The social worker should never assume that he or she knows about a client's beliefs and practices when all that the worker really knows is that the client identifies with a particular religion. Within a religion there are usually numerous subgroups or branches that differ in a variety of ways. For example, within Christianity there are numerous denominations and within each of these there are usually further divisions along a conservative–progressive continuum. Further complicating this situation is the fact that the beliefs, practices, and traditions of a religion or faith community are often intertwined with a particular nationality, culture, or ethnic group.

- A social worker must be prepared to respond to questions that a client may ask about the worker's religion or spirituality. A client may have several motives for asking such questions. As a general rule, people are most at ease with those who have beliefs, values, and life experiences similar to their own. Thus, a client may want to know if the social worker is capable of understanding his or her spiritual and religious beliefs and practices and perhaps whether the worker is accepting or disapproving. Some clients may ask about the worker's religion simply because they are curious about how the social worker has approached the questions of life's meaning. Still other clients may be trying to manipulate the worker into taking their side in a family conflict. How a social worker responds to such questions will depend on why the client is asking and how various answers might affect the professional relationship and their ongoing work together. (See Item 8.4 for guidance on responding to personal questions.)

Selected Bibliography

Canda, Edward, and Leola Furman. *Spiritual Diversity in Social Work Practice,* 2nd ed. New York: Oxford, 2009.

Cunningham, Maddy. *Integrating Spirituality in Clinical Social Work Practice.* Upper Saddle River, NJ: Pearson, 2012.

Derezotes, David. *Spiritually-Oriented Social Work Practice.* Upper Saddle River, NJ: Pearson, 2006.

Van Hook, Mary, Beryl Hugen, and Marian Aguilar. *Spirituality within Religious Traditions in Social Work.* Independence, KY: Cengage, 2002.

15.19 THE CLIENT WHO IS IMPACTED BY THE CRIMINAL JUSTICE SYSTEM

In every practice setting, social workers will meet people who have had their lives changed and disrupted by crime. Some are the victims of crime, some have committed crimes, and some have a child, spouse, parent, or friend serving a sentence in a correctional program. Increasingly, social workers are employed in probation and parole, juvenile courts, pre-release centers, halfway houses, diversion programs, and prisons. In these settings they learn firsthand about the complexity and problems within in the criminal justice system.

The United States has a serious crime problem and an extremely high rate of incarceration. With about 5 percent of the world's population, the United States has nearly 25 percent of the world's prisoners. At times, one of every 100 adults is in jail or prison while many others are on probation and parole. Of those who are incarcerated, most are males, most are economically disadvantaged, and a disproportionate number are members of a racial or ethnic minority. Most of those in prison have low levels or education and few job skills. Many, but certainly not all, grew up in fractured or dysfunctional families. About one-half of those entering a prison are between the ages of 18 and 27. Many are nonviolent drug offenders. Many struggle with a mental illness.

The victim

Many of the clients known to social workers have been harmed (physically, emotionally, and economically) by a crime such as an assault, rape, homicide, robbery, fraud, drunken driving, identity theft, and extortion. Whole neighborhoods and communities are impacted by crime. For example, those living in a high-crime neighborhood are often afraid to leave their homes to visit friends, do their shopping, and attend school. Local businesses are challenged to continue operating when their expenses are increased by vandalism, robberies, and extortion. The victims of crime have a very personal interest in the operation of the criminal justice system and in the actions and decisions of those who work within this system. They typically want increased police protection, stricter laws, and stern courts, and they want offenders convicted and imprisoned so they cannot harm others.

When working with a client who has been injured or traumatized by a crime, the social worker should be aware that most states have some type of a victim compensation program. If an individual meets the eligibility requirements, such a program may provide assistance in paying for medical expenses, mental health counseling, loss of income, and funeral or burial expenses. Individuals who have been traumatized by crime will usually benefit from counseling, therapy, and self-help or support groups.

Increasingly, communities are developing programs of *restorative justice* that focus attention on the personal harm caused by crime rather than only on the laws that have broken. These programs are designed to give the victim an opportunity to speak to the offender and explain how she or he has been harmed. The program gives the offender an opportunity to learn about the consequences of his or her crime, take responsibility, provide restitution, and offer an apology. Programs of restorative justice promote healing by both the victim and the offender. They are a supplement to ordinary court activity and punishments, not a substitute.

The offender

Crimes are committed by many different types of people and for a wide variety of motives. A significant number of crimes are related, directly or indirectly, to the use of drugs and alcohol and to the distribution of illegal drugs. Some crimes are very deliberate and calculated acts. Others are thoughtless and impulsive. Some people who commit a crime, even minor crime, experience intense feelings of guilt and remorse. On the other extreme are those who seem devoid of guilt and only regret that they got caught. Some who have committed even terrible crimes appear to be fundamentally good, truthful, and compassionate people. Others consistently display a tendency toward dishonesty, violence, and even cruelty.

Social workers employed in noncorrectional settings and also private practitioners will occasionally have a client who is arrested and drawn into the criminal justice system. When a worker's client (e.g., an individual who has been receiving counseling from the worker) is arrested, the worker should do what is possible to ensure that the client secures competent legal representation. If the accused is held in jail, a visit and discussion by the social worker may assist him or her to better cope with the situation and make good decisions about how to proceed.

Those who are poor are at a distinct disadvantage within the judicial system. Because they cannot afford a private defense attorney, they must rely on an overburdened public defender. If offered the opportunity to be released on bail, a poor person may not be able to raise the money needed for making bail and consequently he or she may spend months in jail awaiting a trial date or a plea bargain agreement.

It is important to understand that vast majority of those who are charged with a crime do not go to trial. Rather, the prosecutor and the defense attorney negotiate a plea bargain. Typically, the accused agrees to plead guilty in return for a minimum sentence or he or she agrees to plead guilty to a lesser crime that carries a less severe punishment. A judge must approve the terms of a negotiated plea bargain. Plea bargains are necessary for the court system to function. The system does not have the personnel, time, or money necessary to provide all of the accused with a trial. Only the most serious crimes are likely to go to trial. Some who are accused of a crime may accept a plea bargain, even if innocent, because they fear that a jury will find them guilty and they will end up with a punishment more severe that that offered by the plea bargain.

Classification

All who enter the correctional system are subjected to some type of assessment and classification. For example, on one extreme are *situational offenders*, those for whom the criminal act was unexpected and out of character. On the other extreme are the *habitual offenders* or career criminals who have a long history of criminal behavior. A career criminal may view time in jail as simply the "cost of doing business." The situational offender is probably a good candidate for rehabilitation; the habitual offender is probably not.

Those who administer the correctional system have little choice but to use classifications and categories in order to manage programs and prisoners. However, when a person is placed in and treated as a category or a class, individualization is sacrificed. Correctional programs seldom have the capacity or resources to adequately address such problems as inadequate education, lack of job skills, lack of reading ability and language skills, substance abuse, learning disabilities, mental disorders, and so on.

Probation and parole

If an individual is placed on *probation* or *parole,* he or she must maintain regular contact with a probation or parole officer and adhere to a set of rules and conditions such as keeping the officer informed of living arrangement and employment status; at the discretion of the officer, submit to drug testing, a body search, and/or home search; avoid contact with known felons; stay away from places that sell alcohol or display pornography; secure and utilize treatment for an addiction or mental health problem; avoid contact with the victim of the crime; and adhere to a curfew. A violation of these rules may result in the imposition of an additional sentence or a return to prison.

Prison environments

The physical and social surroundings of a prison will vary greatly depending on whether it is a minimum-security facility, a maximum-security prison, or something in between. When an individual enters a *maximum-security prison* he or she encounters a frightening and disorienting environment. These prisons are designed to hold persons for whom violence, intimidation, and manipulation are a way of life. Within such an institution one finds among the prisoners a status hierarchy, a code of conduct, and an economic system that governs the distribution of goods, services, and opportunities. Like all people, inmates want to be respected and taken seriously, but in this degrading environment being feared by others is a substitute for genuine respect. A new inmate may want to just serve out the sentence and be left alone. But that seldom works. New inmates are typically tested and challenged and they usually need to join a group for self-protection. Inmate groups typically divide along racial and ethnic lines, or by gang affiliation.

By contrast, a *minimum-security correctional facility* will typically have a very different atmosphere. The inmates usually feel fairly safe and have more privacy, freedom, and choice within the prison. They also have more access to visits by friends and family.

The impact of imprisonment

Most people sent to a correctional facility are eventually released after serving a sentence. They then return to their community and to their family, if they have one. Ideally, their time of incarceration is a time of positive change and rehabilitation, a time of making the best of a very difficult situation, and a time to prepare for life that follows prison. For that to occur, two elements must be present. First, the facility must offer a wide variety of educational, training, and therapeutic programs. Second, the inmate must have the motivation and the capacity to make use of those programs.

All too often, time spent in a prison is a negative and damaging experience that reinforces and solidifies criminal thinking and activity. It causes many to feel embittered and angry. Many inmates come to believe that they have been treated unfairly when they hear of others who committed the same crime but received a lesser sentence.

The time spent in prison will often weaken the inmate's already fragile ties to family. When finally released and returned to the community, the "ex-cons" are usually poorly prepared for the job market and are frequently feared and avoided by ordinary citizens. Having a criminal record makes it difficult to find a decent job, obtain housing, and enter into a positive and helpful social network.

Of critical importance are rehabilitation programs that help inmates examine and understand their behavioral patterns and habitual ways of thinking (see next heading); identify their personal goals; and construct a framework of moral and ethical principles to be used in making choices and decisions. For many inmates, reducing the chance of recidivism means making significant changes in their lifestyle and social network. Once released, they need to create and maintain a set of healthy and pro-social friendships that provide guidance, encouragement, and support.

For some prison inmates, faith-based programs are attractive and beneficial. Such programs can offer the individual a new set of values, a new way of understanding his or her life, and a sense of purpose, hope, and identity. When the individual is released, these programs can provide valuable social support and encouragement, help in finding a job and housing, and counseling.

Criminal thinking

Many repeat offenders and career criminals have a way of thinking and an outlook on life that is significantly different from that of situational offenders and law-abiding citizens. The existence of this cognitive pattern helps to explain why they persist in criminal activity. Basically, *criminal thinking* is a set of erroneous beliefs and distorted values. Below are the key components of criminal thinking:

- Playing down or dismissing the seriousness of their crimes and blaming others or circumstances for their criminal behavior.
- A lack of empathy and compassion for their victims. They experience little or no remorse or guilt for the harm they inflict on others.
- A belief that their victims got what they deserve because the victims are naïve, stupid, or weak.
- A persistent belief that they are above the law and can violate laws because the laws are stupid and unfair and because they have a right to take a share of the good things in life, if necessary by deceit or force.

- Frequent use of lies, deception, manipulation, and intimidation to get what they want. They have no hesitation to use, abuse, and discard people if it serves their purposes or gets them what they want.
- Their manipulations often take the form of charming and endearing themselves to others by presenting themselves as helpful and generous so as to win trust and secure the emotional leverage they need to exert influence and control.
- A strong desire to exert power and control over others. When not in control, they feel nervous, weak, and frustrated. Interpersonal conflicts are resolved by threats and shouting rather than by respectful discussions and compromise.
- They are impulsive in decision making. They take action without anticipating or appreciating the likely consequences. Decisions are made in response to current circumstances and opportunities rather than on the basis of fundamental moral and ethical principles. In many cases, this mode of decision-making style reflects a real lack of reasoning and critical thinking skills.
- They have trouble sticking with a plan and following through on the commitments and promises they have voiced. They are easily influenced and swayed by the current or immediate situation.
- They assume that they can get away with their crimes and are too smart to get caught. Over time they may become overconfident and feel invulnerable. When their self-confidence begins to weaken, drugs and alcohol are often used to pump up their courage or cover their fears.

Unless this pattern of criminal thinking can be changed, the chances for rehabilitation are quite low. For additional information on distorted thinking patterns and persons who are manipulative and dangerous, see Items 10.8, 10.9, and 13.7.

The offender's family and children

When an individual is convicted of a crime and sent to a correctional program or prison, his or her family usually experiences emotional turmoil and economic hardships. Feelings of frustration, grief, loss, shame, embarrassment, anger, guilt, self-blame, and regret are common. Some family members may be angry with the offender for getting in trouble, whereas others feel guilty because they could not keep the offender out of trouble, or perhaps because they did not protect him or her from getting caught. Many family members worry about the offender's safety and mental health, especially if he or she is in a maximum-security prison.

Separation by imprisonment places great strain on a marriage or partner relationship. The spouse or partner left behind may seek professional help in deciding whether to pursue a divorce and end the relationship. The spouse or partner may need help with practical problems such as finding a less expensive place to live, securing health care, adjusting the family budget, arranging child care, finding a job, and so on.

Children react in various ways to the incarceration of a parent. For most, it will be a confusing and troubling experience. For some, however, such as those who have been abused by the parent, the parent's removal provides a sense of safety. A variety of factors will determine how a child is affected: the child's relationship and closeness to the incarcerated parent, age at time of separation, temperament and personality, prior separations, length of separation, strength of family, reactions by the other parent and family members, nature of parent's crime, reactions to crime by community, and so on. These children often experience humiliation, teasing from other children, social isolation, difficulties in school, and various other problems such as mood swings, developmental delays and regressions, depression, outbursts of anger, and violence. Studies suggest that the children of imprisoned parents are at increased risk of poor school performance, school dropout, drug abuse, early pregnancy, and gang involvement. A social worker in contact with these children should make sure that they have access to appropriate counseling. Mentoring programs and Big Brother/Big Sister programs are important for these children.

Family visitation of an inmate

When a social worker is providing services to the family of an inmate, the worker needs to give attention to several issues related to visitation. Visits by family and friends help the inmate cope with the loneliness and stress of confinement and they maintain some semblance of family bonds and communication. Encouragement from family is an added incentive for the inmate to utilize existing programs of education and training as preparation for life after prison, if an eventual parole is possible. Visiting can reassure family members that the person they care for is doing as well as can be expected and it helps them work through their mixed-up thoughts and feelings about what has happened and why. Visits and regular communication can help the family make informed decisions such as those related to personal finance and interactions with the children. And visits help family members visualize and anticipate the challenges that lay ahead if and when the inmate is released.

The effect on children of their visits to a parent in prison has not been well researched. Needless to say, the physical structure of the prison and the security procedures can be frightening to a child. It is disturbing to see one's parent in that environment. However, many child welfare specialists suggest that visiting by a child is usually beneficial because the visits help the child recognize, understand, and gradually accept the realities of the situation. It is better for a child to struggle with and adjust to a painful reality (e.g., Daddy is in prison because he hurt someone) than to live with a fantasy or a deception (e.g., Daddy is a soldier and living in a foreign country). Visits can reassure the child that she or he has not been abandoned by the parent and is not responsible for the parent leaving home. If the child's caregiver is unsure about whether a child should visit the parent in prison, he or she should request guidance from prison personnel (e.g., prison psychologist, prison social worker) and/or specialist in child development.

A child visitor, like all visitors, must be on the prison's list of approved visitors. The parent, foster parent, or other adult who will be taking the child to the prison should have visited the inmate one or two times before taking the child to the prison so the caregiver knows what to expect and can prepare the child.

Basically there are two types of visits. In a *noncontact visit* the visitor and inmate are separated by glass or wire mesh. In a *contact visit* the visitor and inmate share the same space and are allowed to offer a brief hug and touch. All who wish to visit an inmate—whether a family member, friend, or social worker—must submit to prison officials the required application to visit. Only those on the list of approved visitors can enter the visiting area. Persons with a criminal record may be denied permission to visit. Most institutions allow visiting only on certain days and times. The rules that govern visitation can be obtained by mail or from the prison website. Visitors should know the rules before they arrive at the facility. The visitation rules in a maximum-security facility are very strict. For example:

- Only those listed on a pre-approved visitor's list are allowed to visit. The falsification of an application to visit will result in the suspension of the visiting privilege.

- Visitors must clear a metal detector (shoes with metal parts, jewelry, and bras containing wire will set off the alarms and may need to be removed before a visit).
- Visitors are subject to the search of their person, belongings, and vehicle.
- Visitors are prohibited from bringing food items, cameras, cell phones, and other electronic equipment to the visiting area.
- Visitors and inmates must remain seated during the visit.
- Visitors are not permitted access to inmate restrooms.
- Visitors caught with illegal contraband will have their visiting privileges suspended and may be referred for possible criminal prosecution.
- Visitors who use inappropriate, foul, or abusive language will be removed from the visiting area.
- Sexually provocative behavior and sexual contact such as petting, fondling, prolonged kissing, and bodily contact are prohibited.
- Visitors must be fully clothed, buttons and zippers must remain fastened, and female visitors must wear a bra and undergarments.
- Children who are visiting are not allowed to use restrooms without supervision by the visiting parent or another approved adult.

It is important for all visitors to understand that prison officials view visiting as a privilege and not a right. Moreover, they are usually ambivalent about visitation. On the positive side, visitation improves inmate morale and creates a better prison environment. On the negative side, visitation programs are difficult to manage and visitors are the main source of contraband such as drugs and weapons entering a prison. Visits can be disappointing and highly emotional. Sometimes a visitor does not show up as the inmate had expected. Sometimes an inmate refuses to meet with the visitor. Sometimes a family argument erupts. Sometimes an inmate will ridicule or humiliate other visitors in the room. Sometimes a last-minute security concern will cancel a scheduled visit.

Prison officials are concerned that some of inmates will seek out and cultivate a manipulative relationship with naïve and gullible pen-pals, prison ministry personnel, and volunteers who "just want to help." Some inmates convince sympathetic visitors to bring them drugs and money or carry messages. Some visitors, knowingly or unknowingly, assist inmates to continue operating their criminal enterprises.

Those who intend to visit an inmate should prepare themselves mentally and emotionally before they go. For example, seeing a family member or loved one in shackles and behind glass, bars, and wires can be upsetting. Crying or emotional outbursts by family members may make the inmates feel worse than they already do. The space available for visiting varies widely among prisons. A visitor should anticipate a lack of privacy and surveillance by the prison staff.

Issues related to social work records and confidentiality

If a social worker's client (or a former client) is convicted of a crime, an officer of the court (e.g., a probation officer) may contact the social worker and request information needed to prepare a pre-sentence investigation report. In addition, the defense attorney may request information from the social worker that might help secure a more lenient sentence for the defendant. How is the social worker to respond?

In such situations, the ordinary *rules of client confidentiality* still apply (see Item 10.5). Client data should not be released unless the client has authorized it by signing a proper release of information or a formal court order requires the social worker to release the information. A judge's routine request for a pre-sentence investigation does not, by itself, authorize a social worker to release client information to the officer of the court.

The same principles on the handling of client records and information will apply if, at a later date, correctional program staff invites a social worker to participate in a case conference aimed at formulating a rehabilitation or treatment plan for a former social work client now in a correctional program.

Selected Bibliography

Alder, Freda, Gerhard Mueller, and William Laufer. *Criminal Justice*, 6th ed. New York: McGraw-Hill, 2012.

Coggins, Kim, and J. Eli Fresquez. *Working with Clients in Correctional Settings*. Peosta, IA: Eddie Bowers, 2007.

Sharp, Boyd. *Changing Criminal Thinking: A Treatment Program*, 2nd ed. Alexandria, VA: American Correctional Association, 2010.

Walsh, Anthony, and Mary Stohr. *Correctional Assessment, Casework, and Counseling*, 5th ed. Alexandria, VA: American Correctional Association, 2010.

Wright, Lois, and Cynthia Seymour. *Working with Children and Families Separated by Incarceration: A Handbook for Child Welfare Agencies*. Washington, DC: Child Welfare League of America, 2000.

15.20 THE CLIENT OR FAMILY AFFECTED BY WAR

Since 1941, when the United States entered World War II, this country has been at war over 55 percent of that time. When a nation is at war, nearly every person and every social institution is affected in some way. At the macro level, U.S. culture has been impacted, for example, by the increased taxes and the allocation of resources to support the war effort instead of human needs such as poverty and health care, or by the eroding international status of the United States in the eyes of many throughout the world. At the micro level, it is estimated that during those 70 plus years, more than 500,000 U.S. military personnel (Army, Navy, Marine, Air Force, Coast Guard) have been killed in combat and nearly one million men and women have been seriously wounded. Most certainly, the families and friends of those who are killed or injured are impacted in a most profound manner. These countless individuals experience many years or a whole lifetime of pain, grief, and distress. All of these people—the dead, the injured and their families, and U.S. society as a whole—are casualties of war.

Social workers, both those serving in the military and those employed in virtually every type of human services agency, have a role to perform in serving the casualties of war. To effectively address these issues, social workers must understand the stress war places on military personnel and the sacrifices made by their families, friends, and other loved ones. To support professional practice with this population, the National Association of Social Workers has created a webpage of resources and information at http:www.socialworkers.org/ military.asp.

STRESS ON INDIVIDUALS AND FAMILIES ASSOCIATED WITH MILITARY SERVICE

In a war, military personnel are called on to commit acts that challenge the conventional notion of morality—acts that if committed by civilians in other circumstances would be considered both criminal and immoral. The social worker should understand that the emotional drain of this contradiction on the service member is substantial and recognize that those who have experienced the horrors of combat are usually reluctant to talk about it, except possibly with other combat veterans. They may be justifiably proud for having served their country but deep within they may not be proud of what they had to do in order to serve their country. They sometimes carry vivid and disturbing memories of what they have seen, heard, smelled, tasted, and felt, as well as guilt about what they did and what they may have failed to do.

In the extraordinarily stressful and chaotic environment of combat, military personnel discover many things about themselves. For example, they may have discovered that they could perform under extreme pressure and were surprisingly loyal and devoted to their comrades. On the other hand, they may have discovered that they could be immobilized by fear and were capable of extreme brutality and perhaps other behaviors that they view as shameful. Not infrequently they feel some degree of guilt, regret, and remorse over what they think they should have done, but did not or could not do. Such feelings are especially intense if they feel somehow responsible for the death or injury of a comrade in arms.

It is not uncommon for families and friends to report that the returning veteran has changed and is not the same person who left them for military duty. The veteran of combat may seem distant, detached, and preoccupied, or perhaps he or she drinks too much and appears depressed, angry, or reckless. Those coming home from war need the understanding and support of family and friends, but their families and friends can never fully appreciate what the veteran actually experienced and are often unsure of what they should or should not be doing in order to make things better. Both the veteran and his or her family may feel frustrated and confused. They may worry and wonder if they will ever again have a normal life.

SERVICES PROVIDED BY SOCIAL WORKERS

Most social workers, regardless of practice setting, will have some veterans and/or their family members as clients. However, the social workers who are part of the military or employed by the Department of Veterans Affairs (VA) will regularly provide services to this population. The social work skills of referral, case management, counseling, crisis intervention, advocacy, the creation and facilitation of support groups, program development, and community organization are especially relevant to serving these clients.

Evidence-based practice research and guidelines developed by the military and the VA are indispensable resources to the social worker. The following programs and guidelines should be kept in mind by these social workers.

Prevention

Increasingly, efforts are being made to help soldiers and their families anticipate the adjustments and challenges they may encounter when the service person returns homes from war. For example, the veteran returning home on leave or being discharged should be helped by a social worker to give careful thought to how he or she will handle questions from family members and curious friends about war experiences. If such recall is harmful, the soldier should be encouraged to simply announce, "I don't want to talk about the war. So please do not ask me any questions." Family members should be prepared to avoid such questions and to ask others not to discuss these matters unless the subject is introduced by the veteran. However, unless the veteran can find a safe place to talk about these matters (e.g., a veteran's support group, individual therapy), she or he or will remain at risk for emotional problems.

Preparing family members for the absence of military personnel during a duty tour is another important professional intervention. If a mother or father is to be away from the family for an extended period of time, plans must be made and assistance provided for assuming family roles for parenting and child care, home maintenance, management of the family's finances, and so on. When the service person returns, these roles again must be renegotiated. Failure to attend to these matters is one reason military families experience a high divorce rate. The deployed person's spouse or partner should be encouraged to maintain supportive contact with other service families and perhaps to participate in a formal support group.

Advancing technology is allowing deployed personnel to stay in closer contact with loved ones back home, which can help to decrease the number of devastating "Dear John/Jane" letters announcing the unexpected end of a relationship. Nevertheless, social workers have a role to play in addressing both the maintenance and dissolution of relationships strained by military duty.

Disrupted families

It is evident that military families experience numerous changes and disruptions while the service person is away on duty. In addition to dealing with their own issues of coping with separation, family members will worry about the military person's safety, especially if the he or she is stationed in a combat zone. However, families can gain some comfort and reassurance through friendships with other families facing similar concerns. An experienced and compassionate social worker might arrange and facilitate such friendships. The family, including older children, should be encouraged to join and participate in support groups so they have an opportunity to feel understood and know they are not alone in their worries.

When facing deployment, it is critically important for the parents to spend time with their children to explain what is happening and assure the children that they are loved, even though the parent must leave for military duty. Young children, in particular, may sense the parents' anxiety and become anxious themselves or perhaps misinterpret why the deployed parent has gone away and thus feel abandoned. The child's other parent or caregiver should be helped to explain to the child, at the child's level of understanding, what has happened and that the parent's departure is not a sign that the child is not loved.

Military families not only miss the person's parenting and other contributions to family life, but they usually also experience high levels of worry and stress during the deployment. One indicator of this stress is found in a study indicating that child maltreatment was three times greater among Army wives during the husbands' deployment than when not deployed (Savitsky, Illingworth, and DuLaney, 2009). Reduction in income can be another stressor. For families of deployed Reservists or members of the National Guard who must leave a nonmilitary job, the income reduction can be substantial and the family's lifestyle severely impacted. Sufficient income may not be available, for example, to cover mortgages or car payments to which the family is legally obligated.

Death

Sadly, military personnel are killed in battle or duty-related accidents. Others may die of illness or suicide. Spouses, partners, children, parents, and other loved ones will feel this painful loss for years and possibly for the rest of their lives. Depending on their practice setting, social workers may have a significant role in helping these individuals deal with their immediate crisis and grief reactions, their eventual adjustments, and possible related mental health problems (see Items 13.14 and 15.17).

Suicide is a significant cause of death for military personnel, especially those who have been in combat and those with multiple deployments. It has been estimated that veterans are twice as likely to commit suicide as nonveterans. The method of suicide is frequently by gunshot, as these weapons often have been an intimate part of the person's existence while in the military. In addition to the suicide risk factors described in Item 15.7, there are some warning signs that are unique to military veterans: increased frequency of cleaning or handling a weapon, staying up at night to "watch over" the house and a preoccupation with home security measures, frequent visits to military cemeteries, wearing a uniform or part of the uniform in civilian life, contacting old military friends to indirectly say good-bye, speaking frequently about the honor of military service, obsession with news coverage of war, and becoming overprotective of children.

Physical injury

The tactics and armor used in modern warfare result in fewer combat deaths than in previous wars. Concurrently, there has been a dramatic increase in the number of individuals who have survived combat but are left with a severe disability. Social workers in VA hospital settings will be part of the team working with the veterans during long, painful, and frustrating periods of rehabilitation. Adjusting to disfigurement, amputations, use of prosthetics, and changes in self-image are always serious challenges. The veteran's loved ones will struggle in their acceptance and adjustment to these same concerns (see Item 15.10).

Many veterans experience traumatic brain injury, or TBI (see Item 15.9). Depending on the location of the injury in the brain, the veteran may develop a pattern of rigid black-or-white thinking, experience seizures, have memory difficulty, and have other cognitive functioning problems. Rehabilitation programs can be helpful for persons experiencing TBI, and the social worker should be prepared to link that person to such programs.

Psychological injury

There is no such thing as getting used to combat—the longer and more intense the exposure, the more serious its impact. Some veterans will say something like, "Well, I was in combat and it didn't affect me." Often associated with that belief is the feeling: "I'm strong. I could handle it. I could tough it out. I'm not a whiner." In reality, no one really escapes the effects of combat. It is not a question of *whether*, but rather *when* the effects of this intense stress and trauma will surface. For some veterans, the effects are delayed and do not emerge until years later.

The social worker should be alert for the cluster of symptoms that signal post-traumatic stress disorder (PTSD). The forms of war-related PTSD include sleep disturbance, intrusive thoughts, flashbacks, nightmares, night sweats, startle reaction, survivor guilt, emotional numbness, wanting to be alone, eruptions of rage or fear, feeling isolated, inability to concentrate, anxiety, depression, and sexual dysfunction. In order to deal with these distressing symptoms, many with PTSD will medicate themselves with alcohol or drugs. The seriousness of PTSD and its symptoms will vary from person to person. Living with a loved one with PTSD is extraordinary stressful.

Flashbacks are one of the many delayed reactions to combat stress. They are a very frightening experience. If you are working with a veteran who is in the midst of a flashback, simply wait for the flashback to be over. Given time, they will come out of it but afterward they may be angry, scared, and embarrassed that it happened. It might be helpful to encourage the veteran to view PTSD and a symptom like a flashback as something like an infected cut that does not heal and periodically breaks open. This infection needs to be cleaned out before it can properly heal. Talking about the trauma is the necessary, but painful, cleansing process.

Sleep disturbance and nightmares are other common symptoms of PTSD. Some veterans will try to avoid sleeping in order to escape recurring nightmares. Some will stay up all night and can sleep only in daylight because their experiences of combat in the dark of night were especially terrifying. A long-term lack of sleep has a devastating effect on one's physical and mental health and exacerbates other PTSD symptoms.

If the post-traumatic stress disorder is not recognized and treated, it can have long-term negative effects on a person's life and functioning. An individual with PTSD is at increased risk of substance abuse, committing domestic violence, and suicide. Treatment of this disorder usually involves the application of cognitive and behavior modification therapies, psychotropic medications, arousal reduction and anxiety management, stress reduction techniques, or exposure therapy. In exposure therapy, a specially trained social worker or other therapist encourages and assists clients to repeatedly talk about their traumatic experiences and confront the very thoughts and feelings they are trying to avoid. The goal of this therapy is to gradually gain control over disturbing thoughts and learn that they need not be afraid of those memories. Support groups composed of veterans are another effective means of helping veterans come to terms with their experiences and make a successful transition back into civilian life.

Other conditions with a strong emotional component to which social workers should be alert when serving military veterans are chronic pain, sexual trauma, and sleep disorders.

Military to civilian transition

In order to understand some of the adjustment problems of combat veterans after their discharge from the military, it is helpful to think of this separation as a loss experience. Even those who voluntarily leave the military may feel ambivalence. They may be glad to be out of harm's way and happy to rejoin their families, but recognize that they are also giving up a sense of identity, purpose, structure, and comradeship found in the military. Even giving up one's weapon that has been a constant companion and source of protection is no small matter.

An individual with military experience typically has developed a strong work ethic and the qualities of self-discipline and goal-directedness. Consequently, he or she becomes a valued employee in civilian jobs. However, the transition from the military to the civilian employment sector can be difficult. For example, the military attitude and job skills may not translate easily into a civilian context. Whereas the military is highly regimented and one's work assignments are a matter of following the orders issued by a superior, in civilian life, work assignments are often flexible and even open to negotiation. Social workers may be able to help veterans anticipate, recognize, and adjust to these different expectations in the work environment.

At present, the United States has an all-volunteer military. By contrast, a military draft forced individuals into World War II, the Korean War, and the Vietnam War. Today's military personnel have deliberately chosen to serve their country and many entered the military with an eye on making it a career, a training ground for civilian jobs, or a route to support for attaining higher education. Thus, if an injury forces them out of the military, it has also disrupted their career plans, identity, and sense of belonging. For the veteran's spouse and children, leaving the military means losing the mutual support and sense of community that exists among military families. Such social and emotional losses add to the crisis and adjustment problems related to a veteran's physical or psychological injury.

Too often the emotional scars from military service make it difficult for many veterans to function well in the private life. For example, it is estimated that one-third of the adult homeless population in the United States are veterans of wars dating back to World War II. Furthermore, the domestic violence rate in military families is high.

Referral

Veterans often need access to many different services. The VA offers a vast array of services, including over 50 hospitals and 900 local points of contact. Services in rural areas are sparse, although advances in technology are starting to reduce this problem. Eligibility for veteran-related service is very complex to determine and depends on such factors as the time and place of one's military assignments, the risks involved in that assignment, and whether the veteran was in the regular military, the National Guard, or the Reserves. Because different programs use somewhat different eligibility criteria, it is often a lengthy process for a veteran to identify and enroll in needed services. The social worker should help the veteran find needed information and negotiate this complex sometimes frustrating system. One good entry point for these services is the VA benefits telephone number (1-800-827-1000). Another first step is to contact a state Office of Veterans Affairs or one of the many local veterans' services organizations (e.g., American Legion, Veterans of Foreign Wars, Vet Center).

Military families, too, should be encouraged to make use of services and programs that will be especially knowledgeable and sensitive to their concerns. These would include, for example, their military base's Family Assistance Center, Deployment Support Groups, Family Advocacy Program, Military Medical Clinic, Military Mental Health Services, and Military Chaplains.

Selected Bibliography

Clancy, Joanne E., and Bradford W. Sheafor, "Social Work with U.S. Casualties of the Middle East Wars." In *Social Work: A Profession of Many Faces,* 12th rev. ed. Bradford W. Sheafor, Armando T. Morales, and Malcolm E. Scott. Upper Saddle River, NJ: Pearson, 2012, pp. 185–198.

Iraq War Clinician Guide, 2nd ed., National Center for Post-Traumatic Stress Disorder. http://www.ptsd.va.gov/professional/manuals/manual-pdf/iwcg/iraq_clinician_guide_v2.pdf (June 2004).

Rubin, Allen, Eugenia L. Weiss, and Jose E. Coll, eds. *Handbook of Military Social Work.* Hoboken, NJ: Wiley & Sons, 2013.

Savitsky, Laura, Maria Illingworth, and Megan DuLaney. "Civilian Social Work: Serving the Military and Veteran Populations." *Social Work,* , no. 4 (2009): 327–339.

Snyder, Douglas K., and Candice M. Monson, eds. *Couple-Based Interventions for Military and Veteran Families: A Practitioner's Guide.* New York: Guilford, 2012.

Whealin, Julia M., Lorie T. DeCarvalho, and Edward M. Vega. *Clinician's Guide to Treating Stress after War: Education and Coping Interventions for Veterans.* Hoboken, NJ: Wiley & Sons, 2008.

15.21 THE CLIENT OR FAMILY EXPERIENCING AN ADOPTION

Social work is most likely to be the profession involved in facilitating adoptions and providing support for adoptive children and their families. Adoption is the legal transfer of responsibility for a child to a new family that will substantially impact both the child and the family. Thus, familiarity with the more common issues experienced by adopted children and their families before, during, and after the adoption is important knowledge for the social worker.

LEGAL CONSIDERATIONS IN ADOPTION

From a legal perspective, an *adoption* is a court-ordered transfer of parental rights and parental responsibilities from one person to another, typically from the child's natural or biological parent(s) to the adoptive parent(s). From a social work perspective, adoption is not so much an event that concludes with the adoption, but rather is a process of building and supporting a particular form of family that carries with it some unique challenges.

Prior to the adoption there must be termination of the natural parents' legal rights and responsibilities. There are two forms of termination: voluntary and involuntary. In a *voluntary termination* the child's parents elect to surrender their legal rights and responsibilities. In an *involuntary termination* a court orders the severance of those rights and responsibilities, often because the child was abused, neglected, or abandoned and reasonable efforts to help the parents provide adequate care have failed.

Legally, an adoption is different from foster care. In *foster care*, the rights and responsibilities are retained by the child's natural parent(s), by the court, or by a child welfare agency that has been assigned custody of the child by a court. A foster parent becomes the child's caregiver but not his or her legal parent. (For a listing of basic parental rights and responsibilities, see Item 15.4.)

There are two types of adoptive placements: open and closed. In an *open adoption* the child's biological parent(s) and the adoptive parent(s) agree to have ongoing communication and/or contact after the adoption is legally finalized. Such an arrangement allows the child to know her or his biological parent(s) and allows the bio-parent to participate the child's life, at least to some degree. In a *closed adoption* there is no contact between the adoptee and his or her bio-parents. Open adoptions are increasingly common, especially in instances of voluntary termination, but rare in situations of court-ordered involuntary termination.

SERVICES TO ADOPTIVE CHILDREN AND PARENTS

Broadly speaking, the adoption-related services provided by social workers fall into three time periods: pre-adoption, placement, and post-adoption.

The pre-adoption period

During *pre-adoption* the social worker helps prospective adoptive parents explore in-depth their interest in adoption and come to an informed decision on whether adoption is a good choice for them. For some, this might involve discussion of their reasons for wanting to assume or expand their parenting role; for others, it could focus on how they dealt with and grieved their infertility. Also typically explored at this time is the question of whether the adoption of an older child or a *special needs child* (e.g., one with a mental or physical disability) is an option. In addition, the prospective adoptive parents are given information about the adoption process and about special issues typically experienced by adopted children and adoptive families. Often, potential adoptive parents are provided with opportunities to visit with and learn from experienced adoptive parents, older adoptees, and bio-parents that at one time relinquished a child for adoption.

The placement period

The services provided during the *placement period* focus mostly on initial adjustments within the family and on legal procedures that lead up to a judge issuing a *Decree of Adoption*, a court order that finalizes the adoption. Depending on a state's law, the child must usually live with the prospective adoptive parents for 6 to 12 months before a judge can issue the Decree.

The social worker and family should expect to address several factors during this initial period of joining the child and the adoptive family. Being moved out of one environment and into another is stressful for all children, even infants. Regardless of the reasons why a child became available for adoption, the child will continue to have at least a biological connection with those parents and severing that genetic link is a significant loss. Often, too, there is an interim placement in foster care where emotional connections are initiated and then dissolved by an adoption. Additional stress is experienced by the child if there is an international adoption or adoption by a family speaking a different language than the language the child experienced during infancy. The social worker should be aware that these experiences could affect the child's physical and emotional development.

During this period the adoptive parents are expected to become the predictable adult figures in the child's life. The social worker's primary goal should be to encourage and support a gradually deepening relationship between the child and each adoptive parent. One indicator of a satisfactory parent–child relationship is evidence of a high level of attachment and bonding between the parents and child. *Attachment* is a condition in which a child forms lasting loving relationships with the adoptive parents and other people in his or her immediate environment. Although the language is used inconsistently in the literature, *bonding* implies that the parent(s) have returned the loving relationship to the child. The significance of this distinction is to emphasize that the relationship is a two-way street involving a deep emotional connection from the child to the parents and from the parents to the child.

It is thought that problems in attachment take two forms. In one form the child seeks to establish a safe and reassuring environment by constantly engaging in attention-getting behaviors to test the adoptive parents' commitment and willingness to care for the child—even when the child's behavior is provocative and irritating. A second type of attachment problem is when the child withdraws from interaction because she or he fears the pain of a possible rejection. At either extreme, as well as various points in between, the adoptive parents face challenges in adequately bonding with the child.

In short, attachment and bonding do not occur automatically. It takes time, resilience, and thoughtful effort to successfully achieve a healthy level of attachment and bonding. Initially, with an infant, the parents need to become the predominant people in the child's life by performing such essential tasks as feeding, diaper changing, and holding/cuddling the child. For an older child, the parents demonstrate that they are safe, caring, and predictable figures in the child's life by, for example, providing meals, clean clothes, reading to the child or helping with homework, playing games, and being present at naptime and bedtime for needed snuggling. Other people, such as family, friends, and relatives, might perform these tasks after the existence of attachment/bonding is evident, but initially the adoptive parents should clearly be the child's primary caregivers. If indications of attachment/bonding are not apparent after several months, referral of the parents and child to professionals with expertise and training in specialized therapies for dealing with attachment should be considered.

The post-adoption period

The services offered during the *post-adoption* period will usually take the form of counseling and guidance related to the questions and problems that may arise in adoptive families. Many child-placing agencies offer support groups and parent training to help adoptive parents anticipate and address these issues.

There are times when adoption-related problems are most likely to surface, and when the social worker needs to help the adoptive parents provide the child with age-appropriate information. For example, around preschool age, children become interested in where babies come from and begin to request information about their own birth. It is important at this life stage to be clear and unapologetic about the fact that the child was adopted. The social worker should recognize, however, that some parents believe the fact of adoption should be kept secret, although the downside of that bias toward secrecy is that the child often feels there must be something wrong about adoption if it must be kept secret. The child then may feel shame and tend to develop a diminished self-image. The social worker should help the parents interpret adoption as simply one way that families are created. Adoptive family support groups provide the parents with a safe arena in which they can voice their feelings and concerns and learn how other adoptive parents deal with the common challenges of adoption.

One effective means of helping the adopted child better understand his or her roots and connections to birth parents, and possibly to foster parents, is for the adoptive parents to maintain for the child a scrapbook or photo album that contains information about all the people who have been an important part of the child's life. **"The Life Book" a deleted item from the 6th edition** Consistent with the narrative practice model (see Chapter 6), building this record helps to tell the whole story of the child's life.

By the time they enter elementary school, adopted children usually begin to be more curious about their birth parents and why they were placed for adoption. Often for the first time the child is faced with numerous questions about her or his place of birth, name, parents, and brothers and sisters. At this time the child realizes that he or she is somehow "different" than most school classmates in that they were not adopted. This raises new questions about the child's bio-parents and the circumstances surrounding of the adoption. For example, the child may wonder: "Was I somehow flawed or did I do something 'bad?'" If so, might my adoptive parents want to 'unadopt' me at some point?"

Over time, the adoptive parents may have new questions about the birth parents related to their motives, behavior, and life circumstances. The social worker needs to help them maintain perspective, live with unanswerable questions, and especially avoid judging the bio-parents. One interpretation the social worker and adoptive parents might use, when appropriate, is to praise the birth parent(s) for making the choice to place the child with another family when they were not prepared to provide the needed care.

Another critical period is during the adoptee's adolescence when there are the usual strains or conflicts in the parent–child relationship and when the adolescent is struggling to form a personal identity apart from family. This task is especially complex for the adopted child because it involves psychologically separating from two sets of parents—birth and adoptive parents. For the adopted child, the quest to answer the question "Who am I?" at this life stage may reignite feelings that he or she was rejected or abandoned by the birth parents, which may further complicate the process of developing a clear identity. The adoptive parents, too, may find this especially stressful by experiencing the fear that the child is abandoning them and may even wish to return to the birth parents (who are often idealized in the child's mind) as the primary source of parenting. Also, because of an awakening interest in sex, the teenage adoptee may have new and unanswerable questions about the sexual behavior of his or her bio-parents and may develop an intense interest in finding his or her bio-parents to getting answers to such questions.

Early adulthood is another time when adoption-related issues are likely to arise with some intensity. When the adult-age adoptees marry and have children, they are reminded that they know little about their bio-parents and other blood relatives. They recognize that they lack important health-related and genetic information and when they become a parent for the first time are awestruck by the attachment and love they feel toward their child. New questions arise about how any parent, regardless of circumstances, could ever part with a child and what led to that drastic step for the bio-parents. Some adult adoptees, then, enter into a search process intended to discover the identity of their biological parents.

Many adoption agencies and social workers offer assistance to adopted persons who want to fill in the felt gaps in their personal identity and to secure desired information about their medical history and genetic background. Most adopted persons are especially interested in learning about the circumstances that led up to a termination of parental rights and their own placement in an adoptive home. If the agency is able to locate and contact the biological parent, this parent is informed of the adopted person's desire for communication. Both the adopted person and the biological parent must give their consent before there is an exchange of information or a physical meeting is arranged. When an actual reunion takes place, the reported outcomes have been mixed. In some cases it proves helpful by providing information and healing for both the adoptee and the bio-parent(s). In other cases it is upsetting to one or both. Nevertheless, most adult-age adoptees report achieving a greater sense of contentment and closure as a result of meeting their bio-parents and learning more about their history and circumstances of their birth. Many bio-parents report feeling relieved and reassured that their child has been safe and well cared for.

SPECIAL ADOPTION CIRCUMSTANCES

Although no adoption is routine, some circumstances require the social worker and adoptive parents to address some additional issues.

The older child

Adoptive placements are especially complex and challenging when the child is older (e.g., school age) when placed in an adoptive home. That usually indicates that the child was legally freed for adoption by the court action of involuntary termination due to severe and long-standing abuse or neglect by the biological parent(s). Moreover, the older child probably experienced one or more moves from foster-home placements prior to the court's action and prior to the adoptive placement. Such disruptions in a child's life make successful attachment and bonding even more difficult.

The special needs child

The adoption of a child with special needs (e.g., a child with a mental illness or severe behavioral problems, a child with a missing limb) presents the adoptive parents with a special set of challenges, especially in the areas of parenting skills and in accessing and paying for medical care and other treatment, as well as educational services needed by the child.

The foster child

Child welfare and child development specialists have documented the deleterious effects of having to move a child from one home to another. Clearly, multiple placements should be avoided but for a variety of reasons this is not always possible. The term *fos-adopt placement* refers to the placement of a child with foster parents who will legally adopt this child if the court eventually decides to terminate the parents' rights and legally free the child for adoption. A fos-adopt placement has the advantage of preventing multiple placements prior to child's adoption. However, with such a placement there can be no assurance that the court will decide to free the child for adoption. The judge might instead decide to return the child to her or his bio-parents or place the child with relatives.

In most states some type of *adoption subsidy* will be available to adoptive parents who adopt a child from the foster-care system. The subsidy may take the form of direct financial assistance, eligibility for Medicaid, respite care, home modifications, legal assistance, and so forth.

The Native American child

When working with Native American families regarding adoption, the social worker should be aware of the unique provisions of the Indian Child Welfare Act. This act is intended to protect Native American culture by giving tribes a role in deciding any adoptions and the placement of Native American children. Usually, placement with members of the child's tribe is given priority over placement with non-Indian families.

International adoptions

Similar to the preference for in-tribe adoptions for Native American children in the United States, in-country adoptions are preferred by most countries. Countries must balance the desire to retain its children within its culture against the possibility of an improved quality of life for the child. The laws regarding the severing of parental rights for the purpose of foreign adoption vary considerably from country to country and may even vary from year to year within any country. When an international adoption is being considered, the specific laws and regulations of each country must be carefully examined.

In sum, the adoptive experience creates a distinct form of family that has special challenges for both the child and the parents. There must be a realignment of emotional attachments that will be negotiated and tested until the new family patterns are firmly established. The social worker should play an important role in helping the adoptive parents anticipate these challenges and plan to address them when they arise.

Selected Bibliography

Dore, Martha, ed. *The Post-Adoption Experience: Adoptive Families' Service Needs and Service Outcomes.* Washington, DC: Child Welfare League of America, 2006.

Freundich, Madelyn. *Adoption Ethics, Volume 3: The Impact of Adoption on Members of the Triad.* Washington, DC: Child Welfare League of America, 2000.

Gibbons, Judith L., and Karen Smith Rotabi. *Intercountry Adoption: Policies, Practices, and Outcomes.* Burlington, VT: Ashgate, 2012.

Hart, Angie, and Barry Loukock. *Developing Adoption Support and Therapy: New Approaches for Practice.* Philadelphia: Jessica Kingsley, 2004.

Hughes, Daniel. *Facilitating Developmental Attachment: The Road to Emotional Recovery and Behavioral Change in Foster and Adopted Children.* Oxford, England: Rowman and Littlefield, 1997.

Javier, Rafael A., Amanda L. Baden, Frank A. Biafora, and Alina Camacho-Gingerich. *The Handbook of Adoption: Implications for Researchers, Practitioners, and Families.* Thousand Oaks, CA: Sage, 2007.

MacLeod, Jean, and Sheen Macrae, eds. *Adoption Parenting.* Warren, NJ: EMK Press, 2007.

15.22 THE CLIENT WHO IS AN IMMIGRANT OR REFUGEE

A significant number of the people in need of health and human services have the designation of being an immigrant or refugee, thus a social worker must acquire at least a basic knowledge of the problems they face and how their special status might affect access and eligibility for human services.

The United States has been described as a country of immigrants and refugees. Nearly all U.S. citizens have a family genealogy that leads back to another nation and culture. Many people reading this book have parents, grandparents, or great-grandparents who were born in another country. Throughout its history, the United States has been a sought-after destination for persons migrating from countries that have fewer freedoms and opportunities. The United States has been a safe haven for those who sought escape from political and religious oppression and from other forms of injustice.

The rich immigrant history of the United States belies the challenges actually experienced by many who enter the United States as immigrants or refugees. Whether from Europe, Africa, Asia, or parts of the Western Hemisphere, these individuals commonly experience personal, social, and economic problems because of the inherent difficulty of adapting to a new culture; many lack language facility and/or job skills relevant to the American economy. Many live in or near poverty. In addition, some encounter increasing hostility because segments of society perceive newcomers as a threat and disruption to the status quo, an added competition for jobs and housing, and an additional tax burden. Social workers often feel caught between a grudging public that wants to deny services to the new arrivals and the immigrants and refugees themselves who often face extraordinary problems and clearly need the help of educational, health, and social programs.

THE IMMIGRANT/REFUGEE POPULATION

Based on data from the "Current Population Survey" by the U.S. Census Bureau (2012, pp. 2, 5), the foreign-born population in the United States had reached a total of 40.2 million persons by 2010. Included in this population were approximately 14.9 million naturalized citizens; 12.4 million currently legal permanent residents; 1.7 million legal temporary residents. In addition there were 11.2 million unauthorized migrants—some entering clandestinely or with fraudulent documents and others overstaying their visas. Among the foreign-born population 53.1 percent were from Latin American and the Caribbean area (i.e., 29 percent from Mexico and 24.1 percent from other Latin American countries), 28.2 percent from Asian countries, 12.1 percent from Europe, 4 percent from Africa, and .5 percent from other areas. Over one-half of this population was located in the states of California, New York, Texas, and Florida.

Social workers are particularly concerned with various social factors experienced by the foreign-born population when compared to the U.S. native population. The U.S. Census Bureau (2012, pp. 16–21) found the foreign-born population to have higher labor force participation, particularly in service and blue-collar jobs; less formal education; lower median income; less likely to be covered by health insurance; and higher rates of poverty.

The term *immigrant* refers to any person who voluntarily leaves one country in order to permanently settle in another country. However, as part of an effort to limit the allocation of resources to immigrants, various laws and regulations contain additional distinctions and definitions. Some immigrants, for example, have been declared *legal permanent residents* as a means of recognizing those who have legally entered the country through the existing structure. Congress has established quotas for the maximum number of immigrants from each country, facilitating the entry of those who have certain job skills or close ties to family members already living in the United States. Legal permanent residents can, after a period of time and a demonstration that they possess knowledge of U.S. law and culture, become naturalized citizens. The average family income of legal permanent residents is comparable to native families and the 18- to 24-year-old youth are slightly more likely than resident youth to attend college (Pew, 2005). This part of the immigrant population, then, is unlikely to make more of a demand on human services than other U.S. residents.

Some persons receive permission to temporarily enter the United States to attend school or perform certain needed jobs. When the visas of these *temporary legal residents* (also known as *nonimmigrants*) expire, they must return to their homelands. Generally speaking, this segment of the immigrant population has only limited income and few benefits. Social workers may meet persons from this group in hospitals and clinics, mental health centers, schools, and in child welfare agencies (Garrett and Herman, 2006).

People who have entered the country illegally—that is, without meeting the immigration requirements—fare rather badly in the United States. These *unauthorized immigrants* tend to be young, have limited education, live in crowded housing, and yet have high employment rates in farming, cleaning, construction, and food preparation jobs. These families have low income ($27,400 per year), 39.9 percent of the children live in poverty, and 53 percent have no health coverage (Pew, 2005). Although taxes are withheld from their paychecks and they pay sales taxes, these unauthorized immigrants must live under the radar of government scrutiny, are not eligible for Temporary Assistance for Needy Families (TANF) and most other government programs, have few legal rights, and risk deportation at any time (400,000 are deported each year). For social workers, this population is difficult to serve. Many of the usual health and welfare resources are not accessible due to the legal status of such clients. Moreover, unauthorized immigrants often are reluctant to ask for services due to the risk of deportation if their status is discovered.

The Personal Responsibility and Work Opportunity and Reconciliation Act of 1996, referred to as PRWORA, resulted in denying most public benefits to nondocumented immigrants. Specifically, that federal law bars most immigrants from receiving food stamps and Supplemental Security Income (SSI) and also blocks use of "federal means-tested benefits" for five years from their date of arrival in the United States, including TANF, Medicaid, and the Child Health Insurance Program (CHIP).

In addition, PRWORA gives states the option to deny immigrants who arrived in the United States prior to August 22, 1996, from receiving TANF, Medicaid, and services under the Social Security Block Grant. It also allows individual states the right to bar immigrants who arrived in the United States after August 22, 1996, from TANF and Medicaid, following the mandatory five-year ban. This federal legislation, in effect, denies unauthorized immigrants access to all federal public benefits, and grants to the states the legal right to discriminate through restrictive eligibility criteria for federal, state, and locally funded social services.

Refugees enter the United States under a different set of circumstances. They have been victims of oppressive conditions in their home countries and have fled persecution, usually without time to gain legal immigration status or to plan for the disposition and transfer of their property and financial resources. Often, families are not able to escape together and may temporarily relocate in one or more countries before finally arriving at their final destination. Refugee status provides a temporary legal means of entering the United States and can be a first step toward becoming a legal immigrant. Social work practice with refugee populations requires that practitioners explore client problems from two interrelated dimensions: (1) issues originating from the individual's perceptions and interpretations that are a result of culture, values, or "ethnic reality" influences and (2) the aftereffects of the individual's migration journey and reception by the host country.

Because of federal legislation such as the Refugee Act of 1980, most refugees are eligible for public health and human services programs, including cash and medical assistance, social services, and preventive health services. A social worker should be alert to the possibility that other organizations and social agencies working with an individual who is a refugee may not understand his or her cultural background and special immigration status and might have policies and procedures that unwittingly deny their services to refugees (see Item 8.8). In such a situation, interagency negotiation or perhaps client advocacy or class advocacy may be necessary (see Items 13.17 and 13.32). When working with refugees, social workers need to be especially sensitive to the interplay of such factors as the client's ethnicity, religion, nationality, legal and immigration status, age, gender, family context and characteristics, education, economic situation, and acceptance in the community (Puig, 2001).

GUIDELINES FOR ASSISTING IMMIGRANTS AND REFUGEES

Depending on the social worker's job responsibility and agency context, a worker may have a role in assisting individuals and families in planning a migration or escaping as a refugee to a different country; the social worker might also assist those who have entered the country in successfully resettling and adapting to life in the United States.

- *Migration.* When clients are preparing to migrate, social workers should help them focus on several concerns. For example, clients should be helped to address the probable economic and social impact on the family members who leave, as well as on those staying behind. Will there be a loss of income? Can they cope with the emotional pain of a separation and loneliness? Can they successfully adjust to a strange culture and new environment? Can they negotiate a language barrier? Is it safe to make this journey? How can they stay in communication with family and friends? Might this migration require detainment in a refugee camp? Does the migration require waiting for an official decision by the foreign government? If so, how long will the wait be, and what financial and other resources will be needed during the wait for an official decision? What if the person is refused entry?

- *Resettlement.* When clients are new to this country, social workers should help them adjust to the new environment and learn how to secure employment, housing, health care, social relationships, and so on. In addition, social workers should help clients examine such issues as their *acculturation* (i.e., changes in beliefs toward those of the host society), *assimilation* (i.e., the degree of adoption of the values, norms, and behaviors that dominate the society), and *adaptation* (i.e., the ability to adjust one's way of life to fit into the new country). More specifically, workers should help clients consider and address possible discrepancies between their expectations and reality, the degree of stress encountered throughout the migration experience, and the effects on friends and loved ones left behind. Some other factors that social workers should help clients consider as possible impediments to or supports for successful adjustment to the new culture include the following:
  - Language and the individual's degree of bilingualism
  - Differences in expected housing or living arrangements between the cultures
  - Variations in work patterns and expectations by employers
  - The degree of commonality between values and social norms of the old and new cultures and societies
  - The availability of cultural mediators or teachers for new arrivals

- Corrective feedback (positive and negative) needed to assist adaptation
- Tension between adapting to a new environment while holding on to important elements of the original culture
- The degree of similarity or dissimilarity in physical appearance with the dominant population groups in the culture

- *Guiding the Path to Naturalization.* Both legal permanent residents and refugees may require the assistance of the social worker in attaining naturalization. Typically, the social worker helps by informing the person(s) of the naturalization process and assisting in making connections to resources that help accomplish the various steps of the process. The requirements for *naturalization* (the process of awarding U.S. citizenship to a person after birth) include the following. The individual must:

  - Be at least 18 years of age
  - Have resided continuously in the United States for at least five years (three years for the spouse of a U.S. citizen)
  - Have demonstrated good moral character as determined by the absence of conviction of any criminal offenses
  - Be able to read, write, and speak English well enough to understand commonly used English words and phrases, and
  - Demonstrate the ability to pass a citizenship exam in U.S. government and history

Selected Bibliography

Balgopal, Pallassana, ed. *Social Work Practice with Immigrants and Refugees.* New York: Columbia University Press, 2000.

Garrett, Kendra J., and W. Randolph Herman. "Foreign-Born Students in Baccalaureate Social Work Programs: Meeting the Challenges." *The Journal of Baccalaureate Social Work,* 12 (Fall 2006): 24–38.

Pew Hispanic Center. "Unauthorized Migrants: Numbers and Characteristics." www.pewhispanic.org/files/reports/46.pdf. June 14, 2005.

Puig, Maria. "Organizations and Community Intervention Skills with Hispanic Americans." In *Culturally Competent Practice: Skills, Interventions, and Evaluations.* Edited by Rowena Fong and Sharlene Furuto. Boston: Allyn and Bacon, 2001, pp. 269–284.

U.S. Bureau of Census. *Foreign-Born Population in the United States, 2012.* http://www.census.gov/prod/2012pubs/acs-19.pdf

Tartakovsky, Eugene, ed. *Immigration: Policies, Challenges, and Impact.* New York: Nova, 2013.

Zimmerman, Wendy, and Tumlin, Karen C. *Patchwork Policies: State Assistance for Immigrants under Welfare Reform.* Washington, DC: Urban Institute, 1999.

15.23 THE CLIENT OR COMMUNITY EXPERIENCING AN EMERGENCY OR DISASTER

Natural disasters and catastrophic events have the potential to disrupt whole communities and inflict death, injury, trauma, and financial hardship on large numbers of people. Examples include earthquakes, floods, hurricanes, tornadoes, forest fires, airline crashes, terrorist attacks, spills of toxic chemicals, and war-related invasions and bombings.

The defining characteristics of a **disaster** are that it affects many people simultaneously and that its scale requires a highly organized and disciplined emergency response by a range of governmental and private organizations. The roles and activities of social workers at the site of a disaster must fit within an organized rescue and emergency response—one characterized by a military type of decision making and coordinating structure. The leaders of emergency response organizations will have certain objectives and priorities and these will determine what types of human services are most needed and when, where, and to whom they will be provided. In the immediate aftermath of a disaster, the highest priorities are the following:

- Rescue or evacuate people in danger, provide medical treatment to the injured, prevent an outbreak of contagious diseases through proper care of the dead, and inoculations.
- Address the immediate physical needs of the survivors by providing shelter, water, food, blankets, cots, toilets, and the like.
- Maintain public order to prevent panic, looting, and riots. (This requires police or military units.)

After these priorities have been addressed, the emergency response organization will attempt to deal with the psychological, social, and spiritual needs of the survivors by dispatching mental health, social services, and pastoral personnel.

INDIVIDUAL AND FAMILY RESPONSES

How an individual responds to a disaster is related, in part, to the nature of the disaster and whether he or she had time to prepare for what was coming. For example, people who have lost their homes to a flood, hurricane, or forest fire will usually have had a day or two of advance warnings and some opportunity to plan an escape, save some possessions, and share their fears with family and friends. By contrast, an earthquake, terrorist bombing, or plane crash is a complete surprise and much more disorienting. Those exposed to a disaster or catastrophic event will experience some or all of the following:

- Overwhelming feelings of shock, fear, horror, and grief
- Preoccupation the sights and sounds of persons with severe injuries, people dying, and corpses
- Preoccupation with what they have lost, such as a loved one, a house, important papers, pets, and other possessions
- Worry and fear that they may never be able to reestablish a normal life or manage financially
- Feeling that they survived at the expense of those who died (i.e., survivor guilt)
- Feelings of helplessness and a loss of trust, self-confidence, and control

Responses to a disaster often unfold in three stages: impact, recoil, and post-trauma. During the first stage, *acute impact*, people are just absorbing the reality of what has happened. During this initial phase, which usually lasts for up to a few hours, people respond in a variety of ways, particularly when some are still in danger. A few survivors manage to remain surprisingly calm, make rational decisions, and care for themselves and others, but most will be in a state of emotional shock and disorientation. They will experience intense fear and anxiety and have physical symptoms such as sweating, trembling, and stomach upset. They are, however, able to communicate and follow the instructions given by emergency personnel. Of all those caught up in the disaster, a small percentage will be hysterical or paralyzed by their fear, unable to make rational choices and will behave in ways that are dangerous to themselves and others.

During the second phase, the *recoil phase*, survivors realize more clearly what they have been through. Typically, this phase begins several hours after the disaster has hit. At this point, many of the survivors are in a state of emotional exhaustion and many will break down and weep. Many will have an intense need to talk about their experience. Attention must be given to meeting the immediate needs for clean drinking water, food, shelter, and sleeping arrangements. Many will need help to gain access to communication networks so they can contact worried relatives and friends, help replacing critical items such as prescription medications and eyeglasses, and help securing the items needed for basic personal hygiene. Mental health counseling and crisis intervention work should begin in this phase (see Item 13.14).

The third phase of adjustment to a disaster or catastrophic event is termed the *post-trauma phase*. The major challenges faced by individuals and families are grieving for their losses, rebuilding their lives, and reestablishing ordinary and predictable patterns of living. This phase may last for months, years, or the rest of a person's life, depending in part on the adequacy of the crisis intervention services (see Item 15.17).

COMMUNITY RESPONSES

Following a disaster whole communities typically move through four rather predicable phases: heroism, honeymoon, disillusionment, and reconstruction. The *heroism phase* occurs begins soon after the disaster has hit. At this time the people of the community will usually bond together, provide mutual support, and display cooperative behavior. Former divisions of social and economic class, race, and ethnicity are set aside. During this phase, people often experience a positive sense of community and belonging. They take great pride in how they have been helpful to each other and in how well they are working together.

During a second phase, the *honeymoon*, the community feels hopeful and confident that it can and will recover and perhaps become even stronger than before. Prior conflicts, tensions, political disputes, and power struggles within the community are temporarily forgotten.

The honeymoon gradually gives way to a sense of disappointment, known as the *disillusionment phase.* At this point, the people of the community recognize the enormity and complexity of rebuilding. Typically, the available emergency relief programs are time limited and provide much less than what people need or expected. Program limitations and the associated eligibility rules and regulations may elicit anger and a sense of unfairness. It is during this phase that former community conflicts and divisions resurface and people begin to fragment into competing groups. Rumors and misinformation are special problems during this phase. Thus, community meetings that disseminate accurate information are critically important.

Eventually, the community moves beyond its disillusionment and enters the long and difficult phase of *reconstruction*. Some communities are successful in rebuilding after a disaster, whereas others never fully recover. Among the variables that affect a community's capacity for and level of recovery are the extent of the destruction, the community's economic base, the community's prior level of cohesion, the availability of needed resources, and leadership.

GUIDELINES FOR A DISASTER RESPONSE

The following guidelines will help social workers respond to the human needs and problems created by a disaster or catastrophic event:

- Representatives of human services agencies and social work organizations, such as the National Association of Social Workers (NASW), should be involved in local and statewide disaster-planning activities. In order to provide appropriate services at the time of a disaster, social workers and agencies must understand how emergency and disaster relief organizations will respond and function. And long before a disaster occurs, each agency should have formulated a plan as to how it can and will respond and how it will coordinate its work with the emergency response organization and with disaster relief organizations such as the American Red Cross. Social workers who expect to work at the site of a disaster must first secure the proper authorization from those directing and coordinating the emergency response.

- In the first hours and perhaps days following a disaster, the collection of accurate information is of critical importance to rescue operations and other emergency responses. It is important to identify who is still missing and who has been killed or injured. Also, it is important to document where each survivor is now located (e.g., whether the person was taken to a shelter, transferred to a hospital). Having accurate and complete information will reduce the level of confusion, facilitate communication between the survivors and their worried relatives and friends, and allow for the reunification of families.

- Certain individuals will require special attention, even if they have escaped physical injury. This includes young children, the elderly, those with a physical or mental illness or disability, and those without access to family or a social support network. Because children are especially vulnerable to turmoil and social disruption, they should not be separated from their families at times of crisis. If at all possible, families should be evacuated as units and housed together in emergency shelters.

- Information and referral services are especially important in the months that follow a disaster. Thus, social workers in contact with survivors should be familiar with the state and federal disaster assistance programs and related agencies that may provide direct money grants, low-cost loans, temporary housing, and other resources. Regularly scheduled informational meetings with the people affected by the disaster can prevent the formation of destructive rumors and help them keep abreast of actions and plans by disaster relief organizations.

- For every individual who might die in a disaster, hundreds of survivors must face the loss of a loved one—as well as cope with the loss of property and possessions, the loss of their job because their place of work was destroyed, and a fundamental disruption to their usual way of life. Many who live through a disaster will experience adjustment problems and psychological symptoms for many months and even years after the event. Some will develop post-traumatic stress disorder (see Item 13.14). Increased levels of financial problems, depression and anxiety, suicide and homicide, domestic violence, problem drinking and drug use, psychosomatic illness, poor job performance, and the like can be anticipated, as well. Thus, mental health and social services agencies should formulate plans to address an increased need for their services and engage in case finding and active outreach to those who may need them.

- When possible and feasible, the survivors of a disaster that has caused extensive property damage should be directly involved in the cleanup and rebuilding effort. This puts them in direct contact with other survivors and becomes a vehicle for offering emotional and social support. In addition, the cleanup effort can sometimes provide needed jobs and income and also helps the people regain a sense of control and self-confidence.

- Be alert to the possibility that a professional or emergency worker may develop a condition known as *vicarious trauma*. After repeated exposures to people who have been traumatized, social workers and other helpers may themselves develop symptoms of trauma, such as intrusive thoughts and images, sleeplessness, bystander guilt, and feelings of vulnerability, helplessness, self-doubt, and rage. Workers who previously suffered severe emotional trauma and those who are inexperienced in disaster-related work are especially vulnerable to developing these symptoms. Ongoing self-care, including the opportunity to talk about one's experiences and feelings and receive reassurance and support from other professionals, is of critical importance in helping social workers cope with the stress of disaster-related work.

Selected Bibliography

Halpern, James, and Mary Tramontin. *Disaster Mental Health*. Independence, KY: Cengage, 2007.

Miller, Joshua. *Psychosocial Capacity Building in Response to Disasters*. New York: Columbia University Press, 2012.

Ritchie, Elspeth, Patricia Watson, and Matthew Friedman, eds. *Interventions Following Mass Violence and Disasters*. New York: Guilford, 2006.

Rosenfeld, Lawrence, Joanne Caye, Mooli Lahad, and Robin Gurwitch. *When Their World Falls Apart: Helping Families and Children Manage the Effects of Disasters,* 2nd ed. Washington, DC: NASW, 2010.

Webber, Jane, and J. Barry Mascari. *Terrorism, Trauma, and Tragedies: A Counselor's Guide to Preparing and Responding,* 3rd ed. Alexander, VA: American Counseling Association, 2010.

16

Techniques for Sustaining Social Work Practice

LEARNING OBJECTIVES

At the conclusion of this chapter, the reader should be prepared to:

- Discuss the expectations of a social worker to be proficient in taking competency and licensing exams, as well as being knowledgeable of other requirements for becoming a competitive job applicant.
- Exhibit accurate self-perception regarding factors that may affect a social worker's practice decisions including one's personal values, experience of burn-out or compassion fatigue, and sensitivity to the unequal power relationships with clients.
- Recognize precautions a social worker should take to prevent or address legal suits regarding malpractice or negligence, as well as guidelines for testifying or providing expert testimony in a court of law.
- Discuss the importance of obtaining sound supervision and making use of mentoring by an experienced social worker during a social work career.
- Recognize that a professional social worker is expected to be a good consumer of and also a contributor to social work knowledge and should possess skill in both activities.
- Describe the challenges of social workers assuming leadership roles to improve social conditions and achieve greater social justice, as well as to improve the social work image as perceived by the general public.

Social work is a demanding profession but also a rewarding one. However, the rewards are mostly intrinsic. By selecting social work as a career, one is virtually assured of never attaining wealth or prestige. Rather, social work is about caring, sharing, and social responsibility; these are not the values rewarded by our economic system that emphasizes individualism, competition, and the acquisition of things.

From its beginnings, the social work profession has demonstrated special concern for those who are powerless, stigmatized, and devalued—the people who most others tend to avoid or ignore. Because social workers encounter so many people who are desperate and in need, they see firsthand the inadequacy of available professional, agency, and societal resources. Social workers also frequently experience the anguish of knowing that no matter how hard they work, many people will not receive the services they need and deserve. This is a frustration with which social workers must learn to live.

Because many clients are economically poor, most social work jobs are within some type of human services organization. This chapter provides guidance for developing the needed skills for dealing with work-related tasks in these organizations. It offers background information on finding a social work job, taking competence exams, dealing with job-related stress, making use of and contributing to professional literature and making presentations, and serving in leadership roles. In addition, the chapter provides guidance on testifying in court, avoiding malpractice suits, addressing sexual misconduct, and developing mentoring relationships.

16.1 GETTING A SOCIAL WORK JOB

After a social worker has completed her or his professional education, the next task is to secure employment. That usually takes time and effort, as human services agencies are necessarily careful in their selection of staff to serve their clientele. (To examine this process from the viewpoint of the agency, see Item 10.13.)

The first step in finding employment is to identify the job openings. In most communities, several sources of information might be examined. Agencies will typically advertise their positions; thus, job seekers should read the classified advertisements in the local newspaper, visit agency websites, and watch for openings on bulletin boards. In addition, informal networks among professionals are an excellent source of information. Attending local NASW meetings is a good way to tap into the professional network in most communities.

Once an open position is located, the application materials must be prepared. An application typically has two parts: a cover letter and a professional resumé, although sometimes an application form must also be completed. The **cover letter** should focus on the particular job being applied for and stress the applicant's qualifications for that position. It should be approximately one page in length and must be carefully written with no spelling, punctuation, or grammatical errors. The letter should indicate that it and the resumé represent an application for the position, describe why the applicant is interested in that job, and discuss qualifications for the position. The cover letter is not the place to discuss salary expectations or reasons for leaving past jobs. Indicate that a list of references will be provided on request (unless the job announcement asks that references be supplied as part of the application). Be sure to obtain permission in advance from anyone named as a reference. The letter should be upbeat about the position for which one is applying.

The **professional resumé** is more generic than a cover letter and often the same resumé can be used when applying for several different positions. Basically, a resumé is an organized summary of one's professional qualifications and experience. Its purpose is to present the applicant's background in a manner that will persuade the employer to invite her or him for an interview. There is no prescribed format or style for a resumé. Rather, use a creative approach to attract the attention of members of a screening committee who are responsible for selecting a few finalists from a large pool of applications; however, avoid being cute or clever. Often, photocopy shops provide layout consultation, have high-quality printers available, and can recommend easy-to-read fonts, making it relatively inexpensive to prepare an attractive resumé. In addition, many colleges or universities have offices that provide workshops and consultation to students in preparing job applications.

At a minimum, a resumé should include the following information; other items may be added at one's discretion:

- *Personal data.* Include your name, street address, email address, and a phone number where you can be easily reached to facilitate scheduling an interview.

- *Education.* Give the name of your degree(s), your major, the colleges or universities you attended, and graduation dates. List all schools you have attended (listing in reverse order) and possibly add grade-point average, honors, special projects, or any special skills or training that might be relevant to a social work job (e.g., computer savvy, foreign language competence).

- *Experience.* List employment in reverse order (i.e., beginning with your current or most recent job), giving the job title, name of organization, dates of employment, and job duties. It is also helpful to list any practicum and volunteer experience that might have contributed to your social work competencies.

- *Activities and interests.* Identify your professional interests as well as those that extend beyond social work. Note membership in professional organizations, your participation in various clubs or organizations and any offices held, and any hobbies or special interests.

- *References.* A statement such as "References Available on Request" is usually best. If a job announcement calls for references, they should be listed in the cover letter. This flexibility allows you to list the most appropriate references for each position. In general, the persons selected as references should be able to comment on your skills and might include a faculty member, a field instructor, and/or job supervisors or persons who supervised volunteer experiences. In many instances an agency will prefer to contact the references directly, so be sure to provide their telephone numbers and email addresses.

- *Other information.* It may be desirable to add other information such as publications and any unique experiences (e.g., Peace Corps volunteer) that may enhance your competence as a social worker.

If the application is successful, the applicant will be invited to an interview. Typically, the interview process will involve appearing before a panel of interviewers, although there will usually be some one-to-one discussions, as well. Many review panels will present the applicant with hypothetical situations or case vignettes and ask how he or she would handle the situation. The interviewing procedures used by government agencies are usually highly structured and many will require a written exam (see Item 16.2) in addition to oral interviews.

Preparation is essential. First, research the agency thoroughly. Know the services it offers, its target clientele, and something about its organizational structure and goals. This information might be obtained by stopping by the agency in advance to pick up informational materials, by visiting the agency's website, or by discussing the agency with other social workers in the community. Second, dress professionally and be as relaxed as possible during the interview process. Third, be prepared for questions about your personal and professional interests, as well as your preparation for the specific job duties.

Here are some examples of questions that are commonly asked in an interview:

- What are your qualifications for this job?
- What are your strengths? Your weaknesses?
- Why do you want this job?
- What are your career goals?
- Why should we hire you?
- As a social worker employed by this agency, how would you handle the following situation? (For example: A client tells you he plans to take his own life. How would you respond?)

Also be prepared with questions you would like to ask about the agency and the job. An interview is a two-way street—both the applicant and the agency are deciding if there is a good match between your skills and interests and the requirements of the job.

If offered the position, you will then negotiate the salary or other benefits. Before you accept the position, be sure that you understand the job description. Also, before accepting the position, you should (1) obtain a letter of appointment that states the starting salary, duties, and other pertinent information; and (2) review the agency's personnel manual to be sure that you understand the working conditions and benefits.

Selected Bibliography

Doelling, Carol. *Career Development: A Handbook for Job Hunting and Career Planning*, 2nd ed. Washington, DC: NASW, 2005.

Sidell, Nancy, and Denice Smiley. *Professional Communication Skills in Social Work*. Boston: Allyn and Bacon, 2008.

16.2 PREPARING FOR SOCIAL WORK COMPETENCY EXAMS

Test taking does not end when one secures a BSW or MSW degree. At some time in her or his career, most social workers will need to complete a competency examination. Passing an exam is often a part of applying for a job and/or a step in obtaining a sought-after credential, such as securing a state license to practice social work or becoming a private (independent) practitioner. Although occasionally oral exams are used as part of the job application process, state licensing exams are typically made up of multiple-choice questions on a paper-and-pencil or computerized test.

Examinations developed at the agency or state level typically focus on the knowledge and skills relevant to the performance of a specific job. For example, if a state agency test is part of an application process for securing a job as a child protection worker, the exam questions will focus on such matters as relevant state laws, testifying in court, signs of abuse and neglect, understanding child development, and methods of working with abusive and neglecting parents. By contrast, the licensing exams are constructed for statewide or nationwide use, such as those developed by the Association of Social Work Boards (ASWB), and focus more broadly on the range of activities typically performed by social workers regardless of practice setting. Four ASWB tests are available: BSW, MSW, advanced generalist MSW, and the clinical MSW.

Although data is not available on the pass rates for state or agency developed tests, the 2012 pass rates for persons taking ASWB's national licensing tests were: Bachelor's level, 77.1 percent; Master's level, 83.6 percent; Advanced Generalist, 63.3%; and Clinical, 76.3 percent (ASWB Website, 2013). Because the failure to pass a test can prevent a person from qualifying for employment, the courts have ruled that the test questions must be representative of the work required for the typical jobs at the professional level being tested. In order to write relevant test questions and construct a fair test, a formal research effort is periodically conducted that identifies the frequency and importance of tasks performed by social workers. This task analysis provides a "blueprint" for each exam and determines the percentage of the exam questions that will focus on a specific topic or content area. Although a much more detailed list of content for each exam appears on the ASWB website (www.ASWB.org), the following weights reflect the content on each exam (slightly adjusted to make the areas compatible).

Percent of Content Tested on Exam	BSW	MSW	Adv. Gen.	Clinical
• Human Development and Behavior in the Environment	14%	18%	10%	22%
• Issues in Diversity	7	7	5	6
• Assessment and Diagnosis	20	11	24	16
• Direct and Indirect Practice Clinical: Psychopathology & Clinical	21	22	16	16
• Communication	10	7	7	8
• Professional Relationships Clinical: Therapeutic Relationship	5	5	5	7
• Professional Values and Ethics	13	11	12	10
• Supervision/Administration/Policy Clinical: Supervision, Consultation, Staff Development	3	8	6	4
• Practice Evaluation and Utilization of Research	2	2	4	1
• Service Delivery	5	9	11	5
• Clinical Practice and Management	–	–	–	5

When preparing for an exam, the social worker should allocate his or her study time and effort somewhat in the proportion to the number of questions expected in each content area. For example, given the above percentages, one could anticipate that on a 150-question BSW exam there will be 30 questions (.20 × 150 = 30) focusing on understanding of biological, psychological, and societal factors related to human development and people's behavior in the environment (i.e., concepts related to individuals, families, groups, organizations, and communities). Note that there will be 170 questions on the exam to be answered within four hours, but 20 are being pretested for future exams and will not count in your score.

Test questions fall into three categories: recall, application, and problem solving. At the *recall level* (e.g., "Which of the following is the *most accurate* definition of domestic violence?" or "Who was the author of the eight stages of human development?"), the respondent is asked to remember information about the topic. However, *application-level* questions (e.g., "If a school social worker suspects a child has been abused, her or his *first* action should be: _____" or "Which of the following would be the *most effective* technique when presenting numerical data at a professional conference?") expect the respondent to know the information and use it to inform a practice decision. In the *problem-solving questions* (e.g., "Which of the following criterion *best* differentiates between persons with low income from those who live in poverty?" or "Select from the following cultural competencies the one that is *most immediately* applicable when working with an immigrant family that is experiencing…"), knowledge, practice experience, and critical thinking are required to select the correct answer. In general, expect the exams tied to lower levels of required education to have more recall questions and the clinical exam to have more problem-solving questions.

When answering questions, it is instructive to understand the language and concepts used in developing the questions. When questions are composed, the item writer begins by identifying the content area the question is intended to address. Next, a *stem* or the stimulus for the answers (i.e., the opening statement) is prepared. It is important to read and think about the stem very carefully when answering the question, as it provides the focus for selecting an answer. Look for such words as *most, first, best*, and others that emphasize what the question is looking for and that will clue you to address frequency, sequence, priority, and so on in selecting the correct answer. The correct answer is known as the *key*. When the question is pre-tested, the key should be most frequently selected and also chosen by those who score well on the overall test; otherwise the question is not used as a test question. Finally, the item writer prepares (usually) three distractors. *Distractors* are answers that may seem plausible if the test-taker is guessing or not truly knowledgeable about the topic, and is clearly not as good an answer as the key. When taking an exam, it is best to read the stem and answer "A" together, then read the stem again and answer "B," and so on through the several answers. By that time you should be fully familiar with the stem and its intent and should be able to rule out answers that are clearly not the best answer. Typically, that will leave only one or two answers in consideration. This is the time to apply critical thinking skills (see Chapter 7) to work out which answer you will select as your final choice.

There are two schools of thought regarding when one ideally should take such exams. One position is that a person should sit for these exams as soon as possible after completing a social work degree program—while the content of that education is still fresh and the person is accustomed to taking exams. This is especially true when preparing for the bachelor's and master's exams because these tests have a greater proportion of recall and application items. The alternative view suggests waiting until the social worker has more experience. With a year or two of practice experience, one learns a great deal about how various concepts play out in work with people and agencies. Thus, the more experienced worker is better able to apply critical thinking when answering the test questions.

The *NASW News* usually carries advertisements for schools of social work or entrepreneurial companies that offer written materials, workshops, flash cards, and other tools for licensing exam preparation. Like most marketed items, it is difficult to judge the merits of these offerings and sometimes they are quite expensive. A useful and not too costly preparation source can be found at www.aswb.org, the website for the Association of Social Work Boards (ASWB). At this site study materials and practice exams are available that also provide the reasons the key is considered correct and the distractors are not the *best* answers for the questions. Also, the ASWB maintains a list of recommended books (usually textbooks) that one might review in preparation for each level of licensing exam.

Selected Bibliography

Association of Social Work Boards, website, http://www.aswb.org.

DeAngelis, Donna. "Social Work Licensing Examinations in the United States and Canada: Development and Administration." In *Social Workers' Desk Reference,* 2nd ed. Edited by Albert R. Roberts. New York: Oxford University Press, 2009.

_____ . "Licensing." In *Encyclopedia of Social Work,* 20th ed. Edited by Terry Mizrahi and Larry E. Davis. New York: Oxford University Press, 2008.

16.3 DEVELOPING SELF-AWARENESS

Professional social workers emphasize the need to develop self-insight and self-understanding in order to serve others effectively. The term **self-awareness** refers to an accurate perception of one's own beliefs, values, attitudes, and habits and how they might influence worker's decisions and practice behavior. Efforts to develop self-awareness should focus on identifying both strengths and limitations. Many of the strengths that are of importance in social work practice are discussed in other parts of this book. Chapter 3, for example, describes the qualities of courage, compassion, hopefulness, empathy, genuineness, warmth, creativity, imagination, flexibility, energy, good judgment, knowledge, and so on (also see Chapters 2 and 8). The worker can increase his or her self-awareness through activities such as the following:

- Keep a daily journal or log that helps you sort out and think about successful and unsuccessful practice activities and the practice situations that are especially upsetting and distressful.
- Ask for constructive criticism. Seek feedback and evaluations from trusted and experienced colleagues familiar with your performance, responsibilities, and agency setting.
- Obtain and then study audio or video recordings of your interviews, group sessions, and other work-related meetings. (*Note:* Secure permission from others before making such a recording; clients should sign a written authorization.)
- Practice and evaluate your performance in simulated role-play sessions that focus on or act out situations that are especially difficult.

Many individuals are drawn to the helping professions because they believe the problems they have faced in life give them a special understanding or sensitivity to the problems of others. Indeed, life's problems can be a powerful teacher and provide a degree of empathy that others may not have. However, this will be the case only after one has honestly examined those experiences and successfully worked through the residual painful memories and feelings associated with them.

When a social worker becomes aware of some personal characteristic or limitation that interferes with his or her ability to provide services to clients, he or she must be willing to correct the problem or, if change is not possible, to seek a practice setting where this factor will not have a negative impact on clients. Below are some of the factors that can interfere with the formation of a positive professional helping relationship and client service:

- *Personal issues.* To a considerable degree, our core beliefs and attitudes toward people and toward life in general have been shaped by childhood and family experiences. Most people carry a certain amount of emotional baggage into their adult lives, including unresolved parent–child conflicts, prejudice, aftereffects of traumatic events, and so on. Sometimes this baggage is carried to the workplace, where it has a negative impact on clients and work performances—for example:

- Preoccupation with personal problems, resulting in an inability to give one's full attention to the client
- Inability to control one's reactions or exercise self-discipline when in an emotionally charged situation or when under the ordinary pressures associated with social work practice
- Inability to demonstrate warmth, empathy, and genuine caring for clients served by the agency
- Inability to work cooperatively with persons in positions of authority (e.g., judges, physicians, administrators, supervisors)
- Difficulty separating personal experience (e.g., having been a victim of child abuse, growing up with alcoholic parents) from the concerns and problems presented by clients
- Defensiveness that prevents a critical examination of one's job performance
- Avoiding certain clients or especially difficult tasks
- Personalization of client anger and frustrations (i.e., inability to maintain an appropriate level of objectivity)
- Imposing one's values, political beliefs, religious beliefs, or lifestyle on clients
- Inability to respect the religious beliefs and cultural values of a client
- Alcohol or drug abuse
- Misuse or abuse of one's authority or position (see Item 10.11)
- Extreme level of shyness or nonassertiveness resulting in an inability to express opinions and engage in the give-and-take of client work, peer supervision, and teamwork

- *Appearance, clothing, and grooming.* To a large extent, people form their impressions of others—especially the powerful first impression—on the basis of appearance. Thus, the social worker must pay attention to his or her clothing and grooming because it matters to clients and will affect how they respond to the worker and their utilization of agency services. Of course, what is offensive to one client may be acceptable to another, and what is appropriate dress in one agency setting may be inappropriate in another. The staff in a particular setting must make decisions on what is appropriate. Many agencies and most hospitals establish dress codes as a way of providing guidance to staff. When examining your appearance and its possible impact on clients, remember these guidelines:

- Some choices of clothing, hairstyle, perfume, makeup, body decoration, or jewelry may offend or distract clients served by the agency.
- Deficiencies in grooming and personal hygiene may offend clients.
- Uncovered infections, skin irritations, frequent coughing, and similar conditions may distract the client or cause him or her worry and anxiety.

- *Behaviors that devalue others.* Social work values dictate that every client should be treated with dignity and respect. The social worker must avoid behaviors that are disrespectful, including the following:

- Using words, phrases, or gestures that are in bad taste or known to offend clients and staff (e.g., cursing, sexual overtones)
- Telling sexist or ethnic jokes
- Discriminating or showing prejudice against particular client groups
- Making sarcastic, insulting, cruel, or disrespectful comments about clients

- *Distracting personal habits.* Most people have some undesirable mannerisms and habits that their friends and families have learned to accept. However, the social worker must be willing to modify habits that may annoy clients, such as:
  - Fidgeting, pencil tapping, knuckle cracking, nail biting
  - Pulling or twisting hair
  - Chewing gum or tobacco and smoking
  - Scowling, frowning, or other facial gestures that seem to express scorn
  - Excessive nervous laughter, frequent clearing of throat, or other distracting mannerisms

- *Difficulties in cognitive functioning.* A social worker must absorb information quickly and apply complex principles. A capacity for abstract thinking is essential. The following examples illustrate insufficient cognitive functioning:
  - Cognitive deficits that interfere with attention, memory, and judgment
  - Inability to explain the reasons behind one's judgments, conclusions, and decisions
  - Difficulty processing new information, drawing logical inferences, and solving problems
  - Lack of reading speed and comprehension needed to understand records and reports, agency policy, and professional books and journals

- *Difficulties in verbal communication.* The social worker's verbal communication must be understandable to clients and other professional persons. Problems such as these could hamper work with clients:
  - Mumbling, speaking inaudibly, loud or penetrating voice tones, halting or hesitant speech, rapid speech
  - Frequent use of slang not understood by or offensive to clients
  - Errors of grammar or awkward sentence construction that confuse clients
  - Inability to adjust vocabulary to client's age or educational level
  - Uncorrected vision or hearing problems

- *Problems in written communication.* Because so much of the social worker's service to a client involves the exchange of information with other professionals, the worker must be able to communicate in writing. If letters, reports, emails, and agency records are carelessly written and difficult to understand, those attempting to read them will be frustrated and conclude either that the worker does not care enough to communicate clearly or is incompetent. The worker's reputation and effectiveness is seriously damaged if the client or other professional persons form such negative impressions. Serious writing problems that merit correction include the following:
  - Inability to prepare letters, reports, and records that are understandable to clients, agency staff, and other professionals (see Chapter 9)
  - Not recognizing and correcting errors of spelling, grammar, and syntax
  - Difficulty selecting words that adequately express thoughts
  - Inability to write at a speed sufficient to manage required paperwork

- *Poor work habits.* Poor work habits may have a direct or indirect impact on the clients served by an agency. Here are some examples:
  - Being late for client appointments, team meetings, case conferences, and other scheduled events
  - Missing deadlines for the completion of written reports that are important to clients or agencies and professionals serving the client

- Incomplete or sloppy recordkeeping and documentation
- Lack of preparation for meetings with clients and other professionals
- Not following through on assignments or tasks
- Distracting other staff members or keeping them from their work
- Unwillingness to seek and utilize direction from a supervisor
- Blaming clients or others for one's own ineffectiveness; unwillingness to acknowledge mistakes or limitations of knowledge and skill
- Refusal to follow established agency policies and procedures
- Behaviors occurring outside work hours that draw negative attention and thereby lessen client and public respect for the social agency and/or the worker

In order to grow in self-awareness, we need to examine our values, beliefs, assumptions, and behavioral patterns. We must remember, however, that our most significant advancements in self-awareness will not come from self-scrutiny but rather are "gifts" from others, such as comments made by our clients, the constructive criticism offered by a supervisor, professional peers, and others who care about us and our performance as social workers.

Selected Bibliography

Fox, Raymond. *Elements of the Helping Process: A Guide for Clinicians*, 3rd ed. New York: Routledge, 2013.

Hurley, John, and Paul Linsley (eds.). *Emotional Intelligence in Health and Social Care: A Guide for Improving Human Relationships*. New York, Radcliffe, 2012.

16.4 AVOIDING COMPASSION FATIGUE AND STRESS MANAGEMENT

Job-related stress can have three sources. First, there is the stress that is simply a part of a particular job. Everyone placed in a high-stress job will feel stressed—it comes with the territory. Second, there is stress caused by a lack of skills necessary to do the job. For example, a particular job may not be stressful for most people, but will be for the individual who does not have the requisite knowledge and skill. Third, some individuals create their own stress because they have unrealistic expectations or take on an excessive number of responsibilities.

Every social worker responds to the demands of the profession and his or her job in a unique manner; some thrive while others grow weary. There are two especially maladaptive reactions to job stress: compassion fatigue and burnout. The term **compassion fatigue** (also known as *secondary trauma* and *vicarious trauma*) describes a set of reactions that may develop when a professional is helping persons who have just experienced some extremely traumatic event, such as an earthquake, train wreck, or terrorist bombing. The *symptoms* that arise in the helper include recurring images of the suffering and injured people, guilt over not being able to help certain victims, self-doubt, a dread of returning to work, anxiety, anger, difficulty sleeping, depression, and hypervigliance. The onset of those symptoms is relatively rapid and clearly connected with a particular event or experience. Efforts to treat this condition involve the opportunity to discuss in detail the distressing or frightening events with others who also experienced it, education about the phenomena of compassion fatigue, emotional support and reassurance, and individual counseling (see Item 15.23).

The term **burnout** refers to a state of physical, mental, and emotional exhaustion caused by an inability to adequately cope with the demands and stress of a job. A professional experiencing burnout often feels emotionally disconnected and numb, has lost interest in his or her job, dislikes going to work, is irritable and cynical, and treats clients in a routine and insensitive manner. Burnout develops gradually, often over a period of years. An affected professional may feel that something is not right about her or his job performance and attitude toward clients but usually does not recognize or acknowledge the problem. Counseling and perhaps a job change may be necessary to reverse burnout. Burnout is not inevitable; it can be prevented if the professional is committed to self-care and to developing a strategy for stress management. The following guidelines suggest ways to handle job-related stress:

- The key to preventing negative stress reactions is to find your proper niche in the world of work. There must be a good fit or match between you as a person and the demands of your job. As a social worker, you must feel positive about your chosen profession and feel that you are effective in what you do. Before stress reactions were studied as a problematic human condition, an unknown author wisely stated, "In order that people may be happy in their work, these three things are needed: they must be fit for it, they must not do too much of it, and they must have a sense of success in it."

- Examine the fit between your work and your values. Are you spending your time and energy on activities you consider important and worthwhile? For example, if you value relationships with your family and friends, are you making choices that enable you to be with them? On the other hand, if you find that your job is more important and exciting than your family life, then that too must be faced with honesty. As a general rule, people find time for what they really want to do and for that which they truly value. Part of stress management is to become clear about what you value.

- Make an honest attempt to recognize stress in your life. Listen to those who care about you for clues that you are under more stress than you realized (e.g., "You're so crabby when you get home," "You're not as much fun as you used to be," "You never go anywhere anymore," and "You look so tired"). Possible signs of dangerous levels of stress include frequent colds and sore throats, skin eruptions, persistent soreness in muscles and joints, frequent low-level headaches, inability to relax or sleep, fatigue, sluggishness that lingers from day to day, frequent stomach upset, weight loss, diarrhea or constipation, nervousness, depression, irritability, unexplained drop in job performance, and a loss of interest in what had been interesting hobbies and exciting activities.

- Regular exercise, proper nutrition, and adequate sleep help to reduce stress and build natural defenses against the harmful effects of stress. Take several simple and brief physical exercise breaks during the workday (e.g., take a walk at lunchtime, do some isometric exercises, or climb a few flights of stairs). Reduce or eliminate the use of alcohol, nicotine, caffeine, and other drugs. Obtain regular medical checkups. If you are having personal or family problems, seek help from trusted friends or professionals.

- A major source of stress is the feeling that your work and responsibilities are excessive and beyond your control. In such a situation, you must start making some changes or the problem will likely get worse. Learning to manage your time is of critical importance. Time management is, in effect, stress management. When we use our time wisely we accomplish more and are more effective, and that contributes to a feeling of satisfaction and achievement (see Item 9.6). Consult with experienced peers who seem to effectively manage their workload and enjoy what they do. Like a distance runner, set a pace in your work activity that you can maintain without wearing down. Arrange work activity so you will accomplish at least one really important thing each day, for this can produce a surprising amount of job satisfaction. It is usually more satisfying to have done a few things well rather than to have done many things poorly.

- Recognize that perfection is not required or possible in most work-related tasks. Avoid placing unrealistically high expectations on yourself and on others. Also, avoid dwelling on the negatives and on what is lacking in your work. Take time to enjoy the positives in both your personal and professional lives. Help yourself recover from setbacks by recalling your prior accomplishments and maintaining a realistic perspective on your disappointments.

- Build a support group of friends or colleagues with whom you are able to share your frustrations. Find enjoyable ways to spend time together—hike, visit a museum, eat out, see a movie, or travel together. Also, develop hobbies and outside interests that lead you into activities that are significantly different from what you do at work. Doing something that is new and different is like a mini-vacation.

"Building Support Networks" from 3rd edition

- Apply to yourself the techniques you use with clients. For example, when faced with a stressful interpersonal task, use behavioral rehearsal to reduce anxiety and build confidence (see Item 13.4). As a technique for handling your fears, try exaggerating them out of proportion. Exaggerating your fears to the point of being ludicrous may help you laugh at yourself and put your fear into perspective.

- Apply problem-solving and organizational change techniques to the stressors common to most work settings: including poor working conditions, unreasonable deadlines, heavy workloads, interruptions, and problems with co-workers and supervisors. Serious problems in a work environment require careful analysis and intervention. They will not go away without doing something about them!

"Coping with a Bureaucracy" from 8th edition

- Visitors to the United States observe that the lifestyle of its people is characterized by a fast pace, competition, materialism, and a coolness or emotional distance in human interactions. These characteristics also contribute to the stress we experience, but we are not often aware of their effect on us. Look for ways to simplify your life and slow its pace. For example, simplify your wardrobe and your meals so you have fewer decisions to make about what to wear and what and where to eat. Give up nonessential possessions and activities that demand your attention and consume your time but provide little in the way of joy and relaxation. Replace unpleasant things in your life with meaningful and positive relationships with family and friends.

Selected Bibliography

Cox, Kathleen, and Sue Steiner. *Self-Care in Social Work: A Guide for Practitioners, Supervisors, and Administrators.* Washington, DC: NASW Press, 2013.

Mathieu, Francoise. *The Compassion Fatigue Workbook: Creative Tools for Transforming Compassion Fatigue into Vicarious Traumatization.* New York: Routledge, 2011.

Meisinger, Sarah E. *Stories of Pain, Trauma, and Survival: A Social Worker's Experiences and Insights from the Field*. Washington, DC: NASW Press, 2009.

Rothschild, Babette. *Help for the Helper: The Psychophysiology of Compassion Fatigue and Vicarious Trauma*. New York: Norton, 2006.

16.5 DEALING WITH SEXUAL MISCONDUCT

The structure of professional relationships is inherently unequal, making clients vulnerable to exploitation. Clients enter these relationships in order to receive assistance from a competent professional and they trust the social workers to treat their needs and interests as primary. It is expected that the professional will avoid any misuse of this trust and will not exploit the client in any form (i.e., financial, sexual, or in any other way for personal gain). In addition to worker–client interactions, professional responsibility requires that any social worker in a position of power must avoid taking personal advantage of any relationships in a work situation. For example, a supervisor should not seek favors from a supervisee, an administrator should not take advantage of workers, and a teacher or a field instructor should not exploit a student.

Sexual misconduct is any unwelcome sexual advance, request for sexual favors, or other verbal or physical conduct of a sexual nature—either of a heterosexual or homosexual nature. There is an awareness that a potential for sexual exploitation in the human services is high. Consequently, professions take firm and punitive measures when sexual misconduct does occur. Section 1.09 of the *NASW Code of Ethics* (1999) is explicit in prohibiting sexual contact with clients or former clients, the relatives of clients, as well as not providing services to persons with whom the social worker has previously had a sexual relationship. In addition, Section 2.07 of the *NASW Code of Ethics* clearly prohibits sexually exploiting colleagues in a vulnerable position in the workplace.

It is important that human services agencies and universities placing students for internships in human services agencies have clear rules and guidelines related to sexual misconduct concerning student interactions with clients or former clients. Further, clients, family members of clients, and other professionals can file a complaint of sexual misconduct with the NASW as a violation of the *Code of Ethics*—potentially leading to disciplinary action against the worker or student.

In the workplace, sexual misconduct is termed **sexual harassment**. Federal law recognizes two forms of sexual harassment. One form, **quid pro quo harassment**, occurs when an employee is required to tolerate sexual harassment in order to obtain or keep his or her job or to receive a job benefit, salary increase, or promotion. Although a complaint can be filed related to a single incident, usually a successful outcome requires documentation of a consistent pattern of harassment.

The second form of workplace harassment, labeled **hostile work environment harassment**, relates to harassment at work that unreasonably interferes with the employee's work performance, or creates a hostile, abusive or offensive work environment. Such complaints should first be addressed within the organization. Depending on state law, if the person complaining is not satisfied, the process could advance to a complaint with the appropriate state agency or the federal Equal Employment Opportunity Commission.

STRATEGIES FOR PREVENTING AND ADDRESSING SEXUAL MISCONDUCT

At the *organizational level*, it is important to create agency policy that clearly prohibits sexual harassment and identifies procedures for making a complaint. That policy should be published in the agency's personnel manual, and the agency director should periodically post or circulate the statement. Regular training, too, helps sensitize all staff to the problem and can help prevent harassment.

At the *individual level*, if you feel that you are being harassed, you should first speak directly to the harasser, insisting that he or she stop the offensive behaviors. If you are not able to directly confront the harasser, an effective strategy is to send a letter that specifies the nature of the harassing incidents and when they occurred, how you were affected, and how the conduct should change in the future. If the harassment persists, it is advisable to keep a diary of events and a list of any witnesses, as well as consulting with other workers, informing your supervisor or the agency administrator, and seeking resolution using agency procedures. (*Note:* Some employers require an official complaint within 30 or 60 days of an incident.) If the situation is not resolved within the agency, consultation with a lawyer is suggested. Other options include contacting your state human rights commission or the U.S. Equal Employment Opportunity Commission. Federal law requires making an official complaint within 180 days of the incident. If you file a complaint, be prepared for possible negative reactions from the harasser and others in the organization.

Selected Bibliography

Equal Employment Opportunity Commission. "Guidelines on Discrimination Because of Sex, Title VII, Section 703." *Federal Register, 45* (11 April 1980): 2505.

Gutheil, Thomas G., and Archie Brodsky. *Preventing Boundary Violations in Clinical Practice.* New York: Guilford, 2008.

Lindeman, Barbara T., and David D. Kadue. *Workplace Harassment Law*, 2nd ed. Arlington, VA: BNA Books, 2012.

National Association of Social Workers. *Code of Ethics.* Washington, DC: NASW, 1999.

16.6 AVOIDING MALPRACTICE SUITS

Many social workers underestimate their legal vulnerability. In fact, a growing number are being sued for malpractice or professional negligence. Broadly speaking, a worker may be held liable if he or she has done something or neglected to do something that resulted in causing harm or injury to a client.

In this type of lawsuit, the person who files the lawsuit and alleges malpractice or negligence is termed the *plaintiff*. The person who is being accused of malpractice or negligence is termed the *defendant*. In order to win the lawsuit, the plaintiff must prove four points:

1. The defendant (e.g., the social worker) was obligated to provide the plaintiff with a particular standard of care or professional conduct.

2. The worker was derelict because she or he breached that obligation (or duty) by some act or omission that had a foreseeable consequence.

3. The client suffered some injury or harm (physical, financial, emotional, etc.).

4. The worker's conduct was a direct or proximate cause of that injury or harm.

Whether a breach of duty has occurred is determined by measuring the allegedly harmful act or omission against published standards of practice, agency policy, and the performance of social workers in similar settings. The plaintiff's (e.g., client's) injury must be one that would not have occurred had it not been for the social worker's action or negligence. Despite the traditional proximate cause requirement, juries are increasingly finding liability without fault (i.e., finding providers of services negligent even when they were not a proximate cause of the injury).

The professional duties that, if breached, place social workers and social agencies at greatest risk of legal liability include the following:

- Duty to avoid sexual misconduct
- Duty to warn others when a client discloses intent to harm them
- Duty to prevent a client's suicide
- Duty to properly assess, diagnose, and treat a client
- Duty to ensure continuity of service to a client under the care of a worker or agency
- Duty to maintain and protect confidentiality
- Duty to maintain accurate professional records and a proper and legal accounting of any money payments and reimbursements

In addition to allegations of misconduct based on the preceding duties, other allegations may give rise to a lawsuit:

- Failing to report or properly investigate suspected abuse or neglect
- Placing or contributing to the placement of a client into a facility or foster home in which he or she is subsequently abused, neglected, or injured (i.e., failing to properly select or supervise the placement)
- Inappropriately placing of a child or adult into foster care, an institution, a hospital, or jail
- Inappropriately or prematurely releasing a client from foster care, a hospital, an institution, or another protective setting
- Failing to supervise a child or a person with a mental or physical disability while he or she is participating in an agency program
- Failing to supervise the work of others, including the work of volunteers and students
- Providing or arranging the transportation that involves a client in a vehicular accident causing bodily injury
- Practicing social work while impaired by the use of drugs or alcohol or failure to report a colleague known to be impaired and a danger to clients
- Failing to inform a client of eligibility rules or regulations, resulting in avoidable financial costs or hardship to the client
- Failing to consult with or refer a client to a specialist
- Failing to recognize an obvious medical problem and not referring the client to a physician
- Practicing medicine without a license (e.g., suggesting changes in the client's use of medications)
- Misrepresenting one's professional training and qualifications
- Using a radical or untested approach, technique, or procedure
- Providing inaccurate information or advice to a client
- Providing birth control information or abortion counseling to a minor without consent of the parent

- Acting in a prejudicial manner in the selection of an adoptive home or in the licensing of a foster home, child-care facility, or the like
- Failing to be available to a client when needed (e.g., failing to provide professional coverage during the worker's vacation)
- Inappropriately or prematurely terminating a treatment relationship
- Causing alienation between parent and child or husband and wife

Of course, there is a very big difference between being accused of some wrongdoing and being found negligent by a jury. But even if the lawsuit is eventually dropped or dismissed for a lack of evidence, the social worker and/or the agency will have incurred legal expenses and will have experienced the emotional turmoil of being accused and sued. Usually malpractice lawsuits do not go to trial but are settled out of court.

Most lawsuits name as defendants both the social worker and the employing agency because the agency is assumed to be indirectly responsible for the harm caused by an employee. A social worker employed by an agency can be found personally liable, although this is not likely if the worker was acting within his or her job description, was following agency policy, and did nothing of a criminal nature.

In some cases, a social worker is held liable for harm caused by a person under his or her supervision (e.g., another social worker, volunteer, or student). Also, a worker might be held liable if he or she somehow contributed to the harm caused by another professional. An example of this is when a worker refers a client to an incompetent professional or when a worker provides a social assessment report to a psychiatrist who then makes a poor decision based in part on that report.

If named in a malpractice suit, the social worker should immediately contact an attorney (the worker's agency may provide legal representation) and also notify his or her supervisor, agency administrator, and insurance company. The social worker should not speak with anyone about the allegations before securing legal counsel. The worker must never alter case records or other documents related to the case. Such alterations are easily detected and may constitute a crime. An attempt to alter a client record after being named in a lawsuit will be viewed as an effort to destroy evidence and cover up a wrongdoing.

Legal experts note that the key to avoiding a malpractice suit is adherence to reasonable, ordinary, and prudent practices. In order to defend one's self against allegations, the worker must show that her or his actions were fair, in good faith, and consistent with how other professionals would behave under similar circumstances. One of the best defenses is to be able to show that the client gave his or her informed consent to the professional's intervention. This underscores the need to document client involvement in problem identification, assessment, and case planning and the value of written service agreements (see Item 12.5).

By following a number of additional guidelines, the social worker can avoid a malpractice suit or at least minimize its damage:

- Always adhere to the *NASW Code of Ethics* and the *NASW Standards of Professional Practice* relevant to your area of practice and guidance from the NASW Legal Defense Fund (www.socialworkers.org/ldf). Also, adhere to your agency's policies and procedures, as well as state and federal laws affecting your agency's program and services.
- Do not enter into dual relationships. A **dual relationship** is one in which a second set of obligations or expectations is introduced into the social worker–client

relationship. Examples include dating a client, renting an apartment to or from a client, loaning money to or borrowing money from a client, hiring a client to perform some service (e.g., repair worker's car), selling some item or product to a client, and so on. Dual relationships must also be avoided in supervisor–worker and faculty–student interaction.

- Do not become sexually or romantically involved with a client. Sexual misconduct toward a client is one of the most common allegations giving rise to malpractice suits in social work. Any sexual involvement with a client is a clear violation of the *NASW Code of Ethics*, a violation of state professional licensing statutes, and, in some states, a violation of criminal law. Avoid situations that could be misinterpreted as sexually inappropriate or give rise to false allegations of sexual misconduct. For example, male workers should be very cautious about visiting a female client in her home. A third party (potential witness) should be within earshot whenever a male worker interviews a female adult or a child.

- Before providing services to a child or adolescent, be certain that your program or agency has secured the proper authorization from the parent or guardian and that it is lawful for you to provide these services to the minor in question. As a general rule, the parent has the legal right to control and consent to the medical care and other professional services provided to his or her minor-age child. However, the laws of most states allow for some exceptions to this principle. For example, minors may be allowed to consent to their own medical care in regard to pregnancy, sexually transmitted disease, mental illness, and substance abuse. When in doubt, consult with your agency's attorney.

- Know your level of skill and conduct your practice within those limitations. Secure the training and supervision needed to perform job-related tasks responsibly. Become aware of the types of clients or situations that touch your "hot button" personal issues and lessen your ability to be objective. Obtain supervision and/or consultation when you are having unusual difficulties with a client. Always consult with your peers, supervisor, and/or attorney when faced with difficult ethical or legal issues.

- Be especially vigilant when dealing with situations that present high legal risk. Examples include clients who may attempt suicide, clients who are violent and a threat to others, clients who have a history of filing lawsuits, clients who are very manipulative, and clients who quickly find fault or perceive bad intentions in the behavior of others. Be very cautious about giving advice that will impact the client's health or finances (e.g., advising a client to get a divorce, suggesting how a client should invest money, telling a client that her or his physical symptom is of no significance).

- Base your practice on a professionally recognized and accepted approach or model. Keep your client fully informed of decisions, plans, and any risks associated with the intervention. Be careful not to give your client false hope about what you will be able to do. Convey a realistic picture of what you and your agency's services can accomplish. Maintain records that document your actions and decisions and any events or circumstances that have a significant impact on the client.

- Inform clients of any circumstances that may affect confidentiality. Confidentiality must be broken in order to report suspected abuse or neglect, to warn others of your client's intention to harm them, and to alert others of your client's intention to commit suicide.

- Reach out to the client who has been angered by your actions and attempt to rebuild the relationship and address his or her complaint. Many malpractice suits could have been prevented if only the worker or agency had followed up on the client's complaints. If you work for a fee-charging agency, make sure that financial arrangements are handled in a completely business-like manner so as to minimize the possibility of misunderstanding regarding cost and the collection of insurance payments.

- If served a *subpoena* to release client records, consult immediately with an attorney and your agency supervisor. It is important to understand that you must respond to the subpoena, but one possible response by your attorney is to claim confidentiality and to contest the request to release the records. Contesting the request will result in a court hearing and a decision by the judge on whether your claim is valid or if you must indeed turn over the records (see Items 9.4 and 10.5).

- Adhere to agency policy whenever a client presents you with a gift. As a general rule, food and inexpensive gifts valued at not more than a few dollars can be accepted as a matter of common courtesy and etiquette, but a more expensive gift should not be accepted before consulting with your supervisor. Do not transport a client in your private car unless this is in keeping with agency procedures and allowed under your auto insurance policy.

- Do not agree to an interview with a malpractice attorney or an investigator who is seeking information about one of your clients before first consulting with your supervisor or attorney. (It is a common practice for attorneys to attempt to secure statements or information before you are aware that you are the potential target of a lawsuit.)

- The social worker should secure malpractice insurance. It can be purchased through the National Association of Social Workers by NASW members and from some insurance companies. Before accepting a job with an agency, check into the agency's policy regarding providing legal defense for employees who are named in a lawsuit.

Selected Bibliography

Houston-Vega, Mary Kay, Elaine Nuehring, and Elizabeth Daguio. *Prudent Practice: A Guide for Managing Malpractice Risks*. Washington, DC: NASW Press, 1996.

Reamer, Frederic. *Social Work Malpractice and Liability: Strategies for Prevention*, 2nd ed. New York: Columbia University Press, 2003.

Reamer, Frederic. "Risk Management in Social Work." In *Social Workers' Desk Reference*, 2nd ed. Edited by Albert Roberts. New York: Oxford University Press, 2008.

Slater, Lyn. *Social Work Practice and the Law*. New York: Springer, 2011.

16.7 TESTIFYING IN COURT

Social workers employed in protective services, probation, and parole settings testify frequently in court and sooner or later most social workers are called on to provide testimony. Following guidelines such as these can help the worker perform effectively on the witness stand:

- Prepare for the court appearance. Consult with the attorney who will call you as a witness and learn of the questions she or he expects to ask you, as well as the questions you are likely to be asked by the opposing attorney who will do a cross-examination.

- Inform the attorney representing the side for which you may testify of any uncertainty, inconsistency, or gaps in information that will become apparent in your testimony. He or she should know of these concerns before you are called to testify. It is well to remember that attorneys are taught to never ask a witness a question for which they do not already know the answer.

- A social worker's testimony will probably fall into one of three categories: personal observations, reading from a client's case file, and expert testimony. If you are testifying as to your *personal observations,* you should be prepared to do so orally with few, if any, references to notes. If your testimony consists of numerous observations that occurred over a long period of time, you should prepare an outline or chronology of key events to refresh your memory and keep your recollections organized. The opposing counsel and judge will probably look at your notes but the written notes will not usually be introduced as evidence unless their content differs significantly from your oral testimony. Memorize the facts, but avoid sounding as though you are giving a recitation.

    If portions of a *client's case record* or other agency documents such as letters or reports have been admitted into evidence, you may be asked to read aloud the words that you wrote. You should be able to explain why you placed these particular words into the document. Prepare by being thoroughly familiar with the content and organization of the record. Also be prepared to describe the method for producing, transcribing, and storing a case file or document in your office.

    In some situations a social worker may be qualified in court to offer *expert testimony.* An individual who the judge has designated as an expert witness is permitted to offer opinions as to the meaning or significance of certain facts and observations. All other witnesses must confine their testimony to what they themselves observed or experienced. Opposing attorneys will often argue over whether a particular person should be qualified as an expert witness. If an attorney plans to qualify you as an expert, be prepared to explain: (1) your professional qualifications (e.g., degrees, license, certifications, experience, special training, publications), (2) the knowledge base and method used in forming an opinion, and (3) your mode of practice and how it is similar to or different from that of other social workers or professionals in your field of practice or area of expertise.

- Remember that you are under oath. Always tell the truth. Lying under oath constitutes the crime of perjury. Any attempts to avoid having to tell the truth will probably be discovered and exposed and your creditability as a witness will suffer.

- Appearance and demeanor are critical in a court. You should be properly dressed and well-groomed to reflect the solemnity of the courtroom. When seated in the witness chair, you should be attentive, courteous, and serious-minded at all times.

- Listen carefully to the questions you are asked. If you do not understand a question, ask that it be rephrased or explained. If you do not know the answer, say so. Never speculate or guess. Answer only the question that is asked. Answer questions in a respectful and confident manner. Speak clearly and avoid using slang and jargon.

- If an objection is made during the course of your testimony, stop speaking immediately. If the judge overrules the objection, you will be instructed to answer the question. If the objection is sustained, you will not answer the question and a new one question will be asked.

- When being cross-examined by the opposing attorney, keep in mind that he or she is not your friend. Even a polite and friendly cross-examiner is looking for ways to trip you up and to discredit your testimony. Do not volunteer information that is not requested. Do not explain why you know something unless you are asked. And finally, remember that the attorney offering your testimony has a chance to follow up and ask additional questions after the other attorney's cross-examination. This may help clear up any problems in your testimony.

- When being cross-examined, do not lose your temper at questions you consider impertinent or offensive. Exercise self-control. If you maintain your composure, you will be less likely to become confused and inconsistent. If the questioning is truly improper, your attorney will object. Pause before answering a provocative question to allow the objection to be made. Judges are very familiar with the histrionics of some trial attorneys and are rarely impressed by them.

- Do not get caught in the "yes-or-no" trap. If, on cross-examination, the opposing attorney asks a question and ends it with, "Answer yes or no," don't feel obliged to do so if you believe such an answer will be misleading. Instead, begin your answer with something like "Well, that needs explaining" or "That question cannot be answered with a simple yes or no." The attorney may again insist that you to answer either yes or no and the judge may require you to give a yes or no answer, but the judge and jury will at least understand your dilemma and look forward to your explanation when your attorney clarifies the situation on redirect examination.

- Many times, cross-examiners ask compound questions. When responding to a compound question, divide it into sections and then answer each part. Do not agree with a partially untrue statement, because the opposing attorney may cut you off and not allow you to complete your response, thus giving an erroneous impression of your actions or beliefs.

- A witness is sometimes asked a question regarding her or his sympathy for one side or the other in the case. If asked, honestly admit your sympathies. You might preface your answer with something like "On the basis of the information I have, I believe...." A thoughtful and authentic acknowledgment of personal views will not discredit a witness. The judge and the attorneys assume that that all witnesses have beliefs and values and that none can be completely impartial.

Selected Bibliography

Barsky, Allan E. *Clinicians in Court: A Guide to Subpoenas, Depositions, Testifying, and Everything Else You Need to Know*, 2nd ed. New York: Guilford, 2012.

Gutheil, Thomas G., and Eric Y. Drogin. *The Mental Health Professional in Court: A Survival Guide.* Washington, DC: American Psychiatric Publications, 2012.

National Association of Social Workers. *Social Workers and Subpoenas.* Washington, DC: NASW Press, 2011.

16.8 PROVIDING AND RECEIVING SUPERVISION

Throughout most of its history, the social work profession has considered supervision critical to the preparation of new practitioners, as well as a means of quality control in the delivery of services. Unlike those professions in which the private practice model of service delivery is dominant, social work extends supervision well beyond the worker's period of training. As primarily an agency-based profession, social work depends on supervision as a layer of the agency's administrative structure to continue training new workers and provide ongoing professional guidance. Thus, social workers must learn how to use the supervisory process to enhance their own professional development.

The supervisor plays dual roles. The first, **administrative supervision**, involves monitoring the work of supervisees to assure that it meets agency standards. Thus, supervisors are part of an agency's middle-management team and play an important role in agency policy, program, and personnel decisions. The second role is called **supportive supervision**. In this capacity, the supervisor is concerned with workers' job satisfaction, morale, and development of job-related knowledge, values, and skills. New social workers often move rather quickly into roles supervising other staff and volunteers because the basic helping skills they acquire in social work education translate into the skills needed by supervisors.

There are two sides in the supervisory process: the provider and the user, or the supervisor and the supervisee. As students and new workers, social workers will need to know how to make good use of supervision. Later in their careers, they must be adept at providing supervision in order to assist others in their professional development.

Both supervisors and supervisees should recognize that supervision must be carefully planned and the process adapted to the individual supervisor–supervisee situation. Here are the most typical ways in which supervision is given and received:

- *Individual supervision.* These one-on-one meetings between the supervisor and supervisee are the most prevalent form of interaction. Every supervisee needs and deserves regularly scheduled private time with his or her supervisor during which the worker's performance can be candidly examined with sufficient emotional safety to address practice successes and failures.

- *Group supervision.* Holding regularly scheduled meetings between a supervisor and a small group of supervisees provides a time-efficient opportunity for new workers or volunteers to process their experiences with clients, share information and perceptions, and help each other gain knowledge and skill in service provision and meeting agency expectations.

- *Ad hoc supervision.* These brief and unscheduled meetings respond to questions and issues as they arise during daily practice activities. *Ad hoc* meetings are particularly useful for preventing problems and capturing so-called teachable moments.

- *Formal case presentations.* At regularly scheduled meetings, one or more supervisees present in-depth descriptions of their work on specific cases and projects. The supervisor and other participants then offer advice and guidance on how the presenter's performance and client services could be improved.

GUIDELINES FOR USING SUPERVISION

Remembering guidelines such as the following can help the social worker make appropriate and effective use of supervision:

- Realize that your supervisor will expect you to do these things:

  - Follow agency policies, procedures, and specific instructions.
  - Demonstrate an eagerness to learn the details of your job, become more efficient and effective, and accept constructive criticism and suggestions on how you could improve the quality of your work.
  - Take initiative and assume responsibility for work that needs to be done.
  - Consult with your supervisor when you are unsure about how to proceed or when a course of action is raising unforeseen issues or encountering unexpected problems.
  - Immediately inform your supervisor when you become aware of an ethical, legal, or procedural violation that could give rise to a formal complaint or in some way harm the agency or its clients.
  - Work cooperatively with and be respectful of colleagues and promote behaviors that improve staff morale.
  - Maintain accurate and up-to-date records of your work with clients.

- Expect your supervisors to do the following:

  - Evaluate your performance on a regular basis and offer specific suggestions on how it can be improved.
  - Provide or arrange needed on-the-job training.
  - Provide encouragement and support when your work is particularly difficult and frustrating.
  - Keep you informed of changes in agency policies or procedures.
  - Give you a clear warning when your performance falls below standards.

- Establish a regularly scheduled time to meet with your supervisor. This should be at least once a week. Having adequate time to discuss work and job-related concerns is of critical importance.

- Seek your supervisor's assistance in formulating an individualized professional development plan that will build on your strengths and address limitations in your performance. Such a plan should be in writing. It should identify specific tasks and objectives to be accomplished over the next 6 and 12 months, and list specific learning activities (reading, study, conferences, workshops, etc.) to help accomplish the objectives.

- Recognize that there are some intangibles that your supervisor will look for and would come into play if she or he is making a recommendation for a promotion or move to another position. For example, a supervisor is likely to be especially attentive to the quality and quantity of your work, your understanding of the agency and the work to be done, your ability to formulate a feasible plan and carry it out, your leadership skills and the ability to win the respect of others, your time-management skills, your capacity to learn and adapt to change, your initiative and willingness to assume responsibility, and your emotional stability and dependability.

GUIDELINES FOR SOCIAL WORK STUDENTS

Horejsi and Garthwait (2002, pp. 12–13) explain that the social work student has the following special set of responsibilities to his or her practicum agency:

- Meet with the practicum instructor (field instructor) on a regular basis (at least weekly).
- Prepare for all meetings with the practicum instructor and inform him or her of the topics that need to be discussed during the upcoming meeting.
- Be present at the agency on days and at times agreed on by the student and practicum instructor. If unable to attend, notify the agency prior to or at the start of the workday.
- Behave in a professional manner, taking responsibility to understand and carry out assigned duties, meet all deadlines, and seek direction when needed.
- Carry out agency-related assignments, tasks, and responsibilities in a manner consistent with agency policy and procedures and prepare all records and reports in accord with the prescribed format.
- Identify learning needs and, if required, prepare a written agreement that describes learning objectives and learning activities.
- Complete all practicum monitoring and evaluation forms and reports required by the agency and school (e.g., time sheets).
- Discuss with the practicum instructor and/or the school's practicum coordinator any areas of significant disagreement, dissatisfaction, or confusion related to the practicum experience.

GUIDELINES FOR PROVIDING SUPERVISION

Assuming the role of supervising other workers or volunteers is a substantial step in a social worker's career. This is an important responsibility because the supervisees count on the supervisor to guide their own development and because the clients being served by these supervisees trust that the services they receive will be properly monitored and that their interests will be protected. The following guidelines should assist the new supervisor in carrying out his or her responsibilities:

- Social workers who assume the role of supervisor have special ethical obligations. For example, they should be well prepared to provide supervision, which means setting appropriate boundaries, being culturally sensitive, and providing fair and unbiased evaluations of the supervisee's performance.
- Reward good performance. Because supervisors in human services agencies can seldom offer monetary rewards, they must be creative in utilizing other types of rewards such as recognition, offering desirable or stimulating work assignments, and other special privileges.
- Hold supervisees accountable for their performance. When it is necessary to correct or discipline a supervisee, do so immediately after the infraction is discovered and in private. Disciplinary actions must be fair, decisive, very clear, and based on facts. Communicate to the supervisee exactly what is expected in the future and the consequences if performance is not improved. Should there eventually be litigation regarding a termination, this instruction and warning to the supervisee should be in writing. A failure to hold a supervisee accountable for his or her performance can frustrate and demoralize other agency staff and create personnel problems that consume an inordinate amount of a supervisor's time and energy.

- Remember that example is the best teacher. The supervisor must constantly model the values, attitudes, and behavior she or he expects of supervisees.

- Make sure that work assignments are clear and appropriate to the supervisee's level of knowledge, skill, and experience. The supervisee should be helped to learn job-related skills and obtain the training he or she needs to perform at a high level. Adjust the frequency and intensity of the supervisory process to the supervisees' level of competency and to their job responsibilities.

- If dismissal of the employee is a possibility, the supervisor must understand and strictly adhere to the relevant procedures outlined in the agency's personnel manual. Such procedures should reflect state and federal law on employee–employer relations. These procedures typically require that the employee be given written warnings of possible termination, a written description of his or her unacceptable performance, and a reasonable opportunity to improve his or her performance prior to termination. When attempting to terminate the employment of an individual, the supervisor must operate with the expectation that the individual may file a lawsuit and that the dismissal will have to be explained and justified in court. Some behaviors by the employee are so serious that they should result in an immediate move to terminate employment. These include:

  - Clear and serious violations of the *NASW Code of Ethics* (e.g., sexual relations with a client, verbal abuse of a client, or sexual harassment of staff)
  - Theft of agency money, equipment, or property
  - Concealing, consuming, or selling drugs on agency premises
  - Reckless or threatening actions that place clients or staff at risk of harm
  - Deliberate withholding of information from a supervisor or agency personnel that they need to know in order to properly serve clients and maintain the integrity and reputation of the agency and its programs
  - Falsification of agency records and reports
  - Solicitation or acceptance of gifts or favors from clients in exchange for preferential treatment
  - Clear and repeated insubordination

Selected Bibliography

Horejsi, Charles, and Cynthia Garthwait. *The Social Work Practicum,* 2nd ed. Boston: Allyn and Bacon, 2002.

National Association of Social Workers. *NASW Code of Ethics.* Washington, DC: NASW, 1999.

Shulman, Lawrence. *Interactional Supervision,* 3rd ed. Washington, DC: NASW Press, 2010.

Summers, Nancy. *Managing Social Service Staff for Excellence: Five Keys to Exceptional Supervision.* New York: Wiley, 2010.

Taibbi, Robert. *Clinical Social Work Supervision: Practice and Process.* Upper Saddle River, NJ: Pearson, 2013.

16.9 BUILDING AND MAINTAINING MENTORING RELATIONSHIPS

In a **mentoring relationship** an experienced professional and/or seasoned agency employee guides a less experienced colleague in learning how to successfully navigate the practice setting and teaches what one must do to grow and develop as a professional. The experienced colleague is termed the *mentor;* the less experienced one is often termed the *protégé* or *mentee.*

Elements of mentoring exist within a supervisor–supervisee relationship (see Item 16.8). However, in a true mentoring relationship, the mentor is not the protégé's administrative supervisor and does not assign work to him or her, oversee his or her daily work activities, or conduct the agency's formal evaluation of the protégé's job performance. A mentoring relationship is characterized by friendship and mutual trust, rather than by the chain of command.

BENEFITS OF MENTORING TO THE PROTÉGÉ

From the vantage point of the protégé, having a positive mentoring relationship can provide these five benefits:

1. *Support and understanding.* Beginning a new job or assuming a new set of responsibilities can be a time of uncertainty and self-doubt. During such a time, a wise and seasoned employee or professional can be of considerable help to a new or less experienced employee. A mentor's support, empathy, advice, and encouragement can boost the confidence of a protégé and calm her or his fears and anxieties.

2. *Orientation to and assimilation into the agency.* A mentor can help a protégé learn about the practice setting or agency as an environment of professional activity. The mentor can orient the protégé to the organization's culture, history, and traditions as well as help with understanding "office politics" and avoiding political pitfalls. A new employee who is mentored tends to learn the job faster, is more easily socialized into the organization, and is more likely to succeed.

3. *Access to important "insider" information.* A mentor is a valuable source of insider information that the protégé could not easily obtain through other means. Examples include information related to the key events that have shaped the organization, informal policies and procedures that do not appear in written manuals, patterns and personality traits of other colleagues, ongoing interpersonal conflicts within the organization, and the like. The protégé must honor the expectation of confidentiality and trust inherent in the sharing of this information and be prudent and discreet in using it.

4. *Career guidance.* Mentors can help protégés plan their careers, set goals, and develop the skills they need for career and professional advancement. Mentors can also help protégés connect to professional organizations, select professional learning experiences, and participate in community groups.

5. *Role modeling.* An intangible benefit of the mentoring relationship is that the mentor becomes an important role model for the protégé. Much of the protégé's learning and development will occur as a result of observing and imitating her or his mentor.

BENEFITS OF MENTORING FOR THE MENTOR

Mentoring is a two-way interaction, and the mentor should derive at least four benefits from the mentoring relationship:

1. *Professional stimulation.* Social work practice is far from repetitious. Nonetheless, a certain amount of routine develops in agency practice, and it is

easy for workers to fall into the pattern of approaching practice on a "business as usual" basis. The fresh perspectives and insights brought by the protégé can challenge the mentor to examine his or her practice through a different lens and thus stimulate his or her own professional growth.

2. *Updated knowledge.* The protégé can help the mentor learn about and stay abreast of new developments in the field. Likewise, the protégé can motivate the mentor to reexamine old assumptions and update any outdated knowledge and skills.

3. *Agency information.* The mentor can often obtain information from the protégé about personnel, problems, and issues in the organization that other employees might be reluctant to share with a senior staff member.

4. *Professional contribution.* Helping others make the most of their potential is the primary reason most social workers enter this profession. As the protégé grows in competence and effectiveness, the mentor will have the satisfaction of contributing to the growth and development of a colleague. What's more, the mentor may become more valued and respected by others in the organization based on the success achieved by the protégé.

MATCHING THE PROTÉGÉ AND THE MENTOR

Within most organizations, mentors voluntarily take on the mentoring role because they care about or are interested in the professional development of particular individuals. However, in some organizations, mentoring is encouraged by policy and the organization sets up formal mentoring assignments that match new employees with more experienced ones. It is not uncommon for an organization to create mentoring relationships in order to assist employees who may face unique challenges in performing some organizational roles or where role models are in short supply.

When there are cross-gender or gay/lesbian mentoring matches, some potential problems must be considered. For example, others in the organization may perceive such a mentoring relationship as a romantic involvement. Mentors, protégés, and the organization as a whole must be aware of these possible complications and make sure that mentoring facilitates, rather than impedes, professional development and advancement.

GUIDELINES FOR MENTORING RELATIONSHIPS

A social worker who is seeking a mentor or is responsible for matching a mentor and mentee should keep the following guidelines in mind:

- Pick or assign a mentor with great care. Seek a mentor who has a reputation for competence and effectiveness within the agency or practice setting. The mentor must possess the knowledge and skills the protégé hopes to learn.

- The mentor–mentee relationship must be comfortable and safe, take place in an environment of open discussion and mutual trust, and maintain an atmosphere in which the protégé can freely accept or reject advice and constructive criticism.

- The mentor and protégé must commit sufficient time and energy to the relationship. Some mentor–mentee relationships work best with regularly scheduled meetings; others work well on an on-call basis. Expectations about how the interactions will occur should be clearly established at the start of the relationship.

Social workers who are interested in mentoring or providing guidance to a protégé should keep the following points in mind:

- Pick a protégé with great care. A protégé should be someone whom you genuinely care about and someone you want to see advance within the agency and the profession.

- Above all else, be willing and able to separate your own goals and values from those of your protégé. He or she is a unique individual, and you must recognize and honor individual differences. Do not enter a mentoring relationship expecting to create a clone of yourself.

- Listen carefully to your protégé's questions and concerns. Do not assume that she or he has exactly the same concerns that you had at a particular stage in your professional development. The younger generation of professionals grew up in a different time, received a somewhat different type of professional education, and may have a set of personal and family concerns quite different from your own.

Selected Bibliography

Edelson, Marilyn. *Values-Based Coaching: A Guide for Social Workers and Other Human Service Professionals.* Washington, DC: NASW Press, 2010.

Wilson, Pamela P., Deborah Valentine, and Angela Pereira. "Perceptions of New Social Work Faculty about Mentoring Experiences." *Journal of Social Work Education, 38* (Spring–Summer 2002): 317–333.

16.10 CONSUMING AND CONTRIBUTING TO PROFESSIONAL KNOWLEDGE

The professional social worker is committed to engage in *evidence-based practice*. When consuming available knowledge, the worker must carefully select and adapt that knowledge to the unique client and practice situation. Thus, social work needs a strong body of literature as a resource for practitioners, and practitioners need the ability to sort through and draw from that literature. At the same time, the social worker has an obligation to contribute her or his knowledge to other social workers through both writing and presenting her or his insights to professional colleagues.

CONSUMING THE LITERATURE

The worker is obligated to locate the most relevant literature and carefully examine that material for the facts and ideas that may be most useful in work with his or her clients.

"Building the Professional Library" from 3rd edition

Doing so may be difficult for many social workers because of their heavy and time-consuming caseloads, leaving little time for reading and study. Moreover, up-to-date libraries are inaccessible to many social workers.

Fortunately, an increasing amount of helpful information is available online, and articles can readily be obtained and downloaded from one's own computer. When relevant articles and research reports have been identified, the social worker must decide if the information is reliable and trustworthy enough to use as a basis for practice decisions. An online abstract of such information may not contain enough information on which to base a conclusive decision, but will usually be sufficient to inform a decision on whether the complete article or report should be secured.

When reviewing published research, it is important to identify the basic design of the study. Although some studies combine quantitative and qualitative designs, most can be characterized as using just one of these. **Quantitative research** typically involves collecting a large amount of data from a representative sample of respondents. Statistical analysis may then be used to summarize and reduce the data to understandable generalizations and to identify relationships among the data. **Qualitative research**, by contrast, has the capacity to produce a more in-depth understanding of the thoughts, values, and experiences of a smaller number of respondents. Qualitative research is most appropriate when the basic characteristics of the phenomenon being studied are unclear or poorly defined.

A reader of *qualitative research* literature should be aware of these research characteristics:

- Data collection is a highly interactive process. The qualitative researcher involves the respondents in interviews, focus groups, and other interactive processes, in which the respondent is given stimulus materials. Through the use of questions and other efforts at clarification, understanding of the phenomenon is deepened.

- The researcher delays making an in-depth literature review until the data is collected in an effort to prevent researcher bias from affecting the data. Typically, the researcher will connect the findings to the literature only after the data has been collected.

- Because the researcher interacts with respondents and can be biased in how he or she asks questions or interprets the information gathered, the researcher is expected to acknowledge his or her perspective on the matter under study. In doing so, he or she gives consumers of the research clues to researcher bias that may have entered the process.

- Sample size is not a significant consideration in qualitative research. Although the respondents should be representative of the population that is interested in the topic, the goal is to secure more in-depth information from a small number of respondents rather than more general information from a large number. Often, 5 to 10 respondents are seen as a sufficient sample size in a qualitative study.

- Methods used in qualitative research include (1) gathering information directly from respondents through interviews and focus groups, (2) case study analysis to evolve themes and patterns from case observations, and (3) ethnographic research, in which the researcher becomes immersed in the respondent's physical, social, cultural, and work environment to gain in-depth understanding of that person's perspectives and experiences.

- The information collected is recorded as fully as possible, which is sometimes called the *thick documentation method*. It is then necessary to identify and code the themes and subthemes that appear in order to sort, organize, and reorganize the data and thus better understand the phenomenon being studied. Several computer software programs are available to facilitate this manipulation of data.

- A central concept that guides the interpretation and analysis of qualitative data is *triangulation*, or applying multiple data-gathering methods, multiple observers or investigators, and/or multiple perspectives to the same data set. If those results are in agreement, there can be greater confidence in the validity of the information.

When consuming qualitative research, the social worker should be especially concerned about how researcher bias may affect the conclusions drawn. As noted earlier, because the researcher usually interacts with the respondents, it is relatively easy for her or him to slant the data and/or the interpretation of what the data means.

Quantitative research is the more customary form of knowledge development and testing in Western society. It is patterned after the scientific method used in the physical sciences. If studying the success of an intervention approach, for example, the researcher might engage in the following:

- Review the literature and determine the current state of knowledge about that approach.
- Formulate a hypothesis about the impact of the intervention.
- Identify, define, and isolate the various factors and elements that must be examined in order to test the hypothesis.
- Select a statistically valid sample from the population being studied.
- Utilize control groups to hold constant the influence of extraneous factors.
- Apply the intervention to the experimental group.
- Collect and apply appropriate statistical analysis to the data.
- Draw conclusions.

Although this scientific process works well under laboratory conditions where many variables can be controlled, it is much more difficult (and sometimes inappropriate) in working with people. For example, can one ethically encourage or even require a person to remain in an abusive family in order to be part of a control group during the study of a domestic violence intervention? It is possible, however, to examine natural experimental and control groups (e.g., clients who did and did not receive a particular intervention) and then arrive at some conclusions about the merits of the intervention.

Much of the strength of quantitative social science comes from the statistical analysis of the data. **Statistics** are the numerical representations of the characteristics of individual cases—in social work, the characteristics of the people the researcher has chosen to study. The group of cases selected for study may be either a *sample* (i.e., part of a population) or the *population* itself (i.e., the complete group of cases to which the researcher may want to generalize the results). The consumer of this research must have confidence that the sample is indeed representative of the population in order to consider the findings valid.

The consumer must also be confident that statistical analysis was rigorous and appropriate. *Statistical analysis* involves assembling, analyzing, summarizing, and interpreting numerical data in order to inform thinking. Three general questions should guide the social worker in considering the validity of the statistical analysis conducted in a quantitative study:

1. *What was the purpose of the statistical procedure?* Some statistics simply help to reduce data to numerical indicators. These **descriptive statistics** include frequency distributions, percentages, measures of central tendency (i.e., reflections of the most typical response, such as mean, median, or mode), and measures of variability (i.e., descriptions of the spread or disbursement of the data, such as the range or standard deviation of responses).

   A more complex set of statistical tools, **inferential statistics**, allows the researcher to draw conclusions from a sample regarding the degree to which the sample is different from the population. One set of inferential statistics, *measures of difference*, project the likelihood that the differences occurred because of the intervention or other factors being studied, rather than simply by chance.

For example, in the social sciences, the typical criterion for accepting a finding as significant is $p < 0.05$, meaning the probability is less than 5 in 100 that the outcome would occur by chance.

A second group of inferential statistics known as *measures of association* identify the correlation between two or more variables. In social research, it is seldom possible to establish a clear cause-and-effect relationship, but it is possible to identify patterns of interaction among variables. If the relationship between two variables is completely random, or a zero (0.00) correlation, the variables are considered unrelated. However, if one variable increases when the other increases (i.e., a positive correlation), the correlation coefficient will be somewhere between +0.01 and +1.00. Similarly, in a negative correlation, where one variable increases as the other decreases, the scores might vary from –0.01 to –1.00. When interpreting measures of association, a correlation coefficient (either + or –) of less than 0.30 is considered a weak relationship, one from 0.30 to 0.70 is moderate, and one above 0.70 is strong. Other statistical tests reflect the relationships among more than two variables. These *multivariate statistical procedures* include multiple regression analysis, analysis of variance (ANOVA), cluster analysis, and factor analysis.

2. *Was the statistical test appropriate for the level of measurement?* The application of many statistical tests depends on the level of the data being analyzed. The three levels are nominal, ordinal, and interval or ratio. **Nominal data**, the most basic level, is a construction of mutually exclusive categories. Gender, ethnicity, and various yes or no questions (e.g., parent or nonparent) are examples. One category is not considered to have more or less value than another, just different. The next level, **ordinal data**, represents information that can be ranked from low to high, but for which it would not be reasonable to assume that there is the same amount of difference between each category. For example, many scales used in the social work literature are three- or five-point ratings of a factor (e.g., frequently, occasionally, seldom) but there is no assumption of equal intervals between ratings—only indication of more or less, or higher or lower. In other words, a rating scale may be used to indicate that Client A has higher self-esteem than Client B, but in measuring a variable like self-esteem, one is not able to say that Client A has three times more self-esteem than Client B. **Interval or ratio data**, the most precise level of measurement, assumes the categories are divided into equal units and thus permit more exact measures. Examples would be age, population density per square mile, and the number of school children who have been immunized. As the consumer of a research report or article, it is important to be sure that the statistical procedures selected were appropriate for the level of data collected in the study. Otherwise, the statistic may misrepresent the outcome.

3. *Was the type of sample correct for the statistical test used?* The type of sample (in combination with the level of measurement) determines which statistical procedures can be appropriately used. The most powerful (i.e., more rigorous in a mathematical sense) statistical tests are **parametric tests**, which require independent or random samples and interval- or ratio-level data for at least one variable. For a sample to meet the sampling criteria for parametric tests, the different cases being compared must have been independently assigned to groups or randomly selected and there must also be reason to assume that the population from which the sample was drawn has a normal distribution. **Nonparametric statistics**, in contrast, are less powerful predictors but allow work with data

that is nominal and ordinal. Also, since they compare the outcomes observed with expected outcomes for those respondents, they do not assume a normal distribution. Nonparametric statistics fit almost all research situations and are frequently used in social work research.

Like the ability to communicate in a foreign language, a person's facility with statistics quickly diminishes if he or she does not work with these procedures on a regular basis. Thus, making judgments regarding the correct application and interpretation of statistical data is often perplexing for the social worker who seldom uses them. To help such a worker, Figure 16.1 provides a "crib sheet" for use in examining

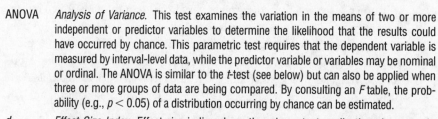

ANOVA　*Analysis of Variance.* This test examines the variation in the means of two or more independent or predictor variables to determine the likelihood that the results could have occurred by chance. This parametric test requires that the dependent variable is measured by interval-level data, while the predictor variable or variables may be nominal or ordinal. The ANOVA is similar to the *t*-test (see below) but can also be applied when three or more groups of data are being compared. By consulting an *F* table, the probability (e.g., $p < 0.05$) of a distribution occurring by chance can be estimated.

d　*Effect Size Index.* Effect size indices have three important applications in research. First, they indicate the strength of the relationship between the independent and dependent variables. This is particularly important in describing results of a complex research study because statistical significance only indicates a relationship between two variables. Second, they are used as a summary statistic when many articles are combined as in a meta-analysis. Last, they are part of the process of computing statistical power prior to performing a study—in most cases determining how large a sample is needed to reject a false null hypothesis. When interpreting the value of *d*, a general rule of thumb for the social sciences is that 0.2 represents a small effect on the dependent variable, 0.5 suggests a medium effect, and 0.8 or greater indicates a large effect. A similar result can be obtained using the *r* value from a Pearson Product-Moment Correlation (see below), although the interpretation must be adjusted in that 0.1 suggests a small effect, 0.3 indicates a medium effect, and 0.5 or larger reflects a large effect of the independent variable on the dependent variable.

DF　*Degrees of Freedom.* *DF* indicates the number of ceils in a set of data that are free to vary. This freedom to vary is an important factor in estimating the probability of an outcome occurring by chance. *DF* is computed by multiplying the number of rows minus one in a table by the number of columns minus one. Thus a 2×3 table would have 2 *DF*, whereas a 3×4 table would have 6 *DF*. *DF* is a necessary number when the researcher interprets the probability tables for the different statistical tests.

f　*Frequency.* An *f* will usually be reported in a table and simply reflects the number of responses in each category or interval.

F-ratio　*F.* Usually based on an ANOVA or a multiple regression analysis, this parametric test of significance is a measure of variability that requires interval or ratio data. It tests for difference between the standard deviations of two variables or samples. The *F*-ratio compares estimates of variance *between* the samples with variance *within* the samples. If the between-group variance is higher than the within-group variance, increasing the likelihood that the variance did not occur by chance, the *F*-ratio will be larger. The *F* value has little meaning until it is applied to a table that identifies the probability of that distribution occurring by chance.

Mdn　*Median.* This is a measure of central tendency that may be used with ordinal- or interval-level data. It is the midpoint in a distribution (i.e., the score above which and below which 50 percent of the cases lie).

(Continued)

Figure 16.1
Statistical Notations Frequently Used in Social Work Literature

Mo	*Mode*. This is a measure of central tendency that may be used with all levels of data. It reflects the category that includes the most cases in a distribution and thus can be applied to nominal data. In some distributions more than one category may have the same number of cases, resulting in a bimodal or multimodal distribution.
N	*Number*. The *N* reports the total number of cases that are being considered in the statistical procedure. The *N* may vary in different analyses of a data set due to incomplete responses or test requirements that may necessitate the exclusion of some cases.
%	*Percent*. A percentage is a reflection of the share of the cases that would fall into a category if the total were 100. It is computed by dividing the frequency (*f*) in a category by the total number of cases (*N*) and multiplying by 100.
p	*Probability*. A *p*-value reports the likelihood of a particular distribution occurring by chance if a normal distribution is assumed. Thus, the lower the likelihood of a distribution occurring by chance, the more confidence can be placed in the assumption that the variables being tested indeed affected the outcome.
r	*Pearson Product-Moment Correlation Coefficient*. The *r* is a correlation coefficient (i.e., a number that represents the association between two variables). It reflects the tendency of high or low scores for one variable to regularly be associated with high or low scores for another variable. Therefore, it is possible to predict the value of one set of scores by knowing another. The nearer the *r*-score is to $+1.00$ or -1.00, the greater is the likelihood that the items vary together (i.e., are associated with each other). The r is a parametric test that requires interval-level data. (*Note: The Spearman Rank Order Correlation Coefficient* (r_s) is a similar nonparametric test that can be applied to ordinal or ranked data. It examines the association between pairs of variables and can be computed with a relatively small number of pairs [i.e., less than 30] in the sample.)
Range	*Range*. The range is a measure of variability that reports the span between the lowest and highest scores of the cases in the sample. Data must be at least ordinal to compute the range.
SD	*Standard Deviation*. SD tells how much dispersion from the mean exists in the scores of the sample or population being studied. The more the scores deviate from the mean, the greater the standard deviation score. When comparing samples or groups as part of a study, the ones with the largest SD scores have the greatest variability in distribution, whereas the respondents in groups with smaller SDs are more like the mean (or average) and thus are more homogeneous. In a normal distribution, about 68 percent of all cases fall within one standard deviation from the mean (34 percent above and 34 percent below) and 95 percent fall within two standard deviations from the mean.
t-test	*Student's t*. The *t*-test is a parametric test of significant difference between the means of two samples (or a sample and the population from which the sample was drawn). At times it is also used to test the significance of the difference between two coefficients of correlation. If the means differ substantially (i.e., a higher score), it is likely that the difference was not a result of sampling error or chance, and it is reasonable to assume that the difference is associated with actual variations in the factors being examined. A *t* table provides statistical estimates of the probability that the results might be due to chance (e.g., $p < 0.05$).
$\bar{X}$	*Mean*. The arithmetic mean is a measure of central tendency that requires interval- or ratio-level data. It is the sum of the values for a variable divided by the number (*N*) of cases.
χ^2	*Chi Square*. χ^2 is a nonparametric test of significance that may be applied with nominal data. In essence, it compares the observed and expected frequencies for a variable to determine if the differences found could be explained by chance. χ^2 can also be used to test the relationship between two nominal variables, such as gender and political party affiliation. Until the chi square value is translated to a probability score (e.g., $p < 0.05$), it has little meaning.

Figure 16.1
Continued

quantitative research–based literature. It identifies several commonly used statistical procedures by the symbol commonly used in the literature and gives a brief description of its purpose.

CONTRIBUTING TO THE PROFESSION'S KNOWLEDGE

Social workers are not just consumers of professional literature; they are also obligated by the *NASW Code of Ethics* to build the knowledge base and make it available to other social workers (NASW, 1999). This knowledge usually is made available through conference presentations or preparing written materials to be made available through either online or published journal articles. Determining the best way to transmit one's knowledge to professional colleagues depends somewhat on the nature of information to be communicated, the interaction one wants with an audience, and the number of professionals one wants to reach. Figure 16.2 compares these forms of knowledge transmission.

Presenter/Author Viewpoint	Conference Presentation	Journal Article
Ability to shape how audience consumes the information	Presenter has complete control. Audience can leave the room, but otherwise must accept the presenter's structure. Presenter must anticipate audience ability to consume information.	Reader has complete control. Reader can skim, change order of material, or turn to another article. Author must capture and hold the reader's interest in the topic.
Relationship with person receiving the information	Presenter is face-to-face with the audience and can adjust presentation based on verbal and non-verbal audience reaction.	Author has no personal interaction with the reader and must anticipate the reader's beginning knowledge of the subject matter and interest in more depth on the topic.
Delivering numerical or detailed information	Power-point and overhead transparencies can help audience navigate the organization of the presentation and examine any detailed Information. Hard-copy handouts allow the audience to take home the information for further study.	Reader can change the order of the presentation to fit his or her learning style. All information must be contained in the article narrative and associated figures that the reader can examine at will.
Size of audience	Audience size is limited to the capacity of the room where the presentation is made. Typically this is a small number.	Subscriptions to social work journals range from a few hundred to 160,000 for *Social Work*. It is not possible to know how many articles are actually read.
Process for selection	A conference announcement invites an abstract and a committee screens and selects presenters. The full presentation is usually not developed until the paper has been selected. The conference is usually within 4 to 6 months after selection.	The full paper is developed and submitted to an appropriate journal for consideration. Committee and editor select articles to be published. Acceptance rate varies by journal, but the typical range is 15 to 20 percent of submissions published. Once selected, an article may take 1 to 2 years before it is published.

Figure 16.2
Comparison of Methods for Sharing Professional Knowledge

Making oral presentations

It is important for social workers to develop skill in public speaking, not only for conference presentations but also for addressing community groups and legislators in advocacy efforts. The nature of the presentation can vary considerably. At one extreme is an off-the-cuff presentation and at the other extreme is reading from a prepared paper. Neither is usually very effective. Unless one is a charismatic speaker, the former is likely to be difficult to follow and the latter can easily lull the audience to sleep. Somewhere between the two extremes is the recipe for an effective oral presentation.

The presenter must carefully plan the speech so the intended message is accurately received by the audience. A presenter should always remember that the listening audience does not have the opportunity to reread something that is not understood. Thus, clarity is of critical importance and some repetition of key points is appropriate. The following guidelines may help to plan a successful speech.

Step 1: *Know the content and be familiar with the audience.* When presenting at a conference, remember that the audience will usually have several choices of presentations to attend at any one time. A title in the program that both reflects your topic and yet shows a little pizzazz helps to attract an audience. When a conference participant selects your session, the expectation is that you will know your subject matter thoroughly and have important information to transmit in an interesting way.

Step 2: *Select and adapt the content to your audience.* For example, a presentation on measuring client change during an intervention would be quite different if presenting to a group of social work practitioners, as opposed to presenting to presenting to the local Rotary Club. It is helpful to visualize a person who might be like people you anticipate will be in the audience and prepare as if you are speaking to that person.

Step 3: *Carefully organize the flow of information.* In broad terms, the speech should include three major components: a preview of the topic, the main body of the speech, and a summary pointing out the conclusions reached about the topic. Be prepared with visual aids (e.g., PowerPoint) to help the audience follow the flow of the presentation, and hand out hard copies of detailed information to minimize the need for note taking. Organize the materials so that sufficient background information has been presented to support the audience understanding the conclusions or summary you make at the end of the presentation.

Step 4: *Select creative ways to make the presentation interesting.* Your enthusiasm for the topic and confidence in your conclusions will go a long way in keeping the audience interested. In addition, using case examples can help the audience understand how they can apply that information. Such case examples must, of course, be altered to protect client confidentiality. Presenting two sides of an issue with a point/counterpoint format might assist an audience in considering a topic from different perspectives.

Step 5: *Prepare your notes to help maintain the planned organization of the presentation.* Notes may be prepared as a script of what you have to say with key words highlighted or in a set of note cards. In either case, these notes should be viewed as reminders of what you want to say and when you want to say it. Never read aloud from these notes. The pages of a script and your note cards should be numbered in case they get out of order.

Step 6: *Be as relaxed and comfortable as possible when presenting.* Careful preparation is a prerequisite to building confidence in making a speech. To reduce anxiety further, go to the room where you are presenting 15 to 20 minutes ahead of the session to be sure any audiovisual equipment is working and the room is arranged in an appropriate way for your presentation (e.g., chairs in a circle, a table where you can place your notes). Also, it is helpful to mingle with the audience before the session begins. Introducing oneself to a few audience members who arrive early, asking what they hope to get from the session, and simply cultivating a few familiar and responsive faces in the audience can increase the comfort level of the presenter considerably.

Step 7: *Be aware of your mannerisms while speaking.* Words and phrases such as *you know* and *uh* are annoying and distracting, as are physical mannerisms such as elaborate gestures or excessive pacing while presenting. Practice delivering the speech in front of a mirror to get a sense of the time required (although the time it takes to deliver a speech is often underestimated). Also, be sure to dress appropriately for the nature of the meeting, as attire that is out of place can be distracting to the audience.

Step 8: *Leave time for discussion.* Conference schedules rarely leave a speaker with all the time she or he would want to fully develop a topic, and the tendency is to fill every minute with what you want to present. However, an advantage of a conference setting over written materials (e.g., a journal article) is the opportunity for interaction with the audience. Give them a chance to ask for clarification, to identify areas that they want discussed in more detail, and the opportunity to express their own opinions about the topic. In that way it can become a learning experience for both the audience and the presenter.

Preparing a journal article or other written work

When preparing written material, it is important to remember that whether it is accessed online or through the hard copy of a journal, the reader ultimately decides if the material will be read at all and, if so, how it will be approached. Many readers will use the title as their first decision for continuing to read, asking themselves, "Does this appear interesting enough to spend my time reading this material?" Some readers will begin with the first paragraph and read each word as the author has presented the material. Some will first skim the whole article and return to read more carefully the parts that interest them. Others may read the introduction and conclusion and, if their interest is not captured, move on to other materials. Armed with this information, the author must write to help the reader determine if she or he will read the article.

The following steps should be followed when preparing written materials:

Step 1: *Have a clear and important message.* Although some journal readings are built on original ideas and data, most articles update and expand existing information, synthesize or combine available knowledge in a unique way, or simply express something already known in a form that makes it more understandable. Since article manuscripts are limited in length (usually 15 to 20 double-spaced pages), the scope of the article cannot be too broad nor the content too complex. A good test of scope is to see if the key ideas can be stated in a single paragraph. If it is not possible to be this succinct, the topic is probably too broad and may need to be broken into subparts and presented in more than one article.

Step 2: *Select an appropriate journal.* A large number of journals address matters of interest to social workers. Some publish articles on a wide range of topics, but most specialize. NASW's *Author's Guide to Social Work Journals* (2010) contains information about publishing requirements for over 200 different journals. Each has its own focus and will attract a specific readership.

Before beginning to write, examine several issues of the journal(s) most appropriate for your content and make an assessment of the probable readership, type of articles published, and typical format of the articles (e.g., research-based, theory development, case applications). Each issue of a journal or the journal's website will usually include a statement of its publishing requirements and provide information on preferred topics, length, and procedures for submitting articles, such as electronic or hard copy submission. Social work journals typically require that materials be submitted in the APA style (*Publication Manual of the American Psychological Association*, 2010). Remember, too, that it is considered unethical to submit the same article to more than one journal at a time.

Step 3: *Picture the audience.* It is often helpful to imagine that you are writing to some specific individual. Select someone who would be likely to read the article, and write to that person. Use language that communicates your ideas clearly to him or her, and use concepts you expect would be familiar to that person.

Step 4: *Prepare an abstract.* Most journals require a 75- to 100-word abstract to accompany the article. Although it is often easier to write an abstract after the article is completed, preparing a first draft of the abstract before writing the article can help focus attention on the most important points. The final abstract should be clear, concise, and factual, as it may ultimately appear in databases where potential readers are searching for specific information.

Step 5: *Develop an outline.* The reader's ability to comprehend the information in the article will be influenced by how well it is organized. Think through the logical connections between elements to be included. Preparing an outline will help you ensure that smooth and understandable transitions are provided to link the various parts of the article in a coherent fashion.

Step 6: *Write the introduction.* The opening two or three paragraphs should tell the reader what the article is about, explain why it is important, and suggest which social workers might be especially interested in this material. Tying the subject to a current issue or including a short case example related to the topic may help the reader recognize the benefit in reading the entire article. For many writers, getting started is the most difficult part of writing. Do not let frustration over the introduction block the process. Some writers find it helpful to write a rough introduction with the intent of completely rewriting it later.

Step 7: *Set the context or background.* It is important to let the reader know where this material fits in social work (e.g., practice theory, practice techniques, social welfare policy issues). The reader also needs to know the theoretical context in which this material is placed. A *literature review* that summarizes what is known or unknown about the topic indicates to the reader that you understand the current thinking about the topic. It also provides the background for judging the importance of your contribution to the topic. Due to limitations in the maximum length of an article, the literature review cannot be extensive and must be focused clearly on literature that is most relevant to the topic of the article.

Step 8: *Prepare the body of the article.* Concisely report the facts and observations that are the heart of the article. It is helpful to supplement narrative material with alternative means of presenting the information (e.g., charts, figures, tables, and lists). If case examples are used, be sure that they are presented in a way that helps the reader generalize from that example to other situations.

Make frequent use of headings and subheadings so the reader can easily follow the flow of ideas and information. Articles are most readable when they contain short paragraphs with clearly focused content. Write simply and clearly and avoid social work jargon. Omit gender-specific language and any terms that might reflect bias or stereotyping based on race, ethnicity, gender, age, handicapping conditions, or sexual orientation.

Step 9: *Prepare a summary and/or conclusion.* End the article with a short statement that pulls together the key points and presents conclusions that can be drawn from this material. If relevant, point out additional research that is needed to further develop the subject.

Step 10: *Collect and format references.* Using the format appropriate for the selected journal, list the references that support the ideas and information presented.

Step 11: *Rewrite, rewrite, rewrite.* Expect to revise and rewrite a number of times before determining that the article is completed. Polishing the structure, content, and language time and time again is an essential part of good written communication. It sometimes helps to read the manuscript aloud, thinking about how it might sound to someone else and checking for any errors that might have been overlooked.

Step 12: *Let it cool.* Avoid sending an article to a journal as soon as it comes out of your printer. A few days or a week away from the material provides a fresh perspective and may yield alternative ideas for presenting the material or strengthening the way ideas are expressed. It may be helpful to use this time to get colleagues to review the work and offer comments. Remember, however, that it is your article, and you must own the final result. Do not feel obligated to incorporate all suggested changes. Also, do not allow this cooling period to become an excuse for procrastination. You may never be completely satisfied with your writing, but you must stop refining it at some point.

Step 13: *Be prepared for acceptance or rejection.* Typically, the editor of a journal will send your manuscript to three or four reviewers. It often takes six or more months for the reviews to be completed and the editor to determine if the article is to be included in an upcoming issue of the journal. Online journals usually have a shorter time line. Reviewers conclude their work with a recommendation to (1) reject, (2) accept if revised in specific ways, or (3) accept for publication without major changes. Some journals will, on request, provide the reviewers' comments if the article is rejected. If that occurs, seriously consider those comments and either revise and resubmit the article, send it to another journal, or drop your plan to publish.

Step 14: *Finalize the manuscript.* If the article is accepted, you will work with professional editors who will offer suggestions for strengthening the presentation. You will have the opportunity to be sure that their editing does not distort or misrepresent the content. In addition, when an article is accepted, the author will be required to assign the legal rights to this material to the publisher. It will then be necessary for the publisher to approve any subsequent reprinting or extensive quoting of the article in other books or articles, including your own.

Selected Bibliography

American Psychological Association. *Publication Manual of the American Psychological Association*, 6th ed. Washington, DC: APA, 2010.

Atkinson, John M. *Lend Me Your Ears: All You Need to Know about Making Speeches and Presentations*. New York: Oxford University Press, 2005.

Furman, Rich. *Practical Tips for Publishing Scholarly Articles: Writing and Publishing in the Helping Professions*. Chicago: Lyceum, 2007.

National Association of Social Workers. *Author's Guide to Social Work Journals*, 5th ed. Washington, DC: NASW Press, 2010.

Szuchman, Lenore T., and Barbara Thomlison. *Writing with Style: APA Style for Social Work*. Belmont, CA: Brooks-Cole, 2004.

Thyer, Bruce A. *Preparing Research Articles*. New York: Oxford University Press, 2008.

16.11 IMPROVING THE SOCIAL WORK IMAGE

The typical citizen has little understanding of what social workers actually do. On TV and in the movies, the social worker is often portrayed as either a judgmental and mindless busybody or someone who breaks up families by removing children for no good reason. All too often, the only newspaper or magazine articles that mention social workers are ones describing how the acts or omissions of an agency or a social worker contributed to a client's harm or distress. Additional image problems are created when the media use the term *social worker* in a generic manner and apply it to any person who is working or volunteering in the human services field.

If they are to make their maximum contributions to improving the society, social workers must actively work to create a more positive image. The image will change in a positive direction when it becomes evident to the public that social workers are truly experts in what they do and are able to get results that nonsocial workers are unable to match. The financial rewards and the status associated with certain other professions (e.g., medicine, dentistry) came about not through exhortation but rather because their members completed long and difficult training, acquired a definite and identifiable expertise, and promoted legislation providing clients with legal protections concerning the outcome of their decisions and actions.

In order to promote a greater public understanding, social workers should adhere to certain guidelines:

- Assume a personal responsibility for improving the profession's image. Three actions are essential. First, provide to all of your clients the highest quality service possible. Second, behave in a highly professional and completely responsible manner when dealing with clients and the public. Third, remind those observing your performance that you are a social worker.

- Use the title of *social worker*. If you must also use a descriptor such as *counselor* or *psychotherapist* to clarify your role, describe yourself, for example, in this manner: "I am a social worker who provides psychotherapy to troubled youth," "I am a social worker specializing in the planning and development of services for persons with AIDS," "I am a social worker who administers a family support program," "I am a social worker who teaches at a university," and so on.

- When being interviewed for a news story, make sure the reporter understands that you are a social worker, that you have a degree in social work, and perhaps describe the special training that has prepared you for the work you do. Always operate on the assumption that reporters and the public at large have little or no idea that social work is a distinct profession. Otherwise, you will probably be called a *sociologist, welfare worker, counselor,* or *agency employee.*

- Speak of your work with respect. If you truly value what you do, others are more likely to adopt a positive attitude toward both you and your work. Avoid any action or association that would detract from the profession or damage your credibility and trustworthiness.

- Work with other social workers, possibly through the local NASW chapter, to plan and implement a media and public relations campaign aimed at educating the public about social work and social workers in your community. March is designated as "Social Work Month," but a strong local campaign should be conducted throughout the year.

- Whenever a news story uses the term *social work* or *social worker* in an erroneous manner, send the newspaper, magazine, or radio or TV station a letter that explains the error. Also send a packet of informational materials that describes the nature of the profession and social work activities.

Selected Bibliography

Hallman, Patsy Johnson. *Creating Positive Personal Images for Professional Success,* 2nd ed. Lanham, MD: Rowman & Littlefield Education, 2012.

Whitaker, Tracy. *Who Wants to Be a Social Worker? Career Influences and Timing.* Washington, DC: National Association of Social Workers (NASW Center for Workforce Studies), 2008. http://workforce.socialworkers.org/studies/BeaSocialWorker.pdf

Whitaker, Tracy. *The Results Are In: What Social Workers Say about Social Work.* Washington, DC: NASW Press, 2009.

16.12 BECOMING A LEADER

Social workers encounter many situations of social and economic injustice that cry out for attention and change. These injustices may occur in their own agencies, where modifications in policies, programs, and practices are needed in their communities, or in the larger society. In order to change these situations, the social worker must be willing to step forward and assume the role and responsibilities of leadership. Desirable change does not happen by accident. Rather, it is set in motion by people who assert themselves, articulate their concerns, and take on the hard work of leading.

Most efforts to define **leadership** speak of it as a process of using authority and interpersonal influence to guide people through a course of action and toward a particular goal. An effective leader draws on his or her own sense of mission to create a climate and foster the attitudes that move a group or organization toward a desired end. The exercise of leadership always occurs within a context of competing and conflicting forces.

Leadership should not be equated with administration or organizational management. *Leadership* is the process of bringing about some significant change by inspiring people to let go of what is familiar and to embrace a new vision or mission. By contrast, the process of *management* seeks to bring about order and consistency within an organization through the use of various administrative tools and procedures, such as planning, budgeting, and coordinating staff. Not all who occupy administrative positions are effective leaders—nor are all leaders effective managers.

Although certain characteristics—such as intelligence, dependability, verbal ability, adaptability, and even physical height and attractiveness appear to be associated with leadership, no one set of traits predicts who will become a leader. Research does not support the belief that some people are so-called born leaders. In order to become an effective leader, one must build on her or his strengths and learn and practice the skills of leadership, just as she or he would develop any other set of skills. An aspiring leader must consciously cultivate the development of those qualities as well as the thought processes, attitudes, and interpersonal skills associated with leadership. Consider these guidelines:

- *Have a clear vision about what you want to accomplish.* Leaders must go beyond what was and what is and articulate a vision of what could be. It is the leader's vision that provides a critically important sense of purpose and direction and infuses the change effort with the confidence not only to make difficult decisions but also to act on those decisions. However, leadership is about much more than having ideas. In fact, effective leaders are seldom the most creative and innovative thinkers. People who are attracted primarily to ideas and theory seldom make good leaders because they often move too quickly, become impatient with the slowness of change, and get frustrated with the hesitations and limitations of those they seek to lead.

- *Articulate your vision for your followers.* This vision must be one that can be translated into clear language and achievable objectives and plans that are feasible within the existing political, economic, and cultural environment.

- *Lead by example.* A leader cannot ask others to do what he or she is unwilling to do. Followers are inspired and motivated by the resolve, courage, hard work, and sacrifices of an effective leader. Leaders must exhibit the behaviors and attitudes they want to see in their followers.

- *Cultivate a group of followers.* In order to attract and retain followers, leaders must respect and demonstrate genuine concern for the wishes, values, and abilities of those they want to lead. Leaders must be willing and able to curtail some of their own hopes in order to avoid moving too far ahead of their followers.

- *Maintain clear and continuing communication with your followers.* This communication must keep followers focused on the desired goal while also attending to the concerns, fears, and ambivalence they may have about investing their time, energy, and money in working toward this goal.

- *Be prepared to make difficult decisions.* The social, political, economic, and organizational environments are constantly changing, and leaders must be willing to take calculated risks, cope with uncertainty, and manage situations that are inherently unpredictable. Nothing destroys the capacity to lead more quickly than indecisiveness and inability to take action when action is clearly necessary. It is often said that "It is better for a leader to occasionally make a bad decision than to be perceived as someone who cannot make a difficult decision."

- *Develop and maintain a positive personal and professional reputation.* The capacity to lead is often tied to having a favorable reputation within one's organization or community, to possessing special knowledge of and prior experience with the issue that has drawn people together, and to having a well-developed network of personal and professional contacts.

- *Develop the art of building consensus and coalitions.* Leaders create networks among individuals and organizations and facilitate their cooperation and collaboration. They reward others for their cooperation and share credit, even with those with whom they may disagree. Leaders must also be willing to compromise when doing so is a necessary step toward reaching a sought-after goal.

- *Work to identify and understand the various motivations of followers.* Leaders should anticipate possible disagreements among followers and take steps to prevent or resolve these conflicts before they distract from achieving the goal and splinter the followers into competing factions. At the same time, leaders must be willing to diminish or counter the influence of those individuals or groups that are creating unnecessary conflict or roadblocks to achieving goals.

- *Use your influence in a thoughtful and deliberate manner.* The type of power and influence available to a leader will vary, depending on the type of group or organization she or he is leading. In most situations, a social worker providing leadership will possess only the influence that comes from being a person who commands respect and attracts a following because of his or her personal charisma, attractiveness to others, and knowledge or expertise. If the leader happens to occupy an administrative position within a formal organization (e.g., executive director, high-level administrator, or elected official), she or he will possess the power of authority and legitimacy associated with that position. A leader who possesses administrative authority may also have the power to reward or punish the actions of others and can initially increase their level or cooperation or decrease their level of resistance to a proposed change. However, such a leader must avoid imposing acquiescence or superficial agreement that dissolves at a later point in the change process.

- *Develop a high level of self-awareness.* Leaders must understand their own strengths and limitations and constantly examine their own motives and behaviors. When leading, the focus should be on the goals, not on the leader. Some potential leaders destroy their capacity to lead by letting their own need for public recognition and admiration shape their decisions and actions.

The following are some qualities and characteristics that have also been found to be important to effective leadership:

- The capacity to critically evaluate various ideas and proposals, including one's own decisions, plans, and actions
- The capacity to speak and write clearly so as to articulate a vision and purpose in ways people can understand
- Perseverance even in the face of disappointment and criticism
- The ability to delegate responsibility and to teach or empower others to perform as well as they can
- Willingness to take personal responsibility for one's decisions and actions
- Openness to new ideas and acceptance of persons with various abilities and diverse backgrounds
- The ability to create a sense of camaraderie and feeling of community among one's followers
- The ability to make effective use of available time and get things done

Selected Bibliography

Breshears, Elizabeth M., and Roger Dean Volker. *Facilitative Leadership in Social Work Practice.* New York: Springer, 2013.

Bryman, Alan, ed. *The SAGE Handbook of Leadership.* Thousand Oaks, CA: Sage, 2011.

Burghardt, Steve, and Willie Tolliver. *Stories of Transformative Leadership in the Human Services: Why the Glass Is Always Full.* Los Angeles: Sage, 2010.

Gardella, Lorrie Greenhouse, and Karen S. Haynes. *A Dream and a Plan: A Woman's Path to Leadership in Human Services.* Washington, DC: NASW Press, 2004.

Ledlow, Gerald R., and M. Nicholas Coppola. *Leadership for Health Professionals: Theory, Skills, and Applications,* 2nd ed. Burlington, MA: Jones and Bartlett Learning, 2014.

Author Index

Subject Index

Note: The bold locators refer to key terms